The Power of
Money Dynamics

The Power of
Money Dynamics

Venita VanCaspel, CFP

President,
VanCaspel & Co., Inc.
1540 Post Oak Tower
5051 Westheimer
Houston, Texas 77056
(713) 621-9733

Reston Publishing Company, Inc.
A Prentice-Hall Company
Reston, Virginia

Drawings by Jan Smulcer

Library of Congress Cataloging in Publication Data

VanCaspel, Venita
   The power of money dynamics.

   Includes index.
   1. Finance, Personal.   I. Title.
HG179.V364   1983   332.024   82-16535
ISBN 0-8359-5570-2

Editorial/production supervision and
interior design by Linda Zuk

The final typesetting was done on a TEXSET 1000 system in Reston
Virginia, using a Mergenthaler Omnitech/2100. The galleys and page
makeup were also done on the TEXSET 1000 system using a Canon LBP-
10 Laser Printer for page proofs.

TEXSET 1000 is a trademark of TEX Corporation

© 1983 by Venita VanCaspel and
Reston Publishing Company, Inc.
A Prentice-Hall Company
Reston, Virginia 22090

10   9   8   7   6   5   4   3

Printed in the United States of America

*To the VanCaspel Team, whose daily dedication
and delightful spirit make it possible
for me to help others become financially independent.*

Contents

Chapter 3 Dow Power to 3000   59

Chapter 4 Professional Power for Your Money   97

Chapter 5 The Infallible Way to Invest   147

Preface

You are living in an era of tremendous change! Dynamic, challenging, and frustrating change is taking place in family relationships, international affairs, living styles, technology, and especially in the nurture and investment of your money. To win the money game in this decade—and win you must—you will have to develop a special kind of expertise, mental attitude, agility, diversity, and determination.

It will not be change, but rather your reaction to change, that will determine your financial future. Change can greatly enhance your fortune, or it can destroy it; make you a millionaire or a pauper; delight you or disappoint you; exhilarate you or depress you. Change brings with it heightened potential and devastating crevices of danger.

How you cope with this inevitable change will determine whether you'll win or lose the vital money game. The money game is not like any other game. You cannot choose whether you'll play, for the money game is the only game in town. Since you have no choice but to play, it behooves you to learn to play the game very well, for losing could mean spending your life in a state of frustrating, devastating financial insecurity.

Financial independence can be yours if you have an average ability to earn and a little discipline to save, if you apply the information you'll learn in this book, and if you are granted enough time. You have control over the first three variables.

There is probably nothing that you'll ever learn to do that will become as easy and as exhilarating as making money once you've mastered the rules. You'll find that there will be an investment for every season, but there will be no investment for all seasons. Agility and diversification will become your keystones as you learn from this book how to take advantage of the dynamics of the Economic Recovery Tax Act of 1981 (ERTA) and how to position your assets effectively where demand is greater than supply in order to compound your money rapidly.

This is a personal book. Financial planning must of necessity be personal, for you are different from any other person. You are a unique creation and have developed in your own unique way. You have different financial objectives, assets, tax bracket, temperament, emotions, and time schedules than even your closest friend. Your financial program, therefore, must be designed for you and for you alone.

If you and I could sit down and plan your financial future, I would ask you many pertinent questions about you and your money. I would then endeavor to design a program that fits not only your financial needs, but your emotional needs as well. Designing a program for your financial needs is relatively simple, once I know all the facts; but mapping a course that fits your temperament and your prejudices and then communicating these ideas to you in such a way that you will understand and then act upon them is a continuous challenge.

Since you and I may never have the opportunity to sit and discuss your financial plans, I have designed this book to give you a step-by-step guide to use in designing your own financial blueprint and keeping it updated constantly to fit these dynamic times.

I will be sharing with you the knowledge I have acquired over the past twenty years as a Certified Financial Planner. During that time it has been my joy to watch the assets of my clients grow and to see their dimension for living expand through the application of the money and living skills that I have taught them and helped them to apply. Added to these people I have helped personally have been the vast numbers who have read my last three books: *Money Dynamics, The New Money Dynamics,* and *Money Dynamics for the 1980s.* My daily mail enthusiastically detailing successful results is an avalanche of joy to me, for nothing delights me more than receiving testimonials of success from my readers and valued clients.

It continues to be my privilege to be in daily contact with some of our nation's top policymakers, the most expert observers of the money scene, our leading financial planners, and a large number of successful business and professional people who make decisions that affect us all.

From this vast exposure to information, my training, and my years of experience, I have developed a certain expertise.

Through my seminars, speeches, books, and counseling, I feel that I have helped raise the level of financial independence of my fellow Texans, and through the enormous sale and use of my past three books, the financial independence of a nation. Financial Planners, stockbrokers, and enthusiastic readers across the nation continue to recommend to their clients and friends my books, my national Public Broadcast Television series ("The Moneymakers," carried by 182 stations nationwide), and my national *Money Dynamics Letter.* These are helping Americans learn how to profit from owning a part of American industry, real estate, energy, and a vast number of other areas of our free enterprise system. Such ownership is vitally important, for if they do not own and participate in the fruits of the system, Americans will vote to destroy it, resulting in one of the world's greatest tragedies. We know that the free enterprise system is not perfect, but it is the best system yet devised. It has brought the greatest good to the greatest number of people.

Now, reach out your hands and let me grasp them firmly as I lead you down the road toward financial independence. To provide you with a solid foundation it will be necessary at the beginning of this book to introduce you to some tables that may not be as exciting as we would both like for them to be. But do persevere, devour them, and let them seep deeply into your subconscious mind. You'll find them invaluable in the attainment of your predetermined worthwhile goal. Now, let's begin our exciting journey together toward your financial independence.

Acknowledgments

So many have touched my life and helped me toward my goals that this page could not possibly cover them all. I would like to express my special thanks to Helen Fourmy, who has been my faithful, motivating, and excellent associate for many years; to JoLieta Davis, whose immense talent and personal dedication smooth the ripples of my personal and business life; and to her very talented and beautiful assistant, Yvonne Ingram, who is changing roles to become my valued secretary; to Donah Shaw, who has for years been my delightful and efficient secretary, bringing order and fun into my life; to Susan Streich, whose calm and lovely presence gives me a sense of continuity; to Betty Henderson, whose enthusiasm for the task at hand makes being around her a delight; to Allison Hunt, Linda Gaskill, Beverly Jackson, Nancy Claire, Kristen Genitempo, Betty McLeod and Diana Owen, who make the VanCaspel Team of Financial Planners hum with the greatest efficiency; to John Weatherston, who brings us the wise maturity that comes from experience; and most especially to Walt Burton, Wally Garrett, Terry Albin, Mike Thompson, and Rick Madden, who, along with Helen, make up the most talented team of financial planners in the country today.

The Power of
Money Dynamics

Chapter 1

Your Keys to Money Power

Welcome to the exciting world of money and its marvelous kaleidoscope of change—changes that will force your old strategies into obsolescence and bring you new opportunities in abundance!

Don't be discouraged if you are discovering that all the old money rules your parents taught you aren't working, for there are many more productive ways to put your money to work today. You can now own the thing that owns the thing. You can see a need and fill it. You can be an owner of a vast combination of productive assets and participate in their growth while sheltering a large portion of this growth and the income it produces from the devastation of taxation.

You are truly fortunate to be living in this exciting period of investment history. In my many years as a Certified Financial Planner I have never seen so many viable investment opportunities for both large and small investors.

The application of the techniques clearly defined in this book will make the next ten years the most profitable you've ever experienced.

Money Has No Gender

Throughout this book I will use the masculine pronoun in a neutral way to mean "he or she." I have found that God has been very fair in His apportionment of brains. He has made women as intelligent and as capable as men, so in this book I'll not bother myself with all this "he-she" business, but rather will devote myself to the order of the day: helping you make your money work effectively for you.

The same money rules apply to women as to men. If you are a woman, don't ever think it is your inalienable right that a man should take care of your financial security. The single state—whether it is through choice, circumstances, death, or divorce—will probably be your lot for at least a part or all of your life. Even if you marry, you have an obligation to be a financial partner to your husband and to be as well informed as you can about money. I have found that love is not so much looking into each other's eyes, but looking in the same direction—and the same is certainly true when it comes to money.

In the past, too many women have been taught "It's not nice to talk about money." You'd better believe it is nice to talk about money—and to learn about money—or you won't have any. The sweet damsel who sits around waiting for Prince Charming to come riding into her life on the proverbial white horse and take care of all her financial needs may very well find herself cleaning up after his steed.

Dear Investor

My greeting to you is "Dear Investor" because you are an investor. You are either investing all of your wealth in today's goods and services or you are reserving a portion of it to invest in tomorrow's goods and services. You do not have the choice of whether you will invest, but you do have the choice of how you will invest. The wisdom you bring to bear on these choices will have a greater influence on your financial future than the amount of money that comes your way.

Do you want to consume all that you earn today and hope that somehow tomorrow will take care of itself? As short-sighted as this may seem, it is the course being taken by the vast majority of your fellow citizens.

Three Sources of Income

If you'll stand back and objectively analyze your potential sources of future income, you will find that there are three chief sources.

The first is you at work. However, there will come a time when, regardless of how badly you want to work, the world will not let you. It will retire you.

The second source is your money at work. If you make proper preparation and turn some of your income into growing investments, a time will come when you will no longer have to work for your money, but you will be able to trade places with your money and let your money work for you. I have found that income from capital is immensely more secure than income from labor.

The third source of income is charity.

Man at work, money at work, charity—which source do you want to depend on when you retire? Since "man at work" may not be an option open to you and "charity" has rarely brought happiness, apply your intelligence toward assuring yourself that there is sufficient "money at work" to retire in financial dignity.

Why do so many fail to become financially independent? During my years as a financial planner I have searched for the answers, for I have been convinced that if I could discover these answers, I could help thousands of people avoid living twenty to thirty years of their lives in the tragic state of financial insecurity and enable them to retire in financial dignity.

Six Reasons So Many Fail

I believe I have found the reasons. There are six, and here they are: (1) procrastination; (2) failure to establish a definite financial goal; (3) ignorance of what money must do to accomplish that goal; (4) failure to understand and apply our tax laws; (5) being sold the wrong kind of life insurance; and (6) failure to develop a winning mental attitude about money. When you have completed reading this book, you will know how to avoid all these reasons for failure and you will have a definite blueprint for financial success.

Procrastination

Procrastination can be the greatest deterrent to reaching your goal of financial independence. Time can be your greatest ally. If you have a sufficient amount of time, you will not need as much money to put to work. The less time you have, the more money it will take. Do not waste this precious commodity—a commodity that is distributed to each of us equally.

Procrastination is a deadly enemy of your obligation to retire in financial dignity. Sometimes you may confuse goals and obligations. A larger home, a boat, travel to foreign lands—all of these can be your goals. But preparing to retire in financial dignity is more than a goal. It is your obligation, a debt that you owe yourself and others—your family, your community, and other taxpayers. With proper financial planning and sound money management, it is a debt that you can pay, so as to make your retirement years happy instead of haphazard, comfortable instead of dependent.

I have observed that in the early years of life, when spending habits are formed, thoughts of retirement are far away and have little relationship to current needs and even less to future needs. The habit becomes reinforced with the same passing of time that brings retirement closer. Then when retirement time is so near as to be of immediate concern, it is often too late to make adequate preparation.

Procrastination often stands in the shadows, awaiting its opportunity to spoil your chance for success. You may even be procrastinating because you fear success. You will probably go through life as a failure if you wait for the "time to be right" to start doing something worthwhile. Do not wait. The time will never be "just right" to start your journey down the road to financial independence. Life is a journey, not a destination. Take all your "someday I'll do it" ideas and put them to work now. There is no such thing as a future decision. There are only present decisions that affect the future.

Make "Do It Now" your slogan for the rest of your life! And, always aim high. If you aim for the stars, you certainly should not end up with a handful of mud.

Failure to Establish a Goal

The second reason that many fail to become financially independent is that they fail to establish a goal. If you aim at nothing in life, you are liable to hit nothing. I've never had anyone come to me and say, "Venita, I plan to fail." Yet I've observed many who failed to plan and who unfortunately met with the same dismal results.

After moderating "Successful Texans" and "The Moneymakers" and after listening to the life stories of the other recipients who were honored, as I was, with the Horatio Alger Award for Distinguished Americans—and who have attained success under our free enterprise system—I have reached some conclusions about the necessary ingredients for success in life and in money matters. Successful people differ in appearance, voice, height, weight, education, and family background, but they all have one thing in common: they know where they are going. Each has a goal. If anything sidetracks one of them, or if something doesn't work the way they planned, they just dust themselves off and go right back in the direction of their goal. After many years of observation, I am in complete agreement with the famous psychologist William James, who said, "Anything the mind can believe and conceive, it can achieve."

Visualize your financial goal right now. Your mind will not let you conceive what you cannot achieve. Write out your immediate, intermediate, and distant goals in a clear and concise manner, stating exactly what your goals are and your timetable for accomplishing each of them. This will crystallize your dreams and cause you to develop a different life-style in which more power and energy are devoted to each day's activities. You will become a different person. Problems will be looked upon in a different light and you will find you can focus on the solution. A by-product of goal setting will be determination. It is already a force inside of you and goal setting releases the power of determination so that it can propel you to financial levels that were heretofore beyond your reach.

Success in money management is not a will-o'-the-wisp that comes to some and not to others because of fate, chance, or luck. Success in money management can be predicted, if you have a plan and if you follow that plan.

If you give a blueprint to a skillful builder, do you think that it will be a matter of chance, or luck, that he will complete the structure successfully? Of course not. He merely begins at the beginning and follows the plan step by step to its completion.

This book is your blueprint for success. If you follow it, financial independence will be yours.

Ignorance about Money

A third reason for failing is ignorance of what money must do to accomplish a financial goal.

There is an educational void in our nation. We are raising a generation of financial illiterates. Even our college graduates cannot figure simple percentages.

The tragic mistakes they are making because of these deficiencies in our system are destroying their dreams, their hopes, their families, and their pride in themselves and their country. Their hoped-for rewards from their talents and skills are disappearing like vapor. From my years as a stockbroker and later a certified financial planner, I have observed daily the devastating effect of this void.

Our schools are doing a tremendous job of teaching the know-how of a vocation. They are offering their students a vast array of

opportunities to prepare themselves for the career of their choice, from basic mechanics to electronics. They are offering them the opportunity to acquire knowledge in a wide variety of fields such as engineering, chemistry, computer technology, sales, distribution, management, and accounting. They are also offering students courses that will prepare them to live enriched lives through the study of music and the various arts.

Yet our schools are not teaching students the one subject that they will need to live well in our free enterprise system—and that is how to manage their money. This vacuum is so great that the average couple cannot begin to defend themselves against the financial uncertainties and multitude of choices they face in our complex society.

This lack of financial know-how is not only destroying the American dream, but can lead these financially illiterate citizens to vote to destroy our free enterprise system. Any person will be against something that he does not understand or that he feels he cannot participate in. The destruction of this system would be one of the greatest tragedies to beset our world.

The free enterprise system is not perfect by any stretch of the imagination, but it is the best system yet devised for bringing the greatest good to the greatest number of people.

I find that people are frightened today. All the old money rules are not working. For the first time, they have taken their money out of the bank and they probably won't put it back. They've put it in money market mutual funds (which I'll discuss later), but this is a temporary home and they will need to search for more rewarding investments to survive.

Failure to Learn our Tax Laws

The fourth reason many fail to achieve financial independence is that they fail to learn and apply our tax laws. The only money you'll ever get to spend at the grocery store is what the government lets you keep. Every investment you make must be carefully correlated with your tax bracket or you are making the wrong investment. You must learn to avoid taxes—not evade them. Learn to defer taxes, convert to classifications where the taxes are lower, and learn to think in terms of tax equivalents. Throughout this book you'll find how to invest for "keepable" income.

Contrary to any misleading headlines you may read, your total tax bill will not be cut appreciably in the decade of the 1980s. Even with the so-called tax cut provided by the Economic Recovery Tax Act of 1981, tax-bracket creep and the added Social Security taxes will probably make your total tax bill higher than it was before the cut and the purchasing power of what is left lower. The massive tax increase in the guise of a mislabeled "windfall-profits tax" (on which there can be and often is a tax without a profit) is really a sales tax on gasoline, heating oil, and other petroleum products. It was called "windfall profits" to deceive a public ignorant of basic economics.

The real burden of taxes is what the government spends. If the government spends more than it takes in, you and I pay the difference in the form of inflation and the interest expense on the national debt.

The Economic Recovery Act of 1981

ERTA, as it has come to be called, was designed by its originators to facilitate the reindustrialization of the United States and to increase personal savings. Our congressional process greatly dulled its effectiveness by making the cuts in taxes come too slowly to accomplish the maximum good. Now we must wait to see whether Congress and the American public will give the changes time to heal the damages caused by many years of excessive government spending and costly red tape combined with punitive disincentive tax laws for individuals and business. As a nation, we've come to expect instant solutions—the quick fix. After all, every night on television we solve major problems in an hour, with six breaks for the good life.

On October 2, 1981, I was a guest on a television show and the host said to me, "Well, Reaganomics certainly isn't working is it?" My answer to him was, "The program only became effective yesterday. Don't you think we should give it more than twenty-four hours before we pass judgment?" Thirty years of moving away from productivity and the incentives to be productive cannot be changed in a few hours or a few years. But in time, the direction can be changed through productive investments in plants and equipment and through the reduction of unwise increases in federal spending and the money supply. These measures could move us toward a balanced budget, wages that reflect productivity, and a lowering of interest rates, which in turn should allow our industries to produce products that can compete nationally and abroad.

If you have not read the highlights of ERTA, do so now. My favorite reference book is *Research Institute Master Federal Tax Manual* (it can be obtained by writing to the address in the Appendix). It is written in lay language. How can you play the money and tax game if you don't know the rules? No better than you can play any other game. You are playing the very serious game of financial power and survival, and this book will teach you how to win.

The Wrong Kind of Life Insurance

The fifth reason that people fail to become financially independent is that they have been sold the wrong kind of life insurance. I say "sold" because if they had received sufficient information about the purpose of life insurance and how each policy was put together, they would not have made the tragic mistakes that they have made.

My publisher excerpted and made available for distribution Chapter 13, "Life Insurance—The Great National Consumer Fraud," from my two previous books. Over 2 million copies are now in circulation across the United States. I am delighted with the fantastic impact this chapter has made and is continuing to make on the whole insurance industry, and the number of families that will have a better opportunity to achieve financial independence because they have followed my instructions. I have changed the title of this chapter slightly for this book because those who profit so handsomely from selling the wrong kind of insurance have been able to get it banned or its use curtailed in eight states. It is my hope that the change from "fraud" to "dilemma" will somewhat reduce their success and make it possible for more families to benefit from the information it contains. You'll learn what you need to know about life insurance when you read Chapter 13 of this book.

Failure to Develop a Winning Mentality

The sixth reason that people fail to win the money game is that they fail to develop a winning mentality. The demarcation line between success and failure is often very narrow and can be crossed if the desire can be stimulated, if competent guidance can be made available, and if sufficient encouragement and incentive are provided.

There are many vital parts to the psychology of winning. Some of the most important for financial independence are attitude, effort, lack of prejudice, persistence and enthusiasm.

Attitude. There is a truly magic word that you should place not only in your vocabulary, but also in the very fiber of your being if you desire to be successful in the realm of money or in any other important area of your life. That magic word is ATTITUDE!

Everything in life operates according to the law of cause and effect. You must produce the causes; the rewards will take care of themselves. A good attitude leads to good results; a fair attitude, to fair results; a bad attitude, to bad results.

You will shape your own financial life by the attitudes that you hold each day. If you have a poor attitude toward learning about money management, you will not learn very much until you change your attitude. If you have an attitude of failure, you are defeated before you start.

Sometimes a prospective client will say, "If I invest, the market will go down. I've never made any money in the market." Until he can change his attitude, he will not become a successful investor. I have found that truly prepared, working optimists always make money. I have also found that pessimists rarely do.

Look around you. Study successful people. You'll find that they go sailing through life from one success to another. These people have the attitude that they can accomplish whatever they set out to do. Because of this attitude, they do accomplish their goals. They achieve some remarkable things and the world calls them successful, brilliant, lucky, and so on.

Luck. As you may guess, I do not believe in luck. Luck happens when preparedness and opportunity get together. If you are prepared, you will be lucky. A close friend of mine, who is a well-known and respected business consultant, studied a particular company and bought shares of stock while it was still in its infancy. These shares have now grown in value tremendously and have made him a very wealthy man. There are those who would scoff and say, "I should be so lucky." It wasn't just luck. He was prepared.

When he and his wife were first married, they scrimped and saved and lived in a modest apartment. They even sold their car and rode the bus to work so they could save a nest egg. It was this nest egg, which they had so painfully saved, that was used to make their "lucky" investment. Had they not prepared, they would not have had the means of availing themselves of all this "luck."

Prejudice. We all have prejudices, but we should continually work to rid ourselves of them. In counseling, I sometimes encounter a couple who seem to be saying to me, "Please don't confuse us with facts." They do not want to know the truth. The truth will not make them free, regardless of how carefully or intelligently it may be presented to them.

Lack of Concentrated Efforts. To become a good investor, you must seriously apply your intelligence, use your ability to acquire knowledge, and give your attention to details and timing. If you cannot, will not, or do not have the ability to do these things successfully for yourself, do not take a distorted ego trip by not admitting that someone may be able to do something better than you can do it. Put the professionals to work for you.

Desiring Something for Nothing. If I were to distill all the wisdom I've ever learned into nine words, they would be: There is no such thing as a free lunch. I have observed two drives where this is evident. One is the gambling instinct, which has driven many to failure in the market. Investing, properly approached with constant supervision, is in my opinion the safest long-term thing that can be done with money. Speculation, on the other hand, can be risky. This desire for a "free lunch" is often seen working in the opposite manner by those who will leave their funds in a savings institution because they refuse to pay a brokerage commission to get their funds invested. The money that they "save" is often very costly.

In making an investment decision, the important factor is not what it "costs." You do not care what it costs, but you are truly concerned with what it pays.

Lack of Enthusiasm. I do believe I can forgive almost any shortcoming a person may have except lack of enthusiasm; and it is especially essential in the acquisition of money. Enthusiasm is contagious; if you have it in sufficient quantities, others will welcome you into their group. You will be more in touch with the needs and thinking of the people around you, and you can profit from the investment opportunities that will become obvious to you.

Guessing Instead of Thinking. Information is available about almost any subject you need. Don't let indifference or plain laziness keep you from acquiring the facts essential to making good judgments. Acquire the major points of information you need—you'll never have "all" the information. If you wait that long, you'll probably make your decision too late for maximum profit. I find that most decisions are made too late rather than too soon. We all have a tendency to have a good laugh when someone says, "Do something, even if it's wrong." I have found that there is usually more merit in this than is apparent on first blush. As Ralph Waldo Emerson said, "Do the thing and you will have the power."

Lack of Capital. Build up your nest egg, and do it while you are young. Remember to pay yourself first and then don't spend the nest egg, but use it as collateral for levering a larger egg and then a larger one. Never consider any earnings on your investments as spendable until you have reached your goal of financial independence. This is how you develop your money power. Your banker will welcome you with open arms if you have collateral to back your bankable idea.

Being Overinfluenced by the Opinions of Others. I have observed that those who fail to accumulate sufficient amounts of money are easily influenced by the opinions of other people. Opinions are cheap. You will find them everywhere. There are always those who are just waiting to foist their opinions on you if you will accept them. If you let others overinfluence you when you are reaching decisions about your money, you will not succeed.

Lack of Persistence. Are you a good "starter" and a poor "finisher," as so many are? Each year we must close our reservations early for our January financial planning seminars because we cannot seat all those who want to come. This year our overflow seminar in addition to our regular three-session seminar had 700 people in it.

If you begin a financial planning program and happen to experience a temporary setback, do not give up. I've observed this at times when a client starts a monthly investment program. If the market goes up after he starts his program, he'll happily put in his investment each month, but if the market goes down, he'll abandon the program, regardless of how I've tried to explain that dollar-cost-averaging results can benefit from stock market fluctuations. There is no substitute for persistence. If you make persistence your watchword, you'll discover that "old man failure" will finally become weary of you and will make his exit. Failure cannot cope with persistence.

During my twenty years as a financial planner, I've searched for the common denominator of success. I've noticed that one particular characteristic seems to run through each life—the successful person has formed the habit of doing the things that failures do not like to do.

Perhaps you think that you have certain dislikes that are peculiar to you, and that successful people don't have these dislikes but like to do the very things that you don't like to do. This isn't true. They don't like to do them any more than you do. These successful people are doing these very things they don't like to do in order to accomplish the things they want to accomplish. Successful people are motivated by the desire for pleasing results. Failures search for pleasing experiences and are satisfied with results that can be obtained by doing things they like to do.

Inability to Make a Decision. I have found over and over again that those who succeed in making large sums of money reach decisions promptly and change them, if at all, very slowly. I have also found that those who fail to make money reach decisions very slowly, if at all, and change them frequently and quickly. Procrastination and indecision are twins. Pluck this grim pair out of your life before they bind you to the treadmill of financial failure.

Yesterday is past, tomorrow is only a promise. Only today is legal tender. Only this moment of time is yours. Where you will be financially next year or ten years from now will depend on the decision that you make today—or the ones you don't make.

Of the many studies of successful people, near the top of the list of characteristics is their ability to be decisive. Of the many studies of failures, at the top of the list of reasons for their failure is procrastination. Study, think, plan, act!

Making a Decision is a Privilege. No one can make your decisions for you. You will find that free advice about your money is always available. It's usually those who lean back and give you the most "positive" advice whose finances are bordering on catastrophe. They are often wrong, but never in doubt.

There have been times when I, or one of our team of financial planners, has counseled a couple who have attended all three sessions of our investment seminar and thus have listened to me for at least five hours. They have asked for an appointment, and one of us has spent two hours with them in uninterrupted personal conference. When it comes time to apply this information to their own personal finances, they will say, "This sounds fine, but let us go home and think it over." On the surface this sounds like a prudent, sensible thing to do, doesn't it? However, I find that it usually is not. They already have all the information they need. They will not be "thinking it over" after they leave. Dozens of other matters will require their attention. They are trying to avoid making a decision, not realizing that no decision is a decision. They are deciding that where their money is now is the best place for it to be—for that is the result brought about by their lack of action. Always remember, indecision is decision—usually against you.

Overcaution. The person who takes no chances generally must take whatever is left over after others have finished choosing. Overcaution is as bad, if not worse, than lack of caution. Both should be avoided. Life will always contain an element of chance. Not to win is not a sin. But not to try is a tragedy.

There is no reward without risk. If you've never missed when investing, you've not been in there trying, or you've been holding your losers far too long for maximum profits. Play the money game well, but never safely. Avoid a life of no hits, no runs, no errors!

The reason many are not successful investors is that they are afraid to do anything with their money, so they leave it in the bank or savings and loan for years, where inflation destroys it. That's not playing it safe. That's playing it dumb.

Lack of Self-Discipline. Another cause of failure is lack of self-discipline. The secret of financial independence is not brilliance or luck, but the discipline to save a part of all you earn and to put it to work in shares of industry, real estate, natural resources, tangible assets, and so on.

To be a winner, you must practice self-discipline. Self-discipline achieves goals. There are those who think of self-discipline as "doing without." To me, it is "doing within." It's a mental and physical process. It's your own vivid visualization of financial independence. Winners are those who are doing within while they are doing without.

Expectations. The successful people with whom I have visited seem to find their accomplishments not too difficult and often surprisingly easy, simply because it seems so few are really trying.

Winners look at life as a game—one they expect to win, are prepared to win, desire to win, and know how to win. They have conscientiously nurtured and developed the habit of winning. They affirm and reaffirm to themselves each day that they are self-determined.

Acquire Equity. Again, I emphasize, own the thing that owns the thing! Own the assets that create the wealth. If you are, or remain a lender, you will receive only the crumbs and the owners will be the winners. This book will teach you how to be an owner.

Money. Rid yourself of the old myth, if it has been plaguing you, that money is not important. It is important—vitally important! It is just as important as the food it buys, the shelter it provides, the doctor bills it pays, and the education it helps to procure. Money is important to you as you live in a civilized society. To split hairs and say that it is not as important as other things is just arguing for the sake of the exercise. Nothing will take the place of money in areas in which money works.

What is money? Money is the harvest of your production. The amount of money you will receive will always be in direct ratio to the need for what you do, your ability to do it, and the difficulty of replacing you.

I'm amazed at the number of people who tell me that they want money but don't want to take the time and trouble to qualify for it. Until they qualify for it, there's no way they can earn it.

All you need is a plan—a road map—and the courage to arrive at your destination, knowing in advance that there will be problems and setbacks, but knowing also that nothing can stand in the way of your completing your plan if it is backed by persistence and determination.

Keep money in its proper place. It is a servant, nothing more. It is a tool with which you can live better and see more of the world around you. Money is necessary in your modern life. But you need only so much of it to live comfortably, securely, and well. Too much emphasis on money can reverse your whole picture and make you the servant and your money your master.

You do want to have money and the things it can buy, but you also must check up continually to make sure that you haven't lost the things that money cannot buy.

Three Financial Periods

Now let's look at your financial life. It will most likely be composed of three periods: the "Learning Period"; the "Earning Period"; and the "Yearning" or "Golden Period," depending on the decisions you make in your earning period.

Let's examine each of these financial periods.

3 Financial Periods

Age 1-25	25-65	65–?
LEARN	EARN	YEARN or GOLDEN

The Learning Period

I hope that you begin learning at birth and never cease to learn until you bid this world good-bye. The fact that you are reading this book indicates that you are. However, your formal learning period will probably last for your first twenty-five years, depending on your vocation.

If you are considering whether a college education is a good investment for yourself, your children, or your grandchildren, the answer is yes. It will cost between $15,000 and $50,000, depending on your choice of schools, vocation, and number of years before entering college. But the investment can yield a good return. Studies show that a college graduate earns $250,000 to $400,000 more during his life than does a person with only a high school diploma. Time, money, and effort invested in education increase the productivity of the individual. This investment in human capital is similar to an investment in capital equipment for a plant that increases productivity, which in turn yields an increase in profits. A college education can bring more than just financial rewards. The ability to think and to plan is stimulated in college. There are fewer divorces among college graduates. A college education can add a greatly enlarged dimension to life. And it is an asset that cannot be confiscated through taxation or other means.

There are many who want to believe that financial gains come by luck. I do not believe in luck. "Luck" comes when preparedness and opportunity get together. I have found that the more I place myself in the path of opportunity, the luckier I become. I have never learned a new tax law or mastered a new investment concept that I haven't had an opportunity to use advantageously immediately.

As I observe many around me, I am reminded of the man who stood in front of a wood burning stove and said, "Give me some heat and I'll give you some wood." But that's just not the nature of the wood burning stove. The wood must come first. The same is true of preparation, so do not skimp on this important ingredient. Put adequate wood in your burner, and it will yield the warmth of financial security.

However, never make the mistake of thinking that you can rest on your laurels of accumulated knowledge, for you are living in a dynamic world of change that makes it absolutely essential to obtain new information every day. I hope you did not end your education upon your graduation, but that yours was truly a commencement exercise whereupon you began your education.

The Earning Period

The second period of your financial life will be your "earning" period. This will probably last for around forty years, from age twenty-five to age sixty-five. This is when you apply the vocation that you have learned during the first period of your life.

Have you ever thought of how much money will come your way during those forty earning years, or have you just thought of your earnings as so much money a month? Add it up and you'll see that a tremendous amount of money will pass your way. Even if you never earn more than $525 a month, over a quarter of a million dollars will pass your way. If you earn $1,050 a month, over half a million dollars will pass your way. If you earn as much as $2,500 a month, over a million dollars will pass your way.

Monthly Income	10 Years	20 Years	30 Years	40 Years
$ 500	$ 60,000	$120,000	$ 180,000	$240,000
600	72,000	144,000	216,000	288,000
800	96,000	192,000	288,000	384,000
1,000	120,000	240,000	360,000	480,000
1,500	180,000	360,000	540,000	720,000
2,000	240,000	480,000	720,000	960,000
2,500	300,000	600,000	900,000	1,200,000
3,000	360,000	720,000	1,080,000	1,440,000

As you can see from the above chart, there is no question that a lot of money will come your way. What's the problem? It's how to keep some of it from passing through your fingers, isn't it?

. . . at only $2000 per month, $960,000 will pass through your hands during your earning years . . .

The Secret of Accumulation of Wealth

Let me share with you a very simple secret for the accumulation of wealth. The secret has only ten words in it and is so simple you will be tempted to discard it. But if you remember it and put it to use, it will be of great value to you for the remainder of your life. The secret is this: "A part of all I earn is mine to keep."

You may be tempted to say, "Everything I earn is mine to keep." It isn't so, is it? It belongs to the IRS, the baker, the butcher, the mortgage company, the church. If you were to place in a line, in the order of their importance to you, all those whom you wanted to receive a portion of your paycheck, would you place yourself at the head of the line? Is that where you have been putting yourself? If you are like so many others, you've put yourself at the end of the line, trying to save what is left over and finding that your ability to spend up to and beyond your income is utterly amazing. You must learn to pay yourself first or, if not first, at least along with the others.

If you were to save one-tenth of all you earned and did it for ten years, how much money would you have? A whole year's salary at one time, of course. And that's not all, for you would put this money to work, and before long you would have much more working for you.

The Yearning or Golden Years

The third period in your life will be your retirement years. These will be either your "yearning" years or your "golden" years, depending on the financial decisions you make during your "earning" years.

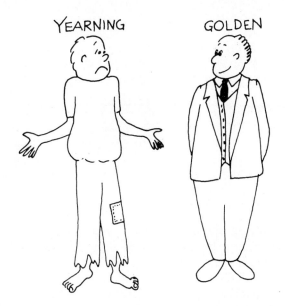

YEARNING   GOLDEN

If you are a male of age sixty-five, you will probably live to around seventy-nine years of age. If one of us females makes it to sixty-five, please be prepared to have us for a very long time. You can hardly kill off an old woman—we are sturdy! My oldest client is ninety-six years of age. Three years ago I got her to quit investing for growth!

Will this period of your life take care of itself? The answer is NO. The future belongs to those who prepare for it—and how tragically few are preparing!

Why, in a nation with a high per capita income and unparalleled prosperity, do 98 percent of our citizens reach sixty-five without having made adequate preparation for retiring in financial dignity?

Perhaps they—and you—have been lulled into a false sense of security by the cozy sound of the words Social Security. (Social Security, especially if you say it softly and slowly, does sound like a warm puppy.) You may find out all too soon that it should have been called "Social Insecurity." By that time it may be too late to alter your financial fate.

Actually, Social Security was never meant to provide you with financial independence. It was designed to prevent mass destitution. If you count on it at all, which I don't recommend, treat it as a very miniscule part of your financial plan, for the probability of it making a meaningful contribution to your retirement is slim.

It may surprise you to learn that when you reach the age to qualify for Social Security benefits, if your income from it and other sources is insufficient for you to live in financial dignity, making it necessary for

you to continue to work, you will forfeit all or most of your Social Security benefits over $6,000 (scheduled to go to $6,480) until you reach age seventy.

Today, 3.6 million of our citizens over sixty-five are caught in this financial trap and are forced to lose Social Security benefits; 1.1 million of these have reduced benefits; and 2.5 million are working but do not earn enough to lose benefits.

Most of them paid their hard-earned dollars into the system all of their working years. But they are disqualified from receiving benefits because these are not enough to keep body and soul together, for their average Social Security payment is only $385.51 per month.

If they had made provisions outside of Social Security, they could now be receiving unlimited income from capital in the form of dividends, rents, interest, and royalties and still be receiving their Social Security checks.

You may live a long time; yet longevity may be a mixed blessing. You may decide how long you will work, or it may be decided for you, but the decision of how long you will live is not in your hands.

Present-day medical science is getting so good at making us live longer that for every ten years we live, they add another four years to our life expectancy. Medical science may be adding years to your life, but it is still up to you to add some life to those years. Money is a necessity. It will not of itself bring you happiness—it will only give you options. However, I have yet to meet a person who found joy in poverty.

Never confuse piety and poverty. Until you are financially independent, you are an economic slave. Slavery does not bring the self-esteem each of us must possess. I believe our Maker wants us all to prosper and be in good health.

Have you ever considered what the difference is between an "old man" and an "elderly gentleman" in the eyes of the world? It's no other than income.

How Much Money Will You Need?

Since one of your objectives is to have sufficient funds to retire in financial dignity, you might ask how much will it take? I really don't know, but let's see if we can get a bit of a handle on the situation.

The amount of money you will need at retirement time will depend on the standard of living you wish to maintain, the number of years before you retire, the destruction inflation will have brought to the purchasing power of money, your ability and willingness to apply what you'll learn in this book to produce the maximum income and growth during retirement, and the number of years you will live.

To get some idea of the amount that may be required, let's begin

Table 1-1. Additional Income Needed (in Dollars)
at Retirement, with Various Inflation Rates

Years Until Retirement	5%	8%	10%	12%	15%
10	1.63	2.16	2.59	3.11	4.05
11	1.71	2.33	2.85	2.48	4.65
12	1.80	2.52	3.14	3.90	5.35
13	1.89	2.72	3.45	4.36	6.15
14	1.98	2.94	3.80	4.89	7.08
15	2.08	3.17	4.18	5.47	8.14
16	2.18	3.43	4.60	6.13	9.36
17	2.29	3.70	5.05	6.87	10.77
18	2.41	4.00	5.56	7.69	12.38
19	2.53	4.32	6.12	8.61	14.23
20	2.65	4.66	6.73	9.65	16.37
21	2.79	5.03	7.40	10.80	18.82
22	2.93	5.44	8.14	12.10	21.64
23	3.07	5.87	8.95	13.55	24.89
24	3.23	6.34	9.85	15.18	28.63
25	3.39	6.85	10.83	17.00	32.92
26	3.56	7.40	11.92	19.04	37.86
27	3.73	7.99	13.11	21.32	43.54
28	3.92	8.63	14.42	23.88	50.07
29	4.12	9.32	15.86	26.75	57.58
30	4.32	10.06	17.45	29.96	66.22
31	4.54	10.87	19.19	33.56	76.14
32	4.76	11.74	21.11	37.58	87.57
33	5.00	12.68	23.23	42.09	100.70
34	5.25	13.69	25.55	47.14	115.80
35	5.52	14.79	28.10	52.80	133.18

with what you would need if you were retiring today and then adjust your figures by what you think the future rate of inflation will be.

Table 1-1 shows rates of inflation from 5 to 15 percent. I cannot tell you what future inflation rates will be. They could subside with the change in mental attitude that is occurring across the nation—people are beginning to question the validity of trying to carry one another around on their backs. This is a judgment you must make for yourself. Table 1-1 can help you relate that judgment to dollars. Subtract your age from sixty-five to obtain the number of years before retirement (if this is the age at which you plan to retire). Read across the top and find the rate of inflation you think it is safe for you to assume. There you will find how many dollars it will take then to buy the same amount of groceries that a dollar buys today.

For example, assume that you would need $2,000 per month if you were retiring today, that you are age forty-five, that you plan to retire in twenty years at age sixty-five, and that you think the government can slow inflation to 5 percent. Go down the left-hand column to 20 and across four columns to 2.65, your adjustment factor. Now let's adjust: $2,000 x 2.65 = $5,300. This would be the amount you would need per month in twenty years to obtain the same housing, food, and clothing as you do with $2,000 today.

Inflation will probably not accommodate you by stopping when you retire, so you should plan for an additional amount to cover continued inflation.

How Much Capital Does This Require?

How much capital will it take to produce $5,300 per month?

Shall we use a 6 percent yield? If so, you will need $1,060,000 of capital ($5,300 x 200 = $1,060,000). At an 8 percent yield, you can reduce this amount to $795,000; at a 12 percent yield you can lower the amount to $530,000. That's a lot of capital. Before you become discouraged, remember that you have twenty years before you need it, and if you decide to use a portion of your principal each month during retirement, this amount can be reduced. There is nothing sacred about principal. The sacred thing is to make you and it come out together!

Incidentally, since my first book was published back in 1975, we have received thousands of calls asking why I multiplied the monthly income desired by 200 to obtain the amount of capital required. If you'll take 12 and divide by the rate of return and multiply your answer by the monthly amount, it will give you the amount of capital required to produce that monthly income. For example, 12 ÷ .06 = 200; $5,300 x 200 = $1,060,000, the capital needed to produce $5,300 per month at 6 percent. At 8 percent, you would multiply by 150 (12 ÷ .08).

Monthly Savings Needed

How much will you need to invest each month if you average 6 percent on your investment (see Table 1-2)? (Surely when you've completed this book you will be able to double that amount.)

As you can see, time is a powerful ally in accomplishing your goal. If your goal is $300,000 and you begin when you are twenty-five, you can reach it by saving $153 per month. If you wait until forty, you will need to save $429 per month.

If you put your money to work at 12 percent, and you must do that well, you can either reduce the amount you must invest by half; or better, you can increase your goal to $600,000.

Table 1-2. Monthly Savings Needed at 6% Interest
(Compounded Annually) to Attain Predetermined
Amount of Capital

AGE NOW	YEARS TO RETIRE- MENT	MONTHS TO RETIRE- MENT	*Desired Amount*			
			$200,000	$300,000	$500,000	$1,000,000
25	40	480	$ 102	$ 153	$ 255	$ 510
30	35	420	140	210	350	700
35	30	360	198	297	495	990
40	25	300	286	429	715	1430
45	20	240	426	639	1065	2130
50	15	180	674	1011	1685	3370
55	10	120	1192	1788	2980	5960

Time, Not Instant Pudding

Time can be a great ally in accomplishing your financial goal. Use it to your advantage, rather than trying to reach your goal fast, as tempting as that may be.

You will be tempted, for we live in an age of "instants." We drink instant coffee, eat instant pudding, spoon instant soup. Do not make the mistake of trying to carry this over to your money world. It takes time to accumulate a living estate. Many have difficulty accepting this fact of life. Many of our citizens have adopted an attitude of impatience, perhaps at the cost of serenity and physical and mental well-being. On the other hand, impatience to get things done deserves much of the credit for the achievements of Americans in building one of the wealthiest nations in the world.

Time is important. As a matter of fact, it is the first ingredient of my formula for financial independence.

Formula for Financial Independence

This is the formula that I have used over the years and that has been so valuable to me and my clients:

Time + Money + American free enterprise =
Opportunity to become financially independent

Let's take a good look at what effect time, the rate of return, and the amount of money you have to put to work will have in accomplishing your financial goal.

Time—The First Ingredient. If you are young and have only a small amount of money to invest, don't despair, for you possess one of the most important ingredients for financial independence—the ingredient of TIME. It doesn't take much money to compound to a tidy sum if you have time for it to grow. A savings of $30 per month started at age twenty-five is equivalent to $90 a month started at age thirty-five, $300 at age forty-five, and $1,275 at age fifty-five (as indicated in Figure 1-2, page 31).

Or, if we calculate the importance of time in reverse, a savings of $50 a month for ten years at 12 percent is less than $25 a month for fifteen years.

Perhaps you have a lump sum of $10,000. Let's look at the difference time makes in your results:

Years	At 12 Percent
10	$31,058
20	96,462
30	299,599
40	930,509

These figures point out the importance of starting as early as you can to reach your predetermined goal. I hope you are granted a large amount of this first ingredient, and that you learn early the importance of putting each day of it to maximum use.

Money—The Second Ingredient. This is an ingredient that you have every payday or that you have acquired through previous paydays of your own or your industrious and generous forefathers.

Your next challenge is to put this money to work for yourself as hard as you no doubt had to work to get it. To become financially independent, you must save and let your money grow. Unfortunately, I observe many people who save and let savings institutions grow, building magnificent skyscrapers that add impressively to our skyline.

Rate of Return

The rate of return that you receive on your funds will be determined by how skillfully you put your money to work under our free enterprise system.

You have looked at how important time is in the accomplishment of your goal; now let's introduce another important factor, the rate of return, and look at the difference an additional 5 percent can make:

$10,000 Lump Sum Invested at 10 Percent and 15 Percent

Years	At 10 Percent	At 15 Percent	Difference
10	$ 25,937	$ 40,455	$ 14,518
20	67,274	163,665	96,391
30	174,494	662,117	487,623
40	452,592	2,678,635	2,226,043

If we assume that you can invest $100 per month, your results would be:

$100 Per Month Invested at 10 Percent and 15 Percent

Years	Amount Invested	At 10 Percent	At 15 Percent	Difference
10	$ 12,000	$ 21,037	$ 28,018	$ 6,981
20	24,000	75,602	141,372	65,770
30	36,000	217,131	599,948	382,817
40	48,000	584,222	2,455,144	1,870,922

Don't Fight the Battle Alone. Are you amazed at the difference an additional 5 percent can make in your results?

At 10 percent you contributed $58,000 in forty years, and the savings institution contributed $978,814 from their profits by investing your money in American industry, real estate, and natural resources.

On the other hand, if you obtained 15 percent on your investment, you contributed $58,000, and you let American industry, real estate, and natural resources contribute $5,075,779 to your wealth, for a difference of $4,038,965.

It is not necessary to fight the battle alone if you will apply the information contained in this book so that American free enterprise can be of help to you.

The Eighth Wonder

One of the best ways to obtain a graphic picture of the importance of the rate of return is to study compound interest tables. Compound interest tables are fascinating. In my opinion, the "eighth wonder of the world" is not the Astrodome, but compound interest. Tables 1 through 6 in the Appendix show compound interest results and will be of immeasurable help to you in your financial programming. Don't yield to the temptation of saying, "Oh, I probably can't understand them," and flip casually by. Take a moment now to study them and you'll be surprised to find some real jewels of information. I'll help you apply the information so you won't have to go it alone.

Lump-Sum Investment

Appendix Table 1 will show you how much a $10,000 lump sum will grow over the years at varying rates of return. If you haven't yet saved $10,000, just keep dropping zeros until you reach your category. If you are fortunate enough to have $100,000, just add a zero.

For example, if you have $10,000 to invest for a goal that is twenty years away and you can average 12 percent on your money, you will have $96,462 when that time arrives, exclusive of taxes. If you have thirty years, that $10,000 will grow to $299,599; in forty years it will be $930,509.

Monthly Investment Results

Let's assume you do not have a lump sum, but can invest $1,200 a year, for an average of $100 per month.

If you average 12 percent over a twenty-year period, your results will be $96,838; in thirty years, $324,351; and in forty years, $1,030,970. As you can see, the secret of financial independence is not brilliance or luck, but the discipline to save a portion of all you earn and to put it to work aggressively (see Appendix Table 2).

Annual Investment Required

In the Appendix you'll find two other very interesting compound interest, or yield, tables. Table 3 enables you to determine how much you'll need to save per year to accomplish your predetermined goal. This table is based on a $100,000 investment. Just multiply to adjust to your goal. For example, you've determined you'll need $500,000 when you retire in twenty years, and you think you can average a minimum of 12 percent on your investments. That means that you must save $6,195, or $516 per month, to accomplish your goal.

If you started thirty years before retirement, you could reduce this to $154 per month.

Lump Sum Required

Further, let's assume you would like to know what lump sum you would need to invest at various rates of return to equal a given amount at the end of a specified period (see Appendix Table 4).

Again, if you have twenty years before retirement and you can average 12 percent on your investments and desire $500,000, you will need to make a lump-sum investment of $51,835. To point out the importance of time, if you had started thirty years before you would only need a lump-sum investment of $16,700.

Three Things You Can Do With a Dollar

There are only three things you can do with a dollar—spend, loan, or own. If you decide to spend your dollars, I hope you've had a good time, but you have cut off our conversation. The only money that I can help you invest is the money you decide to keep. If you decide you are not going to spend it now, but are going to keep it to spend at a later date—not that you are never going to spend it, since that's just too cruel a thought—there are only two things you can do with a dollar: loan or own.

You may "loan" it to a savings institution, placing it in what is commonly called a "guaranteed" fixed position. We'll look at ways this can be done in a later chapter.

You may also place your dollars in a position so that you can "own." You may own shares of American industry, real estate, commodities, energy, cinema, precious metals, precious gems, rare stamps, art objects, antiques, and so on. We shall discuss the many ways that you can "own" throughout this book.

Let me now share with you the Rule of 72. It's a very simple one that you can use without elaborate compound interest tables.

The Rule of 72

I have a degree in economics and finance, yet I was never taught this rule in college. It's an extremely valuable rule and you'll find it very useful. The Rule of 72 gives you the answer to the question of how long it will take to double your money—to make $1 become $2—at various rates of return.

If you obtain 1 percent on your money, it will take 72 years for $1 to become $2. If you obtain 1.3 percent, it will take 55.4 years; if you obtain 6 percent, it will take 12 years; if you obtain 12 percent, it will take six years; at 18 percent, four years; and at 24 percent it takes three years (see Figure 1-1).

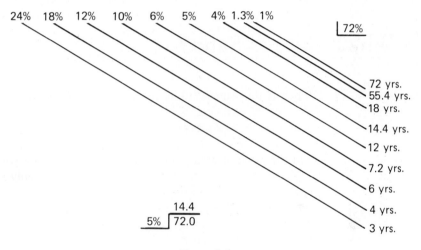

Figure 1-1.

When you came to 1.3 percent in the example above, did you say to yourself, "In these enlightened times no one would loan money at 1.3 percent." Unless you are one of the informed minority who have read and applied Chapter 13 of my last two books, you are probably loaning your money at 1.3 percent or less on the cash surrender value portion of your life insurance.

With the Rule of 72, you can see that at 6 percent $1,000 becomes:

$2,000 in 12 years
4,000 in 24 years
8,000 in 36 years

At 12 percent, $1,000 becomes:

$ 2,000 in   6 years
4,000 in 12 years
8,000 in 18 years
16,000 in 24 years
32,000 in 30 years
64,000 in 36 years

As you can see, it does make a difference how well you invest your money.

Which Rate Is Safer?

Which is the "safest" thing to do with your money—"loan" or "own"?

In the past, has it been safer to "loan" your money to a savings institution at 4–6 percent (or even for brief periods of time at 18 percent), or to "own" shares of American industry, real estate, and energy, with the hope of averaging 15 to 40 percent or higher? We shall take an in-depth look in this book at which way has truly been the "safest" long-term approach to money management. Suffice it to say here that if you have to wait eighteen years at 4 percent or twelve years at 6 percent for $1 to become $2, you have lost the fight, because inflation has more than doubled your cost of living—to say nothing of your loss through the tax bite.

Even at 10 percent your exercise has been similar to that of the little frog who was trying to hop out of the well. Every time he hopped up one foot, he slid back two. If you ignore change, inflation, and taxes, your money exercises may prove to parallel those of the little frog in the fairy tale of the frog and the princess, but without the kiss of the princess to miraculously make you an affluent prince.

"Stability" vs. "Safety"

In a later chapter I'll discuss the matter of stability and safety in more detail, but suffice it to say here that one of the most common mistakes made in the investment of money is that people confuse two very similar words that have very different meanings. These two words are "stability" and "safety." Stability is the return of the same number of dollars at a point of time in the future. "Safety" is the return of the same amount of food, clothing, and shelter. You can be "stable" and be far from "safe." This book is dedicated to helping you be a "safe" investor.

The $300,000 Estate

I encourage my clients to have as their minimum goal a $300,000 estate. I'll have to admit as soon as they reach it, I raise the ante. Your goal should be a minimum of this amount; and the younger you are, the higher your goal must be because inflation will continue to erode your purchasing power. A 6 percent yield on $300,000 is only $1,500 per month, and that's not easy street today. A 12 percent yield is $3,000.

Figure 1-2 is a handy chart showing how much you need to invest annually or monthly to reach a goal of $300,000 at 12 percent.

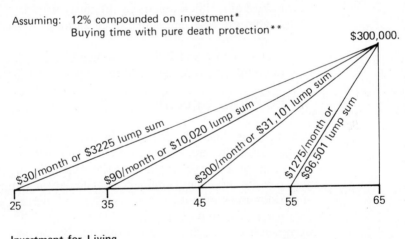

Assuming: 12% compounded on investment*
Buying time with pure death protection**

Investment for Living		
Age	Monthly or Lump Sum	Monthly Cost for $300,000 Death Insurance
25	$ 30 $ 3,225	$27
35	90 10,020	28
45	300 31,101	52
55	$1275 $96,501	113

*University of Michigan, Bureau of Business Research, Common Stocks & Yields.
**Based on rates of a leading insurance company.

Figure 1-2.

To all my good engineering friends, let me say that I am quite aware that money does not compound in a straight line, but in a curve. However, I have learned that only a few people can relate to a curve, but almost everyone can relate to a straight line— hence the straight lines. You will find a chart with the proper curves in Chapter 13, "Life Insurance—The Great National Consumer Dilemma. In that chapter, I also tell you how to buy time.

Pennies Become Millions

You may have seen this vivid illustration before, but let me repeat it, for it is such a graphic example of compounding.

Let's assume you had a choice of working thirty-five days with a pay of $1,000 per day or working for a penny the first day and doubling the amount each day for thirty-five days. Which job offer would you take?

If you took the first choice, at the end of the thirty-fifth day you would have received $35,000. What would you have received if you had made the second choice? You would have received $339,456,652.80. As you can see, one penny compounded at 100 percent per day produces over a third of a billion dollars by the thirty-fifth day. I realize this is an exaggerated example, but your rate of earnings is very important today in your quest for financial independence.

Get to know and fully comprehend interest rates, leverage, and how to compound your capital through good investments.

To Be More Specific

Perhaps your timetable does not fit into neat little five- and ten-year segments, and the money you have to invest is not in blocks of a $10,000 lump sum or $100 per month. In the Appendix you'll find tables that give you the necessary numbers to calculate a lump-sum investment at various rates of return from 2-1/2 to 15 percent and from one to fifty years. The first, Appendix Table 5, is titled "One Dollar Principal Compounded Annually." For example, if you have seventeen years before retirement and have $14,000 to put to work for that purpose, and you think you can average 12 percent, your factor would be 6.8660: $14,000 x 6.8660 = $96,124.

Let's assume that you can invest an additional $160 per month. Look at Appendix Table 6, titled "One Dollar Per Annum Compounded Annually." Go down the 12 percent column until you are opposite seventeen years and you will find your factor of 54.7497; $160 per month, times 12, times 54.7497 is $105,119.

So in seventeen years with a $10,000 lump-sum investment to which you have added $160 per month, you would have $201,243 (exclusive of taxes).

In 1748 Benjamin Franklin wrote, "Money is of a prolific, generating nature. Money can beget money, and its offspring can beget more." His was a definition and joyous explanation of the nature of money and one that can be of great value to you. Franklin's words "Money is of a prolific, generating nature" have a biblical ring to them, and well they may, because the Bible makes us aware that we are required to be good stewards of money.

You Are the Steward

I firmly believe that every dollar that comes your way comes there for a purpose. A portion of that dollar should be spent for the necessities of life, a portion for luxuries, a portion should be given away, and a portion should be invested for tomorrow's goods and services. I am also thoroughly convinced that you are the steward of every dollar that comes your way, and if you are not a good steward of that money it will be taken away from you.

The story of the talents in the Bible are as true today as they were when they were recorded. In Matthew 25:14-29 you will find these words:

> Again, the Kingdom of Heaven can be illustrated by the story of a man going into another country, who called together his servants and loaned them money to invest for him while he was gone. He gave $5,000 to one, $2,000 to another, and $1,000 to the last—dividing it in proportion to their abilities—and then left on his trip. The man who received the $5,000 began immediately to buy and sell with it and soon earned another $5,000. The man with $2,000 went right to work, too, and earned another $2,000.
>
> But the man who received the $1,000 dug a hole in the ground and hid the money for safekeeping. After a long time their master returned from his trip and called them to him to account for his money. The man to whom he had entrusted the $5,000 brought him $10,000.
>
> His master praised him for good work. "You have been faithful in handling this small amount," he told him, "so now I will give you many more responsibilities. Begin the joyous tasks I have assigned to you."
>
> Next came the man who had received $2,000, with the report, "Sir, you gave me $2,000 to use, and I have doubled it."

"Good work," his master said. "You are a good and faithful servant. You have been faithful over this small amount, so now I will give you much more."

Then the man with the $1,000 came and said, "Sir, I knew you were a hard man, and I was afraid you would rob me of what I earned, so I hid your money in the earth and here it is." But his master replied, "Wicked man! Lazy slave! Since you knew I would demand your profit, you should at least have put my money into the bank so I could have some interest. Take the money from this man and give it to the man with the $10,000. For the man who uses well what he is given shall be given more, and he shall have abundance. But from the man who is unfaithful, even what little responsibility he has shall be taken from him."

Let's analyze what the master considered good stewardship. He praised the two who "bought and sold" with the money entrusted to them, and gave them more. He severely reprimanded the one who dug a hole and buried the money, saying, "You should at least have put the money into the bank so I could have some interest." Note, however, that this was not what he recommended. Had the

Table 1-3. Interest Rates (Percent) Paid by Savings
and Loan Associations and by Banks

Year	Savings Accounts in Savings Associations	Deposits in Commercial Banks
1947	2.3%	0.9%
1948	2.3	0.9
1949	2.4	0.9
1950	2.5	0.9
1951	2.6	1.1
1952	2.7	1.2
1953	2.8	1.2
1954	2.9	1.3
1955	2.9	1.4
1956	3.0	1.6
1957	3.3	2.1
1958	3.38	2.21
1959	3.53	2.36
1960	3.86	2.56
1961	3.90	2.71
1962	4.08	3.18
1963	4.17	3.31
1964	4.19	3.42
1965	4.23	3.69
1966	4.45	4.04
1967	4.67	4.24
1968	4.68	4.48
1969	4.80	4.87
1970	5.06	4.95
1971	5.33	4.78
1972	5.40	4.65
1973	5.50	5.12
1974	5.55	5.15
1975	5.25	5.00
1976	5.25	5.00
1977	5.25	5.00
1978	5.50	5.25
1979	5.50	5.25
1980	5.50	5.25
1981	5.50	5.25

servant lived in the United States during the period when our banks paid 3 percent interest, in order for the money to have doubled, the master would have to have taken a twenty-four-year trip. Even if he had earned up to 5 percent, it would have taken 14.4 years. And at 8 percent it would have been a nine-year trip. By most standards, these would be very long trips.

Table 1-3 shows the rates paid by savings and loan associations and by banks from 1947 through 1981 for passbook savings.

Summary

In this first chapter you and I have come a long way toward determining what your goal must be to attain financial independence. We've had to cover a few charts and tables to give perspective to your challenge and to give you the assurance that you'll win the money game.

You've already seen that it will be necessary for you to save for the future so that you can fulfill your obligation to yourself, to your family, and to society. But you've also seen that you have all the requirements for financial independence and that you will not have to fight this battle alone. Your dollars can have fantastic earning power. Throughout the pages of this book you'll find your own personal powerpack.

Application

All the knowledge in the world will do you no good unless you apply it to your own particular set of circumstances. So at the end of each chapter I'll give you some questions to answer, some financial data to collect, and some specific tasks to perform.

May I suggest that you obtain a loose-leaf notebook and that you paste these words on the outside:

___(Your name)'s___ Progress Report Toward Financial Independence

Begin your notebook by listing the following questions and your answers to them. This notebook is for your eyes only, or for yours and those of your spouse if you are married, so be very honest with yourself and very specific.

1. What source or sources of income do I want to depend on at age 65?

2. How many years before I plan to retire?

3. What monthly income would I like to have if I were retiring today?

4. What inflation factor should I use?

5. How much will I need per month at retirement?
6. If I choose the guaranteed route, how much capital will be required?
7. What rate of growth on my investments is my minimum objective?
8. If I choose the variable route, how much capital will be required?
9. How much can I put to work today: (a) lump sum, (b) monthly?
10. What books am I going to read to assure myself that I'll develop and keep a winning attitude about money? You will find a recommended list in the Appendix.

Chapter 2

The New Math of Inflation

There are four prime reasons you must learn to invest:

1. To put inflation to work for you.
2. To increase your income.
3. To make your capital grow.
4. To learn to turn your tax liabilities into assets.

In this chapter we'll take an unemotional look at inflation and the devastating path it has cut across the face of the United States, bringing havoc to many a financial plan.

Inflation, the Robin Hood of the 1980s

Inflation was the Robin Hood of the 1970s and will continue to be the Super Robin Hood of the 1980s. Through the efforts of the Reagan administration. its rate of growth can decrease, but the direction is still upward even if at a decreasing rate. Nine percent inflation is admittedly better than 15 percent, but even at that rate our cost of living will double in eight years.

Accept this fact of life and make your decisions about money accordingly. If I can leave only one thought with you, after you have read this book, it is this: deal with life as it truly is and not the way you wish it were. This chapter will give you the facts about inflation. This book will enlighten you as to ways that you can make inflation work for you rather than against you. There is probably nothing in your economic life that can make as much money for you as inflation if you understand how it works, learn to embrace it rather than fear it, and harness its energy.

Inflation does not destroy wealth. It does not reduce the number of houses that builders can build, the amount of wheat that farmers can produce, or the number of telephones that Ma Bell can install. Inflation redistributes wealth. It takes it from those who do not understand how it works and gives it to those who do.

Inflation takes from the ignorant and gives to the well informed. You will be either its victim or its beneficiary. It will make you a winner or a loser. The choice is yours. It's much more fun being a winner. All you need to do is recognize that inflation is a fact of your life—an economic force in the world in which you live—and that you must protect yourself against it or suffer its dire consequences. Inflation has been your constant companion since the day you were born, and from all indications it will continue to be with you for the remainder of your life. This problem does not belong to the United States alone, but has been felt worldwide. Tolstoy chronicled that every civilized nation that has ever existed has experienced the ravages of inflation.

Poor Richard Hits the Fan

I was raised in the dust bowl of Oklahoma under the Puritan ethic embodied in *Poor Richard's Almanac*—"Work hard, be thrifty, don't borrow."

Were you raised under Poor Richard's guidelines? If you were, throw off his shackles this very minute. He'll drag you down to the bottom of inflation's ocean, and you won't surface in time for resuscitation.

Have you been exposed for years to the "Prudent Man's Rule," so dear to the hearts of regulatory agencies that decide whether you have prudently managed pension funds under your trusteeship or other fiduciary responsibilities? If you have, and have faithfully followed the old guidelines of 40 percent in corporate bonds and the remainder in very, very blue chip common stocks, you and the beneficiaries of your pension plan have been losers and from all indications will continue to be losers. With the continued battering of inflation, the "Prudent Man's Rule" has now become the "Stupid Man's Rule."

You will find the "Poor Richard" and "Prudent Man's" philosophy very hard to escape, for it is all around you. Today as you drive down the freeway to work, strategically positioned at a curve in the road, in brilliant lights, you may see a billboard emblazoned in bold print that reads:

"INVEST IN SERIES E BONDS TO GUARANTEE YOUR FUTURE"

Is this false advertising? Can you name a ten-year period in the past thirty years when investing in a Series E bond has "guaranteed your future"? Can you name even one year in the past decade when, after inflation (and later after taxes), your money maintained the only value worth maintaining—its purchasing power?

I read about an interview recently in which the U.S. Savings Bonds people were asked, "Does it pay to save when the inflation rates have been exceeding the rates on Savings Bonds?" And the added question was put to them, "Under these circumstances can you really say you are saving?"

The Savings Bond spokesman's reply was, "Yes, for if you didn't save, you'd be that much farther behind." It would appear that he was conceding that a loss was involved, but he insisted a loss could be a gain.

If it doesn't pay to save, you might be asking, does it pay to spend? Often it does, if you have exchanged your paper money for something more durable that has an opportunity to retain its value—in other words, if you have moved your money out of paper and into things. Once you have brought yourself to making this decision, you have opened yourself to a wide range of other decisions: Which things? When? At what price? At what location? This book should give you some of the answers.

You live in a world of change. Every day is a new day. That's why my profession as a Certified Financial Planner is such an exciting one and why I love it so much. That's why this book has "dynamics" in its title. Financial survival requires the best use of your intelligence, experience, agility, continuous study, daily diligence, and discipline. But your rewards can be so great that the investment of your time and energy in this endeavor can make it all worthwhile. There will be times, if you are not always on guard, when you may be lulled into a false sense of security, and you'll temporarily let down your defenses. You may hear one of the government's "inflation fighters" make an optimistic announcement, or you may have received something comparable to the big WIN button we were given back in the Ford administration to wear, but don't be deceived. Inflation will continue. (In case you've forgotten, WIN stood for Whip Inflation Now.)

What Causes Inflation?

Your government itself is the chief cause of inflation. It does this not by trying to give you what you hate, but by trying to give you the goodies you want—such as full employment, health insurance that you won't buy for yourself, "entitlement," a word that has been bandied around in recent years. Many politicians equate entitlement to being "entitled to" support from the cradle to the grave, often without any relationship to effort on the part of the recipient, just because they were fortunate enough to have been born in the United States.

If our forefathers were writing the Bill of Rights today, after having lived in our environment for a number of years, they would add a clause to the bill saying that every person is entitled to a job. Before World War II this was not a commonly held belief. Before then, prices went up, but they also went down, so prices remained essentially stable. Now that so many believe in their right to job security and are abetted by the philosophy of a host of congressional members that you can solve any problem if you'll just cover it with enough appropriations, inflation has gone on a rampage, not only here but abroad, for we have exported this concept.

The year after World War II, Congress passed the "full employment act," which declared that our government would vigorously promote both price stability and full employment. Even a college freshman with no more exposure to economics than Economics 101 should know that those are two inconsistent goals.

The Employment Act of 1946 was to be the embodiment of utopia, and brilliant government administrators would do a balancing act whereby high employment rates could be generated by accepting higher inflation. But what has the implementation of this theory wrought? We have found that employment that results from inflation lasts for only a short period of time, and in order to restimulate employment, inflation must again be accelerated. Always remember that full employment brings the politicians more votes than does licking inflation; therefore the majority of politicians will opt for full employment.

Inflation also makes it easier to meet any economic liquidity crises that may occur. For example, look at what happened to Penn Central and Franklin National Bank. There was a time when bankruptcies, like unemployment, were natural phenomena. Today, Washington abhors such occurrences, so it lends money to Lockheed, becomes Franklin National Bank's low-cost supplier of funds, and guarantees Chrysler's loans and New York City's bonds.

It is incongruous that a government of what is billed as a capitalistic free-enterprise system took badly needed capital from other areas of our economy and subsidized Chrysler, one of our worst-managed companies. This was done in the name of preservation of jobs, when that same amount of money put to work in more efficient areas would have created more jobs. To add to this unbelievable situation, the support came at a time when one of the most efficiently run industries, the oil industry, was being criticized and penalized for making profits. When we reward the inefficient and penalize the efficient, we increase inflation by disrupting the natural forces of supply and demand. We also put more pressure on government to deficit-spend and these deficits lead directly to more inflation.

Dilution

If you will learn to substitute the word *dilution* every time you see the word *inflation,* you will come to have a better understanding of inflation. As Congress votes to expand currency and credit to finance bail-outs of the automobile industry, the housing industry, and welfare, it in turn dilutes the purchasing power of your money. As you can readily see, if another million dollars of currency were to be printed and circulated for every million already in circulation, twice as many dollars would be chasing the same amount of goods and services, so they would rise to twice their original price. The true value of goods and services has not risen. The value of the currency has been cut in half by doubling its quantity—hence dilutions have occurred.

The U.S. Inflation Rate

What has been the rate of inflation in the United States? Let's examine the past by beginning at the turn of the century—1900. Figure 2-1 plots the purchasing power of our dollar from 1900 through 1981.

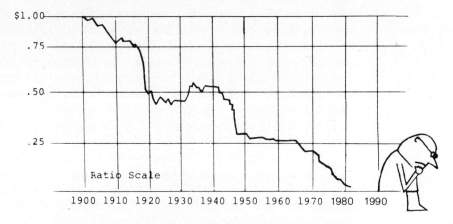

Figure 2-1. Purchasing power of the dollar.

A more graphic way of looking at the effect of inflation is to look at a dollar composed of quarters that you have held since 1900. You now go to the grocery store to make a purchase. How much do you think your dollar will buy in the form of goods and services in comparison with what it bought in 1900?

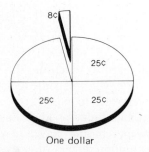

One dollar

Your dollar has lost 92 percent of the only value it has—what it will buy. A dollar has no value in and of itself. Its only value is what you can exchange it for in the marketplace. What you want to store for the future is not so many dollars, but so many pairs of shoes, tubes of lipstick, and hamburgers.

Think of Bread

In 1940, you could go to your local grocery store and buy ten loaves of bread for $1. By 1950, you could buy only six loaves. By 1960, you could buy only four, by 1970 only three, and by 1980 only one. How many will your dollar buy today? It is the same dollar, but it has lost the major portion of its only value.

If I can do nothing else for you in this book but help you to convert your thinking from dollars into bread, I will have done you an immense favor. I warn you, it is an emotional transition that only a few can make. If you can make it, you will be in the minority—but remember, it's only the minority that become financially independent.

Between 1940 and 1979, the dollar held its own in only two years, and then by less than 1 percent. Not even a professional gambler would accept those odds. Yet, if you are holding a dollar today, you are betting against those odds. If you are a saver, placing your savings in a "guaranteed" position, you are a gambler, and if the past is any indication of the future, you are "guaranteed" to lose!

What if I were to say to you, "I want to recommend a stock for your serious consideration. I know that its record has not been very good, but I have faith that it will improve. It was selling for $100 in 1952; by 1957 it had dropped to $96; by 1962 to $88; by 1967 to $79; by 1972 to $63; and by 1977 it was $44. Today it is at $28, but don't let that discourage you. I still have faith in this investment, and I want you to invest in it." If I were to make such a "buy" recommendation to you, what would you say to me? Before you say, "You've got to be kidding!" I want you to know that this investment is recommended by most of our state and national banks, by all of our savings and loan companies, by all of the nation's life insurance companies that sell cash surrender value policies, by your city, and by the federal government itself. What is this investment? It is the U.S. dollar! (See Figure 2-2.)

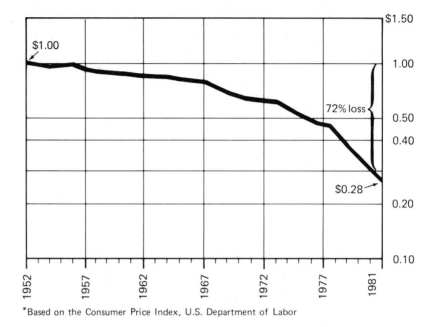

*Based on the Consumer Price Index, U.S. Department of Labor

Figure 2-2. Purchasing power of the U.S. dollar, 1952-1981.

It Is the U.S. Dollar

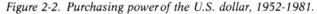

"Guaranteed" dollars are recommended as a good, "safe" investment for you by all savings institutions and insurance companies that sell cash surrender value life insurance; yet they never want a "guaranteed" dol-

" IT IS THE U.S. DOLLAR!"

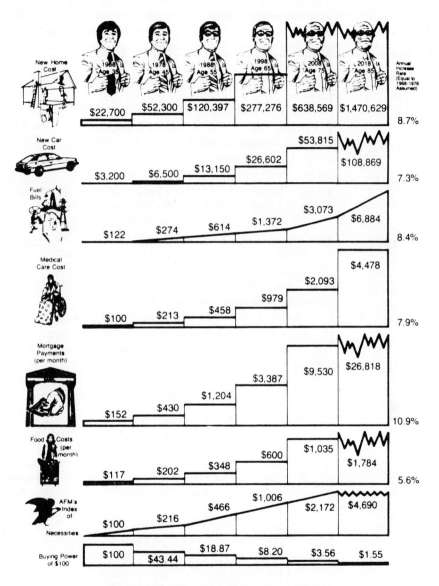

Figure 2-3. Effect of inflation on purchases.

lar for themselves. They want to "guarantee" your principal, "guarantee" your rate of return, and "guarantee" that your dollar will work for them—usually harder than it works for you. You will receive a "guarantee" that you can always get back each deflating dollar you have placed with them (excluding "your" savings account with the life insurance company). You are also guaranteed that you will never receive any more than that dollar, plus any compound interest you may have left with them, regardless of how much your money has earned for the institution to which you loaned it, and regardless of what the cost of living has become.

In my seminars I sometimes hand out the chart shown in Figure 2-3 because it gives a picture of inflation as it relates to the things we buy. I remember a lady looking at it and saying, "I think these figures are exaggerated and I just can't accept them." I asked her if she could accept the 1968-78 figures. Her answer was, "Oh yes, because they actually happened." These figures are only an extrapolation of what happened from 1968 to 1978. You may use them as you see fit.

If you are still in a state of shock, Table 2-1 will not help you regain your composure. If you assume an annual inflation rate of 7 percent in the 1980s and also assume that the tax bracket creep won't push you into a higher bracket, Table 2-1 shows what you must earn in 1990 to keep pace with what you had to earn in 1970 and 1980 in order to maintain your same standard of living.

Inflation averaged 2 percent in the 1950s, 2.3 percent in the 1960s, 6.1 percent in the first half of the 1970s, 8.8 percent the latter part of the 1970s, and reached an intermittent high of 19 percent in the early 1980s.

Table 2-1. Inflation's Effect on Incomes

If you had this income in 1970	You needed this much to be as well off in 1980	You will need this much (if inflation runs at the same pace) in 1990
$ 5,000	$ 10,676	$ 25,697
7,500	16,188	39,188
10,000	22,552	55,941
20,000	34,349	87,708
25,000	59,855	188,689
30,000	73,171	148,658
35,000	86,036	204,795
40,000	98,356	231,024
50,000	121,556	280,417
100,000	221,677	493,574

*Source: *U.S. News and World Report*, July 14, 1980.

Long-Term Inflation Outlook

What will inflation be during the remainder of the 1980s? Much depends on the growth of federal spending over the next few years. If Reaganomics is allowed to reduce goverment spending as a percentage of our nation's economic output (our Gross National Product), then there is hope that inflation will drop. If his program, or a similar program, is not carried out, the inflationary spiral will worsen.

Here is a graph that shows the correlation between inflation and government spending. As you will note, the trend has been upward since 1956 and took a big jump during the Vietnam era, as shown by the trendlines B and D. Federal encroachment on the private sector as well as inflation reached a climax in the 1974-1981 period, as you will note from trendlines A and C.

Where do we go from here? Will the trendline go back to the 1965 figure by 1983? If so, inflation should drop to 6 percent or lower, according to trendline D. Will that happen? Watch Congress and the President closely for signs of which direction inflation will take.

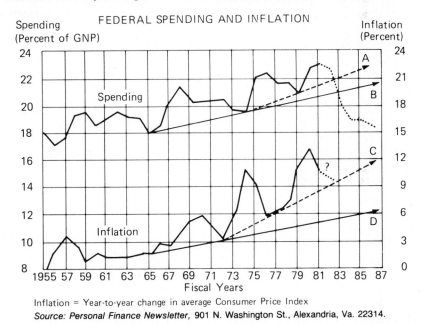

Inflation = Year-to-year change in average Consumer Price Index
Source: Personal Finance Newsletter, 901 N. Washington St., Alexandria, Va. 22314.

If inflation should get back to 6 percent, before you rejoice do realize that in 12 years you'll lose one-half of the only value your money has, its purchasing power. At 7 percent you lose it in 10; at 12 percent in 6 and at 17 percent, which some knowledgeable economists are projecting, in a brief 4.24 years.

Table 2-2. 8% Inflation

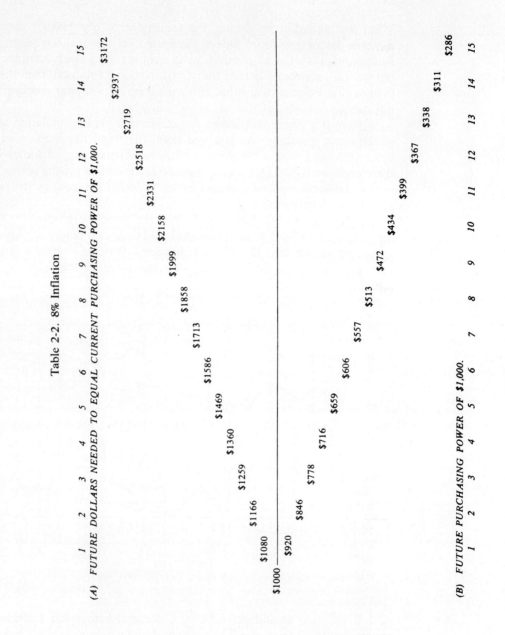

(A) FUTURE DOLLARS NEEDED TO EQUAL CURRENT PURCHASING POWER OF $1,000.

1	2	3	4	5	6	7	8	9	10	11	12	13	14	15
														$3172
													$2937	
												$2719		
											$2518			
										$2331				
									$2158					
								$1999						
							$1858							
						$1713								
					$1586									
				$1469										
			$1360											
		$1259												
	$1166													
$1080														

$1000

(B) FUTURE PURCHASING POWER OF $1,000.

1	2	3	4	5	6	7	8	9	10	11	12	13	14	15
$920														
	$846													
		$778												
			$716											
				$659										
					$606									
						$557								
							$513							
								$472						
									$434					
										$399				
											$367			
												$338		
													$311	
														$286

50

"Guaranteed Income for Life"

Avoid being enticed by advertisements for endowment policies that proclaim "an income that you can never outlive" when that income is $1,000 a month. Let's assume we can slow inflation to 8 percent. What future dollars would you need to equal the current purchasing power of $1,000? (A on Table 2-2.) Or looking at it in another way, what will be the future purchasing power of $1,000? (B on Table 2-2.)

Obtaining a Real Income of 2 Percent

If you were to say to me, "Venita, I think I deserve a 'real' income after income taxes and inflation of 2 percent," how much would you have to obtain on your investment to reach what you have decided you deserve?

My answer to you will be influenced by two factors: the rate of inflation and your tax bracket. Table 2-3 will probably be an eye opener to you. As you will see, if we can slow inflation to 8 percent and you are in a 20 percent tax bracket (I jokingly tell my seminar audiences that they're at least in a 20 percent bracket if they're warm), you must re-

Table 2-3. Rate of Return Required to Produce a "Real"
2% Income After Income Taxes and Inflation

INCOME TAX RATE	Inflation Rate										
	2%	3%	4%	5%	6%	7%	8%	9%	10%	11%	12%
50%	8.0	10.0	12.0	14.0	16.0	18.0	20.0	22.0	24.0	26.0	28.0
40%	6.7	8.3	10.0	11.6	13.3	15.0	16.7	18.4	20.0	21.7	23.3
30%	5.7	7.1	8.6	10.0	11.4	12.9	14.3	15.7	17.1	18.6	20.0
20%	5.0	6.3	7.5	8.8	10.0	11.3	12.5	13.8	15.0	16.3	17.5

INSTRUCTIONS:
1. First, select the column which matches the inflation rate (2% to 12%).
2. Second, select the line which matches the income tax rate (20% to 50%).
3. The number which appears at the intersection of the column and line indicates the rate of return necessary to offset the combined effect of income taxes and inflation. (For example, if you assume inflation will be 6%, a 50% taxpayer must earn a 16% rate of return per annum in order to show a 2% real growth after adjusting for both income taxes and inflation. At 10% it goes to 24%.)

ceive 12.5 percent on your money. If you are in a 30 percent bracket and we have inflation at 10 percent, you must earn 17.1 percent. In a 40 percent bracket and at 11 percent inflation you must earn 21.7 percent; and in a 50 percent bracket and 12 percent inflation you must earn 28 percent. As you can see, you really have to run very fast today to be 2 percent ahead. If you are brave enough to want 5 percent real income after taxes and inflation, look in the Appendix.

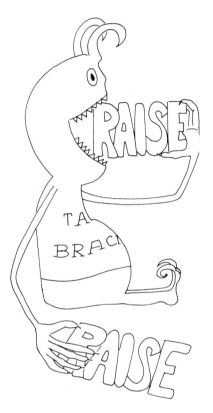

The Tax Bracket Creeper

There is a hideous monster lurking in the Internal Revenue Service tax rate schedule that you may not be aware of that can bring devastation to your financial planning. It's not the "Cookie Monster"; it is the "Bracket Creeper Monster." This monster hides out in the fine print of the IRS tax schedule, and it feeds especially on inflation. In the past ten years, the prices you have had to pay for your daily living expenses have doubled, but you may not think they are affecting you because you've been receiving cost-of-living raises to help you maintain your purchasing power. What you have failed to notice is the "Bracket Creeper Monster." Your higher income has pushed you into a higher tax bracket. For example, if your taxable income was $20,000 and you filed a joint return ten years ago, you paid $4,380 in federal income taxes, and had $15,620 left after taxes to enable you to keep pace with inflation. Your employer has by now raised your salary until your taxable income is $40,000, making you owe a federal income tax of $9,195 and leaving you $30,805 after taxes. But to keep even, you would need $61,610. Your federal income taxes increased 110 percent while your cost of living increased 100 percent.

The average working couple earning $35,200 a year will pay more than one-third of their income in taxes. On a national level, federal and state income taxes after all exemptions and deductions will average 11.6 percent of personal income; but other taxes such as sales, excise, customs, property, Social Security, and franchise more than triple the bite.

Taxes have risen a massive 46 percent as a share of personal income in the past three decades. Americans today are taxed 26 cents for every dollar earned. Social Security is our fastest rising federal tax.

The Reagan tax "cut" under ERTA cut the rate of taxation for the first time since the Kennedy administration. This does not mean that the average American will be taxed less; it only means that he would have paid even more without the rate reduction.

Under ERTA, indexing to dull the effect of the "Bracket Creeper Monster" is supposed to begin in 1985. Few believe that politicians will let this happen, because it will greatly reduce their aura of magnificent largess.

U.S. federal tax collections from citizens who do not take steps to protect themselves through proper planning increase an average of 16 percent for every 10 percent of increase in personal income. If you live in a state with progressive state income taxes, such as California and New York, inflation causes an increase in the state tax bite as well. As a result, the government has a vested interest in maintaining inflation, since our laws permit a windfall tax bonus every year we have inflation.

The New Math of Inflation

Poor Richard advised "don't borrow," but inflation has made his advice obsolete. Inflation rewards those who owe money, not those who pay cash. I'm not talking about plastic money—your VISA, MasterCard, or American Express cards. Never charge anything you can't pay for in thirty days. Never borrow for your daily living or luxuries. Only borrow long-term for investing—never for spending.

Let's look at the balance sheet of three families and see which family was the most prudent in an inflationary economy.

The Anderson family's balance sheet looks like this:

Cash	$ 10,000	Mortgage	$ 5,000
Home	10,000	Net worth	$15,000

Net worth is the difference between your assets and your liabilities and is a measure of how rich you are.

Now let's assume that prices double. The Andersons' balance sheet will now look like this:

Cash	$ 10,000	Mortgage	$ 5,000
Home	20,000	Net worth	25,000

The Andersons' net worth has now increased from $15,000 to $25,000, which at first glance appears good; however, their net worth has not doubled, as prices did. Therefore, this family has fallen behind in the inflation race. Their wealth or purchasing power has been reduced by inflation.

Now let's examine the Barton family's balance sheet:

Cash	$ 5,000	Mortgage	$ 5,000
Home	10,000	Net worth	10,000

A doubling of prices has this effect on their balance sheet:

Cash	$ 5,000	Mortgage	$ 5,000
Home	20,000	Net worth	20,000

The Bartons have held their own. They have exactly kept pace with inflation.

Now let's look at the Calloway family's balance sheet:

Cash	$ 3,000	Mortgage	$10,000
Home	12,000	Net worth	5,000

When prices doubled the Calloways' net worth looked like this:

Cash	$ 3,000	Mortgage	$10,000
Home	24,000	Net worth	17,000

The Calloways' net worth increased from $5,000 to $17,000, or more than tripled, while prices only doubled. The Calloways beat inflation.

What lesson about inflation have you learned from these three families? Is it this sad commentary: "Inflation often rewards those who owe long-term debt, not those who pay cash"?

This does not mean that you should overleverage. The inflation rate also fluctuates, and there will be times when it is increasing at a decreasing rate. When you receive such indications, reduce your leveraging until the trend reverses.

You don't have to be on the verge of bankruptcy to benefit from inflation. You can and should have cash, but you will want to have a large amount of your assets invested in things that can inflate with the cost of living. Again, I emphasize, own the thing that owns the thing. To win the inflation game in the years ahead, you will have to learn to use leverage wisely. Your assets must be primarily in investments that can rise as fast as the general price levels at each stage of the inflation cycle. There was a time when families did not feel comfortable unless they had cash in the bank. Today families feel uncomfortable with money in the bank. For the first time in our history, a large number of our citizens have taken their money from banks. Indications are that they are not going to put it back. This means that more and more of our citizens will be searching for better ways to store their future purchasing power.

Inflation Does Not Hurt the Knowledgeable

Inflation will not hurt you if you become knowledgeable and act to protect yourself from it. But you will be saddened as you look around and see the tragic faces of the hard-working, thrifty, sacrificing persons who have faithfully saved and put their money where they have been told it would be safe and have lost their money's only true value—its purchasing power. With it they have also lost the privilege of retiring in financial dignity. At least the spendthrifts had the fun of spending their money until they got off the inflation train. During their working years, their raises usually matched or exceeded their cost-of-living increases. But when they got off the inflation train and it went on without them, they had no chance of keeping up with the inflationary spiral.

The Total Portfolio

To take advantage of the transfers that inflation makes in wealth, you must begin by thinking in terms of a total portfolio that you will have positioned efficiently at the proper time to beat inflation. Your portfolio must maximize your after-tax return balanced against a level of risk that provides you with peace of mind. You will want to avoid fads unless you are equipped emotionally to act rapidly. As inflation pushes up the price of your assets, faddists will start jumping in with both feet. At this point prices will begin to overdiscount inflation. The faddist will be

selling as prices drop. You will want to be in a position to buy at that time.

To beat inflation, you will always want to be holding the right combination of assets. There is an investment for each season, but not an investment for all seasons. This means that nothing you have can be just put away in your safe-deposit box and forgotten. You must learn to be flexible and alert.

You should classify all the investment vehicles available to you as to their appropriateness for accelerating inflation or decelerating inflation. Then decide whether inflation is about to accelerate or decelerate.

Many who come to me for financial counseling have already accumulated sufficient assets, or could easily do so within a few years, to enable them to reach or work toward financial independence, if these assets were properly put to work. This may be true for you. You may be working extremely hard for your money, but unfortunately once it is obtained, instead of putting it to work for yourself, you have unknowingly given away its earning power. You cannot afford to have your money working for others. If you do, you'll lose the money and the tax game!

Summary

Inflation will be a part of your life for as long as you live. You can fear it, hide your head in the sand, and say that it doesn't exist or that it will go away, but you are only kidding yourself and inviting financial disappointments. Inflation can be your valuable ally. You can use it to increase your wealth by applying your intelligence and energy to studying the inflation cycles and positioning your assets at the proper location at the proper time. You must face the reality that you will probably never own an asset that is immune to the inflation cycle.

The facing of this reality and your determination to use these forces can be a challenging and profitable undertaking.

Application

1. Have you mentally made the necessary transition from dollars into bread?

2. Go to the library and check out a 1940 *Life* magazine or *Saturday Evening Post* and study the ads.

3. Do you think the Full Employment Act of 1946 will be repealed?

4. Are you still living under the *Poor Richard's Almanac* theory of working hard, saving, and not borrowing?

5. What steps will you take today to throw off Poor Richard's shackles and move into the real world?

6. What steps will you take to intelligently and legally cut your tax burden?

7. What steps will you take to put inflation to work for you rather than against you?

Chapter 3

Dow Power to 3000

In the first chapter of this book you learned my formula for financial independence:

Time + Money + American free enterprise =
Opportunity for financial independence

In this chapter let's substitute "American industry" for "free enterprise." Once you've done that, your next questions are: Which companies are in those industries? What performance can I reasonably expect from my money? and How much of my assets should I commit to the market?

In my opinion the timing for this book could not be better! I firmly believe that we are entering a bull market environment unprecedented in the last sixteen years and that the Dow Jones Industrial Average will be above 3000 before the end of this decade. I have never claimed to have a crystal ball, nor do I now, but I see the future convergence of so many factors that are already in motion that I can reach no other conclusion.

Now let's go about the business of learning how the stock market functions, and then at the end of the chapter I'll give you my reasons for being so enthusiastic.

Playing the Market

I often have people come up to me at our seminars or at social occasions and say almost smugly, "I play the market," as if the market were a game. They seem to think I should be pleased and should give them a loving pat on the head.

Investing is not a game. It is a very exacting science that requires skill, training, knowledge, and discipline. Even with these qualifications you will not always be right. This dynamic and fast-moving world we live in changes every minute of every day. Successful investing is a skill that you must either learn yourself or hire the professionals to do for you. You have no choice.

The Language of Investing

To become a successful investor, you'll need to know the language of investing and the kinds of securities that you'll find in the marketplace.

There are four basic types of securities. They are:

1. Common stock
2. Preferred stock
3. Bonds or debentures
4. Options

Common Stock

All corporations have common stock. If you organized a corporation for the purpose of buying a popcorn stand at the corner of Main Street and First, and sold one share of common stock to nine persons at $100 per share and one share to yourself at $100, the corporation would be capitalized at $1,000 and would have ten stockholders. In buying one of these shares, you became a shareholder of the corporation. You took an equity position and will participate in the future gains or lack of gains of the corporation for as long as you hold your share.

Preferred Stock

Preferred stock is a stock on which a fixed dividend must be paid before the common shareholder is entitled to a dividend each year. The dividend is usually higher, and if it is a cumulative preferred stock, any past dividends that have been omitted must be paid before the common shareholder is entitled to a dividend. If the preferred is also convertible, it will have a conversion ratio into the common.

There is much confusion about preferred stock. The uninitiated seem to think that "preferred" means "better." This is rarely true. Unless it's convertible, it has neither the growth potential of a common stock nor the relative stability of a bond. The word "preferred" relates to dividend precedence only. I personally believe there are better ways for an individual to invest.

Bonds or Debentures

The third type of securities is bonds or debentures. A corporate bond may be a mortgage bond. For example, if you were to invest in equipment trust certificates, you would hold a mortgage on specific freight cars.

A much larger area of the bond market is debentures. Your security for this type of bond is the general credit rating of the issuing corporation. For example, you may buy an American Telephone and Telegraph debenture at 8.70 percent due in 2002. In this instance, you do not acquire a mortgage on specific telephones, but instead your security is based on the tremendous assets and credit of AT&T.

Characteristics of common stocks and bonds can be oversimplified by stating them in this manner:

Stocks

1. Not guaranteed as to principal.
2. Not guaranteed as to rate of return.
3. Guaranteed to participate in the future destiny of the company.

Bonds

1. "Guaranteed" as to principal if assets are available at maturity.
2. "Guaranteed" as to rate of return if funds are available.
3. Not guaranteed to grow, regardless of any increase in the profits of the corporation.

I cover bonds in more detail in a later chapter.

Convertibles

There are those who think that convertible bonds give the best of two worlds—offering you the third characteristic under stocks, and the first two under bonds; however, they frequently fall short on both scores.

A convertible bond is a bond that usually carries a lower interest rate than a regular corporate bond, but is convertible into common at a specified ratio. For example, if a convertible is bought at par, which in a bond is usually $1,000, and is convertible into 100 shares of common at the holder's option and the common is selling at $10, there would be no incentive to exchange, for the bond will usually carry a higher yield than the common. However, if the market price of the common should increase to $15, you would now have a bond with a value of $1,500. If, on the other hand, the common goes below $10, you still have your bond with its higher yield acting as a cushion under the bond.

How have they performed? Not well enough for any gold stars. The size and quality of the convertible market have left much to be desired. In severe market declines, they have suffered along with their common neighbors. My emphasis in this chapter will be on common stocks. They will offer you the greatest potential for gain (or loss). You will find a vast array of them in the marketplace, which may seem confusing at first. However, we'll take a step-by-step approach, and your learning should progress rapidly. (If it does not, the next chapter teaches you how to let the professionals in the market do your investing for you.)

To be successful in the stock market, you will need to know how to use the mass network of facilities available to you for trading securities.

And you need to keep accurate records; Figures 1 and 2 in the Appendix are suggested forms for keeping records of your buys, sells, and dividends.

Listed Stocks

Stocks that are publicly held are classified as either listed or unlisted (commonly referred to as over-the-counter). "Listed" means that a stock is listed on a national or regional exchange. Listed stocks represent, in dollar assets, the largest segment of the American economy. There is probably no asset that you will ever own that you can so readily turn into cash as a stock that is listed on a national exchange. It offers almost instant liquidity.

Our four largest exchanges are the New York Stock Exchange, the American Stock Exchange, the Pacific Stock Exchange, and the Midwest Stock Exchange.

The Big Board

The New York Stock Exchange is the oldest and largest. It began very informally near the time of the birth of our nation. Our first secretary of the Treasury needed to set up a monetary system. To have a monetary system in this new nation, he needed to establish banks. To establish banks, he needed stockholders who were willing to invest capital. However, no one was willing to invest capital in bank stocks if there was no way to sell their shares. To make a market for these bank stocks and other issues, a group of eleven men used to meet under a buttonwood tree at the foot of a street called Wall, and trade among themselves and as agents for their clients. They eventually moved inside, and from this humble beginning grew the mighty New York Stock Exchange.

How Wall Street Got Its Name

It might interest you to know how Wall Street got its name. The Dutch, who first settled Manhattan Island, were very fond of pork, so they brought hogs from the Netherlands. To confine the hogs they built a wall to make a pig pen—hence the name Wall Street. It's fun to note that some of our stock market history goes back to pigs and hogs.

Unfortunately, we still have a few investors who get piggish. It is always good to remember an old saying, "In Wall Street, the bulls sometimes make it and the bears sometimes make it, but the hogs never do."*

The Over-the-Counter Market

Another vast area of the stock market is the "unlisted" market, called the over-the-counter (OTC) market, that has no "counter" or meeting place. Once, I had a lady become confused and ask me for an "under-the-counter" stock. After she told me which stock she had in mind,

---

*Evan Esar, *Twenty Thousand Quips and Quotes* (New York: Doubleday, 1968).

I decided she had accidentally hit on a good description. It was a very speculative stock.

The over-the-counter market is a vast negotiated market. For many years there was no central marketplace for these stocks. Various brokerage houses would "make a market" in a particular stock. This means that they would inventory the stock they bought and sold. There are now over 50,000 stocks traded in the over-the-counter market through a network of telephone and teletype wires linking the various brokerage houses. There is a daily "pink sheet" giving "bid" and "asked" quotations of the market makers from the previous day reporting to the National Daily Quotation Service. ("Bid" means what someone is willing to pay for the stock. "Asked" is the amount for which someone is willing to sell, subject to confirmation or change in price.) When you see a market report on a listed stock in the paper, you know that a trade actually took place at that price. In the over-the-counter market, you could have a quote with no trade taking place.

There is a wide range of quality in the stocks traded in the over-the-counter market. Traditionally, bank and insurance company stocks have been traded there, even though they have substantial assets. On the opposite end are "penny stocks" (those that sell for a nominal amount per share), which also trade there.

Often a stock is traded over-the-counter for years, and as it grows in assets and popularity, it may apply for listing on a national exchange and be accepted.

In the past, I have warned that if you are new to the market, you probably should avoid the over-the-counter market until you become more knowledgeable, but with the establishment of the National Association of Security Dealers Advanced Quotations (NASDAQ), the whole complexion of this market has changed.

NASDAQ

In February 1971, NASDAQ appeared on the scene. Various market makers of OTC stocks feed in the changes in their markets to Bunker-Ramo Central Control, which updates the "bid" and "asked" quotes on each issue every five minutes, showing the best "bid" and "asked" offers available.

NASDAQ has had a profound effect on the OTC market, making current markets available to all parts of the country at the same time and enabling dealers to give prompt and accurate service.

Your Brokerage Account

How do you use this mass network of facilities? How do you open an account with a stockbroker? It's just as easy as opening a charge account. As a matter of fact, your prospective broker will probably ask fewer questions than the department store where you applied for your last charge account. He will need to know your address, home and office telephone numbers, occupation and company for which you work, spouse's name (if married), social security number, and bank reference; and he will also want to know if you are over 21, if you are a U.S. citizen, and how you want your stocks registered.

A good financial planner will ask much more information about your assets, your age, your tax bracket, your financial objective, and your temperament. (A financial planner is a stockbroker, but a stockbroker is not necessarily a financial planner—unless he or she is trained to treat your complete financial planning needs.) If in doubt, you may want to choose one who is a member of the International Association of Financial Planners and perhaps has earned the certified financial planner designation. You'll learn more about this growing profession in a later chapter.

When you make a purchase or sale, it is a firm commitment, regardless of whether the stock goes up or down. A confirmation is mailed to you showing the number of shares of stock purchased or sold, price, commission and fees, net amount due, and settlement date. Within five business days from the trade date, you must pay for stocks you have bought. If you have sold a stock, you must deliver your stock certificate within the same period of time, and receive payment.

Commissions Are Low

Stocks carry one of the lowest commission rates for the exchange of property in the United States. Remember the commission you paid when you sold your last house? Was it 6 percent to the realtor, plus all the closing costs, making your total between 10 percent and 12 percent? You can sell 100 shares of a $40 listed stock for a commission of around 1-3/4 percent, and this rate will probably go lower. Quite a difference, isn't it?

How Your Order is Executed

After your account has been opened, you may place your orders by telephone with your broker and ask him to buy or sell securities for you. For example, let's assume that you place an order to buy 100 shares of General Widgets "at the market." Your broker then gives the order to his company's trader. The trader immediately contacts its floor broker on the floor of the exchange, who quickly walks (it's against the rules to run) to the post where General Widgets is traded. Since you want to buy, the floor broker tries to buy at the lowest price.

At the same time, there may be a farmer in Vermont who must have funds to pay for his son's college tuition. He contacts his broker, his broker contacts his floor broker, and the two of them meet at the General Widgets post. The exchange is an auction market, and bids and offers are made by outcry. That's why the floor of the exchange is so noisy and may look and sound like a madhouse. Your company's floor broker will be trying to buy for you at, say, $50 per share. The farmer's broker will be trying to sell at $50-1/4. Your broker finally decides he can't buy for you at $50, and the Vermont farmer's broker decides he can't obtain $50-1/4, so $50-1/8 is agreed upon. Millions of dollars of stock change hands daily. However, no contracts are signed, and there is no shaking of hands. In this business, your word is your bond; and when it isn't, you're no longer in this business.

A record of the trade is written on a slip of paper and handed to a runner, who places the slip in a pneumatic tube that carries it to the tape operator. Within approximately three minutes, if you are sitting in front of a tape in a brokerage office, you will see your trade coming across the screen: GWI 50-1/8. This is for 100 shares. If the trade had been for 200 shares, it would have shown GWI 2s 50-1/8. If the trade was for 1,000 shares, it would appear GWI 1,000s 50-1/8.

Round Lot, Odd Lot

All transactions shown on the tape and reported in the financial section of your newspaper are for round lots (100-share trades or multiples of 100). This does not mean, however, that if you want to own some shares of General Widgets, you have to have $5,012.50 plus commission. For instance, if you want to buy ten shares, you certainly may. You would give your ten-share order to the broker, who would contact the odd-lot broker. The odd-lot broker buys in round lots on the exchange and divides it into odd lots. You pay an odd-lot differential for his service. In this example, it would be an additional 1/8 of a point, or $.125 per share. This is not a commission. It is an odd-lot differential. Your commission would be in addition to the differential.

The amount you pay per share for your odd-lot purchase is determined by the price of the next round-lot trade after your order is received. For example, if the next round-lot trade is $50-1/8, you would pay $50-1/4.

If you buy an odd lot on a round lot—for example, 125 shares—you pay an odd-lot differential on the 25 shares if you trade on the American Stock Exchange. If the stock is traded on the Pacific Stock Exchange or New York Stock Exchange, it trades with the round lot without the odd-lot differential. No odd lot differential is charged on orders entered before the market opens. As you can see, the odd lot charge does not make enough difference to discourage you from buying in odd lots.

Ratios

Ratios can be quite confusing to the investor who is new to the marketplace. To give you a better understanding of them, let's examine two well-managed companies, X and Y. They both manufacture an excellent product for which there has been an increasing demand. For ease of comparison, assume that the stock of both companies sells for $10 per share, that both earn $1 per share, and that both manufacture a product we all want and need.

Stock X pays a 50¢ dividend, and stock Y pays a 10¢ dividend. What is the yield of each, and what is the price-earning ratio?

Stock	Market Price	Earnings per Share	Dividend	Yield	Price-Earnings Ratio
X	$10	$1	50¢	5%	10:1
Y	$10	$1	10¢	1%	10:1

Yield is the relationship of the dividend to the market price. Therefore, a 50¢ yield on a $10 stock would be 5 percent per annum. A 10¢ dividend would then be a 1 percent yield.

The *price-earnings ratio*, often referred to as the P/E, is the relationship of the market price to the earnings. It indicates how much the investing public is willing to pay for $1 of earnings. In both stocks, the amount is $10, making the P/E ratio 10:1.

Which Stock Is Best?

Which stock should you buy? When I ask this question in the seminars, the majority choose stock X. The savings institutions' advertising campaigns have made them very income-conscious.

Did you answer *X* or *Y*? The correct answer for you depends on your financial objective. Do you need income now, or do you need income later? If you need it now, you may want to choose stock *X*; if you need it later, you should choose stock *Y*. If the company pays out 50¢ to you and you are in a 30 percent tax bracket, you lose 15¢ to Washington. If you are in a 50 percent bracket, you lose 25¢. If your need is for income later, then you very well may come out better if the company plows back the 90¢ into enlarged plants and facilities, with the hope that some day stock *Y* will grow in value to perhaps $15 per share. Sometimes it's better to get your eyes off the extra 4 percent income and on to the 50 percent potential in capital gains.

There is often another factor to be considered, and that is your temperament. There is a triangle in finance as there may be in romance. Let's look at the financial triangle and see where you should place yourself for your mental comfort and for the best correlation with your financial objectives.

Triangle of Finance

At the top of the triangle I have placed Growth, at the left Income, and at the right Stability. (I used to call this corner Safety, but with our present rate of inflation if you are "stable," you are certainly not "safe," so I have changed it to Stability.) By stability, I mean a guarantee of the same number of dollars at a future date, not the return of the same purchasing power.

As you can see, the farther you move toward Growth, the farther you move from Stability and Income. You may be young enough to invest for Growth, but when you move in that direction, you could have increased volatility. This may disturb your peace of mind, and peace of mind is a good investment, too. If you were my client, I would try to

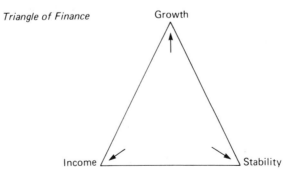

Triangle of Finance

Growth

Income

Stability

determine your peace-of-mind level, because regardless of how well the investment fits your financial objective, if you are uncomfortable with it, it's not right for you and you may abandon it before it has had time to achieve the desired goal.

Let's assume your chief reason for investing in stocks is for income. What characteristics should be of importance to you?

How To Select Income Stocks

Income stocks are relatively easy to select as compared to growth stocks. However, there are some important points you'll want to consider before you give your broker a buy order.

Good Dividends That Keep Increasing

You want stocks that not only pay good dividends, but also have a good record of increasing their dividends rather consistently. If you are dependent on your dividends for your groceries and if the price of food continues to rise, you must increase your income or reduce your intake. Most of us would probably be a lot healthier if we did the latter, but we have a tendency to reject this alternative.

Dividends That Are Earned

You should carefully determine if the corporation is earning the dividend. Years ago many of the bank trust departments were putting shares of Sinclair Oil in trust accounts that they managed for widows who needed income. Sinclair was paying a liberal dividend. Unfortunately, the trust officers did not look to see if the company was earning the amount they were paying. They were not. The day of reckoning came, as it usually does, the dividend was cut, and many a widow's account suffered capital losses. Do not reach too far for yield and jeopardize your capital.

Often I have calls from someone who is going through a *Standard & Poor's Stock Guide* and spots a stock paying a 12–14 percent yield. They'll excitedly call to buy it, assuming that no one else has been so observant as to have spotted this bonanza. Usually the reason for the high yield is the poor evaluation that the market has given to the future prospects of the company.

Resistance to Business Cycles

A characteristic of all good income stocks should be that they have a good measure of resistance against cyclical waves in the economy. The consumer demand for the products produced by these companies should continue through all phases of the economic cycle.

Long Dividend Record

In selecting stocks for dependable income, it is obvious that you will want to choose quality issues, since younger, less tested companies have not been around long enough to establish an extended dividend payment record.

Income stocks usually pay out 65–75 percent of their net earnings in cash dividends. Once a regular dividend rate has been established, it is unlikely that it will be reduced because of poor earnings in a single year.

During times of market corrections, I often have calls from less sophisticated holders of income stocks who are worried that their dividend will be cut because the market price is down. If all is well with their company, I try to calm them with the explanation that short-term market prices often have no relationship to earnings. (In the long term they usually do.)

Who Decides the Amount of the Dividend?

The amount remaining after the expenses and taxes have been paid by a company is the amount available for dividends. The decision as to whether a dividend should be paid and how much it should be is made by the board of directors. The amount of the earnings, the need for retained earnings, and the past dividend record all influence the directors' decision.

Yield on Original Purchase Price

As you learned above, the yield on a stock is the relationship of the dividend to the market price. Every shareholder is entitled to the same dividend per share. However, the market price paid by one shareholder may be different from that paid by another. If you paid $50 for a share of stock and the dividend is $2, your yield on your original investment is 4 percent ($2 divided by $50). If you paid $35, the $2 represents a return, or yield, on your original investment of slightly more than 5.7 percent.

Most yields, however, are calculated on current market price. If the price per share is now $60, still with a $2 dividend, the yield would be slightly over 3.3 percent.

Looking Ahead

If you do not need income now, consider companies with slightly lower yields. Often these companies are plowing back a larger portion of their earnings into expanded facilities that should in time yield higher earnings that would allow them to pay out higher dividends. Over a ten- to fifteen-year period, many growth stocks have actually had a larger cash pay-out than income stock. One percent on $10,000 is only $100. But let's assume the growth stock continues to grow and reaches a value of $100,000. (One percent on $100,000 is $1,000, or 10 percent on your original investment.)

A booklet that you may find of help if you are interested in selecting stocks for income is one published by the New York Stock Exchange, entitled "Investment Facts—Cash Dividends Every Three Months from 25 to 100 Years." The booklet points out that the widespread ownership of stocks listed on the New York Stock Exchange is due in large part to a growing awareness that surplus dollars can be put to work in investments that will reflect the ever-changing economic conditions of our country.

The ability of common stocks to mirror these developments constitutes their greatest attribute. Of course, it is also their greatest risk. On the plus side is the fact that over the years the yields from good common stocks often have helped their owners keep in step with living costs. There is no such phenomenon as a "sure thing," and past performance does not guarantee the future. But the facts that history has recorded may serve as a clue to the future. If so, it may be of help to look at the long-time dividend payers listed in this booklet.

The booklet lists recent prices of the stock, the dividend record, and its yield. Of these common stocks, 466 have paid a cash dividend every single quarter for 25 years, and 100 have paid a dividend for every quarter for 50 to over 100 years.

Preferred Stocks

Preferred stocks are equities senior to the common, but junior to indebtedness of the issuer. Eighty-five percent of the dividends from an American corporation is exempt from taxation when received by another American corporation. This tends to raise the market price of the higher yielding preferreds, making them less attractive to you for your individual investment program. You will normally receive a higher rate of return from a high-quality corporate bond than from a preferred stock.

Blue Chips, Red Chips, White Chips? The stocks I have described above would generally be called blue chips. What is a "blue chip" stock? First, the name can be traced to the game of poker, in which there are three colors of chips: blue for the highest value, red for next in rank, and white for the lowest value.

Sometimes people will come up to me after a seminar or a television appearance and say, "I only invest in blue chip stocks and throw them in the drawer and forget about them." They stand there seemingly anticipating my approval. I consider this approach a risky one. I would prefer to see them invest in more volatile stocks and watch them carefully than to have them plant their garden and not tend it. The blue chips of today may be the red chips of tomorrow, the white chips of the next day, or merely the buffalo chips. (I'm a rancher—you do know what pasture frisbee is, don't you?)

However, there are some characteristics of the so-called blue chips that are worthy of your consideration, such as:

1. A long history of cash dividend payments in bad times and good.

2. A long history of good earnings in both booms and recessions.

3. Leadership in an established industry.

Income vs. Growth

The equities market provides a wide spectrum of alternatives with respect to rates of return. When investing in growth companies, you must pay a premium in terms of P/E relationship and, therefore, receive less in the way of current income. Growth companies have an opportunity to reinvest their earnings at higher rates than are available to you as a stockholder if the earnings were paid out to you and you had only the after-tax amount to invest. Therefore, growth companies have very low payout ratios.

It is too simplistic, but there is some truth in the fact that the highest-yielding common stocks have lower expectations of future growth and, therefore, lower P/Es.

If you do not expect growth of the company, you should ask yourself why the price is so low, making the yield so high. Is the company in serious financial straits? Is the company likely to cut its dividends? Is the regulatory environment likely to be adverse so that the company may have to reduce its dividend to conserve its cash for working capital needs? What is the outlook for the industry?

It is clear that investing for income is not without risk. If you had bought certain steel company issues a few years ago for income, you would have had your dividends reduced and in some instances eliminated. Not only did the income go down, but the principal loss was also substantial. It is also clear, however, that investing for high income can have its rewards. In periods of high merger activity some cash-rich income stock companies became the targets of acquiring companies. Some of those acquired had spectacular rises in their prices, and if you had sold your shares at the proper time, you could have realized substantial capital gains.

In summary, if your desire is for income:

1. Look for companies that have a long unbroken dividend record.

2. Don't reach too far for yield and jeopardize principal.

3. Remember that too high a yield can be dangerous and misleading.

4. Favor companies producing consumer goods and services.

5. Select sound companies that continue to increase their dividends.

Income stocks are not too difficult to select after you've conscientiously done your homework. However, selecting growth stocks can be one of the greatest challenges you have ever undertaken.

Growth Stocks—The Royal Road To Riches

During the surging 1960s, the magic word on Wall Street, Main Street, Podunk Street, or almost any street you happened to be traveling at the time, was "Growth"! Investing in "growth" stocks was the royal highway to riches. So greatly did some "investors" become enamored of that magic word that they were willing to pay fantastic prices for new and relatively untested electronic and scientific issues. So unrealistic did they become that they actually paid as high as seventy times earnings. In some instances, there were no earnings at all.

Growth Stocks—What Are They?

What are growth stocks, and why should you consider investing in them?

A growth company is usually one that is increasing its sales and earnings at a faster rate than the growth of the national population and business in general. The long-term annual growth rate of our population has been about 3 percent. A growth company, as a rule of thumb, should be increasing its sales and net earnings at least as fast as the combination of the two, and preferably much faster.

Growth companies are usually producing goods and/or services in dynamic and new industries. The 1940s saw the surge of oil stocks, television shares, and pharmaceutical companies. The 1950s continued the drug stocks' popularity, with flurries in uranium, cameras, electronics, missiles, and automation.

The 1960s saw leisure-time industries; baby products; continued popularity of electronics, with computer-oriented stocks keeping pace; technology-related industries; life insurance companies; drugs; retail; convenience goods; soft drinks; and, most especially, the surge of the conglomerates trying to leverage their balance sheets, many times using what became known as "funny money." Ling-Tempco-Vought, Gulf and Western, Textron, and International Telephone and Telegraph all brought visions of investor "sugar plums" during their heydays of mergers and acquisitions. There was a short period of time when there were jokes in the investment community of investment decisions becoming a matter of which one of the few conglomerates to choose. The tinsel began to tarnish, the craze passed, and we returned to sound investment evaluation based on realities rather than the new math of Wall Street, which seemed to say that 2 plus 2 equals 5.

During the first part of the 1970s, the market suffered a major correction. This correction was much more extensive than the widely followed Dow Jones Industrial Average revealed. The decline of the Dow, though sizable, was not bad enough to explain the awful sense of despair that gripped Wall Street during the latter part of 1973 and on through 1974 and 1975. It did not tell how hard the overall stock market was hit. The only averages that showed declines approaching the true magnitude were the superbroad unweighted ones, such as the *Value Line Composite* and the *Indicator Digest* average.

The bull market of the 1960s was in the supergrowth stocks—the franchises, the computer leasers, and the like—not the staid, less volatile Dow 30. The Dow went up during those years, but the broader averages went up more rapidly and also went down more rapidly when the high flyers fell out of favor.

Why was the market plunge so severe in 1973 and 1974? There are many reasons, all interrelated. Let's look at a few of them.

Many market declines are in direct relationship to the junk some stockbrokers "peddle" on the way up. Being a broker is a volatile vocation, but it is made more so by the short memories of a large portion of its personnel. It was another case of too much sizzle and not enough steak.

The Federal Reserve Board instituted extremely restrictive money policies in an effort to slow down runaway inflation. The results of its actions could be compared to taking a man who has been accustomed to three gourmet meals a day and throwing him into solitary confinement, giving him only bread and water, and then beating him with a stick. The market must have a steady flow of money to function properly. Historical studies show a direct relation between the supply of money in the economy and stock market prices.

The ugliness of Watergate disillusioned the American public as nothing else had in many a decade. Their faith in their leaders was badly shaken. A sense of uneasiness and gloom settled over our nation.

During the Ford administration, a certain confidence was renewed and continued for the first part of the Carter administration. But as faith in Carter's leadership declined, and with the administration's capitulation of the direction of the economy to what many consider the ill-advised and counterproductive actions of the Federal Reserve Board, the market again was thrust down. When people feel bad inside, they sell their stocks. When they feel good, they buy. Gut-level feelings have no correlation with earnings. Human emotion took over, and they sold and sold.

It is at times such as those that we need to read these words: "even in the general moment of gloom in which this . . . is written, when many begin to wonder if declines will never halt, the appropriate abracadabra may be: 'They always did.'"*

How to Spot Growth Stocks

To become good at selecting for growth, you must be aware of current events: current trends, supply, demand, psychology, and money markets. In fact, you must be truly current. One of the most stimulating

---

*Bernard M. Baruch, October 1932.

characteristics of being a financial planner is that every day is a new day in the market. Nothing remains static. There is no way you can be a truly top-notch investor by buying blue chips and throwing them in a drawer and forgetting them. This only increases your risk and lowers your opportunity for gain.

Be in the Right Industry

If I were to choose the most important consideration for selecting growth stocks, I would have to say that it is to be in the right industry at the right time. There is always an industry moving up, regardless of the general overall trend of the market. You should endeavor to predict a trend before it happens and move out before the trend runs out. You should try to be aware of technological changes and opinions of the buying public. It will not pay you to be right if nobody cares. Sitting with money in a stagnant "correct" situation while other stocks are moving up just doesn't take the place of making money.

Fantasy Stocks

Do not buy what I call fantasy stocks—stocks based on an idea yet to come. The idea may be great—even correct—but how do you know there will be adequate financing, good and honest management, marketing ability, and public acceptance of the product? (What people want and what they need are different things.) You might say, "But look at Haloid that later became Xerox." There is no way that those who

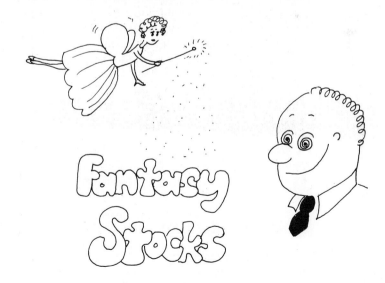

bought Haloid could have known it would become one of the best-managed sales organizations that the country had seen for many a year. Also, you could have bought Xerox many times since its beginning and made just as much money with proper timing on buys and sells. If you will wait until some of the results are in, it may save you some heartaches. (Of course, you will also need to be astute enough to avoid getting on at the front of the bus while the informed are getting off at the back.)

This is different from a story stock from which good results have already been realized, but even better results are expected. The best story is the "Good Earnings Story."

Management Is the Key

There is no substitute for energetic, intelligent, dedicated, and enthusiastic management. They should be a stock-minded management team that is interested in increasing the market price of their stock, and this can only be sustained in the long term by increased earnings.

With good management and an average product, it is possible to make money. A superior product with poor management may well yield very disappointing results. The key is good management and a superior product together.

Self-Generating Earnings

Select a company that has self-generating rising earnings and reserves with expectations for continued increases over the foreseeable future. Few companies really shine solely by acquisitions, as many seemed to believe during the conglomerate era of mergers. Pretax earnings on assets of growth companies should be between 10 and 30 percent.

Technological Research and Development Are Musts

A growth company must retain a large portion of its earnings for research and development that will produce a salable product that offers excellence in quality, design, or performance, and preferably all three.

Flair for Salesmanship

A growth company must have a dynamic, aggressive sales department. A good example of salesmanship is Revlon's success at selling

"hope in a jar." Revlon's ads are so compelling that it takes restraint to read the brilliant magazine ads and not dash to the nearest cosmetic counter.

Consistently Superior Growth of Earnings

A growth stock is not just a stock that has gone up in price. You want stocks that have shown a consistent, year-after-year, superior growth in earnings even in the face of business reverses and that have a consistent year-in, year-out market for their products or services.

Leaders in a Fast-growing Field

You will want to search for the companies that dominate their markets or are leaders in fast-growing fields. These can be companies in emerging fields or companies that have developed new ideas in established fields.

Cyclical Stocks

Most short-term speculators use the so-called "cyclical" stocks. These stocks are found in those industries most sensitive to swings in the business cycle. They include the heavily capitalized industries such as steel and heavy machinery. These areas are traditionally strongest in periods of prosperity and at a low ebb in times of recession. The trick is to buy cyclical stocks in the early stages of a business upturn and sell them as closely as possible to the crest. This is not easy.

Popular Favorites

Another trading technique is to move along with the popular stocks of the moment. You can make as much money, short term, on what others think a stock is worth, as on what it is really worth. In the long term we have always returned to basics.

Following the fashions in finance is hazardous. However, if by using good logic you are convinced that a new industry is about to boom, then cautious selections of a stock in that industry may prove rewarding. The trick is to buy early and then, when everyone is clamoring for shares in that industry, sell! Almost invariably the stock market darlings, at the height of their popularity, will sell above sensible valuations.

Special Situations

Another area of speculation is the area of special situations. This can cover a great many areas: mergers, sudden increase in the price of a valuable asset, a new mineral find, a new venture, and so on. Your success will depend greatly on your getting accurate information ahead of the pack. Is the product or service in the mainstream of a rapidly growing demand? Is the demand likely to last? If it is a new venture,

"That valve controls the Dow Jones Average"

determine if it is well capitalized. At least half of all new ventures fold because they run out of capital before they can get into full-fledged operation.

Who will be managing the company? Innovators may have a highly functional idea or patent, but they'll fail because they do not know how to run a business. Creative design people often are very poor at manufacturing techniques, cost control, merchandising, financing, and record keeping. Check to see if those who will run the business are personally solvent and have adequate practical or technical background. The key man may be a fantastic salesman and a poor production man, or vice versa. He may know sales promotion but have no idea about cost controls.

The third thing to consider in a new company is superiority of product or service. New products should be advanced, unusual, and ahead of the field.

Finally, can you afford to lose everything you put into the new company and not miss the money?

On the record, the chances of a new company's growing from zero to great substance are very slim. But if this kind of speculation adds zest to your life and you can afford it, happy hunting!

Investor or Speculator

We have covered some of the basic characteristics that you must consider in becoming an investor for growth. Should you ever speculate in the stock market? Are there categories between being an investor and being a rank speculator?

The Trader

In even the most valid growth stock selection, there is a time to buy and a time to sell. However, there is another area of the stock market that I would classify between the growth stock investor and the rank gambler. It is that of the trader. I must admit that the line of demarcation does get hazy at times.

There appear to be at least three classes of people who fit this category. If you do not have ample capital, I hope you will resist the temptation to join their ranks, as most out-and-out traders lose money. These three classes are:

1. The constitutional speculators: not necessarily gamblers, but people willing to "take a chance"—to take big risks in hope of great gain.

2. Those who truly think they can supplement their income by modest trading in and out of the market.

3. People with large amounts of income to whom fully taxable income is unattractive, but to whom long-term capital gains are more alluring.

Don't Be Greedy

One characteristic that I have observed about the timing of all good traders is that they never try to squeeze out the last point in a stock. When the great financier Bernard Baruch was questioned on how he made so much money in the stock market, he answered, "I always sold too soon." He always tried to leave a little in it for the next buyer.

Cut Losses Quickly

In trading, it is absolutely necessary to cut your losses quickly. If you've made an error in judgment, don't wait around to find out just how wrong you really were. You can't afford an ego trip. If a 20 percent drop occurs, go back and review your homework and be sure you have all the information you need. It may be that the market is just wrong or it may be that you've made an error in your calculations.

Some of my clients act as if the stock knew they owned it or what they paid for it. The stock doesn't even know that your cousin, once removed, works for the company.

Don't think about an impending dividend, or that you have a loss in the stock, or that you just bought it. Also, don't hesitate to buy it back, even at a higher price, if you made a mistake in selling. Above all, don't fall in love with a stock—don't marry it. Be objective. Be flexible. Don't be guilty of prejudices in stock. We all have them occasionally, but the sooner you recognize them and shed stocks that hinder your investment judgment, the better investor you'll become.

Tax considerations should be the furthest from your mind. You are only trying to use $1 to make $2, not to do tax planning while in front of a stock board watching the "horses" run.

Don't Cry

Two other cardinal rules are "Don't cry" and "Don't look back." Lick your wounds and charge forward.

Flexibility in Selecting Stocks

Common sense will be your greatest ally. You probably will not be able to produce a superior investment performance all of the time. Some of the most respected professionals do not, and they occasionally lag behind the averages. First of all, you'll want to search for bargains. If you can buy stocks at a fraction of what you think they are worth, in the long run most of them should turn out better than if you had paid all you thought they were worth.

To decide what a stock is worth, you will want to use what is called security analysis. The best book on this subject is *Security Analysis* by Graham and Dodd. After you've used standard security analysis to decide the value of a stock, you'll want to compare it with the price of other stocks and buy those stocks that have the lowest price in relation to what you think they are worth.

You will also need to be flexible. There are those who will only buy famous stocks. I know others who will buy only those stocks that the analyst designates as fast-growth stocks.

The fact that you have been in the right kind of securities for several years does not mean that they will be the right kind for the future. You'll be tempted when you've had unusually favorable performance to be self-satisfied and think you've found the answer to stock selections and continue with those stocks. But if a particular security or industry has had a superior performance for five years, it may be time to get out of it. It probably won't be in the right industry for the next five years. Flexibility must be your policy. To achieve this, look around to find the cheapest stock in relation to value.

It is extremely difficult to buy a bargain if you are buying what other people are buying. If you want to buy the same thing that is popular with your friends or popular with the other investment security analysts, you won't get a bargain. If you buy the same things they buy, you'll have the same performance they'll have. If you're going to have a superior performance, you've got to buy what other people are not buying, or even what other people are selling. Therefore, you'll want to search for those areas that are extremely unpopular and then determine if that unpopularity is permanent. Things don't get low for no reason at all. They get low because other people are selling them. You'll want to search for those stocks that other people are selling, and then if you determine that this problem or adverse outlook is temporary, you will want to buy them and patiently hold them until the public changes its mind. Some of the ancestors of the Rothschilds of Europe were asked questions on this subject and they said, "We always buy cheap and sell dear." You'll want to become a philanthropist. If people are extremely anxious to sell things and trying to find a buyer at any price, you accommodate them; and at other times when people are extraordinarily anxious to buy something and bid it up to a high price, you'll again accommodate them by selling to them.

Should You Buy on Margin?

From years of observing margin account investors, my answer to you is no. Leave this area to the large, sophisticated—whatever that means—investors who are active in the market and who understand the risks as well as the rewards of this type of account. I find that it is usually best if you discipline yourself to the use of only your investable funds. To lose some of your savings in the market is one thing. To lose your future savings as well is another. Yes, I know if it goes the other way your potential for gain is greatly enhanced. It's not that I don't believe in leverage. I believe very strongly in using leverage in real estate and other areas, and in using stock as collateral for funds to purchase capital items.

If after these warnings you still want to open a margin account, here is how it works. First, the Federal Reserve Board sets the margin requirements. These requirements have ranged from 50 to 100 percent in the post-World War II period. For example, if the margin rate is 70 percent, it means that if you want to buy $10,000 worth of stock you would need to put up $7,000 in order to make the purchase. You would deposit the required cash or securities with your broker within five business days after the purchase.

You will pay interest for the amount you have borrowed. This has ranged from 6-1/2 to 20-1/2 percent. The amount of interest will be posted on your statement monthly.

To open the account you deposit $2,000, or whatever minimum your brokerage firm requires, and sign a margin agreement and a securities loan consent form. This agreement gives your broker the power to pledge or lend your securities. Your securities will be held in what is called "street name," meaning that they are registered in the name of the brokerage house and you do not receive delivery of the certificates. Your broker will, however, credit you with all the dividends received, send you all the reports, and vote your stock in the manner that you direct. You must also abide by the margin maintenance requirements. This usually requires that your margin equity be at least 25 percent. For example, if you bought $10,000 worth of stock with an initial margin requirement of 70 percent, you put up $7,000 and received credit of $3,000. Let's assume the stock drops to the point where it is worth $4,000. Since you owe your broker $3,000, your equity in the securities is only $1,000 and you are right at the 25 percent limit. At this point you will receive a margin call and you'll be asked to put up more cash or securities. If you cannot meet the call, he will sell your securities, retain the $3,000 you owe him, and credit you with the balance.

Should You Buy or Sell Options?

The use of options has increased greatly in the past ten years. You may have attended a seminar, read newspaper ads, or received a call from an aggressive broker extolling options as the way to lock in additional income if you are on the selling side and to make a large return on a small investment if you are on the buying side.

Buying Options

It's not all that easy, but in order for you to not feel left out when the conversation turns to "puts" and "calls," let's take a brief look at the world of options.

A "call" option is a contract that gives you the right to buy 100 shares of a given stock at a fixed price for a fixed period of time. The period of time usually runs nine months and ten days (for tax reasons), but you can run 30, 90, 120 days or other lengths of time. The premium that you pay for the option usually runs about 10–15 percent of the value of the stock.

A "put" option is the reverse of a "call" option. You now have the privilege of selling 100 shares of the stock at a fixed price within the option period. These usually cost a few percentage points less than call options and are not as popular.

Why would you ever buy an option? The main reason is that it gives you a chance to make a sizable profit on the move of a stock while limiting the amount of possible loss. For example, you think that General Widgets Company stock selling at $40 may surge to $80. It would cost you $4,000 to buy the shares, and you may not want to risk $4,000 or you may not have $4,000 to invest. Still, you would like to take the chance that General Widgets will jump and as a result you'd make a large profit. In this case you might go the option route, buying an option for $400. Let's assume your anticipations are correct and the stock hits $70 within the option period. You exercise your option, buy the 100 shares at $40, and then turn around and sell the shares for $70.

You have received $7,000 from the sale of the shares. From this you would subtract the $4,000 you paid for them, the $400 premium for the option, and about $110 for the brokerage commissions, and you would wind up with a profit of $2,490.

Now let's assume that your expectations did not materialize and General Widgets goes to $30. What do you do? You do nothing. You simply let your option expire. You are out $400. Your loss is limited to the cost of your option and you are thankful that you didn't buy 100 shares at $4,000 and watch your investment shrink.

"Put" options work in reverse. (There are also some very fancy devices called "straddles"—a combination of a put and a call; "strips," which are composed of two puts and one call; and "straps," which are one put and two calls.)

Selling Options

What is a call option? It is a contract that allows the buyer of the option the right to purchase a particular stock at a specific price during a defined period of time, regardless of the market price of the stock. A covered call option is an option written by a seller who owns the underlying security. When you write a covered call option, you receive an option premium and also continue to receive any dividends on the underlying portfolio stock.

The combination of the income from the option premium plus the dividends from your stock may be two or three times the amount of dividend income alone. Option writing can substantially increase your income from the stock without a commensurate increase in risk.

You may also lock in a profit. If you have bought a block of stock with the goal of making $5 per share profit and sell an option at $5, you lock in that profit.

Your overall objective when you sell call options is to utilize various strategies to produce higher current income, lessen your portfolio's volatility, and reduce your risks in down markets.

Now let's return to portfolio basics.

A Profitable Portfolio

There are three important areas in choosing and maintaining a profitable portfolio of stocks: diversification, proper selection, and constant supervision. Let's examine the first, diversification. Diversification means spreading the risk. The old adage of not putting all your eggs in one basket has considerable merit in assembling a good investment portfolio.

Diversification

Don't put all your faith in only one company, for it may disappoint you. You may be well informed on sales figures, competitive situations, or whatever, but always be prepared for a disaster. Going for broke on a winner could make you rich, but no one knows which stock will be the big winner. If you buy a diversified group of fundamentally sound stocks with good earnings, the chances are that in a good market you will catch at least some of the big winners. Most big money in a diversified portfolio comes from one or two big winners.

Don't be deceived into thinking that ten oil stocks is diversification; it is not. You should have a portfolio covering a wider range of industries. For example, you may have some stocks in the soft drink industry, the retail area, drugs, home furnishings, electrical equipment, brewing, agricultural machinery, gold mining, and others.

When managing your own portfolio, you may find it extremely helpful to limit yourself to ten stocks, regardless of the amount of money you have to invest. I'm surprised to find that investors think they can only own 100 shares of each company's stock. If the capital you have available for investing is sufficiently large, perhaps you should consider owning 1,000 shares of each stock.

Moving to Strength

Don't overdiversify because you may find that you are unable to truly be current on a large number of companies. If you limit your holdings to fifteen to twenty stocks and a stock comes to your attention that you feel you should buy, what will this force you to do? To eliminate one. So you go down through your list and sell the one that is doing the poorest job for you. Now, won't you? I wish this were true of all my clients. Many go through and pick out their winner to sell and smugly say, "You'll never go broke taking a profit." They are keeping their losers and selling their winners. That's not the way to upgrade a portfolio. Sell the poorest performer. This allows you the possibility of continuously moving to a position of strength.

Timing Is the Key

There is a time to buy and a time to sell. The old adage about buying low and selling high is easy to say and very hard to do. Often you never know what the high or low is until it's too late for maximum advantage.

But how do you determine when to buy and when to sell? Let's look at buying first.

When to Buy. Buy stocks only when you think you can make a profit. The only reason to be in the market is to make money. Buy only when you anticipate a substantial rise within one year. Look for 25 percent appreciation per year. Buy for investment gain, not dividends.

To make money in the market you may have to learn to buy ice cubes in the winter—in other words learn not to run with the pack. Learn to buy the stocks others are selling and sell what others are buying. You may find it extremely hard to go against the crowd.

When to Sell. I have a very simple rule for judging when to sell a stock I own. It's so simple you'll probably dismiss the whole idea. However, I've found over the years that it has helped me cut through the tinsel and fog and to reach good decisions as to when to sell.

I do not look at what price I paid for a stock unless selling it would cause me to incur a large capital gains tax liability. I simply ask myself, "If I had the money this stock would bring in my hands at this moment, would I buy this stock at this price?" If my answer is yes, I hold. If it is no, I sell. The only difference between my owning this stock and having the money is a small amount of commission which I should not let affect my judgment.

You may have great difficulty selling. Most people do. If you have a gain, you may not be able to bear the thought of selling and paying the capital gains tax. When you analyze the situation, there are only two ways to avoid eventually paying it, neither of which you are going to like. You can hold it until it goes back to what you paid for it; or hold it until your death, and let your heirs worry about the tax when they sell it.

On the other hand, if you have a loss, you may say, "I won't sell, for I just can't afford to take a loss." You already have the loss. There are only two questions now that you should ask yourself. Can you deduct the loss advantageously on your income tax, and where are you most likely to make up your losses—where you are or in another stock?

Lay your hand over the cost basis of your stocks and judge them individually on their potential over the next six months.

When you no longer anticipate a worthwhile rise, when the outlook for earnings is no longer favorable, when the stock is clearly overpriced in relation to its normal price–earnings multiple or to that of companies of similar quality in the same industry, sell.

Don't Average Down

I am not in agreement with a large number of stockbrokers who advise their clients to average down. What is meant by averaging down?

Let's assume that you bought 100 shares of a stock at $30 per share, and that it has dropped in price to $20.   There are those who recommend that you buy another 100 shares at $20. This would give you an average cost per share of $25 on the 200 shares.

I feel you can average yourself right into the basement of the poorhouse. I never mind paying a higher price than my original purchase price if there is earnings justification. It just means the market has confirmed my own good judgment.

There will be exceptions, so go back and redo your homework and monitor this stock very closely.

The Institutional Investor

The institutional investor is one who usually buys in large blocks at advantageously lower negotiated commissions. He is the large life insurance company, the large bank, the large pension fund manager, the large college endowment fund manager, the large mutual fund.

Logic would seem to indicate that this much money in the hands of trained, informed, unemotional money managers would lend a high degree of stability to the market. I'm sorry to say that I don't think this is what will be happening. Their equipment for becoming better informed has reached a high degree of electronic sophistication. Unfortunately, they all seem to be availing themselves of the same tools. They are all reading the same computer printouts from their very advanced monitoring equipment. This shows all of them the same buy and sell signals at the same time, causing simultaneous buying and selling that results in sudden and often precipitous price changes.

An example might be found in the stock of Wrigley. Their commercials may have been a bit staid—"double your pleasure, double your fun"—but you always knew Wrigley was there. Then suddenly at 1 P.M. on that fateful day in October, trading was halted by the New York Stock Exchange. When it reopened around 2:30, there was no pleasure and no fun. Wrigley was off 27 points, almost a 20 percent drop. Just like that. By year's end it had shed another 15 points.

Had the bottom suddenly fallen out of the chewing gum market? No, as a matter of fact, third-quarter earnings were well above the previous year's earnings, but they were not what Wall Street expected. Wall Street becomes nervous when its expectations are not met, and 20,000 shares were dumped. That is what is called "bombing" a stock.

You Can Compete

Can you as an individual investor compete with so many institutional buyers in the market?

Yes, you can probably beat all but the well-managed mutual funds if you will conscientiously do your homework and keep reasonably calm. One of your greatest assets is flexibility. There will be times when the economy is such that you can't make money in the stock market. At such times, get out.

It may be more difficult for the professional money manager to unload a block of 200,000 shares of the kinds of stocks institutions hold without depressing the market in that stock.

For example, suppose you decide that IBM's multiple (the stock's price relative to its earnings per share) is too high, and you'd like to sell your 50 shares. Fine—no problem. But if Morgan Guaranty held $2 billion of IBM stock, could they do the same? No, they are locked in, unless they want to see their last shares sold at prices much lower than their first.

Very often, the way to make big money in the market is to find small, well-managed, rapidly growing companies. Most institutions are too big to be able to take advantage of that strategy. You can buy meaningful positions in smaller companies that the "big boys" cannot touch. You would hope, however, that as the company grew, the institutions would be able to move in, which in turn should help move up the price of the stock you "discovered."

The 1980s

As I stated in the opening of this chapter, I'm excited about the stock market for the decade of the 1980s and I am convinced we'll see a Dow above 3000. There are many reasons for these convictions. Let me give you the chief ones.

Price–Earnings Ratio. The price-earnings ratio of our stocks are around seven. Over the past ninety years the average has been fourteen times earnings. Indications are that we should return to this P/E ratio. While the market values of the majority of stocks have not increased, the corporations behind them have prospered, and their earnings have climbed. There are many sound and profitable companies selling at drastic discounts.

Stocks are bargains when compared to other investment possibilities. Over the past decade, real estate, oil and gas, precious metals, and certain hard assets (all of which we'll discuss as we progress through the book) have provided a hedge against inflation because their prices have increased. Stocks have not participated. Yet these stocks aren't just pieces of paper called stock certificates; they represent shares of ownership in real businesses that have assets that can produce growing earnings and dividends.

Earnings. If we average 9 percent inflation during the 1980s, the sales volume of corporations will double in eight years, even if they don't produce any more goods. Nine percent a year for eight years compounded doubles the sales volume. If they produce more goods, which I believe they will, they will double in a shorter length of time. Therefore if sales double and price–earnings return to normal, share prices would be four times what they are now. Four times today's prices is above 3000 on the Dow.

Shares Below Book Value. There have only been three times in history when prices were below book value and all three of those times proved to be very short and great times to load up on stocks. These were 1932, 1942, and 1948. Shares are now approximately 16 percent below book value.

Replacement Book Value. Because of inflation, it costs approximately 70 percent above stated book value to replace most American plants and equipment. On the basis of replacement value alone, this would increase the Dow to around 1700. Because shares have been selling below replacement costs, many corporations are now buying the shares of other corporations as a cheaper way of acquiring plants and equipment than building and acquiring new ones.

Corporations Are Repurchasing Their Stocks

Some of the smartest and best qualified investors in the world know that these stocks are a bargain. How do I know? I know because these same businessmen are repurchasing their own stocks.

Even in the Great Depression, on the market's worst day, stocks were not as cheap in relation to replacement value. That is why the people who know their companies best are using their cash to buy their own shares at a fraction of what they know they are worth.

Political Environment. With the passage of the Economic Recovery Act of 1981, our country has officially entered into a new era. No longer will it be the government's role to solve everyone's economic problems. It has attempted to do this for the past twenty years and in the process has consumed an ever increasing share of our finite productive resources. I believe that "free enterprise" is being given a second chance and that the government is creating a supportive environment by decreasing government intervention in the system and by reducing the uncertainties over government policies with which business has been faced.

ERTA is an important part of this program and should have an enormous positive effect on the stock market as additional incentives to invest and save become a reality. These incentives to invest should encourage corporations to build new facilities or modernize old ones, and these efforts should, in turn, increase worker productivity.

As important as the new tax policies are for the well-being of the economy, the implications for the securities markets are even greater. It is through the stock market that increased savings will be channeled into industry for plant equipment. It is through the markets that the necessary research and development for technological advances and productivity enhancement will be financed.

The reduction of the capital gains tax and the elimination of the distinction between earned and unearned income and the other incentives to earn and invest should provide a powerful thrust to the securities market.

Movement from Hard Assets. It appears that inflation, though still present, will be increasing at a decreasing rate. In the past, for every 1 percent increase in inflation, $100 billion went out of stocks and into various hard assets and tangibles. When inflation declines, the reverse occurs and the funds flow back into the securities market.

Deleveraging. Our economy is in the process of being deleveraged; that means future growth will be financed with equity rather than with debt. No longer will it be the government's role to solve everyone's economic problems. It will now be up to the private sector to do so by utilizing the profit incentive.

ERTA will be an important component of this program and will have a great influence on the success of the stock market.

Demographics. We are entering a period of labor shortages, which in turn will accelerate technology. (The Baby Boom will have passed through the pipe.) A new phase of the industrial revolution based on a technology of substituting capital for labor is getting under way.

Semiconductor—"The Chip". "The Chip" will be the basis for this revolution in productivity. The "chip" could very well become as important a factor in our economy as was the development of the steam engine and mass production in their times.

Allocation of Capital. Funds for the reindustrialization of the United States must come from the securities market. The principal role of the market has always been to allocate capital. Every economic system requires investment choices. In a planned economy, such as socialism or communism, capital decisions are made by the bureaucrats. In a free enterprise, capitalistic economy, the markets make those choices. The markets determine which industries and companies will get capital and which will not. The principal difference between the United States and the Soviet Union is the stock market.

Pension Funds. Private pension plans alone are projected to be $3 trillion in fifteen years, and the public pension funds could add another $2 trillion. If only 50 percent of the private pensions (historically it has averaged 55 percent) goes into common stocks, that would amount to $1.5 trillion, and there are only around $1.25 trillion worth of stocks in the United States.

Property and Casualty Companies

Property and casualty companies are usually enormous holders of common stocks. They began the decade with only 15 percent of their assets in common stocks. That's the lowest in twenty-five years.

Foreign Investors

There is an enormous amount of foreign money available for investment in the United States. Foreign investors' interest is twofold. Our stocks are attractive values, and our U.S. dollar is depressed in comparison to many other currencies.

There has also been a change in foreign legislation. Prime Minister Margaret Thatcher was able to change restrictions in England so that Englishmen can invest more easily in foreign securities. Now they can invest in what they choose where they choose. Japan is now allowing its pension funds to go outside the country to make 10 percent of its investments.

Individual Investors

Money Market Mutual Funds. At present $190 billion are parked in mutual money market funds, a large portion of which is poised to go back into the stock market.

Individual Retirement Accounts. Now every person who has earned income can set up for himself his own pension fund, called an "Individual Retirement Account," (discussed later) and can contribute 100 percent of income up to a maximum of $2,000; he can deduct the contribution from taxable income and have the earnings compound tax-deferred. Around 100 million people are eligible. If one-fourth participate (that is, 25 million people) at $2,000 per participant, that is $50 billion per year. If only one-half of this amount goes into common stocks, that is $25 billion of new money. Since that's more than the new supply of common stocks, this alone could have a large effect on pushing stock prices higher.

This may very well be the beginning of people's capitalism. Instead of only 33 million people in our country who own shares, we may soon have 60 million people who own shares. As our citizens invest their money in common stocks, I have great hope that they will gradually begin to learn the meaning of private enterprise and the problems of businesses and that this increased intelligence will be manifested at the voting booth. One of the reasons that I have devoted so many years of my life to helping as many people as I can to become financially independent is that I believe that it is imperative for Americans to own a part of American industry. If they do not own a part of it and do not understand how the system works, they will vote to destroy it. This would be one of the world's greatest tragedies. We all know the system isn't perfect, but it is the best system yet devised and it has brought the greatest good to the greatest number of people.

I believe we are approaching an era of harmony and prosperity.

Be prepared to participate in it to the fullest, for the decade ahead will offer you a dynamic challenge—a challenge that you cannot afford to turn down. It is a challenge you must accept. Do so with intelligence, knowledge, vigor, and enthusiasm!

Application

1. A good way to become knowledgeable about growth industries is to be alert to current trends. In which areas should you be attuned as you read the daily newspaper?

2. How will you become informed about the management of the corporations in the industries that you feel offer the most growth potential?

3. How do you determine the right time to invest?

4. How will you time your sales?

5. What is the Gross National Product today?

6. What is your prediction of what the GNP will be in ten years?

7. What is your prediction of the price-earnings ratio of the stocks on the Dow in ten years?

8. What action will you take to apply your predictions to benefit your own financial future?

    a.

    b.

    c.

9. Sit down and draw the financial triangle. Place yourself on the triangle. Are you emphasizing income when your real objective is growth of capital?

10. Order the booklets "Investment Facts—Cash Dividends Every Three Months From 25 to 100 Years," "The Language of Investing," and "How to Get Help When You Invest" from the New York Stock Exchange, 11 Wall Street, New York, N.Y. 10005.

Chapter 4

Professional Power
for Your Money

Now that you've had a good look at some of the basic requirements for becoming a successful investor in the stock market, you may be saying to me, "I'm an engineer (or accountant or salesman or doctor). I'm good at what I do because I devote many hours a day to my vocation, but I have neither the time nor inclination to study the stock market. Yet I know that I need to have my money working for me. I may have children who will need funds to go to college and I'll need to have funds to retire in financial dignity someday. What can I do?" If you don't have what I call the three *T*s and an *M*, put professional money managers to work for you.

Time

The first *T* is for time. Do you truly have the time to study the market trends? I'm not asking if you have a moment before you settle down to watch the next murder mystery or police or hospital drama on TV to take a quick glance at the evening newspaper to learn whether your stocks went up or down during the day.

Do you really have the time to spend studying balance sheets, profit and loss statements, market trends, economic indicators, changes in monetary policies, increases in government expenditures, decreases in other areas of government expenditures, shortages, surpluses, consumer buying trends, international competition due to lower labor costs, access to raw materials, and so forth?

If you can answer that you do have this time and feel that it would be more rewarding financially and emotionally to spend this time being a professional in the market than spending it developing more expertise in your profession, pursuing a hobby, or engaging in recreational activities, then you have the first *T*.

Training

The second *T* is for training. What is your educational background— accounting, statistical analysis, money and banking, marketing, economics, finance, psychology? Even if you have the first *T* of time, can you properly translate this knowledge into action? If you can, and if you are thoroughly schooled in these areas and have developed some reasonable expertise in them, you qualify for the second *T*.

Temperament

The third *T* is for temperament. Are you temperamentally suited for successful investing in the stock market? Have you worked very hard for your money? Were you a child of the Depression? Does your memory of hard times make you squeeze every dollar until the eagle screams loudly?

In my counseling I have observed that those from such a background tend to make their emotional decisions about money more black and white than they should be. Money decisions must often be various shades of gray. I find that if a person has experienced bad times, he either clutches a dollar very tightly to his bosom for fear of losing it, or decides that once he gets a dollar, he is going to put it to work aggressively to see if he can turn that dollar into an additional dollar. My reaction to not having any money has been the latter. It's not that I enjoy hoarding money or even spending it. My challenge has been to take one dollar and make two, and then take the two and make four, and so on. Money is like a flower. If you squeeze it, you will crush the life out of it. You must let it blossom forth to reveal its full beauty.

Analyze your own personality. This is not an easy thing to do. Some basic books on psychology may be of help to you. One I have enjoyed is Dr. Muriel James's book on transactional analysis entitled *Born to Win*. I also recommend Dr. Maxwell Maltz's book, *Psycho-Cybernetics*. The whole field of psychology can be fascinating, and through it you may discover why you and others react to certain stimuli and conditions the way you do. In the world of finance, this knowledge can pay handsome dividends.

Can you act when you have reasonable facts before you? You'll never know all the facts. If you wait until you are 100 percent sure, your decision will invariably be too late. I find that most investment decisions are made far too late rather than too soon. Don't ever deceive yourself into thinking that if you don't make a decision, you haven't made a decision. You have. You have decided that where your money is right now is the best place for it to be.

I've found the difference between mediocre and superb performance in the market is the ability to evaluate and then take the appropriate action quickly.

I observe many who plant good fruit trees in the form of good stocks and refuse to harvest the fruit, letting it rot on the trees.

Don't become enamored with a stock because it has been good to you by making you an unrealized capital gain (meaning it went up). Don't be afraid of taking a profit if it appears that the stock has topped out and will probably be flat for six months to a year. Don't back off from taking a profit just because you'll have a capital gains tax to pay.

There is a time to buy and a time to sell—regardless of which stocks you own. Can you unemotionally move when it's time to do so? If so, you have the third *T*, temperament.

Money

You have analyzed your three *T*s. Now let's look at how you fit the *M*, which represents money. Do you have enough money to diversify your holdings? Diversification is one of the first rules of successful investing. Do you have sufficient funds to enable you not to put all your eggs in one basket, but to have at least ten baskets—one basket for office equipment, another for natural resources, still another for beverages, another for retail stores, another for technology stocks, and so on?

It is difficult to obtain adequate diversification with less than $100,000. There are many institutions and other fiduciaries who do

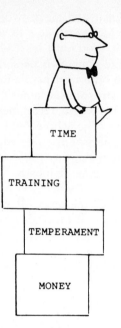

not consider sufficient diversification can be obtained with less than $250,000.

You may feel the need to subscribe to an advisory service. You should calculate this cost in money and in the time needed to digest and apply the contents.

If you have the three *T*s and an *M*, you will find being your own pro fun and rewarding. Therefore, you should plan to devote considerable time and energy to this important facet of your financial future. If not, let the pros do it for you.

Letting the Pros Do It

You may find letting the professionals do your investing for you very hard to do. It is especially hard for some professionals. You would think it would be otherwise, since they are very aware of how much time, training, and experience it took to bring them to their present level of proficiency. The admission that someone else can do something better than they can do it often is just too hard an admission for some persons to make. The same doctor who would be aghast if I should suggest diagnosing my own pains will hop into the stock market arena without any more preparation.

Even when the professional becomes a pro in the market, I usually find that the good full-time pros outperform the part-time pros.

Let's assume that you are willing to let the professionals help you. What choices are available to you?

Private Professional Management

There are two ways to obtain professional management. If you have a large amount of money to invest, you may qualify for private professional management through an investment advisory service. There are some that will accept as small an account as $50,000 for a fee of 1 percent of the net assets per annum. Most of the top services will not accept an account of less than $250,000. Some services will not accept a private account of less than $20 million. Management charges run from 1/2 to 1 or 2 percent, usually depending on the size of the account.

Let's assume that you have sufficient funds to qualify for private professional management. What should you do?

First, do an in-depth study of the professional teams available. Become acquainted with their personnel, and take a good hard look at their past performance. After all, you are buying brains. You might as well get the best "brains" you can for the money you are paying.

Second, you will sign an agreement giving the management service discretionary power to buy and sell for your account. This can be cancelled or amended at your discretion. In the agreement you should designate the stockbroker of your choice.

Third, you will need to transfer the agreed amount of money or stocks to the bank or broker that is to act as the custodian of the assets in the account. They will then make the proper delivery of stocks and money at the direction of the advisors.

After these necessary steps have been taken, you will begin to receive confirmations from your broker on each buy and sell. Your service will also make a monthly or quarterly report to you, giving you a resume of all transactions, a report on gains and losses, and often a comparison of your portfolio's performance against that of the popular averages. You may withdraw the account at any time.

Public Professional Management

If the amount you have for investment in equities is less than $250,000, you should consider using public professional management, through the investment medium of the investment company trusts, commonly called mutual funds.

I would prefer calling them by another name. Not that the term "mutual fund" does not give an indication of their nature, but I find that so many confuse them with mutual savings and loan or mutual insurance companies, and worry that they can be assessed accordingly, which of course is not true.

The Feeling Is Mutual. "Mutual" means you may mutually benefit from pooling your resources with others. For example, let's say you have $1,000. Alone you could not obtain diversification or professional management. But let's assume there are 999 others who each have $1,000 and have the same financial objective that you do. If all of you pooled your funds, you would have a million dollars. With a million dollars, you would have sufficient money to spread your risk among a number of different industries. You would also have enough money to hire some top professional money managers to select and constantly supervise your holdings. A mutual fund, then, should do for you what you would do for yourself if you had sufficient time, the proper training, the right temperament, and sufficient money to diversify. It offers the same advantages to the small investor that the wealthy have always had. The wealthy have enough money to diversify and enough money to hire the pros.

There are now 17.5 million shareholders investing $250 billion in mutual funds. They are the fourth largest type of financial institution in the United States.

In a previous chapter, we concluded that there are three basic requirements for successful investing: diversification, proper selection, and constant supervision. Let's examine these three to see if a quality mutual fund with excellent management could fulfill these requirements. There is a wide range of expertise in mutual fund managements. There are a large number of them that I would not use. There is a select group of management teams that have consistently produced superior performance. You should spend considerable time and study in choosing the one or ones you will use.

The Seminar Fund

For the past twenty years I have conducted financial planning seminars in Houston, Texas. At the second session of each seminar, I discuss mutual funds and how they work. As an example, but not necessarily as a recommendation, I usually use the same mutual fund. It is middle of the road in its financial objectives, has a good forty-eight-year record, and has averaged approximately 12 percent compound over its lifetime with all distributions reinvested. It's not the top performer among funds, but its record is consistently good.

I always use a fund that has averaged at least 12 percent over the long term, for I'm convinced that that's the minimum long-term performance you should accept on your money. With inflation and taxes, this 12 percent would not be enough to keep ahead today, although during this forty-eight-year period it would have. I'll show you a system that we use today that should still keep you considerably ahead.

In this book I'll call this fund the Seminar Fund. That's not its real name. If I were to use its real name, I would have to hand you a prospectus before I could tell you about it, and send you a new one each year. I do encourage you to go to your broker and get the prospectus of a real fund. Most prospectuses are pretty much the same. The funds they describe differ as to financial objective, investment advisors, and performance, but their fees, commission, and structure are similar.

In our chapter on selecting stocks, we agreed that one of the first requirements of successful investing was diversification—spreading your risk. Mutual funds fulfill this requirement.

Diversification. The Investment Company Act of 1940 provides that a mutual fund may not have more than 5 percent of its assets in any one company nor own more than 10 percent of the outstanding shares of any one company. Because of this regulation, if you own a mutual fund you know that you will always have at least twenty stocks in your fund's portfolio, and also that any one of the twenty will not represent more than 10 percent of the outstanding shares of that company. This in itself ensures a fair degree of diversification.

You will find as you explore the large number of funds available that most of them have from 100 to 150 different stocks in their portfolio, and that they cover a wide spectrum of industry groups.

For example, Table 4-1 shows the way $10,000 would have been spread if you had invested in the Seminar Fund on December 31, 1981, and it lists the ten largest individual holdings separately.

Sometimes in the seminar in describing the diversification, I mention Philip Morris and note that the fund had its largest holding there on December 31. I tell my audience about the time when the first tobacco warning was issued by the surgeon general and one of my lady clients called to see if she should sell her Philip Morris stock. My answer to her was, "No, never sell sin short." I then go on to comment that they've added another popular "sin"—Miller's High Life Beer.

Diversification such as this can permit you to own your slice of the U.S. economy by becoming a part owner of the major companies whose products and services you use regularly. At the end of 1981, the Seminar Fund's portfolio was diversified into 112 common stocks.

Such diversification is essential if you want to build a prudent investment portfolio. Even if you had many thousands of dollars to invest, you would find it difficult to achieve this broad a diversification.

Table 4-1. Largest Individual Holdings

Philip Morris	$444	Union Oil of California	179
International Business Machines	314	NCR	173
SmithKline	225	Atlantic Richfield	159
Capital Cities Communications	195	Phillips Petroleum	158
General Electric	194	Boeing	143

Other Portfolio Securities in the Seminar Fund

AMP	$ 70	International Paper	$86
Abbott Laboratories	61	K Mart	82
Ahmanson(H.F.)	28	Kaiser Aluminum & Chemical	86
Alcan Aluminium	29	Knight-Ridder Newspapers	108
Alco Standard	49	MCA	127
Aluminum Company of America	51	Manufacturers Hanover	27
American Airlines	45	Masco	70
American Broadcasting	43	McDermott	51
American Telephone	1	McDonald's	129
Amfac	8	Minnesota Mining & Manufacturing	21
Anheuser-Busch	78	Monsanto	84
Avery International	66	Morgan(J.P.)	74
BankAmerica	62	Motorola	4
Bethlehem Steel	30	Northwest Airlines	127
Boise Cascade	31	Northwestern National Life	
Bristol-Myers	77	Insurance	29
Canadian Pacific	71	Owens-Corning Fiberglas	11
Carolina Power & Light	45	Owens-Illinois	85
Caterpillar Tractor	84	Penney(J.C.)	89
Colt Industries	42	Pitney-Bowes	63
Communications Satellite	92	Polaroid	99
Delta Air Lines	37	Reynolds Metals	23
Digital Equipment	108	Roadway Express	24
Disney Productions	82	Rohm & Haas	115
Duke Power	57	St.Paul Companies	92
du Pont	25	Searle(G.D.)	102
Eastman Kodak	78	Sears, Roebuck	65
Federated Department Stores	139	Shell Oil	133
Firestone Tire & Rubber	28	Southern Railway	32
First Charter Financial	21	Sperry	23
First Chicago	24	Standard Oil of California	40
Ford Motor	37	Sterling Drug	109
Foremost-McKesson	54	Texas Utilities	96
General Dynamics	52	Tidewater	53
General Motors	95	Time, Inc	106
Goodyear Tire & Rubber	31	Times Mirror	137
Great Northern Nekoosa	73	Transway International	29
Great Western Financial	58	UAL	71
Halliburton	109	Westinghouse Electric	111
Hanna Mining	39	Westvaco	61
Hart Schaffner & Marx	14	Weyerhaeuser	24
Hilton Hotels	84	Xerox	91
Hitachi Ltd.	57	Other Stocks	160
Holiday Inns	70		
Honeywell	22	Total Stocks	7,839
Host International	36	Net Cash and Equivalents	2,161
Inco	13	Total	$10,000

To purchase 100 shares each of just ten of the largest holdings in the Seminar Fund would have cost nearly $51,000 at year-end.

I'm sure you'll agree that this array of values plus a few other stocks and cash and cash equivalents should fulfill the first requirement for successful investing—diversification.

Proper Selection and Constant Supervision. The Seminar Fund often has a picture in its guidebook of some very learned looking men and women sitting around a large conference table with research reports in front of them. They are having one of their daily conferences to determine which stocks to add and which to take out of the portfolio, or to determine which stocks they presently hold fulfill the requirements that the shareholders designated when they chose this particular fund.

A staff of analysts, each a specialist in his own field, constantly reports to this committee. There will be specialists in the oils, the chemicals, the technologies, and so forth. Not only do they read, analyze, and project figures on each company in their industry specialty, but they also make on-the-spot studies and conduct fact-finding interviews with the top officers of these companies. They often have research staffs worldwide.

I remember an officer of an oil company calling me to invest in a particular fund after one of the fund's analysts had called on him. He was very impressed with the analyst's thorough knowledge of the oil industry and especially of his company.

Successful investing is a full-time job. In a dynamic and competitive economy, the fortunes of individual companies—and often entire industries—can change very rapidly. Professionals who can stay abreast of these changes and capitalize on them are likely to achieve superior results.

These financial analysts log hundreds of thousands of miles a year visiting corporations and talking with their key executives, their competitors, their suppliers, their bankers, and their customers. The analysts also study the industry, as well as the economic and regulatory climate in which each company operates. They review trade publications, company reports, and financial journals; confer with leading business consultants and economists; and analyze reports from scores of investment and statistical services. The information gathered by these financial professionals flows continuously into their offices, where it is evaluated and converted into investment decisions.

Successful investing is a continuous problem-solving process. As in any problem-solving situation, the individual or group who, first, has access to the best information concerning the problem and, second, can apply the best combination of judgment, experience, imagination, and financial resources to this information is the one most likely to consistently come up with the best solutions.

The thoroughness and training of these specialists fulfill the two other requirements of successful investing—proper selection and constant supervision.

In addition to these three requirements of successful investing, the properly selected mutual fund can provide other valuable benefits. These benefits include:

1. Convenience
2. Dollar-cost averaging
3. Ease of record keeping
4. Matching your financial objectives
5. Passing on professional management
6. Ease of estate settlement
7. Lower costs
8. Quantity discounts and rights of accumulation
9. Exchange privilege
10. Timing
11. Performance
12. A check a month

Convenience, an Essential Ingredient. The first is convenience. We all do what is convenient for us. Mutual funds can offer this convenience with a plan that will fit almost any pocketbook. You may start an investment program in a mutual fund with a relatively small amount of money; in fact, some funds have no minimum initial investment. Others will accept as small an amount as $100. You may then add funds in any amount which may be as low as $25. In addition, you have the privilege of automatically reinvesting both your dividends and your capital gains, usually without commission. Some funds charge to reinvest dividends. None charge to reinvest capital gains. If you were to receive these same dividends from individual stocks in your private portfolio and you realized capital gains from your buys and sells and wanted to reinvest, you would be charged a commission. Since a mutual fund permits immediate reinvestment of small or large amounts of money, it gives you an opportunity to speed up your compounding potential.

Dollar-Cost-Averaging As You Earn. The second item in the list of twelve additional advantages that a mutual fund may offer is that you can truly dollar-cost average. This means putting the same amount of money into the same security at the same interval. One certainty of the stock market is that it will fluctuate. So put this characteristic to work for you instead of worrying so much about it. Choose an amount you can comfortably invest each month (not too comfortably or you may not save anything) and invest that amount on the same day each month.

Many funds provide a bank draft authorization so that the bank can automatically draft your account each month. I find this to be an extremely satisfactory arrangement for my clients. Banks never forget! I find my clients often do.

The mutual funds will carry your share purchase out to the third decimal point, which allows you to truly dollar-cost-average. This makes this investment medium a good one to use for this purpose.

Chapter 5 covers this point in more detail.

Recordkeeping Made Easy. Another characteristic of the mutual fund is that you have professionals doing your recordkeeping. You will have five choices when you open an account. Regardless of which choice you make, the fund will provide you a historical record of your account.

1. Reinvest all distributions.

2. Reinvest all distributions, and you may add amounts systematically or when you desire.

3. Receive dividends in cash and reinvest capital gains.

4. Receive dividends and capital gains in cash.

5. Receive a check a month.

All you need to do is keep the last confirmation you receive that year, and you will have a complete record of your account. The mutual fund also will send you (and IRS) a Form 1099, showing the dividends and capital gains paid to you for the year. This you will want to keep and attach to your federal income tax return.

You will receive a confirmation statement every time there is any activity in your account. You do not need to worry about the safety of your share certificates. They will be held for you by the fund's transfer agent, or sent to you if you wish.

Where Do You Fit on the Triangle? Do you remember our triangle of finance that we used when we were discussing individual stocks? It is applicable here, too. A fund must state in its prospectus its financial objective. This objective cannot be changed without the consent of the shareholders. The fund rarely changes its objective. If it is at present an income fund and management also desires to manage a growth fund, they will establish a new fund and add it to their family of funds. The financial triangle would look something like this:

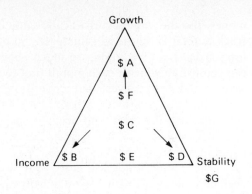

As you can see, you can't be a Paul Revere who hops on his horse and rides off in all directions. You must decide in which direction you want to go. When you maximize Income you move farther from Growth. The same is true if you select Stability as your primary concern.

A fund management group may have a family of funds, attempting to provide a fund on each place on the triangle, or it may have only one or two.

Kinds of Mutual Funds

There are approximately eleven kinds of mutual funds: growth (aggressive, quality with income), income, tax-advantaged trusts, corporate bond, balanced, convertible bond, specialty funds, option, municipal bond, and money market funds.

Growth Funds

Under the growth designation you could have four subheadings: "go-go," very aggressive growth, quality growth, and growth with income funds.

If you invest in a quality growth fund, you will be placing your dollar nearer to the top of the triangle at *A*, because its objective is long-term growth. Intermittent volatility should not be of great concern. Nor should you be interested in dividends. As a matter of fact, if it were possible for the fund managers to select stocks that paid no dividends and just grew in value, with no need to buy and sell and realize capital gains, this would be ideal for you. What you really want is for $1 to grow to at least $3 in ten years. You would prefer not to have any tax liability in the meantime if this were possible.

When I've asked a prospective client his financial objective and he has answered that it is growth, I may recommend a particular quality growth fund to him. When he asks me, "How much does it pay?" meaning what are the dividends, I know I have not conveyed what a growth fund is designed to do.

Common Stock Funds

The middle-of-the-road fund that seeks growth with income is the strong-hold of the mutual fund industry. It would fit in the middle of your triangle and is the place where most investors feel the greatest comfort.

When deciding where you should be on the triangle, you should remember that your temperament is important in your investment program. I find in my counseling that once I have sufficient information about a client's time schedule, assets, and tax bracket, it is not difficult to choose the investment that would fulfill his needs financially, but it may not fit his temperament. Regardless of how much I think he should invest for maximum growth, if I detect that volatility would disturb his peace of mind, then the best investment for him will probably be in the middle. Peace of mind is a good investment, too.

Our Seminar Fund fits in the middle, and it is letter F on the triangle. Let's say that F stands for "just fine" for most investors. Trying to make it too fast is what causes most failures. Remember, those who make it to their goal of financial independence have usually done it slowly. If you select your fund well from this category, you should be able to obtain your 12 percent compounded over a twenty-year period. (12 percent is $96,462.) The Seminar Fund has in the past averaged 12 percent or better in seventeen of the twenty-nine twenty-year periods. The entire record appears in Table 7 of the Appendix.

In this category also are funds that invest in stocks only from the list that are legal for investment of trust funds in the District of Columbia and that meet the "prudent man's rule" for investing. This means that an attorney, a fiduciary, or you could place an orphan child's money in it, and that it would be difficult to question you as to whether you had acted as a prudent fiduciary.

Income Funds

There are a number of quality income funds. Their portfolio managers choose stocks that have paid good dividends in the past, have a record of increasing dividends, and have a reasonable expectation of continuing good dividends and market stability of their shares. If your need is for income now, rather than later, this is the type of fund you may want to consider. Your location on the triangle would be *B*.

Bond Funds

When you invest in a bond fund, you are placing your dollar in the lower right-hand side of the triangle (*D*). Bond funds have been around for many years; however, during the growth craze of the 1960s, they attracted very little attention. With the agonizing reappraisals in the stock market in the 1970s they became popular again.

Bond funds invest most of their funds in debt-type securities. These are corporate bonds and debentures, perhaps a few convertible bonds, treasuries, or commercial paper. Instead of taking an equity position in the market, you become a lender of money when you choose these funds.

When you invest in a bond fund, do not think that the price of the shares will remain fixed. It will not. It will fluctuate with interest rates.

If your fund is composed of bonds with an average yield of 12 percent and the going interest rate is 14 percent, then the fund will not be able to sell its bonds at par; therefore, the price of your shares would decline. On the other hand, if the going rate drops to 10 percent, the fund probably can sell the bonds at a premium (above par) and the price of your shares will increase. If a bond was purchased at par (usually $1,000) and carries a rate of 9 percent, and if it matures January 1, 2000, this does not mean that the fund must hold the bond until the year 2000 to turn it into cash. It means that on January 1, 2000, the person holding the bond is guaranteed $1,000. Between now and that date, the value will usually fluctuate with the country's going interest rate. If you have owned a bond fund over the past few years, you have a loss in it today. I would suggest, if it is part of a family of funds, that you exchange it for one of the more growth-oriented funds and charge the loss off on your tax return.

Balanced Funds

In position *C* on the triangle, you will find balanced funds. These are funds that invest approximately 60 percent of their funds in high-quality bonds and the remainder in high-quality, income-producing "blue-chip" stocks. In periods of market decline, if that decline has not been caused by extraordinarily high interest rates, they could experience less volatility than the growth funds. Conversely, in a rising market they usually lag behind.

Convertible Bond Funds

In an effort to obtain the best of two worlds, some management groups a few years ago established convertible bond funds. These funds were designed to have a relatively good yield and some potential for growth. Any dollars you have placed in these funds would be placed around *E* on the triangle. As discussed earlier, convertible bonds are supposed to offer you the best of two worlds: the guarantee of principal and rate of return of a bond, and the potential for growth of common stock.

The theory runs that, even though you may be placing a bit of a damper on maximum growth potential, there is down-side protection, for the convertible bond should drop in price only to a level where it will take on the characteristics of a bond yielding the current interest level. Unfortunately, we've had wildly gyrating and unusually escalating interest rates that have made these funds more volatile.

The limited number of quality convertible bonds available in the marketplace has tended to make for a thin market (not enough traders to make it competitive). Also, many of the firms who offered convertible bonds in the past were not the blue-chip companies. They had to offer convertibles to "sweeten the kitty" to sell their bonds. Because the convertible bonds have been tied to less stable securities, they have been more volatile than some shareholders have been willing to accept.

Specialty Funds

Specialty funds may concentrate on insurance, bank, utilities, or gold stock. I have not placed them on the triangle because their characteristics are not easily categorized. Utility shares may be popular from time to time for those who want income. Gold stocks can be a very interesting approach in times of worldwide economic instability.

Tax-Managed Trusts

In recent years a new type of fund that has attracted some attention is one that elects to be taxed as a corporation rather than act as a conduit, as a regular mutual fund does. You are not given a choice of whether or not you will receive your dividends in cash. They are reinvested for you. The fund pays the tax, if any is due. Usually the fund can avoid the tax by conscientious portfolio management. If you've held your shares for over a year and want some cash distribution, just liquidate some shares. The gain will be treated as a capital gain for tax purposes.

One of these funds will let you exchange publicly traded securities you may hold, both stocks and bonds, for shares of the trust, and thereby you will avoid the commission on their sale.

Flexible Funds

There is another category of funds that is difficult to place in any one position. Their chief characteristic is that they are allowed by charter to invest all or a portion of their funds outside the United States. This can be a valuable feature because there are times when there are good buys in other countries and not here. The majority of the few funds following this approach have done very well.

Municipal Bond Funds

These are covered in more detail in a later chapter. They provide tax-free income, permit additions in small amounts, and provide reinvestment privileges to allow you to compound tax-free. If you have had the misfortune to have invested in any bond fund over the past several years, you probably have a rather substantial loss. Should you establish your loss by selling your municipal bond fund? The answer is probably yes.

Money Market Mutual Funds

In my opinion, there are only two places to have guaranteed liquid dollars: in a checking account or a money market mutual fund. You need funds in a checking account for convenience. Money market mutual funds have made passbook savings accounts and certificates of deposit obsolete.

Money market mutual funds came about during the mid-1970s when high interest rates became available to those who had $100,000 to put into savings. You probably remember seeing ads back in 1974 offering 12 percent on $100,000 certificates of deposit. Well, some people didn't have $100,000, so some of the funds established money market funds whereby investors with as little as $1,000 could take advantage of these higher rates by pooling their money with others in the fund.

When you deposit money into one of these accounts, there is no cost to put it in and no cost to take it out, it compounds daily, your rate will usually be comparable to that on a million-dollar certificate of deposit, you can write a check for $500 or more, and you can even draw interest while it is clearing. If you don't think your check will be processed for a few days, you should certainly use your money market mutual fund check-writing privilege. Money has tremendous earning power and you'll always want it working for you rather than someone else.

Your regular money market fund will be invested in large-denomination, short-term money market instruments issued by the Treasury, government agencies, banks, and corporations.

There are also money market mutual funds that must have 100 percent of their assets invested in either Treasury, federal agency obligations, or reposits backed by them. Their yield is generally 1/2 to 1 percent less, and some of them are exempt from state and local taxes.

A few years ago Americans who did not have large amounts of savings had to accept the small percentage that was available on savings accounts because of Regulation Q. It was great for the banking industry but deprived many a depositor of a decent return on his money. The money market funds came to the rescue of the small saver.

I can see six advantages to money market mutual funds (don't confuse these with the so-called money market certificates issued by some savings and loans). They are: (1) higher yields; (2) instant liquidity; (3) check-writing privileges; (4) funds draw interest until a check is cleared; (5) more safety; and (6) more privacy.

The "more safety" I've mentioned above may have surprised you. I know the argument that deposits in banks are protected by the FDIC (up to $100,000) while there is technically no insurance for money market funds. However, if there should be a run on the banks, the $100,000 would be hard to deliver. If that should occur, only about 2 percent of all bank deposits could probably be paid off under the guarantee.

On the other hand, if you want added safety, you may use the funds that only invest in U.S. government paper, which is backed by the people who print the money.

I personally use the regular money market mutual funds, but I do avoid those that invest heavily in commercial paper.

Learn to use money market mutual funds for your business and personal use. You'll need accounts with two different managements. You'll know why when I discuss "timing."

On the triangle I have represented money market mutual funds by the letter *G* and have placed it outside the triangle since it would be out of the market. Here *G* could represent "Good" if money is tight and is attracting interest rates of 13 to 20 percent.

"Will Some Brains"

Another characteristic of a mutual fund is that it allows you to choose professional management for those dependent on you. I have a client who has been an excellent stock trader for years. We have made very good profits together. He has thoroughly enjoyed the challenge of predicting trends before they happened, buying the leading stocks in those industries, moving out of them before the trends ran out, and moving into the next trend ahead of the other traders. A few years ago he said that he wanted to invest in a particular mutual fund. Since he had never shown any interest in mutual funds over the years that he had been my client, and since he obviously was very good at selecting his own portfolio, I asked him why he had now decided to avail himself of outside professional management. He said, "I want to will some brains to my wife and daughter." He was not being derogatory. He described his wife and daughter to me. He obviously loved them very much and was proud of their accomplishments. Then he added, "They know nothing about money management. It's probably my own fault. Stock analysis and projections have been my avocation for many years, but I've never attempted to share this information with them. On the other hand, I don't really think it's their cup of tea. They are both creative, artistic, very social people who have taken delight in the luxuries my talent has provided for them, but I don't think they have ever given much thought to the source of the funds that provide these luxuries. I'm getting up in years now and want to will some brains to my wife and daughter so that they may continue to have professional management of their money in the event that I'm not here to provide it for them."

The selection he made was good, and his reasoning was sound. He selected a management team with a long consistent record of good performance.

You may want to consider if professional management is something you desire to have readily available to members of your family.

Ease of Estate Settlement

Another reason that my client chose to place some of his funds under professional management as he grew older was the ease of estate settlement. He knew that upon his death the individual stocks in his portfolio would be frozen and could only be changed with the permission of the courts.

For example, let's say that shares of U.S. Steel had been in this portfolio at the time of steel's confrontation with the Kennedy administration, when for all practical purposes they were told they would not be allowed to make a profit. There had been earlier storm warnings on the horizon. Quick action to sell looked prudent. But if the estate had not been probated, the shares could not have been sold quickly enough to protect the estate.

Now let's assume that U.S. Steel had been in the portfolio of his fund. The fund's portfolio managers were free to sell U.S. Steel from the fund and replace it with another stock. The shares of the fund were frozen in the estate, but not the securities that made up the portfolio of the fund. Therefore, the mutual fund could have provided professional management of the assets while awaiting settlement of the estate, which can take several years.

Diversification Maintained After Probate

Another advantage that the fund makes available is the ease with which an estate can be divided with no disruption of diversification. Let's assume that there were four heirs instead of two, that the benefactor wanted them to share and share alike, and that the securities in the estate were in the form of 4,000 shares of the Seminar Fund. Each heir would receive 1,000 shares. There would be no disruption of diversification in each of the four portfolios. Each would still own a proportionate share of 100 to 150 stocks, all professionally selected and managed as if they belonged to one billionaire.

Lower Cost

Mutual funds should not be used as trading vehicles, for the initial commission can be higher to buy than for individual stocks. However, there is no commission to sell regardless of how much the shares may have grown in value. Also, most funds do not have a commission to reinvest dividends or capital gains.

A study conducted by the National Association of Security Dealers indicated that an investment of $5,000 in sixteen individual issues, which is what they deem necessary for adequate diversification, would cost 7 percent in commissions, assuming an "in and out" transaction in listed securities. If you conclude that dividend reinvestment at asset value is worth 1 percent to the average investor, that rights of accumulation are worth 0.5 percent, and that the exchange privilege is worth 0.4 percent, the commission of individual stocks would be 8.9 percent. This study also found that the average charge on fund sales is only 4.4 percent because of the discounts obtained on purchases of over $10,000 and cumulative discounts.

On the basis of prevailing commission rates, $5,000 invested into twenty different stocks at $25 per share would pay commissions around $474 each time, or 9.5 percent of the amount involved. The average fund has over 100 stocks, or five times this diversification, plus a team of professionals selecting the stocks.

For example, a $100,000 investment in a fund with 100 stocks in its portfolio would carry a 3-1/2 percent cost in and no cost to come out. Compared to purchasing and selling 100 shares of a $20 stock, the commission would be around $102, or a little over 2-1/2 percent. That's for just one trip and one stock. It's difficult to trade for as low a cost. The funds also pay commissions, but with negotiated rates you would find it difficult to match their lower costs.

Also, the Seminar Fund over a fifteen-year period would have reinvested more distributions for you without charge than your original investment on which you paid a commission. So you might feel you had your second go-around for free.

What Does It Pay?

I find that many people get hung up on what something costs them. I hope you do not. I never worry about what something "costs" me, but I am vitally concerned about what it "pays" me. It makes no difference what it "costs."

Let's assume that you turn over $1 to me to manage for you. I charge you no sales charge to do this. I will charge you, however, one-half of 1 percent yearly management fee. At the end of ten years, I return to you $2 net after all costs are taken out.

Now let's assume that you turn over another $1 to me, and on the $1 I charge you 8-1/2 pennies. Again I charge you one-half of 1 percent yearly management fee and at the end of ten years I return to you $3. Which was the best investment for you? Which really cost you the most? Did your efforts to save 8-1/2 pennies "cost" you $1?

Distilling the Wisdom of the Ages

If I were to distill all the wisdom that I have acquired over the years reading, interviewing, and observing, I could put it all in just nine words. "There is no such thing as a free lunch."

For example, let's assume you had $10,000. A savings institution would not have charged you to open a savings account with them. As a matter of fact, they may have given you a handy Teflon skillet or a fuzzy wuzzy blanket for doing so. But how much did it cost? Thirty years later, your $10,000 would have grown to $42,706 with the savings

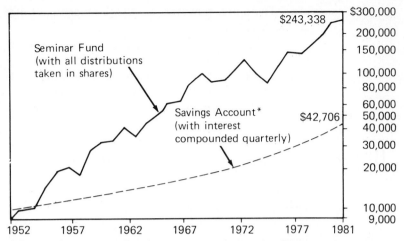

Figure 4-1. Growth of a $10,000 investment in the Seminar Fund and in a savings account.

institution, if all distributions had been reinvested. However, in that same period, had your $10,000 been in the Seminar Fund with all distributions reinvested, your results would have been $243,338 (see Figure 4-1). Which would you rather have—4 times your original capital, as in the savings account, or 24 times your original capital in the Seminar Fund? (I'm required by regulation to put in this disclaimer about it being a period of "rising stock prices" and "may be no indication of the future." Incidentally, the Dow Jones Average was not up but down 1.7 percent over the past ten years.) Most investors do not beat any of the popular averages. Bankers are now trying to "index," which means their trust departments are trying to do as well as the indexes by investing in the same stocks.

"Opportunity Fee"

I call the mutual funds sales charge an opportunity fee. My reason for doing so is this: Let's assume that you want to travel from Houston to Dallas. You find that the only way to get there is by bus. You go to the bus station; the clerk writes out your ticket and says, "That will be $14.65, please." You answer: "I'm not going to pay that." If you don't, you're just not going to Dallas. It's not what something costs you, but what it pays you that should be your chief concern.

There are, however, a few well-managed funds that do not make a sales charge.

Carefully examine their performance, too. Remember, though, you will not have the help of a financial planner in selecting your fund and in timing their purchase of exchange, and lack of cash flow may affect their performance. You will be buying from them very much as you would a suit of clothes from a mail order catalogue or Sunday supplement of your newspaper.

Buying Brains at a Discount

Earlier I said that mutual funds enabled the smaller investor to obtain the same advantages as the wealthier investor. The investor who has larger amounts does obtain quantity discounts on his original purchases. Table 4-2 gives some typical acquisition costs.

Table 4-2. Typical Acquisition Costs

Amount of Purchase	Total Acquisition Cost
Under $10,000	8.50%
$ 10,000 but less than $ 25,000	7.50%
$ 25,000 but less than $ 50,000	6.00%
$ 50,000 but less than $ 100,000	4.50%
$ 100,000 but less than $ 250,000	3.50%
$ 250,000 but less than $ 500,000	2.50%
$ 500,000 but less than $1,000,000	2.00%
$1,000,000 but less than $2,000,000	1.50%
$2,000,000 and more	1.00%

Letter of Intent

Perhaps you do not have a sufficiently large sum today to cross one of the discounts, but you will during the next thirteen months. Then you may want to consider buying under a letter of intent. The letter of intent is not a commitment to buy, but a privilege to buy at a discount during the thirteen-month period. For example, let's assume that you have $10,000 to invest today, but anticipate having an additional $15,000 to invest during the coming thirteen months. You would then invest under a $25,000 letter of intent. When you do that, you receive the same discount on your $10,000 purchase as if you had invested $25,000. The custodian bank then escrows some of your shares. When the additional $15,000 is added, the custodian releases your shares. If you decide you do not want to add the remaining $15,000, that is your privilege. If the thirteen months pass and you have not completed your letter, you have two choices: return the discount, which you would not have received anyway without the letter, or the custodian bank will sell enough of your escrowed shares to return to the fund the second discount you received and will send you the remaining shares. Your discount would be adjusted back to the $10,000 level. Therefore, the letter of intent never costs you more and can save you money. You are not required to return the dividends and capital gains on the extra shares you received during the period they were in escrow.

The Large Investor

As you looked at the $500,000 level in Table 4-1, you may have said, "Big deal. Who has that kind of money?" Contrary to what many people think, many large investors buy mutual funds. Many financial planners report that their clients' average mutual fund purchase is over $27,000. Many pension funds invest far in excess of a million dollars with the funds and receive the original discount while continuing to receive additional discounts. The Seminar Fund has many large investors with more than $5 million invested, and one company has $27 million in the fund.

Adding More at a Discount

Under what is called "rights of accumulation," you may also qualify for additional discounts. Let's assume that you own shares that have a value of $20,000 and that you have $5,000 you would like to add to your account. You may do so under the "rights of accumulation" at the $25,000 discount level. As your account grows, you may continue to add at progressively smaller opportunity fees as you cross each discount. Pension and profit-sharing plans use mutual fund shares because of their lower cost of acquisition, diversification, ease of record keeping, and because they meet the "prudent man" rule and fiduciary requirements.

The Exchange Privilege

An important characteristic of most mutual funds is that they offer you the privilege of exchanging one of their funds for another one of their funds. There would be no commission and there would either be no charge or a $5 exchange fee that would go to the transfer agent for his expense in doing this for you. This privilege could be of interest to you if your financial objective has changed.

For instance, if your financial objective has been growth but you are retiring, you may now be more interested in income. You have the privilege of changing from one fund to the other without a sales charge. You should be aware, however, that if you realize a gain on your shares, the IRS considers this a sale, and you'll have to pay a capital gains tax on your profit. A better way may be for you to just begin receiving your check a month from your growth fund, hoping that appreciation will replace the value of the shares redeemed.

You may also establish a loss for tax purposes using the exchange privilege. Let's assume that the market has dropped below your cost. You are still confident of the investment ability of the management team and believe that temporary market conditions have adversely affected anticipated performance. You are nearing the end of the year and have some capital gains already established for the year through the sale of some property. You may want to exchange the fund that you own for one of their other funds, thereby establishing a loss for tax purposes. Even without a capital gain, you could establish a $6,000 loss to be used against $3,000 of ordinary income. If you do not use all of the loss in that year, you may carry it forward indefinitely until you have used all of it.

You would need to wait at least thirty-one days before moving back to your original fund, or the IRS would disallow the deduction, calling it a "wash sale." Again, there is no commission to exchange it back to your original position.

Timing

The greatest advantage to the exchange privilege is that it gives you the opportunity to move in and out of the market without a commission. If the Federal Reserve is severely tightening the money supply, which looks as if it will choke the market, and your fund is part of a family of funds that has a money market fund, you may want to move over to this safer harbor, ride out the storm, and draw a tidy interest in the meantime.

You may be wondering why the fund managers do not take this action for you. They do move into as defensive a position as they can under the regulations by which they must abide. However, to qualify as a regulated investment company, which is important to you in terms of your taxes, less than 30 percent of their gross income in any fiscal year can be derived from holding securities less than three months. This regulation may inhibit moving from stock to cash on a short-term basis, which for your purposes may be the most prudent action to take. The exchange privilege gives you the opportunity to take advantage of the strengths of top professional management while avoiding the weakness caused by these regulations. This can make it possible for you to exploit their offensive ability by holding their funds during rising markets and avoiding what may be short-term weakness by moving out of the funds entirely during down markets.

Timing Services

You can attempt to time your own moves in and out of the market or you can use a timing service to do this for you. Our firm makes timing services available to our clients. Timing services have become very viable considerations during the past few years, because the Federal Reserve has been "playing with" the money supply and causing great volatility in interest rates and available capital.

During the twenty-year period between 1946 and 1966, we experienced an era of stability in our economy. Inflation was moderate, the fiscal authorities were not tampering unduly with the money supply, and for the most part the United States was dedicated to the profit system under free enterprise. Our standard of living was going up, and our gross national production was increasing steadily. Then in 1966, the Johnson administration attempted welfare and warfare without the courage to increase taxes. It wanted to create the Great Society without paying for it. This ended the era of stability and launched us into the era of pendulum economics.

Up until that time our stock market indexes resembled the man with the yo-yo walking up the stairs. If you got your eyes off the yo-yo, the man eventually climbed the stairs. With the coming of pendulum economics, the market became like the man with a yo-yo standing on the stairs. You'd make it and lose it, make it and lose it. It became more and more obvious that there were times when it might be too risky to be in the market and other times when it was risky to be out of it. If the drops could be avoided, the gains could be accelerated. This brought the birth of the timing services.

A sketch of this might look something like this:

Era of Stability   Era of Pendulum Economics

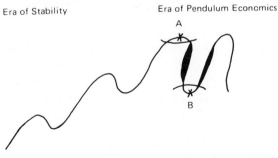

Our company and others went out to find a service that would get you out at point *A* and back in at point *B*. I wish I could report to you that we found one. We did not. But we did find more than one that had a good record of getting you out in the *A* area and back in around the *B* area. Obviously, this would not guarantee you against a loss. For example, if you went in at the high at $10 and the timing service triggered you out at $9, you would have suffered a $1 loss. What the timing service attempts to do is to avoid your investment going to say $6 before you start your climb up again. Even if your climb starts at $9, your potential is greater than if you had come down to $6 before starting up again.

Timing services are not a panacea. In sideways markets they can be very disappointing. They should be used, if you so choose to use them, over at least a four-year period. Figure 4-2 shows the hypothetical results of using a particular timing service with a growth fund in the same family of funds as the Seminar Fund. As you will note, $100,000 during the eight years and five months grew on a buy/hold basis to $349,357, or 15.5 percent a year, and to $495,722 with timing, or 20.3 percent. This is a difference of $146,365 or $17,219 per year average. The future may be better or it may be worse.

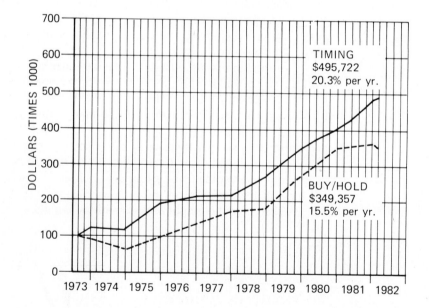

Figure 4-2. *Results of using timing service with growth fund in the same family of funds as the Seminar Fund with all dividends and capital gains reinvested.*

What Kinds of Funds Work Best With Timing?

If you are convinced that the timing service can help in keeping you out of the market when you ought to be out and in the market when you ought to be in, then your logical choice would seem to be an aggressive high-quality growth fund. It should go up faster in an up market when you are in and should go down faster in a down market when you are out.

Charges for Timing

Fees charged by the various timing services usually average about 2 percent of the net asset value per year.

The performance shown for the fund above is before the 2 percent fee; however only a 5 percent figure was used for income while out of the market from August 3, 1973, through December 31, 1980, and interest rates during some of those periods ran up to 10–20 percent in the money market funds where the money was placed when out of the market. Actual rates were used for the period after January 1, 1981. Over the past four years we have averaged around 24 percent.

If you are interested in timing, you should select a family of funds that has an aggressive growth fund and a money market fund. The timing service will then move your funds between the two.

Disadvantages of Timing Services

First, they can only try to get you out near the top and back in near the bottom. They will not be infallible. Though the fund does not charge a commission to make the exchange, the IRS does get into the act. If a gain has occurred, you will have realized either a long- or a short-term capital gain, and they'll want what they think is their share. However, if you are using timing with a tax-sheltered vehicle such as a Keogh, Individual Retirement Account, IRA rollover, pension or profit-sharing plan, all of these compound tax-sheltered, and no tax will be due.

Performance

You've heard the expression, "It doesn't mean a thing unless you pull that string." The same is true of your mutual fund. What has been its past performance (knowing that whatever it has been, there is no guar-

"TOTAL RETURN"

A meaningful way to compare the return on an investment in the Seminar Fund with the return on other investments.

"Total return" is simply a percentage figure which shows the change in the value of an investment when income dividends and capital gain distributions are taken in additional shares; it is a combination of income return and capital results.

Income return is represented by income dividends. Capital results are the change in net asset value of shares, adjusted for capital gain distributions.

Together, these add up to a percentage return that can be compared to those provided by other investments.

The chart below illustrates an assumed $10,000 investment from January 1, 1934 through December 31, 1981. The table depicts the Fund's total return in each of those 48 years.

The boxed figures in the lower right-hand corner sum up the entire lifetime of the Fund. They show

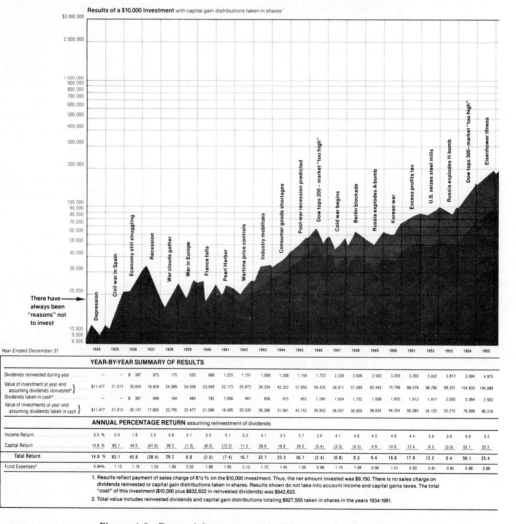

Results of a $10,000 Investment with capital gain distributions taken in shares¹

Chart labels (left to right): Depression · Civil war in Spain · Economy still struggling · Recession · War clouds gather · War in Europe · France falls · Pearl Harbor · Wartime price controls · Industry mobilizes · Consumer goods shortages · Post-war recession predicted · Dow tops 200 – market "too high" · Cold war begins · Berlin blockade · Russia explodes A-bomb · Korean war · Excess profits tax · U.S. seizes steel mills · Russia explodes H-bomb · Dow tops 300–market "too high" · Eisenhower illness

There have always been "reasons" not to invest

Year Ended December 31		1934	1935	1936	1937	1938	1939	1940	1941	1942	1943	1944	1945	1946	1947	1948	1949	1950	1951	1952	1953	1954	1955
YEAR-BY-YEAR SUMMARY OF RESULTS																							
Dividends reinvested during year		—	— $	387	975	175	520	866	1,225	1,151	1,068	1,206	1,156	1,723	2,339	2,606	2,583	3,059	3,293	3,432	3,812	3,984	4,975
Value of investment at year-end assuming dividends reinvested² }		$11,477	21,013	30,640	18,859	24,369	24,558	23,949	22,173	25,872	34,334	42,322	57,850	56,435	56,911	57,089	62,442	74,789	88,078	98,790	99,201	154,833	194,089
Dividends taken in cash³		—	— $	387	948	164	484	782	1,056	941	836	915	852	1,240	1,624	1,732	1,638	1,855	1,913	1,917	2,050	2,064	2,503
Value of investments at year-end assuming dividends taken in cash }		$11,477	21,013	30,137	17,805	22,795	22,477	21,096	18,495	20,535	26,396	31,561	42,152	39,903	38,557	36,959	38,634	44,254	50,085	54,125	52,210	79,008	96,316
ANNUAL PERCENTAGE RETURN assuming reinvestment of dividends																							
Income Return		0.0 %	0.0	1.8	3.2	0.9	2.1	3.5	5.1	5.2	4.1	3.5	2.7	3.0	4.1	4.6	4.5	4.9	4.4	3.9	3.9	4.0	3.2
Capital Return		14.8 %	83.1	44.0	(41.6)	28.3	(1.3)	(6.0)	(12.5)	11.5	28.6	19.8	34.0	(5.4)	(3.3)	(4.3)	4.9	14.9	13.4	8.3	(3.5)	52.1	22.2
Total Return		14.8 %	83.1	45.8	(38.4)	29.2	0.8	(2.5)	(7.4)	16.7	32.7	23.3	36.7	(2.4)	(0.8)	0.3	9.4	19.8	17.8	12.2	0.4	56.1	25.4
Fund Expenses⁴		0.94%	1.13	1.19	1.53	1.89	2.02	1.88	1.95	2.13	1.72	1.45	1.06	0.98	1.10	1.08	0.96	1.01	0.93	0.81	0.85	0.88	0.86

1. Results reflect payment of sales charge of 8½ % on the $10,000 investment. Thus, the net amount invested was $9,150. There is no sales charge on dividends reinvested or capital gain distributions taken in shares. Results shown do not take into account income and capital gains taxes. The total "cost" of this investment ($10,000 plus $832,622 in reinvested dividends) was $842,622.

2. Total value includes reinvested dividends and capital gain distributions totaling $827,555 taken in shares in the years 1934-1981.

Figure 4-3. Forty-eight-year record of Seminar Fund without timing service.

that an investment has provided a compound annual investment return of 12.03%.

One more point. If you look at the third line of the table ("Dividends taken in cash"), you will see that shareholders who have chosen to take their dividends in cash have received a growing stream of income that has more than offset the constantly rising cost of living.

During the period illustrated, stock prices fluctuated and were higher at the end than at the beginning. These results should not be considered as a representation of the dividend income or capital gain or loss which may be realized from an investment made in the Fund today.

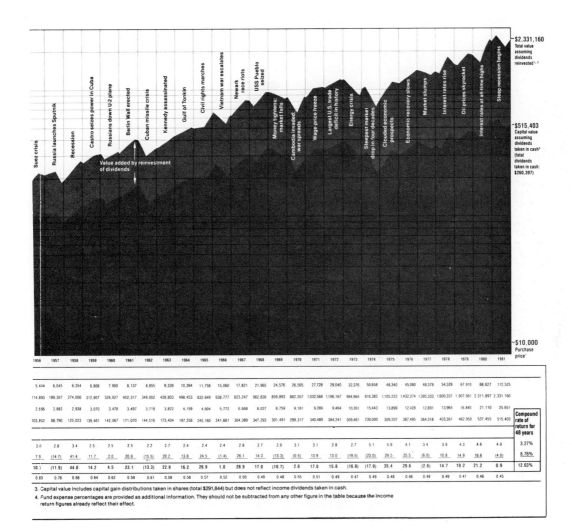

Right-side chart labels:
- $2,331,160 — Total value assuming dividends reinvested[1,2]
- $515,403 — Capital value assuming dividends taken in cash[3] (total dividends taken in cash: $260,397)
- $10,000 — Purchase price[1]

Year	Line 1	Line 2	Dividends taken in cash	Line 4
1956	5.444	114.893	2.656	103.892
1957	6.045	189.307	2.882	88.790
1958	6.354	274.006	2.938	125.023
1959	6.808	312.807	3.070	139.461
1960	7.900	326.927	3.478	142.067
1961	8.137	402.317	3.497	171.070
1962	8.855	349.002	3.719	144.516
1963	9.339	428.803	3.822	173.404
1964	10.394	498.453	4.159	197.256
1965	11.758	632.649	4.604	245.160
1966	15.060	638.777	5.772	241.661
1967	17.821	823.247	6.668	304.389
1968	21.965	962.836	8.027	347.293
1969	24.576	859.893	8.759	301.491
1970	26.505	882.357	9.161	299.317
1971	27.728	1,032.568	9.289	340.489
1972	29.040	1,196.167	9.464	384.241
1973	32.376	994.964	10.261	309.461
1974	50.658	816.385	15.443	239.000
1975	48.340	1,105.222	13.899	309.207
1976	45.080	1,432.274	12.428	387.495
1977	48.378	1,395.333	12.891	364.318
1978	54.328	1,800.337	13.965	403.361
1979	67.910	1,907.061	16.840	462.959
1980	88.627	2,311.897	21.110	537.455
1981	112.525	2,331.160	25.651	515.403

Compound rate of return for 48 years

Year	Income return	Capital return	Total return	Expense %
1956	2.8	7.9	10.7	0.80
1957	2.8	(14.7)	(11.9)	0.76
1958	3.4	41.4	44.8	0.68
1959	2.5	11.7	14.2	0.64
1960	2.5	2.0	4.5	0.62
1961	2.5	20.6	23.1	0.59
1962	2.2	(15.5)	(13.3)	0.61
1963	2.7	20.2	22.9	0.59
1964	2.4	13.8	16.2	0.58
1965	2.4	24.5	26.9	0.57
1966	2.4	(1.4)	1.0	0.52
1967	2.8	26.1	28.9	0.50
1968	2.7	14.3	17.0	0.49
1969	2.6	(13.3)	(10.7)	0.48
1970	3.1	(0.5)	2.6	0.55
1971	3.1	13.9	17.0	0.51
1972	2.8	13.0	15.8	0.49
1973	2.7	(19.5)	(16.8)	0.47
1974	5.1	(23.0)	(17.9)	0.49
1975	5.9	29.5	35.4	0.49
1976	4.1	25.5	29.6	0.48
1977	3.4	(6.0)	(2.6)	0.46
1978	3.9	10.8	14.7	0.49
1979	4.3	14.9	19.2	0.47
1980	4.6	16.6	21.2	0.46
1981	4.9	(4.0)	0.9	0.45
Compound rate	**3.27%**	**8.76%**	**12.03%**	

3. Capital value includes capital gain distributions taken in shares (total $291,844) but does not reflect income dividends taken in cash.

4. Fund expense percentages are provided as additional information. They should not be subtracted from any other figure in the table because the income return figures already reflect their effect.

Figure 4-3

125

antee it will be the same in the future)? But perhaps you can obtain some wisdom from the past.

I will be disappointed if it does not average in excess of 12 percent compounded over the next ten years.

There will no doubt be times when this will be an unattainable goal and other times when you'll vastly outperform this objective. Figure 4-3 shows the forty-eight-year record of the Seminar Fund without super-imposing a timing service, but using the expertise of their professional management. During this period, many seemingly catastrophic events have occurred, as you can see by the notations titled "There have always been 'reasons' not to invest." You will note, however, during its forty-eight years from January 1, 1934, to December 31, 1981, it had a compound rate of return of 12.03 percent. You can see for yourself the years it did that well and the years it did not. As a matter of fact, nineteen one-year periods were below that average and twenty-nine one-year periods were above that average.

Is Its Performance Guaranteed?

As you look at this record you may be asking, "Is this investment guaranteed?" I'm happy to tell you it is not! If you want a "guaranteed" dollar, you should take it to an institution that has a gold emblem on the door that declares that your funds are "guaranteed" (up to $100,000) by the FDIC. What does FDIC stand for? That's right—the Federal Deposit *Insurance* Corporation, a guaranteeing arm of the government. (They also bring to you the post office and Amtrak.)

Have you ever bought an insurance policy for which you did not pay a premium? What if I came to you and said, "I want to guarantee that you can always have your $10,000 back at any time regardless of what increases may have occurred in your cost of living and regardless of how much money I have made on your money, and all I want to charge you is $877.44 per month every month you leave it with me, or $10,529 per year?" What would you say to me? You'd say "The cost is too high," wouldn't you? That's what would have been your average per-month cost the past forty-eight years to have had your $10,000 guaranteed. A guaranteed dollar rarely pays. Most of the time it costs, and costs dearly.

To calculate this cost for yourself, note that the $10,000 has grown to $515,403 with no reinvestment of dividends. (You're taking the interest in cash from your guaranteed investment, too.) Subtract $10,000, your original investment, and this leaves $505,403. Divide this number by 576 (48 years x 12 months per year) to obtain $877.44 per month.

To get a visual picture of the difference between the "guaranteed" and the nonguaranteed, take your pencil and start at the left side of the

chart at $10,000 and draw a line to the right side at $10,000 and you
will note that the difference is $505,403.

The Yo-Yo and the Stairs

Now that you've studied the chart of the Seminar Fund, what are your
reactions? Remember, it covers a long period of time—forty-eight years
from 1934 through 1981. Do you agree that this is a fairly graphic
picture of a man with a yo-yo going up the stairs? What difference
did it make to him how many times the yo-yo yo-yo'd during the life
of the fund? The stairs he climbed reached quite a height. If you
had invested $10,000 on January 1, 1934, reinvested all your capital-
gains distribution (classified as part of capital by regulation), and on
December 31, 1981, decided to cash in your shares, you would have
received $515,403 net to you after all costs had been taken out, with the
exception of your federal and state income tax responsibility. If you had
reinvested both your capital gains and dividends, your $10,000 would
have grown to $2,331,160.

Just think how many life insurance policies, by contrast, have been
sold to men age seventeen or to their parents or grandparents with the
idea that the $10,000 placed in the cash value would be growing for their
retirement incomes at age sixty-five. For example, if they had placed
$10,000 into an insurance contract with one of our largest companies
forty-eight years ago, the guaranteed cash value by December 31, 1981,
would have been $27,322. In addition, their projected dividends (not
guaranteed) were $15,394, for a total of $42,716. To give you a point
of reference, $10,000 compounded at 2-1/2 percent for forty-eight years
is $32,715; at 3 percent it is $41,323; at 5 percent it is $104,013; and
at 12 percent it is $2,303,908. You can make these calculations for
yourself by looking in the Appendix at Table 5, "One Dollar Principal
Compounded Annually."

We, of course, do not know what the next forty-eight years will
bring, but if our economy is no better or no worse than the past forty-
eight years, surely this performance can be one of the possibilities you
should consider.

What About Inflation?

Inflation is the economist's way of saying "rising prices." The experts
can all explain how it happened and what it means, but no one has been
able to make it go away. To keep even with rising prices, you will

need a constantly rising income. How much income will you need in the future? One word tells it all: more. You will need more take-home pay from your job and more dividends from your investments.

Under the mountain chart you've just been studying, look at the line entitled "Dividends taken in cash." It shows how much cash, in income dividends, your $10,000 investment with capital gains reinvested would have generated during each of the past forty-eight years. Note that in forty-two of the past forty-eight years, the dividends paid by the Seminar Fund increased over the prior year. From a modest $387 paid in 1936, the dividend payments have increased to $25,651 in 1981— that's more than 2.5 times your original investment. This increase in income would not have been possible from a like amount invested in bonds or placed in a savings account.

The Berkleys and the Campbells

Another way to examine the cost of the guarantee is to take the hypothetical case of Sally and Jim Berkley and Vicki and Jack Campbell. Both inherited $30,000 on January 1, 1952, and each couple invested their $30,000 for retirement and for some income to help with current expenses.

The Berkleys placed theirs in a guaranteed position where they could obtain a 12 percent return with the principal guaranteed. (This was no small feat, since the rate being paid by savings and loans in the United States in 1954 was 2.5 percent. Perhaps they invested in Lower Slobovia Sewer Bonds.) The first year and every year thereafter they earned $3,600 interest on their investment—$300 a month, never less, never more. The Berkleys felt safe and said, "With an investment that pays 12 percent a year, we have no worries. We are safe for life."

But were they really? What happened to their purchasing power? In 1952 they could have bought a new Cadillac for $3,600. Today they would have to spend that much on a used Volkswagen.

Of course, they still have their original nest egg, but that, too, will buy only a fraction of what it used to. The Berkleys didn't understand how savagely inflation could eat away at the purchasing power of their dollars. Their "safe" investment had turned out to be not so safe after all. I know of no fixed-income investment available today with a yield high enough to offset long-term inflation.

The Campbells, on the other hand, understood that the only "safe" investment was one that would protect their purchasing power. They realized they would need more and more income in the years ahead and that their original investment would also need to grow. The Campbells decided to invest in the Seminar Fund. Like the Berkleys, they took their income in cash.

The Campbells knew that the value of their investment and the size of their income dividends would fluctuate. But they recognized the fact that a rising income is the best hedge against rising prices. And they felt that, over the long haul, an investment in the Seminar Fund and the income that it produced should continue to grow, reflecting the growing earnings and dividends of the companies in which the Fund invested.

Figure 4-4a & b shows what happened. Year after year, the Campbells received more income—rising income to help them keep pace with the rising cost of living. By 1966, their dividends for the year totaled $3,278; by 1971, they totaled $5,378; by 1976, they were up to $7,058; and in 1981, while the Berkleys were still getting only $3,600 a year, the Campbells received $14,565 in dividends from their Seminar Fund.

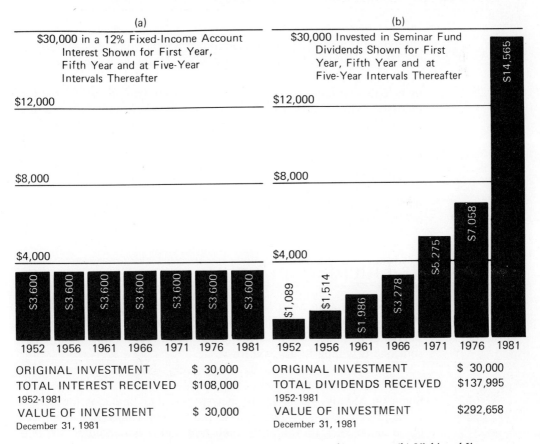

Figure 4-4. (a) Sally and Jim Berkley's "guaranteed" account; (b) Vicki and Jim Campbell's investment account.

The Campbells had another enormous advantage over the Berkleys. At the end of 1981, the Berkleys' investment was still worth only $30,000, but the Campbells' investment in the Seminar Fund had grown to more than $292,658!

Perhaps you should think about the Berkleys and the Campbells as you plan your financial future. Remember that a fixed return—no matter how high it is—is never "safe." Not as long as prices keep going up.

Do you believe that prices will continue to rise? Do you believe you'll need a rising income to offset those rising prices?

Should some of your investment dollars be put to work in an investment like the Seminar Fund?

Direct or Indirect Investing?

All money is invested in American industry either directly or indirectly. The direct method can be accomplished by putting your money to work in an investment similar to the Seminar Fund. An indirect method would be to lend your funds to a savings institution and let it invest in American industry. When you choose the latter method, you in effect place a filter along that $10,000 line in our example. The screen in that filter has in the past been equipped with a very fine mesh, and very little has filtered through to you.

Remember, to become financially independent you must save and let your money grow. Many save and let savings institutions grow. To participate in the profits of American industry, you must get your eyes off the yo-yo and on the stairs.

All Assets Fluctuate in Value

Why should you let daily fluctuations bother you? Everything you own fluctuates in value. The market value of any asset you own is only what someone is willing to pay you for it.

Your home fluctuates in value every day, but the newspaper doesn't carry a market page quoting its value. What if it did? You come home on Monday, pick up the newspaper, and find that the market value of your house is quoted at $70,000. On Thursday evening you come home, pick up the paper, and find that it is quoted at $62,000. Would you panic and begin crying? Would you be alarmed and begin to weep over your $8,000 loss? The loss is just as real if you need to sell.

Fortunately for your peace of mind, the values of your home and other assets are not published every day; therefore, you are unaware of their fluctuation in value, and you are saved the agony of existing in a state of panic as some do when they own securities.

Don't succumb to the yo-yo panic! If you do, you may find it very costly.

Consistency of Performance

Table 7 in the Appendix is a record of four time periods of the Seminar Fund. It shows the span in each that was the best, the worst, and the median period.

For our purposes here, let's consider the median to be fairly typical. Here are the compound growth rates for each of the median periods shown:

Median Period	Ending Value	Compound Rate
10 years (1941-50)	$28,746	11.1%
15 years (1946-60)	52,022	11.6
20 years (1942-61)	167,493	12.4
25 years (1943-67)	293,762	11.8
Lifetime		
48 years (1934-81)	$827,555	12.0

In today's environment of unusually high interest rates, 12 percent may not seem high. But remember that the current level of interest rates is a very recent phenomenon.

Mutual Funds for Your IRA Account

Mutual funds should make an excellent vehicle for your IRA account. It's simple to establish by completing an application form. The custodian cost is usually around $6.00. As you know, you may now contribute 100 percent of your earned income up to a maximum of $2,000, deduct it from your taxable income, and let the earnings compound tax-deferred. If you have a nonworking spouse, $2,250 can be contributed if at least $250 is registered in the latter's name. If both are working, each can contribute $2,000.

You may make your contribution any time before you file your federal income tax return for the year you are making the contribution.

If you have the $2,000 at the beginning of the year, you should consider making it then. In that way you'll have the whole amount compounding all year tax-sheltered. If you need to invest as you earn, the mutual fund is especially adaptable to this plan in that you can add relatively small amounts, and if you contribute the same amount each month or each quarter, you can get the mathematical advantage of dollar-cost averaging. (Explained more fully later.)

If you invested $2,000 per year and averaged 15 percent a year on your investments, you would have the following assets in your IRA account:

Year	Amount
$2,000/year	
10	$ 46,699.00
20	235,620.00
30	999,914.00
40	4,091,908.00
$2,250/year	
10	52,536.00
20	265,072.00
30	1,124,903.00
40	4,603,396.00
$4,000/year	
10	93,398.00
20	471,240.00
30	1,999,828.00
40	8,183,816.00

How to Receive a Check a Month

Let's assume you began investing in the Seminar Fund on January 1, 1952, by beginning with a lump sum of $10,000, and that you added $100 a month for the next twenty years. By December 31, 1971, you would have invested $33,900, plus dividends and capital gains, and you would own 27,900 shares with a market value of $195,163 (details in Appendix Table 8).

Let's now assume you are ready to start enjoying the fruits of your labor and investment program. You would then deposit your shares with the transfer agent (or you may have left them with him all along as unissued shares), and you would complete and send the fund a withdrawal application stating how much a month or quarter you would like to receive. You would begin receiving a check each month or quarter. You are free to increase, decrease, stop, and start whenever you like. Each time, your check will be accompanied by a complete report on the status of your account.

If you had started a 6 percent withdrawal on December 31, 1971 you would have received monthly withdrawals of $975.81, or $11,709.72 per year. Ten years later, on December 31, 1981, you would have withdrawn a total of $117,100, and your remaining shares would have had a value of $233,786.

Your net results would have been:

Amount withdrawn	$117,100
Amount remaining	233,786
	$350,886
Amount you contributed over 20 years	33,900
American industry contributed	$316,986

(See the Appendix for details.)

Again, you don't have to fight the battle alone if you'll let American industry work for you.

Source of Your Monthly Check

Your monthly checks may come from one or a combination of four sources. These are:

1. Dividends
2. Realized capital gains
3. Unrealized capital gains
4. Original investment

If the amount you requested the fund to send each month is more than the dividends the fund is earning, the second source of funds would be your realized capital gains—the profits the fund has made buying and selling stocks. If your withdrawal is more than these two, they will need to use some of your unrealized gains. (This occurs when the fund has bought a stock, and it has increased in value, but they have not yet sold it. Thus the gain is unrealized.) If the amount per month you have requested is greater than these three, you will then start using a portion of your original investment. But don't be overly concerned about doing so. You have saved it for this purpose. Your concern should be with making you and it come out together.

The check a month can be an excellent way to use your accumulation in an orderly fashion while keeping the remainder at work in a diversified, continuously managed portfolio of common stocks.

As hard as it may be for you to believe, it was not until the mid-1960s that mutual funds were allowed by our regulatory agencies to show a check-a-month withdrawal record.

The Kettle of Nutritious Broth

You might picture your withdrawal program as a kettle filled with nutritious broth. This broth represents housing, clothing, food, and so on for your retirement years.

Your kettle might look something like this:

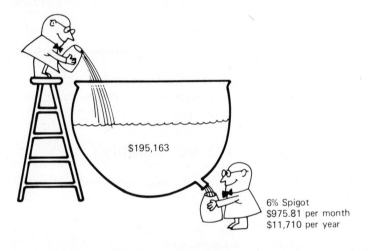

$195,163

6% Spigot
$975.81 per month
$11,710 per year

As the fund needs dollars to send you your check each month, it will redeem shares. When the fund distributes dividends or capital gains, it reinvests them into additional shares. Therefore, the number of shares you own will change with any activity in your account. This is the reason that you deposit your shares with the transfer agent when you begin your withdrawal program. Your concern should not be with the number of total shares in your account, but with the net asset value of the shares in the account.

Your performance record, if you begin it today, may be better or it may not be as good. But don't you like to visualize American industry ladling in the nutritious broth at the top while you withdraw at the bottom?

How Long Will Capital Last?

Let's assume that instead of the level of the kettle increasing, it decreased. There is nothing sacred about principal. There is nothing that says you are obligated to leave an estate to your heirs.

If you used capital at 7 percent while it was only earning 6 percent, do you know how long your capital would last? Thirty-three years! If you begin your withdrawal at sixty-five, in thirty-three years you'll be ninety-eight years of age!

Figure 4-5 is a handy chart to use in programming how long capital will last:

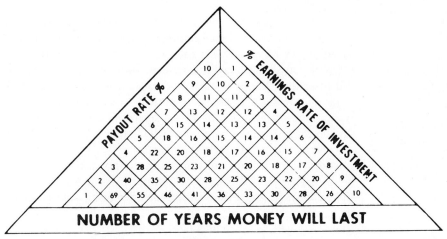

Figure 4-5

Another way to visualize how long capital will last is to use Table 4-3.

Table 4-3. How Long Will Your Money Last?

PERCENTAGE OF ORIGINAL PRINCIPAL WITHDRAWN PER ANNUM	*Total return per annum on balance of principal*						
	3%	4%	5%	6%	7%	8%	9%
	PRINCIPAL WILL LAST . . .						
4%	46 yr						
5	30	41 yr					
6	23	28	36 yr				
7	18	21	25	33 yr			
8	15	17	20	23	30 yr		
9	13	14	16	18	22	28 yr	
10	12	13	14	15	17	20	26 yr

Suppose you have $100,000 that is growing at the rate of 7 percent a year, and you withdraw at an annual rate of 8 percent—$8,000 a year or $666.67 per month. Look at the box where these two percentage figures intersect, and you will see that principal will last thirty years.

You're Not Spending, But Repositioning

I find that often a prospective client thinks he is spending his money when he makes an investment.

If you make an investment by withdrawing funds from a savings account, you are not spending your money but repositioning it, so that it will work for you rather than for the savings institution.

If you should desire to redeem your shares, you may do so on any business day. You may cash in all or part of your shares. When you sell your shares back to the fund, you will receive an amount representing your share of the value of all the securities and other assets of the fund at the time. It could be more or less than your cost. The amount you receive will depend on the investment performance of the fund and the market value of the stocks in the fund's portfolio that day.

If your need for money is temporary or if it is not a favorable time in the market, you may want to consider using your shares as collateral at your bank. You can usually rent time in this way with the hope that the value will increase at a later date.

Even if the market is progressing nicely, you may decide to borrow against the value of the stocks instead of disturbing the goose that you feel is producing satisfactory eggs.

The rent (interest) is deductible on your federal income tax return.

Who Invests in Mutual Funds?

A recent New York Stock Exchange study compared twenty-two million investors who owned only common stocks with nine million investors who owned mutual funds. (Five million owned both mutual funds and common stocks; four million owned funds only.) It contrasted the "stock only" investors with the fund investors and found:

1. Fund investors are the better-educated clients; 65 percent are college graduates vs. 50 percent of the "stock only" clients.

2. Fund investors are the wealthiest clients, with the largest assets; 23 percent have portfolios of more than $25,000 vs. 15 percent of the other clients.

3. Fund investors are the highest-income clients. Nearly 50 percent have incomes of $15,000 vs. only 33-1/3 percent of the other clients.

4. And finally, to put away the idea that mutual fund investors lock up their money forever, fund investors are the most active clients, with 25 percent making more than six transactions per year vs. only 10 percent of other clients.[*]

If It's a "Better Mousetrap"

If quality mutual funds have performed in the way I've indicated in my examples, why haven't investors embraced them with great enthusiasm and in massive numbers?

The chief reason is that state securities boards, the Securities and Exchange Commission, and the National Association of Securities Dealers have prohibited them from telling their story. About all they have allowed those recommending mutual funds as a valid way to invest to do legally is to warn you that you might lose your money. That's not the best way to spread the good word, I'm sure you will agree. It has been said that it is easier to get an ad for pornographic literature approved than it is an ad for a mutual fund.

A mutual fund prospectus giving full disclosure of all pertinent facts was rejected by one of the states because it showed a loaf of bread in color. Even though it had in bold print on the front of the prospectus these words:

THESE SECURITIES HAVE NOT BEEN APPROVED OR DISAPPROVED BY THE SECURITIES AND EXCHANGE COMMISSION, NOR HAS THE COMMISSION PASSED UPON THE ACCURACY OR ADEQUACY OF THIS PROSPECTUS. ANY REPRESENTATION TO THE CONTRARY IS A CRIMINAL OFFENSE.

I've had many panic-stricken clients call when they reread the packet of material after they had made an investment and saw this caption in bold print. One in particular was a lady for whom I had made an investment in a fund that contains shares only in common stocks and/or securities convertible into common stocks that are legal for the investment of trust funds in the District of Columbia. It is a fund that qualifies under "the prudent man rule" and is often used by attorneys who are in a fiduciary capacity.

---

*We are indebted to *Wiesenberger Financial Services Marketer* (an excellent publication) for this breakdown on mutual fund clients.

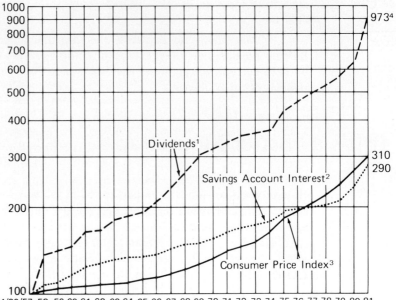

Figure 4-6. Dividends vs. savings account and the cost of living.

After reading this caption, she called and was incensed that I would have the audacity to recommend an investment that was not "approved by the Securities and Exchange Commission." No amount of explaining ever convinced her that the SEC neither approved nor disapproved, so we canceled the trade. What she missed in income is pictured in Figure 4-6.

I pride myself on having informed investors, but a prospectus has often been a deterrent to intelligent investing.

The regulatory agencies also have not allowed sales literature that pictures people showing any signs of reasonable solvency. I remember one brochure that was rejected because the man had cuff links in the cuffs of his shirt. They were not diamond-studded but looked more like the dime-store variety.

Perspective on Performance

With respect to performance, the mutual fund industry's long-term record has been very good, even when we add to the industry total the dismal record of the go-go funds. There is no question that you should be selective in your choice of fund management, just as you are with any investment. Some managements have historically outperformed others. Your charge for management will be approximately the same for each, so choose the ones that have depth of management, an excellent long record of past performance, and a fund or funds that fit your financial objectives. You may also want to consider having some of your money under one management and some additional funds under another. There is great merit in your considering diversification of "brains". Don't get hung up on an extra 1 percent or so cost for the "opportunity fee." Diversification can add safety and perhaps increase your net worth.

Compared to What?

A few years ago, it became fashionable among financial writers to give a sharp jab to the stomach of the mutual fund industry. There were at least two reasons for this. First, I think the writers just got tired of reporting the same old news each day, which in substance said the market went down again. Second, the mutual fund industry had been a knight in shining armor. When spots of tarnish began to show, it was much more fun to kick the knight than to polish away the tarnish to let the shining metal beneath show through.

The incongruous part of this development was that these same financial writers were the ones who had placed the crown of victory on the heads of some of the "go-go" fund managers with such headlines as "_____ Fund up 113 percent for the Year!" (Regulations require that I omit the name of the fund.)

Headlines such as these and interviews quoting the "bright" young men who were managing a very small number of "hot" funds brought on a performance race like we've never seen before and, it is to be hoped, will never see again. The older, well-managed funds, with seasoned money managers at the helm and with true dedication to sound investment principles, did not engage in these wild excesses as did the few gunslingers who had their field day in the speculative heat of 1967.

I'm convinced, as I've mentioned, that many of the agonizing reappraisals we have had in the stock market (that's stockbroker jargon for saying that the market went down) are in direct proportion to the amount of junk peddled by stockbrokers during speculative periods.

As a financial planner dedicated to faithfully helping my clients accomplish their long-range plans, I had one whale of a time trying to justify why I recommended a fund that only increased 39 percent in 1967, after they have read a headline that year stating " Fund up 113 Percent." My warning about "letter stock" (stock that could not be sold until a certain time had elapsed) fell on deaf ears. I had to either sell the fund to the client or know that he would buy it from some other broker. We could at least tell him when we saw the storm warnings.

Did You Know the Dow-Jones' Average Is Not for Sale?

In some financial publications, you may find mutual fund performances lumped together and actually compared to the Standard & Poor's 500 Stock Index, as if the index were for sale. It's not for sale. Neither is the Dow Jones Industrial Average.

Your problem may be not what the Dow has done performance-wise, but how you can intelligently put to work $10,000.

The most common comparison I've seen in the press matches Standard & Poor's 500 Stock Index and the Lipper Average of 530 mutual funds. All the comparisons I've seen ignore the critical fact that the S&P index is weighted by the value of each company's common stock. Twenty-five giant "blue chips" account for about one-half of the weight of the index, and the 475 remaining securities account for the other half.

The Hindsight Game

Let's play a game to test your performance in stock selections. I'm even going to let you choose the winner after the race has been run. Below are the thirty stocks in the Dow Jones Industrial Average. I grant you $30,000. You are to select three stocks and invest $10,000 in each as of December 31, 1933. Now go down the list and make your selections.

Now look at Table 9 in the Appendix and you will find the amount each of your stocks would have grown to in that period of time. Add up their totals and divide by three to get your average. What is your figure? How close does it come to $515,403, the performance figure for $10,000 invested in the Seminar Fund? Are you surprised to find that only four stocks out of the thirty in the Dow Jones Industrial Average outperformed the Seminar Fund? Minnesota Mining & Manufacturing

Dow Jones Industrial Stock	Your Selection	Estimated Market Value
Allied Corporation	_____	_____
Aluminum Company of America	_____	_____
American Brands	_____	_____
American Can	_____	_____
American Telephone and Telegraph	_____	_____
Bethlehem Steel	_____	_____
duPont	_____	_____
Eastman Kodak	_____	_____
Exxon	_____	_____
General Electric	_____	_____
General Foods	_____	_____
General Motors	_____	_____
Goodyear Tire & Rubber	_____	_____
INCO	_____	_____
International Business Machines	_____	_____
International Harvester	_____	_____
International Paper	_____	_____
Manville Corporation	_____	_____
Merck	_____	_____
Minnesota Mining & Manufacturing	_____	_____
Owens-Illinois	_____	_____
Procter & Gamble	_____	_____
Sears, Roebuck	_____	_____
Standard Oil Company of California	_____	_____
Texaco	_____	_____
Union Carbide	_____	_____
United States Steel	_____	_____
United Technologies	_____	_____
Westinghouse Electric	_____	_____
Woolworth, F. W.	_____	_____

was the top performer of all. Ten thousand dollars in it grew to $6,540,000, or 65,300 percent. The second best performer was Merck, which grew to $3,813,753. The poorest only grew to $10,688. The third was International Business Machines, which grew to $2,704,208, and the fourth was Eastman Kodak, which grew to $569,533.

If you had been an investor at the end of 1933, do you think you would have chosen any one of these four stocks? Probably not, because Minnesota Mining & Manufacturing was a small manufacturer of sandpaper with one plant in St. Paul; Merck was a very closely held family business that was several payments behind in dividends to preferred stockholders; International Business Machines was a stodgy manufacturer of adding machines, typewriters, and other office equipment whose net worth and profits had been declining for four years in a row; and Eastman Kodak's dividends to stockholders by then had been cut by two-thirds and much of its business was outside the United States.

The Seminar Fund during this time outperformed all but these four of the thirty stocks on the Dow Jones Average and your $10,000 would have grown to $515,403 without reinvestment of dividends, and $2,331,160 with reinvestment. Investing in common stocks does require skill.

Income

At this point you might be saying, so much for growth, income is the important thing. Let's look at the dividends. Have you ever said, "If I had just invested in General Motors or American Telephone and Telegraph, I would have received a lot of cash dividends." After all, AT&T is the most widely held stock in the country and General Motors is second. However, had you been an investor in the Seminar Fund for the same period of time, you would have received more dividends. Here are the figures, assuming a $10,000 investment made on December 31, 1933:

	Market Value 12/31/81	Total Cash Dividends	Total Results
The Seminar Fund	$515,403	$260,397	$775,800
General Motors	65,070	196,041	261,041
AT&T	31,579	55,849	87,428

When someone tells you he wished his grandfather had set aside some shares of GM or AT&T for him in the 1930s, tell him you would have preferred that your grandfather had put the same amount of money into shares of the Seminar Fund.

Can You Beat Dow-Jones?

The average person does not do as well as the Dow-Jones Industrial Average when investing on his own. This does not mean, of course, that you are average. You should use the system which best serves your temperament, lifestyle, and pocketbook.

Let's take a look at Table 4-4 and see how the Dow-Jones Average of 30 Industrial Stocks, the Standard & Poor's 500 Composite Index, and the New York Stock Exchange Composite Index did in comparison to the Seminar Fund.

You can compare the Seminar Fund's performance each year for the past forty-eight years by looking at Table 10 in the Appendix.

Table 4-4

Summary	Latest 10 Years (to 12/31/81)	Latest 20 Years (to 12/31/81)	Latest 30 Years (to 12/31/81)	Latest 48 Years (to 12/31/81)
The Seminar Fund	+ 38.9%	+ 176.9%	+ 849.4%	+ 5,054.0%
Standard & Poor's 500 Composite Index	+ 20.0	+ 71.3	+ 415.6	+ 1,113.4
Dow-Jones Average of 30 Industrial Stocks	- 1.7	+ 19.7	+ 225.0	+ 775.9
New York Stock Exchange Composite Index	+ 26.0	+ 129.8	+ 422.9	NA

When the Pros Fail You

Look for depth of management and performance over long periods of time when you select your family of mutual funds. But what if you have been faithful about doing your homework and have selected a family of funds that has had a good past performance record of good management, but the management changes. They lose some of their top pros, or they are bought out by an industry that has more experience in managing debt instruments than equities. What do you do? If, after you have given the new management a reasonable amount of time to prove their professional management abilities, they are failing to perform, get out. Deal with reality—not with what you hoped would be or will be.

I should warn you that regulatory agencies may make it very difficult for even the most dedicated and conscientious financial planner to be of maximum help to you. The regulatory personnel may not be trained in money management, may look only at cost, not results, and may reprimand him for moving you from a "sacred" investment. (It becomes "sacred" to them when you pay a commission.) Ask the planner, before you become his client, if his first allegiance is to you, or if his fear of being questioned on "suitability" will make him leave you in an investment that has changed in suitability for your purposes.

Underlying Value Is the Key

I personally believe that the 1980s hold tremendous promise because the Dow-Jones Industrial Average was selling by 1982 at only seven times earnings.

To put this into perspective, if you could buy all the outstanding stock of a company that's selling at five times earnings, you'd be getting a 20 percent return on your investment. Even if you were to assume a decline of 25 percent, this would still mean a price-earnings ratio of only 6.7, or an earnings return of 15 percent.

Companies create wealth, and, in the past, successful investing in common stocks has resulted from becoming one of the owners of the companies creating this wealth. Stock prices in the long term are determined by the earnings and assets of these companies.

Do not make the mistake so many investors do of taking the short-term view of the stock market when providing for your long-term goals. I find that many predict the future by making straight-line extrapolations of the latest three- or five-year periods. When the market has gone down over a period of several years, instead of welcoming it as a buying opportunity, they sit on their hands. When the market has been going up for a period of years, they assume the opposite and eagerly jump in with the full anticipation that this happy condition will continue for the next three to five years.

Watch for times in the market when good solid values are available, and have the courage to buy at bargain prices.

Summary

A mutual fund can do for you what you would do for yourself if you had sufficient time, training, and money to diversify, plus the temperament to stand back from your money and make rational decisions. It should make available to you what the very wealthy have always had: sufficient money to diversify and sufficient money to buy some of the best brains in the country.

If you can do better than the professionals and can spare the necessary time from your full-time vocation, by all means do your own buying and selling. If not, don't let your ego keep you from hiring these professionals to work for you for $5 per thousand or less.

Application

1. How much can you invest today in a lump sum to begin your journey toward a minimum $300,000 living estate?

2. Should your goal be higher? $400,000, $500,000?

3. What amount can you invest each month?

4. Should you use the convenience of the bank draft system so that your investment schedule will be systematic? The bank never forgets. You might.

5. Analyze your performance record on your stocks, using a record similar to the one in Figures 1 and 2 in the Appendix. What has been your percentage of gain?

	Your Record	Your Chosen Fund's Record
Last year		
Last 5 years		
Last 10 years		
Last 15 years		
Last 20 years		

6. Rate yourself with regard to the three *T*s and an *M* as they relate to investments:

	Excellent	Good	Poor
Temperament			
Time			
Training			
Money to diversify			

7. Which type of fund best fits your financial objective and temperament?

Aggressive growth	
Growth	
Growth with income	
Income	
Corporate	
Convertible bond	
Balanced	
Specialty	
Tax-advantaged trust	
Municipal bond	
Money market	

8. Should you hire a timing service?

9. Write to the Investment Company Institute, 1775 K Street, Washington, D.C. 20006, Telephone 202-293-7700, and ask them for their booklets describing the various uses for mutual funds. They are an excellent source of information and will provide you without charge a complete list of all funds keyed to their investment category. This list will include addresses and in many instances toll-free telephone numbers.

10. The address of Wiesenberger Financial Services is 870 Seventh Avenue, New York, New York 10019. Telephone 212-977-7453.

Chapter 5

The Infallible Way
to Invest

Dollar-Cost-Averaging

Is there an infallible way to invest in the stock market? Perhaps not. But then, what in life is infallible? However, there is one way of investing I've found that comes closer than any other. It's called dollar-cost-averaging.

This concept has been widely practiced by astute investors for years. Instead of trying to time the "highs" and "lows" for their purchases (which, as we've learned already, is a lot easier said than done, since you never seem to know what the low is until it's too late to do anything about it), they have learned the value of investing a fixed amount of money on a regular schedule and letting the principle of dollar-cost-averaging work for them.

This plan does not require brilliance or luck, but the discipline to save and invest over a long period of time. How dull—no brilliance or luck, just discipline. That doesn't make your adrenal glands surge, make bells ring in your cerebrum, or bring a sparkle to your eyes. Nor will it lend itself to sharing enticing tidbits at the "happy hour" about your marvelous astuteness in the market.

But let's assume that you are going to get your kicks in other ways and that you feel becoming financially independent does have some compensating features. Just what is dollar-cost-averaging, and why should you consider it one method for attempting to build your living estate?

When you dollar-cost-average, as you will remember, you invest the same amount of money in the same security at the same interval over a long period of time, with the assumption that the stock market will fluctuate and eventually go up. (These two things have always happened in the past. We don't know what the future holds.)

Let's assume that you can discipline yourself to save $100 a month, or a quarter, or at any regular interval, and that you have the earning capacity and the discipline to do this for a long period of time. Then get started immediately, because it makes little or no difference in your end results whether the market is going up, down, or sideways when you start.

If you are paralyzed into a state of inertia as to when to buy, what to buy, and when to sell, which has caused you to be in the delay-linger-wait syndrome, skip buying a particular stock and choose a family of mutual funds that has an excellent reputation for good management and a commendable record of past performance and that has an aggressive growth fund and a money market fund. A fund is especially adaptable to dollar-cost-averaging because under an accumulation plan you can buy fractional shares carried out to the third decimal point. You may also invest monthly or quarterly in a Monthly Investment Program (MIP) Plan in a stock listed on the New York Stock Exchange. However, you may find the MIP Plan in the end more costly and without sufficient diversification.

Let's assume you have $100 per quarter to invest. For the sake of simplicity, we will assume that you have chosen a mutual fund and it is selling at $10 per share. You invest $100 and receive ten shares. Then a correction occurs in the market and the fund in which you are investing goes down to $5 per share. You will plop in your $100 for the quarter. (You're not masterminding this program once you've made your decision regarding the investment to be used; but you are investing each quarter, regardless of what the market is doing.) At $5 per share you would receive twenty shares for your $100. Let's assume by the next quarter the market has returned to where it was when you started and is now selling at $10 per share. You will now receive ten shares for your $100.

An overly simplified illustration would look something like this:

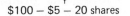

$100 – $10 – 10 shares $100 – $10 – 10 shares

$100 – $5 – 20 shares

Let's take an inventory:

	Regular Investment	Share Price	Shares Acquired
	$100	$10	10
	100	5	20
	100	10	10
Totals	$300	$25	40

Results: Total invested $300. Total shares owned 40.
Ending market price per share $10: 40 X $10 = $400.

You may have made a $100 gain with the market dropping 50 percent and only returning to where it started. Average price per share (25/3) = $8.33. Average cost per share ($300/40) = $7.50. You bought more shares (20) at a low cost ($5) than at a high cost ($10) and received an average cost for your securities.

If you are investing in a mutual fund, it should have a tendency to fluctuate with the market because of its wide diversification, and if our long-term upward trend continues, you should benefit from this fluctuation.

If you are one of those who enjoy playing with numbers, here are three hypothetical examples started at different points in varying business cycles. I've simplified and somewhat exaggerated the examples to demonstrate more clearly the principles of dollar-cost-averaging. In actual application you should take into consideration the period of your overall program.

In a Declining Market

	Regular Investment	Share Price	Shares Acquired
	$300	$25	12
	300	15	20
	300	20	15
	300	10	30
	300	5	60
Totals	$1,500	$75	137

Average price per share ($75/5) = $15.00
Dollar-cost-average per share ($1,500/137) = $10.95

This example shows the importance of continuing your investment program throughout a declining market. When the share value dropped from $25 to $5, the greatest number of shares was acquired. So any recovery above the dollar-cost-average of $10.95 would establish a profit.

In a Steady Market

	Regular Investment	Share Price	Shares Acquired
	$300	$12	25
	300	15	20
	300	12	25
	300	15	20
	300	12	25
Totals	$1,500	$66	115

Average price per share ($66/5) = $13.20
Dollar-cost-average per share ($1,500/115) = $13.04

Even in a relatively steady market, dollar-cost-averaging can work to your advantage. As the example above shows, the actual per share cost is 16¢ less than the average price of $13.20 per share.

In a Rising Market

	Regular Investment	Share Price	Shares Acquired
	$ 300	$ 5	60
	300	15	20
	300	10	30
	300	15	20
	300	25	12
Totals	$1,500	$70	142

Average price per share ($70/5) = $14.00
Dollar-cost-average per share ($1,500/142) = $10.57

As the above example shows, the dollar-cost-average per share of the five figure investments is $10.57. When compared with the current $25 per share value, it does demonstrate the importance of fluctuations in prices to the success of dollar-cost-averaging.

The practice of dollar-cost-averaging does not remove the possibility of loss when the market is below the average cost, but it clearly demonstrates that the successful pursuit of the system will lessen the amount of loss in a declining market and increase the opportunity of greater profit in a rising market.

So you see, dollar-cost-averaging doesn't give you the fun of sharing your brilliance at the coffee klatch; but if it helps you to increase your assets, it could make it possible for you to enjoy a fattening gooey Danish pastry later.

If your real reason for investing is to make money, dollar-cost-averaging is the most infallible way that I have found to approach the market.

Investing for Gain?

You would be surprised how many people are in the market not to make money but for the thrill it offers!

One afternoon a dentist and his wife came to my office to open a brokerage account. They said they did not expect or want my advice. All they would require of me were good executions. They explained that his profession kept him extremely busy with little time off and "playing the market" would be their diversion. Their chief goal was not to make money but use their brokerage account as a mini-Las Vegas. (This type of account brings joy to the heart of a broker who enjoys receiving a good income. No investment responsibilities, just the delight of taking the commission checks to the bank.)

This case history reminds me of another. One of my young CPA clients stopped me on the street one day to tell me he would be calling me in about a month to make an investment of some funds he would be receiving. A month passed; then two months passed. One afternoon our paths crossed again, and I asked, "Tommy, have you received your money yet?" A sheepish grin appeared on his face. He said, "Yes, but tax time was so busy, we just couldn't get away for our planned trip to Las Vegas, so I put the money in the commodity market and lost it."

I'm going to assume that you are reading this book because you want to become financially independent and not for the kicks gambling may give you.

Ego, the Deterrent

Let me again remind you that one of the greatest deterrents to successful investing is the three-letter word EGO. Dollar-cost-averaging will not do a thing to bolster your ego. Ego causes investors to hold a stock long after it has gone sour because their ego will not let them admit that they could have made a mistake. They harbor the hope that by some miracle it will return to what they paid for it; then, they tell me, "I'll sell." Don't say to me, "I've never had a loss," and expect me to be impressed. It means to me that you've probably never been in there trying or that your ego made you hold long past the time when you should have let go. When you make a mistake in the market, don't just hold. If you do, you may find out just how wrong you really were.

One of the major reasons many refuse to use professional management is that it's an admission that someone can do something better than they can do it. Again, EGO.

Let's assume that your masculine or feminine prowess is not threatened by the admission that someone can do something better than you and that you've decided to let the professionals managing the Seminar Fund do your investing for you.

John Worked for the Telephone Company

Let me share with you the account of John and Martha. John worked for the telephone company and he reached the historic day when he turned fifty. His wife, Martha, gave a big birthday party for him, and loads of friends came to help him celebrate. They had a great time that evening.

However, the next day, John began to have some somber thoughts. "I'm fifty. I'll retire from the company in fifteen years. We haven't saved much toward retirement. I wonder what my pension will be?" John went to the personnel office the next day to inquire about his pension and found it would be only $350 per month.

That night, as they sat at the kitchen table, John told Martha of his unhappy findings and said, "Martha, even with Social Security, our pension will not be enough to allow us to retire in dignity."

The children were all out on their own by then, and, after scrutinizing their budget, they decided they could save $100 a month. So each month after that John sent the custodian of the Seminar Fund a check for $100 and requested that the custodian invest it for him in shares of the fund.

John and Martha did this for fifteen years. Then came John's happy retirement day, and on that day he sat down at the same kitchen table and wrote a letter to the same custodian, saying, "I've been sending you a check for $100 a month, but I'm retiring now and won't be able to send you any more money. Would you be so kind as to now send me a check for my dividends each quarter and to also send me any capital gains you make each year." This the bank did. John lived twenty more years, and when he was eighty-five he departed this life.

A few weeks later, Martha's friend Julia also lost her husband. She came to Martha saying, "I've received these life insurance proceeds, and I have such a strong sense of stewardship about their use that I'm endeavoring to invest these funds as prudently as I can. I've been considering a particular mutual fund and remembered that you and John owned it. I need to know if you have been happy with the results?" Martha said, "Oh yes, and I still own the fund." Julia answered, "I know it's a personal matter, but would you tell me how well you have done?"

Martha began walking toward a drawer in the kitchen saying, "I don't mind sharing this information with you at all. John kept excellent records, so let's take a look."

When they looked at John's records, this is what they found. John and Martha had received $48,395 in dividends and $54,325 in capital gains distribution during the twenty years of John's retirement. Martha said, "I especially remember these capital gains distributions because John liked them the best. He kept reminding me that they were 'half tax-free' and of course, if he were living now they would be 60 percent tax-free." Then she added, "Would you believe that I still have all the shares we had at the time John retired? We often looked up their net asset value in the paper together, so I know how to calculate their value."

When Martha and Julia multiplied the number of shares times the net asset value per share, they found they had a value of $93,961.

All John and Martha had ever done was save $100 a month from age fifty to sixty-five!

Table 11 in the Appendix gives the record of the Seminar Fund, showing a beginning investment of $250, adding $100 per month for fifteen years for a total investment of $18,150, and then taking in cash the dividends and capital gains for the next twenty years.

Perhaps you are five years older than John and have only ten years before you reach retirement age. Let's assume that you can begin with

$250 and can faithfully add $100 a month, rain or shine, market going up, market going down, Elliot Janeway's predictions of bust, or Kiplinger's *Changing Times* headline of "Boom Ahead!" For 119 additional months, you faithfully send in your money to the custodian. How will you come out? I don't know. I can show you in Table 12 in the Appendix how you would have done during each of the thirty-nine ten-year periods between 1934 and 1981 using the Seminar Fund. The last column on the right shows the results.

Age Forty-five

If you are forty-five years of age, five years younger than John, you can see the twenty-nine twenty-year periods of the fund in the Appendix. Again, the last column shows each twenty-year period.

Does Life Begin at Forty?

Perhaps you are only a tender forty. Does life begin at forty? I don't know that it does, but I do know that if you have come to me at that age and do not plan to retire until sixty-five, I have twenty-five years to be of help to you.

In the last forty-five years, there have been twenty-four twenty-five year periods, and Table 12 in the Appendix shows what happened during each of those twenty-five year periods. Again, the right-hand column tells the results.

Are You a Tender Seventeen?

Let's Assume that you are a mere seventeen years of age. Table 13 in the Appendix is the total record that was attained by dollar-cost-averaging over a forty-eight year period. The total from January 1, 1934 to December 31, 1981, after all costs were taken out with the exception of federal income taxes, was $1,963,312—almost two million dollars from dollar-cost-averaging with $100 per month.

The secret of financial independence is not brilliance or luck, but the discipline to save a part of all you own and to put it to work in a good cross-section of American industry, energy, and real estate.

Sam Steady and George Genius

Are you asking yourself, "Is this the right time to invest? If I wait, could I buy at a cheaper price?"

Let's look at two investors and, just for fun, let's call them Sam Steady and George Genius. Sam Steady began investing $100 each month, reinvesting all his dividends and capital gains for thirty years. When he calculated his results on December 31, 1981, he found that he had invested $36,000 and he held shares with a market value of $217,662.

George Genius, on the other hand, was truly a genius. After long tedious hours of study and agonizing decision making, he successfully picked the absolute low of the year each year for thirty years and invested $1200 at this point beginning on March 13, 1950. When he calculated his results he found that he had invested $36,000 and that his value was $243,905. He was sure his performance would be so far superior to Sam Steady's that he was eager to tell him about it. When they sat down to compare their results, George was deflated to learn he had outperformed Sam by only $26,243, or around 4/10 percent per year and that Sam had done no agonizing and had enjoyed many hours of leisure that he had not had. In Table 14 in the Appendix, you can see Sam and George's record.

When is the best time to start a monthly investment program? Answer: As soon as possible.

Use a Bank Draft Authorization

The most successful program of dollar-cost-averaging we have used for our clients is based on bank draft authorization. Under this system you complete the bank draft authorization form of the fund for the amount you want to invest each month (this can later be increased, decreased, or stopped) and attach a blank check across which you have marked "void" (the computer picks out those numbers on the bottom left-hand corner with special ink); then each month the bank automatically drafts your account and sends the money to the fund. We find the bank rarely forgets, whereas sometimes our clients do. There are certain decisions one needs to make in life and move on—such as a systematic investing program (or exercise program).

Lump-Sum Investing

You can also use dollar-cost-averaging for larger lump-sum investments. For example, you have $25,000 to invest, but you are uncertain whether this is the right time to commit so large a portion of your assets to the market and you have opted not to use a timing device to move you from the stock growth fund to the money market fund.

You may select the fund or list of stocks that fits your financial objective. If you are using a fund, you may file a Letter of Intent with the fund, as discussed in Chapter 4. This gives you the privilege of investing at two discounts over the full offering price. There is usually a discount at $10,000 and a second one at $25,000. You have thirteen months to cross one of these discounts.

The lump-sum method is also helpful when you do not have the $25,000 now but will have it within the thirteen month period. You may be selling some of your assets at a capital gain or cashing in some government bonds with a large amount of accrued interest. If you space their disposition over two tax years, you may be able to save some tax dollars.

Realize that dollar-cost-averaging takes time because it means placing your investment dollars in chosen securities month after month, year after year, sweating out recessions, confidence crises, and so forth. Compared to the horse races or a turn at the crap table, it's disgustingly dull. If the thought of retiring in financial dignity and enjoying the Golden Years brings you joy, perhaps dollar-cost-averaging is for you.

Our formula still remains:

Time + Money + American free enterprise =
Opportunity to retire in financial dignity

Summary

You will find as you go through life that there are very few things that you can consistently count on to be true over long periods of time. But I am convinced that if you have the ability to earn a reasonable income, have the discipline to systematically save and invest the same amount of that income each month, have the intelligence to select a fund as good as or better than the Seminar Fund, are granted a sufficient number of years, and if our economy is no better or no worse than it has been in the past, you should become financially independent. Substitute DCA (dollar-cost-averaging) for EGO and do it NOW. Again I repeat: The secret of financial independence is not brilliance or luck, but discipline!

Application

1. How many years do you have before retirement?
2. How much can you save each month for this purpose?
3. Which day of the month is most convenient for you to make your investment?

4. Should you send in your check each month or let the bank draft your account automatically?

5. If you decide to use mutual funds, which fund best fits your objectives?

6. What other method have you found to attain financial independence that has a greater likelihood for success?

7. What is the secret of financial independence?

Chapter 6

The Real Power of Real Estate

There are three major areas you should consider when determining how best to employ your investment dollars. The first area is shares of American industry. You have looked at the criteria you must learn and follow to realize success in this area. The second major area is real estate, which we will examine in this chapter. The third is natural resources, with which you will become more familiar in a later chapter.

In times of uncertainty, investors tend to "return to the earth." This phenomenon exhibits itself in revived interest in investments closely allied with the land—either under, in, or attached to the land. Let's first consider which, if any, of these areas offers a valid investment medium for you.

Raw Land—The Glamour Investment

Often a young couple who has attended one of my seminars will come to our office for counseling, as each person who attends a seminar is entitled to do. They are usually very starry-eyed about their future and

say, "We want to invest in land. They're not making any more of it, you know."

Yes, I know they're not making any more of it—with perhaps the exception of the Dutch reclamation from the sea. That does not mean, however, that land is a valid investment consideration for them. To begin with, young couples usually have no more than $5,000 in liquid assets, they frequently have two or more children, and they have a very small equity in their home. It will be very difficult for them to take a meaningful position in raw land. Larger tracts—which they do not have the resources to secure—offer the best profit potential. Taxes must be paid while they wait for the land to "mature"—meaning waiting for the ultimate commercial user. Also, if they borrow money to finance the purchase, interest payments must be paid. Because of their lower tax bracket, the deductible characteristic of interest is not of significant help. They must also forego liquidity while waiting. Investing in "land" becomes more of a wistful dream than a valid investment possibility for this couple.

Your financial situation may be quite different. You may possess liquid assets and have a high cash flow from other income sources to service the interest on the loan and to pay taxes while you wait. You may be in a higher tax bracket, which allows you to shift a significant portion of the carrying charges to the IRS. This makes an investment in raw land a valid possibility for you. Your next consideration should be whether to invest on an individual basis or to join others in a land syndication.

Historical Perspective

Although the United States has built most of its cities, building is still going on at a rapid pace. Far more vacant land remains available than you might think. Not counting reserves of government property or the Alaskan wilderness, there are more than five acres of land per person in the United States. Much of this land is usable and accessible.

Our present land boom began after World War II and appears to have years to run. Most of the war babies who made such a great demand on school facilities in the 1950s and the colleges in the 1960s now have families of their own and need shelter. As well, the increase in divorce, the choice of marrying later or not at all, and the increased longevity of our children have created additional demands for housing and for land upon which to build. Demand for housing is steadily increasing and should continue to do so for the next decade. Housing construction brings other real estate activities. Shopping centers, office buildings, and industry follow new centers of population into expanding suburbs. There are many indications that land and its development hold great profit potential throughout the 1980s.

Land has always been the glamour growth area of real estate. It comes unfettered of buildings to manage and tenants to satisfy. However, you must also realize that an investment in empty land can be a speculative venture.

Principles to Follow

If you decide that investing in raw land is for you, there are six basic principles you should remember. The first principle is: Don't follow the population. Get out in front of it. Put your dollars in advance of a population or business trend. The second is to realize that timing of land purchases is all-important. The third is to be prepared financially to service your holdings. The cost of property taxes, liability insurance, and interest on financing makes it necessary to have around a 20 percent a year increase in the price of the land just to cover expenses, to say nothing of what the money you have invested could be earning in another investment.

It is important that you fully comprehend the nature of the ultimate land use, which will determine what a developer can afford to pay for your property. It is also necessary for you to understand the timing of the return of your invested capital. For a property to double in value may seem to be good; however, if the property should take twenty years to double, it will not be quite so attractive. (Remember our Rule of

72. You've only averaged 3.6 per annum percent on your money.) Successful real estate investment requires a forward-looking investigation and an understanding of the nature and character of the property being considered.

Fourth, keep your down payment low—paying down as little cash as possible. Sellers are often willing to take a smaller down payment and to finance the remainder in order to reduce their capital gains taxes.

If you want to take the risk of maximum leverage, you should endeavor to negotiate the smallest down payment you can get—perhaps as low as 10 percent. If you take this course, you will need to obtain a much higher appreciation—the amount necessary being determined by the interest rate you might pay and the potential for gain offered by other investment opportunities.

Fifth, be prepared to wait. The price of raw land seldom climbs steadily over a long period. Instead, values tend to remain fairly level for years.

When prices are rising, it may be easy to sell land, but if the price doesn't rise, money invested in land may be tied up for years while the expenses of ownership roll on. Even if a buyer can be found, financing may be difficult for long periods of time. Many banks will not carry mortgages on undeveloped land. You, the seller, may have to finance the buyer over a period of years. This may very well make land the least liquid of investments.

Some of the saddest plights I have seen have been widows who've come to me for financial advice when they could not find a buyer for their raw land and had to sacrifice essentials to pay the taxes and interest.

Sixth, if you make a land purchase and incur a large debt, be sure to buy adequate term life insurance to cover the indebtedness to avoid a possible hardship on your heirs. Even if you own the land outright, without any indebtedness, land is not liquid. Insurance proceeds will allow your heirs to have enough ready cash to pay inheritance taxes and avoid a forced sale at the wrong time.

If you have already accumulated a substantial net worth with some liquidity, raw land may very well be a viable investment consideration for your investment dollars. If not, as glamorous as owning raw land may appear, you should probably pass up the temptation.

Raw Land Syndications

In recent years raw land syndications have enjoyed considerable popularity. Should you consider owning a small interest in a syndication? It all depends. Here are some criteria you should examine carefully:

1. Who is the general partner or syndicator? What is his track record? Is it excellent or just fair? Syndications can be good or very poor depending on the know-how of the syndicator to buy right and to find a satisfactory buyer when it's time to sell.

2. Who are the other investors? Can they meet their portion of the payments on principal, interest, and taxes when they are due? If they can't, and you and the other syndicators can't pick up the tab, the property will revert back to the mortgage holder.

3. Ask yourself, "Is it a good investment?" If the answer is yes, then look at the tax savings potential. Too many syndications are structured to save taxes and have slim chances of earning you a good return on your invested dollar. Do look at comparable sales and appraisals in the area. Too many syndications have also been put together on the "greater fool theory"—meaning, "I'll find a greater fool than I am and sell it to him"—and then got caught without the proverbial chair when the music quit playing. Raw land can become an alligator—an alligator that eats money. Avoid alligators.

4. Examine what your after-tax cost will be on the investment, and then calculate what you think your yearly return will be on your cost basis.

Recreational Lots or Condominiums for Investment

Should you buy recreational lots or condominiums at the seashore, on the lakes, in the desert, in the mountains? Probably not in most instances. Some work out well, but the majority have been marked up so much before being offered to the investor that the opportunity to sell at a profit is minimal. Liquidity is a definite problem after all the lots have been sold, the aggressive sales force has moved on to other developments, and there is no one left around to sell yours.

Investing in Commercial Income-Producing Real Estate

Indirect Investing

It has been an interesting psychological study to me during my many years as a financial planner to find that many who make deposits in savings and loan institutions are convinced that the officers of those institutions are rigidly standing there, guarding their little nest egg to guarantee its safety. It never seems to occur to them that while they are depositing their hard-earned money at the teller's window, the loan officer at a desk a few steps away in normal times is lending out the same money to be invested directly into real estate.

If you are a depositor in a savings and loan association, you are an indirect investor in real estate. You are "guaranteed" your sliver of the interest the borrower pays plus your original deposit, and the institution is entitled to what in the past has been the larger portion of the pie. Let's say, for example, that you have $100,000 and you place it in a savings and loan and are willing to leave it there for one year in a certificate of deposit. Also, let's assume that you are in a 40 percent tax bracket. Your mathematics at the end of the year could look something like this:

$100,000	Deposit
10,000	Interest for one year
$110,000	Total at the end of the year
4,000	Taxes due at 40%
$106,000	Net after taxes
6%	After-tax return

And what was the rate of inflation the past few years? Any time it is greater than 6 percent you were like the little frog that hopped up one step and slid back two; you didn't make it out of the financial well.

Direct Investing in a Nonmortgaged Building

Let's say instead that you become a direct investor by taking the same $100,000 and buying and paying cash for a building. You then lease that building for $13,000, or 13 percent per year, under an arrangement that is called a triple-net lease or a net-net lease. In triple-net lease, you would be a nonoperating owner, and the leaseholder would be the operator and would pay all variable costs such as taxes, insurance, and maintenance (from whence comes the triple name), as well as a lease rental each month.

The company doing the leasing may find this arrangement advantageous, for it frees capital for inventory, expansion, or other activities related to the company's business. It may also offer tax advantages. You as the owner, on the other hand, may like the arrangement because you have no variable costs to surprise you and you should have a predictable income stream from the lease for a period of years. With escalation clauses, your rentals will increase with inflation and the gross volume of the lessee to give you an inflation hedge in your annual income plus any appreciation that has occurred when you sell the property.

As a direct investor, not only do you place yourself in a position to obtain the full earning power of your money, but you introduce the vital ingredient of tax shelter on all or a portion of your cash flow owing to allowable depreciation.

Depreciation

Depreciation deductions for income tax purposes are allowed as if the building were decreasing in value with use. This may be true. Often the contrary is true. In fact, it may actually be increasing in value as replacement costs escalate. Depreciation is a bookkeeping entry. No checks are sent, and it does not reduce the actual cash flow.

There are varying kinds of depreciation schedules, but let's assume that you are using what is called straight-line depreciation over a fifteen-year period. (You are not permitted to depreciate the land on which the building is built.) Let's see how allowable depreciation affects the taxation of your cash flow.

Your mathematics might run something like this if you had purchased land and building for $100,000, with a cash flow of $13,000, or 13 percent, and your accountant had set a value of $75,000 on the building. He allocated $25,000 as the cost of the land. The example below is grossly oversimplified, but should introduce to you the basic effects of depreciation on your taxable cash flow. In this example I've assumed a tax bracket of 40 percent.

Hypothetical Example of a $100,000
Nonleveraged Building, Triple-Net-Leased

$100,000 at 13% cash flow	$13,000
Building $75,000—depreciation	5,000
Taxable cash flow	8,000
Taxes at 40%	3,200
Cash flow	$13,000
Minus taxes	3,200
Net after taxes	$ 9,800 or 9.8%

At an after-tax return of 9.8 percent, you've improved your situation, but considering our present rate of inflation, you may feel you are just holding on with your bare knuckles if you include any appreciation that may have occurred.

Direct Investing in a Mortgaged Building

Again let's buy a building for $100,000, but this time let's only put down $25,000 of your money and borrow the remaining $75,000 from a life insurance company, and let's assume we can borrow the money at 16 percent interest per annum (or you might assume an existing lower interest mortgage). You have now introduced another deductible item—interest expense.

Your savings from this deduction will be determined by your tax bracket. In our example, you are in a 40 percent bracket, so the IRS picks up 40 percent and you pick up the remaining 60 percent. In other words, you have been able to shift a portion of the burden of carrying the mortgage. Shifting the burden back to the IRS is a vital lesson that you must learn in order to survive financially.

In addition to being able to deduct interest payments, you are also allowed to deduct depreciation on the entire $75,000 allocated to the price of the building, not just on that portion represented by your $25,000 down payment.

Let's look at some possible mathematics that illustrate the possible effects of depreciation and interest deductions. (This is intentionally oversimplified with amortization of the loan and salvage value omitted.)

Hypothetical Example of a $100,000
Leveraged Building, Triple-Net-Leased

$100,000 at 13%—cash flow	$13,000
$25,000 down payment	
$75,000 mortgage at 16% interest	12,000
Net cash flow after interest	$ 1,000
Minus depreciation	5,000
Taxable income (loss)	(4,000)
Net after-tax cash flow	1,000 Cash
Tax savings	1,600 (4,000 x 40%)
Net after-tax return	$ 2,600

At 10.4 percent ($2,600 ÷ $25,000) after-tax cash flow, you are beginning to make progress.

After studying the above mathematics, you may have been inspired to look for a building to buy and then lease. After long searching, you may have come away bewildered, finding that you lack the expertise to select the building or sufficient funds to make an economically viable investment in a commercially leasable building. If this has occurred, don't give up the idea of investing in triple-net-leased buildings, because the shortage of capital for business expansion that is a current condition in our economy today makes this type of investing one that you should consider.

Let me now introduce you to a method of investing that may offer you one of the best approaches to investing today under our present tax laws. This method is called the limited partnership. The more you learn about the limited partnership approach to investing, the more you will probably want to use this method.

Limited Partnership

A limited partnership is composed of one or more general partners who have professional expertise and who are willing to assume unlimited liability and several or a large number of limited partners, usually without expertise, but with some investable funds, who do not want liability beyond the extent of their investment. The limited partners are treated, from the standpoint of taxes and income, as individuals, with all the benefits flowing directly through to them, if certain IRS criteria are met. This is called the *conduit principle*.

A limited partnership may be diagrammed in this manner.

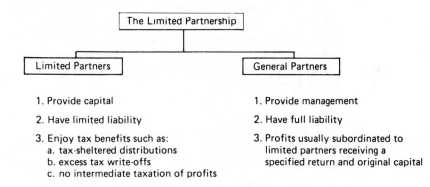

Registered Limited Partnerships

A limited partnership offering made on a national public basis must be registered with the Securities and Exchange Commission and with the Securities Commission of any state where it is offered.

The Securities and Exchange Commission neither approves nor disapproves the offering. The SEC does not rule on its investment merits, but attempts to see that those making the offering make "full disclosure" of all material facts relative to the offering in the prospectus, which may be interpreted by the particular SEC examiner as full disclosure of all the possible negatives that could possibly occur. (In a later chapter you will become painfully aware of the difficulty you may have in obtaining a clear understanding of just what is being offered.) You will rarely become aware of any of the positive attributes of the offering from reading the prospectus, especially if you do not read to the end of what is usually a very long document, and have advanced degrees and extensive experience in financial real estate analysis. After reading it, you may be completely stunned and wonder how your financial planner ever had the audacity to recommend such a "risky" investment. Don't stop there. Continue to investigate and study, and find out if there are merits to the investment that may outweigh the negatives. Look to see if these are truly negatives. Often you will find they are not, despite the prospectus. The other day a regulatory officer declined to let an issuer use a copy of an article that was an extremely informative and true account of the investment because there were only a few negative comments about the investment. You will usually be allowed to learn only the negatives—none of the attributes. Personally, I think "full disclosure" should include both.

Some states, in addition to determining if there has been full disclosure, will attempt to judge the merits of the offering and also to determine suitability guidelines for the residents of their state. Some government employees are empowered to take it upon themselves to decide "what is good for you," or what is "fair, just, and equitable," what is the minimum you can invest, and what assets you must own for it to be "suitable" for you.

It may appear ironic to you that the proverbial little old lady in tennis shoes can open a trading account with a swinging brokerage firm, can trade in such commodities as pork bellies and cocoa futures, can trade options—naked or covered—and can speculate in computer and uranium stocks, with or without any hope of future earnings. But when the same little old lady wants to invest in a limited partnership that invests in a diversified portfolio of professionally selected triple-net-leased buildings from corporations that have assets of millions of dollars and are publicly traded, such as General Motors, Sears, and Safeway, she must in most states have $30,000 in income and $30,000 in net worth (or $75,000 of net worth) exclusive of home and furnishings for her to be a "suitable" investor. In other states, she may be required to have assets in excess of $100,000 for it to be "suitable" for her to make an investment of as small an amount as $2,500.

You should carefully consider the limited partnership as an investment medium. Under the expert management of the *right* general partners, in the *right* investment area, at the *right* time, you may find that it offers excellent potential for tax-sheltered cash flow, excess deductions to shelter other income, equity buildup, and appreciation. This is not to say that all limited partnerships are without risk. Everything that has to do with investing or not investing money has risk. Doing nothing with your funds during periods of accelerated inflation is extremely risky.

You should look into publicly registered income-producing triple-net-lease limited partnerships:

1. If you are willing to give your investment a bit of time to mature.

2. If you do not demand instant liquidity on all assets.

3. If you do not have an emotional need to tally up your net worth daily by looking up quotations in the daily newspaper.

4. If you are in a tax bracket of 24 percent or above.

5. If you are willing to forego ego and admit that there might be those who, through economy of scale and expertise, can do your real estate investing for you better than you can do it for yourself.

These real estate limited partnerships usually can be divided into two broad classifications: nonoperating and operating. Each offers different types of properties, different potential benefits, and different exposures to risk. Let's first look at the nonoperating partnerships.

Nonoperating Partnerships
Sale/Leaseback Transactions

In 1973 and again in the early 1980s the Federal Reserve Board adopted a very restrictive money supply policy with a stated desire of slowing inflation. These restrictive periods brought about such shortages of capital that even corporations with the assets of a company like International Business Machines could not go into the market and successfully float a bond issue, even at very high interest rates. This left many large, very credit-worthy corporations that had expansion plans already on the drawing boards with no or limited access to capital needed for these plans. In order to continue their pattern of growth, these corporations began selling their buildings and then leasing them back under a triple-net-lease arrangement. This freed their capital to continue their expansion and inventory as they had originally planned.

Triple-Net Leases

Let's look at how triple-net leases have worked in the past, since we may return to similar money conditions in the future. Let's say that the J.C. Penney Company built a building for $3 million, paid $1 million down, and obtained a $2 million mortgage. They now want to open another location in a new regional shopping mall but the government has already siphoned off all the country's savings to cover the increasing interest bill on the federal deficit, leaving no funds for private enterprise. J.C. Penney would then sell its building to a limited partnership and lease it back under a triple-net-lease arrangement, whereby J.C. Penney agrees to pay the partnership a monthly lease payment and also agrees to pay all the variable costs, such as taxes, upkeep, and insurance. J.C. Penney would also agree to escalate these payments, giving the purchaser a hedge against inflation.

In addition to J.C. Penney, such companies as Sears, Safeway, Federated Department Stores, and others also want to open new stores, so they do likewise. With so many companies taking this approach, a demand is then created for large pools of capital.

To fill this need, an organization of real estate experts whom I highly respect register with the SEC each year for national distribution units of a large limited partnership to invest in the triple-net leases of these major U.S. corporations. For a company's building to be eligible for purchase by this partnership, the company must have a sizable net worth, be credit-worthy, and be publicly traded. Eighteen to twenty of these buildings are placed in each partnership. The partnerships are divided into $500 units, and investors are allowed to purchase as few as five units ($2,500). This management team now has an eleven-year record, which is detailed in their prospectus.

Each offering has been for around $60 million of equity capital, which allowed them to invest approximately $180 million in triple-net-leased buildings each year.

When the restrictive and expensive money policies of the Federal Reserve were put into effect during the latter part of 1981, this partnership began to pay all cash for its buildings with the intent of financing them at a later date when money might be more available.

Actually, the investments are made in these properties as the money comes in. If you make an investment in this type of partnership, early in the offering you may not know which buildings will be purchased. The general partners will notify you as purchases are made. This procedure is known as investing in nonspecified properties, or a "blind pool."

Blind Pool

"Blind pool" means you do not know which General Motors building or which J.C. Penney's building the general partner will buy. I prefer a blind pool because the general partner has much more bargaining power with the money in hand when going in to negotiate a purchase. For example, let's assume the partnership has found the building that meets its investment criteria but the owner knows the sale will be contingent on the general partner's ability to raise the capital to make the purchase. What kind of hard negotiating do you think they'll be able to do? But, let's assume they enter the bargaining room with millions of dollars already in hand. Do you think they are in a more advantageous bargaining position? I do. So when you are investing with a general partner with an excellent past performance record, I believe it will be to your advantage to choose a blind pool offering, despite the HIGH RISK caption the SEC requires on the front cover of the prospectus.

Leverage

If there are any long-term mortgages used in the investment, this will also trigger the HIGH RISK caption. Sure, leverage can work against you in adverse circumstances, but remember what Bernard Baruch said when they asked him how he made so much money. He said "OPM"—"Other People's Money." Also, inflation rewards those who owe money, not those who pay cash, because the borrower is allowed in an inflationary economy to repay the debt with cheaper and cheaper dollars. (I'm not advocating short-term debt, only long-term secured debt, so put away your credit cards.) You are solvent as long as what you own is greater than what you owe.

I have often wondered if money market instruments such as U.S. government bonds and certificates of deposit of large commercial banks and savings institutions were to be the investment, but at the time the investor made the investment he did not know which instruments, and if leverage was going to be used, whether the caption HIGH RISK would be required on the front of the prospectus.

In my opinion, this type of investment is not high risk. I would personally rather own J.C. Penney's buildings than own its bonds. Any court in the land will throw out a tenant for nonpayment of the rent. Of course, recourse is also available to a bondholder if the interest is not paid when due, but this is a much slower process, and there is less potential for full recovery. Also, there is not a specific building that can be rented to another tenant in the meantime.

The potential benefits of an investment in a nonoperating real estate limited partnership are:

1. Potential cash distributions paid quarterly or monthly.
2. Current tax shelter of a portion or all of your cash flow.
3. Equity buildup (mortgage paydown).
4. Appreciation.

Let's look at some oversimplified mathematics that could occur if the partnership that I've been using for my clients continues to meet its financial objectives. It has in the past, but it may not in the future. Let's assume that after careful study you think this investment meets your financial objectives and fits your temperament. Let's further assume the following: You make a $10,000 investment; the partnership, on the average, pays you a 9 percent cash distribution each year, with 75 to 100 percent of it tax-sheltered; the properties are held for ten years, and they appreciate 1 percent per year.

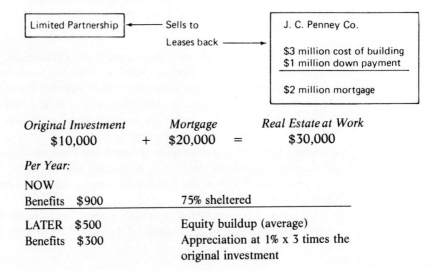

Original Investment		Mortgage		Real Estate at Work
$10,000	+	$20,000	=	$30,000

Per Year:

NOW
Benefits $900   75% sheltered

LATER $500   Equity buildup (average)
Benefits $300   Appreciation at 1% x 3 times the original investment

Or, if we use percentages, here's another way of picturing their objectives for you:

	Quarterly Cash Distributions	Excess Deductions
NOW	9% (cumulative average)	
Benefits	(75% tax sheltered)	0
	Equity Buildup	Appreciation
LATER		
Benefits	4–6%	3–9%
		(1% to 3% × 3
		of leverage)

In this oversimplified example, the mortgages the partnership assumed would add an additional $20,000 to your $10,000 investment, for a total of $30,000 in real estate working for you.

Let's further assume that you are in the 29 percent tax bracket. If your cash distributions are $900 per year and 75 percent is tax-sheltered, the remaining $225 will be taxed. At 29 percent, you would lose $65.25 to Washington, leaving you with $834.25, or an 8.34 percent after-tax cash flow. (You would have to earn 11.74 percent fully taxable to equal this return.) This would be your NOW benefit.

Later Benefits

Equity Buildup

Every month when the lessees pay the rent, the general partner in turn pays a portion to the mortgage company. This builds up your equity.

Equity buildup through the reduction of mortgage balances is one of the primary sources of your potential gain in this type of partnership. This is the reason that the partnerships usually hold properties long enough to provide a meaningful reduction of the mortgage balances. You do not, of course, receive this equity buildup until the building is sold for a profit, or for at least the original purchase price. However, a big plus for you is the fact that any buildup that occurs does so from funds paid by the lessee and is not taxable until the buildings are sold and then at the capital gains rate, or a maximum of 20 percent.

Let's look at the mathematics in our first example if the partnership in which you may have invested sells all the buildings in its portfolio in ten years and is able to sell them for just their original purchase price:

Hypothetical Example of Possible Results

	Investment		Mortgage		Real Estate
	$10,000	+	20,000	=	$30,000

NOW

Benefits	9,000	Cash distributions ($900 x 10 years)

LATER

Benefits	5,000	Equity buildup ($500 x 10 years)

Total

Benefits	$24,000	Total cash distributions, equity buildup and original capital before capital gains taxes

Over the ten years you would have received a total of $9,000 cash distributions paid out on a quarterly basis, and would now cash in on your equity buildup of $5,000. This plus your original investment of $10,000 would total $24,000. Therefore, your benefits would have been 9 percent NOW and 5 percent LATER, or a total of 14 percent per year before taxes.

Appreciation

The example above does not include any appreciation. Let's now assume that some appreciation occurs because of escalating replacement costs and the increased cost of strategically located commercial land. If the buildings appreciate 1 percent a year and you are leveraged three-to-one (meaning you invested $10,000 and the general partner borrowed $20,000 on your behalf), this would provide you with another $300 per year, for a total of $3,000 appreciation in ten years. This sum added to the $24,000 would bring your total to $27,000. If a 2 percent appreciation occurs, this would add $6,000, for a total of $30,000. Capital gains taxes would then be due on the amount that your sales price exceeds your adjusted cost basis. Adjusted cost basis is arrived at by taking your original investment, which was $10,000, and subtracting any cash distributions on which you did not pay a tax and any excess deductions you have received.

The government never forgives a tax, but it will allow you to defer it and oftentimes it can be turned into the more favorable capital gains. It is usually to your advantage to defer taxes for a number of reasons. The chief reason is inflation, and you can pay it off with cheaper and cheaper dollars. At only 7 percent inflation and a 40 percent tax bracket, in ten years you could pay off the original $1 tax liability with a 48¢ dollar; and if you can then convert it to a capital gain, which real estate lends itself to doing, you can pay it off with a 19¢ dollar. The game you must learn to play if you are to survive financially is the D.C. Game. You'll either be sending your money to Washington, D.C. or you'll learn to defer and convert! You'll learn more about this very important game later.

The above has been happening until recently, but toward the end of 1981 the Federal Reserve began a program of very restrictive money supply that has led to high interest rates and a scarcity of capital. This management's new approach will probably be as follows:

Investment	10,000
Cash flow, 12% x 10 years	12,000
Finance property in 5 years and distribute $4,000	4,000
Profits from sale in 10 years	2,500
Total benefits	$28,500

In this example you have received your investment back in five years, if they do very modest financing at that time ($1,200 x 5 yrs. = $6,000 plus $4,000 borrowed = $10,000). You could put this amount to work again (which should greatly increase your internal rate of return) and still own the property after leveraging.

Possible Disadvantages

You should be aware that the long-term triple-net leases that contribute so much to the dependability of your cash distributions can have an adverse effect on appreciation potential. The partnership may not be in a position to raise rentals quickly and current cash flow is the most important item in determining the sales price of your property when it is sold. (However, nearly all of the leases now contain escalation clauses that can greatly enhance their inflation protection potential.)

This type of partnership will usually use a fifteen-year straight-line depreciation schedule; therefore, the distributions may be only partially sheltered and may not produce any excess deductions that save taxes on income from other sources.

Investing in triple-net-leased properties is not without risk. While the management need not be concerned with fluctuations in occupancy rates and operating expenses, nor with variation in rent schedules, it does need to be concerned with the credit-worthiness of its corporate tenants. Great expertise is necessary to evaluate the properties as well as the financial strength of the corporate tenant.

If you are a conservative, income-seeking investor desiring some tax shelter and some opportunity for appreciation to hedge against inflation, you should consider committing some of your investment dollars to this type of partnership.

We've been appraising here the characteristics of partnerships that are nonoperating. Let's now turn our attention to those partnerships in which the general partners actually operate the properties purchased.

Operating Limited Partnerships

An operating partnership usually invests in multi-tenanted properties, such as apartment buildings, office buildings, and shopping centers, and operates these properties. In this type of real estate investment, leases are generally of shorter duration, which can be a major advantage. Rents can be raised as the leases are renewed. This provides appreciation potential. However, it can also be a major disadvantage if the buildings do not stay fully rented. If the vacancy factor goes up, the cash flow goes down and can go down to the point where there is no income. This can occur when 20 percent or more of the units are vacant and there are large mortgage payments to be met.

Multifamily Housing

I know of no area today where demand does, and from all indications will continue to, outstrip supply more than in the area of multifamily housing.

There are a host of reasons why this particular investment media should yield excellent results over the next three to six years. Let's look at some of them.

Average Family Priced Out of the Home Market

Because of the sharp increase in construction and land costs, the average family can no longer qualify for a mortgage on the average American home. The average family income today is approximately $21,000, the average existing home costs $66,000, and the average new home is $86,700 (in many areas such as San Francisco, it is higher). With mortgage interest rates ranging from 15 to 18 percent today, only a few families can afford to buy homes. The National Association of Home Builders estimates that only 7 percent of the families in this country can qualify for a 15 percent thirty-year conventional mortgage on $60,000. This leaves them only three choices: to live in mobile homes, to live with relatives, or to rent garden-type apartments. If these families want to live in the more desirable areas of their city, want access to such facilities as swimming pools, tennis courts, and recreation centers, they have no other option but to live in garden-type apartments. They may be frustrated potential homeowners, but home ownership is not one of the options open to them, unless they are able to purchase one of the lower cost condominiums.

Cheaper to Rent Than to Own

From 1970 to 1982 the cost of home ownership escalated 186 percent, while the cost of apartment rents escalated approximately 98 percent, making rents a better buy during that period than home ownership (unadjusted for any capital increase in the value of the home). In Appendix Table 15 you'll find a year-by-year study. (Incidentally, the consumer price index increased 143 percent during that period.)

The "Opportunity Spread"

One of the major financial indicators that predicts the increase in rents is the relationship between present rates and what they will have to be to support new construction, known as "replacement rents."

In 1974, market rents were 20 cents per square foot per month, which is equivalent to $160 per month for an 800-square-foot apartment unit. The replacement rents necessary to prompt builders to build was 28 cents or a per apartment discrepancy of $64 per month, or 40 percent between market rents and replacement rents. As long as this disparity existed, apartment projects were protected from competition. Only as rents rose to 28 cents did it make sense for builders to start new construction.

By 1982, rents averaged 35 cents a square foot but replacement rents were 61 cents, so that rents would have to go up 26 cents or 74 percent over the current market price before new construction would occur. In 1974 the difference between market rents and replacement rents was 40 percent, and property prices since then have doubled despite a 10-15 percent national vacancy factor in 1974. At present vacancies are below 4.5 percent and the "opportunity spread" is 74 percent—almost double that of 1974. This indicates that apartment rents will have to increase $208 per month before any new apartment construction will take place. No new construction should translate into sharply increased rents and increased value for owners of existing properties.

How Can You Benefit?

Now that you have been apprised of this situation, how can you best turn this knowledge into a profit? Should you go out and buy some apartments? Probably not, unless you have a large amount of money to invest, because economy of scale is often necessary for maximum profitability. Probably not, unless you are either very talented at repair and upkeep, or have the ability to supervise others, and truly want to be bothered about repairing a renter's commode. You may very well enjoy a larger return on your money by investing, along with a large number of others, in very selected limited partnerships that invest in garden-type apartments, with chief emphasis on the Sun Belt. In this way, you can invest as small an amount as $5,000 ($2,500 for some partnerships and $2,000 for Individual Retirement Accounts—IRAs) or in multiples of $500 above that amount, and can have the potential for quarterly distributions, tax-sheltered. You also may have excess deductions to save taxes on other income, equity buildup, and possible appreciation with no effort on your part but to deposit the hoped-for quarterly distributions into your bank account and to enter the proper amounts for excess deductions in the proper place on your income tax return each year. You do not have to report as income your tax-sheltered quarterly distribution.

Management Is the Key

For many years, I have recommended to my clients several registered offerings by general partners whose expertise I greatly respect and with whom my clients and I are very comfortable. These partnerships have an offering each year that allows them to acquire in excess of $100 million of properties. Their past performance has been excellent. They have exhibited the ability to buy excellent properties at the right price and location, and have been able to manage these properties with outstanding expertise and to sell them profitably at the right time for maximum profits. This may or may not continue, but the quality and depth of their personnel, their very conservative approach to financing, and their stringent reserve requirements encourage me to think that this trend will continue.

You As An Investor

Let's assume that you are in the 29 percent tax bracket. Let's further assume that you have $10,000 you do not need to grab back over the next four to seven years, and that you are investing in a limited part-

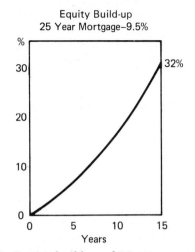

Equity Build-up
25 Year Mortgage–9.5%

Figure 6-1. Equity buildup of 25-year mortgage at 9.5%.

nership that has leverage of around three to one and has as its objective a 3–8 percent cash flow. In this type of investment, your cash flow may vary. You are investing in an operating business, and like other business operations, cash flow can fluctuate. Some months, for example, a carport may need to be added to enhance a property or other improvements may need to be made. It's not like the partnership investing in triple-net leases, where all the costs are paid by the lessees. Here they are paid by the partnership. Cash flow should not be your chief concern, but your goal should be appreciation from their plowing back the cash to improve the property and increase the rents so they can obtain a higher sales price later. If current cash flow is important to you, the triple-net lease may be best for you.

Let's further assume that not only will the cash flow be sheltered from current taxation, but that there will be excess deductions of 10–20 percent that you can use to save taxes on other income.

These quarterly distributions and excess deductions can provide you with your NOW benefits. Your LATER benefits can come from equity buildup (mortgage paydown) and appreciation. Equity buildup in these partnerships will probably be smaller per year than in the triple-net-lease partnerships, because the properties are usually held for shorter periods of time. If you've ever looked at the amortization table on your own home, you will have discovered that equity buildup occurs in a curve. It is small at the beginning, with most of your payment going to interest, and larger as you get further into the schedule. Figure 6-1 gives you a picture of how equity buildup escalates the longer the property is held.

The equity buildup may be around 3.5 percent if the apartments are held for briefer periods of time and more if they are held longer.

This type of partnership offers greater appreciation potential than the triple-net leases. Sears, Safeway, General Motors, and others have tremendous bargaining power when it comes to negotiating lease terms. Apartment renters, in sharp contrast, have no bargaining power at all when there is a shortage of housing. Because current vacancy rates are at the lowest level they have been in the thirty years records have been kept, the apartment owners should be able to raise the rents to keep up with or ahead of inflation. This should increase the cash flow, which, in turn, usually increases the sales price.

Multiple-Tenant Mathematics

If we assume a 6 percent cash flow, a 10 percent excess deduction, a 3-1/2 percent equity buildup, a conservative 6 percent inflation, your tax bracket at 29 percent, a $10,000 investment, and four-to-one leverage, your mathematics could look something like this each year while investing in this type of partnership:

Hypothetical Example of $10,000 Invested in a
Limited Partnership Investing in Multiple-Tenant Real Estate

Original Investment			Mortgage		Real Estate
$10,000		+	30,000	=	$40,000
NOW	600		Tax-sheltered, paid quarterly		
Benefits	290		10% excess deduction ($1,000 x 29%)		
	$ 890		Current after-tax benefit (or 8.9%)		

LATER	350		Equity buildup (mortgage paydown)	
Benefits	2,400		Appreciation ($600 x 4 of leverage)	

Using percentages, the following might give you a better visual picture of what the partnership hopes to accomplish:

Hypothetical Example of the Above Using Percentages

	Quarterly Cash Distributions Tax Sheltered	Excess Deductions
NOW Benefits	3- 6%	10–20%

	Equity Buildup	Appreciation
LATER Benefits	2.5–3.5%	10–24%

NOW Benefits

Your $500 cash distribution, tax sheltered, plus your excess deductions would make up your NOW benefits. In a 29 percent tax bracket, you would keep $600 plus another $290 if depreciation, interest expenses, and so on, brought you a total of a 10 percent excess deduction. This would provide you with a total after-tax benefit of $890 (the $600 they paid to you plus the $290 you did not have to send to Washington). How much would you have to earn on $10,000 to have $890 left after taxes? You would have to earn $1,253 taxable income, or 12.53 percent per annum, to obtain an equivalent to your current keepable income here. In a 39 percent bracket, you would have to earn $1,622 or 16.2 percent, and in a 50 percent bracket, $2,200 or 22 percent. Don't set your sights only on cash flow unless you need current income, but on your total after-tax results. Let me demonstrate by assuming only a 3 percent cash flow and a 20 percent excess deduction your first year. Your after-tax results would be almost the same in the lower brackets and greater in the higher:

$300   cash flow
580   (20% excess deduction in 29% bracket)
880   Total—equivalent to 12.39% taxable ($2,000 ÷ .71)

In a 39% bracket the equivalent would be 17.7 percent, and in a 50 percent bracket 26 percent. In the future years you could anticipate an increase in the cash flow and a decrease in your excess deductions.

These would be your NOW benefits, and they could be most attractive. However, your chief reason for investing should be your LATER benefits when the apartments are sold and you hope to cash in on the equity buildup and appreciation.

Later Benefits

When the properties are sold for as much or more than the original purchase price, and only then, do you reap any later benefits. Various payout arrangements are provided by the general partners, so you should study each carefully to see which ones appear to give you the fairest return. A typical arrangement may be that when you have received back your original investment plus 12 percent per year, the general partner then receives 10 percent of the profits in excess of your original capital contribution, and you and the other limited partners receive the other 90 percent. Other programs may provide that this split or other arrangements, such as an 85–15 percent split, shall occur once you've received back your original investment plus 10 percent. Your net results may be as great in one as the other. It all depends on the sale price.

On receiving your proportionate part of the sales proceeds, you will owe a capital gains tax (and perhaps a small ordinary income tax if accelerated depreciation has been taken) on any gain above your adjusted cost basis unless you take steps to shelter it again. Remember all those distributions that you have been receiving without current taxation and the excess deductions that have saved you taxes on your other income? Now the IRS wants its due. Taxes are rarely forgiven, but they can be postponed with good tax planning. In the interim you have the earning power of the money, and when and if you do have to pay, you can make the payment with cheaper dollars if inflation continues. Also, it gives you time to plan with the hopes of converting ordinary income into capital gains, lowering your tax bite, and giving you time to figure out how to postpone paying the tax until an even further point in the future. Tax avoidance or postponement must be a vital part of your program for economic survival.

Nonleveraged Multifamily Housing

In 1981 a management team that heretofore had established an excellent performance record by offering leveraged programs became aware that "cash was king" and added an all-cash offering along with their leveraged offering. They found they were able to buy at substantial discounts because builders could not obtain permanent financing and were suffering from very high interim financing costs. These costs were making what should have been profitable complexes unprofitable ones.

When the capital markets ease, they plan to finance the projects. Even if this does not occur, inflation should cause the properties to appreciate. A typical cash flow anticipation could be:

Year 1: 8% sheltered, 3% excess deduction

Year 2: 9–10% sheltered, 3% excess deduction

Year 3: 10–12% most of cash sheltered

If the properties are then financed, a proportional part would then be paid out to you, if you are an investor. It will not be taxable to you and you would have all or a large part of your money back to invest again and still own your proportionate part of the partnership.

In a nonleveraged program your immediate quarterly cash flow will be greater and your risk of negative cash flow on a property will be reduced, since there is no mortgage to service. However, you have fewer deductions because there is no interest to deduct and you have a lower base for obtaining depreciation deductions. If inflation is at a relatively high level and mortgages are not placed on the properties, your appreciation will not multiply as quickly as it would if there was leverage. However, if the opposite occurs, or if we have a recession, you are in a more comfortable position.

Community Home Parks

Another area of real estate investing you'll want to seriously consider is a registered limited partnership that invests in community home parks. As we have said, escalating building costs have made the traditional home unaffordable by a large segment of our population, but energy costs have also escalated, especially for those living in the North. As a result, the southern climate has become more appealing. Remember, too, that ERTA has increased the capital gains exemption permitted for those over fifty-five on the sale of their home. Under this provision, if the taxpayer is fifty-five years of age or older when he sells or exchanges property that he has owned and used as his principal residence for periods aggregating three years or more during the five-year period ending on the date of the sale or exchange, he can elect to exclude from his gross income up to $125,000 ($62,500 on a separate return) of gain on the sale.

This provision has greatly stimulated the interest of older couples living in the North to look at community home parks in the South and the West.

What could you anticipate if you were to invest in such a partnership, which you can do for $1,000 per unit (minimum units 5 or $5,000)? From my observations, I believe some reasonable expectations could be:

Year	Cash Flow	Excess Deductions
1	4%	12%
2	5	9
3	7	7
4	8	5
5	10	4
6	12	3
7	13	0

Private Placements

If you are in the 50 percent tax bracket, have assets in excess of $100,000 excluding home and furnishings, and your temperament does not require the greater safety of diversification, you may want to consider investing in a private placement of an apartment complex or other income-producing real estate if it is offered by a general partner with high integrity, a very large net worth, and a long and excellent performance record. Never, never invest in one that does not meet these criteria. A private placement is offered under SEC Regulation D (formerly Rule 146) and can, under certain provisions, qualify for exemption from registration. However, the private placement documents, called the offering memorandum, must disclose all pertinent information, as they would if they were registered. They may contain even more.

An SEC regulator will not have scrutinized the offering memorandum, but our laws are such that all the negatives and disaster possibilities that regulators can possibly think of will be in the offering memorandum, and it will be a very long and weighty document with pages and pages of dire warnings.

The number of investors will be limited and they must be "sophisticated and wealthy" or have a "sophisticated offeree's representative and be wealthy."

A private placement usually contains only one property. One in which I invested on August 8, 1977, required that I make investments over a three-year period. The first year I invested $13,062.50, writing off 55.4 percent of the investment. The second year I invested $13,433.33, writing off 99.7 percent, and the third year $14,473.33, writing off 64.5 percent for a total investment of $40,000 plus 969.16 of interest. Write-offs were projected to continue over another six years and to be 122 percent of the amount I invested. This made my average investment approximately $13,670 per year over the three-year period.

My cash flow the second year was projected to be 3.2 percent tax-sheltered (in reality it was over 5 percent, since this was 3.2 percent on the total three-year investment and I did not make the third-year investment until the third year and was actually earning on the funds in another position) with equity buildup at 4.2 percent. By the fourth year, tax-sheltered cash flow was projected to move up to 8 percent, and the equity buildup to 4.9 percent.

By the end of the third year I calculated that my benefits in a 50 percent tax bracket had been:

	Year	Cash Distribution Tax-Sheltered	Tax Savings From Excess Deductions
	1	Minimal	3,637
NOW	2	1,262	6,480
	3	2,614	4,190
		3,876	14,307

	Year	Equity Buildup	Appreciation
	1	$48	
LATER	2	155	?
	3	169	

My first three years:

> $3,876 Cash distributions received
> 14,307 Tax savings from write-offs
> 372 Equity buildup
> $18,555 ÷ 3 years = $6,185 average benefits per year.

The average benefits per year, $6,185, divided by $13,670, the average investment per year, gave me 45 percent average *after-tax* benefit per year. To obtain the same current equivalent net after-tax benefit on a taxable cash flow, I would have had to earn 90 percent annually on a certificate of deposit in a 50 percent tax bracket. In addition, I anticipated six more years of tax write-offs without any additional investment and tax-sheltered cash distributions of 8 percent or more plus capital appreciation. We are now into our fourth year. The cash flow is $9,673 per year or 24.18 percent, and we have received an offer of sale at a very handsome profit.

There can be negatives to this type of investment. Chief among them is lack of diversification. I do not have ten to fifteen properties, as I would have had in a good diversified public offering. If, for example, the area should suffer a sharp decline in employment, as has happened in Seattle and Detroit, I could suffer a negative cash flow. For that reason, I must be sure I have staying power—meaning other funds to carry me through if this should happen.

Deductions

Perhaps you already know how "write-offs" or deductions occur, but let's look at the four most important sources for my deductions in the above investments:

1. *Depreciation.* I was allowed my proportionate part of the depreciation of the apartment complex's total purchase price (less the amount allocated to the land), even though the mortgage company provided approximately four times as much capital as I did. The building is being depreciated on a 125 percent depreciation schedule, since we are a second owner of a multifamily housing investment. As well, we can use component-part depreciation for drapes, carpets, and so on. A new owner can now use 175 percent and a fifteen-year life, which enhances the value of the property.

2. *Interest expense.* Interest payments on the mortgage (subject to some restrictions) are also allowable deductions.

3. *Operating losses,* if any should occur.

4. *Charges that can be legitimately expensed in the year paid.*

Because of borrowed funds, I will be allowed to deduct more than I have invested. (The Revenue Act of 1978 modified the at-risk rule to apply to all activities except real estate investment. This is another plus for investing in real estate.)

Another private placement we recommended to our clients called for an investment of $86,000 over a four-year period in an apartment complex in Houston. The projections were as follows:

Payment	Year	Tax Savings 50% bracket
12,800	1979 (late)	4,844
25,000	1980	14,013
20,000	1981	25,345
28,700	1982	

This apartment building was sold in less than 2-1/2 years before it was necessary to make the $28,700 payment. Clients received back $50,000 ($5,000 to be received later), as well as tax savings of $44,202 on their $57,800 investment. In 1990 they will receive another check for $60,000 plus $1,200 per year interest semiannually until that time.

If you are financially able to assume greater risks and you meet the suitability requirements, private placements by the right general partners are investments you should consider. They can be structured for greater tax benefits so that you can invest some "soft" before-tax dollars, and the burdensome expense of registration can be reduced.

Performance: Past and Projected

Past performance of the partnerships my clients have used have been most gratifying. I do not know the future. However, I do know that this performance was obtained when our country was experiencing lower rates of inflation and excessive overbuilding. We are now experiencing well-documented underbuilding and continued inflation. We have underbuilding, and we have no rent control in the areas in which these partnerships purchase properties. The partnerships are still able to buy properties on the basis of current cash flow rather than replacement costs, and these are rapidly escalating. Rent is still one of our best buys, and I think there will have to be an increase of $100 to $200 an apartment before sufficient new building will occur. This should allow the partnerships to continue to make substantial rent increases while maintaining high occupancies. You should consider investing some of your "hard" after-tax dollars in large, well- managed limited partnerships investing in multifamily housing.

You may want to use this type of partnership or the triple-net lease, or you may use both, as many of my clients choose to do. The triple-net lease and the all-cash multifamily limited partnership are the more conservative and should pay out higher current cash distributions. The latter should pay out completely tax-sheltered distributions, with excess deductions to save taxes on other income. If growth of capital is your primary objective, multifamily housing and multiple-tenant properties should offer you greater potential.

Shopping Centers and Office Buildings

In a number of the registered limited partnerships investing chiefly in multifamily apartments, the general partners have often included quality office buildings and shopping centers. This practice may continue, or, because of the more favorable depreciation provisions for the housing, they may begin placing these in separate offerings.

Investing in shopping centers and office buildings can be most rewarding and can offer excellent tax-sheltered cash flow and equity buildup and appreciation potential. The general partner will usually diversify the portfolio as to kinds of properties and their locations. Past results on these have been very pleasing to our clients. Your leverage would be similar to the multifamily housing partnerships. Some are structured with some first-year write-offs going in. Others are not.

Choose management with an excellent past performance record. That doesn't give you a guarantee for the future, but it gives me a lot of comfort when I'm making this type of investment, which I do in both registered and private placements.

For several years we've done all the equity financing through private placements for a particular office and shopping center building in Houston with superb results. Our holding periods have usually been 2 1/2 to 3 years, at which time we have taken our gains and invested these funds into the next office complex being developed.

Hotels

There is also an excellent registered limited partnership available that invests portions of the partnership funds into tax-quality hotels along with apartments, office buildings, and shopping centers. Hotels are probably the most inflation-sensitive type of income-producing real estate because room rates can be raised twice a day. The average "lease" is 2.4 days, which is the average stay in a hotel. (The story is often told of the business traveler who visited Chile, which at that time was experiencing runaway inflation. During his five-day stay, the room rates were raised three times). Hotels do have the advantage of more easily passing along escalating costs, and so have the potential for ultimately being capitalized out in increased property value. This characteristic greatly enhances their appreciation potential.

Budget Motels

We have also recommended that our clients consider budget motels through a registered limited partnership where the general partner is one that heads a fast-growing budget motel chain.

As inflation continues, the commercial traveler's cost for transportation, food, and lodging is escalating. According to one of the national CPA firms that specializes in the lodging industry, budget motels have been able to capitalize on the accelerating inflation rates and energy problems, establishing a solid market base on which to grow in the 1980s. As older, full-service motor hotels are forced to increase their room rates, the market for budget properties should become more attractive.

You can become an investor for as small an amount as $2,500 in units of $500. Cash flow projections are excellent beginning the second year. You should only anticipate bank interest or less during the first year while the motels are being constructed. They may be constructed for cash and, after a steady cash flow has developed over two to three years, a mortgage may be obtained on the motels. These funds could be used to increase the number of rooms of the original motels or to build additional motels in other selected locations.

Since the demand for budget motels should continue to increase, this is an investment you may want to consider if you are interested in cash flow with some tax shelter and the potential for appreciation.

Miniwarehouses

From all indications, the 1980s will bring to you many investment opportunities. One type that has had particular appeal to our clients over the past six years has been the registered limited partnership that invests in miniwarehouses. Private placements in these areas had been available previous to this, but there were no registered ones that could be purchased by the average investor in small units.

Again we return to our demand-supply criteria. Why has demand for miniwarehouses greatly escalated? And why do I think that this demand will continue?

As home prices continue to rise, many would-be buyers are being priced out of the market and forced to live in apartments. Even those who are able to buy must settle for smaller houses or condominiums. The cost of constructing new office buildings also has escalated, limiting more and more businesses in the amount of space they can afford to rent. Manufacturing representatives likewise are finding conventional warehouse space costly or nonexistent.

These factors have combined to create a need for temporary storage space, opening the way for investment opportunities in miniwarehouses. These structures are inexpensive to construct and designed to offer accessible storage space for personal and business use at a relatively low cost. Space may be required on a long-term or short-term basis, but the typical rental period is less than one year, and spaces are rented usually on a month-to-month basis.

Miniwarehouses are ordinarily built in locations that are highly visible from main roads and expressways. They have brightly painted doors, neon signs in eye-catching positions, easy access to and from well-travelled roads and densely populated areas. Several complexes can be situated within a metropolitan area. Managers who live in the complexes provide security and ongoing rental information and services.

The cost per square foot to build a miniwarehouse is roughly half that of an apartment building. But a miniwarehouse can be rented for a comparable amount of money per square foot, and it has a much lower operating cost.

By investing in units of a public offering, you can become an investor in as many as eighteen to twenty miniwarehouse complexes in four to five major "metroplexes" with as small an amount as $2,500. The units are usually $500 and most offerings require a minimum investment of five units.

As investments are made in the units, the general partner obtains land and builds the miniwarehouses with no financing. The elimination of interim financing costs and mortgage payments makes it possible for miniwarehouses to produce a positive cash flow with only a 30 percent occupancy. In a good location, this level is often reached within 60 days of completion of the facility.

At 95 percent occupancy, miniwarehouses can begin producing a cash flow of 12 percent or more by the fifteenth month. Some of our programs already have a 19 percent cash flow. As an owner, you receive your proportionate part of the depreciation that is allowed on the warehouses, which could shelter 35-40 percent of your cash flow from taxes.

Also, your cash flow has the potential of increasing annually. I have found that management in the past has been able to escalate rents approximately 10 percent per year without causing the renters to move. This 10 percent usually can be translated into a 2 percent increase per year in cash flow to our investors. (We are a nation of packrats, and a 10 percent increase in cost usually is not enough to make us move our junk.) Since leases are on a month-to-month basis, they are very inflation responsive in that rents can be raised monthly.

Most partnerships are set up with the arrangement that when you have received your original investment back, the general partner can mortgage the building. If they obtain a mortgage, you will receive your proportionate part of these borrowed funds. These funds will not be taxable to you since they are borrowed. You will still own your proportionate part of the warehouses, less the mortgages, so you should continue to receive some cash flow after mortgage payments.

The primary objective of the partnership is to buy prime metropolitan real estate in the growth sectors of the United States. This makes it possible for the partnership to create a land bank while producing a good cash flow. Later it is anticipated that developers will pay an appreciated price for the land, demolish the miniwarehouses, and erect office buildings, high rises, and condos. This higher and better use should yield exceptional capital appreciation.

Possible Disadvantages of Real Estate Limited Partnerships

What are some of the risks and disadvantages of investing in registered limited partnerships that invest in real estate?

First, there can be delays between the time you make your investment and the time the money is actually invested in properties. During the interim you will receive interest comparable to the rate you would have been receiving in a money market mutual fund, but you will not be receiving tax-sheltered cash flow from real estate.

Second, partnership units can only be transferred with the consent of the general partner. (In the past this has not been withheld unreasonably.) Therefore, there will usually be no public market for the units; however, the National Association of Security Dealers is now studying the feasibility of such a market. Third, as a limited partner you cannot participate in the selection and management of the properties without losing your limited partnership status.

Beneficial Effects of the Economic Recovery Tax Act (ERTA)

The Economic Recovery Tax Act of 1981 greatly enhanced the profit and tax savings potential of good commercial and residential income property. Heretofore, the owners of both commercial buildings and apartments estimated the depreciation according to what they thought the life of the building would be.

In apartments, owners generally chose twenty-five to thirty years. In commercial buildings, forty, forty-five, fifty years and sometimes an even longer span were chosen. There was nothing carved in stone for realtors by the IRS. This put the owners in an adversarial position with the government, which is not exactly a positive situation for attracting investments.

ERTA in one fell swoop has allowed owners to take a straight-line depreciation for fifteen years, and the depreciation situation has been made audit-proof and nonarguable.

What does this change mean to you if you are an investor? Before ERTA, on an average $10,000 investment you would have received a deduction of around $3,000 over a five-year period. Now you will receive a $5,500 deduction. The $3,000 formerly was arguable by the IRS. The $5,500 is nonarguable.

This shorter fifteen-year depreciation schedule on commercial real estate ("Accelerated Cost Recovery System") adds significantly to the rate of return you can receive. Moreover, for residential real estate, including multifamily housing, the fifteen-year schedule together with the new liberalized 175 percent accelerated depreciation rate increases the tax write-offs by more than 300 percent over the old IRS guidelines. These materially increased tax losses permit you to recover your investment in the form of tax savings much sooner than in past years. Under

ERTA, as an investor in a multifamily real estate limited partnership, you can write off 70–80 percent of your investment in the first five years, compared with 30–40 percent under the old law.

ERTA is also beneficial upon the sale of the property because it reduces both individual and capital gains rates. Individual rates, as you know, were reduced 23 percent, the full effect to be felt in 1984. The maximum rate was reduced from 70 to 50 percent and the capital gains rate dropped to 20 percent. Also, you may benefit from the new recapture provision of the act, with far less recapture or none at all, if the transaction is structured properly.

Another feature of the act liberalized the provision regarding "unrelated business taxable income" for pension and profit-sharing plans. Before the passage of ERTA, U.S. pension plans were the smallest investors in real estate, on a percentage basis, of any of the countries in the free world because of this provision. Only 3 percent of retirement funds were in real estate, whereas other countries invested close to 40 percent. The reason was the IRS did not allow tax-exempt status to income or gains from the leveraged part of real estate that was bought. ERTA altered this.

Institutions make up one of the largest single pools of assets in this country. There are now over $700 billion of assets in pension funds and they are growing between 10 and 15 percent a year.

The new tax law, the new attitude toward rent control, the greater fluidity in selling real estate, the greater keepable cash flow through depreciation, and the new demand that is being unleashed without a correspondingly greater supply, to me bodes well for the future appreciation of well-selected, well-managed commercial and residential multifamily housing.

You will probably find that the structure of a limited partnership is the best way to put our tax laws and economic shortages to work for you to enhance your net worth.

Real Estate Investment Trusts (REITs)

All of the types of participation in commercial income-producing real estate we have discussed so far may appeal to you, but at this point in your financial life you may not meet all the suitability requirements, or you may not choose to invest this amount of money in a less liquid limited partnership. By suitability I mean that the regulatory agencies may require that investors in limited partnership offerings have an income of $30,000 and $30,000 net worth, exclusive of home and furnishings, or a net worth of $75,000 with no income requirements.

Are there ways you can participate with smaller amounts of money? Yes, you can, through what are known as real estate investment trusts. This type of real estate investment was developed in response to the needs of those who wanted to invest small amounts of money in the profit potentials that real estate investing had to offer, but who wanted at the same time to maintain the liquidity of a stock. To fulfill this desire, the modern equity trust was created to acquire and hold income properties of all types, yet have the shares publicly traded.

The Real Estate Investment Trust (REIT) industry expanded greatly in the late 1960s and early 1970s, when many financial institutions, with the encouragement of Wall Street, established affiliated mortgage trusts in order to provide additional sources of capital. Though a few trusts used little leverage, many aggressively sought higher yields by lending to builders for construction. Their yields, together with their price per share, escalated and they became the darlings of the brokerage industry and of our largest national banks. Some of these REITs bore the prestigious names of such banking institutions as Chase Manhattan Bank and Bank of America. The nation's largest brokerage firms brought forth underwritings in REITs and held many public seminars extolling their virtues. Unfortunately, neither they nor others ever anticipated the drastic steps that would be taken by the Federal Reserve Board shortly thereafter to restrict the nation's money supply, and that would cause a disastrous money crunch, sending interest rates reeling skyward. Many of the mortgage REITs had loaned funds for longer terms while borrowing for short terms and making a tidy sum on the spread between the two. But suddenly their cost to borrow money escalated beyond the rates at which they had made their loans. This spelled immediate and devastating trouble.

Even in less perilous times, REITs may have a rough time. A REIT, for example, may have made an excellent purchase of property, but it may be what is known as a "turn-around situation." During the period when needed improvements are being made, the REIT's earnings may be lower. A drop in earnings of a stock frightens traders and often causes them to virtually bomb a stock, driving down its price and causing general chaos and disappointment to the investor.

I'm convinced that my beloved Wall Street has never really understood real estate investing and that, properly structured, REITs can offer a valid investment opportunity for those who want to participate in commercial income real estate while being able to maintain liquidity.

REITs may fit your needs. Their shares can be freely transferable, in contrast to limited partnership interests. The trust must by regulation be a passive entity and must employ outside agents to perform required services. So long as it meets certain asset and income tests and distributes at least 95 percent of its net taxable income each year, it will not be separately taxed. However, distributions may be partially or wholly tax-sheltered, but net operating losses cannot be passed through to you as an investor to be used to shelter income from other sources, as can occur under the limited partnership arrangement.

You may find the operation of a REIT very much like that of a limited partnership, except that more emphasis will be placed on cash flow and equity buildup because of its inability to pass through excess tax losses. However, the increased liquidity of shares and the restrictions on resale of properties may encourage REITs to periodically refinance their properties, which in turn could allow current realization of some of the equity buildup.

Open-End REITs

A major partnership sponsor that we use now offers a REIT that invests in mortgages and land under established real estate. The shares participate in a percentage of the rent from the buildings plus a base rental. Total return is projected at 20 percent annually and you have the privilege of reinvesting your cash flow in additional shares, which should give you a compounding effect.

It is estimated that this could result in 9.5 times your investment over twelve years if you reinvest, and around 2.1 times if you do not. This product was designed for purchase by qualified pension plans (IRA, Keogh, pension and profit sharing) but you may also want to consider it if your financial objective is predictable income with an inflation hedge and liquidity that you can have in five days. The shares are $25.00 per share and the minimum investment is $1,000.

Figure 6-2 is a hypothetical illustration of the possible benefit with and without a reinvestment plan.

Farmlands

Should you consider investing in farmlands? Your answer probably depends on the amount of money you have to invest, your tax bracket, your temperament, and what you enjoy doing. Farmland properly bought and financed in the right location has in the past enjoyed excellent price appreciation.

In addition to inflation, there are other factors that can cause an increase in farmland values. Some of these are:

1. Increasing demand and ability to pay for food that can be produced from farming the land.

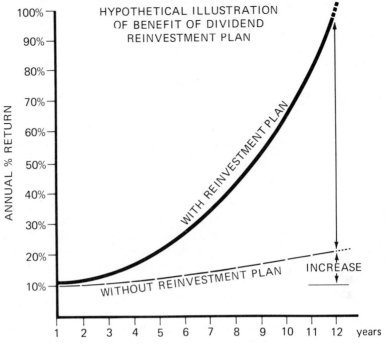

Assumptions:
1. An initial lump sum investment.
2. Distributions are paid each quarter each year.
3. Initial annual dividend rate of 11.3% increasing to 21% by the 12th year.
4. Dividend reinvestment share price is original share price (no increase in price of shares).
5. Of course, the "Without Reinvestment Plan" curve does not take into consideration the additional benefit of using dividends to acquire other investments.

Figure 6-2

2. The scarcity of good crop-growing land. This scarcity increases as urbanization takes more and more farmland and converts it to housing subdivisions.

3. Increasing demand for U.S. food items and commodities, especially by the OPEC countries as we enrich their coffers.

Should you consider investing monies in farmland as an inflationary hedge and to produce an income stream? If so, what investment strategy should you use?

If you are knowledgeable about farming, have sufficient time and the desire, and can emotionally and financially weather bad crop years, you may want to consider buying some farmland and putting it into production. This takes great expertise, usually fairly large amounts of money, and may not offer you the amount of diversification needed to reduce risks.

Producing Orchards and Vineyards

What about producing orchards and vineyards? Again, this activity will take great expertise and a fairly large amount of capital unless you become a limited partner in a large operation. ERTA has introduced some favorable tax advantages, for you would be allowed to completely depreciate the original cost of any trees, vines, and irrigation systems, including pumps and wells, over a five-year period. Since the trees and vines usually represent the greatest allocation of the total value per acre, the tax advantages can be attractive. Since investment tax credit is also allowed, you can receive in excess of a 150 percent write-off over a five-year period.

An example of how this might work could be a 175-acre fig ranch that is four years old and in its first year of production, and that is purchased for $7,700 per acre including land, fig trees, pumps, and wells. The down payment could be $1,985 per acre. Farming costs, taxes, and other expenses could account for an additional $421 per acre in the first year.

The purchase price of $7,700 per acre could be allocated as follows:

	Cost Per Acre
Land	$2,000
Land preparation	150
Pumps and wells	300
Irrigation system	800
Fig trees	4,450

If the trees are in the first year of commercial production, ITC of $445 per acre is available. The pumps and wells and irrigation system are "used," so the ITC is limited to 10 percent of the first $125,000 of value (assuming the investor had not otherwise reached his limits for used ITC), which in this situation means another $110 per acre of ITC. In addition, another $833 per acre of depreciation can be taken plus all the operating farming costs of perhaps an additional $421 per acre. Total deductions could be $1,253 per acre plus the ITC of $555 per acre.

Over the next four years, as an investor you would make additional cash contributions, which would decrease each year as the fig trees moved toward stabilized production. During this period you would have been allowed to completely depreciate the trees and irrigation system. If we assume an 8 percent inflation rate per year, the fig orchard could sell for $17,888 per acre in ten years. That would mean a 32.5 percent after-tax, internal rate of return, after taking into consideration the recapture of all of the depreciation as ordinary income.

The Ideal Investment?

I have never found an ideal investment. If you do, please let me know. However, I have found that the right kind of commercial income-producing real estate limited partnerships under the guidance and management of the right general partners has in the past contained some of the characteristics of an ideal investment. These are

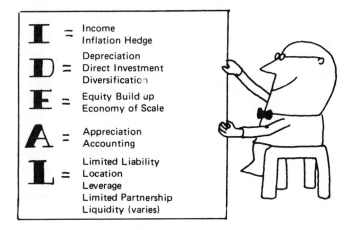

I =	Income Inflation Hedge
D =	Depreciation Direct Investment Diversification
E =	Equity Build up Economy of Scale
A =	Appreciation Accounting
L =	Limited Liability Location Leverage Limited Partnership Liquidity (varies)

Let's consider each in summary.

Income With Tax Shelter

The only money you'll ever spend at the grocery store is what the IRS lets you keep. Income-producing real estate limited partnerships investing in triple-net leases have in the past paid out cash flow quarterly with the major portion sheltered. This has come about because they are allowed to pass through to the limited partners the depreciation and interest expense on the properties. Those investing in multiple-tenant properties have been able not only to shelter the cash distributions paid quarterly, but to provide excess deductions to save taxes on income from other sources.

Inflation Hedge

If you have received no other message from this book, I do hope the one you have not missed is the absolute reality that inflation came thundering in with our government's dedication to full employment and "entitlement programs" and that it will never go away until this philosophy is changed. My advice to you is to quit worrying about inflation and get on the right side of it. Inflation can make you a lot of money if you place your funds intelligently in those areas where demand is greater than supply.

Depreciation

The limited partnership form of investing permits the pass-through of the depreciation expense deduction allowed by the IRS. Another important characteristic of real estate is that depreciation is allowed on the total cost of the building—not just on your investment. You may have only put in $10,000 and the mortgage company $30,000, but your depreciation is based on the total $40,000. You are allowed a deduction for depreciation even when your asset is actually growing in value.

Direct Investing

All money placed in a savings and loan association is invested in real estate. If you are a depositor, you are an indirect investor in real estate investment. If you invest in a limited partnership, the partnership may borrow the mortgage money from the savings and loan, but you have a direct investment and are in a position to receive your money's full earning power (but you also give up the fixed dollar guarantees). In my opinion, your only hope of staying even after inflation and taxes is to be a direct investor. Own the thing that owns the thing.

Diversification of Risks

One of the first rules of successful investing is diversification. Never put all your eggs in the proverbial one basket. Spread your precious eggs out in several baskets of various kinds of real estate and in various locations. Ten properties located in ten locations should offer more safety than one property in one location.

Equity Buildup

If you own your home on which you have a mortgage, you are already familiar with equity buildup (mortgage paydown). The difference be-

tween the equity buildup in your home and the equity buildup in the commercial properties of the limited partnerships is that you had to build up the equity in your home by your monthly mortgage payments, but in the limited partnerships the tenants build up your equity through a portion of their monthly rent payments. Equity also builds up without being taxed as long as deductions are sufficient to shelter at least part of the cash flow.

Economy of Scale

I can't emphasize enough how important economy of scale can be in the purchase, management, and sale of commercial real estate. Most of the truly significant profits are made on the very large real estate properties. There are fewer buyers to compete and they can also buy the carpeting, paint, refrigerators, stoves, and so on, directly from the factory. As a limited partner, you have the opportunity to participate in a proportionate part of larger properties than you may be able to do on an individual basis.

Appreciation

"Capital gains" have always been and still remain the golden words of the investment world. No federal income taxes are paid on the appreciation of real estate until the properties are sold. The properties can just sit there and grow in value without taxes. (They can go down in value, too.) Appreciation is realized when and if the properties are sold for a larger amount than was paid for their purchase. If the properties have been held for over a year, the profit on the sale is considered a capital gain and only 40 percent of it is taxable, with a maximum tax of 20 percent.

As inflation pushes up replacement costs, appreciation in real estate has a good likelihood of occurring.

Accounting

My clients especially enjoy the accounting done for them by the general partners for their real estate investments. They are sent a completed Schedule K-1 (schedule used for limited partnership), as well as a blank one to complete and attach to their income tax returns, plus a guide with red lines and arrows stating, "Put this figure on this line." By following the detailed instructions, the clients can complete their own returns if they desire. (However, I find that truly competent and creative CPAs can be worth much more than they cost.)

Leverage

Again, as mentioned before, remember Bernard Baruch and his answer to the question of how he made so much money: "O.P.M.—Other People's Money." Let other people's money work for you. Inflation rewards those who owe money, not those who pay cash. (I am talking about long-term real estate mortgages, not revolving charge accounts.) When and if appreciation occurs, the total value of the building appreciates, including the borrowed portion. Leverage can work for you if properly used. It can spell disaster if it is abused or if the economy of the area turns against you.

Limited Liability

As a limited partner, you could not be called upon for additional funds. You have limited your liability.

Liquidity

Real estate investment trusts provide you with liquidity. Many of the other forms of investing in real estate curtail liquidity. Do not place funds into real estate that you want to be free to grab back on very short notice.

Location

The three most important rules in selecting the right piece of real estate are location, location, location (and in periods of tight money I would add terms, terms, terms). Your objective should be to be a proportionate owner of a diversified portfolio of properties selected and managed by top professionals who have established a long record of success and who have large pools of money for investing. This enables them to purchase properties that have the necessary characteristics of good location and the right terms.

Summary

If you are willing to give up instant liquidity, are in a 24 percent tax bracket or above, and can forego the pleasure of looking up the market value of your properties in the paper each day, you may find that the limited partnership is a good way to prevent double taxation and to allow you to participate in investments that, if made individually, would require large amounts of capital.

Investing in real estate should be considered in any program designed to build financial independence. In my opinion, the opportunity for relatively high leverage with relatively low risk makes it a viable inflation hedge. Unusual tax benefits also can enhance its attractiveness, but they should not be your principal motivation.

Current tax-sheltered cash distributions can also be attractive. If your income stream needs to be steady, then be prepared to sacrifice some of the growth potential. If current income is not your chief objective, then look at the operating leveraged partnerships where income may fluctuate but where the potential for appreciation is greater.

Our formula for financial independence should now add real estate and might read this way:

Time + Money + Real estate =
Opportunity for Financial Independence

Application

1. Which areas of real estate investing best fit your tax bracket and your temperament?
2. List the steps you will take to become better informed about investment alternatives.
3. Make a list of all your alternative investment possibilities. Calculate your expected rate of return, your loss to taxes, your keepable funds after taxes, your potential to hedge against inflation, and your potential for equity buildup and growth of capital.

Your Worksheet for Comparing Real Estate Investing
With Other Types

$_____ investment, _____ % tax bracket.

Indirect Investing

	In-come	Taxes	Keep-able	Infla-tion Hedge	Equity Build-Up	Appreci-ation
Savings & loan						
Corporate bonds						
Municipal bonds						
Single-premium deferred annuity						

Direct Investing

Triple-net leases _____

Multiple tenant _____

4. List here the areas of our economy where you think demand will be greater than supply over the next three years:

   a.

   b.

   c.

   d.

5. List here the course of action you plan to take to profit from these shortages:

   a.

   b.

   c.

   d.

Chapter 7

Home Sweet Home—
To Rent or Buy?

There is one kind of real estate about which you have no option; you must have a place to live during every period of you life. You do, however, have a number of choices about how you allocate your funds to meet this and other needs.

Food, clothing, shelter—the three essentials of life! That's what you learned in grade school, and as an adult you probably do not question these necessities. Since shelter is a necessity, but only one of your necessities, it behooves you to approach its provision as coolly and economically as possible, for you will want to have funds left over for a few of the other goodies that put a bit of frosting on the cake of life.

There is much fuzzy thinking about the best way to provide shelter. Many couples, particularly young ones, hate to rent even for a short period of time. They are convinced that rent receipts are pure waste, not realizing that rent money is no more wasted than the money spent for food or medicine. Many view house payments as almost pure "savings" and rent money in terms of a leaky faucet.

You may be one of those who are deliberately closing their minds to economic realities in order to own their own home.

Single-Family Dwelling—Hobby or Investment?

To put this matter of renting versus owning into proper perspective, let's look at the landlord-tenant relationship. A landlord renting a one-family dwelling would probably earn a net of 6 percent on this equity—the market value of the home less the mortgage. This could happen only if he kept the home rented most of the time and the renter paid the rent promptly. (He may, however, be enjoying considerable tax shelter by way of depreciation while owning an appreciating asset.)

If the landlord has a $10,000 equity in a $50,000 home, he might hope to net a cash flow of around 6 percent on his $10,000 each year, which is $600, or $50 per month. Or, put in another way, if you had that much equity in your own $50,000 home, you'd be saving $50 per month by not renting the house from the landlord. However, you may not save that much because you can't claim as many deductions as the landlord.

Real estate ads often cite the fact that homeowners can deduct interest on their house loan and real estate taxes from their income taxes. The ads are right but do not give the whole story. The landlord also can deduct these items, plus many more that the IRS will not allow the homeowner to take. These cover insurance, repairs, painting, the green shrubbery, depreciation, and so on.

Every house has a potential rental value—the sum that could be realized by renting to a tenant. As a rule of thumb, the rental value is about 10 percent per year of the market value. A $50,000 home then has an approximate annual rental value of $5,000, or a little over $400 per month.

A single-family dwelling may not be a good investment, in the real sense of the word, for either the landlords or the homeowners who are in the lower income tax brackets (with the exception of the time between the mid-1970s through the present, when high interest rates and high replacement costs have greatly escalated home values). Homes often are more of a hobby than an investment unless you have chosen a home in what later becomes a growth area where land values accelerate rapidly. This could then be an excellent investment. However, don't go overboard; inflation or a shift in location desirability may not bail you out of a costly real estate purchase. While you're waiting for the property to inflate in value, taxes and interest put a very bad dent in your family budget.

The Real Cost

The real cost of home ownership includes upkeep and repair, fire and homeowner insurance, property taxes, equity investment, and depreciation (value loss). These expenses are just as real for a homeowner as they are for a landlord. The big difference lies in the fact that a landlord usually recognizes them and includes them in the price he charges for the use of his property, whereas you may be tempted as a homeowner to pretend that these expenses do not exist.

The landlord knows that he must get over 10 percent per year in rent on his property to cover his expenses and net him a profit. You, as a potential or present homeowner, would be wise to think as he does.

If you have been living in an apartment, feeling you just must buy your own home and save all that rent money, do slow down and take heart. The drain on your solvency may not be as bad as you have been thinking.

Avoid the Apples and Oranges Comparison

The rather unemotional approach I've given home ownership should do one thing for you, and that is to make you aware that the monthly payments have little to do with the real cost of owning a home.

How do you go about comparing the cost of renting an apartment with the cost of buying a home? One way is to compare the annual rental for an apartment with 10 percent of the value of the home you are thinking of purchasing. If you foolishly compare the monthly payments on the house with the monthly payments on the apartment, you are, in effect, comparing apples and oranges. There is no comparative relationship. Mortgage payments have nothing to do with the cost of home ownership. Mortgage payments only relate to debt reduction.

Study Figure 7-1 and you will see that home ownership costs have escalated rapidly since 1970. While apartment rents have escalated around 89 percent, home ownership costs have escalated around 174 percent. Rent is one of the best buys today, having gone up less than the Consumer Price Index. As you'll note, it has gone up around 134 percent during the same period.

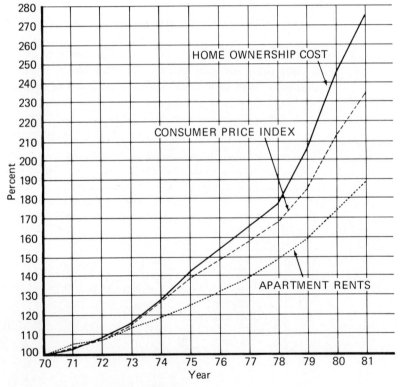

Source: Bureau of Labor Statistics

Figure 7-1. Cost of home ownership, Consumer Price Index, and apartment rents (1970-1981).

Buy or Rent?

Should you buy or rent your shelter? Your answer should be determined by a number of factors. Chief among these would be: your tax bracket, need for space, temperament, life-style, savings in the bank, investment possibilities, familiarity with the various neighborhoods, current home prices, availability of financing, and likelihood of being transferred.

Tax Advantage

Much has been said about the tax advantages of home ownership and there are some excellent advantages, but these advantages are not as clear-cut as they may appear at first. Interest and property taxes have both soared the past few years. Interest rates alone on a typical home are over twice what they were just a few years ago. Because these are allowable deductions on your tax return, they can be important to you if you are in a sufficiently high tax bracket. If you are in a 30 percent bracket, you are able to shift $30 out of every $100 you pay in interest and property taxes back to the IRS. In a 50 percent bracket, it's $50. As you can see, the higher your bracket, the greater the "subsidy" from the government.

This does not mean, however, that renters do not get tax breaks, too. The landlord is permitted to deduct interest and property taxes also. In addition, he is allowed to deduct two other important items the homeowner is not allowed. He can deduct depreciation on a fifteen year basis on the total cost of the property and also operating expenses. We learned how important depreciation deduction can be from Chapter 6. If landlords were required to pay these bills without treating them as expenses, rents would have to be higher. By permitting treatment of these items as operating expenses, renters pay lower rents and find more apartments available.

In the lower tax bracket, the tax relief may be just an illusion. If your income is $20,000 per year, you may not get much of a tax break from the extra deductions. Even if you are in the middle income bracket, you will probably save no more than 20 percent of the net cost of your interest and property taxes by deducting them from gross income.

The IRS allows each family a standard deduction anyway, and unless you have enough deductions to itemize, including interest and property taxes, these last two costs become pure expenses.

If you have ever had a really aggressive real estate agent pull out his form entitled "Analysis of Home Ownership Costs," he may endeavor to persuade you that owning your own house will cost practically nothing, since the monthly charges consist almost entirely of tax-deductible interest and property taxes, and the remainder is your contribution to your equity, which will, of course, increase. He will then proceed to tell you that all you need is a down payment, which will be the best investment you have ever made. He will attempt to persuade you that you should be a wise house hunter and buy, and not a foolish house hunter and rent, with nothing to show for it but rent receipts.

But this arithmetic omits two crucial elements. One of these is the loss of income that the down payment might produce if invested elsewhere. Another is the transfer costs, the expense of buying and selling a house, which can amount to over 8 percent of its value. When these costs are put into your analysis, they can turn the calculations around in favor of renting.

However, our whole U.S. housing system encourages buying, not renting. Spouses, children, pets, neighbors, politicians, and bankers all argue for home ownership. It has become one of those fundamentals we look to as securing the nation. Our tax laws favor ownership. The Brookings Institution estimates that homeowners get $7 billion worth of federal tax breaks annually.

The IRS also exempts you from the capital gains tax when you sell your house, as long as you buy another house that is as expensive within a year or build another within twenty-four months. This all encourages home ownership to become a habit. With exceptions, these rules also apply to a condominium and stock in a cooperative.

Gains that are not taxed reduce the basis on your new home. (Losses are not deductible.)

A second rollover of gain is also permitted without tax if you are an employee or are self-employed and the gain is from the sale of a former residence in connection with starting at a new principal place of work, provided the tests applicable to the deductions allowed for moving expenses are met.

The two-year period is suspended for the time a serviceman-taxpayer is serving on extended active duty after the sale of the residence. The suspension period can't exceed four years after the date of sale, with some exceptions as detailed in Code Sec. 1034(h). Also, if you are fifty-five years of age or older (or your spouse is) before the date of sale of your home, you may elect a one-time exclusion of up to $125,000 of gain if you have owned a home and used it as a principal residence for periods aggregating three years or more during the five-year period ending on the date of your sale.

Mobility—The American Way

Another consideration that may recommend renting is that we are a very mobile society. Renting allows you to move more easily without the worry and delay of selling a home and the expense of sales commissions and horrendous closing costs.

At this point you may be thinking that if you owned a home, you would be building an equity in return for your payments as the years go by, whereas now you have nothing but rent receipts.

But remember, I've been comparing the cost of renting with the cost of owning. You can save money and acquire net worth in other ways than by paying on a mortgage. You can open a money-market mutual fund or start a monthly investment program with the difference.

The Case of Mrs. Bailey

An elderly widow client of mine lives in a house that is debt-free and has a market value of $50,000. She asked if she should sell her house and rent an apartment. I told her that if she would bring me a list of her expenditures for the past year, I would be happy to advise her from a financial point of view. She gave me a list of her utilities, yard-work expenses, house repairs, insurance, and taxes. I then added a 6 percent "guaranteed" return she could obtain on the $50,000 that would be available for investment after the sale of the house, even though we can certainly do better than 6 percent on her money. When we added all of these together, we found that she could live in a $500 per month apartment more cheaply than she could live in her own home. In addition, she did not have to worry about watering her yard or possible vandalism during trips out of town.

I advised her, however, not to rush into selling her home. Answering a question on a financial basis is one thing and answering it on an emotional basis is quite another matter. Sometimes you need to consider that some expenditures are an investment in living.

Your Temperament

Home ownership may have great psychological benefits for you. Pride, a sense of belonging, having a place to put down roots—all of these can be very important. You may change, improve, and convert your home and grounds as you wish.

However, you now have an asset thay may demand much from you. It will take your or someone's time, energy, and money. Home repairs and upkeep can be costly. You have now become your own landlord, garbage man, and repairman. Yards will probably have to be mowed and shrubbery planted, watered, and trimmed. This may take away some of your freedom to play golf and tennis or to travel.

Is your income variable? Could it drop by a large amount? Are you subject to transfer? If so, you could have difficulty selling your home if this happened in a recession or a period when mortgage money had either dried up or had become very expensive. When you rent, your commitment lasts only as long as your lease.

Your Need for Space

If you have a growing family, they may need more space than renting would provide. Small children will need a place to play. The number of apartments that accept children or provide them with sufficient large play areas is limited. Schools may be better and not as crowded in the suburbs. Investigate thoroughly the schools and recreational and cultural facilities.

What Price Home Can You Afford?

If you decide to purchase a home, it may be the largest single investment that you will make in your whole lifetime; therefore, invest carefully and within your budget.

There is no magic rule as to what percentage of your income should be spent for a roof over your head; however, I have found that usually this expenditure should not exceed 30 to 35 percent of your income. We've already concluded that there are other things in life as important as housing. You may desire good clothing, nutritional and tasty food, excellent medical care, a sporty or at least adequate automobile, and an annual vacation. This makes it necessary to apportion your income.

There are certain guidelines lenders will use in determining the maximum mortgage they will grant. A rule of thumb used by many lenders is one-fourth of total income after long-term debt (any debt over ten months). For example, if you were purchasing an $89,000 home, and applying for a 75 percent loan of $66,750, at 16 percent your monthly payments would be $897.78 per month and you would need an income of $3,591 per month after long-term debt, or an annual income of around $44,000. If your earnings are higher, you may want to consider spending less. After all, there are other things you'll want. A large home may not be as important to you as other pleasures and comforts.

These figures only take into consideration the principal and interest mortgage payments, and do not include other housing costs such as insurance, taxes, utilities, maintenance, and repair. Inclusion of these, of course, would mean that you would be required to have a higher annual income to qualify for a loan.

Should You Buy a New or Old Home?

Advantages of the Old

New and used homes appreciate at about the same rate if the neighborhood is good. The rate in recent years has been between 10 and 15 percent a year. The possibility of your buying a used home is greater because more of them are available.

Also, you may be able to buy the older one for less. The rooms may be more spacious. The construction may be of higher quality. It may be nearer shops, schools, churches, and transportation. The neighborhood will be established, and the landscaping has probably been done. Taxes tend to rise less for older homes and you may avoid assessments for such things as utilities and water systems. There has been increased interest in older, close-in homes in recent years as the cost of gasoline has soared and traffic congestion has increased.

Disadvantages of Buying an Older Home

It may be more difficult when purchasing an older home to obtain the maximum mortgage, and the duration of the mortgage could be less. Repairs and remodeling can be expensive. Upkeep can be greater. The older home may lack central air-conditioning and new built-in appliances; adding them now may be costly.

Where to Buy?

I once interviewed the head of the real estate department for Prudential Life Insurance Company. When I asked him what the most important considerations in choosing real estate were, he drew himself up to his quite considerable height and said that there are three requirements you must never forget. They are "location, location, location!" (Another time when I asked a very successful real estate investor this same question, his answer was "terms, terms, terms.")

The same is true in selecting your home. The three requirements you should never forget are neighborhood, neighborhood, neighborhood. (As the cost of money escalates and inflation destroys purchasing power, you may also want to add "terms.") The homes and people around you not only affect the resale value of your home, but also your enjoyment of it.

The Least Expensive in the Neighborhood

Resist the temptation to buy the most expensive home in the neighborhood. It is much wiser to own a modest home in an expensive neighborhood. Your modest home may gain in value by being surrounded by more expensive homes, but an expensive home in a less expensive neighborhood will probably suffer because the mortgage obtainable may be limited in amount to the price of the least expensive home.

Distance from Work

Distance from work should also be seriously considered. Before you yield to the temptation to move far out from town to escape high land and tax costs, consider the cost of driving long distances to work. This cost can easily wipe out any savings.

Savings of $4,500 on the price of a home thirty miles from work could be used up in a few years if it were necessary to drive an extra 1,500 miles a year.

The time required to drive the extra distance should also be of prime consideration. Time is money. Extra time spent in driving may subtract from your earning power and sap your energy.

If you find, after considering all of these factors, that you still want to live farther out, may I suggest that you utilize your commuting time by installing a tape cassette in your automobile. There are excellent educational and motivational tapes on almost any subject. (A list of my favorites is in Appendix Figure 3.)

Premanufactured Housing—The "Mobile Home"

The conventional new or pre-owned home may no longer be a reality moneywise for you, or you may find that there are added amenities and more favorable locations available in a mobile home. I use the term "mobile home" because it is the term most used and understood. However, only 2 percent of such homes are ever moved, so mobility is no longer their major characteristic.

As you begin to study the pros and cons of whether you should consider premanufactured homes, you may discover there are a lot of myths surrounding this increasingly popular form of housing. One that has been prevalent for years is that only senior citizens live in them, but statistics show that half of the buyers are couples under thirty-five years of age.

Another myth is that they are shoddily built. However, a recent study showed that more than 60 percent of mobile homes built twenty or more years ago are still in use today. Still another myth is that the parks are overcrowded, are filled with noisy children, and are distant from shopping centers. Some of them are, but more and more of them are in beautiful surroundings like the ones I discussed under "Community Home Parks" in the previous chapter and are near shopping areas, schools, and medical facilities.

You may be tired of city life and want to move to the country because you enjoy the fresh air and space and have the option of keeping horses or raising cattle, dogs, or other animals. The premanufactured homes may make this choice available to you.

Current surveys show that many individuals and couples with excellent salaries are preferring the economy and ease of maintenance of this type of housing. Also the first-time buyers are finding that the down payment and monthly payments can fit into their budgets more readily than the conventional home.

Since 1976 the federal government has set standards for construction and safety of these homes. This code sets standards higher than those established for conventional housing in many communities.

Housing and Urban Development's National Manufactured Housing Code holds all mobile homes in the United States to a single standard. In the area of energy efficiency, the code specifies standards for heat loss and gain, efficiency of appliances, and minimum-level insulation protection; for fire safety, it requires smoke alarms and pop-out windows in sleeping areas, two exits, plus certain flame-spread standards in walls, ceilings, and cooking areas. Incidence of fire in mobile homes is now slightly less than in site-built homes.

Today's manufactured housing bears practically no resemblence to the old-time trailer. The homes come with peaked and slate roofs, cathedral ceilings, skylights, storm windows, microwaves, sewing areas, wood siding, wet bars, sunken bathtubs, and fireplaces. And they feature shelves and cupboards galore.

Price of Premanufactured Homes

While the cost of the average conventional home has passed $80,000 nationally, that same home made in a factory would cost $35,000 to $45,000. The reason for the price break is the efficiency of the assembly line. To build 1,000 square feet of housing the conventional way requires around 600 man hours. To factory build this same space takes around 250 man hours. When you add to this the more efficient quality control and no interruptions for bad weather or shortages of materials, the savings can add up.

In the past there have been restrictions on financing, locating, zoning, and licensing this type of housing, but these restrictions and hindrances are gradually being removed.

In Houston, for example, one of this country's largest builders of single-family, site-built homes has opened housing developments made up entirely of premanufactured housing. Another builder in California has developed posh double-wide premanufactured homes beginning around $85,000.

The only obstacle that seems to remain in this type of housing is the public image. But, bit by bit, with changes in legislation and zoning and with increased quality of development, this type of housing is moving closer to the mainstream of acceptable housing and may be an option you will want to consider.

Large or Small Down Payment?

If you decide after looking at all the facts that buying a home of your own is best for you economically and emotionally, then should you make a small down payment or a large down payment?

From the point of view of a financial planner, there is no doubt that the down payment should be as low as you possibly can arrange in the money market you find yourself in. There are a number of reasons you should make this choice.

1. Any money tied up in a mortgage is a dead asset. The house doesn't know whether or not it has a high or low down payment on it. It will increase or decrease in value just the same. This is especially true in a state that has a homestead law like Texas. Once you've moved in, you cannot refinance this home and get that equity out. It is locked in until you sell. It's almost like that money sitting in a checking account not drawing interest.

2. Interest is deductible. As you've seen, you don't want to miss this subsidy.

3. Inflation rewards those who owe money, not those who pay cash. You can pay off the mortgage with cheaper and cheaper dollars as inflation continues. (Remember the new math of inflation.)

4. If you need to sell, it's easier to find someone with a small down payment than a large one unless you have a due-on-sale clause when an assumption is made.

5. You have additional funds to invest in other ways and so gain added diversification.

The Allens and the Bakers

To help you make your comparison, let's look at two families. Each found just the right home, and each home cost $89,000 (the national average price for a home in 1981). Each, fortunately, had $89,000, an income of $45,000 a year, and two healthy children of approximately the same ages.

The Allens

The Allens were reared by parents who programmed them with such admonitions as "Always pay cash"; "Never owe money"; "You might come upon hard times, so have your house paid for so you'll have a roof over your head"— the Poor Richard guidelines.

When it was time to close on their home, the Allens believed that the most prudent way was to pay cash, which they did. They then complimented themselves on saving "all that interest" and not having to make house payments each month.

The Bakers

The Bakers were reared by parents who were business oriented and held earning power of a dollar in high respect. They had taught their children to use or rent each dollar they could and to put it to work at its maximum potential. So when it came time to close on their home, they thought that the prudent course for their family was to move in with the minimum down payment and to obtain the best mortgage available.

Then they began shopping for terms and rates. First, they went to a life insurance company—choosing the kind that has enticed its policyholders to do their "banking" with the company in the form of cash surrender value. These companies, consequently, have large sums to lend if they choose to lend them for home mortgages. In the past, they have been the largest single underwriters of real estate mortgage money. During the past few years, however, they have been demanding and obtaining, a sizable portion of the equity in the commercial buildings they are financing.

The Bakers also shopped at savings and loan associations. These funds had been placed on deposit with them by those who wanted a "guarantee" of only a portion of the earning power of their money. These depositors were willing to settle for indirect investing in real estate by investing in the mortgage of the Baker's home. The Bakers found that the rates and terms varied from one savings association to another, depending on the amount of lendable money each had at the particular time and the value judgment of each of their loan officers as to the Bakers' ability to pay.

They also looked at mortgage companies and found that the rates varied by the same criteria as did those of the savings and loans.

The Bakers decided on financing a plan that would allow them to make a $22,500 down payment, with a $66,750 mortgage for thirty years at 16 percent from a life insurance company, with monthly payments of $897.78, principal and interest. (Their taxes were estimated to be around $159 per month and the insurance around $30. This made a total of $1,086.78.)

Assuming a Mortgage

Since the homes were new, it was necessary for the Allens and Bakers either to buy with cash or obtain a mortgage. Had the homes been "used," a third option might have been available and desirable. This is to "assume" a mortgage—that is, to take over responsibility for the mortgage that the seller has on the house. Older mortgages carry a lower interest rate than new mortgages, and the closing costs are considerably less if the home is in a community in which banks charge "points" for a loan (a "point" is 1 percent of the amount of the loan and the average was around 4 points in 1982 for a 75 percent mortgage). The purchaser pays the seller for his "equity" (the difference between the sale price and the mortgage) and then assumes the monthly payments. Ultimate legal responsibility for the mortgage, however, lies with the original buyer, so it is important for the seller to check the buyer carefully. At present, most lenders are requiring that they approve of new buyers and are escalating the interest rate and placing a due-on-sale provision in the deed of trust. If these changes are made, then the original buyer is relieved of the legal responsibility of the loan. If the owner's equity is high, it will usually be advisable to obtain a new loan commitment in order to avoid a high down payment.

Which Couple Made the Right Decision?

Let's look at the Allens. They will not have a monthly house payment, and they will not have to pay interest on $66,750. They reasoned that over the thirty-year period they will "save" $256,450 in interest. They felt smugly proud of their decision.

The Bakers, on the other hand, felt that they had made the right decision.

Which do you think made the right choice? Measure your value system against each of theirs to see where you feel you will be the most comfortable. This will help you to decide which course would be best for you.

But do remember what I said about inflation rewarding those who owe money, not those who pay cash. I realize that this is a sad commentary on life, but it is a fact you must learn to accept. You must learn to be a realist. Look at life the way it truly is, rather than the way you wish it were.

If the government is successful in slowing the rate of inflation to 4 percent (do you really think it will?), you would be paying off your "loaned" dollars in ten years with 60¢ dollars, in fifteen years with 40¢ dollars, and in twenty years with 20¢ dollars.

Think how long your dad had to work for a dollar thirty years ago, and then compare it with the minutes of work you have to do today. Any time you can postpone paying back a dollar that you have obtained on a long-term basis at a reasonable rate, always avail yourself of the opportunity. You must, of course, invest the money you have not paid down on the house in such a way as to earn more than the after-tax cost of renting it.

Making House Payments

The Allens do not have to concern themselves with paying monthly house payments; the Bakers do. The Bakers also have the responsibility of investing $66,750. How should the Bakers invest these funds to provide the extra $897.78 needed monthly for house payments?

There are various investment possibilities that they should consider. By the time you have completed this book you will know they have a wide choice of viable investment alternatives in mutual funds with a systematic withdrawal program, limited partnerships in oil and gas income programs, real estate programs in triple-net leases, multi-family housing, miniwarehouses, cinema, and some other possibilities.

Meeting an Emergency

The Allens paid cash for their home remembering their parents' warning about possible hard times. However, if the Allens have an emergency, they will not be able to redeem a few square feet of their house. If they live in a state with a homestead law, they can't even pledge it as collateral for a loan. The loan-free home may have given them joy at the time of purchase, but if they should have a real emergency, they may find that their home is a dead asset that does not offer liquidity.

The Bakers, on the other hand, could redeem a few shares of their stock or take their shares to the bank and use them for collateral to borrow any needed funds.

Availing Yourself of an Opportunity

In money management, always put yourself in the driver's seat. Leave options open to yourself. Using your stock as collateral at the bank does not necessarily require an emergency. A good business opportunity may present itself. You'll have to pass it up if you don't have available funds. With collateral you can obtain these funds.

Interest is Deductible

To give you an idea of how much of the Baker's monthly payment is interest, which is deductible, the percentage schedule for the first five years of their 16 percent loan was: 99.85 percent, 99.67 percent, 99.47 percent, 99.23 percent, and 98.96 percent. For the first year, .998 x 897.78 x 12 = $10,751.82 interest out of a yearly payment of $10,773.36.

The IRS lets the Bakers deduct interest payments, so if they are in a 40 percent tax bracket, Uncle Sam bears 40 percent of their interest cost.

Of the 16 percent interest they are paying, their net cost is 8.96 percent.

Salability

As we mentioned earlier, one of the reasons you should consider renting is the fact that Americans are a mobile lot. Recent studies show the average family moves every seven years. The letters IBM, in our neighborhood, stand for "I've Been Moved." If moving is necessary, you may find it easier to find a buyer with $22,500 for a down payment than one with $89,000. Of course, the house can be refinanced, but this might cause your buyer to bear points on a new mortgage, which could run several hundred dollars; or refinancing may not be available.

There are reasons other than transfers for moving. If the children have grown and left the nest, a large home may be a burden rather than a necessity. The desirability of the neighborhood may have changed, or your company offices may have moved to another section of town. The reasons for moving can make a lengthy list.

Rate of Gain on Invested Capital

It is estimated that homes have appreciated an average of 10 to 12 percent per year over the past ten years.

The Allens have $89,000 invested in their home. Twelve percent appreciation would increase their net worth by $10,600 per year, or $106,000 in ten years.

The Bakers' $89,000 home has also appreciated the same 12 percent, or to $195,000, but they have had only $22,500 invested. An increase of 471 percent on their invested capital, as compared to the Allens' 119 percent. (The figure for the Bakers must be adjusted for their interest deductions and taxes on their dividends and capital gains on their investments.)

Shopping for Terms

Money is a commodity. It is a commodity like peanuts, warehouses, and even houses. Never be emotional about money. If you do, you won't make rational decisions about it. Put it in its proper commodity status. Therefore, go in a businesslike manner to secure your mortgage.

If you have a contact at a lending institution, be sure to avail yourself of any help this person can give you; it does make a difference whom you know. Do not accept the first loan offered to you. Shop for rates and terms. Each institution's circumstances vary from time to time, so their lending conditions and rates will vary accordingly.

Rates are important; but, as I will discuss later, the down payment and length of payment period far outweigh a slight differential in rates.

What To Do When Mortgage Money Is Tight

In the latter part of 1981, several things happened to virtually dry up mortgage funds. The Federal Reserve Board tightened the money supply to such an extent that almost all mortgage money was dried up. This in turn forced up the rates for borrowing and the cost of money to the savings and loans that had been a large supplier of mortgage money. All this occurred at a time when a large number of our citizens became more savvy about money (thanks to financial planners such as myself writing books, speaking, and appearing on television and radio) and moved their money out of 5-1/2 percent passbook savings accounts, and lower interest-paying certificates, into money market mutual funds.

Another source of funds had been life insurance companies that sold policies with savings programs in them. But these funds began to decrease as more and more people became knowledgeable after reading my books and others and began cashing in their cash surrender value whole-life policies. Also, insurance companies that already had large pools of money found themselves in a very enviable position. Developers of office buildings were in such need of permanent financing that they found they could demand and obtain 50 percent or more equity in the buildings they were financing. This was more profitable than making home loans.

Residential real estate sales consequently slowed to a trickle. Real estate salesman being the creative souls that they are (with the extra nudge of survival) came up with many "creative financing" plans. Most of these plans greatly favor the buyer (it became a buyer's market) and are to the disadvantage of the seller. You may find it necessary to buy or sell during such periods of tight money or chaos in the money markets, so let me introduce you to a few of the terms you'll be coming across.

Graduated Payment Mortgages (GPM)

This type of loan will permit you to pay lower monthly payments in the early years of your mortgage with payments rising in later years to a level sufficient to amortize your entire loan over the term of the loan. With lower initial payments, you may be able to qualify for a home loan with a lower income base, or conversely, buy a more expensive house with the same income. In most instances, your lender will require some good evidence that your future income will increase along with the increasing payments that will be due.

This type of loan will require you to pay more interest over the life of the mortgage because in the early years with your lower payments, very little of your payments are being used to reduce your principal. In fact, in some instances, your early payments are so low that they do not cover the interest, so the accumulated and unpaid interest is added to your principal balance for payment in later years. In this arrangement your principal amount at the end of your first few years will be greater than when you first obtained the loan.

If you decide to use a GPM, run the numbers out for the entire term of the loan to ascertain both the payments you'll need to make and the actual increase of your principal. Only then can you make an intelligent decision.

If you are a young, fresh-out-of-college professional with a long-term increased earning potential, this type of loan may be a viable consideration.

Adjustable Rate Mortgage (ARM)

Adjustable rate mortgages (also called variable rate mortgages or VRMs) have interest rates that move in tandem with agreed upon economic indices. In general, you agree to make payments in one of two ways: monthly payments become larger/smaller, or payments remain equal but differing amounts are allocated to principal and interest, with the possible modification of the term of the loan.

There are some restrictions on the lender: the variation in interest rates must be based on an index over which the lender exerts no control, and the indicator must be readily identifiable by the borrower (such as the six-month Treasury bill rate).

Shop carefully if you're considering an ARM or VRM vehicle. Look particularly for: (1) the index used (don't accept the "cost of funds" index from the Federal Home Loan Bank Board, which has a tendency NOT to fall in tandem with other economic indices); (2) the initial payment amount; (3) how often the payment rate can be changed; and (4) a limit, if possible, on the extent of increase permitted.

Balloon or Short-Term Mortgages

These mortgages usually require monthly payments just as if you were going to amortize your loan over a thirty-year period but they balloon in three to five years and the balance becomes due in full at that time. The thing you don't know with this type of loan is what going interest rates will be when it balloons or if loans will even be available at all.

In some real estate circles these are now being called "bullet loans," meaning someone has a gun to your head on maturity. I heard a new name the other day—"neutron loans." They leave the building standing, but kill the owner.

Assumable Mortgages

In this type of mortgage, as the name implies, you would assume the payment schedule of the original mortgager, which in all probability would be at a lower rate than is available today. If you can find an assumable loan, this may be worthy of your consideration. However, it may require more cash than you have available or that you want to have tied up in equity. Funds unnecessarily tied up in down payments are really dead assets that could usually be working harder for you in a different position.

VA and FHA loans are assumable if the borrower is credit-worthy. Other lenders may put a due-on-sale clause in the mortgage terms calling for the full payment of the balance in the event of a transfer of title. Make sure the lender agrees to an assumption in writing.

Blend

Sometimes you may find that the lender will not allow you to assume the balance due at the original low interest rate, but will allow it at a higher rate that is still lower than the prevailing rate—hence the term "blend" to indicate the blending of the new and old interest rates.

In some instances the lender may even advance funds to make a larger mortgage, thereby reducing the amount of funds needed for a down payment.

Builder financing at lower than the going rates may also surface in times of tight money. Check these carefully, for the builder may be adding this lost interest into the purchase price of the home in order to make the financing package more attractive.

In any event, if you find yourself shopping for a mortgage at such times, do just that—shop, shop, shop. I know it adds another burden to the already heavy burden of making a buying decision on a home or an investment property, but it can greatly affect your standard of living or profit potential for many years to come.

If You Are Selling

If you are selling a home today, you may find your realtor encouraging you to furnish financing in the form of a second mortgage. While this creative financing helps their salespeople preserve their commissions in times of high interest and tight money, it may cause you some serious problems. This form of financing may be based on the selling price of your home, not on the soundness and profitability of the financing arrangement, and may be at low market rates. Interest rates may rise considerably above the rate on the mortgage you are carrying, making you very sorry to be missing these higher rates. If you need to use some of the money tied up in the mortgage, you may not be able to find a buyer, and even if you do, you may have to discount the mortgage by a substantial amount.

Balloon mortgages are also common. This means that in three to five years the total second mortgage becomes due. But when the payment is due, the financial market could be very tight and the courts could rule due-on clauses unenforceable.

Deregulation of financial institutions allows the money market to control the level of interest rates, so the cost of financing may become greater than the rate of inflation. You may have no other choice if you must sell, but if you can avoid seller financing, it is more prudent to do so.

Timing Your Purchase

No doubt, some years are better than others for buying a home. If you buy your home when money is more abundant, your interest costs will be lower, which will result in lower monthly payments for you. The quantity of money, which influences the cost, is regulated by action of the Federal Reserve Board, which in turn is based on consumer borrowing demands and whether the current objective is to try to slow inflation, or to increase employment. If the main thrust is to slow inflation, money will be tighter and interest rates higher. If the latter, credit will be more available and will cost less.

But what if you decide that you've reached that period in your family's life when you should buy a home, and it turns out that this is the time the Federal Reserve Board's money policies are restrictive and have driven money rates to a high level? Should you postpone your purchase?

The answer is probably no. Such Federal Reserve Board action is usually taken with the hope of slowing down inflation (a doubtful premise). This means that you are looking for a house during a period of rising building costs. If you wait until interest rates are lower, the price of the house will by then have inflated, and your monthly payments will just as great or greater. Since the part that is interest is tax deductible and the part that is principal is not, you may be better off with the combination of lower price and slightly higher interest. So if you feel you must buy a home, go ahead regardless of present interest rates.

The Hybrid Homeowner

If you want the advantages of owning your home and the advantages of an apartment, perhaps you should consider owning your own apartment.

This can be done either in a cooperative apartment or townhouse, or a condominium. What's the difference?

In a co-op you buy "shares" in the building and facilities, including recreational facilities. When shares are sold in co-ops, it must be by vote of the majority of the shareholders. You become both landlord and tenant, which means that you take your share of both economic and managerial responsibilities.

Co-op ownership does give the tax advantages of home ownership together with recreational facilities and maintenance at a lower cost than an individual family dwelling.

In a condominium, you own your own apartment and a pro rata share of the facilities rather than stock in the building. This means that you have the same responsibility for common areas, but you may sell your apartment to whomever you wish within the rules you accepted when you made your purchase. The tax and facilities cost advantages are identical to those in the co-op.

The methods of financing for both are similar to financing a one-family home.

What are some of the problems with these forms of home ownership? First, in co-op apartments, owners have occasionally had problems with the co-owner vetoing the sale of their shares, which means, effectively, they could not sell their home. More important, poor maintenance of an apartment complex seriously lowers the value and salability of your apartment, so it is imperative to buy in a well-located, well-maintained building, just as you should buy a home in a well-located and well-maintained neighborhood.

You may need to have an income above $20,000 to approach any meaningful break on your tax return through home ownership.

There are many legitimate reasons for buying a home. You may feel that it is a better place to raise your children. It may give you a sense of security, of belonging, or of status. A lovely home can be a true joy and a prestige symbol that adds to your self-confidence.

However, don't plunge into home ownership only because others are doing it—a kind of follow-the-follower pattern of thinking —without truly weighing the pros and cons. Even though there are a number of valid reasons for home ownership, I find that most of them are sociologic and very few are based on genuine economic facts. Houses should not be bought as investments per se but as places in which to live. Today 66 percent of U.S. families live in houses that they own. This still leaves a substantial minority who rent.

If you truly believe that owning your own home will bring you greater enjoyment of life, will make you a more respectable citizen, and will offer you that additional privacy that may be important to you, then consider buying a home. But if your reasons are to boast about all the money you are saving, be careful not to boast to an economist.

Should You Prepay Your Mortgage?

If the mortgage on your home carries a rate lower than the going rate, you may receive an offer from your mortgage company to give you a substantial discount for early prepayment of your balance. Should you consider such an offer? If you are looking at your decision from a business point of view, and I'm hoping you do treat your money in that way, your answer in most instances will be no. The companies don't give money away. They know it will be more profitable to them to get rid of your low-interest mortgage. This is the same reason you should keep it. You can usually obtain a better return on your money invested in another way. You also give up your liquidity. If you have an emergency, you can redeem a few shares of your stock, cash in your money market mutual fund, or other investments, but you cannot redeem a few square feet of your home. As we have seen, in states like Texas, which have a homestead law, equity in a home is a dead asset. There are also tax reasons. Mortgage discounts are considered capital gains, taxable at a maximum rate of 20 percent.

The only time to accept such an offer is if you must sell your home soon and live in a state where due-on-sale clauses are enforced and you would have to pay it off anyway. If you intend to keep living in your home, do keep your valuable mortgage.

Mortgage Refinancing

Before we summarize some of the highlights regarding home ownership, let's discuss whether you should ever refinance your home. The answer may very well be yes, when mortgage funds are available at the right rate.

Your home could be an excellent source of capital. With your equity increasing each year because of inflation and brisk demand, you may be living in a giant savings account. If you want money to pay for college costs or medical bills or to invest, one way would be to refinance your mortgage. This approach not only frees capital, but it gives you the advantage of paying off your new mortgage with a new level of inflated dollars.

Your home doesn't know whether it has a mortgage on it or not. It will inflate just as much with a small equity or a large, and if you use the funds obtained from refinancing (homestead law prevents this in Texas), you could have two assets escalating with inflation, rather than just one. Always look at the reverse possibility, too.

Summary

1. It can be less or more expensive to rent a multifamily dwelling than to own a single-family dwelling. Rental frees down-payment money for other investments and also allows you mobility to move to larger or smaller quarters or another location quickly and easily.

2. Calculate your true housing costs unemotionally, remembering that the mortgage payment is only one of several major items in your housing costs.

3. Monthly house payments should not exceed one week's earnings.

4. If you anticipate moving, buy a home similar in style to that of your neighbors. This does not do much for your sense of creativity, but

it may help you avoid taking a shellacking on resale. A good rule to remember when making an investment in any asset of considerable value is "Be a conformist." The more conventional you are, the better your chances are of increasing the value of your assets. Preserve some of your individuality, but don't go overboard. You may find it quite expensive if you do.

5. Avoid paying too much for gimmicks. The builder may have spent an extra $1,000 on gadgets for flashy first-impression eye appeal and be able to sell you the house for an extra $3,000. As the years go by, you will want to build in your own charm, and the "gook" the builder originally added may turn out to be a hindrance rather than an enchantment.

6. Avoid paying too much for a view. Surroundings are important, but after a year you'll probably take the view for granted and wish that this extra expenditure had been avoided.

7. Keep your down payment as low as possible; inflation lets you repay with cheaper dollars; resale should be easier; return on invested capital can be higher; and liquidity or pledgability can be available in times of emergency or investment opportunity.

Your home can be your castle or, under unfortunate circumstances, your prison, so use both your heart and your head in choosing how you'll provide that roof over your head.

Application

1. Should you rent or buy?
2. How long do you plan to live there?
3. If you decide to buy, should it be a house, a cluster home, a condominium, or a townhouse?
4. How much is available for a down payment?
5. Emotionally do you identify with the Allens or the Bakers in this chapter?
6. On the basis of our formula, what price home can you afford?
7. What kind of neighborhood best fits your way of life?
8. Is availability of a clubhouse with social facilities, tennis courts, and swimming pools important to you?
9. Whom do you know, or what contacts can you make, to obtain favorable financing?
10. Is the prime interest rate rising or dropping at this time?

11. If you have chosen to make a low down payment, how will you employ the remaining funds?

12. Items to include in your housing checklist:

   a. First and foremost, remember location, location, location. How is the location?

   b. Accessibility to work?

   c. Accessibility to schools?

   d. Accessibility to shopping facilities?

   e. Accessibility to recreational facilities?

   f. Rate of price increase of homes in the neighborhood? Percent per year.

   g. Neighbors?

   h. Traffic patterns?

   i. Noise?

   j. Smells?

   k. How does the cost of the home that you are considering compare with recent sales in the neighborhood?

   l. Conditions of the maintenance fund for upkeep of the neighborhood?

   m. Determine whether or not it is located within the bounds of the 100-year flood plain as determined by the National Flood Insurance Program. (If it is, to obtain a loan you must buy flood insurance for the term of the loan.)

   n. Towns grow and values tend to increase west, north, uphill, and away from rivers. Where is the house in relation to these?

   o. How old is the home?

   p. If the home is ten years old, are you a good handyman on repairs?

   q. Does the home fit your style? Yard work? Entertaining?

13. Cornell University, Cooperative Extension Programs, Martha Van Rensselaer Hall, Ithaca, New York 14853, now offers an analysis of housing costs and benefits that you may find helpful in deciding whether to rent or buy. The fee is $7.00.

Chapter 8

Power-Packing Your Money With Energy

We've concluded that a major requirement for successful investing is to place some of your funds where demand is greater than supply. One commodity that is already in great demand, and most certainly will increase, is energy. The developed nations of the world continue to increase their demands while the emerging Third World nations are rapidly joining the throng.

You will discover as you begin to study energy-related investments that energy is a broad category and not all areas will be viable considerations, especially if your investment funds are limited.

The Energy Crisis—Its Cause

In 1974, the average man on the street came face to face with the fact that energy is not a magical manna that drops from heaven and runs into his electric light switch and into the tank of his automobile. With the Arab oil embargo, he discovered that he could no longer drive into the corner gas station, say, "Fill 'er up." receive a sheet of green trading stamps (double on Tuesdays) plus a drinking glass with the insignia of his local football team, and be merrily on his way in a few minutes.

The "energy crisis" did not just suddenly arrive on the scene, although you may have gotten that impression from the news media. In 1967, interviewed Michel T. Halbouty, a highly respected independent oil producer, on my CBS affiliate television program, "Successful Texans." He warned then, as he had been doing since 1960, of the energy crisis that would occur if steps were not taken to allow a reasonable return on capital invested in the oil industry. At that time, he was making warning speeches across the nation, and he has continued to do so. When I interviewed J. Hugh Liedtke, chairman of the board of Pennzoil, he also warned of the problems that were imminent if proper action was not taken. He quoted extensively from comprehensive government studies on the subject and brought charts to illustrate graphically the seriousness of what would surely happen.

I interviewed George Mitchell, chairman of the board and president of Mitchell Energy and Development. He gave the same warning and continues to do so. (I again interviewed Mr. Mitchell before my trip to the White House on October 4, 1978, where I, along with other community leaders, was briefed by President Carter and his staff regarding the need for the passage by Congress of the Natural Gas Policy Act.)

These knowledgeable oilmen and others with expertise in the industry pointed out over and over again that the flow of new oil could not possibly meet the new and increasing demands.

The need to encourage production seemed obvious to those who were in production, but the opposite view was taken by those who controlled the legislation to fill the need.

The Federal Power Commission continued to hold down the price of natural gas to 10–16¢ per cubic foot, to which they had arbitrarily rolled it back despite the continuous pleas of the oilmen. The commission took the pose of the three little monkeys, put their hands over their eyes, and said, "Hear no evil, see no evil, speak no evil, and all these bad, bad predictions will fade away." Of course, the big bad wolf, called energy shortage, did not fade away.

The attitudes of the eastern congressmen also aggravated the situation as they took the attitude, "How dare you talk of raising the price of the natural gas used to bake the bread for the dear families residing in my state?" And then they added, "and don't you muss our scenic coastlines with refineries either; keep them down in Texas and Louisiana where they belong."

They also insisted that the federal government allow massive amounts of foreign oil to be imported into the United States at prices so low that domestic producers could not compete.

At this time, risk capital to be used to drill oil wells was also in short supply.

In the 1950s, the corporate tax rate was 60–70 percent, and the individual rate could go as high as 90 percent. At these confiscatory levels, there was a tremendous incentive to search for ways of turning tax liabilities into potential capital assets. Oil drilling programs fit this possibility because of the 100 percent write-off potential of intangible drilling costs. Large amounts of risk capital, therefore, were made available.

But in the 1960s, the maximum corporate tax was reduced to around the 48 percent level and the individual's tax to the 50–70 percent level. This greatly reduced the tax incentive. All of these factors combined to reduce the profitability of searching for oil and gas reserves.

The number of independent oil operators dwindled from 35,000 to 5,000, and the number of rig operators from 3,500 to around 900.

As the supply of oil and gas decreased, the demand increased. A collision course was already in the making when the Arab bloc discovered our great vulnerability and decided that their best bargaining tool against Israel was U.S. dependence on their oil.

Will the government take a more intelligent approach throughout the 1980s? To date, the government's batting average has improved, but it still has a long way to go. Instead of taking steps to lessen our dependence on foreign oil, it has concentrated on making the oil companies the scapegoat and blaming them for all of our problems. The explanations of the energy crisis I've heard gushing forth from government officials, newspaper reporters, and TV commentators have been tantamount to blaming the gynecologist for the baby.

Our profit-minded and efficiently run oil companies did not produce the gasoline shortage. Our wasteful consumers did not produce the gasoline shortage. Severely cold winters in the North did not produce the shortage. Not even the OPEC countries produced the gasoline shortage.

The oil industry has been around for a long time and its member companies have always had the obligation to make a profit for their stockholders. Our consumers have not suddenly become more wasteful. The North has had hard winters before. Sheiks have always desired wealth. Why, then, for a century or more before 1971 were there no energy crises, no gasoline shortages, no problems about fuel oil?

We have an energy shortage for only one reason. The government decreed that there would be one. Of course, this was not done openly. The administration didn't send a message to Congress asking it to legislate long gasoline lines. But when President Nixon, on August 15, 1971, imposed wage and price controls, maximum prices on crude oil, gasoline, and other petroleum products were instituted. However, when these controls were later lifted on other commodities, but remained in force on crude oil and its by-products, the journey to shortages was greatly accelerated.

As an economist, there is one thing I have learned very well, and that is how shortages and surpluses are created. If a surplus is desired, all that is necessary is to have the government legislate a minimum price that is *above* the price that would otherwise prevail. That is what has been done to produce surpluses of wheat, sugar, butter, and many other commodities. Perhaps most tragic of all is the creation of a surplus of teenage labor. The minimum wage is a legislated price above the price that would otherwise prevail for the labor of teenagers. Like every minimum price, it enhances the amount supplied and reduces the amount that is demanded, thereby producing a surplus.

If you want a shortage, do the opposite. Have the government legislate a maximum price that is *below* the price that would otherwise prevail. Consider, for example, New York City and other cities that have unwisely legislated rent controls, causing a shortage of rental dwellings. The energy crisis and the gasoline shortage have come to us in the same way. The reduction of controls could provide the incentive to produce the energy needed domestically and stop the unnecessary transfer of our nation's wealth to the sheiks of the Middle East.

The dismantling of the Department of Energy with its $12 billion annual budget could lower the price of gasoline at the pump to around 9 cents per gallon. The DOE has employed more than 20,000 people, and its budget has exceeded the total profits of the ten largest oil companies and more than doubled the profits of the next twenty largest. Its budget has been about the same as the total dollars spent annually by all participants exploring for oil and gas in the United States. This has included all major oil companies, independents, and individuals. It has cost you and me over $3.60 for every barrel of oil produced in the United States just to have the DOE. As a comparison, the average selling price of domestic crude oil was only $3.92 in 1972. This does not include all the costs to comply with all the regulations, allocation requirements, pricing systems, and other overhead generated by the DOE.

The government is the chief beneficiary in the rise of oil prices. It is estimated that for each dollar increase in crude oil prices, the "windfall profit" tax generates one billion dollars in taxes for the United States.

The government's attention has been so preoccupied by "windfall profits" that few, if any, steps have been taken to increase production in order to reduce our dependence on imports from the OPEC countries.

As a matter of fact, the tax bill amounts to protectionism for the Persian Gulf. It's frightening to think that the value of all our Big Board (NYSE) companies is around $900 billion—a value that has taken 200 years to create—and that over the next four years we may be paying half of that to OPEC. This is not a sustainable position. We can't continue a policy whereby much of our real estate, many of our companies, and a large amount of our equities will be bought in exchange for oil.

Over the next few years, more than a trillion dollars will go out of the Western world to pay for oil. I don't believe our national and international monetary system should sustain such a drain.

Turning Lemons Into Lemonade

There is no question that the government's ostrich-like policies created the energy crisis of 1973-1974 and that they have perpetuated its continuation. But intead of wasting our energies condemning government actions, let's examine ways that you may benefit from the existing situation. Let's consider it an "Energy Opportunity" rather than an "Energy Crisis."

How can you best avail yourself of these opportunities? There are three areas that you should consider: investing in energy-related securities, investing in oil and gas producing wells, and investing in oil and gas development and exploration.

Energy Stocks

I believe that we may be at the beginning of a new Sputnik-like era. Our reaction to the Sputnik shock in 1957 caused a big boom in technical equipment. Fortunes were made in semiconductors. A similar opportunity may now exist with regard to energy-related securities. Our petroleum engineers lead the world in hydrocarbon expertise. I have high hopes that those billion-dollar brains at NASA in Houston will soon be turned to alternative energy research. A nation that can put a man on the moon can surely solve its energy problems, especially in view of the fact that we are blessed with an abundance of two additional great energy sources, coal and uranium. With the proper investment incentives, other natural resources such as hydrogen, thermal energy, solar energy, and wind-generating power offer great potential. Unfortunately, the government has floundered to date and, instead of providing sufficient incentives for private investment, it has enacted punitive laws that discourage research and development by industry—especially in oil, gas, coal, and uranium, which are necessary to supply our energy needs until other sources prove significant.

Nuclear power makes the cheapest and best use of our natural resources and, despite some of the emotional outcries against it, our top scientists maintain that with proper safety precautions, it can be a blessing to an energy-demanding world.

Much emphasis has been placed on solar energy and what a boon harnessing it will be to the world. The data I've gathered from energy engineers indicate that this is just a popular pastime for politicians, and that in the near future solar power will have very little impact on the solution of our energy shortage.

The United States has enough uranium to produce significant supplies of nuclear energy. A large number of the oil companies have entered the field. You would think this would delight the government, but, instead, legislation has been proposed to prevent the oil companies from doing so. Uranium may some day overshadow oil as a source of energy.

Another energy source is the gasification of coal, which, if done on a large enough basis, should be no more expensive than importing oil. Likewise, the western United States has vast quantities of oil in the form of shale rock. Concentrated technology should be able to devise economical means of extracting this oil on a basis that would be competitive with the world market of crude oil. If this industry was allowed to develop without governmental intervention, there are strong indications that our gap between domestic oil production and consumption could be narrowed significantly. Additionally, we still have untapped sources of hydroelectricity and geothermal energy.

The industries that will benefit from the new push to be self-sufficient in energy will offer a vast range of investment opportunities. Study each carefully, and pick the leader in the industries you choose.

To take advantage of this rare investment opportunity, you should use the same basic criteria that I outlined earlier for the selection of your stocks. Some of the older, more heavily capitalized companies should fit the income category, if this is your financial objective. The smaller, more aggressive companies may be involved in more venturesome drilling programs or research and development activities that place them in the growth or speculative categories.

Many companies will broaden their base and engage in exploration, production, refining, and distribution. They may even go into the manufacture of products that use petrocarbons as their base.

You should consider not only these companies, but also those that build offshore drilling rigs and those that build refineries. Oil without refineries is of no use.

Management skills, company assets, and consumer demand are vital areas for study, whether you are selecting an oil company or a company in a related field.

Energy Production

We have been examining investing in oil and gas and other energy through the stock market. This is a legitimate consideration for your investment dollars. But let's look at other ways. My favorite way of participating in energy through investing serious after-tax dollars, and one what that I think is worthy of your consideration, is through registered oil and gas income limited partnerships.

To help you decide whether to invest in companies that produce oil and gas or whether to invest directly in production by investing in limited partnerships that buy only producing wells (no drilling), let's take a look at Exxon's figures the year I held my first Energy Seminar.

EXXON 1972 Figures Per Share

22.39	Earnings before depreciation and taxes
4.72	Depletion and depreciation
17.67	Pretax earnings
10.83	Corporate taxes (including minority interest expenses and excise taxes)
6.84	After-tax earnings
3.80	Dividend (taxable to the shareholder, thus double taxation)
3.04	Retained earnings (corporation decides how they will be used)

As you can see, if you had owned a share of Exxon in 1972, only $6.84 of cash flow was left after taxes to allow them to perpetuate the business. Of this amount, $3.80 was paid out to you as a dividend. You probably paid federal income taxes on these dividends, and therefore suffered double taxation. The company retained $3.04. The company did not ask you whether you would like to have these funds reinvested. This was decided for you by the board of directors. You did hope, however, that these funds would be used to find more oil and gas, which should increase the profitability of the company and eventually be reflected in the price of the stock.

Exxon is a corporation; therefore, as an investor, your liability is limited to the amount of your investment. If you have invested $10,000, that is all you can lose, even if the company's stock was to become nonexistent. This stock is also readily salable, since it is listed on the New York Stock Exchange. Its value may fluctuate, but it is a liquid investment.

Is there a way that you can obtain the same limited liability while avoiding some of the double taxation, get the benefits of the depreciation and depletion allowance, and for the minimal sacrifice of accepting some limited liquidity avoid the worry of market fluctuation? Yes, there is, through the investment medium of oil and gas income limited partnerships.

Oil and Gas Income Limited Partnerships

In making any investment decision, you should attempt to find a vehicle that will supply a product that everyone wants, that everyone needs, and that is in short supply. There is no such thing as an ideal investment, but oil and gas income limited partnerships fit a number of the criteria that you will want in your investment program.

Oil and gas drilling programs have been offered to high tax-bracket investors for many years, but it has only been since 1970 that you have had the opportunity to invest in production without the risks of drilling. This is accomplished through a product designed for both the smaller, lower tax-bracket investor as well as the higher tax-bracket investor.

The concept of owning oil and natural gas reserves is more than 100 years old, but before the advent of oil and gas income limited partnerships, ownership in production was limited almost entirely to oil companies, wealthy individuals, and institutional investors.

These oil income partnerships are based on a simple concept. A series of limited partnerships acquire existing, producing oil and gas properties for the income that they generate. The production from these wells is sold, and the income flows back to the limited partners and to the managing general partner. They offer good income potential, which is substantially tax-sheltered in the early years, and a continuing partial shelter in later years, as well as opportunity for appreciation to stay abreast of inflation; some provide first-year deductions that may be used to reduce your other taxable income.

As in real estate limited partnerships, you, the limited partner, have limited your liability to the amount of your investment. The general partner who possesses the management expertise has unlimited liability. He secures the proper producing properties and has the responsibility of operating them on a profitable basis. For doing so, the general partner usually shares from 10 to 15 percent of the costs and the revenues.

Despite the oil business's reputation for riskiness, in my opinion a well-managed oil income program has less risk than most stock investments. This is true because oil income programs are not particularly subject to short-term market fluctuations. The value of the programs depends upon the value of their reserves and the level of income that they produce. The value of the reserves usually stays abreast of inflation. The true income fund partnership does no drilling. If an opportunity exists for in-field drilling, such drilling is contracted for by the general partner on a farmout basis. This means that none of the limited partners' money is subjected to any drilling risk.

The structure of this type of partnership is similar to the diversified concept of a mutual fund, and the oil income programs acquire a variety of already producing oil and natural gas wells for the income or profit they can generate as the natural resource is produced over the economic life of the properties. The properties acquired by the general partner for these programs have generally experienced several years of production. This is desirable because after sufficient time has passed, oil reservoirs have enough production history and reservoir data to allow reasonably accurate estimates of the reserves. Such producing properties can be evaluated within an acceptable margin for error, usually in the 10 percent range. It is at that stage that oil income programs become buyers of producing properties.

If you become an investor in oil and gas income limited partnerships, the major portion of the revenues will flow directly to you. You will receive the depletion and depreciation allowance that shelters part, and sometimes all, of your cash flow. You'll pay taxes only once on the remainder that is not sheltered. To date, we've had almost all of the cash flow sheltered.

Cash Flow Investment Options

Some programs offer three options for the disposition of your quarterly distributions.

The first option is to reinvest all of your quarterly distributions into subsequent partnerships. This gives you the opportunity to increase your capital base if your objective is asset growth rather than current income. (Approximately 75 percent of our clients make this choice.) If your financial objective changes, you are always free to choose one of the other two options.

A second option is to receive a portion of your distributions quarterly or monthly in cash and to reinvest the balance into future partnerships. This method is designed to provide you with a way to use a portion of your income currently while maintaining your capital base. We have found that if you limit your cash withdrawal to no more than 10 to 12 percent, you should be able to maintain your capital and also experience considerable growth on your original investment.

But you might say to your financial planner, "I think my ball of twine is about to unwind, so just send me the total cash distribution." If you choose this third option, you will receive all your distributions in cash quarterly. Each distribution will contain a portion of original capital as well as income earned on the capital.

Past Performance

How would you have fared if you had made an investment of $10,000 in the October 1970 partnership of a typical management company and were appraising your results on December 31, 1981 (see Table 8-1)? (I always use $10,000 in my examples because the math is easier, but you may invest as little as $2,500 on an individual or corporate purchase and as little as $2,000 in an IRA account, and in some of them add as little as $50.)

Investors generally experience a gradual increase in distributions over the first two or three years of a partnership's life. This is due primarily to the amount of time required to invest the partnership's funds in producing properties plus the need to dedicate a part of the cash flow to repay loans made by the partnership to acquire their properties if you are investing in one of the leveraged programs. Since each partnership is a depleting entity, once it has reached its maximum distribution level, you see a gradual decline in your distributable cash flow over its remaining economic life. As Table 8-1 illustrates, to date not only have the reserves not declined in value, but they have increased as has your cash flow (Table 8-2). This has been due to increases in the price of

Table 8-1. Hypothetical Investment of $10,000
in an Oil and Gas Income Program
(As of December 31, 1981)

Option I—All distributions reinvested:	
Distributions reinvested	$ 92,647
Purchase price	182,097
Option II—Accepting 12% withdrawal:	
Distributions in cash	$ 13,200
Distributions reinvested	60,812
Total distributions	74,012
Purchase price	137,931
Option III—All distributions in cash:	
Distributions in cash	$50,931
Purchase price	58,083

oil and gas sold, improved recovery techniques, and expert management of the partnerships.

What Should You Expect Today?

Should you expect to do this well if you were to invest in an oil and gas income limited partnership today? I really don't know. I do know that the 1970 timing was exceptionally good. There is no question that they have reaped the advantage of greatly accelerated oil prices, for which they cannot claim credit. I truly hope that oil prices won't accelerate as rapidly in the future; however, it appears to me that there will still be significant price increases.

I personally invested $25,000 in their April 1977 partnerships and have reinvested my distributions. My repurchase price by the end of 1981 was in excess of $70,000 and my annualized cash flow exceeded 22 percent on my original investment. Some of the other programs in which we invested our clients' funds have done even better. I also made a fairly substantial investment in our pension fund in 1977 and again in 1979 and have been very pleased with the performance. You may wonder why I placed an investment that produces tax-sheltered cash flow in a pension plan that is already tax-sheltered. The reason is performance, which is the goal of any trustee of a pension or profit-sharing plan. I also believe it to be a "prudent" investment—whatever that means in our present world economy.

Leveraged and Nonleveraged Programs

Oil income programs can be of two types: leveraged and nonleveraged. *Leveraged* oil income programs use bank production loans to

Year	Quarter	Amount	Year	Quarter	Amount
1971	first	$ 585	1977	first	$1,621
	second	587		second	1,621
	third	302		third	1,621
	fourth	447		fourth	1,621
1972	first	$ 414	1978	first	$1,621
	second	425		second	1,621
	third	425		third	1,621
	fourth	350		fourth	1,621
1973	first	$ 350	1979	first	$1,621
	second	300		second	1,621
	third	350		third	1,621
	fourth	400		fourth	1,621
1974	first	$ 800	1980	first	$1,621
	second	1000		second	2,161
	third	925		third	2,161
	fourth	900		fourth	2,161
1975	first	$ 900	1981	first	$2,161
	second	875		second	2,161
	third	875		third	2,161
	fourth	825		fourth	2,161
1976	first	$ 750			
	second	650			
	third	650			
	fourth	650			

*Inception to date $50,935

finance a portion of the purchase price. In the first example above, leverage was used; it works something like this. For every $1 that you invest, about 80¢ remains after start-up costs for doing the research on production and general expenses. (It's actually running at about 84¢. Many of the start-up costs are fixed dollar items. So if the general partner can generate sizable subscriptions, the start-up costs, as a percentage of the investor's dollar, are reduced.) This 80¢ may be supplemented by borrowing up to 80¢, to provide total purchasing power of about $1.60 for each gross dollar invested. The bank loans allow the general partner to purchase larger reserves from which to obtain cash flow. The loans are usually paid back to the banks over a period of years, dedicating less than 50 percent of the cash flow from the properties for debt service. For a well-managed program, this should still allow ample cash flow to insure good distributions to the limited partners. You also have the potential for an increase in cash flow after the bank borrowings are repaid. This type of financing can produce favorable results. We all know that our country runs on energy. We also should be aware that the energy business runs on money. Several companies have done a superb job of combining the two.

Nonleveraged programs usually provide a higher cash flow at the beginning than do leveraged programs and they do not have the potential of repayment problems to the bank. If your objective is maximum cash flow now, you should probably choose the nonleveraged program. If your objective is cash flow later, you may want to consider the leveraged programs, where profits could have more of an opportunity to grow and are less sensitive to high interest rates knowing that they will have interest payments to make. Leverages can make a good program even better, but have the opposite effect on a poor one.

Restored Liquidity

Restored liquidity is a difficult concept to understand. This means the amount of your original investment that has been "restored" to you— in other words, how long did it take you to get your money back? For example, if you had invested $10,000 in the first program discussed above, your restored liquidity would be as shown in Table 8-3.

Table 8-3. $10,000 Investment

Year	Annual Cash Flow	Cumulative Cash Flow	Restored Liquidity
2	1921	1921	19.21%
3	1614	3535	35.35
4	1400	4935	49.35
5	3625	8560	85.6
6	3475	10,335	103.3
7	2700	14,735	147.3
8	6484	21,219	212.2
9	6484	27,703	277.0
10	6484	34,187	341.8
11	8104	42,291	422.9
12	8644	50,935	509.4

Perhaps you did not need current income, chose not to reinvest in the next program, and could not think of anything more constructive to do with your checks than to put your quarterly distributions into a passbook savings account at your bank. If you did, by the first quarter of your fourth year you would have put all of your funds back into your savings account, where it would be drawing interest; in addition, you would be receiving cash flow from your oil and gas program.

To Table 8-3 we can now add two additional columns. Column I would show earnings on your cash flow from your program plus 5-1/4 percent interest in your savings account all compounded annually, and Column II would show restored liquidity from the program plus interest from your savings account (although I've used 5-1/4 percent passbook savings, I can't think of anything more obsolete today than a passbook savings account):

	Column I	Column II
1971	0	19.2
1972	100	36.3
1973	190	52.2
1974	274	91.2
1975	478	130.7
1976	686	164.6
1977	864	238.0
1978	1,249	315.3
1979	1,655	396.7
1980	2,082	498.5
1981	2,617	611.1

It's interesting to note that your cash in your savings account would now be $61,130 and your repurchase price for your oil program would be $58,083, for a total of $119,213. You now have the potential for two incomes from the original $10,000. Had you chosen to reinvest in future oil and gas programs instead of withdrawing the cash, your repurchase price would be $182,097, or an additional $62,884. It rarely pays to take a working dollar and make it become a loaned dollar that works for a savings institution.

Compare this restored liquidity with an investment of $10,000 in a corporate bond paying 10 percent. It would have taken you ten years to receive interest checks totaling $10,000 (to say nothing about the loss of purchasing power that has occurred to your principal owing to two-digit inflation). Always keep indelibly pressed on your mind the time use of money. Money received today is always more valuable than the same amount received in the future.

Buying Reserves

How does the general partner determine how much to pay for oil and gas properties? Since oil and natural gas are found in sand and rock formations, the energy cannot be extracted from beneath the earth's surface in a matter of days, months, or, for that matter, sometimes many years. Because of this natural delay, the expected revenue to be returned over time is discounted to present worth when petroleum engineers are determining the price that should be paid for an acquisition.

The first thing the engineers determine is the amount of oil or gas a reservoir will produce annually and the estimated cost of producing that reservoir. They must then determine what price they expect to receive per barrel or per Mcf, which allows them to calculate the gross revenues to be realized over the property's economic life. By subtracting the operation costs from the gross revenues, the operating profits may be determined for each year of the well's economic production.

You wouldn't invest a dollar today for a dollar to be paid back to you at some time many years later. Neither would a petroleum engineer. Consequently, after the general partner has determined his objective rate of return for the partnership, he must discount each year's revenue by that factor to a present worth figure. The total value of each year of revenue's net worth becomes the price that may be paid to achieve the target result. This is the "time-use of money" concept that we've already discussed.

Discounting is nothing more than compounding in reverse. When you learned the "Rule of 72" earlier, you learned that money that is invested and compounded at 12 percent per year will double every six years. Conversely, if we wish to see our money compound at 12 percent per year, we would pay only half today what we would expect to realize in six years. With this in mind, we would be willing to pay only 50¢ for a dollar of net revenue to be realized in six years. If a dollar of revenue would not be realized for twelve years, we would be willing to pay only 25¢ today for that future dollar of revenue. If the dollar of revenue is not to be realized for eighteen years, we would pay only 12-1/2¢ today for that future dollar of revenue. With this formula, we would be willing to pay only 87-1/2¢ for $3 of future revenue that would be realized, $1 in each of the sixth, twelfth, and eighteenth years (see Table 8-4).

For Your Added Protection

For your added protection, the discounting does not stop here; the general partner, who is acquiring the production on your behalf, then begins what is called "haircutting," which is applying a discount for an

Table 8-4. Purchase Price per $1

Years Before Recovery	Amount Would Pay	Reserves
1		
2		
3		
4		
5		
6	$.50	$1.00
7		
8		
9		
10		
11		
12	.25	1.00
13		
14		
15		
16		
17		
18	.12½	1.00
	.87½ for	$3.00

unspecified risk factor. The general partners do this because they know that engineering of reserves is more of a scientific art than an exact science, so they want to build in protection by haircutting what they will pay for reserves. This discounting of future net reserves and haircutting the resulting figures provides a substantial degree of protection to an investor acquiring producing oil and gas properties.

The actual risks hinge on two elements: (1) Is the engineering accurate? (2) Will the energy be sold for the prices anticipated? However, the error in either of these areas would probably have to be extremely large for an investor not to realize a return of his capital over the partnership's life. Therefore, if you are considering this as a viable investment, the real risk is not so much whether you will get your money back, but rather whether the profitability will be as large as anticipated.

Companies offering oil and gas income programs attempt to minimize errors in engineering by using various experts to estimate reserves. If multiple evaluations arrive at comparable results, then the risk of surprises should be minimized.

First, they look at the history of the wells they are considering for purchase for the program. If this looks promising, their in-house engineering staff does an in-depth study. If that looks good, they submit it to one or more independent engineering firms for study and calculation of reserves. Once they, too, think that the properties are attractive, the general partner submits the properties for study to the oil and gas department of the bank that will be doing the matching financing, if leverage is to be used. If all of these agree, then an offer is made at a price that they think will allow them to fulfill their financial objective for their investors.

All of these studies do not guarantee that errors of judgment will not be made, but I do know from discussing this matter with independent oil consultants that they make very conservative estimates for banks and then discount these estimates sometimes as much as 30 percent.

The general partner spreads each partnership's investments into a number of different acquisitions with as many as 150 to 1,000 wells to maximize diversification.

In analyzing the risks you may be taking in any investment, always look at potential supply and demand. From all the projections I have so diligently studied, I am convinced that long-term demand should exceed supply, although there may be temporary periods of oversupply, which in turn should be translated into buying opportunities for ultimately realizing higher oil and gas prices.

Depreciation and Depletion

Depreciation in an oil and gas program is similar to that obtained in a real estate investment. The depreciation schedule for each piece of equipment depends on the depreciation schedule allowed by the IRS.

Depletion allowances are unique to natural resources and have been allowed because the resource is being depleted; therefore, a portion is considered to be a return of capital.

As you are probably aware, percentage (statutory) depletion has been under attack by Congress constantly for several years. With the Tax Reduction Act of 1978, percentage depletion is no longer allowed for those buying already producing oil and gas properties. However, investors are allowed cost depletion.

If Congress continues to chip away further at percentage depletion allowance, then you should anticipate paying even more for gas at the pumps.

Since the oil and gas income funds now use cost depletion instead of statutory or percentage depletion, their tax-shelter benefits should not be greatly affected, particularly in the earlier years.

Tax-Sheltered Cash Flow

What should you anticipate in the way of cash flow if you should invest in an oil and gas program? The figures we presented when we first started recommending these programs are as follows. (We still use the same figures even though results have been far superior to our projections.)

	Cash Flow Investor	Write-offs
1st year	7–9%	Sufficient to shelter cash flow
2nd year on	10–12%	Sufficient to shelter cash flow 2nd year

If your cash flow is greater than 12 percent and you take all your distributions in cash, a portion of your cash flow probably represents a return of your own capital, and you may be gradually liquidating your holdings in oil and gas.

The goal of any investment program is to obtain cash flow, tax-sheltered with appreciation potential. To date, tax-sheltered cash flow has been a delight to many owners of previous income programs. They must realize, though, that the IRS never truly forgives a tax. The limited partners are reducing their tax basis and will have a capital gains tax on selling if the sales price is above the cost basis that is left. My philosophy is to take the tax-sheltered cash flow now. In the meantime, you'll have the time-use of your money, and we will surely be able to think of a way to avoid paying the tax later, or at least reduce it when and if that time should come.

Investment Units

Most states require a minimim investment of $2,500 ($2,000 for IRA accounts). New partnerships are available for investment monthly, quarterly, or yearly, depending on the programs selected. Some states require that the minimum be invested in each new partnership one wishes to invest in, while other states let you add as little as $50 into new partnerships as you go along, once you've met the original minimum in at least one offering. The wells in each partnership are selected for a broad blend of payouts. Some wells may have a high cash flow and deplete more rapidly. Others may deplete over a much longer period of time. The operators work continuously to increase production. The reason for this is that the general partners' interests in these programs parallel those of the limited partners. As they increase productivity for you, they increase their own revenues.

Minimum Repurchase Price

Some programs offer you the guarantee that if within ten years after you invest in one of their partnerships your total distributions plus your repurchase price do not equal 100 percent of your investment, they will add an amount necessary to reach that minimum repurchase price. In my opinion, the general partners should never have to dip into their coffers to meet this guarantee.

Disadvantages of Oil and Gas Income Programs

There are two disadvantages to oil income programs of which you should be aware. These are investment lag time and liquidity.

Oil income programs may raise all of their money before they identify the properties that they intend to buy. (They may also have properties inventoried and ready for placement.) If they do not have the property available, the funds are usually invested in Treasury bills, certificates of deposit, or money market mutual funds while the program management searches for suitable purchases. They may be able to find the right properties immediately, or it may take as long as a year to do so. During that year, you would not be receiving oil income, although you would be receiving interest on your funds. However, in recent years as the amount under management has grown, very large purchases have been made in advance.

A more important disadvantage of some oil income programs is their limited liquidity, since there is no ready market for the limited partnership interests in the absence of a "bugout" provision by the general partner.

You should always view your investment as a long-term one, but of course, you never know when you might need to convert your investment into cash. The general partner of one of the largest of these programs is contractually obligated to repurchase your program from the partnership's inception, subject to its financial ability to do so, at their determined purchase price.

After the acquisitions are completed, the general partner may give you a cash selling price each quarter or each year, depending on the program involved. You may choose to cash in your interests or continue to retain them. Our clients usually choose to retain them, since they do not know of another investment that has offered them a comparable cash flow, with tax shelter and potential for appreciation.

In summary, if you desire a relatively low-risk investment in energy, give serious thought to oil and gas income programs for your "hard" after-tax dollars.

These programs have made it possible for investors to join together and combine their resources in order to acquire a diversified portfolio of producing oil and gas properties that are managed professionally. Typically, the programs are designed for the generation of immediate income, but may, through reinvestment of distributable cash flow, offer an excellent opportunity for asset accumulation.

"Hard" and "Soft" Dollars

Above, I used the term hard dollars. There are two kinds of dollars— "hard" and "soft," as you will learn from Chapter 11, "Turn your Tax Liabilities Into Assets." For now, suffice it to say that your "hard" dollars are the ones that you have left after you have sent to the IRS the portion of your income that they require. "Soft" dollars are the dollars that you are going to lose to taxes if you don't take some constructive steps to prevent the journey.

Every taxpayer who has taxable income has some "soft" dollars; however, our security laws are such that there is very little a financial planner is allowed to do to help you shelter those dollars until you reach the 44 percent tax bracket and have a certain net worth.

You hit the 44 percent bracket at $45,800 in 1982 on a joint return, and you'll have a tax liability of $11,457. If you are single, you'll reach the "magic" number at $34,100, losing $8,812 to taxes. If you have reached this bracket, you may want to consider placing some of your funds into limited partnerships that invest in oil and gas drilling programs.

If your taxable income is below these figures, you may want to skip to the applications at the end of this chapter. If you want to get a preview of the possible tax incentives with which you may want to become familiar when you cross into the 44 percent tax bracket, do read on. As inflation continues its destructive path, more and more of our citizens will move across that line. Inflation is "taxation without representation," and that provoked a little tea party in Boston once upon a time. With inflation, you are thrust into a higher and higher tax bracket even without Congress increasing the tax rate schedule. We are one of the few nations that taxes inflation. "Indexing" has been legislated by Congress for 1985—but few believe that Congress will really bring this discipline upon themselves, for it would slow down the increase of revenues and prevent the proliferation of spending programs so dear to some.

Oil and Gas Drilling Limited Partnerships

Historically, oil drilling programs have raised far more money than income programs. In recent years, public and private drilling programs have attracted more than $1.5 billion per year, whereas the newer income programs have attracted less; but the amount is increasing rapidly as many more investors have received pleasing results as energy prices have risen.

You may be asking, "Isn't it risky to drill for oil and gas?" The answer is, "Yes, it is." Searching for oil does involve considerable risk. (Paying taxes does, too.) Most oil programs attempt to reduce your risk by drilling a large number of holes in different areas on which a large amount of geological study has been done.

Should you invest in a drilling program? Your answer should be determined by your tax bracket, the source and regularity of your income, your temperament, and other tax-sheltered investments that are available to you.

In a drilling program you are usually allowed to write off 60-100 percent of your investment. This means that if you invest $10,000 in a drilling program that entitles you to eventually write off 100 percent, you will be investing $5,000 of your money and $5,000 of the IRS's money. Your question now is, "Am I willing to risk my $5,000 for the potential of keeping IRS's $5,000 and possibly a larger return?" If your answer is "yes," go ahead and make the investment. If it is "no," then you'll be more comfortable paying the tax or seeking other ways to turn your tax liabilities into assets.

Always keep in mind that striking oil is not simply a matter of drilling a hole in the ground whereupon the oil gushes out like a broken water main. Nothing could be further from the truth. Despite the high level of U.S. petroleum technology, there remain many situations in which trial and error is the only method that can be used to determine whether there is oil at that location and whether it can be raised to the surface and transported to the refinery economically.

Exploration Economics

With the emergence of the OPEC cartel in 1973, drastic changes have been forced upon the world scene regarding the supply and cost of energy. Our governmental policies of disincentive discouraged exploration and development, making us more vulnerable than even OPEC realized when they first tested the waters to see if they could make their controls effective. Unfortunately, today we are not much closer to a solution to our energy problem.

Even the most junior student of basic economics should be able to recognize that decontrol of prices must be the cornerstone of any program to increase supply.

Price has always been and will continue to be the only common denominator for the many daily decisions that will have to be made about production and, for that matter, conservation of energy. No government has the omnipotence to make these decisions efficiently. Decontrol can create a climate that will provide the incentive to search for oil and gas.

The Natural Gas Policy Act of 1978 is a good example of what even limited decontrol can accomplish. Although the act is a nightmare of undecipherable regulations, it did allow the price of newly discovered gas to increase to the range of $2 per thousand cubic feet at the wellhead in the early part of 1979 and to $3.10 by 1982.

The resulting improvement in the economics of gas exploration is illustrated in Table 8-5, which shows that in 1970 a 10,000-foot gas well cost $150,000 to drill and $306,700 to produce and sell the gas. At a price of 17¢ Mcf, this well yielded a profit of $373,300, so that the return-risk ratio was approximately 3 to 1. This meant the driller had to hit better than one out of three to pay for the unsuccessful wells. As a result, drilling activity declined.

But gross revenues from the same well at 1982 prices of $3.10 per Mcf will be $12,400,000. Even though drilling costs have quadrupled and royalties and production taxes have increased 2800 percent, the resulting return-risk ratio has increased to 14 to 1.

Table 8-5. Exploration Economics
Typical 10,000 Foot Western Oklahoma Gas Well

Year	Costs	Revenue	Exploration Economics
1970			
Drilling Cost	$ 150,000		
Operating Cost	30,000		
Royalties @12.5%	85,000	4,000,000 MCF	Profit - $ 373,300
Prod. Taxes @7%	41,700	@ $ .17 Per MCF	Risk - $ 150,000
Total	$ 306,700	$ 680,000	Return/Risk Ratio - 3:1
1982			
Drilling Cost	$ 600,000		
Operating Cost	90,000		
Royalties @22%	2,728,000	4,000,000 MCF	Profit - $ 8,015,000
Prod. Taxes @10%	967,000	@ $3.10 Per MCF	Risk - $ 600,000
Total	$ 4,385,000	$ 12,400,000	Return/Risk Ratio - 14:1

*Source: May *Petroleum.*

Exploratory or Development Program?

An *exploratory* drilling program is composed primarily of wildcat wells in areas where there has been no established production. These programs usually spend 100 percent of their initial capital in search of new field discoveries in frontier wildcatting.

Exploratory drilling is usually carried out in locations that are unexplored, often remote, very deep, and that have no pipelines to transport the product, if any is found.

A well is also considered exploratory if it is drilled in an area where production has been established at, say, 5,000 feet and the geologist thinks there might be additional production at 20,000 feet below that level and drills to either prove or disprove his theory. In exploratory drilling, your chances of finding anything commercially profitable are 1 in 20. These programs obviously involve the highest risks, but they may also return the greatest rewards.

Balanced programs balance risk and return, usually spending 50 percent of initial capital on controlled exploratory and other lower risk projects, and 50 percent looking for new fields in known producing areas.

Development programs use their initial capital for drilling extensions to known fields, developmental wells within existing fields, and other lower risk projects. The risks are lower and so are the expected returns. Your success ratio on development wells could move up to 60-70 percent. Of course, if you have to acquire such leases in order to drill, your lease costs will be higher, and thus the wells will be more expensive.

Development programs usually have cash distributions sooner than exploratory ones, because the wells may be shallower and so take less time and money to drill; or the pipelines may already be in place so they can be hooked up for delivery more quickly. Since good roads will probably already have been built, they should greatly speed up transporting the oil if trucks are used for hauling.

In an exploratory program, if oil and gas are found, additional capital may be needed for further development. If all or most of the original capital has already been spent, additional capital must be secured. This can be done by using revenues from the first well, but the process will probably be time consuming. Money can be borrowed from the bank to provide further deductions, but this debt would need to be paid by the cash flow from the productive wells before you began receiving distributions. Thus, you would own an asset but would probably have to wait for cash distributions. Another means is for the general partner to assess the limited partners. If you are one of the limited partners, this may or may not fit your financial circumstances in the year the assessments may be made. As you can see, one of the characteristics of an exploration program may be slow cash flow, but your ultimate returns could be greater.

Importance of Early Cash Flow

Let's make some assumptions so that you can get a picture of how important early cash flow can be to your financial future. Let's assume: that you were in a 50 percent tax bracket in 1979, invested in a drilling program with write-offs of 80 percent in 1979, 10 percent in 1980 and 10 percent in 1981; that your investment would return 2.15 times to 1 over the life of your program; that your cash stream comes in over a ten-year well life declining curve of 10, 15, 20, 15, 10, 8, 7, 6, 5, and 4 percent respectively, over the ten years; and that we continue with our present depletion allowances.

Figure 8-1 gives you a picture of the time-value concept of money. A well that starts a cash return in the first year would yield 25 percent after-tax return. The same program starting a cash return in the fourth year would yield a 12.36 percent after-tax return.

Tax Benefits

There are three important tax benefits available to you if you invest in an oil drilling program. These come from the deduction of intangible drilling costs, the depletion allowance, and the potential for partial longterm capital gains treatment upon the sale of the investment. Your program may also be structured in a way that will provide additional tax benefits through investment tax credits and depreciation of capital equipment.

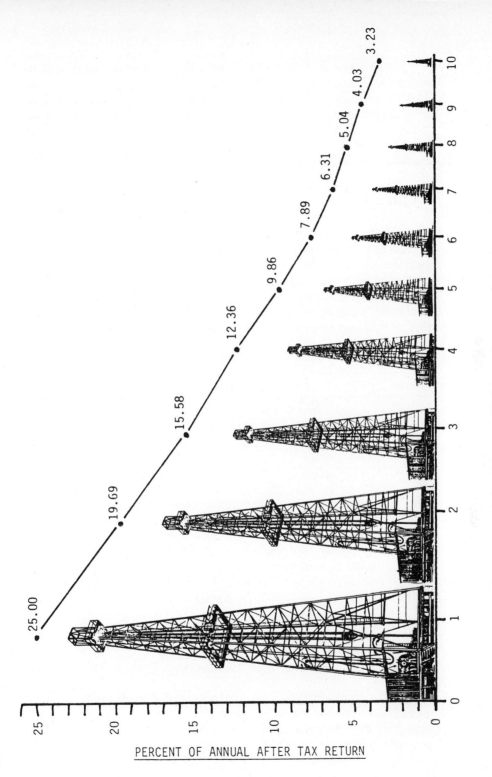

Figure 8-1. Year that well starts providing a cash return to investors.

PERCENT OF ANNUAL AFTER TAX RETURN

25.00

19.69

15.58

12.36

9.86

7.89

6.31

5.04

4.03

3.23

Your major costs in drilling can be expensed as intangible drilling expenses. These include well-site expenses and actual drilling costs. This should mean that from 60 to 90 percent of your investment may be deducted in the year you make the investment and up to 100 percent within two to four years.

The extent of your tax benefit will depend upon the type and amount of your income.

Depletion

The best-known tax benefit is the depletion allowance. This allows for a portion of your income from the sale of oil and gas production to be tax-sheltered provided that you qualify as a small producer. As a limited partner in both the income programs and in the drilling programs, you will usually be classified as a small producer and will also qualify for the minimum "windfall profit" tax. Table 8-6 shows the depletion allowance rate by year and by production volume.

Table 8-6. Depletion Allowance Rate

Year	Production	Exempted	Depletion Rate
1982	1000 barrels a day	6.0 million cu.ft. gas	18%
1983	1000	6.0	16%
1984 and thereafter	1000	6.0	15%

To determine your tax-sheltered amount, apply the depletion rate to your gross income before separating expenses that will result in the tax-free amount (assuming they do not exceed 50 percent of the net income). Typically, 30 percent or so of the cash flow in a drilling program would be tax-sheltered, as the following example illustrates:

Gross income	$2,000
Less separating costs	600
Net income	$1,400
Depletion allowance (18% of gross income)*	360
Taxable income	$1,040 (74.29% of net income)

* 18% in 1982,
16% in 1983, 15% thereafter.

In this example, you would receive a check for $1,400, with $360 or 18 percent of gross income being tax-free because of the depletion allowance. The maximum amount of the depletion allowance that would have to be included as a tax preference item would be $360. But it would not be taxed at the minimum tax rate unless you had other items of tax preference that when added to this would exceed the exclusions ($10,000 or 1/2 tax liabilities). In certain types of program structures, an even larger percentage of income may be tax-free because of depreciating capital expenditures.

Structuring Drilling Programs

There are many ways to structure a program in terms of who bears the cost, who receives the tax advantages, and who receives the income.

The structure of your program is important, but it may not be as important as the strength and technical qualifications of the general partner and the partner's ability to find and develop profitable reserves.

The most frequently used sharing arrangements you will encounter are: (1) functional allocations, (2) reversionary interest, and (3) promoted interest.

Functional Allocation. In this structure all items that are immediately deductible for income tax purposes are paid for out of investor funds, and the general partner pays for all nondeductible (capital) items. Oil and gas revenues are usually shared 60 percent to investors and 40 percent to the general partner. Because investor funds are used only for deductible items, this structure results in the highest deductibility, usually 100 percent of the initial investment. Deductible items are primarily intangible drilling costs, including dry holes and abandoned acreage. This structure transfers all of the deductibility, a disproportionately large share of risk, to the investor. Therefore, it is important that the general partner be required to make some minimum risk investment. Usually this minimum risk is set at 15 percent of the investor subscriptions if the general partner is to earn 40 percent of oil and gas revenue.

Reversionary Interest. Investor subscriptions are used to pay for all costs. The general partner pays for a small portion of the program, usually 1 percent. Investors receive a high percentage of oil and gas revenues (usually 99 percent) until they have recovered their investment on some basis, at which time the investors' share of revenues decreases and the general partner's share increases. The key to this structure is the basis on which investors achieve payout before the sharing of revenues changes. The most desirable basis from the investors' point of view is for the interest to change only after the investors have recovered their entire investment in the program. From the general partner's point of view, the interest reversion should occur as the investors are paid out on each well. As a compromise, most programs are written so that the interest reversion occurs on the payout of each prospect. The difficulty with this is that the general partner decides what constitutes a prospect and will generally lean toward defining each well as a separate prospect. If you are interested in a reversionary interest program, be sure that the payout point is on a prospect or program basis and that the definition of prospect is clearly set out.

Promoted Interest. Investors and the general partner each pay a share of the cost and risk of drilling and acreage, and share oil and gas revenues on a disproportionate basis. Typically, investors pay for 75 percent of all initial drilling and acreage costs to earn 50 percent of revenues, while the general partner pays for 25 percent to earn 50 percent. The general partner is more at risk in this type program, and in return earns more equity.

Table 8-7 summarizes some of the significant characteristics of these three structures.

Table 8-7. Three Types of Drilling Programs

Type of Structure	Deductibility % of investment	General Partner at Risk	% Investor Equity	Remarks
Functional allocation	90–100	Moderate	50–60	Frequently used by established program sponsors for exploratory or balanced programs.
Reversionary interest	50–80	Low	99 before payout	Used mostly by new or financially weak program sponsors for developmental programs.
Promoted interest	50–80	High	50	Frequently used by established program sponsors for exploratory or balanced programs.

Other Features You Should Know

Three technical features of program agreements that you should be aware of are: (1) assessments, (2) liquidity, and (3) conflicts of interest.

Assessments. Drilling programs can be written so that you may or may not be assessed by the general partner for additional funds beyond their initial investment. If a program is assessable, assessments are typically limited to completion and development costs. Assessments are typically limited to 20-50 percent of the initial investment. There is no clear answer as to whether a program should be assessable or nonassessable, and there are many programs in each category.

Liquidity. The liquidity of all drilling program investments is generally poor. These are investments that must be made with a long-term attitude. However, most drilling programs require the general partner to make one or more offers to purchase the limited partner units. Such repurchase offers usually begin two years after the formation of the partnership and are based on independent engineering appraisals of the reserves and cash flow of the partnership at that time. The evaluation formulas used for these repurchase offers are fairly standard within the industry, and they allow for profit to the general partner from the purchase. Many investors decline the repurchase offers and elect to retain their partnership units for future cash flow and potential appreciation in oil and gas prices. Most partnerships allow for limited transfer of ownership in events such as death and gifting with approval of the general partner.

Conflicts of Interest. All program structures and agreements contain potential for conflicts of interest between the general partner and investors. Many of these conflicts are inherent in each structure and cannot be avoided. You should select management on whose integrity you can rely to exercise fiduciary responsibility to the limited partners. However, two major conflict areas to look for and avoid are "marking up" and "proving up." "Marking up" means the general partner provides acreage, materials, or services to the partnership at a marked-up basis above cost. Unless you are very sophisticated and knowledgeable in the oil business, you should stick to programs that prohibit marking up of all types. "Proving up" means the general partner assigns a small amount of acreage to be drilled by the drilling program while he retains substantial adjacent acreage for his own account. Program funds are thus used to prove up the acreage retained by the general partner. To avoid this potential conflict, be certain that the partnership agreement specifically prohibits proving up.

As you can see, you and your financial planner will need to do some in-depth "due diligence" to determine which program best fits your needs and temperament. Choose a program offered by general partners who have good past records or, if no past records exist, become familiar with the expertise of their geological staff, the net worth of the general partners, and the fairness of the "payouts." Determine whether you can make money with the compensation schedule if the drilling programs are successful.

Public or Private Programs?

There are two basic classes of drilling programs, and each of these can be structured in a wide variety of ways.

The majority of the programs you'll be offered will be registered programs, meaning the general partner has gone to the time and considerable expense of registering the program with the Securities and Exchange Commission and the various states in which they will be offered. This means these programs can be offered publicly to those who meet the suitability requirements in those states in which they have been approved for sale. These requirements vary from state to state. Some states only require full disclosure. In other states, securities personnel take it upon themselves to determine what is "good for you."

Public programs are structured as limited partnerships and the oil operators are the general partners. Private programs may be either partnerships or joint ventures. The minimum investment in public programs is usually $5,000 to $10,000.

Most private programs are also considered securities but are exempt from registration. These programs usually require a larger minimum investment and can be structured by using recourse financing that may provide you with a 2 to 1 write-off on the capital you invest that year. Remember, however, that recourse financing means that if the program does not produce sufficient revenues to pay off the note, you must pay the note on its maturity, if the maturity date is not extended, and you must have sufficient funds to pay semi-annual interest payments. Even if the note is paid off for you, it can be taxable to you. Some of the best and some of the worst programs I've seen have been private programs.

Completion Programs

Because of the high cost of money in recent years, a new form of investing in energy, called "completion programs," is now available through registered limited partnerships. The cost of drilling a well is approximately 70 percent of the total cost. The equipment that goes in and on the well after it is drilled amounts to the other 30 percent.

This equipment can be depreciated like any other equipment, and it qualifies for the 10 percent investment tax credit (new limitations on old). The deductions are not as great your first year and must be spread over a longer period of time. However, there is much less risk because the equipment is supplied only to those wells that have already been drilled and deemed commercially feasible.

The equipment also has salvage value and can be moved to another site even if the well is eventually depleted.

The revenue is usually shared in proportion to the amount of the total costs that are incurred in bringing the well into production. In other words, if 70 percent represented the drilling cost and 30 percent the equipment, then the revenues would be shared in that proportion.

You may be wondering why anyone would be willing to give you a percentage of the well after production has been discovered. In every oil well somebody has to put up the money for the equipment. This must be done by the drilling contractor or another group of investors. In times past this was done by the oil operator himself, but with the advent of high interest rates and increased drilling activity, he may have lending limits at the bank and his pockets may be only so deep. If he borrows from the bank, he is usually required to dedicate 100 percent of the production to the reduction of the loan. If he takes in a completion partner, he can split the revenue 70–30 percent without paying 100 percent to the bank.

If you invest in a completion program, your costs can usually be written off in five years and your rewards will be determined by the success of the wells that are equipped.

Royalty Programs

Another approach that you may want to consider is a program that acquires royalties and overriding royalty interests for leases on which others are expected to drill. These royalty payments are generally made to those who hold a working interest. If a dry hole results and the well is plugged and abandoned, the partnership is permitted to write off its investment as an abandonment loss cost; if you are an investor, you receive your proportionate write-off. If the drilling is successful, the partnership capitalizes the investment, and the program is entitled to depletion over the years.

Before investing in any tax shelter, you may want to discuss the matter with your C.P.A., but do find one who has tax savings for you as his chief concern, not just tax tallying.

I have a doctor client in a very high tax bracket who at one time needed some tax-sheltered investments every year. Whenever I suggested a particular shelter to him, he asked that I submit it to his C.P.A., as I was happy to do. Unfortunately, his C.P.A. was an uncreative soul who could tell him to the penny how much he owed in taxes at the end of the year, but who could not imagine taking any "risks" to prevent paying taxes. So the C.P.A. always turned down each proposal. Finally, I told the doctor I would not send any more offerings to his C.P.A., because he was only going to say no and tell him just to pay his taxes. The doctor admitted that this was true and joined with me in investing in the oil and gas drilling program that discovered a major gas field in Louisiana.

Coal in Your Energy Future

Another area of energy is coal. Up to now, the government has only given lip service to its potential for helping to solve our energy problems. The government admits there is a shortage of oil and gas and an abundance of coal, but continues to enforce punitive regulations and disincentives so great that our vast coal reserves are still virtually untapped.

Our country has vast resources of coal. Our domestic coal reserves are equal to one-half of the known reserves in the entire world and have five times the energy value of our domestic recoverable oil and natural gas.

Of a total of 1,600 billion tons of identified coal resources (plus an equal amount believed to exist), reserves of 434 billion tons are considered mineable under today's economic and technological conditions. Yet, we consume and export only about 600 million tons a year.

Technology Development Required

Whether we can continue to maintain a way of life that depends on a high rate of energy consumption will no doubt be determined by how successfully we are able to take advantage of our coal. Today three-fourths of our energy comes from oil and gas. A principal objective of U.S. energy policy should be to develop the technology that will enable us to substitute coal for fuels in short supply.

The United States has enough coal that is recoverable under present economic and technological conditions to last 360 years at current rates of consumption. Moreover, technology now being developed by industry can enable us to recover and use a larger portion of our coal resources. Several forecasts project a tripling of the U.S. demand for coal by the year 2000 if certain technological and environmental problems are overcome.

Substitute for Other Energy

In expanding the use of coal, the primary near-term challenge is to recover and burn more of this fuel with less environmental impact. Electric utilities, which already use almost two-thirds of all U.S. coal produced, also account for 9–10 percent of the oil and 16–17 percent of the natural gas consumption. So generating plants need to rely even more on coal (and nuclear energy) to conserve scarce quantities of domestic oil and gas.

Need for Coal Gasification and Liquefaction

The importance of coal to the nation's energy future will continue to rise during the next quarter of a century.

Projections of our midterm energy needs require the establishment of an industry to make synthetic fuels from coal and oil shale.

How can you make investments that can participate in the development of our needs for coal utilization? This is a difficult question to answer. Some of the private placements offered for coal mining have produced excellent results. Unfortunately, this need has also attracted those who do not have the necessary expertise to select, negotiate, and mine the proper leases. Some of these people have offered private placements that do not appear to me to have economic viability.

Several of our international oil companies emphasize that they are not just in the oil business, but are in the energy business. They are doing vast amounts of research and development on the best ways to mine and use coal as well as process oil shale, capture solar and geothermal energy, and safely use nuclear energy.

Summary

An intelligent approach to financial planning cannot ignore the potential rewards of investing in energy. If you are in the 25–50 percent tax bracket, the oil and gas income programs may best fit your investment needs. Even if you are in a 50 percent bracket you'll still have some "hard" after-tax dollars that you may want to put to work in the income programs.

If you are in the 50 percent bracket and have "soft" dollars to invest, you may want to consider investing some of those dollars in exploration programs. Oil and gas account for three-fourths of all the energy we consume, and the demand is growing at an unprecedented rate, both here and in foreign countries. It is estimated that on a worldwide basis, there will be more oil consumed during the decade of the 1980s than has been consumed since petroleum was discovered.

Do your tax planning early. This gives you an opportunity to look over the many viable possibilities. It also gives the companies time to do the drilling before year end and possibly provide you with a larger write-off for the year. It also gives you the additional benefit of having your annual investment deductible in advance against your estimated quarterly tax liability. Be sure to complete your W-4 form at the beginning of the year claiming all the deductions you'll be entitled to. Money has earning power and it should be in your account and not the IRS's. You should consider investing smaller amounts in several partnerships rather than all of your funds in one. This allows you to spread your risk over a larger number of wells.

Application

1. Should some of your "hard" dollars be invested in oil and gas income-producing programs?
2. What other investments compare favorably for after-tax return and potential for appreciation?
3. What dollar amount should you invest this year?
4. Should you invest in energy stocks? If so, which four offer the greatest potential for price appreciation?

	Stock	Market Price	Yield	Price/Earning Ratio
1.	_____	$_____	_____%	_____
2.	_____	_____	_____	_____
3.	_____	_____	_____	_____
4.	_____	_____	_____	_____

5. If you have some income that will be taxed at 50 percent how much of it should be invested in drilling programs?

Chapter 9

Hedging With Hard Assets and Collectibles

In inflationary times money moves into what is called hard tangible assets that hold the promise of offering some protection from the ravages of inflation. There are a number of such assets with which you may want to become familiar. Chief among these are gold and silver bullion and coins, rare gold and silver coins, junk silver coins, uncirculated silver dollars, mutual funds that invest in gold stocks, diamonds and colored gemstones, rare stamps, and various investment-grade collectibles.

Gold

Gold should be looked at as a store of value, not as a medium of speculation. In the past people accumulated gold not because they thought it would bring them wealth, but because it was a means of representing and preserving the wealth they already had.

The government arbitrarily controlled the price of gold at $35 an ounce for decades while the price for everything else was allowed to rise with inflation. In 1971 the government was literally forced to let the price float freely and it radically went up to regain its price relative to other goods and services. At that time gold became an attractive speculation and went to $200 by 1971. After backing off to $103 in 1976, it climbed to $886 in January of 1980. Once again it backed off and dramatically lost 60 percent of its dollar value.

What does the future hold for gold? I do not know, but you should have some knowledge of this store of value and its place in your portfolio.

Even in normal times gold has held a special attraction. Charles de Gaulle spoke lovingly of "gold, which never changes, can be shaped into ingots, bars, coins, has no nationality, and is eternally and universally accepted as the unalterable fiduciary value." From biblical reference to the gift of the Magi to the gold medals awarded at Olympic competitions, gold has been held in high esteem.

Should gold have a place in your total financial planning? The answer could be yes. Should you use it as your "fail safe" plan in the event other more conventional approaches fail, or regard it as one of the items you should value for its investment merits alone? Should you treat gold as you do fire insurance on your home? If your home doesn't burn down, you probably wouldn't cancel your fire insurance. Or should you treat it as a viable investment for profit? This you will need to answer for yourself.

Let's say you've determined that a portion of your assets should be in gold or gold-related investments. What approach should you take? Should you invest in gold bullion, gold coins, gold medallions, gold jewelry, gold mining stocks, or mutual funds that invest in gold mining stock?

Gold Demand

There are five types of gold demands: the monetary demand, the industrial commercial demand, the political demand, the inflation-hedging demand, and the depression-hedging demand.

Monetary Demand. Even though most politicians condemn the backing of gold or silver for paper currency in circulation as archaic, it does have the advantage of limiting the amount of currency and credit governments can create. The supply of money today is growing worldwide at a compound rate of over 10 percent per year, while the gold supply is increasing only around 1-1/2 percent.

I will not go into how the United States has arrived at this point in our history, nor how our country abrogated the Bretton Woods Treaty on August 15, 1971, when we closed the gold window and refused to exchange any more dollars for gold. Suffice it to say, since that time the world has been pushed into floating exchange rates that have caused highly unstable fluctuating currencies.

Today, in spite of our often repeated U.S. position that gold is being demonetized, European monetary authorities believe the opposite—that gold is being remonetized. Over 50 percent of the monetary reserves of the world's central banks are held in gold bullion. Arab and Japanese central banks have become particularly active in acquiring gold.

Industrial Demand. In 1981 industrial and jewelry demand for gold absorbed over one-half of the world's production. There were only 1,200 tons of newly mined gold. This demand is growing.

Political Demand. This factor could be the most important. Political demand for gold occurs when there is political turmoil in the world as "smart money" of a particular region moves out of the currency of that region and into the world's most liquid and anonymous instrument, gold. We have seen classic examples in recent years of this "slight capital" exiting Vietnam, Iran, and Afghanistan and Central America moving into gold.

Inflation Hedge. In 1938 you could buy a man's suit for a $20 gold coin or a $20 bill. Today, as we know, that bill would only buy a tie whereas the gold coin would still buy the suit. The gold coin has retained its purchasing power.

When inflation is accelerating, or there is a threat that it will, the demand for gold increases. When the prospects for inflation decrease, the price of gold decreases. The correlation became obvious as the Reagan administration became more and more effective in slowing the inflation rate and the price of gold dipped accordingly.

Gold in Times of Depression . What has been the record of gold-related investments during times of depression? There are two kinds of monetary turmoil. One is inflation in which money becomes worth less every day, and which causes people to turn to gold to protect their purchasing power. A second kind of monetary turmoil is depression in which money becomes worth more every day. In such circumstances people fear the loss of their money and can also turn to gold, which many consider the ultimate money.

A bit of history may add some perspective. In the early 1930s President Franklin Roosevelt noticed people taking money out of savings and loan associations because of their fears concerning the solvency of these institutions. They put their money into gold. When the savings and loans appeared to be in danger of collapsing, there was no money available from them for mortgages. To help prevent this from happening, President Roosevelt abolished gold ownership in 1933 in order to stimulate the depositing of currency with savings and loan associations. This is precisely what happened after he abolished gold ownership.

(One footnote, perhaps, about the behavior of governments: President Roosevelt abolished gold ownership in 1933 at the official price of $20.67 an ounce; after all the gold had been turned in, President Roosevelt raised the price of gold to $35.00 an ounce.)

The stock market reached its low in 1932. It took twenty-five years for the Dow Jones Industrial Average to achieve the levels it had reached in 1929. In times of depression people lose confidence in a corporation's ability to produce a profit and pay a dividend, or pay interest on bonds that they have sold previously. They also lose confidence in a municipality's ability to generate sufficient taxes to not only pay interest on bonds but to retire debt as well.

The result is that in a depression people have turned to gold and to gold mining shares as a mechanism for both income and appreciation.

Ways to Invest in Gold

There are five ways you may invest in gold: mutual funds investing in gold mining shares, gold bullion, gold coins, gold futures, and gold mining ventures.

Mutual Funds Investing in Gold Mining Shares. I personally prefer investing in South African gold mining shares through a well-managed mutual fund for a number of reasons. Usually the prices of the stocks lag behind the bullion itself, giving me an opportunity to see the direction gold prices are moving. Most of the time the shares outperform the bullion, and they also pay a dividend, which in the past has run as high as 10 percent. There is daily liquidity by wire or mail. Also, the government could ban the ownership of gold and could require that it be turned in for less than its market value.

South African Political Stability. Many have expressed a fear of political instability in South Africa, and others have expressed a dislike of some of their racial policies. In regard to their political stability, it is interesting to note that almost every nation except South Africa has replaced its political leaders over the past four to five years either by scandal or a vote of no confidence. Also, the Republic of South Africa has never had a bank failure. The government is also trying to improve the standard of living for everyone in the nation.

Patriotism. How patriotic is it to invest in South African gold shares? That's a question you may have and should answer for yourself. You may believe that if we have monetary turmoil and economic disruption, your patriotic duty is to maintain your purchasing power in real money so that you will have the means of helping rebuild our country in the event an economic disruption should occur. Historically, gold-related investments have been effective in the preservation of capital in times of monetary and economic uncertainty.

Each of us must be a steward of all the assets that we have. To preserve buying power is an obligation of all of us who are socially minded because those who have capital always dictate the ethics and morality of our nation through the type of investments that they make.

Gold Bullion (Bars and Wafers). You probably should not consider this way, since it would generally have to be assayed prior to resale. You could consider this method if you are buying a large amount of gold and plan to leave it on deposit at a bank and eventually sell it without ever taking possession.

Gold Coins. One way you might consider, which is the most popular way, is low-premium bullion coins that trade within a few percent of their bullion content. These coins—such as the 1-ounce Krugerrand, the 1-ounce Canadian Maple Leaf, 1.20-ounce Mexican 50 peso, and the .98-ounce Austrian 100 Corona—are very liquid, require no assay upon resale, and are concentrated forms of wealth in a convenient and anonymous bearer form. These can be purchased at a 3 to 7 percent premium above bullion price.

A large network of gold coin dealers is spread across the United States. They make two-way markets in the popular bullion coins (as well as silver coins and bars). A typical commission is 2–3 percent. You should probably avoid margin coin dealers since leveraged positions in gold coins can be wiped out by sharp short-term fluctuations in these markets. Most gold coins are delivered by the dealer directly to the investor, though larger dealers will store the coins for a nominal fee. Most investors keep their coins in a safe-deposit box.

Gold Commodity Futures. These are highly speculative and very difficult to trade successfully. Go this route only if you are willing to take very speculative risks.

Gold Mining Ventures. This is covered later.

Investing in Silver

There was a time when I considered gold to be money and silver a metal. Silver is an industrial metal, but it can offer a hedge against inflation.

In the inflationary surge of the late 1970s, silver rose tenfold from under $5 per ounce to over $50. In the disinflation of 1981 and 1982, it fell back to below $7. If inflation surges again, however, like gold, silver can also be expected to rise.

There are three popular silver investment vehicles in the United States:

1. *Junk Silver Coins.* These are bags of dimes, quarters, and fifty-cent pieces, minted prior to 1965, before the U.S. government replaced the silver in other coinage with plastic and copper. A bag contains $1,000 in face value with a market value of $6,300 in mid-1982.

2. *Silver Bars.* These bars come in sizes of 1, 10, 100, and 1,000-ounce, the 100-ounce bar being by far the most popular. Only bars from well-known refiners, such as Englehard, Johnson Mathy, or Credit Suisse, should be purchased. These well-known bars will not have to be assayed upon repurchase.

3. *Uncirculated Silver Dollars.* These dollars, minted in the late 1800s and early 1900s, were for the most part melted down over the years. The few that remained were held either by collectors or the Federal Reserve Banks until the 1950s and 1960s. Morgan or Peace Silver Dollars have had very favorable price appreciation in recent years

because of both their silver content and their scarcity (or numismatic value). They tend to be much less volatile in price than gold or silver.

Rare Coins

Rare (numismatic) U.S. coins can be another way to preserve capital. They date back to 1793, were coined in gold and silver, and are in low supply owing to the small number originally produced and the subsequent melting that has occurred.

They are a highly concentrated, portable store of wealth and are not subject to governmental regulation or exchange controls; and in the past they have been excluded when government confiscation of gold and silver has occurred.

Over 75 percent of U.S. rare coins are held by long-term investors, a factor that should give underlying price stability.

Numismatic coins are not as liquid as bullion coins but there are over 3,500 U.S. coin dealers.

What Makes a Coin Valuable?

You may ask, What makes a coin valuable? It is more than age, condition, date, type, or metal content. A great deal depends on its rarity and its supply and demand. There are approximately fifteen grades of excellence recognized by the American Numismatic Association, ranging from *Proof*, the mirror-like finish of a coin that was manufactured by the Mint and then carefully preserved from any nicks or scratches, all the way to the fifteenth grade, *Good*, which actually means "Very heavily worn with portions of lettering, date, and legends worn smooth. The date may be barely readable."

Prices of rare coins have been rising steadily, year after year. It appears that this trend will continue, for there is a static supply of coins—and there will never be very many more available than there are now—while there is an increasing demand as more and more collectors crowd into the field. As you've learned by now, when demand is greater than supply, prices tend to rise.

Using price data from the "Coin Dealers Newsletter," a widely read wholesale dealer publication, for four overlapping five-year periods the results were as shown in Figure 9-1.

Here are some of the features and potential benefits that well-selected numismatic coins can offer:

Feature	Possible Benefit
Potential appreciation	Growth, assets increase.
Diversification	Risk spreading can lower losses, allow appreciation in other areas.
Inexpensive entry	Small amount of money needed to initially establish an account.
Anonymity	Maximum protection and discretion.
Long-term capital gain	Gains on coins held one year qualify for long-term capital gains treatment.
Tax-free exchange	When coins are exchanged rather than sold, tax payment is deferred until finally sold for cash.
Durability	No special handling or environmental considerations necessary. Careless handling can be avoided by special coin holders.
Insurable	If lost or stolen, the entire investment is not lost.
Easy maintenance	Cost to maintain is no more than a safe-deposit box.
Relatively high liquidity	Coins may be tendered to a coin dealer at wholesale, or consigned to a commissioned auctioneer.

In the Appendix you'll find a graph (Figure 4) showing the ten-year appreciation of investment-quality rare coins.

Rare Coins Limited Partnership

At this point in our discussion you may have been impressed with the investment potential of rare coins, but do not have the interest or perhaps the time to develop expertise in them. If this is where you find yourself, you may want to consider Rare Coin Limited Partnerships. Each unit is $500 and the minimum purchase is five units, or a minimum investment of $2,500.

MAXIMUM & MINIMUM PERCENTAGE RATES OF INCREASE (DECREASE) IN PRICE: (% HIGHEST − % LOWEST)

	Period 1	Period 2	Period 3	Period 4
Silver Commemoratives				
Highest	78.0	77.1	87.0	91.1
Lowest	14.0	18.3	24.1	22.5
Gold Commemoratives				
Highest	54.0	69.0	82.1	82.1
Lowest	22.0	33.5	40.3	41.8
Type Coins-Proof				
Highest	52.40	79.6	79.9	69.0
Lowest	13.10	35.9	19.6	19.6
Type Coins-Mint State				
Highest	76.0	96.8	91.5	99.1
Lowest	19.0	27.7	30.3	30.3

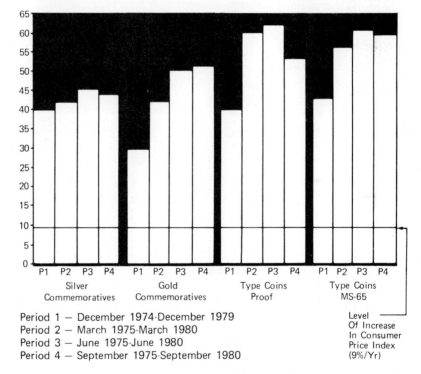

Period 1 — December 1974-December 1979
Period 2 — March 1975-March 1980
Period 3 — June 1975-June 1980
Period 4 — September 1975-September 1980

Level
Of Increase
In Consumer
Price Index
(9%/Yr)

Figure 9-1

271

Rare Stamps

Another area you may want to familiarize yourself with is rare stamp collecting. It is one of the most popular hobbies in our nation, with over twenty million collectors here and fifty million around the world. Most people who collect rare stamps consider it a hobby, but there are growing numbers of persons who are buying stamps as an investment and are finding it very profitable.

Stamp investing, highest quality of course, has yielded about a 12 percent per year rate of return on investment for the past two decades. Philately, as stamp collecting is referred to in trade circles, is a fairly big business. Around a billion dollars in sales occur each year, and it is estimated there are in excess of fifty million collectors worldwide. There appears to be no scarcity of willing investors, but dealers are beginning to complain that they cannot obtain enough quality stamps to sell—again a situation where demand exceeds supply.

The top-priced stamp at present is the British Guyana 1856 one cent, appraised at $280,000.

Some rules you may want to follow when investing in rare stamps are:

1. Begin as a collector, and work into becoming an investor.

2. Diversify in stamps.

3. Choose only top-quality stamps.

4. Look for stamps that are old, clean, undamaged, and of course, rare. If you do not have the inclination or time to do this on your own, work with a financial planner who is knowledgeable in this area.

Why have rare stamps performed so well? Some characteristics that they possess that may be of interest to you are:

1. *Price Appreciation*. Stamps have outdistanced the rate of inflation. Their prices are maintained because of the unflagging interest of fifty million collectors throughout the world.

2. *Safety*. Prices tend to rise in both good and bad times. Stamps are portable and can be used as a shield against political or economic unrest.

3. *Tax Advantage*. An investment in stamps is taxed only when you sell them and then at the lower capital gains rates. You are also allowed to take deductions for any expenses incurred in connection with your investment, such as a safe-deposit box, insurance, and so on.

4. *High Liquidity*. There is a steady, active market for quality stamps. New collectors and investors are constantly entering the market. It may actually be easier to sell rare stamps than to buy them.

5. *Ease of Maintenance.*   Stamps can be easily protected, transported, and insured. When stamps are kept in a safe-deposit box, insurance rates are extremely low.

The Economics of Diamonds

"Diamonds are forever." "Diamonds are a girl's best friend." These are the ads most familiar to us. Are they forever the best investment? The answer is no, not every year, but over the long run the prices of high-quality investment-grade diamonds have kept ahead of inflation.

The brilliance and durability of diamonds have always fascinated humans, and the desire for them has not diminished over the years. However, in the last few decades the beauty of diamonds became secondary, and they began to be viewed more and more in terms of their investment potential. Those who live in the United States have been slow in catching up to the awareness of this potential, but Europeans and Third World businessmen have recognized it for years.

In typical fashion, once alerted to the possibilities, U.S. investors jumped into the market with enthusiasm and vigor, often without sufficient information or the background to make wise decisions.

Since investment-grade diamonds can be considered a viable part of a diversified portfolio, you should become more knowledgeable about this area of investing. The information I'll present here will not be sufficient to make you an expert on the subject, but it should make you more knowledgeable, teach you a few do's and don'ts, and whet your appetite for further information.

Diamonds have long been a haven for some of the assets of the very rich. Worldwide affluence is a relatively recent phenomenon. Europeans have a much longer tradition of mistrust of governments and fiat currencies than do we Americans. Consequently, gemstone investing has a much older history in Europe. This demand has accelerated during the

past few years, raising the prices and pulling the better quality stones to markets outside our country.

Beauty, Durability, Rarity

All gems have three attributes in common. They are beautiful; they are durable; and they are rare. Beauty may be in color, irridescence (as in pearls or opals), or fire (as in diamond). Durability is necessary for a valuable gem—pearls are soft, yet durable. A diamond is the only colorless, transparent gemstone that has all three of these qualities. It stands alone in its ranking of gemstones for its transparent, colorless beauty, as well as its rarity and durability.

Since the nineteenth century, the major mining center for diamonds has shifted from India to South Africa. South Africa experienced a "Diamond Rush" in the 1860s very much like California's Gold Rush. The rarity of diamonds is underlined now by the fact that fewer and fewer of the finest gemstones are being found.

Costly to Mine

Searching for the diamond of high value is not unlike looking for the proverbial needle in the haystack. It is estimated that current procedures may require mining from 45 to 200 tons of rock or sand to uncover one carat (2/10 of 1 gram or 1/142 of an ounce) of quality diamond, an extremely costly and arduous process. Approximately 80 percent of all diamonds found are unsuitable for jewelry or investment and are used for industrial purposes. The industrial diamond, because of its color, structural defects, size, or shape, does not meet the high standards required for gemstones. Of the remaining 20 percent, only about 3 percent are considered to be of investment grade. And of this 3 percent, only 1 percent will yield a gemstone of at least one carat in size.

Today diamonds are mined not only in South Africa, but also in South-West Africa (Namibia), Angola, Australia, Russia (20 percent of the world's supply), Brazil, and India. U.S. production so far has been quite modest.

Monopolistic Control

The major control for distribution of diamonds is by the DeBeers Consolidated Mines of South Africa, Ltd. Since the 1930s, DeBeers has held an ironclad monopoly on the diamond industry that amounts to from 60 to 85 percent of the world's supply. The Central Selling

Organization (CSO), the wholesaler arm of DeBeers, purchases rough diamonds not only from DeBeers mines (18 percent of the world's supply), but also from other producers. The distribution of the diamonds is controlled through "sights" or sales that are held ten times each year by DeBeers. At these sights, packages are made up of the rough high-grade stones, as nearly as possible according to the requirements that have been previously stated to DeBeers, which insures a firm control on the price. DeBeers' stated policy is "to maintain a high degree of price stability for gems and diamonds at all times". While this method of control has been questioned, it has not been broken. Major producers and cutters cooperate with DeBeers because they agree that control and stability are as good for the industry as for DeBeers.

The select group of 230 buyers invited to the "sights" may refuse to purchase a packet, but they rarely do, as hundreds of other buyers could easily replace each one. After the purchase of the parcels from DeBeers, the buyers, if they are dealers, sort the package into categories for their own customers. If they are cutters, they will divide the rough package into the group they plan to sell, and the stones that will be cut under their supervision. Each stone must be evaluated, and the master cutter must use his skill and professional judgment in deciding the most practical shape and size for that particular stone before the work is begun. Then cutting, shaping facets, and polishing will all be a part of the process.

The Four Cs

Cut. The "cut" of a diamond refers to its proportions and dimensions, based on certain measurements. The brilliance of the diamond depends not only on the light reflected from the surface, but on the rays that have been partly absorbed before being refracted. The diamond is exceptionally reflective: about 17 percent of the light falling directly on its surface will be reflected back, accounting for its "life" (compared with about 5 percent of light falling on a transparent glass stone). Diamond will also absorb 80 percent of the light entering before it is refracted, creating the diamond's "fire". The perfectly cut diamond maximizes the amount of light returned to the viewer; hence, the more finely proportioned the stone, the higher the value (see Figure 9-2).

The word "cut" is also used to mean the "shape" of the stone, or the design of its finished form. While unusual shapes may be used, many cutters choose one of the five most popular shapes or cuts (Figure 9-3):

1. The familiar Round-Brilliant with fifty-eight facets has been a favorite in rings and other types of jewelry for centuries. In tiny sizes,

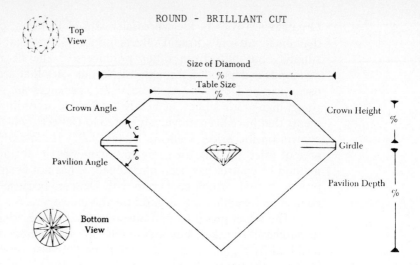

Figure 9-2. *The more finely proportioned the stone, the higher the value.*

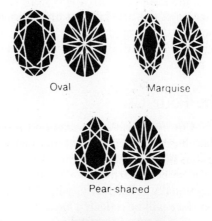

Oval

Marquise

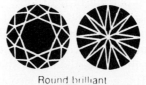

Pear-shaped

Round brilliant

Emerald

Figure 9-3. *The most popular diamond cuts.*

with only eighteen facets, it may be used as a side stone in the setting, when it is called a single cut. Eighty percent of all polished diamonds are Round-Brilliants.

Three modern variations of the Brilliant cut are also among the most often selected:

2. The Marquise-Brilliant is usually long and narrow, in a pointed boat shape. In the setting of a ring, this shape tends to make the fingers look slim. Because of the additional labor required for the cutting, it may be more expensive than a Round-Brilliant stone of the same size and quality. Also, the Marquise may be chosen by the cutter to maximize the unflawed portion of a stone.

3. The Pear-shaped Brilliant is another popular cut for jewelry. The world's largest fashioned diamond, the Cullinan I, or the Great Star of Africa, is pear-shaped. The original size of the rough diamond was 3,106 carats.

4. The Oval-Brilliant is also an adaptation of the Round-Brilliant. It may appear to be even larger than a Round-Brilliant of the same carat weight.

5. The Emerald cut, so called because emeralds are often cut this way, is rectangular or square. Its facets are polished diagonally across the corners.

After the diamond has been cut and polished, the finished product will be sold to importers, wholesalers, or distributors. There are about ten exclusive cash markets, or Bourses, in the world, one of which is the Diamond Dealers Club in New York. The diamond trade is extremely secretive and security conscious. (I still have my security badge with my photograph on it from my trip to the floor of the club.) Once a grudgingly bestowed membership is gained for the clubs, business is conducted on the principles of trust and credit. The loss of that trust by simply refusing to purchase a stone once accepted can ruin the perpetrator forever in diamond circles.

Purchasers select stones from the cutter with the greatest care. Other features in addition to the cut and proportion that increase the value of a gem are the color, clarity, and carat weight.

Color. Diamonds come in a full range of colors, including red, pink, blue, and yellow, with the highest grade of color for a diamond being the whitest possible, or colorless. As color is detected in a stone, its value decreases as the hue deepens. This is true until the diamond reaches the optimum point—when the shade is so rich that the value rises precipitously. This rare and quite valuable color is termed a "Fancy." Fancy diamonds are in great demand for investment stones as well as for jewelry.

Techniques and systems for color grading of polished diamonds may vary to a significant extent among diamond exchanges and dealers throughout the world, but the determination is becoming increasingly scientific because of the spectrophotometer. This instrument measures the nitrogen content of a stone; more nitrogen means a deeper color. The spectrophotometer is an instrument commonly used in research by industry for measuring absorption and directional reflectance. Specially modified for diamond-color grading, it is used to measure specific wave lengths of reflectance, comparing the diamond to pure barium sulphate powder as a standard of whiteness.

Clarity. The third *C* is clarity. The clarity of a stone is another factor that governs its price. Clarity is defined as the degree of internal perfection, or the degree to which the stone possesses inclusions, or irregularities, which may diffuse or scatter light. Undesirable reflections may be caused by the presence of foreign matter within the stone, surface defects, minute cracks, natural strains in the crystals, or certain other imperfections. The method of quantifying clarity is a point system generally based on the size of the inclusion, its position, and the extent to which it interrupts the optimum passage of light. The terminology established by the Gemological Institute of America is generally used: it runs from FLAWLESS to VERY VERY SLIGHT INCLUSIONS, to VERY SLIGHT INCLUSIONS, to IMPERFECT. For a diamond to be regarded as FLAWLESS, it must be free of external blemishes as well as being clean internally. While FLAWLESS is the top grade for clarity, it is something of a misnomer, for rarely if ever is a stone completely flawless. This grade may possess some modest irregularities that cannot be considered to materially affect the brilliance of the diamond. Figures 5 and 6 in the Appendix show a GIA color-grading scale and a chart of color-grading systems for polished diamonds.

Carat. The fourth factor affecting value is the carat weight. This is a familiar standard, but must not be confused with the "karat" used to describe the fineness of gold. The origin of the carat measurement was the seed from the carob tree. This tiny seed was so uniform in weight and shape that Middle Eastern gem traders used it as a gauge in weighing diamonds. The international standard of the carat weight is .2 grams, while each carat is divided into 100 points. For example, a 3/4 carat stone would weigh exactly 75 points, or 75 percent of the weight of one carat, or .15 grams. In determining carat weight, laboratories use extremely accurate caratronal electronic scales that weigh to one-thousandth part of a carat. This sophisticated equipment is believed essential to proper evaluation, since carat size is a prime factor in assessing the value of the diamond.

Cost

The passage of a stone from the cutter to wholesaler to jewelry manufacturer to jewelry wholesaler to retailer creates a chain of markups that escalates the price to the ordinary buyer. Thus the value of a diamond as an investment is best realized when dealing at the cutter's level. Also, the price spread is not linear or predictable by carat weight. A small stone may have a 200–300 percent spread, whereas a large stone of two or more carats may have no more than a 20 percent spread.

Liquidity

Suppose you need to turn your stones into cash. Liquidity of diamonds falls somewhere between that of gold coins and real estate. They are more liquid than real estate but less liquid than gold coins. Diamonds are a relatively long-term investment and should not be purchased with a speculator's eye for quick, overnight profit. On the other hand, diamonds do represent a tremendous opportunity for concentrated wealth that occupies a minimum amount of space and causes a minimum amount of nervousness when reading the financial page of the newspaper each morning.

Inflation Hedge

Have investment-grade diamonds properly bought offered a hedge against inflation? The answer is yes, over the long term, but in the early 1980s they became overpriced and declined in price, even though the long-term outlook seems to be upward. DeBeers sets the price of diamonds against the world's strongest currency, with an eye on the inflation charts. Since the United States accounts for approximately 55 percent of the world's market for diamonds, the rate of inflation in the United States has been a large factor in the pricing. Worldwide inflation, of course, must also be considered. For example, the rate of inflation of countries with major cutting centers, such as Israel, must be taken into account.

Stable Stores of Value

Fundamental to the long-term dependability of the diamond market has been the power of DeBeers. As stated above, the cartel has controlled up to 85 percent of the world's diamond supply through controlled distribution. The percentage is not fixed, however, and has been known to slip to as low as 60 percent. The continued maintenance of stability is based on the belief by the world's suppliers that the cartel serves the best interest of the industry as a whole.

It is difficult to argue with the success of the past, but it is also impossible to predict who will attempt to break the monopoly in the future. The huge outreach of DeBeers makes it unlikely that its grasp will be loosened in the near future, but challengers will be seeking ways to sell independently. One likely development in the next decade will be more companies attempting a vertical control of their own. In trying to crack the market, they could easily flood it with supplies that would send prices tumbling. Once again, it must be emphasized that any investment has its risk. To succeed, DeBeers must continue to balance the needs of producers against those of major cutters, as well as to convince both groups that continued control is in their best interest as well as possible. On balance, the danger of undercutting the cartel is not sufficiently dire to warrant withdrawal from diamond investing. DeBeers has not gained its position without learning how to maintain that status.

The plan of the company is to extend its influence further into the areas of cutting and marketing. Nevertheless, there will continue to be both smuggling operations and small governments' determined efforts to market diamonds independently. DeBeers expects this. You should also.

The wild card in the scenario is the Soviet Union. Up until now, Russians have worked primarily through the cartel. The fine reputation of the Russian polished diamonds, however, creates the possibility of an independent marketing effort on their part or a price war generated by their unilateral offering of rough stones. The Russian intent in marketing diamonds is unpredictable, but it would seem that stability would be in their best interest, since diamonds constitute a major export for them to buy the foodstuffs they have not been able to produce.

The politics of any of the producing countries could potentially affect the diamond market. Past unrest in South Africa created some apprehension on the part of distributors. It should be remembered in this regard that the DeBeers Central Selling Organization has had extensive experience negotiating with many different regimes. A shift in government would not alter the need for marketing, while temporary disruption of the producing mines could only enhance the value of investment diamonds.

Scarcity

A much more crucial future certainty is the eventual depletion of the world's natural diamond supply. While too much may be made of this, since there is obviously a limit to "the world's supply" of any natural resource, the fact remains that diamond supplies are dwindling. The estimate that without new finds the entire world's supply will be marketed by the year 2000, is one of several estimates that vary between twenty to forty years. All are based on known supplies. There have been recent finds in Australia, but to date the amounts produced have been disappointing.

How to Invest

After learning what you have thus far about diamonds, if you feel they are worthy of some of your investment dollars, there are certain criteria to follow and pitfalls to avoid.

First, deal only with reputable persons or firms. This is the first, primary, and essential criterion for choosing wisely. Unfortunately, the recent upsurge of interest in diamonds has brought the usual pack of charlatans who capitalize on consumer fads and naiveté. The publicized stories of zirconium switches and telephone sales tend to make buyers uneasy. But reputable firms do exist. Care should be taken to get recommendations and to investigate past records. A gemstone should not be bought from a person or firm without strong backing. Also, as a general rule, one should not buy an investment stone from a jeweler. The jeweler is at the end of the escalating price chain within the industry and seldom can give the best prices. In addition, most jewelers do not have access to the quality of stone that would be considered investment grade.

Second, the selection of a stone must be made with care. This does not mean merely looking at the beauty of gems displayed on black velvet. It means, rather, the selection of a stone that maximizes the qualities described above (color, clarity, cut, carat weight, and proportion) in line with the amount of money you have to invest. The best investment is still the Round-Brilliant cut, *H* or better color, with at least 1/2 and hopefully one carat or more in size. Once the parameters of the possible choice have been defined, it will be your pleasure to see a selection of stones within these guidelines and appreciate the beauty of the diamond chosen. This, however, is not completely necessary. More important is the transaction with the trusted broker, mentioned above, and the most important aspect, the certification of the stone by an independent laboratory such as the Gemological Institute of America.

Certification

If you have taken the first precaution (in choice of broker), certification will be an automatic procedure, with the cost probably absorbed by the company. You should be very careful in dealing with any sellers who claim to do their own certification. In addition to the independent certification, many companies offer a period of thirty days or more in which a stone may be returned without question. Within that period, if there is reason to want it, you may get a second certification of the stone, which, of course, should duplicate the first description if both are done properly. A possible trend in diamond security is the use of sealed packages for gems, once certified. While this may seem an ideal solution to the potential of switching stones, it really does not eliminate the possibility, since the seal must be broken in any case if verification is absolute, and packets may be switched as easily as stones.

Certification of a polished diamond is one of the most important developments in the industry. It is of special significance for investment goods, since each diamond has its own "fingerprints" which make it unique. The importance of securing independent certification cannot be overemphasized.

Third, you should plan carefully with your financial planner the percentage of your total assets that should be in hard assets.

Fourth, think of diamonds as a long-term investment, not a short speculative venture. Two years should be minimum time for you to consider holding a stone; much longer is better.

Fifth, in case it should be necessary to liquidate your investment in the future, check beforehand how to resell. Many companies make a resale-on-consignment service available to their diamond customers, although they will not guarantee a repurchase because of the risk of having the sale classified as a security by the SEC. Also, diamond marketing is carried on in the United States through computer listings, brokers, and companies that sell investment stones. Just as you should not purchase your investment diamonds from the typical jeweler, neither should you sell them through that avenue.

Sixth, plan to protect your investment through careful maintenance. Diamonds are the easiest of all hard assets to store and care for. Vaults or safe-deposit boxes are available, and adequate insurance is easy to obtain. Of course, careful records and safekeeping of the certificates are vital. Though it's probably best not to do so, if you choose you can have your diamonds mounted and enjoyed as jewelry. Even though we recommend storage in a safe-deposit box, I daresay the majority of owners will be wearing them on their next visit to our offices.

Colored Gemstones

The advisability of investing in investment-quality colored gemstones is also worthy of your study. These stones are from twenty to forty times rarer than diamonds and are available for from 17 to 50 percent of the price per carat. Some guidelines you should consider are:

1. *Purchase top quality.* Every gemstone occurs in a range of quality. For example, a ruby can be opaque, filled with cracks and inclusions, or can be a relatively undesirable color. As such it can sell for as little as $5–10 per carat. However, the very finest ruby has sold in recent months for as much as $100,000 per carat. Between these extremes there is a very wide range of quality, involving color, clarity, cutting quality, and size. Investment grade, therefore, can be simply defined as that quality grade for a given type of gemstone for which the supply does not meet demand, so that the result is an increase in price. In general, the higher the quality grade, the faster the rise in value in a given period of time. The relationship is not necessarily linear. Historically, the rate of increase in value of the very finest gems has been very much greater than the rise in value of stones just a few grades lower in quality.

2. *Keep up to date on the market.* All gemstones do not increase in value at the same rate. Some types of gems are better known than others and the marketplace and their track record for appreciation are better developed. For example, the supplies of rubies are being depleted at a faster rate than those of emeralds causing the supply-demand equation to yield higher prices and a faster rate of growth for rubies.

3. *Deal with a reputable investment company.* Some types of commodities, such as gold and silver bullion coins (for example, Krugerrands), corporate stocks, bonds, and the like are interchangeable. One Krugerrand is almost identical to any other in terms of appearance, weight, and gold content. Therefore, a verbal description of the commodity is sufficient in its marketing. In the case of most collectibles, however, a standard language that is universally accepted for describing such objects does not exist.

4. *Open market.* Purchase investment gems from firms that operate in an open-market system. A major source of liquidity in the gemstone market is the existence of public auctions. Some major auction houses specialize in the sale of fine gemstones and jewelry; items sold in this manner are listed, and sometimes pictured, in widely disseminated catalogs. The auction house gets a commission from both the buyer and seller, but the sale price of the item is determined by the bidders.

The resale of a gemstone is not much different from the sale of any collectible or tangible commodity. In general, such sales are best carried out through brokers.

5. *Certification.* Purchase investment gems with a certificate from an independent laboratory such as AGL, IGI, and United States Geological Survey.

6. *Cyclical.* Be prepared to hold your stones because appreciation can be cyclical.

If you are considering colored gemstones as an investment possibility, I recommend that you become very familiar with them before making any purchases. The gemstones you will want to become familiar with—and probably in this order—are: ruby, sapphire, emerald, topaz, peridot, tourmaline, spinel, aquamarine, tanzanite, tsavorite, garnet, zircon, and chrysoberyl.

Gemstones have been considered a form of money since the beginning of civilization. Their value is known in all societies. Interest in this form of tangible wealth tends to increase in periods of inflation and global affluence, as is reflected in their increased demand.

No individual or group has control over the supply of any colored gemstone. The marketplace is highly structured, yet exceedingly diffuse. The chain of supply is, in most cases, extremely long. Markups tend to be high all along the chain. No government regulates the supply or price of gemstones—the marketplace is one of the last vestiges of free enterprise.

Do be a knowledgeable entrepreneur if you decide to journey forth.

Collectibles

What are collectibles and should you invest in them? I personally do not, but then I'm not a collector and do not relate particularly to collections. But that doesn't mean that they aren't a viable alternative for you. I would recommend that you approach your collecting as something to be enjoyed. You'll probably do a better job of learning about the subject, and even if you don't make money you will have had some fun.

Collectibles include a broad range of tangible goods that usually have in common some degree of: (1) rarity, (2) scarcity, (3) demand, (4) popularity, (5) craftsmanship, (6) antiquity or age, (7) aesthetic qualities of beauty and taste, (8) absolute or classical value to our society and culture. Collectibles include the serious investments such as rare coins, rare stamps, rare books, antiques (furniture, dolls, and classic antique cars), art (oil paintings, prints and sculpture), and oriental rugs and carpets. On the other hand, collectibles also include the more faddish, perhaps less prudent, and yet irresistable nostalgia items—toys, Mickey Mouse watches, beer cans, gum machines, movie magazines, table radios, old opera records, baseball cards, old cameras and "photographia" parts and photos, stock certificates, tea and tobacco tins, Coke signs, Coke trays, penny arcade machines, coin-operated flip-card peep shows, Beatles albums, memorabilia of singers of the 1950s, old *Life* magazines, "Peanuts" memorabilia, patriotic items, cast iron and tin toys, zeppelin toys, old radio giveaways (Tom Mix, Jack

Armstrong, The Lone Ranger, and the like), movie posters, memorabilia of the moon landing, and the list goes on and on.

Investing vs. Collecting

Of course, collecting for investment purposes is an entirely different game from collecting collectibles merely for the sake of collecting. The latter practice is considered more of an exhilarating hobby, a treasure hunt, and a means to exhibit a display case of proud possessions. Investing in collectibles can be a method by which money is made and can be a calculated and serious business. In fact, investing in collectibles has become so common that some large brokerage houses have established a full gamut of services for the collector-investor who wishes to enter the collectibles marketplace. Experts are available to advise their clients on how to make a prudent investment in a collectible specialty area, how to diversify, and how to make profits in collectibles both in the short term and over the long term.

A number of trust companies that manage the finances of many wealthy individuals now recommend that their clients put some of their funds into art, antiquities, and other tangible holdings in order to protect their funds from inflation and taxes.

A partner of an old and highly respected brokerage firm recently said, "Obviously, investors are more impressed with the return on things that continue to outperform traditional investments." In their last study on comparative yields of tangibles, they reported that Chinese ceramics headed the list with a ten-year compound rate of return of 19.2 percent per year. Next in line were high-grade American stamps, producing 15.4 percent per year; then paintings by old masters, yielding 13 percent per year; as well as nongold U.S. coins, producing 13 percent per year, all for a period of ten years.

The Fascination with Tangible Assets

This increasing interest in investing in collectibles and tangibles can be attributed to several factors: affluence, nostalgia, inflation fears, confiscatory taxes, increased leisure time, disenchantment with other forms of investment, and well-publicized accounts of "soaring" prices of collectibles. Much of the fascination with collectibles appears to be as related to stiff taxes as it is to inflation, for profits on them often elude the tax collector, unlike the gains on securities. The collectible marketplace operates in a free-market atmosphere. There is little or no regulation. There is a free wheeling-dealing atmosphere where markets are cornered to make a sale at a profit and where there is no SEC to interfere.

You will find that dealers in collectibles are similar to stockbrokers, except their credentials are not regulated in the conventional stock brokerage ways. You will find a significant number of excellent dealers, both small and large, who are totally honest. However, you must be cautious, for any area as unregulated as this one will also attract the opposite type of dealer—one who is dishonest, one who may even receive your payment without delivering your purchase to you, or who may sell forgeries and counterfeits as if they were the "real things."

American Quilts—An Example

In 1978, I was invited to the White House for the briefing on the president's proposal for deregulation of natural gas. After the meeting, a friend on the staff took me on a tour of the White House. Behind Vice President Walter Mondale's desk was an American antique quilt made by one of the Amish people.

Collecting these quilts and using them for wall hangings has become quite popular since then. If they hold some appeal to you, you may want to consider them as a collectible. Prices begin around $1,000. Most of them are in the somber colors of black, purple, and dark blue and have geometric designs that look striking in modern interiors. The fine stitching and the sophisticated color schemes are their outstanding features. Incidentally, you will find a deliberate mistake in each of them to illustrate that only God is perfect.

A combination of striking design, color harmony, and fine needlecraft are the characteristics most sought after.

Disadvantages vs. Advantages of Investing in Collectibles

Besides the apparent disadvantage of some "wheeler dealers" in the marketplace, there are other disadvantages and pitfalls you'll want to know about before making a commitment of any kind to this type of investing. Because the positives tend to outweigh the negatives, I'll present the disadvantages first:

1. There is no spot price for collectibles—a collectible has a spread between the bid and ask prices which can run as much as 30 percent per item.

2. There is a sales tax on the collectible item added to its price when you keep it in the state in which you purchased it, and this can turn out to be a sizable amount.

3. The extra money spent on the spread and the sales tax means that the collectible must be bought with the idea of holding it for at least eighteen months to two years, and selling it then only if the market is right.

4. Not all collectibles have kept pace with inflation. Generally speaking, high-grade coins and art and antiques, when professionally selected, have done as well as the very best kinds of investments available, and continue to do so.

5. Prices of collectibles can "skid".

6. The collectible market is fraught with fakes and flawed merchandise. When a collectible starts coming into demand, the forgers may grind out reproductions in massive quantities.

7. Many hundreds of "get-rich-quick" and other spurious investment schemes have occurred in the collectibles market. All are risky, some are rip-offs.

8. Collectibles do not pay interest or dividends. They often entail such costs as insurance and storage. They may be difficult to sell within the timetable you have set.

9. Their profits may be a bit deceptive. For instance, the collector-investor may have bought a Victorian clock for $1,000 and sold it at an auction five years later for $1,500. On first blush, that may seem good. But after paying the auction $300, he only has $1,200 left; so his net gain is only $200, or 4 percent a year. So he didn't win the money game.

The Advantages

None of these disadvantages should necessarily discourage you from becoming better informed about collectibles. They can pay off, both in enjoyment as well as in financial rewards.

1. Collectibles have outperformed many more conventional types of investments.

2. With the lifting of exchange controls in Britain, which enables British individual investors and pension funds to invest abroad, there should continue to be a larger number of potential buyers of American collectibles and antiquities. This should help support prices.

3. The willingness on the part of financial planners, banks, investment firms, brokerage houses, and auction houses to inform and advise their clients makes expert advice much more available to you and to others interested in collectibles as investments.

4. The proliferation of investment syndicates formed by doctors, lawyers, and other professional groups in our country has made it possible for quality items to be bought by many more persons than just the wealthiest tycoons in America.

5. The spectacular mega-exhibits on tour in the United States, such as King Tut, have promoted and publicized antiquities and rarities, and are probably accountable for much of the new popularity in rarified Egyptian art treasures. Other exhibits have had similar good effects on art investments.

6. When you sell your collectibles, your profits, if you have held them for a year, will be taxed at the more favorable capital gains rate. Another tax advantage that may fit your tax planning needs and philanthropic nature is to give your collectibles to a museum or a university. This will entitle you to take deductions of as much as 30 percent of your adjusted gross income for up to five years.

7. Because the tangibles' trading market has not been tapped yet by federal regulation, you have greater freedom. This in itself can be very advantageous by affecting their investment potential.

Guidelines on Investing in Collectibles

1. Purchase only what you wish to specialize in; if it is something you like, all the better, as it will maintain your high level of interest over the next ten years and decades thereafter.

2. Buy the best you can afford, even if you must accept limited quantities at first. If possible, purchase your collectibles from a dealer who will guarantee your purchase price back in the future if you trade in for a higher quality.

3. Confine your purchases to collectibles in excellent condition. These will always enjoy outstanding resale value. Look for quality—to be a fine buy, it should be in mint condition. Find out its rarity and its value, as well as its most recent price; verify its date; and determine how many of such items were made.

4. A collectible of any real value should carry a ticket guaranteeing its origin and, in the case of very fine items, its travels as well.

5. The authenticity of the collectible should be guaranteed against a full cash refund.

6. Read as much literature as you can on the subject. The bimonthly newsletter from Sotheby Parke Bernet is an excellent source of information (write Sotheby Parke Bernet, 980 Madison Avenue, New York, New York 10021).

7. Attend auctions, wander through antique stores, talk to people, and familiarize yourself completely with the area of interest before you buy anything. Study your line of collectibles for quality, art form, and all aspects of its category.

8. Buy only from reputable dealers or reputable auctions.

9. Become attuned to holding your collectibles for long periods of time. You must allow time for the markup to cover the difference between wholesale and retail prices.

10. If you are a novice, purchase and specialize in collectibles of known and proven work with a history of regular price appreciation.

11. Be aware of antique shops with large selections and fancy frames. These angles can lead to overvaluation of the piece itself.

12. Undergo a "comparison-shopping" spree before you actually purchase your item. If you are considering a major purchase, call in a professional appraiser.

13. Be informed and up to date on all prevailing economic and political trends that will influence the collectibles market. A rising stock market can result in extra discretionary income for investors and therefore, a likelihood of surplus funds for items such as antiques. The reverse can have the opposite effect.

14. At auctions, try to spot the dealers in the crowd. Generally they bid inconspicuously, but the auctioneer usually knows them. Look for "quick glances" between the auctioneer and his known customer. It may pay to outbid the dealers. They are planning to pay wholesale prices.

15. Regarding sealed bids, bid what you are ready to pay, and don't expect to get the item at a lower price.

16. When bidding from the floor, start high. Continued bidding from a low level stirs up crowd interest. On the other hand, a high bid can knock competition out of the game before the crowd knows what is happening.

17. Don't be afraid to go to the top for advice, even if you are a small investor. Such establishments as Sotheby's and Christie's of New York have been known for their extreme courtesy to all clients, big and small. (Christie's has started a quarterly newsletter. Write Christie, Manson & Woods, Int'l., 502 Park Avenue, New York, New York 10022, and ask to be put on their mailing list.)

18. Always arrange and investigate trucking arrangements, insurance, storage areas such as bank vaults or safe-deposit boxes, storage fees, pick-up terms, burglar alarms, and other security precautions, before buying the actual items.

19. When choosing the collectible you wish to invest in, apply the old truism, "Follow the smart money." This means that one way to find a shrewd investment is to observe the actions of the wealthy, the sophisticated, and those who have demonstrated beyond question their acquisitive abilities.

Collecting Quality Art

Another area that merits your study and research is collecting art. In this area there tends to be agreement among the experts that those who collect art primarily for profit frequently lose, but that those who collect what they love usually make a substantial profit. You will find that collecting art—paintings, drawings, prints and sculpture—can be a delightful, affordable, and profitable investment. Paintings used to be the classic rich man's collectible, that is, the Mellons, the Fricks, and Guggenheims. Now we Americans are behaving much like these millionaires and much like the Europeans—seeking both pleasure and profit in the investment of art.

The necessary components of a good art investment are: rarity, condition, and historical importance. Taste, which is of course subjective, should also be considered. A beautiful picture by a good artist will usually bring more money over a period of years than a great picture that is ugly by a more important artist.

You will probably find as you study this medium that a good art collector is one who buys with both eyes and his heart. Underlying every collection that turns out to be a lucrative investment is almost always an undeniable urge to enjoy art.

Quality art has not ridden the crest of the tangible wave, but it has been a tide unto itself. Fine art, though it doesn't have the liquidity of a stock, can be sold in the New York City art world in not more than

a month at market value. According to a study made by Salomon Brothers, paintings have shown a steady rise since 1968, when they began their survey of price appreciation of tangibles. The result for quality art for the year ending June 1, 1981, was an appreciation of 22.9 percent.

Collecting and Investing in Antiques

Perhaps you have talent for collecting and a love for antiques. Like other collectibles, they can be fun to own and they can turn into a very good investment over the years. They also have an immediate practical value. You can furnish your home today with reasonably good antiques for less than the cost of high-quality new furniture. The irony is that new furniture will immediately depreciate and lose value, whereas antiques will usually retain and appreciate in value.

Antique shops, shows, and garage sales sometimes offer bargains. But if you are a budding collector, you may be better off spending most of your time at auctions. Auctions have three major advantages: (1) volume and variety, (2) no markups, and (3) usually more affordable prices. It is amazing to many people that auction houses such as Sotheby Parke Bernet advertise that in New York, Paris, and London auctions, 75 percent of their items are sold for under $1,000.

Oriental Rugs

Another area you'll want to consider for both their investment potential and beauty is that of oriental rugs. You can rest assured that oriental rugs have reached the investment category when *The Financial Planner Magazine* devotes a large section with pictures in color to this investment media.

Oriental rugs come from one of the six schools considered oriental: (1) Persian (or Iranian), (2) Caucasian, (3) Turkoman, (4) Turkish, (5) Indian, or (6) Chinese. Valuable handcrafted carpets and rugs are named "oriental" because most of the great craftsmen down through history have operated east of Europe.

Rugs of investment quality are handmade and most are fifty years old. The price of a fine antique rug, with dimensions of four feet by six feet, from Turkey, Persia, or the Caucasus, can range from $2,000 to $10,000 and more. It is important for you to know what types of rugs come from which areas; for example, a Turkish village rug is coarser in weave than a Persian rug.

In appraising an oriental rug, experts take into account the following considerations:

1. Age

2. Condition (how are the edges and fringes, and is there any luster?)

3. Knot count (how many per square inch)

4. Tightness of weave (the tighter the weave the more valuable the rug)

5. Definition of pattern (the more definite a pattern, the more valuable the rug)

6. Singularity (How unique is the rug?)

7. Resale value of the rug (What price will the rug command upon resale or trade-in?)

Generally, the rug's resale value depends upon its overall quality as determined by the above criteria.

Summary

You may want to consider getting some of your assets out of paper and into things, but I advise you to go very slowly when you move toward collectibles.

It takes two to three years of concentrated effort to become even a high-class amateur of any collectible. Even then, you will be competing with the old hands, including the "collectiholics," and as with any "_____holic," reason does not always reign supreme. Perhaps one of the best descriptions of a true collector was made by Jules Fleury-Husson, a Parisian collector in the nineteenth century, when he said:

"Do not occupy yourself with politics; never go to the theater; forbid yourself to open a book; scorn the pleasures of family; always have money in your pocket. This will lead to a full life as a perfect collector!"

Diamonds and colored gemstones can be a viable part of your total portfolio of investments. You will not be able to look up their value daily in the newspaper, but you can subscribe to such monthly publications as *Precioustones Newsletter* for diamonds and Kurt Aren's *Gem Market Report* for colored gemstones. Certified diamonds have recognized value the world over; they are the epitome of portability and concentrated wealth; they can bring the added pleasure of rarity and beauty; they are convenient to store and can be bought in small units of measurable value; they can be a hedge against inflation; and the demand for them is increasing.

Being in the right place at the right time will not be easy, but it will be necessary if you are to profit and win the money game. Gold, diamonds, silver, copper, strategic metals, and other tangible assets can play a part in your battle for financial survival in the 1980s, but agility must be your keystone for their price movements can be swift and treacherous.

Application

1. What investment medium best fits your assets, temperament, and time frame?

2. How do you plan to become more knowledgeable about gold?

3. What plan do you have for obtaining additional information about investment-grade diamonds?

4. If you do decide to make an investment in diamonds, should you store them or wear them?

5. Do any of the areas of collectibles interest you? If so, which one or ones?

6. Next time you are in a large city, go to Sotheby Parke Bernet or Christie's. You'll find it enjoyable and perhaps profitable.

7. Are you adding new furnishings to your home? Should you consider using a few pieces of antiques of investment quality and design?

8. Oriental rugs can add beauty to a room and be an appreciating investment at the same time. Go look at them. Even if you don't invest, it should be a pleasurable experience—and that in itself would be an investment in living.

Chapter 10

Your "Guaranteed" Dollars

It is your responsibility to be a good steward of every dollar that comes your way. A part of each dollar will be invested in today's goods and services and used to feed, clothe, house, transport, provide health care, and entertain your family and yourself. A part of each dollar will be given away, and a major portion of your dollar will be taken away by the IRS if you do not take constructive steps to prevent it. A part of your dollar should be saved and invested for tomorrow's goods and services.

In an earlier chapter, you learned that there are only three things you can do with a dollar—spend, loan, or own. You will always need to have some of your funds in a "loaned" position. How much should this be? There was a time when I taught that you should keep three months' expenses in cash reserves. Now I teach that you should keep as much of your funds in an idle position as it takes to give you peace of mind, for peace of mind is a good investment. Your peace of mind may require that you keep idle a lot of what I call "patting money," money that you can mull over and pat like a security blanket. If that is the case, keep it idle. I'll never disturb your peace of mind. I warn you, however, that

I'll try to educate you to such a point that you won't have any peace of mind if you leave too much of your money idle. Determine your level of peace of mind and place those funds into a "loaned" position, knowing full well that they will be working for someone else and that they are guaranteed to lose some of their value with our present rate of inflation and taxation. In this chapter we'll cover the various ways that you can "loan" money.

Never confuse the two similar words "stability" and "safety." "Stability" is the return of the same number of dollars at a point of time in the future. "Safety" is the return of the same amount of food, clothing, and shelter. You can be stable today and not be safe.

Now let's look at some ways you can lend your dollars and place them in a "stable" position.

Your Banker

A very important consideration in your plan to become financially independent is the selection of the right banker. He can play a vital role in the accomplishment of your plan. Take the time and effort to select and establish a close relationship with one who is knowledgeable and creative and whose bank has sufficient assets to finance any bankable project you may want to undertake. Then open your checking account with him.

Checking Accounts

You will always need one or more checking accounts at a bank to be used for convenience and for ease of record keeping. Keep a sufficient amount on deposit to enable you to write a check whenever you choose. Feeling "poor" is not emotionally satisfying and does not contribute to the necessary psychology of winning that you must have to win the money game.

However, do not keep your balance too large. I remember one lady who came in for counseling who had $159,000 in her checking account. I asked if she had a reason for keeping this amount there and she said, "Well, I've been thinking of taking a little trip." I suppressed the desire to ask her which planet was her desired destination.

NOW Accounts

NOW (negotiated order of withdrawals) accounts are similar to checking accounts and are available through both banks and savings and loan associations. A NOW account is different from a traditional checking account because it pays interest of 5-1/4 percent on the balance in your account. However, most NOW accounts have rather large steep monthly or per-check service charges or require a rather large minimum ($500–3,000) balance in the account or some other savings account at the same institution to waive the service charge.

Although NOW accounts may seem attractive compared with checking accounts that earn no interest, you must consider what they are costing you in terms of opportunity to earn a higher return if you placed the dollars required for your minimum balance in some other investment that may yield a far higher rate of return. Also, the service charges for such accounts (if you don't maintain a minimum balance) may be higher than the rather small amount of interest you will earn.

Passbook Savings Accounts

You may open a passbook savings account in any amount at either a bank or a savings and loan association. Interest is earned from date of deposit to date of withdrawal, or to "dividend" date. The maximum rates are fixed by the Federal Reserve System or the Federal Home Loan Bank Board. These rates (usually slightly higher at savings institutions) have ranged in recent years from 5-1/4 to 5-1/2 percent. Deposits and withdrawals can be made at your discretion. Deposits, in most instances, are federally insured to a maximum of $100,000.

If you have as much as $1,000 in savings I cannot think of anything more obsolete than a passbook savings account today.

Other Ways of "Lending"

When you move from a checking and passbook savings account to other ways of "lending" your funds, you will find a wide array of choices. These are commonly called fixed-income instruments. As evidence of your loan to the borrower, you usually receive securities or instruments that represent contracts to pay back your money at a specified time and at a specified rate. These borrowers may be corporations, the federal government, or financial institutions.

Let's examine some of the fixed-income instruments that may be available to you.

Certificates of Deposit

A certificate of deposit (CD) is a deposit account that is usually opened in a minimum amount of $1,000-5,000 and has a fixed rate of interest that will be paid if the certificate is held until maturity. Certificates of deposit are issued by both savings and loan associations and banks, and the maturities range from fourteen days to any number of years.

Personally, I could never feel comfortable with a long-term certificate of deposit. I think that I would be betting against the following four odds with the possibility of losing on one or all of them:

1. I am betting that I will not need the money for the term of the certificate. If I do need the money, my rate will revert back to the passbook rate and I will be penalized. (You can usually borrow against your certificate of deposit at a minimum of 1 percent of net cost. Also, $100,000 certificates can be negotiable, and if they are written by a large, well-known financial institution, they can be sold in the secondary market.)

2. I am betting that long-term interest rates will not rise above the rate of the certificate during the term of the certificate.

3. I am betting that we will not have inflation.

4. I am betting that my after-tax return will be greater than the rate of inflation.

Let's say you were one of the unfortunate people who took out a four-year 7-1/2 percent certificate of deposit three years ago. If only 7 percent inflation had occurred and your tax bracket was 39 percent, your tragic results would be as follows:

DEPOSIT—$10,000

Income		$750.00
Inflation	- 700	- 52.50
Taxes		- 292.50

$ 9,300 + $405.00 = $9,705.00

First year: $10,000 - 9,705 = $295 negative interest
Fourth year: $295 x 4 years = $1,180 negative interest
Results: $10,000 - $1,180 = $8,820 purchasing power

If inflation were double this amount, your results would be:

PRINCIPAL—$10,000

Income		$750.00
Inflation	- 1,400	-105.00
Taxes		- 292.50

$8,600 + $352.50 = $8,952.50

First year: $10,000 - 8,952.50 = $1,047.50 negative interest
Fourth year: $1,047.50 x 4 years = $4,190 negative interest
Results: $10,000 - $4,190 = $5,810

Should you cash in your certificates of deposit in order to put them into a higher yielding investment? The answer depends on how long you have held your certificates, how close to maturity they are, and how much you will be penalized for early withdrawal as part of your agreement. Before you decide, ask the institution where you have your certificate of deposit what your penalty for early withdrawal would be. With that information, you can calculate how much yield you would need to receive on a new investment to enable you to recover the penalty. If you can do better with your money elsewhere, you should seriously consider cashing in your certificate.

Federal Deposit Insurance Corporation (FDIC)

When you place your funds in a checking or NOW account, they may be withdrawn on demand. In a time account the bank can require a thirty-day notification, although this rule is not in force at present.

The bank can, however, refuse to redeem your certificate of deposit until its maturity date regardless of whether you are willing to accept a penalty for early withdrawal. All national banks are required to be members of the Federal Reserve System. National and state banks purchase membership in the Federal Deposit Insurance Corporation. Your account is insured up to $100,000, but not on demand. If your bank goes into receivership, it may take some time for liquidation or reorganization.

Federal Savings and Loan Insurance Corporation (FSLIC)

If you deposit funds in a passbook savings account with a savings institution that is a member of the FSLIC (be sure to check to see if it is), your account has the same basic guarantees as funds in the banks that are members of the FDIC.

Federal Government Obligations

The federal government offers investors numerous possibilities, including savings bonds, Treasury bills, Treasury notes, Treasury bonds, and various federal agency obligations. All of these (with the exception of some federal agency obligations) are guaranteed by the federal government.

Series EE Bonds. The government obligation with which you are probably most familiar is the Series EE bonds. The bonds are issued on a discount basis, which means you pay less than their face value, and their value gradually increases. The difference between what you paid for and what you receive at maturity or redemption is your interest. If you hold the bonds until maturity, which is five years, you will have earned 9 percent a year compounded semiannually. Taxes on the interest are deferred until you cash them in. The interest is usually exempt from state and local income taxes. You have to hold bonds for six months before you are permitted to redeem them. If you redeem them before five years, you will earn less than 9 percent. If you own some Series EE bonds at present and plan to hold some of them, it will be to your advantage to redeem the ones you bought most recently.

Tax deferral does have value, even though the return is meager when you compare it with other fixed-dollar alternatives.

Tax-free savings for children are also made possible by buying the Series EE bonds in the child's name to build a fund for, say, college costs. (Not that I recommend them as a good way to build funds for college. Never try to make a fixed dollar accomplish a variable-dollar job.) File a return the first year establishing the interest as the child's income. If the amount is small, no tax will be due. Also, no state or local taxes are due on government bond interest.

Treasury Bills. Treasury bills have either three- or six-month maturities. The minimum denomination is $10,000, with $5,000 increments thereafter. Bills are issued in original maturities of thirteen, twenty-six, and fifty-two weeks. The first two are auctioned weekly (on Mondays unless that is a holiday, in which case the preceding Friday is used), while the year bill is auctioned every twenty-eight days. A simple way to purchase them, for a small fee, is through a stockbroker or bank.

Treasury bills are issued weekly on a discount basis, under competitive bidding, with the face amount payable at maturity. The investment return on bills is the difference between the cost and the face amount. Bills may be sold prior to maturity at a competitive market rate, which can result in a yield greater or less than the original acquisition rate. The yield on bills, like other short-term money market instruments, can fluctuate greatly.

Treasury Notes. Notes have a fixed maturity from two to ten years and bear interest payable semiannually at fixed rates. They are available in minimum amounts of $1,000 for longer maturities and $5,000 for shorter maturities. Selected notes are auctioned competitively through the Federal Reserve System on a periodic basis. Buyers can subscribe through a commercial bank or a broker. Yields on notes are determined by the acquisition price. These notes may be sold prior to maturity at the current market rate and may result in a yield greater or less than the original acquisition rate at a long- or short-term capital gain or loss. Yields on Treasury notes generally are lower than their corporate counterparts because of the excellent marketability and credit rating of government securities.

Series HH Bonds. Series HH bonds produce current income, and interest checks are sent every six months. If you were buying this type of bond, you would pay the face amount in denominations of $500, $1,000, $5,000, and $10,000 and they would yield 9 percent if held until maturity.

If you own Series E or EE bonds, you may exchange them for HH bonds and continue your tax deferment on the interest that has been accumulating. You'll owe taxes on the HH bond interest that is paid currently, but the tax on your increase in the original value won't be payable until you cash in the HH bonds.

Treasury Bonds. Treasury bonds have a fixed maturity of over ten years and are the longer counterpart of Treasury notes. Yields on Treasury bonds, because they are of longer maturity, are sometimes higher than on Treasury notes, if we assume a "normal," positively sloped yield curve.

Federal Agency Obligations

Agency obligations are issued by federal authorities such as the Federal National Mortgage Association, the Federal Home Loan Bank, the Government National Mortgage Association, and others. These instruments are varied and are tailored to meet the financing needs of the individual issuing agency. Types of issues are similar to U.S. Treasury bills, notes, and bonds. You can acquire these obligations through investment banking houses and banks. For Fannie Maes, the minimum amount available is $1,000; for all others, it is 5,000. Yields on federal agency obligations in normal market circumstances should be marginally higher than corresponding issues of Treasury debt.

There is another group of securities in this category. They were called "mortgage backed securities guaranteed by the Government National Mortgage Association" when they were first established. Since then, they have received the friendlier nickname "Ginny Mae." Ginny Maes offer a number of special attractions, but one in particular is that they pay a fixed return that is often higher than the return paid on a long-term government bond.

Probably the main reason Ginny Maes aren't better known is that when the certificates first appeared in 1970, the minimum unit that you could buy from most brokers was $100,000. Consequently, the buyers were banks, insurance companies, pension funds, and other institutions. Soon thereafter, the minimum purchase was cut back to $25,000. Since then, at least one brokerage firm has created a unit trust that allows individuals to invest in Ginny Maes for as little as $10,000.

Ginny Mae pass-throughs were hatched during the credit crunch of 1969–1970, when mortgage money was tight. The Government

National Mortgage Association (GNMA), established by an act of Congress, said, in effect, to savings and loan associations, banks, and mortgage bankers, "When you have closed enough mortgages, collect them into a pool; then issue certificates, backed by the mortgages, to raise cash so you can loan out more mortgage money. We'll guarantee the pool, so investors will buy the certificates without worry." The packager of the mortgage pool then "passes through" the mortgage payments he receives to certificate holders.

Why should you buy a Ginny Mae pass-through instead of a corporate bond? Well, it does give you a way of spreading a portion of your money into mortgages without any of the worries of collecting payments, defaults, or bookkeeping. Full payments, on time, are "backed by the full faith and credit of the United States Government," and no corporate bond can make that statement. Bonds can be called back by the issuer, some within five years of issue date, and you would lose the high interest return you were counting on. Ginny Mae certificates usually assure their rates for twelve years.

But perhaps most important, you are buying a mortgage, and the pool sponsor sends you a monthly check. Part of the payment represents interest and part return of your principal. (The principal portion, since it is a return of your capital, is not taxed as income.) Of course, you have to wait until a bond matures before your principal is returned. This feature may be of special value to you if you are retired and need a monthly check. If you do not need to use the earnings for monthly expenses, you can reinvest them. The effect of monthly compounding is a return higher than that of a bond that pays the same return but sends you interest checks only twice a year.

A number of firms make a secondary market in Ginny Maes to avoid liquidity problems. There is the risk, however, that interest rates may go up. Therefore, since a prospective buyer can get a higher return if he buys a new pass-through instead of yours, your certificate will bring a lower figure than you paid for it. If the interest rate goes down, the reverse occurs and your pass-through can probably be sold for more than you paid for it.

Should You Invest in Federal Government Instruments?

Will you win by buying any of these government credit instruments? Analyze the possibilities rationally and then formulate your answer. Inflation, which reduces the purchasing power of your money, has the effect of lessening the repayment of your loan. You would seriously protest if you loaned the government $10,000 and it returned $5,000. That's exactly what will happen to you if the rate of inflation is only

7 percent over a ten-year period. Should you demand that in a free economy interest rates fully reflect the inflation rates?

Beginning with the administration of Franklin D. Roosevelt, our federal policy has been to manipulate interest rates in favor of the borrower—and the federal government, of course, has been chief among the borrowers. If you analyze the relation of interest rates to inflation, you will find that since 1940 the investor in Treasury bills has lost money in all but six years. With long-term government bonds, he has lost in all but three years.

Losses by investors in government securities constitute direct gains for Washington. As the purchasing power of your dollar declines, the government can pay you back in cheaper dollars. Moreover, far from being an innocent party, the Federal Reserve plays the key role in generating inflation as a part of its interest-rate manipulation policies.

Since 1940, the Federal Reserve has acquired billions of government obligations, paying for them with checks drawn on itself, thereby converting paper into primary reserve assets of our banking system. As the assets pass through our banking system, which operates on a fractional reserve basis, they are converted into money and credit.

When you lend money to the government, if the rate you are paid is less than the rate of inflation, you have set yourself up for the confiscation of your property.

Our constitution provides that "no person shall be deprived of life, liberty, or property without due process of law." This constitutional right is being violated when interest rates are manipulated for the benefit of the government.

Municipal Bonds

Municipal bonds are issued by local governments (states, cities, various districts, and political subdivisions). Usually, municipal bonds have lower yields than government bonds because of one special feature: the interest paid on these municipal obligations is exempt from federal income tax and usually from state income tax if the owner of the bond is a taxpayer in the state that issued the bond.

Yields on municipal issues are determined by the current level of interest rates, the credit rating of the issuer, and the tax laws.

Most municipal bonds are issued in serial form, some maturing each year for several years, with maturities as high as thirty years. Interest is normally paid semiannually. Investors tend to buy them as they are issued and hold them until maturity. However, municipals, like other bonds, can be sold prior to maturity in the secondary market at the prevailing market rates.

There has been talk from time to time about Congress eliminating the tax-exempt privilege inherent in municipal bonds. If such a change should be legislated, it should not affect those bonds issued prior to the legislation, and their scarcity could easily enhance their value. Before the onerous Tax Reform Act of 1976, we always assumed that the government would not change the rules after the game had been played. Now retroactive legislation has become a reality and a future threat. However, federal taxation of state and municipal bonds does require an amendment to the Constitution ratified by two-thirds of the states. Heavily indebted states are not likely to look favorably on such an amendment.

Another important feature of municipal bonds has been their relative stability. Next to U.S. government bonds, municipal bonds have been the "safest" of all securities. The New York City and Cleveland fiscal debacles placed a cloud on bonds of cities that do not practice prudent financial policies. Puerto Rican bonds also have received lower ratings in recent years.

Types of Municipal Bonds

There are three main types of municipal bonds.

Full faith and credit bonds of a state or political subdivision of the state have the full taxing power of the issuing local government available to pay both the principal and the interest.

Special tax bonds have a designated tax (gasoline, liquor, cigarettes) specifically pledged to pay the interest and principal.

Revenue bonds are backed by the earnings generated in a particular facility and do not have the taxing power of a local government upon which to draw. Many of those bonds are of a very high quality and are often rated equal to or higher than some bonds backed by taxes.

A limited number of hybrid bonds are also paid from both taxes and revenues. As well, industrial revenue bonds have appeared in recent years. These bonds generally are secured by a corporation that has entered into a lease agreement with a community. The bond issuer is normally a public authority that issues the bonds under its municipal title but receives annual installments sufficient to pay the principal and interest on the bonds from the corporation that is using the facility.

How Bonds Are Rated

If you do purchase municipal bonds, you should learn about the quality ratings assigned to the bond issuers. This knowledge is essential if you are going to purchase the bonds yourself. If you are letting professionals select the bonds for you, this knowledge will still be helpful as you study their portfolios.

Bonds are rated by both Moody's Investor Service and Standard & Poor's on the basis of their relative investment qualities. The following definitions for the major rating of municipal bonds are provided by Standard & Poor's (similar definitions apply to corporate bond ratings):

AAA. Prime or highest-grade obligations, possessing the ultimate degree of protection of principal and interest.

AA. High-grade obligations, differing from AAA issues only to a small degree.

A. Upper-medium grade with considerable investment strength, but not entirely free from adverse effects of changes in economic conditions.

BBB. Medium-grade category bonds on the borderline between definitely sound obligations and those in which the speculative element begins to predominate. These bonds have adequate asset coverage and normally are protected by satisfactory revenues. This category is the lowest that qualifies for commercial bank investment.

BB. Lower-medium grade, possessing only minor investment characteristics.

B. Speculative, with payment of interest not assured under difficult economic conditions.

How To Buy Municipal Bonds

If tax-free income fits your financial plans but you do not have the expertise to select, the time to supervise, or sufficient funds to diversify, you should consider investing in a municipal bond trust fund. These funds are usually sold in units of $1,000, plus accrued interest to settlement date. Most of them contain a well-selected diversified portfolio of municipal bonds selected from the top four categories. They provide a tax-exempt yield, which they will pay to you on a monthly basis. The funds are closed-end and self-liquidating, and usually do not carry a management fee (because they are not managed), though a nominal sales charge of around 3-1/2 percent is charged when they are purchased. Although the sponsors are usually not required to do so, they do make a secondary market in the trusts, hereby giving you liquidity if you should so desire.

The Tax Reform Act of 1976 made it possible for brokers to offer municipal bond funds. These are managed funds that allow additions of smaller amounts of money, a check a month, and the various other conveniences of a regular mutual fund, such as redemption at net asset value, reinvestment of distributions, and the like. The municipal bond trust places bonds in a portfolio where they remain until maturity. The bond funds have professional managers who buy and sell bonds in an attempt to maximize yield and safety.

Municipal Bonds and Tax Equivalents

In evaluating a municipal bond, you will find it helpful to consider what another investment with a taxable yield would have to yield to be equivalent to the tax-free yield on a municipal bond. In the 49 percent tax bracket on a joint return, for example, the tax-free yield at different percentages is equivalent to the following taxable yields:

Tax-free Municipal Bond Yield	Taxable Yield Equivalent (at 49% tax bracket)
5%	9.80%
6	11.76
7	13.73
8	15.69
9	17.65
10	19.61
11	21.57
12	23.52

Appendix Table 16 shows two tax equivalent tables for single and joint returns for 19% to 50% tax brackets and for yields of 7 to 16 percent on municipal bonds.

Should You Invest In Municipal Bonds?

When I am asked that question, my answer is, "It depends on what you are going to do with the money if you do not." If you are planning to put it into a savings account or a certificate of deposit, then the tax-free feature of municipal bonds may provide you with a higher after-tax yield. But you must consider whether you can make other investments with higher yields that will leave you with more keepable income, and not jeopardize your principal if you need it before a certain date. As you will note, you would have to receive a yield of 19.61 percent to match a 10 percent tax-exempt yield in a 49 percent tax bracket. I should warn you that if you are considering borrowing money and you own or are planning to buy municipal bonds, the interest you pay on money borrowed to make investments that pay you tax-free income is not deductible. If your investment in tax-exempt bonds is substantial (more than 2 percent of your portfolio), the IRS may examine all your investments to determine whether there is "sufficient direct relationship" between your other borrowing and your investment in tax-exempt municipal bonds.

I think there is really no such thing as tax-free income. The spread between what you can receive on a taxable instrument and a municipal bond is your tax. You've just paid it in advance. When you have to earn $20,000 in a 50 percent bracket to have $10,000 left after taxes to invest in a municipal bond—and at only 7 percent inflation your purchasing power is reduced to $5,000 in ten years—surely we can find a better investment for you. If inflation is lower, you can fare better; if higher, your loss will be greater.

Corporate Bonds

Another way you can lend your money is through the purchase of corporate bonds. Until recently there have been only two main categories of bonds—straight bonds (or debentures) and conventible bonds. Straight corporate bonds, like most government and municipal bonds, pay semiannual interest to maturity, whereupon you receive the principal amount. Convertible bonds offer one additional feature—they can be exchanged, at any time you wish, for a fixed number of shares of the issuing company's common stock. Therefore, convertibles have dual characteristics of fixed-income securities (like any other bonds) and equity securities that may appreciate (or depreciate) in accordance with the price movement of the company's common stock. If a convertible bond trades at a higher price than it would as a straight bond for the same company, the same maturity, and so on, it is usually considered an equity security rather than a bond.

Corporate bonds are usually sold in minimum amounts of $1,000, although there are some $500 bonds. The yield is subject to the current level of interest rates, the maturity, and the credit standing of the issuer. Because no corporation is considered to be as credit-worthy as the federal government, corporate bonds generally pay a slightly higher return (usually 1/2 percent to 2 percent higher) than comparable government bonds. Obviously, when any two corporations are compared, one will be riskier and therefore will have to pay more to borrow money.

Bonds are issued in registered form with "interest mailed to holder" or in bearer form with coupons to be clipped and mailed to a paying agent through the bearer's bank. Many bonds permit the issuing corporation to redeem them early, usually for a price slightly higher than the maturity value. This call privilege gives the borrower an element of protection, in that he can call in his bonds and issue new ones at a lower interest rate if rates have declined since the time the original bonds were issued. Actually, only bonds trading at a premium over par (indicating that interest yields are now lower than they were at time of issue) are liable to be called. Like other bonds, corporates can be sold prior to maturity at prevailing market rates. Bear in mind, however, that if they have a call privilege, this privilege lies only with the issuer and not with you.

Because bonds represent a fixed stream of income, their market value will fall when the general interest rate rises, and their market value will rise when the interest falls.

Suffice it to say that, although most bonds are issued at par of $1,000 and may sell there or at a premium or discount on the day they are issued and will be redeemed at par on the day of maturity, their market value wanders considerably during the interim. Because the cost of money has risen so sharply since the mid-1960s, the market values of virtually all bonds issued prior to that time have declined to well below their $1,000 face values. This kind of market risk in the bond market is very real and exists regardless of the credit-worthiness of the borrower.

Bond interest rates fluctuate for a number of reasons. Probably chief among them during the past few years has been price inflation and expectations of future inflation. Interest rates rise to compensate the saver for the expected erosion in the purchasing power of the dollar.

Another key factor has been the policy of the Federal Reserve to control the supply of money—increasing and decreasing it in an effort either to stimulate or decelerate the economy or to obtain money at a lower rate. In the short run, an acceleration in the rate of growth of the money supply will produce lower interest rates, but over time it promotes a higher rate of inflation that results in higher interest rates.

Fluctuation of economic activity also influences interest rates. The demand for credit rises as economic activity picks up, and therefore interest rates tend to rise; the demand for credit falls as economic activity slows, and this pushes interest rates down.

Bond Ratings

Moody's and Standard & Poor's rate corporate bonds as well as municipal bonds. Their ratings indicate their opinion of the company's ability to meet its principal and interest payments under adverse economic conditions. Two measures of this ability are the amount by which earnings exceed interest payments over a period of years and the amount of stock equity in a corporation in relation to borrowed funds.

If these rating services rate a bond in one of the top four categories, the bond is considered to be of investment-grade quality. Bonds that merit the top rating have a very low speculative element. By the fifth rating, it is significant. By the seventh, it predominates.

Corporate Bond Funds

If you have limited funds, it will be difficult for you to buy and sell small quantities of bonds because of the spread between "bid" and "asked" prices in these small purchases. It is also difficult to diversify adequately. For this reason, if you are considering investing in bonds, you may want to use professionally managed corporate bond funds. They offer a savings of the time and talent required to judge the merits of individual issues, their ratings, their maturities, and coupon rates, and to determine how much to invest in each issue. They also assist in clipping coupons (it has always sounded like fun, but it's really quite a nuisance), watching for called bonds, safekeeping securities, and year-end accounting.

Bonds give us one of the clearest examples of how inflation creates and destroys wealth. Let's take the example of a AAA-rated American Telephone and Telegraph (AT&T) bond issued in 1946 at par ($1,000) with a rate of 2-5/8 percent, maturing in 1986. True to its promise, AT&T has never missed paying $26.25 annually on this bond and in 1986 it will faithfully pay the owner $1,000. However, if the widow needs her funds today, its market price is only $740.

What happened? Why did the AT&T bonds that were recommended as "prudent" investments by banks and trust companies turn out so dismally? AT&T was not trying to take advantage of anyone. It didn't force investors to buy 2-5/8 percent bonds. The corporation itself didn't realize what a bonanza it would reap. The real reason that the widows were hurt and AT&T was helped was that inflation greatly accelerated, bringing disastrous results to the bondholder.

Inflation transfers wealth from the lender to the borrower. The bondholder is hurt in three ways. He receives less in terms of interest than he could on newly issued securities. Also, when the market value of the bond falls, he suffers a decline in wealth. And when he receives back his principal, his purchasing power is less.

Under the Poor Richard rules of yesteryear, bonds were investment vehicles that you put at the bottom of your safe-deposit box; you clipped their coupons semiannually, and you redeemed them on redemption date. Although not exciting, bonds were fine when prices were stable.

History shows that bonds have been a bad buy even if your investment horizons are relatively short. Periods when inflation has accelerated have lasted longer than periods in which inflation rates have decelerated.

During the 1974 market decline, there developed a tremendous interest in bonds and bond funds paying around 9 percent. A large number of both were placed with investors. Table 10-1 shows the long-term effect that inflation can have on these bond yields even if we return to the 5.2 percent inflation rate that prevailed back in 1974. (Appendix Figure 7 is a chart showing what has happened to the prices of high-grade corporate bonds since 1946.)

Table 10-1. Effect of 5.2% Inflation on
Your Purchasing Power

Number of Years	Annual Dividend	Loss of Purchasing Power (%)	Adjusted Purchasing Power of Dividend	Effective Yield (%)
5	$900	30	$630	6.3
10	900	51	441	4.4
15	900	66	308	3.1
20	900	76	216	2.2
25	900	83	151	1.5

If it were possible to have a "floating" or "self-adjusting" yield based on a 5.2 percent annual rate of inflation, what yield would you need to maintain your purchasing power, based on a beginning yield of 9 percent with a 5.2 percent annual inflation rate over twenty-five years? (See Table 10-2.)

For several years, we have cautioned against buying corporate bonds because we believed interest rates would escalate and push down bond prices. A large life insurance holding company in Houston sold the largest bond mutual fund offering that had ever been made right in

Table 10-2. Percentage Yield Needed to
Maintain Purchasing Power
(5.2% annual inflation)

Number of Years	% Increase in Cost of Living	% Yield Needed to Maintain Purchasing Power
5	43	12.9
10	104	18.4
15	192	26.3
20	317	37.5
25	496	53.6

the middle of the time we were expressing this opinion. We did not sell any of the fund and, of course, missed receiving sizable commissions. However, we could not in good conscience encourage the purchase of bonds at a time when interest rates were about to soar. I know our clients are grateful they missed the disastrous debacle that has occurred in the bond market since that date. Had they invested, they would have suffered a 35 percent loss. In just six weeks, a 20 percent skid occurred.

By 1980 the bond market was in such a shambles that major corporations could not easily float a bond issue, and even if they could, they were reluctant to place long-term bonds on their balance sheets at, say, 16 percent because if rates did go down, these high rates would come back to haunt them. Yet, they didn't like being at the mercy of high, short-term money markets.

They began to look at their assets to see what they could sell or borrow against to produce funds and to create some new types of bonds to fit whatever the investor thought future rates might be. Let's look at three of these new types of bonds:

Original Issue Deep-Discount Bonds (OID). If you are of the "rates will come down" school, and want to take your chances with the bond market, you may want to look at the original issue deep-discount bonds, commonly referred to as OID's. These are sold at between 40 percent and 55 percent of face value and pay very low rates of 6–7 percent, and some pay no interest at all. For example, Martin Marietta sold their $1,000 bonds at $538.35, paying 7 percent on the face value, which gave an effective rate of 13.25 percent to maturity. Pepsico and Penney have placed zero coupon bonds paying no interest. These work like a U.S. Savings Bond that you buy for $37.50 and that matures at $50.00.

Floating-Rate Notes. These bonds carry interest rates that are recalculated at fixed intervals according to the level of some publicly announced rate such as six-month Treasury bills. Manufacturers Hanover Corporation sold these seven-year notes in $1,000 denominations. These notes pay interest monthly, but the rate is adjusted weekly and is tied to one-month AA commercial paper rate.

Adjustable Rate Bonds. These bonds change rates more slowly, usually every two or three years.

If You Own Bonds Now

If you own bonds now, what should you do? I personnally do not own any, nor do I have any plans to buy any. But let's say that in 1970 you bought some bonds carrying a coupon of 8 percent that will mature in the year 1995, and let's say that bonds are currently paying 15 percent. Your broker may suggest a swap to a new 15 percent bond so you can establish your loss for tax purposes and get into a higher-yielding bond. It is true that your capital loss can be charged off dollar for dollar against any capital gains you may have. If you have no capital gains, you may charge off $6,000 of loss against $3,000 of ordinary income, and if you still have losses, carry the losses forward. This is better than not establishing the loss. But should you buy bonds again? If you do, you may have to play the same scenario in the future. You will also miss an opportunity for making up your losses.

Let me suggest another possibility. Invest your funds in a registered limited partnership that is buying multifamily housing for all cash. The one we are using is currently paying 8–10 percent tax-sheltered as opposed to your interest on the bond, which is taxable. Your keepable income will increase, and if appreciation occurs you'll have a chance to make up your loss over the next few years.

What if interest rates go up from here? That means that rents and property values will also probably increase. What if rates go down? The partnership will probably put mortgages on the property and send you your money back on a tax-free basis. You would then own your proportionate part of the property and also have your principal back. When the property is sold, there may very well be enough profit to make up your losses on your original bonds.

Table 10-3. Standard and Poor's High-Grade Corporate Bonds

1972–81	−39%
1971–80	−34%
1970–79	−27%
1969–78	−27%
1968–77	−23%
1967–76	−25%
1966–75	−38%
1965–74	−41%
1964–73	−34%
1963–72	−32%
1962–71	−29%
1961–70	−32%
1960–69	−33%
1959–68	−27%
1958–67	−28%
1957–66	−19%
1956–65	−19%
1955–64	−18%
1954–63	−16%
1953–62	−15%
1952–61	−17%
1951–60	−22%
1950–59	−25%
1949–58	−17%
1948–57	−11%
1947–56	−16%
1946–55	− 8%
1945–54	− 2%
Average of 28 periods	−23%

Source: Johnson's Charts, Inc.—bond interest not included.

Should You Ever Buy Bonds?

You should buy bonds only if you are an agile speculator. They certainly are not an instrument to be bought and thrown into a drawer and forgotten, as you can readily see from Table 10-3, which shows what has happened to bond prices over the last twenty-eight ten-year periods.

Commercial Paper

One very specialized way of lending your dollars is through commercial paper. Corporations finance much of their short-term working capital requirements by issuing commercial paper short-term notes with a fixed maturity of 1 to 270 days. Paper is normally issued in a minimum amount of $25,000 or as small as $10,000, and it can be purchased on either a discount or an interest-bearing basis. The investment return is determined by the current level of short-term interest rates and, therefore, can fluctuate significantly over relatively short periods. The returns on commercial paper historically have been about 1/2 percent below the bank prime lending rate. Paper can be purchased with or without arrangements allowing prepayment of the amount initially invested plus a return at the original investment rate. Without such arrangements, paper can be sold in the short-term market at current rates, the yield being greater or less than the acquisition rate.

Traveler's Checks

How would you like to lend a large, well-known company $2,000 for two months, earn no interest on the loan, and in addition pay the company $40 for the privilege of lending it your money? No? This is what happens every time you buy traveler's checks. If you don't use all your checks, you've extended the loan, as they encourage you to do. My purpose in pointing out these features is not to discourage you from using traveler's checks. I just want you to be constantly aware of the time use of money.

Cash Surrender Value Life Insurance

Many people do not realize it, but when they purchase cash surrender value life insurance, they are really lending their money to the insurance company. They are, in effect, banking with a life insurance company by buying protection that contains a savings program. Of all the ways that you can "lend" money, this is perhaps the least rewarding. Although the policy does indicate earnings of 2-1/2 percent to 3-1/2 percent on the cash reserve, if the policyholder dies, his family receives only the face amount of the policy, not the face amount plus the cash reserves, regardless of the amount of savings in the policy. Many people are under the impression that the face amount plus their "savings account" goes to their beneficiary. Estate planner Norman F. Darcey has published a pamphlet entitled, "To the Great Northern Insurance Company I Bequeath the Cash Value of All My Life Insurance Policies" that makes provocative reading. In a later chapter I will explain in more detail the economics of cash surrender value life insurance and why I consider it to be a poor way of lending your dollars. Let me note here, however, the results of a study made by the Federal Trade Commission regarding the rates of return on whole life policies held for various periods of time. For policies held ten years, the study found the rates were a minus 9 percent to a minus 19 percent; for twenty years, a minus 4 percent to a plus 2 percent; and for over twenty years, 2 percent to 4.5 percent. The average for all policies was between 1 and 2 percent.

Annuities

Annuities are another way some have chosen to save for the future. What about annuities? Should you take the beautiful full-page color ads in your weekly magazines seriously and "invest" in an annuity for your happy golden years?

The best answer to this question can be found by looking at the past advertisements of insurance companies trying to entice you to buy an annuity. Go to your local library and request back issues of *Life* magazine. You might start with the February 1, 1943, issue. There you will find a half-page ad with a bold headline that reads, "$150 a Month as Long as You Live." The familiar logo at the bottom reads, "_____ Mutual Retirement Income Plan Guarantees Your Future." The fine print does not say how much you would need to invest to retire at 60 with $150 per month, but it does hint that the smiling couple in the picture began at age 40, twenty years previous to the time it showed them in happy retirement. Now ask the librarian for the January 16, 1950, issue of *Life.* It also carried an ad by the same company headlined, "How We Retired with $200 a Month." The ad shows another mature, well-dressed couple. There is a sandy beach with waving palm trees in the background. This one also does not mention the amount of investment that they would have had to make over that period of time. The same logo appears, however: "_____ Mutual Retirement Income Plan Guarantees Your Future."

Now ask for the January 1, 1951, issue of *Life.* It carried a picture identical to the January 16, 1950, ad and the same copy, except the headline had been changed to, "How We Retired with $250 a Month." Yes, it had the same guarantee at the bottom. The January 23, 1956, *Life* ran another ad by the same insurance company. This headline read "How a Man of 35 Can Retire at 55 with $300 a Month." This time they did not even bother to change the picture of the smiling, delighted couple. The inflation train continues to run faster and faster, but the ad department seems to be able to keep up by increasing the ante each time.

"Retire on $150 a Month" sounded pretty good, so this dollar figure was commonly used in offering fixed-dollar retirement plans. But the story kept changing. The changes in these figures provide evidence that there is no such thing as a "guaranteed, riskless" way to achieve financial independence.

Have you ever wondered why the annuity ads often show a man fishing? Do you think it's because he wants to eat?

Try to imagine what such an ad would be like today. What if someone today guaranteed that you would receive $1,500 a month when you retired twenty-five years from now? Do you really think that amount is going to be enough a quarter century from now? Will it be enough during the twenty to thirty years after you retire?

Single-Premium Deferred Annuities

Single-premium deferred annuities are a different breed entirely from the old annuity contracts, and they can play a part in your "guaranteed" dollar investment program. Income is accrued to your account tax-deferred. For example, if you invest $10,000 in a single-premium deferred annuity that is earning 10 percent, at the end of a year your account will be $11,000. Until you withdraw the $1,000, no tax is due, and it compounds tax-sheltered.

If you want some of your funds guaranteed and do not want the income from these funds to be taxed currently, you may want to consider a single-premium deferred annuity. It offers:

1. Guaranteed principal.

2. Interest guarantees.

3. Tax deferral.

4. Special tax treatment at retirement if annuitized. (I do not recommend annuitizing.)

5. Tax-free exchange from one custodian to another.

6. No tax is payable until the withdrawals equal the full original investment.

7. Probate, with its publicity, delays, and costs, is avoided, with proceeds being paid to the beneficiary.

Some charge an acquisition fee but make no charge for early withdrawals. Others do not charge an acquisition fee, but if you withdraw more than 6—some allow 10—percent in any one year during the first five years, they charge you a percentage on the amount. Table 10-4 gives the after-tax results you would have received in a 50 percent bracket if you had placed $10,000 in a savings and loan at 13.75

Table 10-4. Hypothetical Examples of $10,000 Accounts
Single-Premium Deferred Annuity

Year	Projected Current Rate* 13.75%	Accumulations Guaranteed Rates**	Non Tax-Favored 13.75% Interest Currently Taxed at 50%	Hidden Cost of Taxes
1	$11,375	$11,375	$10,687	$ 688
2	12,939	12,000	11,422	1,517
3	14,718	12,660	12,207	2,511
4	16,741	13,357	13,046	3,695
5	19,044	14,091	13,943	5,101
6	21,662	14,866	14,902	6,760
7	24,641	15,684	15,927	8,714
8	28,029	16,546	17,021	11,008
9	31,883	17,457	18,192	13,691
10	36,267	18,417	19,442	16,825
11	41,253	19,153	20,779	20,474
12	46,926	19,920	22,208	24,718
13	53,378	20,716	23,735	29,643
14	60,718	21,545	25,366	35,352
15	69,067	22,407	27,110	41,957
20	131,531	27,562	37,802	93,729
25	260,487	33,168	52,711	207,776
30	477,026	40,354	73,499	403,527

*Current rate based on 13.75% guaranteed for 1 year and assumed thereafter.
**Guaranteed rates are based on 13.75% guaranteed for the 1st year. 5.50% guaranteed years 2-10 and 4% guaranteed thereafter. If interest rate is ever reduced below 13.0% during the surrender charge period, surrender charges will be waived for a 90 day period.

percent interest, as compared with having placed $10,000 in a single-premium deferred annuity at 13.75 percent, with interest accumulating without current taxes. At 13.75 percent, at the end of ten years, the difference between your tax-deferred account and your taxed account would be $16,825; in twenty years it would be $93,729, and in thirty years $403,527. If you feel you must have your funds guaranteed for your peace of mind and do not plan to disturb your funds for several years, you may want to consider a deferred annuity.

If you are considering lending your money to an insurance company through a single-premium deferred annuity, you will need to determine which type of investment program the company has and which will best fit your needs.

Some companies pool all their money together. If you choose this type, your interest will fluctuate with the going rates. There is another type that puts your money in pockets of investments—meaning all the money received in a particular period of time is invested in a portfolio and stays invested in that pocket. During times of high interest rates, you can lock in these high rates if you choose this type of account.

If you should decide to use a single-premium annuity, then you should decide whether these are rates you want to lock in. If you decide on the "pocket" approach and rates go up, you'll be sorry. If rates go down, you'll be glad you chose this annuity. Since my crystal ball gets a bit hazy, I leave it up to you to decide.

Should You Ever Annuitize an Annuity?

In my opinion, the answer is no. Once you annuitize an annuity, you are locked in to that monthly amount from that time on, so that if inflation continues and you are dependent on this annuity for your essentials, you will have to lower your standard of living every day for as long as you live. If you must have your money guaranteed for your peace of mind, and you don't want to pay taxes as you go along, then go ahead and use a deferred annuity, but don't annuitize it. You can withdraw your original investment without tax (you put in after-tax dollars), and after you have withdrawn that amount, either borrow against the remainder or withdraw portions of it and pay your tax on the amount you withdraw in the year you withdraw it and let the remainder compound tax-deferred.

Don't accept an annuity if you are retiring from your company, if it can possibly be avoided, for the same reasons I've given above. Petition your company for a lump sum and do an IRA rollover or ten-year forward averaging.

Historic Rates of Return

The rate of return that you will receive by "lending" your dollars through most of the major methods we have discussed will vary with economic conditions. Table 10-5 shows yields on various fixed-income instruments over the past forty-seven years.

Mortgages

In recent years, especially as mortgage interest rates have escalated, many people have been lending their money by carrying part or all of the mortgage when they sell their homes or other real estate. For some people, such "creative financing" has been the only way they could

Table 10-5. Average Annual Yield on Selected Types of Investments, 1930–1981

Year	Savings Accounts in Savings Associations	Time & Savings Deposits in Commercial Banks	United States Government Bonds	Corporate (AAA) Bonds
1930	5.3%	3.9%	3.3%	4.6%
1931	5.1	3.8	3.3	4.6
1932	4.1	3.4	3.7	5.0
1933	3.4	3.4	3.3	4.5
1934	3.5	3.0	3.1	4.0
1935	3.1	2.6	2.8	3.6
1936	3.2	2.0	2.6	3.2
1937	3.5	1.8	2.7	3.3
1938	3.5	1.7	2.6	3.2
1939	3.4	1.6	2.4	3.0
1940	3.3	1.3	2.2	2.8
1941	3.1	1.3	2.0	2.8
1942	3.0	1.1	2.5	2.8
1943	2.9	0.9	2.5	2.7
1944	2.8	0.9	2.5	2.7
1945	2.5	0.8	2.4	2.6
1946	2.2	0.8	2.2	2.5
1947	2.3	0.9	2.2	2.6
1948	2.3	0.9	2.4	2.8
1949	2.4	0.9	2.3	2.7
1950	2.5	0.9	2.3	2.6
1951	2.6	1.1	2.6	2.9
1952	2.7	1.2	2.7	3.0
1953	2.8	1.2	2.9	3.2
1954	2.9	1.3	2.6	2.9
1955	2.9	1.4	2.8	3.1
1956	3.0	1.6	3.1	3.4
1957	3.3	2.1	3.5	3.9
1958	3.38	2.21	3.43	3.79
1959	3.53	2.36	4.07	4.38
1960	3.86	2.56	4.01	4.41
1961	3.90	2.71	3.90	4.35
1962	4.08	3.18	3.95	4.33
1963	4.17	3.31	4.00	4.26
1964	4.19	3.42	4.15	4.40

Table 10-5. *(Continued)*

Year	Savings Accounts in Savings Associations	Time & Savings Deposits in Commercial Banks	United States Government Bonds	Corporate (AAA) Bonds
1965	4.23	3.69	4.21	4.49
1966	4.45	4.04	4.66	5.13
1967	4.67	4.24	4.85	5.51
1968	4.68	4.48	5.25	6.18
1969	4.80	4.87	6.10	7.03
1970	5.06	4.95	6.59	8.04
1971	5.33	4.78	5.74	7.39
1972	5.40	4.65	5.63	7.21
1973	5.55	5.71	6.30	7.44
1974	5.98	6.93	6.99	8.57
1975	6.22	5.90	6.98	8.83
1976	5.25	5.00	6.98	8.01
1977	5.25	5.00	6.98	8.08
1978	5.25	10.00	9.95	9.45
1979	5.25	16.00	13.02	13.00
1980	5.50	16.00	13.80	14.70
1981	5.50	16.50	14.00	14.90

Sources: Federal Home Loan Bank Board; United States Savings and Loan League; National Association of Mutual Savings Banks; Federal Reserve Board; Federal Deposit Insurance Corporation; Moody's Investors Service.

sell their homes. So-called creative financing, as discussed earlier, may be great if you are the borrower, but usually that is not the case if you are the seller. The rates are frozen throughout the life of the mortgage, and the mortgage is a nonliquid instrument except when sold at a considerable discount. If during a period of inflation you carry the mortgage after selling your real estate, your wealth will be transferred to the person who bought your real estate.

If you are selling a piece of property and are convinced that the only way you can get the extra few thousand you desire for your property is to take a second lien for that amount, go ahead and do so. If you collect on the loan, fine. If you do not, don't worry, for you could not have sold it for the full amount you desired anyway. I have done this when selling my home on two occasions and have received payment on both second liens ahead of schedule and for the full amount.

Money Market Mutual Funds

We've looked at the various ways in which you can lend your money and found that although many of them carry some guarantees and can offer stability, many of them offer guaranteed losses because they have a low rate of return after taxes and inflation, or because money market conditions would force you to take a loss if you sold before maturity.

Where should you put funds that you need for cash reserves or while waiting for the right investment? In my opinion, the best place is in money market mutual funds.

I've previously described them, but for a brief review, these are mutual funds that invest only in large-denomination short-term money market instruments issued by the Treasury, government agencies, banks, and corporations. The first money market fund was started in 1972. There are now 111 funds with approximately $200 billion of assets.

For years many Americans had no choice but to accept the small return on savings accounts because of a law known as Regulation Q. The only competition for the saver's funds was in the number of teflon skillets and fuzzy-wuzzy blankets offered for new accounts.

The money market funds have come to the rescue of the small saver who does not have enough money to buy a $10,000 Treasury bill or a $100,000 certificate of deposit, which carry market interest rates.

The money market funds offer four major advantages: higher return, instant liquidity, more safety (in the opinion of many), and more privacy.

How do you open a money market mutual fund account? You can go to your financial planner or stockbroker or call one of the 800 numbers given in the ads on the financial pages of your daily newspaper and ask for a prospectus and application blank. Some will accept as little as $1,000, and all as little as $5,000. There is no charge for depositing or taking out funds, the interest compounds daily, you receive approximately the rate of a million dollar certificate of deposit, you can write a check for $500 or more, and even draw interest until your check is processed.

In my opinion, all of these characteristics make the conventional savings accounts and regular certificates of deposit obsolete.

Money Market Funds Invested in U.S. Government Paper

If you feel the need for added protection, there are money market funds that invest only in U.S. government paper. Your rate will usually be 1/2 to 1 percent lower, but your peace of mind may be well worth it in that your underlying paper is issued by those who print it.

Number of Accounts You Should Have

You will probably need at least two money market mutual fund accounts. One should be used as a depository for the liquid funds you need or the funds you are waiting to invest. You should also have another one that is a part of a family of mutual funds that has an aggressive growth fund that you would like to have some of your funds invested in when the market timing is right. Since a computer cannot determine that you do not want all your funds transferred into the market, you'll need two funds. You may also want to have others for your bookkeeping convenience.

Should You Ever Borrow Money?

Should you ever consider reversing the "lending" process and becoming instead the recipient? Of course you should, if you can put the money to work so that your after-tax cost is less than the amount you will earn on the investment you made with the loan. Never borrow for essentials or luxuries. Borrow money only to invest or to leave in place an investment you already have that is doing a good job for you.

In fact, in these days of high taxes it is difficult to accumulate a large estate without borrowing money. The great financier Bernard Baruch, when asked how he made his fortune, replied, "O.P.M.—other people's money." Another well-known real estate tycoon said the most important factor in his real estate acquisitions was "terms, terms, terms." Terms in real estate purchases usually mean little or no down payment and a big, big mortgage—borrowing from those who want "guarantees" and are willing to lend.

Where, when, and how should you borrow money?

If you have collateral in the form of publicly traded stocks, your least expensive source for loans in normal times will usually be your own bank. You should go to the collateral loan department (never to the consumer loan department unless you lack collateral).

Assume that you want to buy an automobile. You own 100 shares of an excellent stock for which you paid $50 a share, and it is now trading at $100 with excellent growth potential for the future. Why kill the goose that is laying the golden egg, and why realize a $5,000 capital gain, 40 percent of which will be taxable?

Take your stock to your banker and pledge it as collateral. You will be required to leave the stock certificate with him and sign a stock power that allows him to sell the stock and keep the amount you owe to him if you do not repay or renew the loan the day it becomes due.

Collateral loans are usually made for 90 days or 180 days. You may pay on the principal in the interim, but you are not required to do so. On the date the loan becomes due, you will be required to send your banker a check for the interest, and you may pay all or part of the loan or send him a letter requesting that he renew the loan. Usually this will be acceptable to your banker, for banks must lend money to earn a profit. They have already made a credit check on you and found you acceptable.

Sometimes you'll get a rookie loan officer who learned at banking school that borrowers should be reducing their principal periodically. However, after a little discussion with him as to how banks make their profit, he will usually agree to renew your note.

Savings Accounts and Certificates of Deposit as Collateral

I often find that a person I'm counseling proudly tells me he has found an inexpensive source for a loan by pledging his savings account as collateral. If you need funds and you have them in a savings account, go ahead and draw them out, and use them. The savings institution is probably paying you 2 percent less than it is charging you; therefore you are 2 percent in the hole by borrowing your own money.

If your funds are in a certificate of deposit and you are near its maturity date, it may very well pay you to use it for collateral and borrow the money until maturity date. Calculate your cost both ways and choose the one that works to your advantage.

If your certificate of deposit or savings account is at a bank, you can usually borrow 100 percent. If it is in a savings and loan, you can usually borrow 90 percent.

Credit Unions

Many people who belong to credit unions through their employers, think their credit union offers the least expensive way to borrow money. You should not automatically assume that this is so. If you have acceptable collateral, you may be able to borrow at a lower cost from your banker. Whenever you borrow money, always check all possible sources and compare the cost of borrowing.

Always go boldly to borrow money—not with head bowed in an apologetic manner. If your banker had a house to rent and you were considering renting one, in what posture would you go to him? In this instance you have come to do him the "favor" of renting his money so that he can make a profit.

Your banker is always happy to rent you money if you can prove you don't need it. What is your proof that you really don't need it?

Your stock certificate, of course, for you obviously could sell the stock and have the money.

Another reason for borrowing on your stock rather than cashing it in is that you are more likely to repay the bank than yourself. For example, you want to buy an automobile, but you don't have that amount in savings. Make a collateral loan to pay for the auto. Then when you finish paying off the loan, you will have your auto and your stock.

Build up your collateral and you'll always have the wherewithal for borrowing money that you can put to work. You may want to consider, if you have the temperament for it, putting your dollars to work 1 and 7/10 times—since 70 percent is what your banker will usually lend you if you have publicly held stock for collateral.

Interest Deductible

Interest is deductible on your income tax return with certain limitations under the Tax Reform Act of 1976. Assume you borrow at 17 percent and are in the 39 percent tax bracket; your net costs after taxes will be 10.4 percent. If you are in the 50 percent backet, net cost is 8.5 percent. Can you invest this money so that your after-tax return will be greater than your after-tax cost? If so, rent the money. If not, your answer is obvious.

Servicing the Loan

You will need sufficient funds or income to pay your interest on your loan when due. There are some investments that have a high after-tax yield that you can use to service your loan while you are enjoying equity buildup and appreciation.

Borrowing Against Cash Value of an Insurance Policy

Many consider borrowing against insurance policies a low-cost source of loans. In my opinion, the only time you should borrow on your cash surrender value is when your health is so poor that you cannot pass a physical for a new policy. If you can pass a physical and obtain pure protection at a lower cost, do so. When you have the new coverage, redeem the old policy. You will then have the cash you need without paying the insurance company to borrow "your own" money,

If your health is such that you cannot pass a physical, borrow the money out each year from your policy and put it to work advantageously. Let's assume that you can borrow the cash surrender value for 5-1/2 percent. Technically, at the same time, the insurance companies claim to be building cash reserves at 2-1/2 percent. This is only a 3 percent spread. In addition, the interest can be deductible if you send a check for the interest to the insurance company each year.

Summary

Should you ever put your dollars in a "loaned" position? Yes, if you need a temporary place for your investment dollars or when interest rates reach astronomical heights. But, you should rarely do so on a long-term basis. You should use fixed-income instruments when it is to your advantage to be out of equities, but do not complacently overstay.

What is your financial objective? To be able to retire in financial dignity? To have funds for your children's college education? Never send a fixed dollar to do a variable dollar job.

On the other hand, should you ever do the reverse and borrow money? The answer is yes, if your return is greater than your after-tax cost and if you can sell your investment for more than you owe. Always be solvent: that means you own more than you owe.

Application

1. Do you currently have enough "patting" money for peace of mind? If not, how much more do you need? What is the best place to put your "patting" money?

2. Is the Federal Reserve expanding or shrinking the money supply at this time? What is the effect on your investments if the money supply is expanding? Shrinking?

3. Are your cash reserves in a money market mutual fund? What is the current rate on money market funds?

4. If you have certificates of deposit, when do they mature? What penalty would you pay for early withdrawal? Can you find some other investment with a higher yield that will recover your early withdrawal penalty?

5. How does the yield on your "guaranteed" investments compare with the rate of inflation?

6. What is the current value of your collateral? Should you have more? If so, what steps will you take to build it up?

7. Can you borrow money and still have peace of mind?

Chapter 11

Turning Your Tax Liabilities Into Assets

Keeping your hard-earned dollars from taking a one-way trip to Washington is worthy of your most dedicated attention. Few other endeavors will add more to your net worth. The only money you'll ever have for investing and spending is what the government lets you keep. I am absolutely dedicated to helping my clients avoid taxes. I believe it is much better stewardship of money to invest these dollars in housing, energy, food, strategic metals, research and development, medical needs, security, entertainment, and transportation than it is to send them through a wasteful bureaucracy with the hope that some day some of the money may filter back into these areas of great need.

Why pay the IRS money you are allowed to keep? You do have a choice as to whether you pay a small or a large amount of income tax. But you must learn the rules each year and abide by them strictly. You will find them always changing, often contradictory, rarely simple, difficult to understand, and challenging to apply. Winning the money and tax game—and win you must—will require maximum dedication in you and your financial planner, a great amount of knowledge aggressively applied, agility, and constant vigilance. The IRS's job is to thwart your every effort. Tax reduction is the enemy of the IRS—which refers to deductions as "costing" the Treasury.

I've heard it said that "anytime Congress is in session, your money is in jeopardy." Perhaps it could be added that "anytime the IRS is in session, your money is in double jeopardy."

Perhaps you have previously shied away from tax-advantaged investments because you have considered them vaguely immoral. If so, you may be confusing tax evasion with tax avoidance. Tax avoidance is using your intelligence. Tax evasion is illegal and severely punishable. But tax avoidance is not only legal, it is also quite proper.

Congress has enacted laws periodically to encourage the shift of funds from taxable sectors of our economy to areas of public need or good by creating tax-free, tax-sheltered, or tax-deferred investments.

There are those who delight in referring to these incentives as loopholes, implying that Congress is not intelligent enough to design a proper tax bill. They fail to recognize that without the incentive of potential gain, no funds would be risked in areas where money is much needed for the welfare of our citizens.

Judge Learned Hand, the famous New York State jurist, once said:

> Anyone may so arrange his affairs that his taxes shall be as low as possible. He is not bound to choose that pattern which best pays the Treasury. Everyone does it, rich and poor alike, and all do right; for nobody owes any public duty to pay more than the law demands.

Senator Byron P. Harrison of Mississippi, former chairman of the Senate Finance Committee, expressed the matter this way: "There's nothing that says a man has to take a toll bridge across a river when there is a free bridge nearby."

Unfortunately, over the years our tax laws have become so complicated that it now takes a great deal of study to avail yourself of some of their benefits. Jerome Kurtz, formerly a Philadelphia lawyer and later the commissioner of the Internal Revenue, told Congress, "Our existing estate and gift tax system could well be characterized as a government levy on poor advice."

So that you will not suffer any more than is absolutely necessary from this government levy, let's look at some of the legitimate ways you can turn your tax liabilities into potential net worth. One of the first games you must learn to play is the "D.C. Game." I like to think of tax reduction as a game that I must win, because it makes the endeavor less grim, more fun, and often profitable. Even if it is not profitable, I will at least have had the satisfaction of knowing I tried.

The D.C. Game

The tragedy of your paying a dollar in taxes is that you not only lose that dollar, but you also lose what that dollar would earn for you if you were allowed to keep it. It is therefore imperative that you learn to play what I call the D.C. Game. This means that you'll either send your money to Washington D.C., or you'll learn to defer and convert these payments.

Technically, the IRS never forgives a tax, but our tax laws do allow you to defer a tax until a later date. If you've chosen certain investments, perhaps you will also convert ordinary income into capital gains, taxed at a maximum of 20 percent.

You may be tempted to say, "If I'm going to pay the tax someday, why don't I just pay it now and that way I won't have to worry about it in the future?" There are five reasons to always defer a tax:

1. *Inflation.* Every year you postpone paying a tax you not only continue to receive the earnings on that money, but when and if you ever do pay the tax, you can pay it with cheaper dollars for which you have worked fewer hours. If you have $1 of taxable income today in a 40 percent bracket, you lose 40¢ of purchasing or earning power if you pay the tax. But if you can postpone the tax for ten years, and if by some miracle the government does change its printing press mentality and inflation slows to 7.2 percent, you can pay the tax with one-half of the purchasing power that you would have to use if you paid it today.

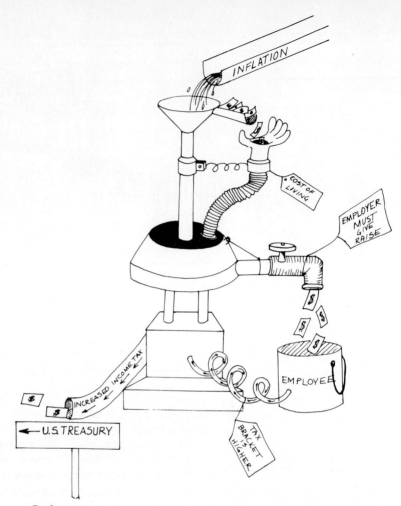

Perhaps you can attain a better grasp of what is happening if you realize that if the printing presses double the amount of money in circulation, the value of your money is cut in half. So when you pay your 40¢ of tax in ten years, it only has the value of 20¢.

2. *Convert to Capital Gains.* Often over this period of time you can convert ordinary income into capital gains. If you can accomplish this you can then reduce your tax liability to 8¢ of purchasing power in ten years—that is, if you quit the money and tax game at that time. You may want to begin the D.C. Game all over and postpone the tax again.

3. *Time Value of Money.* Money has tremendous earning power, so strive to keep it working for you. For example, let's assume you can postpone paying $10 of tax for five years and that you can invest it at 10 percent (and surely we can do better than that). Your results would be as follows:

		Before 50% Tax	*After 50% Tax*
After Year 1	$10 =	$11.00	$10.50
After Year 2	10 =	12.10	11.03
After Year 3	10 =	13.31	11.58
After Year 4	10 =	14.64	12.16
After Year 5	10 =	16.11	12.77
Pay Tax	10 =	6.11	2.77

4. *Declining Tax Rates through 1984.* Not only would you be able to continue to receive return on your money but the tax rate is scheduled to decline through 1984.

5. *Stepped-up Basis.* If your goal is to build an estate for your heirs, on death there is a step-up in your basis and there is a strong possibility that the tax can be completely avoided and it will be a whole new game for your heirs.

So, never bite the bullet until it is absolutely necessary. Put your tax dollars to work as long as you can. At only 7 percent return, in ten years each dollar can gain another 97¢ for you, which would still have a purchasing power of 47¢ even after the erosion of a 7 percent inflation rate.

A Positive Mental Attitude

The first criterion for winning the money and tax game is a positive mental attitude. If you are getting little twinges of doubt right now that you can ever understand our tax laws—do this. Raise your right hand and repeat after me: "I can understand what Venita is going to tell me!" Did you do it? If you didn't, do it now! Of course you can develop the right mental attitude! William James, the great psychologist, said, "The greatest discovery of my generation is that human beings can change their lives by changing their attitudes of mind." Go to work right now on developing a winning mental attitude. Now let's get ready to meet the challenge.

Step One

The first thing you must do is determine what your taxable income will be for the current year. Do this as early in the year as possible so that you can plan your tax and investment strategy in an orderly manner. The quality of tax-advantaged investments is usually much higher in the earlier part of the year than in the later part, and you have time to

investigate and judge the quality of the potential investment without the threat of an immediate deadline, which could force you into a poor decision. Don't find yourself desperately looking for a shelter on December 28.

Taxable Income

Taxable income is the portion that is left after you've made all your permissible deductions. Now that doesn't seem hard to determine, does it? You'll find it a bit more difficult than you think. Perhaps one of the best ways is to take the government tax form itself and fill in the blanks. If all of this is too painful, at least list all the income you anticipate this year on one sheet of paper, and on another sheet list all of your allowable deductions and compute the difference. This will give you an idea of where your problem lies and where we need to start to solve it. Even if you don't take any constructive steps to shelter—and surely you will— the work you've done gathering this information should greatly reduce the number of hours your C.P.A. will bill you for when he prepares your tax return.

Now that you've tallied your income and your deductions and have a figure for your taxable income, look at Table 17 in the Appendix to obtain an indication of your tax bracket and taxes due.

Before the passage of the Economic Recovery Tax Act of 1981 (ERTA) there were two classifications of income: personal service and passive income, which could be further dissected into tax-free, tax-deferred and tax-sheltered income. Passive income was taxed as high as 70 percent. Under the new act, this has been reduced to a maximum of 50 percent. Since the distinction between earned and unearned income has been changed for taxation purposes, we won't need to discuss them, so let's look at tax-free, tax-deferred, and tax-sheltered income.

Tax-Free Income

You can receive tax-free income from municipal bonds, municipal bond funds, and municipal bond trusts. I cover these in another chapter and you should study the tax-equivalent tables. For example, a 10 percent municipal bond equates to a 20 percent pre-tax yield in a 50 percent tax bracket. (Most tax-favored investments that I consider viable produce greater than an after-tax rate of return of 10 percent.)

I'll have to admit, I never buy municipals, even though we make them available to clients who want them, for in my opinion, there is no such thing as tax-free income. The spread between the interest I could receive on a municipal bond and the return I could receive on other investments, I believe is my tax. I would have just paid my tax in advance.

In these inflationary times, the economic viability of having to earn $20,000 in a 50 percent tax bracket in order to have $10,000 left to invest in a municipal bond—which in ten years at only 7 percent inflation would have a purchasing power of $5,000—does not seem to be a promising way to increase true net worth. Do note also what I have to say about the possibility of losing interest deductions if a certain percentage of your portfolio is composed of municipals.

Tax-Deferred Income

In Chapter 10 you were introduced to the single premium tax-deferred annuity. In this type of investment an insurance company guarantees your principal plus a minimum interest rate, and your tax on the interest is deferred until you withdraw the principal. You may withdraw your original investment without tax because after-tax dollars were placed there, so the tax has already been paid. (There may be a penalty imposed by the insurance company on the interest portion for early withdrawal.)

The chief advantage of tax-deferred annuities is that your interest is compounding tax-deferred. Because there is no immediate loss to taxes, you are compounding dollars that would not have been in your account had they been siphoned off by taxes. Again, the tragedy of taxes is not only that you lose the dollars, but you lose the dollars the dollars would earn if they were still in your possession. Also, you have more control over when you can withdraw these funds and pay the tax.

Tax-deferred income is also available through the tax-managed trust funds. These funds usually are invested in high-yield securities that allow income to compound tax-free inside the fund.

In a tax-managed fund dividends and capital gains are not paid to you, but are allowed to compound automatically. When you redeem your shares, they are taxed as long-term capital gains if you have held them for a year. These shares can also fluctuate in value.

Most mutual funds elect to be taxed under the special provisions offered to regulated investment companies. As a result, most funds do not pay corporate taxes on dividends or interest as long as they pass along at least 90 percent of income to their shareholders. In turn, the shareholders pay taxes at their individual rates. Tax-managed funds are operated differently. They have elected corporate tax status and do not plan to distribute realized income and capital gains to shareholders. Since income is not distributed, there is no tax to the shareholders. The funds pay taxes on only 15 percent of dividend income less operating expenses. This is possible because tax law excludes from taxation 85 percent of preferred and common stock dividends paid from one U.S. corporation to another.

You may find that tax-managed funds offer other features that meet your needs. If a regular cash flow is desired, most funds allow for a monthly or quarterly check through a systematic withdrawal plan. Some funds allow for telephone redemptions, which improve liquidity. Social Security (Tax I.D.) numbers are not requested by most funds and no forms are sent to the Internal Revenue Service, because annual income tax reports for the shareholders are not necessary. However, you are responsible for reporting capital gains once shares are redeemed.

Tax-Sheltered Income

You can receive tax-sheltered income from various limited partnership investments and certain individual investments. This type of income, though probably incidental to the reason you made the investment, will most likely become your favorite type of income. The tax is deferred, but you'll remember how important it is to defer a tax and how you can often convert at least a portion of your return into long-term capital gains with the more favorable tax rate. This type of income is discussed in the chapters on energy and real estate. Tax-sheltered income is also treated in this chapter.

Investing Before-Tax Dollars

The main thrust of this chapter is to teach you how to invest some of your before-tax dollars. The tax-sheltered income we've discussed up to now, with the exception of the oil and gas exploration and development drilling programs and the real estate private placements, were obtained by investing after-tax dollars. In a 50 percent bracket, this means that from your last $10,000 of earnings you only had $5,000 left to invest. But the goal of this chapter is to show you ways of using tax-favored investments that will let the IRS bear part or all of the cost. Many of the investments I'll discuss will permit you to invest $10,000 of your $10,000 income and in some instances have more money left than if you had paid the tax.

High Risk

Before I cover deductibility and investing tax dollars, let's discuss risk. You may be saying to me, "But Venita, don't tax-favored investments involve high risk?" My answer to you is, "You'd better believe they do!" As a matter of fact, I will never promise any client that if he makes a tax-favored investment with me he will ever get one penny back. But I am also quick to point out that paying taxes is high risk, too. The return on a tax receipt is zero, and the risk is 100 percent! You may choose. You can invest these funds with me or another financial planner, or you can send them to Washington. All I ever hope to do for any client is attempt to improve his odds.

There are risks. This is the very reason that Congress has provided the tax incentives. They want to encourage you to invest in high-risk areas that provide for the social good of our country.

There are pitfalls in tax-sheltered investments. These consist of economic risks—such as dry holes, cattle deaths, fluctuating markets, unsuccessful research and development projects, lack of sales, and poor management. There is also the risk of being a passive investor. As a limited partner, you cannot participate in the management without losing your limited liability status. This is why it is so important to evaluate management carefully. Because of the risks involved, you should never invest more than you think you are emotionally prepared to lose. You should always analyze the economics of the investment carefully and you should not be tempted by a tax overkill at the price of eventual returns.

You also have tax risks. There are degrees of certainty that deductions will be sustained. Certain areas are probable; others are gray. You also run the risk of changes in the law, and you always face the risk of an audit.

Whose Money Is It?

There was a period when client after prospective client was coming to my office and saying, "My C.P.A. says I'm paying too much in taxes so I should buy some municipal bonds." After a few months of this I decided to conduct a seminar for C.P.A.s and clients about "Whose Money Is It?" I did conduct the seminar and continue to have one every year, and each seminar has been extremely enlightening for those attending. To these seminars I invite specialists in the various tax-favored investment fields to make generic presentations of economic potential and deductibility. (Generic means no investment product is presented.)

At this first seminar I handed out the sheet of paper shown in Figure 11-1. It seemed to help those attending, so I've continued to use

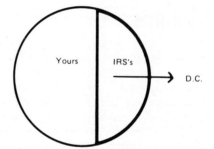

	Deductibility	Approx. 50% Bracket	
		Your Money	IRS's Money
1.	0%	100%	0%
2.	50%	75%	25%
3.	100%	50%	50%
4.	200%	0%	100%
5.	Over 200%	0% + investable funds	100% +

2 Choices:

D.C.—Washington

   or

D.C.—Defer & Convert

Figure 11-1. Whose Money Is It?

it with clients when we are discussing tax-favored investments. Perhaps you will also find it helpful, so here it is.

As you can see from the circle, a portion of your income belongs to the IRS and will be catapulted on its one-way trip if you don't take some action to prevent it. We'll call these your "soft" dollars—the dollars you'll lose to taxes. The ones that are left are your "hard" dollars. (When I was giving this explanation to a very hard-working builder the other day, he protested, "but they are all hard dollars. I've worked so hard for all of them.") Regardless of how hard he worked for them, he would not be permitted to keep those dollars unless he made some tax-favored investments. I find that this concept of hard and soft dollars is a difficult one for clients to comprehend. You must learn to do different things with your soft dollars than you do with your hard dollars. Even after I've carefully explained all this, time and time again a prospective client will tell me, "Oh, I'm a very conservative person who never takes risks, and this sounds like a risky investment." Again, I have to ask them, "How risky is it to send your money to Washington? What rate of return are you expecting from your tax receipt? How much will your tax receipts increase your net worth?" Yes, I know you may have to pay the piper some day, but with time and inflation perhaps you can improve your odds.

Deductibility

Now look again at our diagram and let's discuss deductibility and its effect in a 50 percent tax bracket.

1. *0 Percent Deductible.* All of the investment was made with your money; none of it was IRS's. A good example of this would be a municipal bond or a stock investment.

2. *50 Percent Deductible.* If it's 50 percent deductible, 75 percent is your money, and 25 percent is the IRS's. Good examples of this would be agriculture, marine containers, and certain leasing programs.

3. *100 Percent Deductible.* If its 100 percent deductible, 50 percent is your money, and 50 percent is the IRS's. Good examples of this would be programs of oil and gas drilling, cattle feeding, certain real estate, and so on.

4. *200 Percent Deductible.* In this instance, none of it is your money; all of it is the IRS's. Cable television, mining, research and development, and certain two-tiered real estate programs would be good examples.

5. *Over 200 Percent.* In this investment not only have you not used your money, but you've actually been paid not to do so. Certain mining, video, energy management, medical-related franchises, research and development using recourse financing, and two-tiered real estate in-

vestments entered into early in the year would be examples of this. (Recourse means you are liable.)

Does this give you a better idea of whose money we are talking about?

Progressive Federal Income Tax Rates

You will note from Table 17 in the Appendix that taxes begin at the 12 percent level on your first dollar of taxable income above the "zero bracket amount" and run up to 50 percent. (Zero bracket amount replaced the old standard deduction. It is the amount of taxable income on which no tax is levied, and it is built into the tax tables. This figure is $2,300 for single taxpayers and $3,400 for married individuals filing jointly.)

You reach the 50 percent rate at $41,500 in 1982, $55,300 in 1983, and $81,800 thereafter if you are single, and $85,600 in 1982, $109,400 in 1983, and $162,400 thereafter if you are married and filing a joint return.

We all have some hard dollars and some soft dollars. However, most of the tax-favored investments discussed in this chapter require that some portion of your income be in the 44–50 percent bracket and that you have varying amounts of net worth for investment to be "suitable" in the eyes of the regulatory agencies. I know that if you are in, say, the 40 percent bracket, you don't like paying taxes any more than the person in the 50 percent bracket, but your financial planner's hands will usually be tied by the regulatory agencies, and he'll have to abide by the suitability requirements. But do read on and take hope. We do have some tax-favored investments for the 33 percent bracket investors, and more and more are being added all the time. Qualifications on some are as low as $30,000 of income and $30,000 net worth. With inflation and the tax-bracket creep, you may cross the magic 50 percent mark all too soon.

Deductions and How You Get Them

Most of the people for whom we do tax planning do not understand why or how deductions (write-offs) are allowed against taxable income or against their tax liability. Since this may be true of you also, let's look at some of the characteristics of deductions. These cannot be treated comprehensively in just one chapter, so you'll need to do some in-depth study on your own. I especially recommend that you obtain and read booklets on the Economic Recovery Tax Act of 1981 from your C.P.A., a reputable C.P.A. firm, Prentice-Hall, the Research Institute, or the Commerce Clearing House.

First of all, you need to understand how limited partnerships and, in some respects, subchapter S corporations are treated for tax purposes. The limited partnership investors are treated as individuals, so that all of the tax deductions flow through to the limited partners. The most common sources of these deductions are investment tax credit, depreciation, interest deductions, depletion, royalty and lease payments, and losses due to various causes.

Investment Tax Credit (ITC)

The investment tax credit is a credit against your tax liabilities that is allowed on qualified investments on certain depreciable tangible personal property used in a trade or business or for the production of income in the first year the taxpayer places the property in service. In a 50 percent tax bracket, ITC has twice the value of a write-off. In lower brackets it may be worth three times a write-off. A tax deduction is applied against your gross income and lowers taxable income. An investment tax credit is a credit against the tax itself, so you are allowed to subtract it after you come up with the amount of tax due on your taxable income.

The Economic Recovery Tax Act of 1981 liberalized incentives to encourage investment in both new and used property (with limitations) by establishing new investment credit rules. The new rules apply to property placed in service after 1980.

A 6 percent credit applies to qualified property in the three-year depreciation class; and 10 percent applies to all other qualified property. If you cannot use the credit this year because of lack of taxable income, you may carry it back three years and carry it forward for fifteen years for credits arising in taxable years ending after 1973.

You should become familiar with the various at-risk limitations and recapture provisions.

Energy conservation properties are eligible for an additional 10 percent energy tax credit. Certain expenditures may qualify for both the regular investment tax credit and the energy investment credit if they meet the qualifications for both.

If you dispose of property on which you have taken ITC prior to the close of the recapture period (generally the first full year after the property is placed in service and the succeeding four years, except for three-year property in which the period is reduced by two years), your tax liability will be increased. (Look at the act, for it states exactly what your liability will be.)

Qualified Rehabilitation Expenditures

A new investment credit for qualified rehabilitation expenditures of certain buildings and certified historic structures was added by ERTA. The exact percentages are clearly defined in the act.

Research and Experimentations

A new credit for research expenditures made after June 30, 1981, and prior to January 1, 1986, was made available by the act. Special rules and percentages are presented in detail. Generally, any unused portion of the credit may be carried back three years and forward fifteen years.

Depreciation

If you acquire property for use in your trade or business or for the production of income and the property does not fall within one of the enumerated Accelerated Cost Recovery System (ACRS) classes, you may deduct the entire cost of the property in the year of purchase. However, the cost of machinery, equipment, buildings, or other similar items that do fall within an ACRS class must be deducted over the period of time and in the manner specified by the code and regulations. The amount you deduct each year is called depreciation. You are allowed depreciation on the total cost, even though you may have borrowed part or all of the money to make the investment.

The most important thing you need to know about depreciation is that it is a bookkeeping entry. You do not send anyone a check, though you are permitted to deduct the amount of the allowed depreciation on your income tax return. (Actually, if you are a limited partner, the general partner sends you a K-1 stating your proportionate part of the deduction, and your C.P.A. puts this information on Schedule E of your tax return.)

Depreciation is allowed because buildings, materials, and so on have a limited useful life and must be replaced. Depreciation allows you to set up a reserve to replace the asset.

ERTA attempted to make socially desirable or economic investments more appealing through quicker depreciation or write-offs.

Accelerated Cost Recovery System

ERTA greatly liberalized depreciation schedules by introducing a new system of depreciation called the Accelerated Cost Recovery System (ACRS) effective January 1, 1981. In general, you are allowed to recover your costs on the basis of statutory periods of time that are shorter than the useful life of the asset, or the period for which it is used to produce income. The cost of eligible property is recovered over a three-year, five-year, ten- or fifteen-year period, depending on the classification of the property.

I won't go into further details, for any of the booklets on ERTA will give you the various depreciation schedules that are now allowed. Especially note the provisions regarding real property.

With regard to real estate, our tax laws put it on a pedestal as a favored investment because nonrecourse debt can be used without the disallowance of deductions.

Interest Expense

If you are an investor in a limited partnership, sole proprietorship, or partnership, you may be allowed to deduct your proportionate part of the interest expenses incurred for the investment. Prepaid interest is not deductible. Interest expense occurs any time leverage is used by borrowing funds. (Your deduction for investment interest is limited to your net investment income plus $10,000 if it is not incurred in a business. This limitation may seem grossly unfair to you, as it does to me, since my father didn't set up a multimillion dollar trust from which to receive investment income, as is the case of a particular senator who pushed for this limitation. What about the hard-working entrepreneur who is still trying to make it?)

Let's take a moment to talk about leverage, for the use of leverage generates interest expense and larger depreciation and other deductions per dollar invested.

Leverage

Advantages. Deductions can often be greatly enhanced by the use of borrowed dollars. This is referred to as leverage and is a very important tool in many tax-sheltered investments. Leverage can entitle you to tax deductions in excess of your cash contributions, but you must be "at risk" (except for real estate) meaning you must pay on the due date if the cash flow from the investment has not paid off the indebtedness or if the due date is not extended.

Your basis in your investment determines the amount of deductions that you may take and includes your equity investment, your undistributed revenues, and the proportionate part of any partnership debts for which you are personally liable.

Pitfalls of Leveraging. Repayment of the debt principal creates a call on the shelter's revenue which is not deductible for federal income tax purposes; thus, as the shelter progresses, phantom income is created.

These are dollars you never see because they have gone to repaying funds that were borrowed on your behalf, but they are taxable to you. The taxable income will eventually exceed the cash flow that is available for distribution to you. Despite the high initial deductibility, the excess deductions do not create a permanent tax shelter for you, which leaves only your soft dollars at risk.

Also, you should be aware that the day of reckoning for excess deductions cannot be avoided by making a gift of the property or permitting the loan to be foreclosed. This will be treated as a sale.

This is the reason you should also invest the funds you would have sent to Washington. Do not treat these as spendable, but only as assets to build your net worth and to pay a tax when it becomes due.

Depletion

Certain assets such as timber, oil and gas, and mineral royalties can become depleted. An oil well, for example, will not flow or pump forever. The oil reserves will become depleted. You may qualify for depletion on the basis of the amount of cost or statutory depletion; statutory depletion is generally the higher of the two. This is covered in detail in Chapter 8 on energy.

Losses

Although investment and business losses are almost always deductible, there are certain limitations on the timing if they are capital losses. These limitations are covered in the section "Municipal Bond Swapping" in this chapter. The purpose of investing is rarely to obtain real losses. The tax laws are structured to give you the incentive to invest in areas of need that may show losses at the beginning but that have hopes of gains at a later date. Real losses are to be avoided whenever possible.

Deferral vs. Permanent Shelter

Permanent. Certain forms of tax-sheltered investments generate deductions that are "permanent" in nature. These are: investment tax credit, if the equipment is held for the required time; energy tax credit; research and development credit; and rehabilitation credits.

Deferral. Such items as depreciation, interest, and certain losses defer your taxes, but as we've seen, deferral can be very important. It may permit you to shift to another year and allow you to pay with a cheaper dollar and it may also give you added time to do tax planning. Deferrals reduce your cost basis and when the property is sold, your taxable gain will be based on the difference between your sale price and your adjusted cost. If you are an investor in a partnership, the general partner will provide you with a K-1 form to be used for your tax return and from which you can calculate your cost basis.

Diversification

A vital requirement for any successful investment program you ever undertake should be diversification—the not-all-your-eggs-in-one-basket rule. This rule applies especially to tax-favored investments since most of them are definitely higher risks than investments without tax advantage. It is prudent to spread this risk within the investment area itself as well as among various areas. For example, if you have chosen a general partner who offers a number of oil and gas exploration programs throughout the year, spread your investment throughout several of his programs. Also, spread your tax-favored investments into as wide a variety of industries as is practical.

Spreading your dollars into several offerings allows you to lower your risks and increase your potential for profit. If one tax-favored investment goes sour—and you should go into each of them with the full knowledge that this could and probably will happen sooner or later—don't spend your time crying and moaning and saying, "I'll never try another tax-advantaged investment." You'll really lose if you do that. You're a "big kid," so act like one. You're smart enough to have earned enough money to put you in a higher tax bracket, so do as you've been doing in your business—dust yourself off, and go out and try again. If you do your homework, you'll win most of the time. You know you are going to lose if you capitulate to the IRS.

Most of the tax shelters you will be considering will be structured as limited partnerships, either registered or private placements. Under the limited partnership arrangement, the pooling of funds by a large number of investors provides more funds and thus more diversification. However, the partnership can be structured as a sole proprietorship if the amount of the investment is not too large for one investor.

The advantage of the limited partnership arrangement is that all the tax benefits and revenues flow through the partnership to the individual limited partner. This makes it possible for a person who has investable funds but little or no expertise and who wants to avoid liability beyond his investment to put to work a general partner with expertise who is willing to take liability.

Registered Limited Partnership

In a registered offering, as mentioned earlier, the general partner has gone to considerable expense and time to register the partnership with the Securities and Exchange Commission (SEC), or perhaps if all sales are to be made within one state, only with the state. Even after going to this expense, the partners must also go to each state for clearance. In some states, it may be impossible for citizens living in that state to participate in some excellent investments. Registration allows the general partner to offer the investment through a financial planner or other individuals registered with the National Association of Security Dealers, who are allowed to make public offerings to those who meet the suitability requirements. The offerings are usually quite large and may be for amounts in excess of $100 million. Each unit is usually $500 or $1,000, although some may be as high as $5,000, and the minimum amount of investment is usually from $2,500 (5 units) or $5,000 (10 units) in an individual account and $2,000 (4 units) in an Individual Retirement Account. The offerings are usually open for several months, so you should have ample time to become familiar with an offering, unless you wait until its closing date.

Private Placements

These are limited partnerships that the general partner has not registered with the SEC. From June 10, 1974, to June 1982, these offerings were made under SEC Rule 146, which exempted from registration certain offerings made to thirty-five or fewer "suitable investors." The burden of determining suitability was placed on the general partner and the financial planner.

My interpretation of this rule has been that to be a suitable investor you had to be rich and smart, or be rich and have a smart friend (technically called an "offeree representative"). Because the number of investors was limited to thirty-five (most states did not make you count those who invested $150,000 or more), the size of each unit was often too large for the prospective investor, or the total amount of money to be raised was so small that the whole offering would be placed within a few days and you may not have had time to study its potential in depth.

The SEC has now issued Regulation D to replace Rule 146. The number of permissible investors has been expanded and some of the restrictions removed. You will find more details of this regulation in a later chapter. I am pleased to see some relaxation of the rules in private placements. With the increased scarcity of venture capital, they may prove to be absolutely essential to the maintenance of the free enterprise system in the United States. And I, for one, want to do all I can to maintain it.

In order to solve your tax problem you must have a product. This product must be a business that is "engaged in for profit" to pass the IRS nose test. Large volumes have been written on the various tax-shelter programs available in the marketplace. In this chapter I will cover a few of the ones you are most apt to encounter. The fact that I have not covered a particular shelter does not mean that the one you are offered is not a viable one. Nor does the fact I've covered it relieve you and your financial planner of the responsibility to do your "due diligence," which means try to become as informed as you can.

Real Estate

I must confess that real estate is one of my favorite tax-sheltered investments, and it is also the one most favored by our tax laws. We've already discussed in the real estate chapter the potential for investing your after-tax dollars in registered limited partnerships to produce tax-sheltered cash flow and often excess deductions to save your taxes on your other income. You may want to reread that chapter now to review the various tax advantages that investing in commercial income-producing real estate can offer. Chief among these are the fact that nonrecourse debt can be used without disallowance of deductions. Recourse means that the lending company has a mortgage on the property and must look to the property for obtaining funds rather than having a claim to your assets.

Most of the investment you'll be using for tax-shelter in real estate will be private placement.

You will only have the diversification you do in a public offering because the placement will usually only be one apartment project, rather than the fourteen to fifteen in the public offering, or one shopping center, or one office building.

ERTA Provisions

ERTA has eliminated the use of component depreciation, which was allowed under prior law. This may be a blessing in disguise since the new law eliminates litigation over depreciation methods. Be sure you avoid accelerated depreciation on commercial nonresidential properties because otherwise your gains will be taxed at ordinary income rates on sale. (If the property is held until death, there will be a stepped-up basis.) You can avoid this by using straight-line depreciation over a period of fifteen years. Straight-line depreciation will enable you to get back the depreciation as long-term capital gains with a maximum effective tax rate of 20 percent.

Be sure to read the portion of the offering memorandum that deals with the method of depreciation to determine if it meets your objectives. All depreciation on commercial property is subject to recapture at ordinary rates if ACRS is used. The amount of depreciation in excess of straight-line depreciation is subject to the recapture rules if ACRS is used for residential property. (Subsidized housing has its own set of special rules.)

An Apartment Building Private Offering

Appendix Table 18 is the pro forma page from a particular private placement memorandum for an offering made before the passage of ERTA. Take a moment to study this page. It is a copy of page 89. The 88 pages before this one were for the most part filled with warnings of all the risks in making this investment. This is what is called "full disclosure."

As you will note from the pro forma sheet, you would have invested $6,500, $15,000, $13,000, $12,000, and $10,500, for a total of $57,250 over a five-year period. You'll also note that during a ten-year period it was projected that if you were in a 50 percent bracket, your total benefits from tax savings and cash-sheltered cash flow would be $76,042. At the bottom of the page, three assumptions have been made of possibilities that might occur at the end of ten years: (1) abandonment; (2) selling at the original purchase price; and (3) selling at the general partner's projected market price.

It may be difficult to interpret all the assumptions, but let's look at the bleakest—abandonment, or walking away from the property. At first glance you might think that if you had been an investor in this project and abandonment had occurred, you would have made a serious mistake. But let's examine the situation and see how serious it really would have been.

First of all, you do not receive any sale proceeds. That seems quite discouraging for after all you did invest $57,250. But let's dig a bit deeper. You received benefits each year during those ten years. Let's assume you did what we advise our clients to do and reinvested your tax savings. (You wouldn't have had the money to spend anyway if you had paid your taxes and sent it on that one-way trip.) For simplicity, let's assume you did nothing more creative than place your money into a single-premium deferred annuity at 10 percent. At the end of ten years its value would be $140,299.

On foreclosure you owe the IRS $19,243 in taxes. Incidentally, you won't be able to calculate this from just this one page. If you had the complete memorandum you could. So we now have $140,299 less your tax liability of $19,243, or $121,056—not so bad. In addition, if you invest in another shelter the year of the foreclosure, you may be able to prevent or postpone the $19,243 tax liability.

Also there is no tax to pay on the first $76,042 when you cash in the annuity, because that's a part of your original investment, and only earnings are taxed when withdrawn.

The second assumption made is that the property was sold in ten years and was sold at the exact purchase price—that no appreciation had occurred in ten years. In this instance, after taxes in a 50 percent bracket, you would have sales proceeds of $44,544 and a tax liability of $30,379, for an after-tax benefit of $14,165, plus the $76,043 previous after-tax benefits you had received, for a cumulative after-tax benefit of $91,042. This is for a sale at cost and does not give credit for the value of your tax-sheltered annuity. Even after withdrawing funds to pay for the tax, you would have $140,299 (the value of the annuity), less $30,379 for taxes, or $109,920 plus the $44,544 sales proceeds, or $154,464.

Now let's assume the general partner sold the property at a future market value equal to 3 percent growth in value per year. Your pre-tax sales proceeds would be $87,186. You would have a tax liability in the year of sale (if you do not shelter your gains and are still in a 50 percent bracket) of $41,040. This would give you an after-tax benefit of $46,146 plus your $76,042 previous after-tax benefits, or a cumulative after-tax benefit of $122,188.

In this instance you would have $140,299 from the annuity, less $41,040 taxes on the real estate sale, or $99,259 plus the $87,186 proceeds from the sale of the apartments of $186,445. (You will have some tax on $64,257 of the annuity interest when you withdraw it—but perhaps you won't—or use it for collateral.)

Don't think that the above explanation implies that investing in multifamily housing is riskless. Foreclosure could have come before the ten-year period described above, which would not have given sufficient time for the tax benefits anticipated, nor for the projected cash flow. However, the above is a good example of why you do not want to pay any more taxes any sooner than is absolutely necessary. To repeat what I said at the onset of this chapter, the tragedy of paying taxes is that you not only lose that dollar, but you lose what that dollar would earn if you could keep it.

Recapture

Although *recapture* is a word that sends shivers down the spines of some, it is something that you could live with if it should occur. Let's assume the general partner failed to bring along a property profitably, and a foreclosure occurred in a limited partnership in which you have invested. Let's further assume that you have written off $40,000 on a cash investment of $16,000. You now have a negative cost basis, and upon foreclosure (or sale) this converts to a long-term capital gain. Forty percent of the capital gain would be taxable, or in this instance $9,600. Assuming you are in a 49 percent tax bracket, you would owe $4,900 in taxes, even though you did not receive any cash at the time of foreclosure (or sale). This seems discouraging, doesn't it?

But what is our rule? We don't spend the money that we would have sent to Washington. We invest it so it will be there in the event of just such a reversal.

You should always be aware of the tax consequences of foreclosure, but should not be frightened if you've invested your tax savings; as well, inflation may permit you to pay with a cheaper dollar. The key to any tax-favored investment is whose money you are investing (yours or the IRS's) and what you are doing with your tax savings. I tell my clients that their tax savings belong to me—to invest for them.

Subsidized Housing

I must admit that I've never placed an investor in a subsidized housing program because I have always worried about his not being in a high enough tax bracket for as long a period of time as most programs require. If the investor does not qualify in this respect, he will not reap the maximum tax advantage. Also the potential for capital gains in most programs I've studied is very low because when property is sold the investor can expect to receive only a small amount above the mortgage after twenty to thirty years.

A disturbing factor to me about Section 8 housing is that costs are higher when the government is involved in housing. Average gross rents for Section 8 units are $362 a month compared to $291 for private unsubsidized units. In other words, it would appear that government involvement costs taxpayers $71 a month per apartment unit compared to what the tenant would be able to rent the same apartment for in the private market.

If you are considering a Section 8 offering, be careful to check out the following:

1. Is the developer selling the property to the syndication at a substantial premium?

2. What depreciation schedule is being used?

3. What occupancy rate must the property have to break even? (I've seen those that would require a 98 percent occupancy rate year-round, with the renters paying on time. Unfortunately, many of those renters have no money. That's why the government is taking care of them.)

4. Check out the area. Is it declining or growing?

5. Find out what other Section 8 housing already exists.

6. What are the recapture problems on sale?

If you are a sophisticated investor with a large tax problem and have a battery of sharp advisors and a keen eye for the real estate business, you may be able to profit from a well-structured Section 8 offering designed for the elderly under Section 515 of the Department of Agriculture Farm Home Loan Bank program.

If you don't fit this description, you would probably be happier avoiding subsidized housing.

Renovation of Historic Buildings

Again, I'll have to admit I've never used this type of investment for clients, but I'm willing to look at the numbers.

Although qualifying structures are less plentiful with each passing year, the Economic Recovery Tax Act of 1981 substantially lowers the aftertax cost of rehabilitation of certain older or historic structures. The law allows a 15 percent investment credit for costs of rehabilitating commercial buildings that are thirty to forty years old, a 20 percent credit for buildings that are at least forty years old, and a 25 percent credit for rehabilitating residential or commercial structures that are certified as historic and worthy of preservation by the secretary of the Interior Department. These rules require rehabilitation to be substantial and 75 percent of the existing external walls to be retained.

The credit claimed vests over five years and is claimed in lieu of any regular investment or energy tax credit. Taxpayers claiming the rehabilitation credit must use the straight-line method of depreciation. For other than certified historic structures, the depreciable basis is reduced by the amount of the credit. You may also be entitled to other tax breaks from the city, county, and state.

Oil and Gas Drilling Programs

In Chapter 8 you found information that should help you to determine whether this type of investment dovetails with your tax-planning needs, temperament, and judgment of economic merit so I won't repeat it here. I covered development drilling programs, exploratory programs, combination programs, royalty programs, completion programs, options-to-buy production programs, and income programs. These offerings will be either registered or private placements. The registered programs should allow you to make a smaller investment and should give you more diversification. The private offerings usually require larger minimum investments, but can also be structured to provide larger first-year write-offs using leverage.

What do the 1980s hold for oil and gas exploration programs? I believe the industry will experience a long period of sustained growth. Despite the pressures of inflation; excessive, confusing, counterproductive, and contradictory regulations; political footballing; and punitive tax laws, the oil and gas industry should still be a viable area for your investment consideration. The demand for clean efficient energy is greater than the supply, and this should continue through the decade.

Decontrolled prices must be the cornerstone of our energy policy and we are moving in that direction, but far too slowly. Price is the only common denominator for the millions of daily decisions that we must all make about production and conservation of energy.

In choosing a program for your investment dollars, select one that has a general partner who is well capitalized, has considerable expertise, and has a successful track record. His track record does not guarantee that your program will be successful, but I do like to put my money with people who have a record of being winners. I want the sponsor to have returned at a minimum 100 percent of the investor's cash within four years and 200 percent over ten years. This should add up to a 40 percent per year pretax return. Also, look to see when their leasehold acreage was acquired. If it was before 1979, so much the better. Acreage acquired since then is probably burdened by much higher bonus payments and royalties. The royalty difference can turn a 3:1 well into a 2:1 well. The sponsors should sell the acreage to the partnership for original cost, plus reasonable carrying costs.

Be cautious of "turnkey" drilling where the operator sets a fixed price for drilling the well and agrees to absorb cost overruns. This gives the operator too much latitude for reducing his risks by marking up the cost of drilling.

Early Payout

Do look back at the chapter on energy for a picture of how important it is to receive an early payment from your drilling programs.

Go into programs at the beginning of the year to obtain a larger write-off for the year and give the general partners time for orderly and efficient drilling throughout the year. Drilling rigs and crews may also be more readily obtainable at a lower cost earlier rather than at the end of the year when there are too many out there scrambling for equipment.

Cable Television

Cable television offers considerable potential if the program is structured properly and has top-quality management. Although cable television is a relatively new industry, it has exhibited a consistent growth profile and a remarkable record of stability, and it may offer you a unique investment opportunity. Some analysts project that cable television will be a $20 billion business by 1990.

Traditional cable systems have been in towns that do not have good television reception because of mountainous terrain or long distances from TV stations. A cable system receives TV signals by using a tall tower and distributes the signal throughout the town on a coaxial cable. Subscribers are charged a monthly fee for the service. After the cable system is built in a community, the maintenance and operating expenses are very low in relation to income. The business is generally very predictable and operates much like a utility company.

The capital required to construct or purchase a cable system is substantial, but the investor can leverage his equity investment by using an institutional lender specializing in making first-lien mortgage loans on good cable systems. The collateral on this loan is the cable system itself, and in many cases the personal guarantee of the investor is also required.

The tax shelter is created primarily by the depreciation of the system, the interest on loans, the investment tax credit earned on purchasing the system, and, in the case of a new system, actual operating losses in the first year or two.

A high-quality cable television limited partnership may offer you an investment period of two or three years with an equivalent tax write-off of 200 percent during that period, and with an additional two or three years of tax write-off with no additional investments.

In this same limited partnership, you may look forward to a cash flow starting in the second or third year and continuing throughout the life of the partnership. A total cash return of 200 percent or 250 percent may occur over an eight- to ten-year partnership, in addition to the tax advantages.

One major technological change that has improved the investment's profit potential is the use of satellites and earth receiving stations, which provide additional TV programming. This additional programming attracts more subscribers and so brings in higher monthly revenues.

Some of these programs include uncut movies without commercials, commercial-free entertainment, and sports specials. Because of these Pay-TV channels, cable is proving to be very attractive to residents of larger cities. The demand for cable television is growing in larger metropolitan areas where the housing density and family incomes are higher.

Cable television is regulated by the Federal Communications Commission, and in the past few years there has been a noticeable trend toward deregulation, as there has been in the transportation and trucking industries. Part of this deregulating trend has cleared the way for additional channels via satellite.

One other substantial advantage in these investments is that normal inflation can be expected to inflate the market value of the cable system, therefore offering a potential hedge against inflation, if and when you and the other limited partners choose to sell the system.

Cattle-Feeding Programs

The tax objectives of cattle-feeding can be summarized in two words: tax deferral (postponing a tax liability until a later, more convenient time, or, usually, buying time to figure out a way to avoid the tax altogether). There's no write-off or depreciation on the cattle, but feed costs, interest, and management fees are deductible as they are consumed. Because of the "capital at risk" limitations in the Tax Reform Act of 1976, your deduction will generally be limited to 100 percent or less.

The typical cattle-feeding operation is basically conducted in the following manner. Buyers for the feedlots purchase calves weighing between 400 and 600 pounds. These feeder calves are purchased and placed in feedlot pens of 100 to 200 animals. The feedlot operators feed them a scientifically designed diet in order to maximize their weight gain at the lowest possible cost. In about ten to twelve months, they reach a level referred to as "finished"; they weigh between 900 and 1,100 pounds. Finished cattle are sold quickly at prevailing market prices, since additional feed costs make it uneconomical to hold them after they reach their optimum weight.

The price that the general partner must pay to obtain feeder calves, the cost of feed, and the price of finished fat cattle fluctuate with supply and demand. An investment in only a single feeding program, therefore, could generate a significant profit or a significant loss. This will depend on timing of purchases and sales. Price changes are the main cattle-feeding risk. In recent years, however, many cattle feeders have relied on commodity futures hedging their cattle to lessen the impact of rapid price declines. This is not always an effective hedge.

When the cattle are sold the following year, your net profit—if any, after loan repayment, sponsor's compensation, and operations expenses—is taxed as ordinary income. This allows you to shift taxable income from one year to the next and thereby gives you the flexibility of deferring the tax into a more favorable year. Most of the programs currently being offered are designed to carry over several years in order to allow more flexibility in your tax planning. Almost all cattle-feeding programs employ borrowed funds. If you are a limited partner, your funds are used for the equity purchase of young feeder cattle. The

general partner then borrows additional funds to finance a portion of the cattle purchases, plus the cost of feed for the period.

Cattle feeding is a very cyclical type of investment, but programs that cover several years should give the managers some time to level out some of the peaks and valleys.

Cattle Breeding

Another tax-favored investment you may want to consider is a limited partnership that invests in purebred cattle for breeding purposes. There are two categories of breeders—the purebread breeder and the commercial breeder. The purebred breeder attempts to develop genetically superior breeds of cattle to sell to other purebred breeders or to commercial breeders. The commercial breeder raises unregistered cattle that are intended for slaughter after being grown and fattened.

Purebred breeders concentrate on developing superior seed stock. Champion bulls may sell for ten times more than the average herd sire. The commercial breeder, on the other hand, aims for the greatest number of pounds of acceptable quality beef at the least possible cost to produce.

The purebred programs are the ones usually used in tax shelters and can be just a breeding program or can be combined with a cattle feeding program. Breeding programs can offer you appreciation potential, long-term capital gains, tax deductions, and, if your timing is right, favorable marketing factors.

Tax deductions come from maintenance expenses incurred in connection with building up the breeding herd. These are ordinary expenses and create current tax deductions. The resulting herds of cattle, held for breeding purposes more than two years, are long-term capital assets. The sale of calves from a herd usually results in ordinary income, but the sale of the foundation herd often results in long-term capital gains. When breeding cattle are purchased they are subject to depreciation and investment tax credits. In contrast, when newborn calves are raised through calfhood, many have a zero or near-zero basis for tax purposes; therefore they cannot be depreciated. However, the maintenance expenses incurred in raising such cattle are fully deductible and, of course, convertible into long-term capital gains.

Beef consumption is increasing all over the world because of the increase in population and higher personal incomes. The future outlook is that demand should increase. It is estimated that the United States alone will need to add a million slaughter cattle each year to keep pace with population growth and living standards.

Since 1979, the supply of beef cows has been cut, but what is even more important is that the supply of replacement heifers for beef cattle herds has decreased. This decline means that the future calf crop will decline as old cows leave production and the supply of new heifers becomes inadequate for replacement herds.

Horse Breeding

Another type of tax-favored investment is the breeding of horses—thoroughbreds, quarter horses or trotter and pacer horses for racing, and race horses and Arabian horses for their beauty.

Race Horses

Horse racing is the largest spectator sport in the United States and one of the leading sources of recreation in the entertainment industry. Approximately 95 million Americans go to horse races each year (32 million more than go to baseball games—the second ranking spectator sport). It is larger than the motion picture and record industries on an annual revenue basis. It seems to be truly unaffected by business cycles. In times of prosperity people go to the races because they enjoy themselves there. When economic conditions take a nosedive, people still go in order to forget their worries. The industry is unaffected by price controls and the marketability is enhanced by portability.

Sporting horses have a good record of appreciation. In the Appendix, Figure 8 shows the consumer price index vs. horses. Over the past ten years the average price of thoroughbred yearlings has risen around 15 percent per year. For the period 1976 through 1981, yearling prices in North America increased at a compound rate of 22.2 percent and broodmares at 22.7 percent. In 1981 almost 8,000 thoroughbred yearlings were sold at public auction in the United States at an average price of $35,409—an increase of 19 percent over 1980. The summer "select" sale sold 582 yearlings at an average price in excess of $219,000.

The race itself is only a very small part of the process. It is the culmination of an entire production cycle that is the breeding end of the business. Well-bred colts, fillies, and mares are a highly economic international commodity whose prices have been escalating each year. The chief reason is that in the United States alone there are over 100 race tracks open a total of 7,515 days a year. Last year more than 64,000 horses went to the post over 500,000 times to fill the cards of 68,236 races. England, France, Italy, Germany, Japan, Australia, South Africa, Argentina, Venezuela, Chile, and countries of the Far East also have successful racing programs.

The demand for well-bred horses was further enhanced by ERTA. Under the new tax law, the purchase of (or fractional interest in) a race horse over two years old with good breeding potential lends itself to the following tax treatment:

1. You are allowed a 25 percent depreciation write-off when you place the horse in service during the year; 38 percent depreciation write-off the next year; and 37 percent the next. The rates are subject to certain short taxable year rules.

2. If you start breeding a race horse that is over two years old before the three-year depreciation period is up, you do not have to change to the five-year depreciation period.

3. The capital gains rate has been reduced to 20 percent. If horses are held for at least twenty-four months, some portion of the sales proceeds can be treated as long-term capital gains, except for sales of offspring that will produce ordinary income unless they also are held for twenty-four months and are used for either racing or breeding purposes that will again result in capital gains. Breeding horses over twelve years old when placed in service are also included in the three-year class for depreciation. The younger ones can be depreciated over five years. A two-year-old race horse can be depreciated in three years.

The first-year depreciation rate applies regardless of when you place your horse into service during the first year, be it January or December (unless you have a short tax year). Salvage value is completely eliminated from any computation of depreciation and you are allowed to depreciate them to zero.

Additional incentives are the residual income provided through the state aid programs to thoroughbred breeders. California, Florida, Louisiana, New Jersey, and New York have state-wide organized programs. It is estimated that over $8,000,000 will be available each year to breeders of horses racing in New York State.

Owning race horses was once only for the very rich and was called the "sport of kings." Today, through limited partnerships, the units can be small enough so that even if you only have a small amount to invest you can participate in the fun while enjoying some good tax shelter. (Or you can buy an individual horse and keep it on a farm where there are experts to breed, raise, and race your horse.)

You should select a partnership that is managed by a general partner with a proven record in racing, breeding, and training. The partnership should have the facilities and personnel necessary to breed and raise a foal from a weanling to a yearling or two-year-old.

Racing is a sport, but breeding is the business. Generally, the first two years of an operation are unprofitable. Profits start in the third year when the broodmares drop their foals. Well-bred mares should produce good weanlings, and good weanlings offer the possibility of financial success.

Racing is the other facet of the partnership activities. A winning filly can be worth millions on retirement as a broodmare. The same is true of a winning colt.

Arabian Horses

Investing in Egyptian and Polish Arabian Horses can also provide you with tax advantages and an opportunity to build real capital growth. Owning Arabian horses was once only for the very rich, but, again, through limited partnerships the units can be small enough so that even if you only have a small amount to invest and are only in the 44 percent bracket, you can participate in the fun and at the same time enjoy tax advantages.

As in the case of race horses, you should select a partnership that is managed by a general partner with a proven record in breeding and training. The partnership would have the facilities and personnel necessary to breed and raise a foal from a weanling to a yearling or two-year-old. Here, too, the business requires careful planning, diligent effort, and intelligence.

Generally, the profits start in the third year, as for race horses. The breeding rights for a stallion can be a tidy sum. The breeding rights for Seattle Slew, a thoroughbred, currently run $200,000, and last year I attended a quarter horse sale where the lifetime breeding rights for one stallion syndication brought $30 million.

Because of the complexities of the industry, it can offer an opportunity for substantial risks as well as large rewards.

Most tax shelters are rather boring and you don't get to participate, but this one can be great fun, especially if you can visit the horse farm or go to the races with the hope of seeing your colors pass the finish line first!

Equipment Leasing

Equipment leasing is another area with which you will want to become familiar. You may want to consider becoming a direct purchaser or acquiring an indirect ownership of equipment by investing in a registered limited partnershiip or in a private placement.

Your potential benefits come from tax savings, cash flow and ending value. Tax benefits come through investment tax credits, depreciation of the equipment, and interest deductions on loans. Gains can come from rental payments during the term of the lease. In addition, you may receive residual values when the equipment is sold.

A registered partnership can provide you with the opportunity to pool your capital with a large number of investors. Such a partnership would be able to purchase more equipment than you would be able to acquire on your own. Of course, the number of different purchases that the partnership could make would depend on the funds available to it from the offering.

In the early years it is possible that depreciation may generate tax losses for you in excess of your tax-sheltered distributions. These may be used to offset other taxable income that could defer some tax liability into the future.

Many partnerships have little or no cash flow during the first three years, if they are highly leveraged. If little or no leverage is used, cash flow occurs earlier.

This type of investment is mainly a deferral and should allow you to move some of your income and tax problems from a year of high tax liability to one that is not as high, perhaps after retirement, or this investment may buy you time to carry out additional tax planning. It does not give you the added time-use of money. The investment tax credit, however, is not a deferral; it is a credit against your taxes, and thereby reduces the taxes you pay in the year of purchase. Equipment leasing can offer a dual advantage—tax deferral and tax elimination.

You'll want to check thoroughly the quality of the equipment, the creditworthiness of the lessee, and the possibility of sudden obsolescence. The most promising opportunities for good equipment leases will be in periods of tight and expensive money.

There are three parties to a lease transaction:

1. The *manufacturer* or seller of the equipment

2. The *user* of the equipment

3. The *lease company* or an *investor group* acting as the lease company

All three parties benefit from a lease transaction: the manufacturer or seller is able to make a sale—as a cash transaction; the user puts the equipment to work in his business—sometimes at a better cost to him than available through other financing sources; and the lease company or pool of investors receives some major tax saving and a return on their money.

A registered limited partnership we have used for several years has had a consistently good performance largely because of excellent management, which is a vital part of any leasing partnership. The partnership selects the portfolio of equipment and evaluates the creditworthiness of the users (lessees). Balance is necessary for the added safety of diversification because different types of equipment have different useful lives and tax benefits. The portfolio of equipment might include corporate jets, copy equipment, race cars, oil rigs, over-the-road trailers, and the like. The lessees would usually be one of the Fortune 500 companies or companies that have comparable credit-worthiness. The management is responsible for seeing that the equipment is maintained and that all the rental payments are made on time.

Appendix Table 19 shows typical composite pro formas for a $10,000 investment. The assumption here is that another $10,000 is borrowed from the bank so that $20,000 of equipment is purchased. In the first hypothetical case, it is assumed that the investor is in a 50 percent tax bracket; in the second, that he is in a 30 percent bracket. As you will note, the numbers work very satisfactorily for the lower bracket client.

I have used this type of shelter for clients who are planning to retire in a few years. This gives them write-offs in the early years when they are still working and lets them receive the cash flow when they are not. Remember that equipment leasing is basically a deferral technique.

Marine Containers. One registered offering of interest leases marine containers. These are large boxes with a lockable and sealable opening at one end designed to international standards for the efficient carriage and handling of cargo. The containers are built primarily of steel and come in lengths of 20 and 40 feet. (Statistics are cited in 20-foot equivalent units or TEUs, wherein one 40-foot container is equal to two 20-foot containers.) They are manufactured in industrialized countries throughout the world.

Owing to standardization, containers are intermodal. That means they are compatible with equipment used in the shipment of goods by rail, sea, or highway. The substantial investment in transportation equipment used to accommodate today's standard containers lowers the risk of their becoming obsolete.

There has been tremendous growth in world container fleets because the containers eliminate repetitious cargo handling, reduce handling costs, virtually eliminate theft and pilferage, and reduce cargo transit time. The market outlook for containerized cargo should expand for a number of reasons: only half of the cargo that could be shipped this way is now carried in containers; the inland use of containers is increasing; world trade is expanding; growth in developing areas such as South America, the Middle East, and West Africa is expected to be explosive; and first-generation containers manufactured in the mid-1960s will be phased out and replaced during the next few years.

Standard marine cargo containers lend themselves particularly well to the limited partnership concept for several reasons: they can provide a stream of cash income rentals, and tax benefits can include excess write-offs through accelerated depreciation, interest deductions, and investment tax credit. If you do not need taxable income after depreciation and interest deductions are exhausted (usually after five years on containers), you may be able to avoid such income by gifting your limited partnership interest to your children or others in lower tax brackets. Marine containers are not subject to technological obsolescence and can benefit from increased rental rates and a high residual value, thereby offering the potential for an inflation hedge.

ERTA allows full accelerated depreciation in five years and a 10 percent investment tax credit (ITC) on most containers if the partnership meets certain requirements.

For example, let's assume you invested $10,000 in a typical container-leasing partnership. The partnership would probably borrow an additional $4,600. This would buy five and a half 20-foot containers. If the average daily rental rate was $1.75, if operating expenses and management fees totaled $.55, and debt service was $.45, this would provide $1,500 per year to the limited partner, or a 15 percent before-tax cash flow during the first eight years, assuming there were no increases in rental rates. When the debt is paid off after eight years, the cash flow should increase to $2,000 per year, or 20 percent per year.

Table 20 in the Appendix shows a hypothetical example of how a dollar invested in a container-leasing partnership could return 15¢ per year during the debt repayment period, and 20¢ per year after the debt is repaid.

If you assume a 5 percent annual increase in rental rates (as well as operating expenses), the distribution could be as high as $3,000 per year, or 30 percent by the tenth year. The cash flow would be fully sheltered for the first four years and partially sheltered for the next three years. In addition, an excess write-off between 30 and 50 percent should be available in the first two years of the investment owing to accelerated depreciation and ITC.

At present, used containers built in the 1960s and retired from marine service today are selling for about their original cost. If this trend continues, a significant part of the original investment should be returned when the containers are sold as stationary storage units in twelve to fifteen years.

If the partnership performs as planned—and there is never any guarantee that it will—you should recover your original investment in about six years, obtain attractive income and tax advantages, and provide an inflation hedge.

Computers. The numerous private placement programs available on computer equipment provide excellent income tax deferral benefits in combination with varying degrees of residual value risk of the equipment. Because of the dynamics of the new technology and ever-improving manufacturing techniques, consider those programs that minimize the amount of residual value needed to yield a good economic investment. Those that require material residual value have higher risk. You will find offerings that are structured for an individual and for limited partnerships.

Movies

Public funding of motion pictures is becoming increasingly popular in the present shift away from straight studio financing. Economically structured programs offering benefits from deductions (including depreciation and investment tax credit), distributions from box office, as well as ancillary markets and residual value are available.

Many first-rate producers in Hollywood are today looking for sources of financing outside the studio system. Not only do they desire to retain some creative control over their projects, but they also would like to eliminate that 25 to 30 percent overhead factor built into studio financing. A registered limited partnership that we recommend to our clients has put a 5 percent ceiling on such overhead charges and has contracts with two of Hollywood's finest independent producers to provide the creative expertise for the motion pictures produced by the partnership.

Interest in this industry is being spurred by the new technological revolution that has become the current battleground in the entertainment industry. No longer does the U.S. box office account for 90 percent of revenue to be derived from a motion picture. That percentage is now under 50 percent. Rapidly expanding ancillary markets are more than ever providing a hedge against downside risk.

Of these, network television still generates the most revenue in license fees to the film's owner. Even mediocre movies can command $2.5 million in license fees. Presales calculated on the basis of a major identifiable star in the cast may earn $10 million before the movie is produced. Network TV is now competing more than ever before with the other ancillary markets (cable and pay TV, satellite transmissions, videocassette, and videodisc).

Cable TV now reaches 29.8 percent of U.S. homes and the number of cable households is expected to more than double by 1990. As viewership increases, more money will be available to spend on programming, and as competition increases, bidding for feature films will be driven upward.

The foreign market is an important part of the profit potential, for foreign audiences account for 39 percent of total worldwide rentals, and motion pictures are being put together for their "global appeal." In fact, movies made expressly for television are also finding lucrative foreign box office appeal.

A public partnership that engages in both production and distribution of motion pictures has numerous benefits. It can provide diversification by financing the production of, say, five major, first-run feature films and also can finance the U.S. distribution of up to twenty other completed films.

On the production side, assuming a pool of films exists, the limited partner minimizes his risk through diversification, and owns all revenue rights (network and cable TV, pay TV, syndication, foreign, video, novelization, sound track and nontheatrical). Deductions and investment tax credit can also be taken. The income forecasting method of depreciation allows a greater proportion to be claimed in the first few years of a movie's release. The IRS-recognized ITC formula of 6-2/3 percent (instead of 10 percent) indicates there is no possibility of recapture somewhere down the line if the film's economic life is less than five years. ITC is allowed for a motion picture in the year it is copyrighted. In a pool of several movies, ITC will probably be collected over a two,- to three-year period. In addition, each film has residual value.

On the distribution side, expenditures for prints and advertising can be deducted in the first year. These expenditures are first recouped when a film is released, which could occur within a few months of investment. Quarterly distributions based on theatrical (box office) release of each film the partnership owns usually start coming back within 60 to 120 days of a film's release.

Risk can be further minimized through a lengthy agreement with successful and respected producers.

The joint venture they enter provides for a pool of four to five feature films. Further, before the partnership commits itself to financing a production, it must have written assurance from the producers on one of the following: (1) an agreement with a major distributor for domestic distribution; (2) a presale to some ancillary market covering 40 percent of the budget; or (3) a nonrefundable guarantee from a foreign distributor equal to 40 percent of the budget. The prerequisites further minimize the downside risk to the investor.

The sharing arrangement used by this public offering is: 97 percent to the limited partners and 3 percent to the general partners until the investors recoup their initial investment. However, 2 percent of the general partner's share will be deferred until the limited partners have recouped 100 percent. The ratio will then change to 82 percent to the limited partners and 18 percent to the general partners until 150 percent of their investment has been recouped; then the proceeds will be shared 72 percent to the limited partners and 28 percent to the general partners.

To summarize, we think this partnership offers an entertainment package with limited downside (through ancillary presales) and substantial upside potential (investors own all revenue rights). The economic benefits include deductions, tax-sheltered cash flow, and residual value.

In Appendix Table 21 you will find what we project could be the results using a $10,000 investment in a 40 percent bracket.

If you are planning to retire shortly or want to defer taxable income, this could fit your tax picture very well. You could get the deduction this year and receive its return when you are not working and presumably in a lower bracket.

Producing Orchards and Vineyards

Another area to consider for your tax-sheltered investing is orchards and vineyards.

ERTA introduced some changes in cost recovery that have had a favorable effect on the tax advantages of income-producing tree and vine crops. It is now possible to completely depreciate the original cost of the trees or vines over five years rather than the twenty-five to thirty years, as has been the practice in the past several decades. Likewise, irrigation systems including pumps and wells have a short cost-recovery period of five years. Since the tree or vine components represent the greatest allocation proportionate to the total value per acre, the tax advantages are substantial. This shortened cost recovery period coupled with ITC credit, which is also available for trees or vines and the irrigation systems, can offer you a 150 percent write-off of your original investment over a five-year period.

If you are a first user, you can also take ITC of 10 percent of the total value of your trees or vines or irrigation system. First user is determined by when the asset is put into service, which is represented by the year of installation for the irrigation system and the first year of commercial production for the trees or vines. For most trees and vines, this means the fourth year of production.

I am familiar with a 175-acre fig ranch that is four years old and in its first year of commercial production. The ranch—which includes the land, pumps, and wells; irrigation system; fig trees; and the growing crop—was purchased for $7,700 per acre. The down payment was $1,985 per acre. Farming costs, taxes, and other expenses accounted for an additional $421 per acre in the first year.

The purchase price of $7,700 per acre was allocated as follows:

	Cost ($ per acre)
Land	2,000
Land Preparation	150
Pumps and wells	300
Irrigation system	800
Fig trees	4,450

Since the trees were in the first year of commercial production, ITC of $445 per acre was available. The pumps and wells and irrigation system were "used," so the ITC was limited to 10 percent of the first $125,000 of value (assuming the investor had not otherwise reached his limit for used ITC), which in this situation meant another $110 per acre of ITC. (In addition, depreciation of $833 per acre is now allowable under the ERTA.) Finally, all of the operational farming costs were deducted for an additional $421 per acre. The total deductions were $1,253 per acre plus the ITC of $555 per acre, which, for a 50 percent bracket taxpayer, were equal to a write-off of 95 percent of cash invested.

During the next four years their investors will make additional cash contributions, which decrease each year as the fig trees move toward stabilized production. Investors will be able to completely depreciate the trees and irrigation system during this period and will have achieved tax advantages equal to 19 percent of the invested capital. Assuming 8 percent inflation a year compounded, the fig orchard should sell for $17,888 per acre in ten years. This would result in a 32.5 percent after-tax, internal rate of return, after taking into consideration the recapture of all of the depreciation as ordinary income.

Timber

Another area to consider on an individual or partnership basis is an investment in timber. Some of its profit-potential characteristics are:

1. Low management costs
2. Continuous physical growth
3. Replenishable natural resource
4. Excellent hedge against inflation
5. Actuarial predictability
6. Favorable marketing outlook

A well-tended commercial forest can be a safe and rewarding investment that can provide you with ample cash flow and the potential for excellent capital gains. Trees grow constantly, both in height and in width. One economic benefit of timber is that when the price of timber dips temporarily, the growth in physical volume continues and before long can overcome the effect of the price decline.

It is predicted that the demand for timber will double in the next twenty-five years. By purchasing uneven-aged stands of timber, you may benefit from a harvest of mature trees every five years while benefiting from their growth; with stands of 1,000 acres or more, 100-acre parcels can be scheduled for cutting each year at annual yields of 8-12 percent.

Apart from the future impact of inflation on timber prices, the demand-supply outlook for timber is very favorable and should lead to a rise in prices. The increasing demand for timber for such conventional uses as building materials, as well as for energy needs, is putting additional pressure on the timber industry. Studies are now being made on the possiblity of using "energy plantations" as a cheaper source of fuel.

Timberland offerings are usually structured with agricultural cropping activities to produce a 100 percent write-off, and this form of offering would be more attractive to you as an individual or a major owner of a corporation because of the tax write-off and the tax-free buildup of the investment. A straight timber investment without agricultural cropping activities offers a low tax write-off, usually 10 percent. This type of offering could be a viable consideration for a pension plan.

It can be a conversion shelter in that your gains will be subject to long-term capital gains taxes at a maximum rate of 20 percent. It is usually a one-time investment with no letter of credit or recourse note.

It can also be a comfortable estate builder because it will steadily grow in size and value. Pine trees, for example, grow at an annual rate of 12 percent. Anything that grows at 12 percent, as you will remember from our rule of 72, doubles in size every six years. Should you need income, a cash contract can usually be obtained in thirty days and the lumber cut within ninety days.

As you can see, investing in timberland has some interesting potential. Work with your financial planner and determine if this is an area about which you should be better informed. Carefully examine the offerings, for a strong and experienced general partner is important.

Jojoba Beans

You may not be familiar with this valuable little bean, but as you look for tax relief you may come across a limited partnership for raising these beans on an agricultural basis or one combining cultivation with certain research and development. To date, I have not used one of these partnerships with clients but I am intrigued by the bean and all its properties and hope to find a viable shelter that encompasses some of its possibilities.

The jojoba beans are odd-looking beans that grow in desert areas of the world. They require very little water, sink their roots as deep as 50 feet, and live for hundreds of years. The oil (actually a wax) from these beans is equal or superior to sperm oil in all the traditional applications, and other uses are still being discovered. It seems to be the only source of polyunsaturated wax esters that need no chemical modification. This fact makes it extremely valuable for cosmetics, pharmaceuticals, foods, and for every use of petroleum-based lubricants. Potential demand is so great that it is predicted that the product will be in short supply for the next twenty years.

It will store indefinitely so its extraordinary shelf life makes it very important in everything from cooking oils to cake mixes. It is totally polyunsaturated and is indigestible. However. it will accept fortification by vitamins and flavorings. There could conceivably develop a worldwide market for no-calorie, no-fat, no-cholesterol salad and cooking oils. Medically, it has the ability to dissolve sebum, the fatty substance secreted by the skin and therefore could show promise in treating acne and in reducing some forms of hair loss.

Gas mileage in cars and trucks can be improved by as much as 25 percent when the oil is used in the crankcase, transmission, and the differential gears. It can also extend the useful life of parts three times.

This is only a partial list of the many uses for jojoba oil.

What is the cost of producing jojoba oil? This figure seems to vary considerably. I've seen estimates ranging from $3,400 to $10,000 an acre. Since the jojoba shrubs do not produce beans until their third year, that means a large initial outlay and no income for four or five years. As the plantation grows and matures, the income increases, and by the eighth or ninth year the annual income is projected to equal the original investment.

One partnership offering I've seen used the following projections for a $25,000 investment over a three-year period by an investor in a 50 percent tax bracket, assuming no inflation and a constant price of $1.20 per pound for the beans:

Years	Money Invested	Annual Income	Cumulative Income	Tax Savings
1	$12,000	$0		$6,000
2	9,000	0		4,500
3	4,000	nil		2,000
4		5,250	$5,250	
5		7,250	12,500	
6		11,000	23,500	
7		14,000	37,500	
8		25,000	62,500	
9		25,000	87,500	
	$25,000	$87,500	$228,750	$12,500

The use of jojoba as a viable tax-shelter investment is too new for any precise performance projections. It can be worthy of your study, but do remember that any product with as interesting a potential as jojobas can attract the unscrupulous promoter, so excercise great caution if you are considering this as one of your tax shelters.

Research and Development (R & D)

Though ERTA does provide for some new, nonrefundable 25 percent tax credits for incremental research and development expenditures, the act also includes some very tough rules so that many of the R&D shelters may not qualify. If you are considering such a program, be sure to have adequate tax opinions to give you reasonable assurance that your particular R&D project meets the guidelines.

How do you evaluate a program? First look at the track record of the management of the partnership. Also study what it takes to manufacture and market the product, once the product is developed. Is the company well regarded in the industry? Ask what happens if the money runs out. Budget inadequacy is a major flaw of some R&D programs. Can you be assessed? Is other financing available? If so, how will your interest be diluted?

The capital gains treatment of revenues received after the product is developed is still a gray area. You may be able to claim capital gains, but the IRS may challenge you.

You must be truly at risk to get current deductions. If there is a guaranteed return, the transaction will be treated as a loan.

Some of the offerings will involve the start-up of a new company with the possibility of developing a new product. As an investor, you could share in the proceeds, if there are any, from the new product under development and perhaps a piece of the startup company itself.

Another variation you may find is an existing company that needs funds for R&D. With proper structure, financing for the project can be kept off the books so earnings will not be depressed and the balance sheet won't be laden with debt. In this way, the company gets low-cost funds while the investor gets venture capital opportunities, partly subsidized by tax breaks.

You can make investments in R&D programs late in the year and still obtain deductions.

Today there is a veritable explosion in high technology in the areas of ultrasonics, holographics, computer technology, software technology, and the list goes on and on. So R&D obviously offers an opportunity for exciting upside potential, as well as the potential for loss.

Whenever possible, choose programs that are weighted toward the "D" of the R&D.

Mining

You may want to investigate limited partnerships that focus on the mining of precious metals and other hard rock minerals. There are large mineral reserves today that are too small for development by the major mining companies but that require too much capital for the independent "prospector."

However, it may take a goodly amount of due diligence by you and your planner to find the right offering. Certainly the general partners should have a sound ongoing mining concern; they should have expertise available internally or on a consulting basis; and they should have a very good track record as well as properties in various stages of development. Your write-offs come from such deductible expenses as minimum annual royalties, delay rentals, development expenses, licensing fees, research and development expenses, and depletion allowance.

Another tax benefit is that the partnership can make distributions "in kind." For example, a gold mine could distribute gold nuggets. This would be a tax-deferred event. If you hold the gold for five years, it qualifies for long-term capital gains treatment when sold. Otherwise, it would be taxable as ordinary income when sold. This type of investment could produce portable, liquid, tax-deferred wealth on a pretax basis that can be converted into income in the year most advantageous to you.

Energy Management Systems

Another type of shelter available now is an energy management system. Since the Arab oil embargo of the mid 1970s, our country has been faced with soaring energy cost. We had been the world's greatest waster of energy. In our homes, buildings, and industries, we hadn't been concerned with the amount of purchased energy consumed; it was available and it was cheap. The Oil Producing and Exporting Countries (OPEC) and deregulation changed that thinking not only at the gas pumps but everywhere electricity and natural gas are used.

Escalating energy costs, the demand for energy savings equipment, and the potential for 20 percent tax credits (10 percent investment tax credit and 10 percent energy tax credit) make this an interesting tax-favored investment opportunity. These are structured as limited partnerships, are offered as private placements, and are based on the "shared savings" concept.

"Shared savings" is a plan developed in recent years to provide energy management systems to commercial and industrial companies. Basically, these companies contract for a "free" system; they pay nothing for its acquisition, installation, or maintenance. What they agree to pay is 50 percent of the savings in utility costs generated by their use of the system. Since the cost of utilities in recent years has risen faster than inflation and is predicted to continue to do so over at least the next decade, this "shared savings" concept is profitable for both the user and the owner of the system.

The first type of tax-favored investment opportunity involves primarily the major industrial companies as the users of these systems. These are generally unique systems based upon the reduction of the cost of purchased energy consumed as an integral part of the users' manufacturing process. The first part of your investment in the partnership would be used to research and develop the "know-how" to create a unique system. If that was successful, your partnership would license that "know-how" for an annual royalty payment to the sponsor, who would build, install, and own the system from the sponsor and get the benefits of the "shared savings" contract with the user. That contract may be for a term as long as thirty years.

When your partnership leases that system it gets the benefit of the "pass-through" of the tax credits. You as a partner receive a share of those tax credits and a share of the projected first-year operating loss deduction created by the research and development costs and prepaid rent expense. The equivalent deductions you can take in the first year of your investment can be as much as 230 percent of the cash you invest. You would also have a projected future economic benefit and tax advantage over the lease term and potentially thereafter.

The projected "shared savings" and royalty revenues available to the partnership and distributable to you as cash can be significant beginning in the first full year of operation of the system. As a part of the lease program for those systems, the sponsor has the right to sell the equipment to the partnership at the end of the lease. This feature of the lease allows a large portion of the cash you receive to be received "tax-free" when you get it. This is made possible by using the "Safe Harbor Lease" provision of the Economic Recovery Tax Act of 1981.

ERTA was passed in order to get the country moving again and Safe Harbor Leasing is the part that allows companies that have tax liability to purchase equipment for companies that need the equipment but don't need the tax benefits arising from owning that equipment. Equipment is purchased by the company that needs the tax benefit and leased to the company that needs the equipment. The needs of both companies are taken care of, and these transactions are accorded special tax treatment.

In a Safe Harbor Lease arrangement, if the lessor can sell the leased property to the lessee at the end of the lease, a new deduction arises called "noncash rent." This deduction is the amount the selling price, at the time of the proposed sale, exceeds the fair market value of the leased property to be sold at that time. Fair market value is computed at the beginning of the lease term and is determined without reference to future inflation. This difference is deducted equally over the term of the lease as additional rent, even though it's not actually being paid for in cash. In effect, then, it acts like depreciation by reducing the tax effect of the cash you can receive as a distribution of the partnership's revenue each year.

At the end of the lease term, if your partnership buys the system, it no longer has any rent deduction, but now will have depreciation since it owns the system. Again, a significant portion of the cash distribution you can receive is tax-sheltered by the depreciation.

Calculating the Effect of Using Various Shelters

Appendix Figure 9 is a sample tax-saving worksheet. Make several copies for yourself and make calculations for the various tax-sheltered investments you may be considering. This will graphically show you the effect on your taxable income and the taxes due using various combinations, revealing the net cost of your investment for the current year. If the investment calls for payments over several years, you should make an estimate of effects in those years also.

Pension and Profit-Sharing Plans

If you own or are one of the higher-paid employees of a corporation, an excellent way to shelter funds from taxes is to establish a pension or profit-sharing plan. Have a specialist design the plans that give you the greatest advantage. These are covered in detail in a later chapter.

If you own a closely held corporation and all the conditions are right, probably no other vehicle will provide you with such good shelter without the IRS questioning your deduction. If you follow all the rules, it will give you the flexibility to play the game to your maximum tax advantage. You can balance the funds between the corporation, yourself, and the pension plan.

After a speech I made at the National Conference for Monetary Reform in Acapulco, a gentleman asked me if I knew how to get $1 million out of his closely held corporation without paying taxes on it. My answer was "Yes, sir." When he came in to see me back in Houston, I found that he did indeed have over $1 million in cash inside his corporation, that he had only a small number of employees, that he was the firm's oldest and highest-paid employee, and that he had no defined benefit plan. By establishing a plan, structured properly, we were able to get the million dollars out of his corporation and into the pension plan, with most of the benefits credited to him.

When you establish a plan, not only are your contributions deductible to the corporation, but also all the earnings in your plan compound as tax-sheltered income. Under certain circumstances, it is possible to contribute more than 100 percent of your salary to a defined benefit pension plan. You can be the trustee of your plan and can decide how it is to be invested.

At retirement, you can roll over your IRA to postpone taxes. Funds that are not withdrawn are permitted to continue to compound tax-sheltered. Also, if death should occur, inheritance taxes can be avoided if the plan is set up properly.

These plans can be funded in a variety of ways through the use of mutual funds, stocks, oil and gas income programs, wraparound mortgages, certain real estate partnerships, and so forth.

A very interesting investment in a plan was made by a couple who had a lumber business in the Northwest. They had set up their qualified plan in order to defer some of the corporate income. When it came time to invest the funds in the plan, they bought a colt and hired a trainer paid for by the plan to pursue his racing potential. The colt turned out to be Seattle Slew. They have now sold one-half of the horse to a syndication for over $7 million. All the proceeds from the syndication remain in the plan and the plan still owns 50 percent of Seattle Slew. As mentioned earlier, his stud fees today are going for $200,000.

The trustees of qualified plans must make prudent investments-but whoever said prudent must be dull.

Keogh

I'll cover Keogh plans in detail later, but let me mention that if you are self-employed and do not have a large number of employees, you should consider establishing a Keogh account. Your contribution to your own retirement plan is deductible, and the distributions are allowed to compound tax-sheltered.

Individual Retirement Account (IRA)

I'll cover this account in detail later too, but let me just mention it here. Even if you have a Keogh account and are also covered under a pension/profit-sharing plan, under ERTA every person can now contribute 100 percent of earned income up to a maximum of $2,000, deduct it from taxable income, and let it compound tax-sheltered. If you are married and your spouse receives no compensation, you may contribute and deduct $2,250, but at least $250 must be in the name of the spouse. If your spouse earns at least $2,000, you may contribute $4,000, with $2,000 going into each account. As indicated in Chapter 14, you must be under 70-1/2 through the year to deduct an IRA pay-in. Only cash can be contributed. Contributions can be made to your account at the beginning of each year, which I recommend to give you that additional year of tax-sheltered compounding. However, contributions can be made up to the time you file your tax return.

Capital Gains

Capital gains occur when you sell an asset for more than your cost. If you have held the asset for less than one year, the gain is a short-term capital gain and is taxed as ordinary income if you do not have a long- or short-term capital loss to offset it. If you have held your asset over a year when the sale is made, then 40 percent of the gain is taxable and is added to any other taxable income. The maximum amount that can be lost to tax on capital gain is 20 percent. This may not sound too bad if you say it quickly, but often these assets represent a business or a farm on which a couple have slaved many long hours for many years, and it's often very painful to have so large an amount of these inflated dollars snatched away. If the capital gain exceeds $100,000, it is more difficult to provide acceptable shelter because of the alternative minimum tax legislated by the Tax Revenue Act of 1978.

Alternative Minimum Tax

The reduction of the taxable portion of a long-term capital gain from 50 to 40 percent and the elimination of the untaxable portion as an item of tax preference were steps in the right direction by Congress. But there was a blockbuster in this piece of legislation if you had a capital gain in excess of $100,000 and unusually high itemized deductions.

A worksheet is included in the Appendix (Figure 10) for your use in making your preliminary calculations, but I strongly advise you to consult with your tax advisor before entering into any tax-sheltered investments if you have received in excess of $100,000 of capital gains. Briefly, this act contained two significant factors:

1. Only 40 percent of the gain is taxable income for purposes of computing federal income taxes in the regular way.

2. The other 60 percent of the gain is considered a preference item for purposes of computing the new alternative minimum tax. In most instances, this new alternative tax is computed by: (a) adding one's taxable income to the 60 percent excluded portion of the gain; (b) exempting the first $20,000; and (c) taxing the first $40,000 of the remainder at 10 percent and the remainder at 20 percent. The alternative minimum tax is added to your regular tax in determining your tax liability.

As a result of this interaction, there is a limitation on the amount of a capital gain that can be sheltered.

Minimum Tax on Other Tax-Preference Items

Nearly all tax shelters include certain tax-preference items that may or may not create additional tax liabilities in the form of the add-on minimum tax, which you can compute by using the worksheet in the Appendix (Figure 11).

Tax-preference items for individuals and other noncorporate taxpayers include:

1. ACRS deductions on recovery property (other than fifteen-year real property).

2. Accelerated depreciation on real property.

3. ACRS deductions on fifteen-year real property.

4. Accelerated depreciation on personal property subject to a lease.

5. Amortization-certified pollution control facilities, railroad rolling stock, on-the-job training facilities, and child care facilities.

6. Bargain element in qualified stock options.

7. Excess of percentage depletion over basis.

8. Intangible oil and gas well drilling costs.

9. Historic structures.

The minimum tax is the higher of the alternative minimum tax or the add-on minimum tax.

Stocks

Your chief incentive for investing in stocks should be to make a profit. When you can't make a profit in the market, get out. You should sell when you anticipate that market conditions may become unfavorable or that your stock may have topped out for what appears to be a prolonged period of time. If you sell for more than you paid for the stock and you have held it for over a year, you will trigger a capital gain, 40 percent of which will be taxable unless you have offsetting losses.

For example, let's assume that you bought 1,000 shares of a stock at $5 and that you sold it a year later at $10. You now have a $5000 long-term capital gain, of which 40 pecent is taxable. This $2,000 will be added to your taxable income and will be taxed at your top rate.

If you have realized capital gains and it's toward the end of the year and you have some losses in some of your other stocks, bonds, or other assets, you should consider selling them, establishing your loss, and charging it against your capital gains. Be sure to wait thirty-one days before buying the same asset back or it will be considered a "wash sale" and the loss will be disallowed. If, for exaple, you had a loss in American Telephone & Telegraph, you would not want to buy it back before thirty-one days had lapsed, but you could buy General Telephone the same day and still charge off the loss on the first stock.

Also, don't let the fact that you'll pay a capital gains tax keep you from selling stock that has matured and seemingly reached a plateau. Often I see people plant good fruit trees and let the fruit rot on the trees. Of course, they can avoid the capital gains if they hold it until it goes back to what they paid for it, but this hardly seems like brilliant financial planning.

Dividend Reinvestment of Public Utilities

Public utility stocks are not my favorite investment because utilities are greatly influenced by two things: the cost of capital and the cost of natural resources, both of which could continue to be expensive. Add to this an angry consumer, and you have some real deterrent to growth.

However, you should know about the tax advantage ERTA provides if you own utility stocks. For dividends distributed by a qualified domestic public utility corporation after December 31, 1981, and prior to January 1, 1986, you may elect to take your distributions in newly issued common stock rather than cash and be entitled to deduct up to $750 ($1,500 on a joint return) of the stock dividends per year. The stock dividends that you receive will have a zero basis, and this will be taxed at the full amount when sold. Unless you sell the shares within one year, your sale will be treated as a capital gain. Disposition of any common stock of the issuing public utility before one year from the date of distribution will be considered the disposition of the reinvested dividend shares to the extent that such shares are held.

All-Savers Certificates

In the government's efforts to provide more funds for housing mortgages, ERTA included the provision that for the taxable years ending September 30, 1981, there is a $1,000 ($2,000 for a joint return) lifetime exclusion from gross income for interest earned on qualified depository institution tax-exempt savings certificates. In order to qualify, the certificate must: (1) be issued between these dates by a qualified savings institution (which generally includes banks, mutual savings banks, cooperative banks, savings and loans, credit unions); (2) have a maturity of one year; (3) have a yield equal to 70 percent of the yield on fifty-two week Treasury bills, as determined a week before the certificate is issued; and (4) be available in $500 denominations. With a bit of intelligent planning, surely you can do better with your money.

Income Earned Abroad

If you work for a multi-national corporation or are considering employment abroad, you should also become familiar with the provisions ERTA made for excluding some of your foreign-earned income. If you qualify, you may elect to exclude from gross income foreign-earned income attributable to the period of your foreign residency or presence in the foreign country at an annual rate of $75,000 for taxable years beginning in 1982. This amount will be increased by $5,000 until 1986, when the annual rate will be $95,000.

There is also either an exclusion from gross income for housing cost amounts or a deduction for housing amounts not provided by your employer.

Tax Losses

If you are approaching the end of the year and have losses in your stock or bond portfolio, you probably should establish the loss. You may charge off $1.00 of capital loss against $1.00 of capital gains. If you still have losses you have not used in this manner, you may charge off $2.00 loss against $1.00 of ordinary income up to a maximum of $6,000 of loss against $3,000 of ordinary income. Any excess you have may be carried forward to be used in future years.

Municipal Bond Swapping

If you own some municipal bonds and interest rates have risen since you made your purchase, but you still want to own municipals or corporates, you might consider swapping bonds. You must be sure that the bonds you repurchase are either from a different issuer or of a different issue date or coupon maturity.

The swap could work like this. You own bonds with a par value of $10,000, a coupon rate of 4 percent that is due in ten years, and a market value of $7,200. You sell these bonds and replace them with $10,000 par value bonds carrying a 6.5 percent coupon rate, due in twenty years at a discounted price of $7,200. Your net results would be (1) your yearly income is increased $250 per year; (2) you have established a capital loss of $2,800; and (3) you will recoup your loss in 11.2 years by the increased income of $250 per year. If you have a long-term capital gain to charge your loss against, you'll recoup it sooner. If you do not have a long-term capital gain or if your loss exceeds the gain, $6,000 of your excess can be applied against $3,000 of ordinary income. If your gain is short-term, $3,000 can be applied against $3,000 of ordinary income. If your losses are greater than this, they can be carried forward indefinitely to be applied against future gains and/or applied against $3,000 per year ordinary income.

If your capital loss is considered long-term for each dollar of loss, only one-half can be offset against ordinary income, subject to the $3,000 limitation.

Discount Corporate Bonds

Another way to realize capital gains is to buy discounted bonds such as are often available at the peak of high interest rates. For example, you could have bought:

Alabama Power: 7-1/4% of 2002 at 47-1/2 to yield 16.58%
General Motors: 4-7/8% of 1987 at 63-1/2 to yield 14.20%
Houston Lighting & Power: 3% of 1989 at 47 to yield 15.51%

All of these bonds are high grade and should pay $1,000 per bond at maturity, providing you with a long-term capital gains. For example, par is $1,000 and the current price on Alabama Power is $475.00; therefore you would have a capital gain in the year 2002 of $525.00. (I hope this example also points out the risk of a "riskless" investment— the characteristic often attributed to high-grade corporate bonds by the uninformed.)

An easier way that takes less expertise on your part and that should carry less risk because of their professional management and diversification is to invest in mutual funds investing in deeply discounted bonds. When interest rates go down, bond prices should go up, and the sale would produce a capital gain; or if the discounted bond matured and par value was received, a capital gain would occur.

Subchapter S Corporations

A subchapter S corporation is a small business corporation that has elected not to be taxed as a corporation. A shareholder of a subchapter S corporation must include in his income his pro rata share of the corporation's taxable income, whether the amount was actually distributed to him or not. This can become a tax shelter when lower-income family members are given or sold stock in such a corporation.

Another use may occur when you have a good bankable idea for a new business that will by its very nature probably be operating in the red for its first few years. By setting up the company as a subchapter S corporation, the losses can flow directly to you, and you can charge them off against your ordinary income. Later, when the business becomes profitable, you may or may not want to convert it to a regular corporation. The validity of converting is lessened with ERTA owing to the reduction in maximum rates for individuals from 70 percent to 50 percent. The maximum number of shareholders permissible in a Subchapter S corporation is twenty-five, with certain qualifications. A qualified trust is now allowed to be a shareholder.

Under ERTA, with the maximum personal income tax at 50 percent, there may be more and more regular corporations converting to Sub-chapter S. This could eliminate the hassle with IRS regarding undue compensation to corporate owners.

Home Ownership

If you are in a tax bracket of 40 percent or above, there is considerable merit to owning a home on which you have obtained the maximum mortgage. As explained earlier, interest is deductible; therefore your interest cost is subsidized by the amount of your tax bracket. If your interest is 15 percent and you are in a 40 percent bracket, your net interest cost is 9 percent. If your bracket is 50 percent (and surely you'll make some tax-advantaged investments to lower it), your net interest cost after taxes is 7.5 percent.

Private Annuity

A tool that may fit your financial objective is the private annuity. This type of annuity involves the transfer of your property to a transferee—an individual, a partnership, or a corporation—in exchange for an unsecured promise to make periodic payments to you in fixed amounts for a designated period of time. In most cases, this will be for your lifetime. The assets you may use for this are real property, stocks, bonds, mutual funds, limited partnerships, and so forth.

The advantage to you is that this method can usually increase your cash flow from your assets without substantially increasing your income tax liability. Capital-gains taxation will be spread over the life of your agreement and, as a result, may be reduced in amount.

Since these assets are generally not includable for estate tax purposes, there could be a savings on estate taxes in the event of your premature death. The private annuity can be partly taxable under the estate under certain conditions that your attorney can explain.

There are some disadvantages to the private annuity. Let's assume you transferred this property to your son and you died prior to the completion of the agreement. There is the possibility that your son may be subjected to an adjustment in the basis of that property. If your son held the property for at least a year before selling it, the gain would be treated as a long-term capital gain. If he sold before one year and you died, it could be subject to short-term capital gains treatment. If you live longer than the life expectancy table indicates, the payments may be greater than the original value, but the tax savings and appreciation could more than make up for this. Also, there is no tax deduction accruing to your son for interest paid to you. Another disadvantage is the provision that you are unable to secure the annuity payments by collateralizing through a trust or by mortgage.

How To Fund the Private Annuity

To provide the necessary funds for the monthly payments the buyer will need to make, he should invest the proceeds from the sale of the assets in shares of a high-quality mutual find that is within a family or funds that also has a money market fund; he should also begin a systematic withdrawal program. He might superimpose a market timing service on the fund so he could move in and out of the market as market conditions dictate. In this way diversification could be obtained in a quality cross-section of securities that are professionally managed and still have the custodian bank send you a check each month.

Other investments you should consider are oil and gas income limited partnerships, income real estate limited partnerships, and quality stocks that pay generous dividends.

In summary, the advantages of the private annuity are:

1. Avoids all the costs of probate.

2. Could save on federal estate taxes at death.

3. Could save on state inheritance taxes.

4. Could spread the long-term capital gains tax over a number of years.

5. There is no future appreciation to increase estate valuation.

The Living Trust

The proper use of the living trust (also referred to as the revocable or the *intervivos* trust) can reduce the cost of passing your assets to your heirs.

With the living trust, a pour-over will should be drawn to cover all assets you have not registered to the trust. You should have the trust drawn in the state in which you reside.

Your trust can be written so as to pass your assets as you would do in a will. Some states will allow you to be your own trustee. Some require co-trustees. You may also use a bank or corporate trustee. All of the assets you want to place in the trust should be listed. As changes are made the list should be changed. The trust can offer the following benefits:

1. The cost of probate and administration fees are saved because the trust assets are not probated through the courts.

2. The prolonged probate time can be saved, as the assets can be passed immediately. All creditors must be paid, and the federal estate taxes and the state taxes can be put into an escrow account with the trustee liable.

3. The problem of incapacity is lessened. Generally, under the will method the individual has no document while he is alive, and, should incapacity occur, the court must be petitioned to declare him incapacitated in order to sell any property. The document can state that three doctors can declare the individual incapacitated and the cotrustees or successor trustee assume trustee role.

4. The trust can afford privacy in death as to the amount of assets held in the estate, since it does not go through the probate court. No listing of assets is required, which usually ends up in the local papers.

5. A trust can keep the estate under family control. Since assets such as stock, property, or closely held corporation or businesses are not under court control, these can be sold to raise cash for costs and fees and for state and federal estate taxes.

There are some assets that you should avoid placing in the living trust. Some of these are cars, jewelry, furs, and furnishings. Nor should you place in the trust professional corporation stock, since most states require that the stockholder be of the same profession as the original stockholder.

The transfer of assets into a living trust is not of taxable consequence. (Gift taxes can occur when assets are placed into short-term or irreovocable trust.)

Income Splitting

If you are in a high tax bracket and if you have dependents, you may want to consider income splitting. For example, the interest and dividends you are receiving are being taxed at your higher bracket. If they were shifted to your children, who may have a low or nonexistent bracket, you could reduce the family's overall tax burden. To do this, you will have to transfer the income-producing assets to them either temporarily or permanently.

How should income splitting be done? You probably want to avoid outright gifts or guardianships. Contracts of minors can be voided, and guardianships are cumbersome. Ways you might consider are custodial accounts, special trusts for minors, Clifford trusts, interest-free loans, and gifts.

Custodial Account. As will be discussed in Chapter 15 on financing a college education, you may set up an account with an adult as custodian for your child. You cannot use any of the income for the support of your child, for that is your legal responsibility. This income could be used for such things as summer camp, riding lessons, or college expenses. You will still be entitled to the $1,000 exemption for your child, or each child if you have more than one, as long as the child is either a student or under nineteen years of age. Each child receives up to $1,000 a year tax-free from his own additional exemption added to the $100 dividend exclusion.

You may apply the $10,000 annual gift exclusion for each child and do this each year. If your spouse joins with you, $20,000 each year can be gifted to each child without a gift tax. If you want to avoid having these gifts considered a part of your estate in the event of your death, you should not be the custodian, nor should your spouse if the spouse has joined in the gift.

Special Trust for Minors. Perhaps you think it prudent that your child or children not have access to the principal until age twenty-one. Under the Section 2503 (c) Trust, you may use your $10,000 per child annual gift exclusion ($20,000 if joined by your spouse). These assets and income can be used for the child before age twenty-one. If the trust's assets have not been spent by then, the principal must be paid to the child at age twenty-one.

Clifford Trust. Income can also be split through the use of the Clifford Trust, as discussed in a later chapter. This is a short-term living trust created for a period of the lesser of ten years and a day or the life of the beneficiary. At the end of this period, the trust terminates and your property is returned to you.

A Clifford trust may be used for your dependent children, dependent parents, or others for whom you want to provide income for a period of ten years. Its chief advantage is that it permits you to split income without giving up your asset permanently. (More information appears in a later chapter.)

Interest-Free Loans. Another method of income splitting to save taxes is to make an interest-free loan on a demand note. You would not be required in this arrrangement to give away your assets permanently, not even to relinquish control for ten years, as in a Clifford trust.

This type of program has been vigorously attacked by the IRS for years. But to date they have not won a case. Even if they are eventually successful, the increase in the gift tax exemption from $3,000 to $10,000 ($20,000 if joint) has taken the wind out of their sails. The object is to transfer the use of money without interest from high-bracket taxpayers to low-bracket taxpayers. In order for this plan to work it must have two elements: (1) the note must be payable upon demand, and (2) there should be no pre-arranged plan to forgive the loan at a future time.

Let's assume you have a child ready to go to medical school and your cost will be $10,000 per year. In a 50 percent bracket, you must earn $20,000 to have $10,000 to give to your son. However, if you set up a trust for the benefit of your son and loan the trust $70,000 on a demand interest-free loan, which the trust invests at, say, a 15 percent return, it would produce $10,500 of income that would be taxed in the son's bracket, which should be minimal.

You would have no gift tax on the transfer. You may recover the funds at any time, and appreciation on the investment is removed from your estate. The note would, of course, be part of your estate.

The IRS has been trying valiantly to combat this arrangement. The first case of major signficance in the area of interest-free loans to family members was *Johnson* v. *U.S.* In that case, a parent made an interest-free loan payable on demand to his children. The IRS contended that interest-free loans defeated the purpose of the federal estate tax by reducing the parent's estate by the amount of the interest that could have been charged. However, the district court held that no gift had been made. According to the court, the purpose of the federal estate tax was not defeated, since balance on the loan would be included in the parent's gross estate. The district court also stated that a parent had no obligation to charge interest on a loan to children, or otherwise deal with children at arm's length.

Should you use the interest-free demand note technique? It is worthy of your study and one of the best books on the subject is *Tax Saving Through Interest-Free Loans* by Harry G. Gordon.

Although the details provided in Gordon's book are not very complex (he provides forms, trust agreements, demand notes—almost everything you need), he recommends that you seek competent legal or tax advice before implementing such a plan. I agree. Gordon's forms are flexible enough to require only minor adaptations in the hands of your attorney, which should save you legal tailoring time.

The IRS has intimated that most people who use the method will probably be audited. This probably will not be the case because "interest-free loans just don't show up anywhere on tax forms."

Anyway, if your comfort level is not hampered by the use of this technique, it is worth discussing with your tax consultant.

Making Gifts. You may give $10,000 each year to as many people as you desire without a gift tax. If you and your spouse join in the giving, this amount can be $20,000. Any amount you give above this amount can be taxable and counts against your tax credit. This can have the effect of your prepaying your estate taxes. However, if you are gifting an income property to a person in a low tax bracket this could be a reason for gifting above this amount. Another reason might be that the gift is an appreciating asset. Because it is a gift, the appreciation occurs outside of the estate.

Creative, Knowledgeable C.P.A.

Do find yourself a creative, knowledgeable C.P.A. who is truly dedicated to helping you *not* pay taxes. I've met some who should be on the

IRS payroll. If all your C.P.A. does for you is tally up how much taxes you owe on April 15, the IRS will do this without sending you a bill. You don't want a tax tallier. You want one who conscientiously works for you to lower your taxes. Your greatest single expense last year was probably your tax bill. An excellent C.P.A. is invaluable, and his fees are deductible. Don't, however, shift to him the burden of deciding on the economics of a particular tax-favored investment. That's not his role. I repeat, that's not his function in your life. Your financial planner has that obligation. Your C.P.A. should only be concerned with the tax aspects of the investment to determine if it fits your needs and if he agrees with the tax opinion in the offering memorandum.

If you mistakenly place on him the burden of determining the investment merits of a proposal, he will almost always object. That way he'll never be wrong—of course, he'll never be right either, and you will have condemned yourself to sending your dollars on that one-way trip. Start paying your C.P.A. for helping you not to pay taxes. He must be willing to devote time to your cause. I've seen many C.P.A.s say no just because they did not want to burden themselves with reading and digesting an inch-thick private offering memorandum. Even if they did read it, the offering may have been about an area in which they had little or no experise, but they were embarrassed to admit their ignorance to their client. Then, I've seen others who got their kicks in life by building a reputation as a "deal killer."

Summary

If you are in a 22 to 29 percent tax bracket, you should consider making investments that give you tax-sheltered income, such as registered limited partnerships investing in triple-net leases of commercial real estate and oil and gas income programs. If you are in the 29 to 44 percent bracket, you will also want to consider registered oil and gas income programs and add to those registered offerings of multifamily housing, office buildings, shopping centers, miniwarehouses, motels, and hotels. If you are in the 39 percent bracket, you may want to look at registered programs such as cattle feeding, marine-container leasing and movies. If you are in the 44 percent bracket and above, you will have a wide variety of both registered and private placement instruments to choose from. If you are in this bracket, you may want to turn to Appendix Figure 9 and use the simplified worksheet to calculate the effect of particular tax-favored investments on your taxable income. Unfortunately, under present security regulations, your financial planner will be limited in helping you if you are below the 44 percent tax bracket. You hit that level at $45,800 taxable income on a joint return in 1982 and at $60,000 in 1983.

If you are not earning that amount at present, look around you diligently. There are many exciting career opportunities that will bring you that amount of income and much more. You'll find that if you search with an open mind it is not hard to succeed, because there are so few people out there trying. As you will remember, we've learned that it's not how hard you work or how many hours. Your rewards in life will always be in direct proportion to what you do, your ability to do it, and the difficulty of replacing you. And when you've reached those loftier income levels and are searching for the best tax-favored investment, seek out areas in which demand exceeds supply. Then look for investment packages that have been fairly structured so that if the investment is profitable you will make money. Seek out investments with general partners of unquestioned expertise, high integrity, substantial net worth, and an excellent past performance record. The latter may not always be possible. The area of investment may be a new one. But, if you persist in a spirit of serendipity you should reap great rewards.

As you search for economically sound tax-favored investments, you'll find that you are being joined by an increasingly larger number of your fellow citizens. More and more of them are looking for opportunities to put their hard-earned money into areas of great social need. Also, there is a growing resentment to the ever-increasing tax burden being pressed upon them by the tax-bracket creep—a product of escalating inflation. Because they are faced with a lowering of their standard of living, they are looking for a better way.

As you look for a better way, you should not be foolhardy in your search for tax relief, but neither should you be obsessed by a fear of risk or fear of the IRS. I emphasize again that you don't get a write-off for investing in bonds. (Not that I consider such an investment safe—it's stable but not safe. Remember, our definition of safety is the return of the same amount of food, clothing, and shelter—not the same number of dollars at a point in the future.)

Also remember that it is not safe to pay taxes, either. The probability of your receiving any income from your tax receipt is quite remote. Payment of taxes means a guaranteed loss, and an expected rate of return of zero. Investing in tax-favored investments and tax-sheltered investments also carries risk, but at least you have a fighting chance of turning some of your tax liabilities into assets.

Not only were tax-favored investments put on our law books by Congress to fill a social need, but by your reduction in the amount of taxes you send to Washington, you can hope to force the government to curtail some of its wasteful spending and leave more investment dollars in the private sector to be used to create much needed jobs and consumer products.

Tax-sheltered investments are not gimmicks or loopholes, as some politicians are fond of calling them at election time. The beneficiaries of these investments are you and me and your fellow Americans. You are financing areas of public need much more efficiently than can be done by the federal government. The performance record of free enterprise is far superior. Look around you at government's dismal failures in public housing, job training, energy, postal service, and Amtrak, to name only a few.

Congress made conscious decisions to grant tax incentives for investments in key industries rather than through government subsidies or government-owned-and-operated companies. Tax incentives serve the nation's needs as well as your needs. Congress did not enact tax incentives for the benevolent purpose of reducing your tax bill. When you invest in areas of great social need, you should feel patriotic. You are providing venture capital that benefits the country and that you hope will increase your spendable income and your estate.

Most high-income Americans work hard to earn their money and should be permitted to enjoy the rewards of such hard work. More and more of our high-income citizens are reducing the number of hours they work, often in fields in which there is great need, such as the medical field, because they have not been allowed to keep the fruits of their labor.

You should always keep in mind that, even though the characteristics of the various shelters vary greatly, they are all complex, involve risk, and are usually nonliquid. Even with the tax benefits you may receive, you can lose money as well as make it. Most tax shelters are far removed from the traditional investments such as stocks and bonds, and even if you are an experienced investor, you may find it hard to determine what is glitter and what is gold.

Another characteristic is that they can bring you an adversary—the IRS. This adversary thinking can probably be best described by the answer given by the commissioner of the IRS to the *The National Tax Shelter Digest Magazine* when he was asked to do an interview for the magazine. He stated, "Writing an article about tax shelters would be like a police chief writing an article for a burglary magazine."

The interview request was made at an American Bar Association convention where the commissioner spoke. Attending were many young impressionable C.P.A.s fresh out of college. Can't you envision them sitting there with stacks of regulations in front of them being taught the evils of tax shelters? As the instructors graduate these recruits, you can see them dashing out into the far corners of the country armed with wisdom and guidelines ready to save the government from the dangers of those who have the audacity to try to reduce their tax burdens.

Search for the right tax-favored investment. Work with the knowledgeable pros with the hope of keeping some of your hard-earned dollars from taking that long one-way trip to Washington!

Application

1. Calculate your anticipated taxable income for this year.

2. What is your tax bracket before shelter?

3. Do you have a knowledgeable and concerned financial planner at present who can help you build a living estate? If your answer is no, what steps are your going to take to find one? At the end of the Appendix you'll find the addresses and phone numbers of the International Association for Financial Planners, the College of Financial Planning, and the Institute of Certified Planners. Also, you will find the addresses of *The Financial Planner Magazine*, edited by Forrest Wallace Cato; the *National Tax Shelter Digest*, edited by Marilyn Passell Goldsmith; the *Brennan Reports*, edited by William Brennan; "The Tax Shelter Insider" monthly alert newsletter from America's tax shelter experts; and "The Money Dynamics Letter" edited by me. I recommend that you subscribe to all of them.

4. Do you have a creative, knowledgeable, and competent C.P.A. who cares about your financial future? If not, what steps will you take this week to find one?

5. If your need is for spendable income, compare your after-tax return on municipal bonds, corporate bonds, money market funds, limited partnership programs that invest in oil and gas income, real estate triple-net leases, multifamily housing, marine-container leasing, budget motels, miniwarehouses, and so on.

6. Would a "guaranteed" single-premium deferred annuity using a yearly withdrawal be a good solution? How about a tax-sheltered trust?

7. Which combination of tax-sheltered investments best fits your tax needs? Your temperament?

8. Would you be happier paying the taxes and not worrying about tax shelters? If your answer is no, what constructive steps will you take this year to reduce your taxes?

   (1)

   (2)

   (3)

   (4)

   Happy Tax Avoidance!

Chapter 12

Attaining Millionaire Power

W. Clement Stone was once asked how he would describe the feeling of being so wealthy. His answer was "power"—and then he added, "the power to do good."

Money does give you options in life that you would not have without it. It gives you the option of doing what you consider to be good. If you have a sufficient amount of money, you can greatly influence what books will be printed, what movies will be produced, what television programs will be shown, and what jobs will be created for others.

Do you really want to become a millionaire? If your answer is yes, your next question may be, "Is it still possible to do so today?" The answer to your question is a resounding yes if you have enough time left, if you have a strong desire, and if you are willing to devote sufficient time and effort to pursuing this goal.

To begin, I think it is only fair to tell you I've never helped anyone become wealthy overnight. I've never helped someone with $10,000 turn it quickly into a million. The only people I've ever helped make a million dollars in a relatively brief period of time are those who brought me a million dollars to invest. Remember though, that it takes only an average return of 10 percent compounded to double your money in 7.2 years. At 12 percent it takes 6 years; at 18 percent, 4 years, and at 24 percent, 3 years. My minimum goal for my clients is in excess of 20 percent.

I remember calling the office of Percy Foreman, the nationally known and brilliant criminal lawyer, to invite him to appear on my weekly television program, "Successful Texans." When I asked to speak to him, the receptionist blurted out, "He's in jail." After chuckling over this response, I left word for him to call me when he "got out of jail." Later that afternoon he called, and I invited him to be my guest. He accepted my invitation; and just as I was about to say my goodbye, he said, "Aren't you that lady stockbroker? Can you make me rich?" I answered, "Mr. Foreman, I understand you are already rich; but I believe I can make you richer."

Let's assume that you do not have the elusive million with which to start your high adventure. Is it still possible for you to become a millionaire? The answer is probably yes, if you have the discipline to save, the inclination to study, and a life span of sufficient length.

First, let me say that there are more desirable goals in life than becoming a millionaire. But if this is your desire, there are some very practical ways to approach your objective. To reach any goal, the first step is to divide it into its component parts so that it can be approached one step at a time.

Component Parts of a Million Dollars

What are the component parts of a million dollars? It's $1,000 multiplied by 1,000, isn't it? Trying to reach a million dollars in your lifetime may not be all that difficult to do.

How do you obtain the first $1,000? The most obvious beginning is to save from current income. If you save slightly under $20 per week, you should have your $1,000 in a year. Or if you do not want to wait until you have saved the $1,000, you can start investing as you earn on a weekly or monthly basis from your current income. Another possibility is to borrow the $1,000 from the bank at the beginning and pay the bank back on a monthly basis. This could give you a head start toward your goal.

Therefore, the first requirement for reaching your goal is the ability to set aside the relatively small amount of $20 per week.

Money, Yield, Time

The second requirement is to obtain a high return produced by adherence to aggressive but sound investment practices. These can be readily learned if your desire is strong enough.

The third requirement is a life span of sufficient length.

So you see, the two most important things are time and yield. If you set your sights on a million dollars, you must keep these two factors in mind. Time is something over which you have very little control. But yield is different. I believe that anyone of good intelligence has the potential to earn a high return on his investment, and high returns are absolute musts if you ever expect to become a millionaire.

When we speak of "yield," we ordinarily think of income (dividends or interest) as an annual return on the sum invested, expressed in the form of a percentage. For instance, if you receive $5 at the end of a year on a $100 investment, your yield is 5 percent. However, we shall broaden this definition for the purpose of this chapter and use "yield" to describe any distribution, plus any growth in market value. For example, if $100 grows to $318 in 10 years, we would say its "yield" is 12 percent compounded.

One thing you must be fully aware of is the magic that comes from compounding the rate of return. This means that you are never to treat any income, capital appreciation, or equity buildup as spendable during the period you are building toward your million-dollar goal, but only

Forward March!

as returns that are to be reinvested to increase your accumulation. In other words, don't eat your children. Let them produce more children, and before long you'll have a whole army of dollars working for you. Remember Benjamin Franklin's words, "Money is of a prolific, generating nature. Money can beget money, and its offspring can beget more."

For the purpose of our calculations, any taxes that you must pay on your investments are deemed to have come from another source.

One of the most important things you must remember is how important the rate of return you receive on your investment is to your compounding. For instance, if you can put to work $1,000 each year and can average a compound rate of 10 percent per annum, you will be able to reach your goal in 48.7 years.

However, if you can increase this compound rate to 20 percent per annum, you can reach your goal in 29.2 years. So you see, it does make a great deal of difference what return you obtain on your money.

Diversification—Based on Demand and Supply

Risk in investing can be reduced by following some basic investment principles. In this dynamic world in which we live, the two key concepts you must always keep in the forefront of your thinking are agility and diversification—that means spreading your risks.

In Basic Economics 101 you learned an economic law that you must never forget: the law of supply and demand. Regardless of how diligently governments and economists have tried to repeal it over the years, they have never been able to do so for any length of time. Russia has tried it and failed. England has attempted it and brought a once proud empire of plenty to its knees. Our own Congress continues to attempt to repeal this universal law. Its action has caused shortages and disruptions in energy, beef, housing, labor, utilities, and so on.

In making your determination of where the demand is greater than the supply, be an alert reader of the daily metropolitan newspaper; also read such papers and publications as the *Wall Street Journal, Time, Business Week, U.S. News & World Report, Fortune,* the *National Tax Shelter Digest,* the *Financial Planner* magazine, and *Money* magazine. Also begin to study the St. Louis Federal Reserve Board reports. You'll begin to develop an awareness of demands and shortages.

Avoid the Blue Chip Syndrome

There are those who have the mistaken idea that all one has to do to make money in the stock market is to buy "blue chips," throw them in the drawer, and forget about them. In my opinion, this can be riskier than buying more aggressive stocks and watching them like a hawk. The "blue chips" of today may become the "red chips" or "white chips" or "buffalo chips" of tomorrow. We live in a dynamic, throbbing, changing economy.

Just think back a few years. What car did the "man of distinction" drive? A Packard. I would have had difficulty convincing my father that only a few years later the manufacturers of the Packard automobile would be out of business. What was the chief family home entertainment medium before television? It was radio, wasn't it? And who was the chief manufacturer of that half-egg-shaped wooden box in every home? Atwater-Kent. As you know, the Atwater-Kent Company no longer exists. You live in a world of constant change, and you must always be alert and ahead of this change if you want to become a millionaire through your investment know-how. You must sharpen your talents to predict trends before they happen, and move out before they have run their course.

If the money supply is being greatly restrained in our country, as you've already learned, you will want to develop a more conservative approach to the stock market. As the supply becomes even more diminished, move into money market mutual funds so that you will have adequate liquidity to go back into the market as the money supply is accelerated and also to enjoy the higher yield that money will attract during this period of short supply.

This is not to say you should always avoid the Fortune 500 companies. If there has been an extended decline in the market, the larger better-known companies are often the ones that respond first when the market begins to climb. As it reaches higher levels, you may then want to move out of them into other areas.

Aggressive Growth Mutual Funds with Timing

As discussed earlier, a well-managed family of funds that has an aggressive growth fund and a money market fund with a timing service superimposed on it can also perform very well. Using this system with the aggressive growth fund in the same family as the seminar fund, we have averaged 24 percent (doubling funds in three years) over the past four years.

Investment Advisory Services

I'm also aware of a group that have attained an average annual gain of 54 percent in their aggressive portfolio over the past seven years as an annual increase of 10 percent of the Standard & Poor's index. Their more conservative portfolio has posted a 27.5 percent annual increase. At 54 percent you would have doubled your investment in 1.33 years, and at 27.5 percent in 2.62 years.

Timing

The most important ingredient for success in the stock market is a sharp sense of timing. If you have kept money in the market since 1960, you've probably had a brutally punishing experience. The old advice of buying good stocks and holding them would have been poor advice for recent times.

The Wharton School of Business and Finance conducted a study measuring the results of a particular timing service from 1950 to 1975 and found that an individual could have done 2-1/2 times as well by investing and selling as he would have done pursuing a buy-and-hold strategy.

From 1949 to 1960 the market gained 284 percent, and there were only two intervals of market declines, one of 13 percent and one of 19 percent. But from 1960 to 1981 investors were hit by five landslides during which the Dow-Jones index fell 53 percent; in the first part of 1982 it fell another 20 percent, while technology and energy issues showed losses from 30 to 50 percent.

I believe the stock market will offer you some excellent opportunities for extraordinary gains in the 1980s, but you will need to exercise some agility, or let the timing professionals do it for you.

Dollar-Cost-Averaging

As you've just seen, timing can be a problem, but dollar-cost-averaging in large or small amounts can greatly reduce the need for timing. Such an approach is useful for anyone who has a regular amount to invest over a period of years. Under this plan, you invest the same amount of money in the same security at the same interval. This will always buy you more shares at a low cost than a high cost and give you an average cost for your securities. If the market eventually goes up (so far, it always has), you should increase your capital.

The best way to accomplish this is to select a high-quality mutual fund that is a part of a well-managed family of funds that also has a money market fund. Establish a bank draft for the amount you can invest each month so the fund can draft your account. The advantage of this system is that the fund doesn't forget. I find that sometimes my clients do. Also, you don't have the temptation to skip a month or try to second-guess the market. There are certain decisions in life you need to make and move on—becoming financially independent is one of them.

When the value of your mutual fund reaches $10,000 you may also want to superimpose a timing service that can move it from the aggressive fund to the money market fund and back, as market timing dictates, while you continue your dollar-cost-averaging on the new money you are adding. (Most timing services request a minimum of $10,000.)

This system won't furnish you with fodder for excessive bragging over cocktails, but it has great potential for helping you reach your financial goals.

Capital Shortage

Shortage of capital will probably give you more opportunities for the triple-net leases we discussed in our chapter on investing in real estate. When money is tight, it is difficult even for major corporations to float bond issues at good rates, so they often sell their buildings and then lease them back. This gives them working capital and also provides them with some tax advantages. Triple-net leases of the buildings of major corportions, I believe, offer a much safer investment than their corporate bonds. Any court in the land will evict for nonpayment of rent, but not for nonpayment of interest on bonds. In addition to offering some tax shelter, leases provide equity buildup and appreciation.

Housing Shortage

Another investment potential occurs when housing is in short supply, as it is today.

For example, if you read that the average family income of the nation is $21,000 and the average home is $89,000, then you know that a large number of families will not be able to qualify for a home loan even if they could be granted interest-free mortgages.

I've already shared with you a comprehensive chapter on investing in real estate and you may want to go back and look at it again now. Suffice it to say here that a number of the registered real estate limited partnerships that we have used for our clients for a number of years invest in apartments, office buildings, and shopping centers and average 24–41 percent gain per year on sale. These partnerships have averaged holding periods of 3.5–7 years. At 24 percent you've doubled your money in three years, and at 41 percent in 1.76 years.

The real estate private placements we have used have far exceeded this yield, so if you are a "suitable investor" and there is a private offering by one of the general partners with an excellent track record, you may want to consider this route. Your diversification and therefore your risk will be greater, but your potential for gain will be greater, too. Will the placements do as well if you invest in them today? I really don't know. However, with the housing shortage growing even more acute and in view of the spread between what rents are today and what they must become before any new housing will be built, I believe your gain will exceed the gains of the past. As in the other investments, you would be following our guideline of seeing a need and filling it.

Energy Shortage

The shortage of energy, we know, has created investment opportunities. Here is a product that everyone wants and needs and that is in short supply. If you have the product to supply this need, this should indicate a good investment potential.

As mentioned in Chapter 8, the first $10,000 investment we made for clients in 1970 has now grown to over $182,000, which is around 50 percent compounded annually. A $25,000 investment I made in 1977 now has a value in excess of $72,000. This is in excess of 24 percent. Going back to our Rule of 72, this means I have doubled my capital in three years.

Cinema

We have not used registered limited partnerships that invest in cinema for a sufficient length of time to have a performance record. However, with a projected write-off the first year of around 65 percent together with your original investment and a projection of all your money back in one to two years, as well as trailing ancillary rights, cinema investment should be included in the possible ways of reaching your desired millionaire status.

The list goes on. Suffice it to say that your role is to develop the sense of being able to unemotionally stand back from your money and the investment scene and determine the various areas where the demand exceeds supply, and move your funds into those areas, as long as it appears that that situation will continue.

You can never rest on your laurels. We live in a dynamic world—that's why the title of this book has the words Money Dynamics in it. The world of money changes every day. Every day is a new day! You must meet it with intelligence, energy, gusto, and enthusiasm if you want to have your money in the right place at the right times.

Historic Returns

What skillfully selected investments have offered compound growth rates in excess of 20–30 percent in the past? There is no guarantee the rates will be the same in the future, but a study of past rates can shed some light on areas for you to explore. Those you will want to study are:

1. Carefully managed family businesses or closely held corporations. I consider a profitable, closely held corporation one of the best opportunities for tax shelter and creative financial planning that there is.

2. Well-located real estate: raw land, croplands, ranches, homes, residential and commercial income properties, using leverage when the timing is right. For every $1 you invest, consider borrowing at least another $3 to put with it through long-term mortgages when funds are available at the right price.

3. Carefully and aggressively selected and traded growth common stocks in emerging industries.

4. Selected growth mutual funds, using timing.

5. Selected oil and gas income programs.

6. Investment-quality diamonds and precious jewels, with purchases and sales carefully timed.

7. Antique furniture, art objects, and other collectibles, properly bought and sold.

8. Paintings and sculpture of gifted artists, properly bought and sold.

9. Rare stamps and coins carefully managed.

10. Gold and gold stocks or silver and silver stocks, carefully timed.

11. Commodities, if skillfully handled.

12. Entrepreneural activities.

Reaching a Million Dollars

Let's assume that you are twenty-five years of age, have saved $1,000, can save $50 per month, can maintain an average of 15 percent performance on your investments, and can pay income taxes from another source. Your progress report should then look something like this:

Age 25	$1,000 + $50 per Month
25	$ 1,000
30	8,663
35	18,054
40	40,967
45	87,052
50	179,745
55	466,185
60	741,183
65	1,495,435

If you are thirty years of age and fortunate enough to be able to make a lump-sum investment of $10,000 and can obtain an average return of 15 percent compounded annually, without adding new money to your investment but reinvesting all distributions and paying taxes from another source, your progress report should look something like this over a thirty-five year period:

Age 30	$10,000
35	20,113
40	40,456
45	81,371
50	163,670
55	329,190
60	662,120
65	1,331,800

If you can move up the performance ladder to 30 percent and if you had started with $1,000 and added $50 per month for forty years, your figures would be the following:

Age 25	$1,000
30	17,326
35	36,108
40	81,934
45	174,104
50	359,490
55	932,370
60	1,482,366
65	2,964,732

As you can see, at 30 percent you accomplished your goal in thirty years. With a lump sum of $10,000 at 30 years of age and a 30 percent performance, your progress report would look like this:

Age 30	*$10,000*
35	40,226
40	80,912
45	162,742
50	327,340
55	658,380
60	1,324,240
65	2,648,480

You've accomplished your goal here in less than twenty-five years.

Remember, we are not talking about "guarantees." All we are doing here is obtaining a visual picture of what compounding accomplishes over a period of years if you are able to maintain a 15 percent average and a 30 percent average.

We do not know what our future economy will be. Of one thing we can be certain, however: You will never reach your million-dollar goal with this amount of savings using "guaranteed" dollars. As a matter of fact, you won't keep even after inflation and taxes. If you hope to reach your goal, you must save and let your money grow. Investing your money aggressively and intelligently in well-managed and strategically located U.S. companies that are in the right industry at the right time, real estate expertly selected and intelligently leveraged, and natural resources that are in critical demand will not guarantee you growth of capital, but you will have provided your money with the opportunity to work as hard for you as you had to work to get it. The working dollar is an absolute necessity if your goal is to become a millionaire. Figure 12-1 shows that money compounds in a curve, not a straight line.

Sitting Tight

Do not be tempted to rationalize that because market conditions are unsettled now you should postpone starting your investment program or making investment decisions. When has the outlook been so obvious that you knew exactly what course to follow? If you take this attitude, you might as well dig a hole and bury your money. There is risk in any investment at any time. There is also a risk in a liquid position because of the steady erosion of fixed dollars due to inflation. As a matter of fact, I'll guarantee you at the present time you are going to lose.

As Figure 12-2 illustrates, there are always good reasons for investment inactivity, and our "sitting tight" friend was expert in discovering them. In doing so, he missed an entire lifetime of opportunities. Do the thing, and you will have the power!

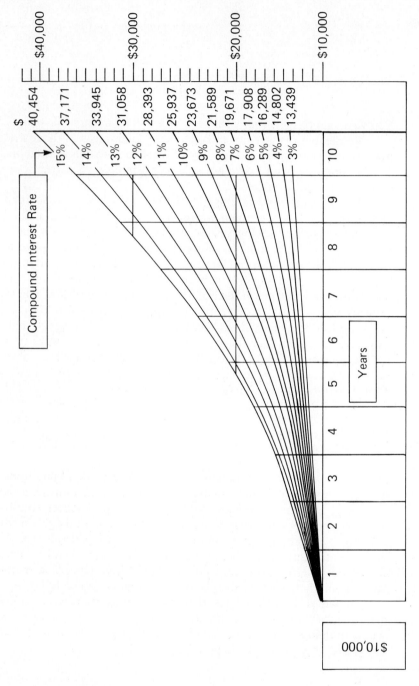

Figure 12-1. *Potential dollar value of $10,000 over a ten-year period at compound interest.*

Market Level

160
140
120
100
80
60
40
20
8
4
2

MARKET
LEVEL
17.46
STOCK PRICES
CLIMBING
TOO FAST
SIT TIGHT

MARKET
LEVEL
11.02
SUDDEN
SET-BACK
IN BUSINESS
RECOVERY
SIT TIGHT

MARKET
LEVEL
15.03
POSTWAR
DEPRESSION
CERTAIN
TO COME
SIT TIGHT

MARKET
LEVEL
40.33
MARKET
MAKING
LITTLE
PROGRESS
SIT TIGHT

MARKET
LEVEL
95.30
VIETNAM
CONFLICT
DIVIDES
AMERICA
SIT TIGHT

MARKET
LEVEL
115.4
WORLDWIDE
UNREST
CLOUDS
OUTLOOK
SIT TIGHT

SITTIN'
TIGHT
1920 – 1980

1927   1937   1947   1957   1967   1980

Figure 12-2.

Reread the first chapter of this book and recognize that to become a millionaire you will need to form the habits of doing things that failures do not like to do. Don't assume that your have certain dislikes peculiar to you and that successful people don't have these dislikes and do things you don't like to do. They don't like to do them any more than you do. These successful people are doing things they do not like to do in order to accomplish the things they want to accomplish. Successful people are motivated by pleasing results. Failures search for pleasing experiences and are satisfied with the results that they can obtain by doing the things they like to do.

Let's assume that your purpose is to become a millionaire—that your purpose is strong enough to make you form the habit of doing things you don't like to do in order to attain this goal.

To have maximum creativity, your body needs to have pure air, wholesome food, aerobic exercise and creative thoughts. When you get home from work, do you grab a can of beer, light up a cigar, and sit in front of the tube to watch a wrestling match or an actor solving one of the three to four murders that occur on television each night? Or do you jog, ride a bicycle, exercise on a treadmill, walk a distance, eat a light nutritious dinner (sans large amounts of simple carbohydrates, sugar, salt, caffeine, saturated fats, and alcohol, but containing complex carbohydrates, vitamins, minerals, and sufficient proteins), and then read the *National Tax Digest, Financial Planner* Magazine, *U.S. News & World Report, U.S. Washington Letter, Money* magazine, *Barrons National Business & Financial Weekly,* the *Wall Street Journal,* and *Business Week?* The successful investor does these things not because he wants to, but because he must in order to accomplish his goals.

You must, too, if you desire to become knowledgeable. Then you must learn to act upon that knowledge. Failures avoid decision making. Successful people know they must act. They have no other choice if they want to reach their goal.

Time plus money plus American free enterprise may make you a millionaire. If it does, fine. If it makes you financially independent, that will be a major accomplishment of which you can be justly proud.

Application

1. What metropolitan newspaper will you subscribe to immediately?
2. What current affairs magazines?
   (1)
   (2)

3. What business publications and newsletter?

    (1)

    (2)

4. What period each week will you faithfully set aside to read and study financial publications?

5. What uninterrupted one-hour period will you set aside each week to contemplate where demand is greater than supply in our country?

    Day of week:

    Time of day:

6. What two-hour period will you spend driving around your city or a city nearby to observe building and land developments?

    Week of the month:

7. What day each year will you take a financial inventory to see your progress dollarwise?

    Month:

    Date:

8. What self-improvement course will you take or what motivational tapes will you order to stimulate your thinking and improve your mental attitude? When?

9. Which books will you read to become better informed about nutrition? (You might start with *Pritikin's Program of Diet and Exercise.*)

10. What exercise program will you faithfully follow to become physically fit? (Dr. Kenneth Cooper's book *The Aerobics Way* is an excellent guide. I am on his aerobics program and heartily recommend it.)

11. What motivational books will you read to help you develop a positive mental attitude? I have found all of Dr. Robert H. Schuler's books and his cassette-tape package entitled "Possibility Thinking" of immense help. Also listen to his "Hour of Power" television program each Sunday, which is broadcast from the Crystal Cathedral in Garden Grove, California. Dr. Denis Waitley's cassette tapes "The Psychology of Winning" and his book by the same title are excellent. Also listen to Mike Vance's cassette album "Creative Thinking" and subscribe to his "Brain Exchange" cassettes. Earl Nightingale's tapes have been a part of my daily life for so many years that his thoughts have long ago been absorbed into mine. I especially like his "Direct Line" series. All of these can be ordered from Nightingale-Conant (address in Appendix Figure 3).

Chapter 13

Life Insurance—The Great National Consumer Dilemma

The Great Mystery

The great mystery of life is the length of it. You should have a plan with the hope that you will live a normal lifetime. You should have a plan in the event that you die before you have had time to accumulate a living estate. You do not know which will occur; therefore, you should prepare for either event. It is not difficult to acquire financial independence if you seek competent advice, apply your talents, and are granted sufficient time.

How can you be sure that you will have this time? You cannot. There is a way to "buy" time, however, and it is called "life insurance." This is the name given to it by life insurance companies who desire to sell it. A better term would be "financial protection for dependents." There is nothing that can insure your life.

The Purpose of Life Insurance

Life insurance is a wonderful thing. There is no substitute for it until a sufficiently large estate has been acquired to protect those dependent upon you. It can provide you with a way to guarantee that your dependents will have the financial means to continue to maintain your targeted standard of living in the event that you should die prematurely. It can be an economic extension of yourself. You should attempt to provide this protection for your dependents before you begin an investment program.

If you have dependents and you have not yet acquired a living estate, you need life insurance to cover the difference between what you have already acquired and what would be needed if you were not here to provide. For example, let's say that you have determined that your dependents would need an income of $2000 per month to maintain them at their present standard of living. At a 6 percent return this would require $400,000 of invested capital; at 9 percent it would require $300,000; at 12 percent $200,000. Let's assume that you have already acquired a living estate of $50,000 and you believe a 9 percent rate of return is reasonable. You would, therefore, need to provide a death estate of $250,000 (exclusive of Social Security) for a total estate of $300,000. As you increase your living estate, if your dependents' requirements have not increased, you can reduce your coverage, reduce this unnecessary expenditure of your money on premiums, and free dollars to be put to work more productively. Your goal is to become self-insured as soon as you can, not to see how much life insurance you can carry. Life insurance premiums are an expense paid with after-tax dollars, and you will want to reduce and eliminate this expense as soon as possible.

The purpose of life insurance is to place over your family's head the umbrella of time—the time to accumulate a living estate.

If you do not have dependents, you obviously do not need to protect dependents whom you don't have. Yet, I am amazed at how many people burden themselves to pay life insurance premiums to protect nonexistent dependents. They would not buy automobile insurance if they did not own an automobile. Therefore, they should apply the same common sense to the purchase of life insurance.

At the beginning of this book I stated that I have found through my many years of financial counseling six main reasons why most of our citizens reach the age of 65 flat broke: (1) procrastination, (2) failure to establish a goal, (3) ignorance of what money must do to attain that goal, (4) lack of a winning attitude, (5) failure to learn and apply our tax laws, and (6) being sold the wrong kind of life insurance. I say "sold" because I believe that had these people been better informed about life insurance, its purpose and cost, they would not have made the mistakes that I continue to see them making.

So that you and your family will not suffer from being sold the wrong kind of life insurance and so that you can change any program that does not make the best use of your money, let's look at the various types of policies and the names given to them. Regardless of what these policies are called, they contain protection alone or protection plus cash surrender value, which is often illegally referred to as a "savings account." As you will readily become aware from reading this chapter, this so-called "savings" element is the culprit that continues to cause all the controversy, confusion, and hostility in the life insurance industry. Premiums on policies that contain a "savings" element must of necessity be higher than those that do not. Since the number of dollars that you have in your budget for insurance is limited, the higher the premiums, the less coverage your dollars will buy. This in turn may cause you to be vastly underinsured so that if death occurs before you have had time to accumulate a living estate, your family may not have sufficient funds to continue to live in financial dignity.

Names Given to Life Insurance Policies

There are four major names given to life insurance policies sold in the United States today: *term, ordinary* or *whole life, limited payment life,* and *endowment.* Each can be participating and nonparticipating (I'll explain this later). In addition, there are special policies that provide combinations of these.

Regardless of what kind of life insurance policy you purchase or what it is called, the true cost of insurance goes up each year. Rates are based on likelihood of death, and each year as you become older you are more apt to die. This is reflected in a standard mortality table.

Term Insurance

There are three basic kinds of term protection: annual renewable term, decreasing term, and level term, plus some special kinds that contain the basic characteristics.

Annual Renewable Term. Let's look first at annual renewable term. If you have this type of policy, the face amount of your insurance remains the same and the rate per thousand increases each year, which it should, for as you grow older you are more likely to die and rates are based on likelihood of death. You can obtain annual renewable term in most states to age 100. This amount of time will adequately take care of any needs that you may have to protect your dependents.

Decreasing Term. Another type of term insurance is decreasing term. In decreasing term the premium remains the same and the amount of insurance decreases. A special form of decreasing term is called mortgage insurance when the rate of decrease matches mortgage amortization at a specified rate of interest. Other forms decrease at specified rates, such as equal percentage or equal amounts of the initial face value.

If knowing that your family will have extra funds to pay off the mortgage on your home gives you greater peace of mind, you can consider mortgage insurance. However, paying off the mortgage may not be the most prudent thing for them to do. They need only to continue making the monthly payments as before.

Decreasing term may serve your purpose very well, but the coverage does diminish each year. Perhaps you should place yourself in the driver's seat, so that you can decide whether or not your coverage should decline rather than have the decision made automatically for you. You can make your annual renewable term policy a decreasing term policy by just dropping the amount of coverage that your family no longer needs.

Level Term. Level term means that the face amount of the policy remains level for the term of time chosen and the premium remains level. The most common periods are 5, 10, 15, 20, 25, and 30 years, and level term to 65. For example, if you chose a 10-year level term, in essence what the insurance company would do is add up the annual renewable term premiums for 10 years and spread the premiums so that you would pay the same premium each year for 10 years. You would be overpaying in the early years and underpaying in the later years.

These are the three basic term policies. In addition, there are two types of policies that are variations of the level term and one type that is a variation of the annual renewable term.

Additional First-Year-Premium Level Term. Additional first-year-premium level term (inappropriately called "deposit level term") is a term policy, usually of 5-, 8-, 10-, 12-, 15-, or 20-year periods, wherein you pay an additional first-year premium to the company as evidence of your intent to retain your policy for the specified period of time. The one most commonly used by financial planners is ten years in duration; is renewable and convertible at your option without evidence of insurability; requires that you add an additional $10 per thousand to your first-year premium; and returns a cash benefit of $20 per thousand at the end of the period, which under current tax laws is not taxable.

For example, if you bought a $100,000 policy, you would add an additional $1000 to the premium the first year, and at the end of the 10 years $2000 would be returned to you. At that time you would have several options without having to provide evidence of insurability: taking out another such policy requiring an additional first-year premium, converting to decreasing term, or a wide variety of other options.

There are also some policies where the additional first-year premium is less than $10 for those who are younger and higher for those who are older.

If you should die during the 10-year period, the death proceeds in some such policies will include an additional amount ranging from the amount of additional first-year premium to the amount that would have been available if the policyholder had lived to the payment period.

The concept was developed because of the high cancellation rate on conventional policies. Reportedly, of every three new policies written today, one is lapsed within two or three years. These lapsed policies are expensive to the insurance company because of the substantial costs to place the policies in force initially. It has paid for your physical examination, paid a sales commission to the agent, and paid numerous other charges in relation to the policy. Accordingly it often charges a higher premium to all policyholders than would be necessary if there were no early lapses or if the company were given some protection against the cost of lapses. By requiring an additional first-year premium, it obtains this protection because, if the policy is dropped before the end of the period, it is entitled to keep all or a part of it.

Modified Premium Whole Life. This is another type of policy that you may encounter. It contains the basic characteristics of additional first-year-premium level term, however, with one major exception. At the end of the stated period of time it automatically converts into whole life, if no other election is made by you. (Whole life will be explained later.) You should exercise other options. (There is an exception: If you purchased a waiver of premium and you become disabled sufficiently to qualify for the waiver, allow the policy to convert to whole life and then consider borrowing out the cash value each year.)

Additional First-Year-Premium Annual Renewable Term. This type of policy has some of the same characteristics as the additional first-year level term policy already described except that, instead of remaining level for the specified period, the premium increases each year from the second through the tenth years. At that time you will have various options from which to choose without evidence of insurability—meaning the necessity of proving you are still healthy.

Whole Life

A whole life policy or ordinary life, as it is commonly called, is a policy where the face amount and the premiums remain the same for the whole life of the policyholder. In order to have a level premium, even though there is an increasing likelihood of death as the policyholder becomes older, the premium charged must be larger than would otherwise be necessary in the earlier periods of the policy so that the same premium can be charged when the policyholder is older.

From Figure 13-1 you will note that the cost-of-insurance line is below the level-premium line for many years and then crosses it around age 65.

As you will note, life expectancy is around age 75; you would have overpaid for 30 years (age 35 to 65) so that you could "underpay" for 10 years (age 65 to 75). A portion of these larger premiums that you

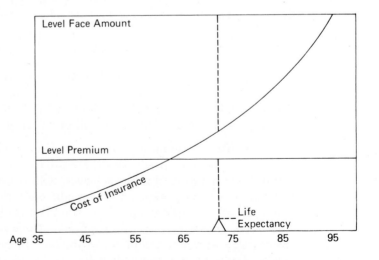

Figure 13-1. Level premium method

would have paid go to build what is called cash surrender value. The building of these values does not increase the amount that will be paid to the beneficiary in the event of your death. As the cash surrender value increases, the net amount at risk for the insurance company decreases; therefore, the policy takes on the characteristics of the decreasing term policy.

Contrary to what most policyholders, and a surprising number of agents believe, the cash surrender value of a policy belongs to the insurance company and it can only be obtained by the policyholder by borrowing against it at interest or by cancelling the policy and thereby losing the coverage.

This policy is also mistakenly referred to by some agents and insurance companies as "permanent" insurance. Anything that is permanent does not disappear. In this policy the "insurance" portion, or net amount at risk, is decreasing each year; therefore, it is not permanent. Only level term protection kept in force until death is permanent insurance.

Limited Payment Life

Another kind of cash value policy is one for which you pay premiums for a limited period of time. This type of coverage is called limited payment life. It provides lifetime coverage, with premiums payable for a specified period of time: 20 years, 30 years, or paid-up at age 65 (which would be a variable number of years depending on your age).

This type of policy offers your family less coverage for the funds spent in the years when they will most likely need the most protection, so that you can pay little or no premiums when your need for protection has lessened and your ability to pay has probably increased. In addition, and especially with our pattern of continued inflation, you have used "expensive" dollars while you were young—meaning dollars for which you had to work many hours—so that you could save less expensive ones later on—meaning dollars for which you had to work fewer hours.

Endowment

Another type of life insurance policy that you may have been sold is endowment. In this kind of policy, the face amount will be paid to you if you are still living on a specified date or to your beneficiary should you die prior to that date. Some are designed to endow in 20 years, others endow at age 65, although I'm amazed at the number of policies I come across that endow at age 80. Yes, 80! In reality, a whole life policy is really an endowment policy that endows at age 100.

In an endowment policy, as well as in other policies that accumulate cash surrender value, you may choose a lump-sum payout or an annuity of a specified amount per month as long as you live. If you make the latter choice, the monthly payments will cease upon your death. You may choose, however, to have your beneficiary continue to receive payments after your death for a set number of years. If you make this choice, you will receive smaller monthly payments. The premiums on an endowment policy, as you might expect, are very high in comparison with other types of policies.

Endowment policies are often sold as retirement programs or college education programs. Since these premiums are paid with after-tax dollars and the cash-surrender values usually compound at a very low rate, they can make an endowment policy an expensive and often quite inadequate way to invest for retirement or for college.

Universal Life

Lately you may have noticed a burst of advertising by a number of insurance companies and stock brokerage firms about a new concept in life insurance called Universal Life. Its proponents present it as the answer to everyone's life insurance and savings problems, offering flexibility both in premiums paid and in death benefits to be received. Universal Life begins with a specified premium and death benefit; but, from that time on, the policyholder may exercise some flexibility as to premiums paid and death benefits.

Although the death benefit is specified at the time the policy is taken out, the policyholder may change the death benefit upward, subject to evidence of insurability requirements, or downward, subject to some minimum. This flexiblity is referred to as "unbundling," meaning that the policy is broken down into three parts: the protection component, the savings component, and the expense component.

As the policyholder makes his payment, a portion of it goes into a savings fund, to yield interest to pay the premium. In effect, the policy puts together term insurance and a tax-sheltered annuity with variable rates, rather than the fixed rates most annuities provide.

Policies vary greatly. A policy for a male 40 years of age might have a first-year premium of $1000 for a death benefit of $100,000. His combined fees and insurance cost that year could use $900 of that premium. The $100 left would be put into a savings fund to earn interest at 4 percent.

The advertising for such a policy may show rates of 10 percent on the savings; but the ad does not specify what portion goes to savings and what portion goes to fees and other charges. The policy may in reality have no net earnings at all the first several years, might break

even in the fourth to fifth years, might go to 8 percent in the tenth year, and might go to the advertised 10 percent by the twentieth year. Also, if a loan is taken out against the policy, a lower rate may be paid on the cash that secures the loan.

Should you consider Universal Life? The answer is no. The guaranteed and illustrated rates of return on the savings portion are not great enough to attract a knowledgeable purchaser.

If you have an extra $2000, for example, you may want to establish an Individual Retirement Account, deduct that amount from your taxable income, thereby lowering your tax liabilities, and have all the income from the account compound tax-deferred. If you desire to have access to your funds before you are 59-1/2 years of age, which is required if you don't want to pay a penalty under IRA, you may invest in a tax-deferred annuity directly yourself, although you would be using after-tax dollars rather than before-tax dollars. This book contains many ways to increase your net worth more rapidly and safely than "bundling" living and dying.

Only One Kind of Life Insurance

There is only one kind of life insurance, and that is pure protection based on a mortality table. All others are pure protection plus a cash value element that I call "funny" banking. Term protection can be a wonderful bargain, and a real necessity for your family if you have not yet had time to acquire a sufficient living estate. Once this has been achieved, you no longer have any need for life insurance: Your need to protect their financial livelihood has already been accomplished. Life insurance is to protect an economic potential. You have either made it financially by 65, or you'll probably never make it.[*]

"Funny" Banking

What do I mean when I use the term "funny" banking in reference to cash value life insurance? Do I mean that a whole life policy is similar to a savings account at a banking institution? Of course not! What I do mean is that the vast majority of people who buy and those who sell cash value life insurance do so because they believe (or are led to believe) that owning such a policy is a good way to save for the future.

---

[*]After you have "made it," you have fulfilled your obligations to your family and yourself. However, at that point you may have another desire. You may want to pass on your estate intact, or at least partially so, to your heirs. You do not have this obligation, but if it is your desire, it is easy to calculate how much insurance will be needed to pay inheritance taxes and retain that amount.

➤ FuNnY BaNkiNg RuLes

1. We may take all the deposits you make into your account the first year.

2. We will charge you to deposit money into your savings account. .

3. We will only pay a specified amount if you die regardless of the amount in your savings account.

4. You will be charged 5½% interest to borrow on your savings

5. If you withdraw your savings, you lose your life insurance policy.

To illustrate the differences between cash value life insurance policies and bank accounts, and why the former has always been such a dismal vehicle for any useful savings program—and is even more so with our present rate of inflation—I invite you to imagine the following scenario. Suppose that you were to go to an institution named "The First Funny Bank of America" and told the polite man inside that you wanted to open a savings account. And suppose he said to you, We're happy to have you, and here are our rules: First, you must buy term life insurance with us to open your account. Second, in addition to what you pay us for the insurance, you must deposit so many dollars into your account for each unit of insurance that you buy. Third, we'll take everything that you deposit into the account the first year. After that, we'll charge you to deposit money into your account. If you want to borrow from this account, we'll charge you 5-1/2 percent to borrow this money. If you should die while this loan is outstanding, we'll subtract it from the amount that we'll pay your beneficiary. If you refuse to pay us for the privilege of borrowing from this account and withdraw the account, we'll cancel your life insurance policy. If you do not borrow from this account and should die, we will not pay your beneficiary the face amount plus the accumulated deposits, but only the face amount.

If the bank had said all of these things to you, would you have opened the account? Think carefully about your answer, because I have just described some of the end results of a typical cash value policy.

The Sales Presentation

In an effort to increase your level of awareness, I feel that it would be helpful at this time if I were to pretend that I am a life insurance agent who has come to sell you the life insurance policy that would

Let's again look at a 20-year endowment policy and look at a common "net cost" presentation on a $10,000 policy:

Total premiums, ages 35–55	$9,000
Maturity value at age 55	10,000
Net profit	$1,000

Again, doesn't this look great? $10,000 of insurance for 20 years, and you get all your money back, plus $1000. Does it appear that the insurance company is actually giving you free protection while paying you $1000? Are you asking yourself if you can afford to turn down this marvelous opportunity? If you truly care about your family's welfare, it appears that it would be prudent to do so. Remember that you lost the use of that money for 20 years and that you could have bought term protection for a fraction of that amount. Incidentally, most states now require an interest-adjusted cost index to accompany all sales presentations like the one above. However, the *true* cost of life insurance depends on a large number of factors, including the rate of inflation during the life of the policy (meaning, if we have inflation, the purchasing power of your dollars would be less when you got them back), available investment vehicles and interest prevailing during the number of years the policy was in force, and, obviously, whether the policy was lapsed, matured, or terminated upon the death of the policyholder.

Minimum Deposit

Minimum deposit insurance plans, affectionately called "mini-dip" by the salesmen who sell them, are whole life or limited-pay life policies (often "participating") that charge a very large premium to create artificially high early-cash-surrender values. If you have this type of insurance, it was your money that produced these high cash values. This type of policy is often presented to those in a 40 percent or above tax bracket, usually in the form of impressive computer printouts that show borrowing out most of the cash values as soon as possible and charging off the interest on their income tax returns.

The impression is often given that the IRS is the one actually financing the insurance program. Even if the interest could be deductible in this plan (and there does seem to be some doubt about the legality of deducting all of it, especially if the policy were purchased after August 6, 1963), it is not brilliant economics to use after-tax dollars to substitute for insurance dollars that can be bought for a few pennies, pay a salesman to put those dollars into cash surrender value, and then pay an insurance company for the privilege of taking these dollars back out of the policy. No interest at all is better than tax-deductible interest.

None of us is in a 100% tax bracket. Only buy "mini-dip" if you have an insurance agent friend whom you want to help prosper and become a member of the Million Dollar Round Table. If your first allegiance is to yourself and the welfare of your family, there is a better way.

Cost Per Thousand Goes Up Each Year

Because of the widespread misunderstanding of this basic fact of life, I reiterate, regardless of what kind of policy you buy, your cost per thousand dollars of coverage increases as you grow older because cost per thousand is based on likelihood of death. There is an increasing cost to insure an increasing risk. As you grow older, you are more likely to die.

The true risk of a whole life policy is shifted from the insurance company over to the cash value portion of the policy a little more each year. This is how the insurance company can afford to provide you with the same death benefit coverage year after year without seeming to charge you any more for it.

Mortality Tables

The mortality table is the initial base for calculating the cost per thousand dollars of coverage of your life insurance policy. Nothing can repeal that table, regardless of how many tantalizing names the advertising industry dreams up to call the various policies. The "insurance" factor is the likelihood of death and is listed by deaths per thousand.

The first table used by insurance companies was the American Experience Table. It was based on statistics gathered between 1843 and 1858. During that time, of 1000 men aged 35, statistically 8.95 died during a given year. That was the death rate in the days of Abraham Lincoln. The second table that the insurance companies were required to use was the Commissioner's 1941 Standard Ordinary Table, based on death statistics gathered between 1930 and 1940—before penicillin. During that period, the death rate had dropped to 4.59 per thousand men aged 35. Later, in 1966, the insurance companies were required to go on the 1958 Commissioner's Standard Ordinary Table, based on statistics from between 1950 and 1954. On this table, the death rate has dropped to 2.51 per thousand. There is now a 1980 CSO Table that has been adopted by some states and the death rate has dropped to 2.11 per thousand.

Insurance companies are not required to go back to old policyholders when a new mortality table becomes available. They, therefore, may continue year after year to charge on the old table.

Table 13-1 is a combination of all three of the mentioned mortality tables, showing deaths per thousand at each age and life expectancy. Study it carefully.

Buy When You Are Young?

Have you ever heard "Buy your insurance while you are young because it's cheaper"? Of course it is. A young man of 25, buying term protection on his life for his 25th year of life, will obviously pay substantially less than a man of 55 buying identical protection for his 55th year. But here is the distinction that many people miss: The fact that an individual has bought coverage early in life has no bearing whatever on what he will pay for that identical coverage when he is older. There are no special mortality tables for people who bought insurance when they were young. They are just as apt to live or die as those people who did not buy coverage at an early age. Those who bought insurance at age 25 will not have a lower cost per thousand at age 55 than those who did not buy at age 25. The same mortality tables apply to everyone. All 55-year-old policyholders pay essentially the same cost per thousand for protection during their 55th year.

Repositioning

During my many years as a financial planner, I have found that the vast majority who come to me actually have some assets. The problem often lies in where these assets are positioned. Many times their assets are working much harder for others than they are for them.

Let me give you an example of a family man, age 35, with a wife and three children, who was carrying an $80,000 paid-up-at-65 life insurance policy that contained $6269 in cash value and for which he was paying an annual premium of $1258. He was in a 44 percent tax bracket. He wanted to set up an Individual Retirement Account, but after paying current expenses he did not have an additional $2000 to invest each year.

Let's take a look at how we greatly increased his living and death estate by just repositioning his assets without increasing his expenditures.

His family was inadequately protected with only $80,000 of life insurance coverage. We obtained a new $200,000 policy, consisting of a $50,000 additional first year premium 10-year-level term policy plus a $150,000 annual renewable term rider. His new premium was $428 and he made a first year additional premium of $500.

Table 13-1. Deaths per 1000 in Three Statutory Mortality Tables

Age	American Experience Table	Commissioners' 1941 Table	Commissioners' 1958 Table	Expectation of Life 1958 Table in Years
20	7.80	2.43	1.79	50.37
21	7.86	2.51	1.83	49.46
22	7.91	2.59	1.86	48.55
23	7.96	2.68	1.89	47.64
24	8.01	2.77	1.91	46.73
25	8.06	2.88	1.93	45.82
26	8.13	2.99	1.96	44.90
27	8.20	3.11	1.99	43.99
28	8.26	3.25	2.03	43.08
29	8.34	3.40	2.08	42.16
30	8.43	3.56	2.13	41.25
31	8.51	3.73	2.19	40.34
32	8.61	3.92	2.25	39.43
33	8.72	4.12	2.32	38.51
34	8.83	4.35	2.40	37.60
35	8.95	4.59	2.51	36.69
36	9.09	4.86	2.64	35.78
37	9.23	5.15	2.80	34.88
38	9.41	5.46	3.01	33.97
39	9.59	5.81	3.25	33.07
40	9.79	6.18	3.53	32.18
41	10.01	6.59	3.84	31.29
42	10.25	7.03	4.17	30.41
43	10.52	7.51	4.53	29.54
44	10.83	8.04	4.92	28.67
45	11.16	8.61	5.35	27.81
46	11.56	9.23	5.83	26.95
47	12.00	9.91	6.36	26.11
48	12.51	10.64	6.95	25.27
49	13.11	11.45	7.60	24.45
50	13.78	12.32	8.32	23.63
51	14.54	13.27	9.11	22.82
52	15.39	14.30	9.96	22.03
53	16.33	15.43	10.89	21.25
54	17.40	16.65	11.90	20.47
55	18.57	17.98	13.00	19.71
56	19.89	19.43	14.21	18.97
57	21.34	21.00	15.24	18.23
58	22.94	22.71	17.00	17.51
59	24.72	24.57	18.59	16.81
60	26.69	26.59	20.34	16.13

We placed the $6269 of cash value in a money market fund which at that time was earning 17.5%.

His premium savings the first year was $330, his tax savings was $880 ($2000 IRA x 44%), leaving $790 to be withdrawn from the money market fund to obtain the $2000 needed for his IRA account. (The second year his premium dropped to $435.50, for a premium savings of $822.50 plus his $880 tax savings, making it necessary to withdraw $297.50 from the fund.)

Now let's tally up to see how his beneficiaries would have fared had he died immediately after we repositioned his assets:

$200,000	Face amount of the policy
500	Additional Death Benefit
2,000	IRA account
5,479	Money Market Fund
$207,979	Living and Death Benefit
80,000	Previous Death Estate
$127,979	Increase in Total Estate

His beneficiaries would have received $127,979 more than they would have before repositioning.

How will they fare if he lives for ten years and then dies? This will depend on the performance of his IRA account and his earnings on his money market mutual fund. Let's make some assumptions. In the first, he averages only 8 percent on his IRA account (shame on him) and 6.72% after taxes on his money market fund. In the second, he averages 15 percent on his IRA and 12% on his money market fund.

Results in 10 years:

at 8% plus 6.72%		at 15% plus 12%	
$200,000	Face Amount	$200,000	
1,000	Matured "deposit"	1,000	
31,291	IRA at 8%	46,699	at 15%
4,017	In savings after taxes	8,731	Before taxes
$236,308	Total	$256,430	Total
80,000	Previous	80,000	Previous
$156,308	Increase	$176,430	Increase

As you can see, in ten years his death and living estate would have increased between $156,308 and $176,430 by repositioning, and his "living estate" would have increased between $36,308 and $56,430.

In ten years his children will be ten years older and their need for protection may have decreased while his living estate has increased. If his children still need protection, his policy is renewable and convertible without evidence of insurability so he has the option of renewing, decreasing, or dropping the coverage as his economic situation at that time dictates.

How Much Life Insurance?

How do you calculate the amount of life insurance that you should carry? First, take your present monthly salary. Let's assume that it is $3000. Multiply this amount by 70 to 75 percent, using 75 percent if you have three or more children. This is about what your family would need to maintain them at their present standard of living if you were not here to provide for them. At 70 percent, $2100 would be needed. Let's assume that your family would be eligible for maximum Social Security. Your wife may receive around $1200 per month until your children reach 18, thus, $2100 less $1200 + $900. How much capital is required to produce $900 per month (given an annual yield of 6 percent)? Just multiply by 200 (12 months ÷ .06) to determine the principal. This calculation gives you $180,000. Let's assume that you have accumulated $20,000 in liquid assets (exclusive of home furnishings and other non-liquid assets). Subtract this amount from $180,000, leaving $160,000 of capital needed.

Calculate the amount that you need, using this method, remembering to add other appropriate expenses such as college costs, etc. Determine if the premiums for this amount of term insurance will fit into your family's budget. If they can, fine. If they cannot, you must reduce the coverage to the amount that you can afford and still live comfortably today.

Double and Triple Indemnities

The question often arises about the amount of accidental death insurance that a young family should carry. In our financial planning, we do not count accidental death policies when calculating the family's need for protection. Even though most young fathers are convinced that if they die, that's the way they'll go, it's not too likely—that's why the rates are low! It's more likely that they'll die from a heart attack while mowing their lawns. It doesn't really matter how you'll die: You are just as dead, and the family's needs are just as real. Buy sufficient life insurance to cover their full needs and don't worry about how you may die.

To Par or Not to Par

A rose is a rose is a rose. But a life insurance dividend is not a dividend is not a dividend! It is a partial return of an overcharge. Those policies that pay "dividends" are often called "participating" policies. (On the front lower left-hand side of the policy you may read "PAR" or "NONPAR.") The words "participating" and "dividends" have a nice ring to them. After all, you certainly enjoy your dividends from your 100 shares of General Motors or Exxon or from your Seminar Fund. But what is a "dividend" from an insurance policy? I refer you to no less authority than the United States Treasury Department Decision No. 1743. When the Tariff Bill of 1911 proposed an income tax on life insurance dividends, representatives of life insurance companies protested the tax. I quote from the decision arrived at after the protest:

> Reduced to final analysis the contentions of the various companies are . . .
>
> That dividends declared by participating companies are not dividends in a commercial sense of the word, but are simply refunds to the policyholder of a portion of the overcharged collected, which overcharge is merely held in trust by the company issuing the policy. Annually, or at stated periods, all, or a portion thereof, is returned to the person holding the policy . . . It was vigorously contended by counsel representing certain of these companies that it was necessary in order to secure new business, to convince the prospective policyholder of the desirability of the same, and that this commercial necessity had resulted in the companies' making misrepresentations of facts as to dividends to prospective purchasers of insurance, and that names and designations, having a single specific meaning in the commercial world and which were therefore attractive to prospective policyholders, had been adopted to represent transactions which they now hold are entirely different from that their name implies and represents, and from which the policyholder himself believed he was receiving and that business necessities had caused a continuance of these misnomers. *It was represented that, in fact, there were no dividends, but merely a refund of overcharges, which for reasons above stated, were usually referred to as dividends.*

Another test as to whether a dividend is a dividend or a partial return of an overcharge, is to ask if you have to pay taxes on it. The answer is no. I'm sure you'll agree that the IRS is never charitable. If it were truly a dividend, it would be taxable.

Participation—How Much Does It Cost?

Carefully study Table 13-2 and you will discover that your cost for "participating" depends on your age. Generally, the younger you are, the more you are overcharged. For example, if you purchased a participating

Table 13-2. Comparative Annual Whole Life Premiums (Par and Nonpar)

Issue Age	Whole Life (Par)	Whole Life (Nonpar)	Amount of Overcharge	Percentage Overcharge
20	$13.60	$ 9.04	$ 4.56	50%
21	13.99	9.40	4.59	49%
22	14.40	9.81	4.59	47%
23	14.82	10.23	4.59	45%
24	15.26	10.67	5.00	47%
25	15.72	11.09	4.63	42%
26	16.20	11.49	4.71	41%
27	16.70	11.88	4.82	41%
28	17.23	12.28	4.95	40%
29	17.77	12.70	5.07	40%
30	18.35	13.16	5.19	39%
31	18.95	13.71	5.24	38%
32	19.58	14.28	5.30	37%
33	20.24	14.87	5.37	36%
34	20.93	15.48	5.45	35%
35	21.67	16.11	5.56	35%
36	22.43	16.77	5.66	38%
37	23.24	17.46	5.78	33%
38	24.10	18.18	5.92	33%
39	24.99	18.94	6.05	32%
40	25.94	19.74	6.20	31%
41	26.93	20.59	6.34	31%
42	27.97	21.48	6.49	30%
43	29.07	22.42	6.65	30%
44	30.22	23.41	6.81	29%
45	31.45	24.45	7.00	29%
46	32.74	25.53	7.21	28%
47	34.10	26.68	7.42	28%
48	35.54	27.88	7.66	27%
49	37.07	29.15	7.92	27%
50	38.69	30.50	8.19	27%
51	40.40	31.93	8.47	27%
52	42.21	33.46	8.75	26%
53	44.14	35.08	9.06	26%
54	46.18	36.80	9.38	25%
55	48.35	38.61	9.74	25%
56	50.66	40.54	10.12	25%
57	53.12	42.59	10.53	25%
58	55.74	44.77	10.97	25%
59	58.53	47.08	11.45	24%
60	61.60	49.53	12.07	24%

policy at age 20 from one of the largest insurance companies, you would have paid $13.60 per thousand dollars of coverage that first year. If you had purchased a nonparticipating policy from another large company using the same mortality table, you could have paid $9.04 that year. The amount of your overcharge was $4.56 per thousand, or 50 percent. At age 35, your overcharge was 35 percent, and at age 50 it was 27 percent.

As the years go by, the insurance company's board of directors can vote to return a portion of this overcharge. In fact, your net premium (premium less "dividend") in later years could even be less than for a nonparticipating policy taken out at the same time. Why do I object then to a participating policy? Because of the time use of money. Money has tremendous earning power. Put it to work for you and your family from day one.

Let's discuss how to take the first step in analyzing your own policies. First, you'll need to get them out of the safe deposit box or wherever you have them stored. Now read them. I'll bet that you never have, even though you've been pouring some of your lifeblood into them.

After you have finished, look on the front of each policy. There you will find the date the policy was acquired. That's its birthdate. Take today's date, less the policy's birthdate, and this gives you the age of the policy. For example, if you acquired your policy in December 1971, and it is now December 1981, it is ten years old. Look toward the back of the policy if you have the "cash value" variety. Go down to the tenth year of the nonforfeiture section. Go across and you will find a "cash surrender" or "loan value." This amount will be for either the face amount or per thousand dollars of coverage. It will state one or the other at the top of the chart. For example, if it's a $10,000 policy and your cash table shows $350 opposite 10 years and the table shows "per $1,000," you would have a cash value of $3,500.

From Whom Should I Buy?

From whom should you buy your protection? Certainly one of the prerequisites is that he not be a member of a captive sales force, meaning that he can write only for the one company to which he is beholden. He cannot be impartial under these conditions. Circumstances will not allow him to be. Also, his company may not even have a policy that fits your needs; if it does have one hidden away, the sales structure in which he works may discourage him from even mentioning it to you.

In my opinion, you should plan your life insurance needs with a financial planner who is dually licensed and is knowledgeable in investments to help you build a living estate and in life insurance to help you buy the time to acquire that estate. These two areas of financial planning are inseparable, since you don't know how long your life will be or how long it will take you to acquire that estate.

I must warn you, however, that dual licensing alone does not ensure that the advice you receive will be objective. Some dually licensed individuals maintain that it will not make any difference to them whether they sell you securities or insurance. Actually, it makes a whale of a difference in their compensation. If they sell you a whole life policy at a cost of $1,000, they may receive as high as 110 percent of that first year's premium (or $1,100) over a two-year period, plus some trail commission from the policy in the future. If they sell you "term" and invest the balance for you in a mutual fund, they would receive only a small fraction of this amount.

Which Life Insurance Company?

Does it make a difference from which legal reserve life insurance company you buy pure protection? No, generally it does not. But you should seek the one that offers the best features at the best rates, designed to help you build a living estate (*beyond* the policy). It should offer policies that are renewable and convertible at your option to a variety of other policies, without evidence of insurability, to a ripe old age. This puts you in the driver's seat, and that's where you should be in designing and carrying out your financial plan.

Life Insurance for Children?

I'm amazed at the amount of money spent each year on premiums for life insurance for children. If you have a policy on the life of your child, ask yourself, "Who is dependent on my child for a livelihood?" You should never make a practice of protecting your liabilities, but only of protecting your assets. As much as you love your child or children, they are financial liabilities until they are old enough and sufficiently prepared to leave your nest.

Should you have enough for burial? You can if you want to, but it's a luxury that I don't recommend. There are limited dollars in the family budget for life insurance, and every dollar spent on life insurance to cover the children means one more dollar taken away from purchasing life insurance on the life of the breadwinner. You may shun such a somber thought, but a child's funeral expenses will be defrayed by the decrease in the cost of caring for the child, while the loss of a wage earner may be a near economic disaster to the family.

If you desire some coverage on your children, you can place a rider on your policy. A common rate is $8.00 per unit, which provides

$1000 of coverage on each child until age 25, at which time it can be converted to $5000 of coverage without evidence of insurability. From five to ten units can usually be obtained.

College Policies

I've seen many endowment policies taken out at the time of a child's birth for the purpose of providing for the expenses of four years of college that did not even cover the cost of the first semester. It makes me sad every time I see an advertisement portraying a beaming youth with a mortarboard jauntily atop his head, proclaiming that his college endowment policy brought him to this happy occasion.

Although you certainly want to plan for your children's education, a college endowment policy is not an effective way to accomplish this worthwhile goal. Planning for this expense is covered in Chapter 15.

A Good "Compulsory" Savings Plan?

First, it should be clear to you by now that life insurance is not the best means available of investing money for the future. You may have been told that life insurance does provide a very convenient way to "set aside" a certain amount each month without the "bother" of setting up a separate savings and investment program. If you have the self-discipline to make premium payments over a period of several years, you can surely manage to invest money in ways that will achieve much more satisfactory results for you.

To further your efforts to gather information in this regard, you may want to read in its entirety the study made by the Federal Trade

Commission and released in July 1979, entitled "Life Insurance Cost Disclosure." In this study, the FTC presented a chart that is its interpretation of rates of return on various investments. This study has since become controversial. I suggest that you read it for yourself and reach your own conclusions. Figure 13-4 is a chart taken from that study.

An Inexpensive Way to Borrow Money?

Sometimes people will proudly point out to me how very bright they have been to have figured out that they can borrow on their policy for 4-1/2 percent to 8 percent instead of from the bank at a higher rate. If you are doing this, you are paying to borrow after-tax dollars that you placed there to begin with. Would you agree to the same arrangement with your bank? Also, you are reducing the amount of your life insurance coverage when you borrow against your policy, because the loan is subtracted from the face amount if it is outstanding at the time of your death. Borrowing against your policies serves only to increase your cost and reduce your coverage. If you are healthy enough to pass a physical, get term protection. If you are not, by all means consider borrowing the cash value out and putting it to work, preferably in an investment with a tax-sheltered cash flow, and write the insurance company a check for the interest each year and deduct the amount on your tax return.

The Six-Month Wait

I've often been asked about the six-month waiting period that can be involved when you request the privilege of borrowing from the cash surrender value of a policy. You might be interested in learning how this came about. During the Depression, many people were cashing in their insurance policies, and many insurance companies were on the verge of bankruptcy. Around that time President Franklin Roosevelt declared a bank holiday saying, in effect, "Sorry about that, but we cannot return to you the funds you have deposited in your bank checking and savings accounts." With this announcement, lights began flashing in the home offices of many insurance companies, and their executives said, "Oh, my goodness! Why didn't we think of that?" They got permission to suspend paying cash value, and ever since that date this six-month waiting period has been in most cash value insurance policies. No recent financial upheaval has led insurance companies to employ this provision; however, you should be aware that the provision is there.

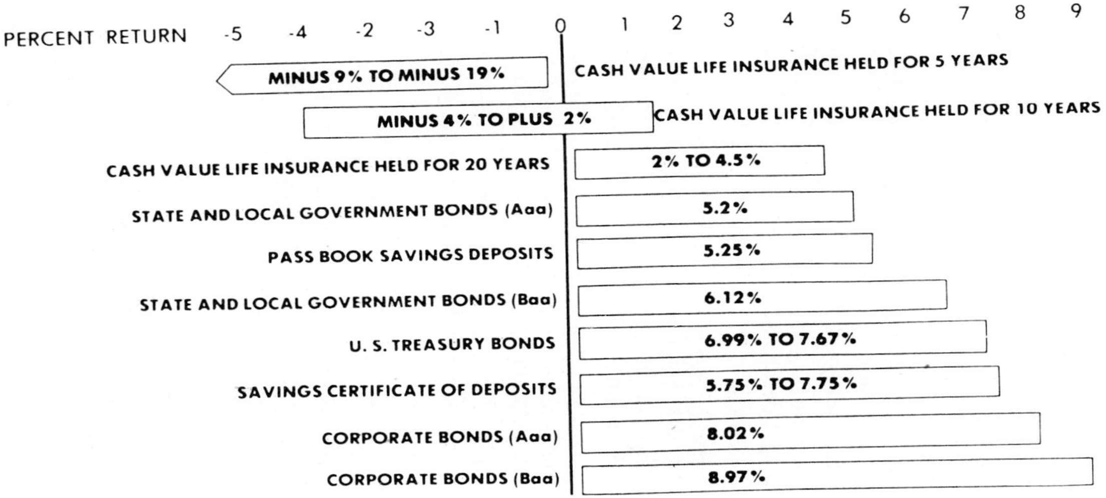

Figure 13-4. *Rates of return on various investments, 1977.*

SOURCE: FEDERAL TRADE COMMISSION

CAVEAT: PURCHASERS SHOULD CONSIDER TAX ADVANTAGES AND DISADVANTAGES OF ALTERNATIVE INVESTMENTS. RETURNS ON CASH VALUE INSURANCE POLICES ARE GENERALLY TAX FREE. SOME BONDS ARE TAX-EXEMPT.

Will You Lose If You Change Your Policies?

The belief that you will lose if you change your insurance policies may have scared you away from the common-sense program of pure protection based on need. Your concern should not be how much you will lose by dropping an existing cash surrender value policy. This money has already been lost. A large portion of total commissions and other acquisition costs were taken out in the early years of your policy, and this money will never come back to you. Your real question is, "How much more will my family and I have if I replace my policy and invest the difference?"

There is nothing sacred about those pieces of paper containing too much fine print glued or stapled together. Life insurance is a commodity. You just naturally get more emotional about something that is related to your life. Why should cash value life insurance be considered a sacred cow? Why is it as good today as it was 100 years ago? Is our rate of inflation the same? Is our overall economy the same? Economics, not emotion, should determine how you protect those dependent upon you.

Look at it this way. Assume that you are a pilot flying to Miami. On calculating your location, you find that you have overshot Miami and are over the Atlantic Ocean. You also find that you have just enough fuel to get back to Miami. If you keep going, you'll run out of fuel and drop into the ocean. If you turn around now, you'll have enough fuel to make it back. Would you bury your error or rationalize it? No. You would change your course and head back toward your destination as soon as possible, for every minute wasted could be costly and catastrophic. Successful financial planning is based on the same principle. If you are heading in the wrong direction, alter your course as soon as possible.

Consider if you will for a moment the viability of the concept that any other financial decision made in our dynamic world should never be changed. Is it logical that the only exception is a cash surrender value life insurance policy? Should you ever be forced to make irreversible long-term financial decisions amidst economic uncertainty? Yet, there are companies that teach their agents that cash surrender value policies are sacred.

Replacement—Benefit or Blasphemy?

As more and more people have become better informed about the potential earning power of their money and also more aware of inflation's devastation to its purchasing power, they have been searching for more productive ways to put their dollars to work. In an attempt to slow this tide of change, some companies have waged very successful campaigns to get regulations passed to require that agents complete and submit lengthy, detailed, and often difficult replacement forms if they recommend the replacement of any policy, regardless of which mortality table was used.

Replacement forms in some states have become so tedious and time-consuming that many a conscientious financial planner has left his client's present insurance program alone, even when it was grossly inadequate and unnecessarily expensive, rather than spend the many hours required to complete these forms.

In Appendix Figure 12 you will find a completed replacement form for one state for an actual case. See if you can calculate the insured's true cost per thousand after you have studied the comparison statement.

Twisting

Some cash value life insurance salesmen refer to a financial planner who recommends term insurance as a "termite," or, if the financial planner has replaced one of their policies, they may call him a "twister." This implies that all who recommend changing your insurance program are "twisters." This is not true. A cash value salesperson *or* a term insurance salesperson is said to be "twisting" if he uses misrepresentation or an incomplete comparison to induce a replacement to the detriment of the policyholder. If he provides an honest complete explanation and disclosure, he is not a "twister."

Some insurance companies, when they receive a notice that one of their cash surrender value policies is going to be replaced, send a dire warning letter and pamphlet to the policyholder, warning him of the serious mistake that he is about to make. Many of the large insurance companies have marshaled their forces to try to put an end to replacement of their policies.

Should You Replace?

Your answer is probably "yes," if you are healthy enough to pass a physical and if any one of these three conditions applies to you:

1. You have more than one policy. A policy fee is charged each year for each policy to pay for administration, in addition to the mortality cost. This fee averages from $10 to $25 per year. If you are carrying six policies and you have a $20 policy fee per policy, you are spending $100 per year unnecessarily. This extra amount could be used for investing or obtaining additional coverage.

2. You have a cash surrender value in your policy. If your bank

had the same requirements as the insurance company, would you do business with it?

3. Your policies are not on a current mortality table.

When Should You Not Replace?

Are there circumstances when you should not replace one or more of your insurance policies? Yes, and here are some of the reasons:

1. You are uninsurable.

2. You cannot lower your cost per thousand by obtaining a new policy.

3. Any of the nonforfeiture provisions of your present policies are important to your current financial planning. These provisions may include paid-up additions and extended-term provisions. Extended term provides that if you quit paying premiums, the company uses the cash surrender values in the policies to extend the period of your coverage. For example, let's say that your cash value was enough to buy you term coverage for ten years. You chose this option and died in the eleventh year. Your family would receive nothing. If you died the second year, they would receive only the extended term amount and the insurance company would keep the nine years of prepaid insurance premiums. There may be income options and annuity options in your present policies that you should examine carefully. Determine if your financial planner can provide you with better alternatives.

4. You are planning to give false information on your new insurance application. There is a two-year contestability period that could result in your heirs receiving only the amount of coverage those premiums would have purchased had you given accurate information.

5. You bought your policies from a friend, and you feel that you would lose him as a friend if you replace them, and a friendship based on his economic benefit is more important to you than the economic future of your family.

6. You cannot withstand the pressure that may be brought to bear on you by your present insurance company or its agent if you attempt to replace.

7. You are planning to commit suicide within the next two years.

My Personal Testimony

From reading this chapter I want to be sure that you have not obtained the impression that I am anti-life insurance. All widows believe in life insurance and I was widowed only eleven months after a conscientious insurance agent had shown us how to obtain more coverage for the dollars that we were spending. Because of the life insurance proceeds I received and my ability to make them grow, I am now financially independent and am writing this book, presenting investment seminars and counseling because I want to and not from economic necessity. I am proud to say that I am a life insurance agent. I receive immense satisfaction from helping families properly buy the time to accumulate a living estate.

Life Insurance—A Very Personal Matter

Your life insurance program should be designed to fit your needs at this particular time. Your needs will change from year to year, so your policies should be reviewed constantly. They are not sacred instruments. Your need for protection may be less, the same, or more each year. Have the effects of inflation made your present coverage inadequate? Is there a new mortality table available? If so, you will want to apply for a new policy if you can get a lower rate. When you have the new policy safely secured (not before), then consider what should be done with your old policies. Policies can be changed and riders can be dropped. Work with a creative financial planner to keep your insurance program finely tuned to your changing needs. A good insurance program should not be expensive, if properly designed, and should be well within your family's budget.

In summary, let me re-emphasize—life insurance is a necessary umbrella until you've had the time to accumulate a living estate. It should be purchased with these ten points in mind:

1. Determine your life insurance needs as if you were going to die today, but also include an extra amount to offset inflation.

2. Life insurance is based on a mortality table; therefore, it should cost you more each year because you are more apt to die. Every time there is a new mortality table, and the rates are lowered, apply for a new policy if doing so can reduce your cost. If you pass the physical and obtain a new policy at a lower rate, redeem or cancel the old one. A life insurance policy is no more sacred than a homeowner's or automobile policy.

3. The purpose of life insurance is to protect those dependent upon you in the event that you do not live long enough to accumulate a living estate. Your goal is to become self-insured by age 65 or sooner. You've either made it by then, or you'll probably never make it financially. (Yes, I know Col. Sanders did!) Life insurance is to protect an economic potential. After 65 your economic potential has greatly diminished. (Yes, I am also aware that insurance proceeds can be used to pay

estate taxes. If your heirs are in that enviable position, hurrah for you! Here we are speaking of bread on the table in the event that you are not able to provide for it. We can obtain term protection to age 100, and that should take care of most situations, even including federal estate taxes.)

4. Life insurance is for dying. Investments are for living. Never ever combine the two.

5. All life insurance policies contain protection alone or protection plus cash surrender value. There is no other kind.

6. Do not do business with an insurance company under conditions that you would not accept from your bank.

7. Only level term insurance on which the premiums are paid each year is "permanent" insurance. Those policies containing cash surrender value contain decreasing "insurance" or net amount at risk.

8. Be sure that your policy is renewable and convertible without evidence of insurability. You should also consider waiver of premium.

9. Normally never have more than one policy (plus your group and your unconverted GI term policy).

10. Avoid participating policies.

My wish for you is that you'll live a long and happy life and that all the life insurance premiums you'll ever pay will be pure waste!

Application

1. Complete Worksheet 1 in the Appendix. Circle in the left-hand column every policy after the first one. Then circle each cash surrender value in (2) and each time you have a policy that is not on the 1958 CSO Mortality Table. Then circle every time you show a "dividend." Each circle that you have made may represent an opportunity for you to lower your cost per thousand and free some of your hard-earned after-tax dollars for serious investing. How many circles did you make?

2. Complete Worksheet 2 in the Appendix. You can obtain all the information that you'll need from Worksheet 1. Is yours a picture of decreasing insurance and increasing "savings"?

3. Complete Worksheet 3 in the Appendix. What is your present cost per thousand?

4. What is the available cost per thousand at your age?

5. What actions do you need to take?

6. When will you take action?

Chapter 14

Money Power for
Your Golden Years

As you have already learned, your financial life can be divided into three periods: the "Learning Period," the "Earning Period," and the "Yearning" or "Golden Period." Whether the third period will be your "Yearning Period" or your "Golden Period" will in all probability be determined by the financial decisions you have made during your "Earning Period." Unfortunately, a large number of your fellow citizens are making the wrong decisions.

What a tragedy—a tragedy that need not happen. And as medical science gets more and more proficient at making us live longer, the number of years spent in this condition will be extended for a vast number of our older citizens. Being broke, especially when you are old, is a devastating experience.

I've sincerely tried through my twenty years of seminars, financial counseling, and three books to raise the level of comprehension of my fellow countrymen about these desperately important financial matters. I feel I've made a tiny dent in Houston, as well as some impact on the nation, because of the wonderful financial planners and stockbrokers who have recommended my books in every state and abroad, the colleges and universities that are using my books, and the enthusiastic reception of my Public Broadcast Series, "The Moneymakers," which is being carried by 181 stations. My goal is to help more and more of our citizens have the means to retire in financial dignity.

Yet I'm saddened to see how many uninformed and frightened people are still trying to cope with a subject for which they have received absolutely no training.

Our educational system continues to send forth our young with so little information about financial matters that they are like time bombs about to destroy their own and their families' economic futures. We are equipping them to earn good incomes and to live the good life. Yet we are not preparing them to know what to do with the money they earn. There are no courses on how to manage their money, to invest their savings so that these savings can grow, or to protect these assets from the risks of casualty or inflation.

Perhaps you, too, have been a victim of this void in our educational system. The fact that you have reached this point in this book tells me you want to fill any void that may be there. Congratulations! Know that I'm delighted to be a channel for your learning. Know that you can fill any educational void you may have. To do this, you must first accept the reality of inflation and high taxes and then resolve to learn to put the former to work for you and avoid the latter. Neither of these will go away, but you do not need to sit by helplessly and let them engulf you.

If you prepare yourself and develop a spirit of serendipity, opportunity will always present itself. Don't just sit idly and say, "God will provide." God gave you talents, a mind, energy, and a strong body. You have all the tools you need to spade the productive loam, but God will not take your spade in hand. Don't sit and say "The government will provide." The government's efforts to provide are what have brought destructive inflation and higher and higher taxation.

I firmly believe that you owe it to yourself, to your family, and to the society in which you live to accumulate the financial means to take care of yourself for all the years you are on this earth. However, I'm equally convinced that you and your spouse, if you are married, do not have an obligation to pass on an estate to your heirs so long as they are physically and mentally fit and you have made an education available to them.

I'm also convinced that if you have a reasonable ability to earn and a little discipline to save a portion of what you earn, and if you apply average intelligence to investing these savings, you can acquire sufficient assets to retire in financial dignity.

If you are male and retiring today at age sixty-five, you can probably look forward to a life expectancy of another fifteen to seventeen years. If you are female, you'll have an average of another eighteen to twenty years. So the sooner you begin, the better your chances are for reaching your retirement years and being financially able to retire in dignity.

As you learned at the outset of this book, there will only be three sources of income at retirement: you at work, your money at work, or charity. Which source do you want to depend on at age sixty-five? Since you at work may not be an option open to you because the world may retire you, and charity will not be fun, that only leaves money at work.

Several means are available to help you prepare for retirement in financial dignity. Let's examine a few of them.

Corporate Retirement Plans

If you are incorporated or work for a corporation, one of the best tax-sheltered ways to prepare for your financial needs at retirement is through either a profit-sharing plan or a pension plan, or a combination of the two. In this way you can get before-tax dollars into the plan and then compound them tax-sheltered. If you are the chief operating officer of a corporation, you will find it most advantageous to have a comprehensive study made by a specialist in the field. He can do a study to determine which type of plan is most advantageous to you while keeping within the IRS guidelines. If you are an employee, however, you may not be permitted to offer any input into that decision.

Technically, profit-sharing and pension plans are designed to attract and hold good employees, which they do if employees are kept adequately informed. However, let's assume you are the chief operating officer or head a closely held corporation. You probably receive higher pay than most of your employees, and the greatest advantage will usually accrue to you. An even greater advantage may accrue to you if you are older than your employees and set up a defined benefit pension plan.

I want to try to make you a pension specialist. Here are a few of the options you and your planner may want to consider.

Defined Benefit Pension Plan

If you are much older than your employees and you pay yourself a relatively high salary compared to theirs, you may want to have a defined benefit plan. This plan can be designed by your specialist to allocate a higher percentage of the contribution to you so that under certain circumstances it is possible to shelter in the plan more than you earn. The only limitation on the dollar amount that can be set as the annual deductible contribution is the amount required to fund the allowable intended annuity when you retire, as determined by an actuary.

If you have employees, the plan cannot discriminate in your favor. Because your employees will generally be younger, however, the cost of funding the pension plan for them should be far lighter proportionally than for you, without being discriminatory.

Your corporation may set aside and deduct sufficient money to fund a straight life annuity on your retirement equal to the lesser of (1) $136,425 or (2) 100 percent of your compensation for your highest consecutive three years of plan participation.

At present there can be provisions in the trust document to permit you to borrow from your own plan under IRS guidelines. This privilege is now being discussed in Congress, so you'll need to check the status of this legislation before making a loan from your plan. If you or your employees do make such a loan, the plan must have a legal ncte with a definite repayment schedule, and you must also pay the going interest rate! (The cost of interest may also be deducted from your taxable income.)

Defined Contribution Plan

Another possibility for you to consider is the defined contribution participant plan with an individual account. The balance in the account determines the benefit a participant will ultimately receive. Subject to adjustments for vesting provisions, the amount contributed remains stable.

These plans include profit-sharing, money-purchase, and target benefit plans. The benefits are derived solely from the contributions made to the various individual accounts. The amount of the contribution is generally based upon a percentage of the annual compensation of each participant or upon a specified dollar amount. The benefits are increased by the earnings attributable to investment of the account and by forfeitures from other participants. The benefits are decreased by the losses attributable to investment of the account.

Profit-Sharing Plan. This plan has a contribution formula that permits the employer to allocate a percentage of its profits to the plan. The actual contribution to the plan is then determined by the employer on the basis of the available profits. If there are no profits, no contribution can be made by the employer.

Most profit-sharing plans have discretionary formulas. A profit-sharing plan may specify, however, that a stated percentage of your company's profits will be contributed to the plan each year.

Once the amount of the contribution is determined, the total contribution is then allocated to the individual account of each participant in the plan. There are a number of possible formulas for determining allocations. The simplest, and perhaps the one used most often, allocates the contribution to the participants on the basis of compensation of each participant compared to the compensation of all participants.

Forfeitures are allocated to the accounts of each of the participants on the same pro rata basis on which contributions are allocated.

The maximum amount that may be added to a participant's account in a profit-sharing plan is the lesser of 25 percent of each participant's annual compensation or $45,475 adjusted for the cost of living. Included in the annual additions that are to be within this maximum amount, are employer contributions, certain employee contributions, and forfeitures.

The amount of contribution deductible may not exceed 15 percent of total covered compensation of all participants.

Money-Purchase Pension Plan. Unlike the profit-sharing plan, the money-purchase pension plan always specifies the formula in the plan document. The formula cannot be discretionary. The contribution formula is stated as a rate or percentage of compensation.

Like the profit-sharing plan, this plan allocates the amounts contributed on a predetermined pro rata basis among the participants. Unlike the profit-sharing plan, the money-purchase plan allows all forfeitures to reduce your company's future contributions.

Generally, the amount deductible in a money-purchase plan is equal to the amount of the required contributions under the provisions of the plan. The annual amount that can be added to a participant's account is the lesser of 25 percent of the participant's compensation or $45,475 adjusted for the cost of living. Included in the annual additions that are to be within this limit are employer contributions, certain employee contributions, and forfeitures.

Target-Benefit Plan. The target-benefit plan is a combination of the defined benefit and money-purchase pension plans. It targets a particular benefit for participants but does not promise to deliver it, as the defined benefit plan does. The company's contributions can thus remain level each year, regardless of the turnover of personnel and the performance of the portfolio.

All of the retirement plans that I have discussed can be integrated with Social Security. This means that you can exclude from the plans all covered compensation up to the Social Security limit and the exclusion may be set at a lower figure. This has the effect of favoring the company's more highly paid employees.

Options When You Terminate Your Plan

As you approach that day when you want to "hang it up" or you want to become an employee of another corporation, for example, you have three options on termination:

1. You can take your funds in an annuity or other installment payout method that will be taxed at ordinary income. At your death, any remaining balance would escape estate taxes if it is properly set up. (This I do not recommend.)

2. You may roll over the entire amount into an Individual Retirement Account (IRA). The entire sum, unreduced by taxes, continues to accumulate tax-deferred until you begin withdrawals. At age 70-1/2 you must start withdrawing.

3. Take the entire balance as a lump-sum distribution. This entitles you to use a special ten-year averaging.

IRA Rollover

You will have only sixty days after receiving a distribution from a retirement program to decide whether to do an IRA rollover or to pay your tax to the IRS.

The rollover was originally designed to give portability to employee pension plans; that is, if you had been working for a company with a retirement program and you decided to move to another company, you could take your vested interest with you and transfer it into an IRA rollover and not be currently taxed on the distribution. The people who have used it most, however, are those who are retiring and want to postpone taxation.

When you receive your distribution, you must first subtract any contributions that you have made. These were contributed with after-tax dollars and are therefore recovered without tax. If you want to withdraw some of the remaining funds, you may do so, but you must pay the tax on these withdrawals at ordinary income rates. The remainder you can roll over without tax and have the funds compound tax-deferred until you begin your withdrawal. You must wait until you are 59-1/2 to start your withdrawal without penalty and you must start at 70-1/2.

You will have a large number of investment choices, but you will be required to use a custodian or trustee that is acceptable to the government. Your choices are:

1. Mutual fund custodial account.

2. Custodial account with a trust company.

3. Commercial bank or savings and loan.

4. Fixed and variable annuities provided by life insurance companies.

Of these choices, I would recommend the first and/or second ones. Let's consider the first option. If you choose a mutual fund that is a part of a family of funds that has a money market fund, you can always have the choice of being in stocks or in a cash equivalent position. You can divide your funds between their growth funds, middle-of-the-road funds, special situation funds, bond funds, and so on, and you can move from one to the other without commission and without tax.

If you choose the second option, you can use any investment that is acceptable to the trust company. This lends itself to a wide array of limited partnerships in oil and gas, real estate, individual stocks, and mutual funds. You can also direct the custodian to increase or decrease these areas as you see fit. I do not recommend the last two options listed above.

Until recently a fifth choice was an Individual Retirement Plan Bond. The Treasury Department has now stopped offering these bonds, but bonds issued prior to April 30, 1982 will still be governed by the terms under which they were issued; that means you are locked in and can't move them.

If you choose a particular custodian and later want to change to another, you may do so. This is called a "transfer of assets" from one custodian to another. This is not a taxable transaction because no "constructive receipt" has occurred. For example, if you previously rolled over your pension plan into certificates of deposit at a bank or savings and loan, you do not have to leave it there. You need only have your financial planner prepare a transfer of asset form for your signature. He can do this easily if you'll give him a copy of one of your confirmations from your present custodian, or you can take receipt of your assets once a year and redeposit them within sixty days with another custodian without tax consequences.

An Actual Case Study

A couple who had attended one of my three-session financial planning seminars requested an appointment, as every attendee is entitled to do. When we sat down for our two-hour uninterrupted personal session in my office, I discovered that he had taken early retirement, had received his distribution fifty days previously, and was faced with a $14,056 tax bill on an $88,201 distribution. I quickly ordered the computer printout shown in Tables 23 and 24 in the Appendix, giving the past results if the funds had not been rolled over and if they had been using the Seminar Fund. I had the computer show a 9 percent withdrawal for eleven years, and, beginning in the twelfth year, use a 21-year self-liquidating program designed to exhaust the principal over their combined expected lifetimes. I had the program done this way even though the couple did not need to start withdrawal immediately. It was the only fair way to compare the two alternatives, because they planned to hold their Exxon stock if they did not choose to rollover.

In reality they had other funds that I recommended they use first if they decided to rollover so that their rolled-over funds could continue to compound tax-sheltered.

In the first printout we assumed that they did not rollover and paid the tax of $14,056, leaving a net of $74,154 to invest in the Seminar Fund. From the 9 percent monthly withdrawals of $556.09, we have deducted 20 percent in taxes on all dividends and 10 percent on capital gains.

As you can see, at the end of eleven years, their after-tax distributions were $73,403, and the remaining value was $115,034. The twelfth year begins a 21-year liquidation. During the 32-year period $388,331 after taxes would have been withdrawn.

Now let's turn and look at the past results, and I emphasize past, that would have resulted from rolling over their pension distribution. As you will note, they had $88,201 to rollover, because they did not owe the $14,056 in taxes that year. Again 9 percent is withdrawn, or $661.51 per month, for eleven years. From these distributions shown under "Annual Total" has been subtracted 20 percent for federal income taxes. By the end of the eleventh year $69,854 after taxes had been withdrawn and the balance of $167,258, shown under the column "Total Value," was still in the account. Again we started a 21-year self-liquidating program designed to exhaust principal. As you will note from the totals, $520,789 was withdrawn. (Incidentally, you are not limited to withdrawing just the annual amount shown. You can make larger withdrawals.)

In the period studied, they would have had $132,458 more distributions ($520,789–$388,331) by rolling over than if they had not rolled over. In reality, it could make an even larger difference because we anticipate their leaving their funds to compound tax-sheltered for several years before making any withdrawals. I also recommend that you postpone withdrawals as long as you can comfortably do so.

Ten-Year Forward Averaging

If the amount of your "lump sum" retirement distribution is relatively small and you are advanced in years, it may be to your advantage not to use an IRA rollover, but to use ten-year forward averaging. Have your financial planner calculate both and then choose the plan that will best accomplish your financial objective.

To make your calculations, begin with the amount of your distribution and deduct any contribution you made with after-tax dollars (this amount you will recover without tax). In other words, the amount you should use is a combination of your employer's contributions, the earnings on the employer's contributions, and the earnings on your contributions.

Now use the tax rate for unmarried individuals, as shown in Table 14-1. The tax is calculated separately from any of your other income, regardless of how much you earned that year or your marital status.

If the amount of your distribution is $20,000 or less, your tax is a flat 6 percent. If your distribution exceeds $20,000, you would use the figures shown in Table 14-2.

Hold tight, and I'll show you how to make your calculation. Let's assume your distribution is $50,000:

1. Compute the lesser of $10,000 or 50 percent of the distribution ($10,000).

2. Compute 20 percent of the amount by which the distribution exceeds $20,000: ($50,000 − $20,000 = $30,000 × 20% = $6,000).

3. Subtract (2) from (1): ($10,000 − $6,000 = $4,000).

4. Subtract the result of (3) from your distribution: ($50,000 − 4,000 = 46,000).

Table 14-1. Federal Income Tax Table - Unmarried Individuals

Income	Tax on Column 1	% on Excess
$ 2,300 (or less)	$ 0	12
3,400	132	14
4,400	272	16
6,500	608	17
8,500	948	19
10,800	1,385	22
12,900	1,847	23
15,000	2,330	27
18,200	3,194	31
23,500	4,837	35
28,800	6,692	40
34,100	8,812	44
41,500	12,068	50

Table 14-2. Selected Examples of Ten-Year Forward Averaging for 1982

Amount of Distribution*	Tax	Percentage of Tax to Distribution
$ 30,000	$2,860	9.6
40,000	4,800	12.0
50,000	6,760	13.52
60,000	8,800	14.67
70,000	11,000	15.71
80,000	12,900	16.13
100,000	17,150	17.15
150,000	29,510	19.67
250,000	61,670	24.67
350,000	102,200	29.20
500,000	174,680	34.94
750,000	299,680	39.96
1,000,000	424,680	42.47

NOTE: It is interesting to note that the tax rate does not reach the 50% rate even when the distribution reaches $1,000,000.
*For distributions of $20,000 and less, use a factor of 6%.

5. Divide the result of (4) by 10: ($46,000 ÷ 10 = $4,600).

6. Take the result of (5) and add: ($2,300[1] + $4,600 = $6,900).

7. Look up the tax on $6,900, which is $676.

8. Multiply this by 10: ($676 × 10 = $6,760). Thus, $6,760 or 13.52 percent would be the tax you would pay on your $50,000 distribution.

After you've done your arithmetic, are there any other factors you should consider? Yes. Your age. For example, if you are seventy years of age and you had opted for an IRA rollover, you would be required to start withdrawing at 70-1/2. The minimum amount of the required withdrawal would be based on the life expectancy of you and your spouse. These withdrawals will be taxed to you at ordinary income rates, which could be higher than the 13.52 percent you would have paid by using the ten-year forward averaging.

If, however, you are forty years of age, the IRA rollover may be a better choice, since it will take a long time for your whole $50,000 to compound tax-deferred. You will be free to switch investments inside the rollover without tax consequences, and the proceeds can pass to your heirs without estate taxes.

Company Termination of Retirement Programs

Perhaps you are not retiring, but your company decides to terminate its retirement plan and makes a lump sum distribution to you. (This has occurred at an alarming rate since the passage of the punitive ERISA bill.) Under this type of rollover, the requirements are exactly the same as above. However, unless you are 59-1/2 or have also terminated your employment, your benefits do not qualify for special ten-year averaging; therefore, the use of a rollover would be even more valuable. Rollovers based on such decisions may later be transferred into a new employer's retirement plan, if the employer's plan permits.

Individual Retirement Account

The Economic Recovery Tax Act of 1981 (ERTA) expanded the amount and eligibility for Individual Retirement Accounts. Under this act every person under the age of 70-1/2 can contribute 100 percent of earned income up to $2,000, deduct that amount from his taxable income, and let the amount compound tax-deferred.

If there is an unemployed spouse, $2,250 can be contributed if no more than $2,000 is placed into any one spouse's account. If both

---

1 The tax table omits the first $2,300 of income.

spouses are earning, each can have a $2,000 account. This applies even if the spouses earn only $2,000. The whole amount can be placed in an IRA. If the amount earned is less, then the total amount can be contributed.

IRA can be considered an admission by the Congress that adequate Social Security may not be there when you are ready for it, or it may be in ailing health, but you'll have no complaint, because you had an opportunity to provide for your own retirement income outside of Social Security.

If you average 15 percent per annum on your money, your results will be:

Years	$2,000	$4,000
10	$ 46,699	$ 93,398
20	235,620	471,240
30	999,914	1,999,828
40	4,091,908	8,183,816

In addition, your contribution will be deductible. In a 33 percent tax bracket ($29,900 joint), your tax savings will be $660 if $2,000 is contributed, and $1,320 if $4,000 is contributed. If you invest this tax savings at 10 percent net after taxes, your results will be as follows:

Tax Savings

Years	$660	$1,320
10	$ 11,570	$ 23,140
20	41,582	83,164
30	119,423	238,846
40	321,322	642,644

If, for example, a working couple age thirty-five establishes an IRA with the above averages, they will have $1,999,828 plus $238,846 or $2,238,674 in their retirement program at age sixty-five. That amount should put a bit of nutritious food on the table and, if the Love Boat is still sailing by then, provide the opportunity for a bit of enjoyable diversion.

When Should Your IRA Be Invested?

If you haven't made your IRA contribution for this year, do it today. Your funds should be compounding inside your IRA tax-deferred rather than be diluted by taxes outside of the plan. You are allowed to make your contribution up to the time you must file your tax return for the past year.

How Should You Invest Your IRA?

We recommend that our clients begin with a well-managed family of mutual funds that has in its stable an aggressive growth fund and a money market mutual fund. Although we offer clients other alternatives, we recommend this approach for three reasons:

1. An account can be opened with as little as $250 (even less in some funds) and can be added to in amounts of $50.00; all dividends and capital gains are automatically reinvested. The custodian fee is modest, usually around $6.00 per year.

2. When the account grows to $10,000, we recommend that the timing service discussed earlier be superimposed on the fund so that the timing service can move the funds as market conditions indicate from the growth fund to their money market fund, or vice versa. There would be no commission for doing this and no tax consequences since the funds are under the tax shelter umbrella of the IRA account.

3. Later, we recommend opening a trust account and using limited partnerships. These partnerships do not usually have reinvestment privileges, so the fund will be a good depository for these cash distributions. In this way, we have all the funds compounding without any funds remaining idle. The Appendix contains the names and addresses of trust companies that have been doing a good job offering trust services.

After your account has been established, you can use a wide range of acceptable investments.

The Cost of Not Having an IRA Account

Table 14-3 shows how much $2,000 a year would grow in a tax-sheltered IRA and how much it would grow without the tax protection of an IRA. All investments are compounded at a rate of 10 percent per year.

Table 14.3. A Comparison of Investment Growth With and Without IRA

	With IRA	Without IRA		
		Tax Bracket		
		29%	39%	49%
	No Current	(Taxable income:	(Taxable income:	(Taxable income:
Years	Taxes	$24,600 to $29,900)	$35,200 to $45,800)	$60,000 to $85,600)
10 years	$ 35,834	$ 21,342	$ 17,279	$ 13,622
15 years	72,298	39,155	30,729	23,503
25 years	229,858	100,488	73,573	52,636
35 years	653,286	234,465	152,062	100,993

Keogh Plans

Are you self-employed as a professional person, a proprietor, or a partner of an unincorporated business? If so, you probably work longer hours than your friend who works for a corporation, but you probably enjoy your freedom and independence. However, when you sit down at the beginning of each year to assess your financial progress and begin to make plans for the new year, you may become painfully aware that the tax bite left you with very little to invest for the golden years of retirement.

At that time, you may look with envy at your friend who works for a corporation with a pension or profit-sharing plan, or who has incorporated his business and set up such a plan. Contributions have been made for his benefit in a retirement plan with before-tax dollars, while you, if you are in a 30 percent tax bracket, had to earn $1.41 to have $1.00 left to set aside to invest for your retirement; and if that $1.00 produced income, you also lost 29 percent of that amount to taxes.

Congressman Eugene J. Keogh considered this an inequitable arrangement, so in 1962, he succeeded in getting Congress to enact the Self-Employed Individuals Tax Retirement Act, HR-10. With the passage of this legislation and later amendments, it became possible for you, if you are self-employed, to establish a Keogh Plan for your retirement.

Your Contributions

The plan allows you as a self-employed individual to set aside 15 percent of your earned income (after expenses and before income taxes) or $15,000, whichever is the smaller of the two. A minimum contribution (and deduction) of the lesser of 100 percent of earned income or $750 is allowed if your total adjusted gross income is $15,000 or less. These contributions are fully deductible, and all earnings accumulate over the years tax-sheltered.

If you have employees, you must also include all full-time employees who have been in your employ for three years. A full-time employee is defined as one who works for you at least 1,000 hours per year (but may drop below this number without elimination).

If you have had your self-employed status less than three years and are setting up a plan for yourself, you must also do the same for each employee who has worked for you the same period of time. Here is a rule that may help you to answer questions you may have with regard to contributions you must also make for employees: "You must do for your employees what you are doing for yourself, if all conditions are the same."

The amount you must contribute for them must be the same percentage you contribute for yourself, with certain variations.

Keogh Calculations

As an example: if your earned income from self-employment is $100,000 for the year, if you have been in business two years, and if you have a full-time employee who has worked for you for those two years, you must include him. If you pay him $12,000 per year, your Keogh contributions would be:

$$\$100,000 \times 15\% = \$15,000 \text{ contribution for yourself}$$
$$\$\ 12,000 \times 15\% = \$\ \underline{1,800} \text{ contribution for your employee}$$
$$\$16,800$$

In a 50 percent bracket, Uncle Sam contributes $8,400 of the $16,800 and you contribute $8,400, making it possible for you to invest $15,000 for your benefit at a cost to you of $8,400.

If, however, you are netting $200,000 annually, and have one employee whom you pay $12,000, you may contribute $15,000 on your behalf, and only have to contribute 7-1/2 percent of the employee's income, or $900, because your $15,000 contribution for yourself is only 7-1/2 percent of your $200,000 income. (When the 15 percent limitation is applied, no more than $200,000 of your self-employed earned income may be taken into account.)

Your investment choices are the same as those under IRA, and in addition, one real estate limited partnership has a leveraged program especially designed for pension/profit-sharing and Keogh plans that qualifies under the new rules of ERTA. This should prove to be an excellent investment medium and well worth your study.

You have the freedom to move from one investment to another under a Keogh Plan without tax consequences. This gives you the flexibility needed for the dynamic world of change.

If you have chosen the mutual fund route, you may want to consider investing monthly as you earn. This gives you the possible benefits of dollar-cost-averaging. For example, if you are contributing $3,600 to the plan, you might invest $300 per month.

You may also consider a lump-sum investment at the beginning of the year, so that your dividends and capital gains, if any, can be compounding throughout the year. Market conditions each year will determine which approach is best.

I find that most of my clients wait until we call to remind them that it's time to make their yearly Keogh contribution. We do this at the end of November and again in March. If you have not set up a Keogh Plan, it must generally be done before December 31 (if you are on a

December 31 tax year). Once you have a Keogh Plan established, you have until you file your tax return to make your contribution.

Understanding Your Benefits

Both Keogh and IRA accounts allow you to invest at a discount. Uncle Sam is paying part of the cost of your retirement program. (At least, he is not taking his amount away from you, so you can have some to set aside.)

Second, the earnings compound tax-sheltered. We are so accustomed to paying taxes that we've forgotten what tax shelter can mean. You may begin withdrawing retirement benefits at 59-1/2 years of age and must begin withdrawals at 70-1/2.

Some self-employed professionals will not set up a Keogh Plan because they can't withdraw these funds until they are 59-1/2 years of age without some penalties. It is usually a blessing that the funds cannot be withdrawn or pledged at the bank for collateral. You would be amazed at the number of professionals who arrive at what was supposed to be their golden years and find themselves scrimping to eke out an existence that is not so golden.

The Magic of Tax-Sheltered Compounding

When you add to the benefit of tax shelter the phenomenon of compounding, you have double forces working for you. Let's assume that you can afford to set aside $15,000 per year and do so for twenty years. (If your contribution is less, adjust by the percentage that $15,000 is of the amount you can invest.)

If you contribute $15,000 per year from age forty-five to age sixty-five, you will have contributed $300,000. (Remember, these are before-tax dollars.) If you average 12 percent on your funds, this sum will grow to $1,210,480. If you move up to 15 percent, this amount will grow to $1,767,151.

In the Appendix (Table 25) you will find the performance record of the growth fund in the same family of the Seminar Fund covering the ten-year period January 1, 1972, through December 31, 1981. The participant would have invested $15,000 per year or $150,000, and the market value as of December 31, 1981, would have been $422,987.

These funds are tax-sheltered instead of tax-free because at retirement you will have several choices as to how you will receive your benefits, and your tax will vary accordingly. These conditions seem to be changing so rapidly that it's difficult to give you any estimates about your tax status in the future. However, after retirement, you may be in a lower tax bracket. Even if the funds were taxed as ordinary income, which can usually be minimized, just the privilege of compounding without taxes for twenty years will make a tremendous difference in your results.

Without Keogh, of course, you are free to withdraw anytime you desire without penalties, and your capital gains distributions enjoy the more favorable capital gains treatment.

With Keogh you cannot begin your withdrawal until 59-1/2 without penalty unless disabled, and you must start withdrawing at 70-1/2 if you are the owner of the business. If you are an employee who is not an owner, you may put off receiving Keogh benefits until you retire, even if that is beyond the time you have reached 70-1/2. If you are the owner, you may continue to make contributions to your plan, but you must also start receiving benefits.

Don't ever be deceived into thinking tax laws are logical. They are not. The other day an engineer client began his comment about some tax law by saying "logically speaking," and I kiddingly told him he had just made his first mistake. Tax laws are not logical. You learn them, apply them, and change when they change.

The Professional Corporation

In 1970 the IRS threw in the sponge in its long fight to keep incorporating professionals from being treated as corporations for tax purposes. By 1973, one-third of the physicians in the United States had incorporated, and it is estimated that at least half have now incorporated their practices. These can be one-man corporations.

The main advantage that you will have if you are self-employed and incorporated is that you will then be considered an employee as well as an owner. As an employee of a corporation, you may participate in retirement and insurance programs on a tax-deductible basis.

Let's assume that you are earning $100,000 as a physician and have incorporated. A comparison under Keogh and under a professional corporation would be as follows.

As a sole practitioner you may deduct $15,000 annually and put it in your Keogh plan.

As a principal of Doctor, Inc., you draw a salary of $100,000 and set up a combined profit-sharing and pension plan. You may now contribute $25,000 (25 percent of $100,000) on a tax-deductible basis to your retirement plan. The corporate retirement plan as well as a Keogh plan may also have estate tax benefits if paid out in a non-lump-sum distribution.

As you can see, the corporate plan would allow you to set aside $10,000 more than would a Keogh plan.

You should also have a specialist compute the figures for a defined benefit plan. You may set aside even more tax deductible income.

There are insurance advantages under the corporate structure. You may also be eligible for substantial life, health, and disability insurance coverages, deductible to the corporation and not taxable as income to you.

Some of the extras you would be entitled to are:

1. Group life insurance—up to $50,000 tax-free. Above that you would pay a nominal tax on term cost of insurance.

2. Group health insurance—hospital, surgical, major medical, and dental.

3. Disability—you would be eligible for long-term disability for life or up to age sixty-five.

4. Key man insurance—the corporation could insure your life as a key employee.

5. You also may elect to set up a nonqualified deferred compensation plan and a medical expense reimbursement plan. The plan also permits a $5,000 federal-income-tax-free death benefit.

You should weigh carefully the pros and cons of incorporation. Your attorney and certified public accountant should be consulted, and the financial and legal possibilities should be studied thoroughly before you take this step.

Do Get Started

While you are studying the pros and cons of incorporation, go ahead and start your Keogh Plan. Even if you incorporate later, this money can be left in your Keogh Plan to grow. If you skip this year, you can never make it up. When they blow the horn to signal a new year, you've passed up this year's tax savings forever.

If you decide to incorporate and also do some consulting on the side, you may have a pension plan, a Keogh Plan, and an IRA, all of which are deductible; as well, the investments are allowed to compound tax-deferred.

Nonqualified Deferred Compensation Plans

A nonqualified deferred compensation plan is a commitment by an employer to pay an employee a predetermined amount of money for a specified period of years upon his retirement or termination of employment.

Let's assume that you are a highly paid executive. You could choose to have your income reduced and have the amount of the reduction become the substance of a deferred compensation plan. You could also have additional amounts deferred in lieu of a salary increase. This would allow you to reduce your current income tax and have an investment compounding under a tax shelter.

When you reach retirement, you will begin to pay income taxes on your withdrawals. At that time you will no doubt be eligible for additional tax exemptions as a retiree, and you will probably be in a lower tax bracket.

The nonqualified plan can be installed without prior approval of the IRS. The rules for adoption and maintenance are few, and the plan can be discriminatory. You may have a deferred plan in addition to a qualified profit-sharing or pension plan.

Your corporation, however, cannot deduct its contributions from its federal income tax. As your taxes on this money come due, then the corporation begins to enjoy a corresponding tax deduction.

Tax-Sheltered Annuities for Employees of Nonprofit Institutions

If you work for a nonprofit institution such as a school, charity, or hospital, you may also qualify for a tax-deferred retirement plan.

Let's assume that you are a school teacher. You may request that the school reduce your salary up to 16-2/3 percent and have the school invest these funds in a qualified annuity program through a life insurance company or a mutual fund custodial account. You thereby avoid paying current taxes on the amount of your reduction. You may also reduce your income sufficiently to reduce the taxes on the remainder.

There are two types of annuities: (1) the fixed and (2) the variable. Many of the older fixed annuities still pay a very low rate of return—many under 3 percent annually. Even with tax shelter, that is not progress at our present rate of inflation. Whether you consider inflation a destructive force, real or pseudo-prosperity, or merely a normal way of life, you must recognize that it will forever be a part of the nation's economic environment.

Despite the foregoing, many people still think that conservative investment requires a "riskless" savings device such as a fixed annuity, and that any nonguaranteed equity investment is automatically speculative. This attitude is dedicated to the proposition that the long-range economy will be deflationary rather than inflationary, and that the world's economy will stand still waiting for one's retirement and will remain so after one's retirement.

History, however, has proved beyond any doubt that basing one's financial security on fixed-guaranteed savings vehicles is the ultimate in absurd speculation. In recent years a few progressive insurance companies have been offering fixed annuities as high as 14-1/2 percent and are also allowing you to move from a fixed to variable position for only a small transfer fee.

Appendix Table 26 is a summary of tax-sheltered retirement plans that lists the type of taxpayer, type of plan, eligibility requirements, maximum annual contributions, financial benefits for the plan holders, benefits for the plan holder's heirs, set-up deadlines, contribution deadlines, and the earliest and latest dates that distributions can start. You may want to take a moment to review these now.

Investing Your Retirement Funds

Certainly a portion of your funds should be invested in mutual funds or individual stocks, if you have the expertise to manage your own portfolio. I am not of the school that adds "and bonds." Bonds have been and, I believe, will continue to be a disappointing choice with our high level of inflation and fluctuating interest rates. If you are talented and agile and are the trustee of your own pension and profit-sharing plan, you might be able to win the discount bond race, but then if you miss you might have the government playing the hindsight game with you and declaring you were not "prudent." The government could even finance a suit against you brought by your employees.

You can select your investments yourself or you can let the professionals do it for you by using an investment advisor, a bank trust department, or an insurance company.

I have not been overly impressed by the results I've seen from a large number of banks and insurance companies.

Mutual Funds

In my opinion, an excellent investment for about a fourth of your retirement money is a well-selected family of mutual funds. Select a management that has a long and high performance record, true depth in its professional personnel, an aggressive fund to be used as your target fund (meaning the fund you'll be in when you are in the market), and a money market fund. Then select a timing service with a good track record and let the timing service move these funds back and forth without commission and without tax consequences. During the very poor market conditions of the past four years, we have averaged 24 percent per year using this system. Not that this performance is all that outstanding, but it is far superior to what a buy-and-hold performance would have been in a number of funds, and it is superior to most other published pension performance records during that period. At 24 percent you will double your money in three years (Rule of 72).

Real Estate

Before ERTA, it was difficult to effectively invest in real estate in a pension plan, especially if you had only relatively small amounts to invest and if the real estate was leveraged, because the IRS held that such investment produced "unrelated business taxable income." ERTA now exempts Keogh and corporate qualified plans from taxation on income from mortgaged real estate as long as certain acquisition rules are followed. An excellent management group whose multifamily limited partnerships we have used for years now offers a limited partnership that invests in a managed portfolio of equity real estate using leverage. The group's investment objectives are:

1. Provide an inflationary hedge by employing conservative investment policies and sound management practices.

2. Provide capital gains through potential appreciation.

3. Provide quarterly cash distributions from partnership operations.

4. Build up equity through the reduction of the principal portion of permanent mortgages on partnership properties.

5. Exclude from unrelated business taxable income the entire portion of any allocations.

Because the partnership will acquire primarily developed commercial and industrial real estate, the fund should enjoy a number of potential advantages. In particular, it will avoid the risks of new construction, the difficulties of obtaining permanent financing, and the uncertainties related to initial leasing. Actual, rather than projected, operating results and engineering studies can be obtained on prospective purchases.

Most properties are expected to be purchased with existing financing in place, often at more favorable terms than are available on new construction today. Rents may be lower than on comparable newly constructed projects, so that existing properties are more likely to be competitive, both now and in the future, as rents and construction costs continue to rise.

It is expected that the partnership, under full capitalization, will own approximately thirteen to sixteen properties throughout the United States. To reduce the risk inherent in the ownership of a single property, the partnership will spread its capital over several properties in different geographical areas. Such diversification will tend to decrease the effects of any local economic fluctuations on the entire partnership.

Investment units are $1,000 with a minimum in corporate plans of ten units or $10,000, and in Keogh Plans of five units or $5,000.

Real Estate Investment Trust. Some excellent real estate investment trusts designed especially for pension plans are also available and are discussed in Chapter 6. One that we use is managed by a team that has a long record of successful registered limited partnerships in real estate. Each share is $25.00, the minimum number of shares is 40 ($1,000), and the minimum additional investment is $100 (4 shares). The funds are invested in land sale or leaseback transactions and participating mortgage loans on improved, income-producing properties. (This is covered in greater depth in Chapter 6.)

Miniwarehouses. Limited partnerships investing in miniwarehouses are another viable pension fund investment. These, too, are described in Chapter 6. They should pay a good cash flow, which can be reinvested in the mutual fund you have in your plan to keep your compounding going, and also offer the potential for land appreciation. The partnerships finance these warehouses once you've received your original investment back through cash flow. When your original funds are returned, they can be invested in another miniwarehouse partnership or another viable investment vehicle.

Wraparound Mortgages. Some limited partnerships invest in a diversified mortgage portfolio consisting primarily of wraparound mortgage loans (a form of junior loan) that are structured to provide equity build-up normally associated with equity ownership. Such loans are selected by the general partner and are placed in the limited partnership for investments by pension and profit-sharing trusts and other organizations exempt from federal income taxes.

Today's market abounds with underleveraged properties that create a demand for mortgage funds at a time when those funds are in short supply.

The object of the wraparound mortgage is not only to generate a high current return but to receive a higher total return over the life of the partnership when the equity build-up is realized in later years.

In wraparound financing, the borrower is offered a new mortgage loan on an existing property (the wraparound loan); the principal amount of this new mortgage equals the balance outstanding on an existing prior mortgage loan on the property plus the amount of the new money loaned.

You may be wondering why the owner of a building would be willing to have his property wrapped in a new mortgage. There can be considerable advantages to the borrower and the lender. Let's assume the borrower is in the 50 percent tax bracket. As you know, interest payments are deductible and principal payments are not. The wraparound mortgage is also being used to fund cost overruns. Let's say that the developer of an enclosed mall shopping center obtained a forward commitment from an insurance company when interest rates were lower than they are at present. It is two years after the original commitment and the developer finds that he is able to lease his space at a substantially higher rent than originally projected. Under the ratios typically used for debt service coverage, he is able to borrow an additional $2 million. When the developer goes back to the original lenders, they will provide the additional funds, but want to increase the rate from 10.5 percent (the original commitment) to 16 percent plus participation. The registered limited partnership management we have been using was able to provide a new $14 million wraparound that gave the developer an additional $2 million to fund cost overruns. The wraparound was at a point higher than the first mortgage (11.5 percent) and so provided sufficient leverage for the partnership to achieve its overall current yield and deferred interest of 19-20 percent.

Energy

Another investment that I have used successfully in our pension plan is the oil and gas income limited partnership. Again, "own the thing that owns the thing." Investments in products that everyone wants and needs and that are in short supply should be profitable to supply. I placed $50,000 in our plan in April of 1977 and another $100,000 in October of 1979. Its current discounted repurchase price is $286,558.

This has been a profitable investment not only in the past, but I believe it will continue to be one. There may be temporary gluts of oil on the market from time to time, but worldwide consumption is increasing and should continue to increase as the Third World countries become more industrialized.

Money Market Mutual Funds

Every pension fund should have a money market mutual fund. In periods of very high interest, it is a safe depository in which funds can compound at good rates. In periods of lower rates, the main portions of the account should be invested in other areas, but the account should be kept open for new contributions to your plan. It can be a depository for the quarterly distributions from your real estate partnerships that do not have reinvestment privileges, or for the funds from stock you have sold when you have not yet decided what stock to replace it with or when the timing may not be favorable to be in the market at all.

The money market fund also provides liquidity for a retiring or departing employee who has vested interest in the plan.

Other Investments

Be on the lookout for other "prudent" investments for your plan, whatever "prudent" may mean today. The race horse Seattle Slew is in a pension plan and all his tremendous earnings have accrued to the benefit of the plan holders and have not been taxed. Remember, however, that if you do use the more exotic investments, they may not turn out to be the bonanza Seattle Slew has been and you may have a government clerk standing in judgment against you and helping your employees sue you for your lack of "fiduciary" behavior.

Avoid Life Insurance in Your Funding

Do not place life insurance in your Keogh, pension, and profit-sharing plans. Do not let an agent convince you that the "incidental" costs of having your insurance inside your plan is incidental. The Appendix contains a PS 58 rate table (Table 28) and another one showing the incidental cost based on issue age (Table 27). Study these two tables carefully. You will note from those tables that if a $100,000 policy was placed in a retirement program at age forty, by age sixty-five the participant would have had to pay taxes on an additional $35,302 of income. When you place life insurance into your plan, you turn a portion of your tax shelter into taxable income.

How Not to Prepare for Retirement

Before closing this chapter, I should caution you against some of the less desirable ways to prepare for your retirement. Let's look at annuities first.

Annuities

Investments are for living. Insurance is for dying. Never combine the two unless you've learned to do both at the same time. This is the lesson we learned in Chapter 13. Figure 13 in the Appendix shows four ads from magazines. The first, printed in 1935, proudly declares that you can live comfortably in the scenic beauty and healthy atmosphere of Hot Springs, Arkansas, for $100 a month. (Have you priced a hot bath there recently?) The 1939 ad declares, "Get $150 a month for life." The ad goes on to say, "You can guard against emergencies; you can avoid investment risks and uncertainties." The ad also says, "Let's assume you are 40 now." What about the uncertainty of what the purchasing power of the dollar will be when it's time to retire? The third ad is titled "How I retired in 15 years with $250 a month." The copy states, "Sometimes I have to smile. It's hard to believe that I'm retired today—retired with a life income." It continues, "And I'm my own boss for keeps." There are some additional sentences that will be of interest: "And the income was guaranteed—whatever happened in the business world—each month, every month, from the day it began as long as I live." From the time I applied for my plan, "I've honestly felt like a rich man. Because I knew I wouldn't just simply live and work and die. I had a future I'd really enjoy. And that's what I'm doing today—with many, many thanks to my (name of insurance company) check for $250 a month that means financial independence for life." Incidentally, it shows the man fishing, I wonder why? The fourth, published in 1966, is titled "How we retired in 15 years with $300 a month." The script is similar. This couple is also fishing. Let's hope the catch is large so they can sell a few to pay for their Florida retirement.

Bonds

Reread Chapter 12, and you'll find that bonds have never been a good long-term investment.

Certificates of Deposit

Your after-tax return usually averages less than the rate of inflation. Therefore, you are back to the example of the little frog moving up one and sliding back two, making it ever so difficult to accomplish your retirement goal.

Social Security

Do you really want to try to live on Social Security? Think of Social Security as social insecurity. That way you won't be deceived into thinking that it will take care of your retirement needs. Social Security was never meant to provide financial independence. It was meant to prevent mass destitution. It was meant to be a base, and you were to build on this base. Even though the Social Security system is for all practical purposes insolvent, you will, if you qualify, receive a check from the government. The question will be whether the proceeds of the check will be sufficient to keep body and soul together.

If they are not and you have to continue working, you may lose many of your benefits. If you are a Social Security beneficiary under sixty-five, $4,080 can be earned before benefits (automatically adjusted after 1981 to reflect increases in average wage levels) are reduced $1 for each $2 of excess earnings this year. If you are sixty-five or older, but not seventy, the limit is $6,000 (also automatically adjusted to reflect increases in wage levels). If you manage to keep from starving before you reach seventy, you can work and not lose any benefits, no matter what you earn.

If your average yearly earnings after 1950 were covered by Social Security, here are estimates of what your monthly Social Security retirement payments should be:

Benefits can be paid to a:	$923 or less	$3,000	$4,000	$5,000	$6,000	$8,000	$10,000
Retired worker at 65	170.25	351.84	413.89	479.94	542.43	674.21	747.04
Retired worker at 62	136.22	281.56	331.15	383.97	434.01	539.43	597.70
Wife or husband at 65	85.18	175.92	206.94	239.97	271.22	337.16	373.52
Wife or husband at 62	63.94	131.99	155.24	180.03	259.10	252.87	280.22
Wife under 65 and one child in her care	85.18	186.15	293.35	405.55	452.36	505.74	560.23
Maximum family payment	255.43	537.99	707.23	885.49	994.80	1,179.94	1,302.27

a. If a person is eligible for both a worker's benefit and a spouse's benefit, the check actually payable is limited to the larger of the two.
b. The maximum amount payable to a family is generally reached when a worker and two family members are eligible.

Appendix Table 29 provides two additional references that will help you project your possible Social Security benefits. Also included (Table 30) is a current life expectancy table.

According to the *Final Report of the 1981 White House Conference on Aging* (Volume 1) in November 1981, the average monthly Social Security benefits paid $376 for a retired worker without dependents and $642 for a retired couple. As of January 1982, an individual whose entire working life was at the minimum wage would have received $355 as a basic benefit, while the worker who had always been at the average wage would have received $535 (the maximum basic benefit was $680).

The same report showed that for the fiscal year 1981 federal expenditures benefiting the elderly were $123,345,000 and amounted to 26.4 percent of the federal budget.

Keep Track of Your Social Security Account

The government does make mistakes in crediting Social Security credits to the proper account. These mistakes can be corrected if they are discovered before three years have elapsed. To avoid future problems, you should write for a copy of your records every two years. If there are errors, they can still be corrected.

To do this, call your Social Security office for Form OAR-7004. It's a postcard that you complete and return. There is no charge.

Should You Take Early Retirement?

Your answer to the question of whether you should take early retirement depends on many things other than Social Security. If everything else is equal, and your income is sufficient with the lower benefits, then go ahead and take your benefits at sixty-two. It will take you many years to make up the income you missed from age sixty-two to sixty-five.

If you retire at age sixty-two, your benefits will be reduced by 20 percent. The closer you are to sixty-five, the smaller your reduction. At sixty-three you would receive 86-2/3 percent, and at age sixty-four you would receive 93-1/3 percent.

If you wait until after sixty-five to retire, you are entitled to an increase of 3 percent in your benefits for each year between sixty-five and seventy-two. So if you wait until seventy to retire, you will get 15 percent more benefits. Here's a convenient table to use if you are considering retiring before sixty-five:

Retirement Age	Percent of Full Benefit	Percent of Full Benefit Lost
62	80%	20%
63	86-2/3	13-1/3
64	93-1/3	6-2/3
65	100	0

If you take early retirement, your benefits do not go up when you reach age sixty-five.

When you become entitled to Social Security benefits, your spouse can collect benefits equal to 50 percent of yours if your spouse is sixty-five, or somewhat lower benefits as early as sixty-two.

Make preparation for your retirement early so that if you receive Social Security it will only be the butter on your bread—not the bread itself. Becoming financially independent will not be an unattainable goal if you begin early, use your intelligence, and don't allow yourself to be enticed by the words "guaranteed" and "no risk" when it comes to investments. Those that seem to have the least risk are often those that guarantee your losses.

The least you can do—not that I consider this enough—is to begin an Individual Retirement Account today. The Individual Retirement Account provisions set up in our tax laws were an admission by Congress that you had better take some steps to fend for yourself if you want your golden years to have any semblance of sparkle and if you do not want to depend on Social Security.

Your Will

You should have a current will drawn by a competent attorney in the state in which you think you are most likely to die. You should have one drawn while you are still young and you should keep it updated. It should certainly be kept current as our laws change. If you already have a will but it was written before September of 1981, go back to your attorney and be sure it complies with your wishes and with ERTA.

I'm a financial planner and do not practice law. Do obtain the services of an attorney with whom you are compatible and in whom you have confidence.

If you begin today to intelligently combine the three ingredients of financial independence, time, and money, with American free enterprise, you can surely reach retirement age with sufficient assets to retire in financial dignity and have the wherewithal to make your retirement years truly golden. Time is your powerful ally, so do take an inventory now and get started.

Application

1. How many years before you retire? _____

2. How much income would you need per month to maintain your present standard of living if you were retiring today? _____

3. What do you think the rate of inflation will be? _____

4. How much will you need by then? _____

5. Your age? _____

6. How many years have you worked? _____

7. What were your total earnings for those years? _____

8. What are your assets now? _____

9. Are your assets sufficient? _____

10. If not, what action do you plan to take this week?

    1. _____

    2. _____

    3. _____

    4. _____

    5. _____

Chapter 15

Capitalizing College Costs

Earlier we discovered that there are three financial periods in almost every life: "the learning period," "the earning period," and the "golden" or "yearning period." Let's discuss how you might finance the "learning" period if you have children who want to go to college. After planning for your own retirement, planning for your children's college education may well be the second largest financial challenge you will face.

Doing precise planning for this cost could be even more difficult than planning for your retirement because there are so many unknowns. First, you do not know where, or even if, your children will want to go to college; second, since costs vary widely among the different types of postsecondary institutions, it is difficult to estimate the amount you will need; third, you will probably have fewer years in which to achieve this particular financial goal; and fourth, you do not know how fast the costs for a college education will escalate.

Despite the many unknowns, it is possible to work out a rough plan to have dollars for those degrees.

A Good Investment?

Is a college education a good investment? There are discussions about this matter from time to time, but from the studies I have seen, it appears that a college degree can add another $250,000 to $400,000 in earning power. Of course, it adds much more. It adds a much larger dimension to life and establishes friendships that lend themselves to business activities later (expecially if you are a Texas Aggie), and reportedly there are fewer divorces among college graduates.

The New Elite

The mass college education that has been occurring over the past fifteen years has produced a new elite in America. This new elite consists of college graduates with skills honed by technology and rapid change. They are not only educated and articulate, but they are permeating every facet of American life, affecting our opinions, our policies and our pleasures.

Every day their influence is becoming more evident in government, business, industry, marketing, and research. "Think tanks" are producing studies for both government and industry. They especially affect the media, which in turn affect a vast number of people through news shows and documentaries.

Costs to Join the "Elite"

Costs will vary according to the type of institution your child attends and the time that will be required to complete his education. Costs are usually lowest at publicly supported, two-year community colleges and highest at four-year private institutions. Four-year state-supported colleges and universities and private two-year colleges generally fall between the two extremes. The amount needed will also depend on whether your child attends a nearby college and continues to live at home or attends a distant college (round-trip air fare two or three times a year can be expensive) and lives on campus or in housing in the surrounding community.

Today total charges for tuition, fees, and room and board are over $11,000 a year at thirteen institutions: Bennington, Harvard, Massachusetts Institute of Technology, Yale, Sarah Lawrence, Princeton, University of Pennsylvania, Brown, Barnard, Tufts, Bard, Dartmouth, and Bryn Mawr.

Average costs per year for resident students by type of institution in the 1981–1982 school year, as reported by the College Board, are as follows:

Type of Institution	Average Costs
Private, four-year	$6,885
Private, two-year	5,604
Public, four-year	3,873
Public, two-year	3,230

Let's assume a modest average annual inflation rate of 5 percent and look at what impact that will have on college costs through the end of the century, as shown in Table 15-1.

Now that you have some indication of what these costs may be, you can use Figure 15-1 to estimate how much college will cost for each child, when you'll need the money, and in what years you'll have an overlap. Your figures can be plotted on a worksheet like the one shown in Figure 15-2.

Financing College

Now let's take our money formula and change it to:

Time + Money + American free enterprise =
Opportunity for college education

Table 15-1. Impact of 5% Inflation on Average College Costs Per Year

| School Year | Type of Institution and Average Costs for 1981-82 School Year | | | |
	Private 4-year $6,885	Private 2-year $5,604	Public 4-year $3,873	Public 2-year $3,230
1982-83	7,229	5,884	4,067	3,392
1983-84	7,591	6,178	4,270	3,561
1984-85	7,970	6,487	4,483	3,739
1985-86	8,369	6,812	4,708	3,926
1986-87	8,787	7,152	4,943	4,122
1987-88	9,227	7,510	5,190	4,329
1988-89	9,688	7,885	5,450	4,545
1989-90	10,173	8,280	5,722	4,772
1990-91	10,681	8,693	6,008	5,011
1991-92	11,215	9,128	6,309	5,261
1992-93	11,775	9,585	6,624	5,524
1993-94	12,365	10,064	6,956	5,801
1994-95	12,982	10,567	7,303	6,090
1995-96	13,632	11,095	7,668	6,395
1996-97	14,313	11,650	8,052	6,715
1997-98	15,029	12,233	8,454	7,051
1998-99	15,780	12,844	8,877	7,403
1999-2000	16,569	13,487	9,321	7,773

As you've already learned, time is a very important element. The more time you have the less money you'll need. For every five years earlier you start, you can reduce the amount you invest by approximately one-half.

But it is also encouraging to learn that you don't have to fight the battle alone, that American free enterprise can contribute a substantial portion if you but provide the time for your money to grow.

Let's take a look at how this element of time could affect your results by assuming you can invest $100 a month for college expenses for your child or children. Let's assume they enter college at age eighteen and that you will average a 15 percent return on your money:

Starting Age	Your Investment	Results	American Industry Contributed
Birth	$21,600	$104,654	$83,054
5	15,600	47,406	31,806
10	9,600	18,943	9,343
15	3,600	4,792	1,192

APPROXIMATE BASIC COSTS

Child will enter college in about:	1983	1984	1985	1986	1987	1988	1989	1990	1991	1992	1993	1994	1995	1996	1997	1998
If your child is now (years of age)	18	17	16	15	14	13	12	11	10	9	8	7	6	5	4	3

Bar values: $6,600; $6,900; $7,200; $7,500; $7,800; $8,100; $8,400; $8,700; $9,000; $9,300; $9,600; $9,900; $10,200; $10,500; $10,800; $11,100

Figure 15-1. Possible annual college costs.

Tax Planning for College

Not only will you need a good rate of return on your investment to achieve your goal, but you will want to do all you can legally to eliminate one of your greatest deterrents to accomplishing your goal, and that is our high tax rate.

Here are some ways you may want to consider to lessen their impact.

Uniform Gifts to Minors

You are permitted to give $10,000 ($20,000 if given jointly with your spouse) without a gift tax to anyone each year. If you are in a fairly high tax bracket, you may want to make a gift to your child and then register the investment in the name of a custodian for the child under the Uniform Gifts to Minors Act. Under this arrangement the dividends and capital gains can compound without tax or at a lower tax, if the child is in a low or no tax bracket. You will still be able to claim your child as a deduction if you supply over 50 percent of his support. You may not, however, use any of these funds for things that you are legally obligated to provide for your child, items such as food and clothing. But you may use the funds for college education.

Figure 15-2. Worksheet for Estimating College Costs:

Entrance Year	Child: Age Now:	Child: Age Now:	Child: Age Now:	Child: Age Now:	Total
	Amount Needed	Amount Needed	Amount Needed	Amount Needed	Amount Needed For Year
19__					
19__					
19__					
19__					
19__					
19__					
19__					
19__					
19__					
19__					
Total					

If your estate is large, you may want to name as custodian someone other than yourself. In the event of your death, the value of the account could be considered a part of your estate for estate tax purposes if you are the custodian.

Clifford Reversionary Trust

As discussed in Chapter 11, another tax savings technique you may want to consider is the Clifford Reversionary Trust. This is an irrevocable trust that must last for at least ten years and one day, or for the lifetime of the income beneficiary (whichever is shorter); it can provide that the income be paid to your child or to a Uniform Gifts to Minors Account for him. At the end of the trust, the capital would revert back to you.

The net result of this arrangement is that the income from the trust can be used or accumulated for college expenses, it can be taxed in your child's lower bracket ($1,000 or more would be tax-free), and you can have your capital returned to you to fund your own retirement program.

If the amount that you place in the trust is $10,000 or less ($20,000 for split gifts), no gift tax is due. Each year the annual excludable amount may be added and no tax will be due on the income if the trust is extended at least ten years beyond the date of the last gift.

Appendix Table 31 shows the amount that can be transferred to a fourteen-year Clifford Trust without adverse gift-tax consequences.

If your gift is in excess of the annual excludable amount, the IRS publishes a table to be used for determining this value and assumes a rate of 6 percent. This table is also in the Appendix.

Interest-Free Loans

I have covered the interest-free loans rather thoroughly in the tax-shelter chapter, but since it is such a good technique for producing funds for college without dilution by taxes, let me briefly review how such loans might be used.

You would lend to your child funds on an interest-free demand note. This means you can demand your money back at any time, and that you do not charge interest for the loan. Your child now has funds to invest and can use the return on the investment to finance his college costs. Because your child will be in a much lower tax bracket or no bracket at all, the tax on the yield would be lowered or eliminated.

For example, you child needs $5,000 a year for college. You lend your child $34,000 on an interest-free demand note. Your child places the funds in a money market mutual fund at 15 percent, which will produce $5,100 per year, the amount needed for his college costs. If you had placed the funds in the money market fund yourself and you were in a 50 percent tax bracket, you would have needed to invest

$68,000 to produce $10,200 to have $5,100 left after taxes. Another approach your child can take is to have a monthly withdrawal program using a family of funds with an aggressive growth fund and a money market fund and superimpose a timing service. Using this arrangement, your son could return your $34,000 and still have some funds left over to launch himself into the business world after graduation.

You can also make an interest-free loan to an irrevocable trust. Let's say you have established such a trust with $1,000 in cash for your children. You can then lend the trust sufficient funds for the trustee to invest to provide the income stream for your children's educational expenses. The trustee can dispense funds as they are needed for each child.

You should be aware that the IRS does not like the interest-free demand note arrangement and brought cases to court on several occasions, but to date has lost all of them. If you are interested in using this technique, I suggest that you have your demand note drawn by a competent tax attorney.

Tax Shelters

If your are in a 39 percent tax bracket or above, another approach is to invest in a tax-sheltered investment. After you have taken the write-offs and before the income begins to flow, give the investment to your child. (If you have a negative cost basis, it is a taxable event. Also refer to the maximum that can be given without a gift tax.) For this purpose you might use an oil and gas development drilling program, a registered limited partnership investing in cinema, or one of the private placements in real estate, cable television, horse breeding, or in some other area.

Other Sources of Financing

Do not overlook other sources of cash for college in the form of scholarships, grants, loans, and work-study programs. There are numerous sources that are not based on financial need.

The Federal Government

President Reagan's attempts to cut federal aid to college students made the headlines, but in reality the programs have not been greatly changed. There are two basic forms of aid: grants and loans. The grants are outright gifts and require no repayment. Pell Grants are available only to students from families with less than $26,000 in adjusted gross income (AGI) and the maximum grant is $1,800 per year.

The Federal Guaranteed Student Loan (GSL) program provides loans at 9 percent, with the government reimbursing lenders for the amount below market rates (there is usually a 5 percent origination fee). The government also pays the interest up to 6 months after graduation, when the student's responsibility begins. Payback periods can be as long as ten years. The maximum loan is $2,500 for undergraduates and $5,000 for graduate students. These loans used to be available to virtually all students, but a 1981 change imposes a needs test for families with an adjusted gross income of more than $30,000. If you are close to a cut-off point, an IRA contribution as well as a Keogh contribution can lower your AGI. Technically, capital, business, and tax-shelter losses can also reduce your AGI below $30,000. Families with rather high income can qualify if they have two children going to expensive private universities, so go ahead and apply at a participating local bank.

Scholarships

Today colleges recruit top students and you may find a surprising amount of scholarship money around. Many are not based on need but are awarded on intellectual ability, athletic skills, or vocational goals, while others are available to children whose parents are members of certain ethnic, religious, union, or other groups. There are a few unusual scholarships for students who are left-handed, who are twins, or who have certain surnames or some unique characteristic.

Sources of Information

Consult with your child's college guidance counselor if your child is in high school and going to college shortly. Once your child has selected the college he wants to attend, meet with the college's financial aid offices.

Some excellent standard college reference guides are: *Barron's Profiles of American Colleges* (Barron's Educational Series, Inc.), *Comparative Guide to American Colleges* (Harper & Row), *Peterson's Annual Guide to Undergraduate Study* (Peterson's Guides), *Lovejoy's College Guide* (Simon & Schuster), *The College Financial Aid Emergency Kit* (Sun Features) *The A's & B's of Academic Scholarships, College Loans from Uncle Sam,* and *Don't Miss Out.* The last three books can be obtained from Octameron Associates, Box 3437, Alexandria, Virginia 22302.

Working Part-Time

Don't be reluctant to let your child work part-time while in college to help meet some of the costs. A number of studies have shown that working students (probably because they have to budget their time more carefully) usually have better grade point averages than students who do not work.

It seems that we humans have two speeds: full speed ahead and dead in the water. The work-study student can tailor his work schedule around his classes so as not to cut off time from study.

I worked my way through college and by trial and error came up with the jobs that best fit my needs. I chose jobs that I could do at times I would ordinarily waste and that required little or no concentration or intensive use of my eyes. By working as the cashier for the faculty and student dining room I didn't stand in line waiting to get my food, but ate ahead of time. This job also provided me with a marvelous opportunity to get to know all the students and in turn led to my being elected president of my class. My other job was to represent the cleaners in my dormitory. This was done at night, right after the dorm closed, which was good time to take a break from my studies. My first job was as a secretary, but this took up every afternoon and was tiring to my eyes. The less glamorous jobs were far superior for my purposes. Even if your child can find part time work, however, you will want to be able to help him meet those college expenses when that time comes. Start early to maximize the first ingredient for having funds for college—and that ingredient is time for your money to grow.

Application

1. Use Figure 15-2 to estimate how much money you will need for the college expenses of each of your children and the years in which you'll need it.

2. Total amount needed for all children: $_____

3. Number of years before first expenses are needed: _____

4.
Year Needed	Amount Needed
19 _____	$_____
19 _____	$_____
19 _____	$_____
19 _____	$_____
19 _____	$_____
19 _____	$_____

5. How much do you now have invested for this purpose? _____

6. Will this be sufficient? If not, how much more will be needed? _____

7. How much can you invest in a lump sum? _____

8. What rate of return will you need? _____%

Chapter 16

The Prospectus—
Power vs. Deterrent

The first rule is—Don't! At least, don't try to read the prospectus from cover to cover as you would a mystery novel. Use the prospectus as you would a handy reference guide. It can be horribly long, confusing, and worthless unless you know beforehand what to look for and who wrote the prospectus.

A prospectus is usually very long and contains many things to which you may not be able to relate. The Securities and Exchange Commission has many bright young people (some in training for top corporate or legal jobs) and many dedicated career servants, but the information that it usually requires a company to transmit to potential investors can at times be extremely confusing, with great emphasis on all the negative aspects, all the possible risks of the offering, and rarely, if ever, any of the possible positive aspects.

If a company wants to offer shares to you and the general public, it must submit a "registration statement" to the SEC, together with a

copy to each state in which shares are to be sold. Nine-tenths of the information called for by the registration statement constitutes the prospectus. It contains information required by a checklist compiled by the SEC. There are about fifteen different forms, each pertaining to a different kind of company. Each form is designed to cover every conceivable type of information about the company. And each time the checklist is revised it gets longer. This has been going on since 1934. By now, the average prospectus contains thirty to fifty pages of fine print, which may cause you to miss seeing the forest because of the many mesquite trees. I hope in the not-too-distant future the prospectus can be shortened to no more than ten pages, free of "legalese." As it is now, it usually takes the proverbial Philadelphia lawyer to make heads or tails of all that mass of fine print, and I suspect he often has difficulty with it, too.

Unduly Long

The undue length of the prospectus does serve one very practical purpose, however. Past experience has shown that small enterprises have a much higher mortality rate than do the larger and older ones. It does cost a great deal of money to gather all the financial data and other information required by the SEC for the prospectus. Small companies are often presented with insurmountable expense hurdles to overcome if they intend to offer their shares publicly. A few have actually gone bankrupt in the attempt. If the SEC wants the company to change the terms of its offering, if it's a new concept, or if it believes the company to be weak, it can delay the offering, require new audits, and increase the burden of expenses. The final draft of the prospectus may, for all intents and purposes, have been edited by SEC examiners to such an extent that it may bear little similarity to the original document presented to them.

The SEC rarely makes any field investigation of a company. Its primary function is to determine that the prospectus contains information required by its rules. These rules do not relate to merits or fairness of the offering (as do the rules of some states), nor to the value of the securities, and the SEC does not check out or investigate the accuracy of the information contained in the prospectus; hence, the disclaimer that appears in bold type on the face of every SEC prospectus:

THESE SECURITIES HAVE NOT BEEN APPROVED OR DISAPPROVED BY THE SECURITIES AND EXCHANGE COMMISSION NOR HAS THE COMMISSION PASSED UPON THE ACCURACY OF THIS PROSPECTUS. ANY REPRESENTATION TO THE CONTRARY IS A CRIMINAL OFFENSE.

This legend must be placed on every prospectus, regardless of the size or quality of the offering, to emphasize the fact that the commission has not approved or disapproved the securities, and that it is a criminal offense to make a representation to the contrary. The term "criminal offense" refers to someone's making a representation that the commission has passed upon the merits of the offering. This applies to any company, whether it be General Motors or a new company offering its stock for sale. Even the most conservative of investment company trusts have this caption in bold, frightening print on the front.

As I mentioned earlier, I once recommended to a prospective woman client a particular mutual fund that has a portfolio of such high quality that the fund invests exclusively in common stocks or securities convertible into common stocks that are legal for the investment of trust funds in the District of Columbia. In keeping with what registered representatives are legally required to do, I gave her the prospectus of the fund with the above in bold print on the front. She called me the next day, absolutely incensed that I had dared recommend to her something that the Securities and Exchange Commission had not approved. I explained the reason, but I was never able to really satisfy her, and she did not make the investment.

This caption has frightened away a host of people who should have become investors. The SEC no doubt is fully aware of the problems of the length and complicated nature of the prospectus. The SEC's theory is that detailed information is required so that the professionals in the investment community can analyze and interpret it for the less sophisticated investor. Unfortunately, it usually does not work out that way. Many brokers have never even read the prospectus and, even if they have, are not sufficiently knowledgeable to discuss such diverse areas in real estate as debt financing, gross rent multipliers, equity buildup, and so on; or in oil and gas, things such as depletion, restored liquidity, intangible drilling costs, tax-preference items, investment tax credit, and depreciation; or in agriculture, things such as crop loan reduction, unamortized loan fees, and prepared cultural costs.

I truly believe in having all my clients completely informed of the nature of the investment they are about to make, the risks involved, and what they may reasonably hope to accomplish if they do decide to invest. But the prospectus as it is now required can be a serious deterrent. My sincere hope is that the Securities and Exchange Commission will make the simplification of the prospectus their top priority for the near future.

Financial Illiterates

I have found that the majority of prospective investors are financial illiterates. If they look at a real estate offering, for example, depreciation shows up as an expense even though no checks were sent. Without a financial planner to explain that the so-called loss is good (meaning it can shelter his quarterly cash flow from taxes, and the excess can shelter a portion of his salary from taxes), the client wonders how the planner dares to recommend an investment that is operating at a loss. Most prospective investors do not have the vaguest idea of how the depreciation pass-through may be equivalent in many instances to an 8 percent after-tax yield with no cash distributions being sent to him.

Management Is the Key

The other important information that doesn't appear in the prospectus concerns the honesty, integrity, and ability of company management. Management is a vital ingredient of success, yet most investors fail to make any independent investigation of the company in which they are investing. I have found that you can take a fair product with good management and make money. I've also found that you can have a superior product with poor management and produce extremely poor results.

Make a Checklist

Let's say you are trying to decide whether to buy shares in a new offering. Your checklist for determining whether a company is a good investment should contain as much of the following as is feasible for you to do.

This will not be easy. If your research is competent and your timing is good (which is vastly important), however, then you may be able to make money on new stock issues by making the following determinations, in order of their importance. (If you are not planning to invest in any new issues, just skip on down to "Registered Limited Partnerships.")

1. Who is really running the business? Find out which persons are actually in day-to-day charge of company affairs. It is usually no more than a handful. Try to determine if the outside directors are "window dressing" or are making a worthwhile contribution to the company by watching over the activities of management. Then independently check out in detail the reputation for honesty, integrity, and ability of the persons who are in charge. You won't find this in the prospectus. But it is worth more than ten prospectuses. Check on these corporate officers as if they were filling out an employment application. After all, if you buy shares in the company they run, they should be working for *you*. If you find any lack of good character, don't invest.

2. Are shares owned by management? If they don't own any, why should you? If they own a bunch, you should make a serious study of the company. Be careful about "dilution." If management owns a lot of shares, that's great. But did they pay 20¢ two years ago for shares they are offering to you for $20? If so, this usually is picked up in the prospectus under a separate paragraph headed "Dilution." It will give you the details.

3. Look at the *size* of the company. This appears in the balance sheet. The smaller the size, usually the more risk involved. For every large company that fails, a hundred small ones go under. You will find the size of the company in the balance sheet. If there are less than seven figures in assets, the company has a high risk. Of course, if you are looking for a long shot that could pay off handsomely, such a company might be for you. Otherwise, pass.

4. Look at the *debt* of the company. This is also in the balance sheet. If shareholder equity is less than 30 percent of total assets, watch out!

5. Age. Time often cures all. The first five years are the biggest risk. Over ten is usually over the hump.

6. Management take. Compare management compensation with other similar companies. Think in terms of percentage of company income. The president of IBM can be paid an enormous sum (which he is) without hurting the percentage. But when a small company pays an enormous sum, then double-check who runs the business and the number of shares they own.

7. Preferred stock and debentures. The safest policy is to put your money in a company with little or no "senior" securities. This is just

another form of debt. Take senior securities into account when figuring debt risk.

8. Earnings. Why does this come last? Because management will think of every accounting possibility to show high earnings during a stock offering. Go back over the past five years and see what the trend has been.

The "Red Herring"

Most brokers mail to prospective investors a preliminary or "red herring" prospectus in advance of a company's offering. This prospectus is used to solicit preliminary orders called "indications of interest." The "red herring" prospectus has not been finally reviewed by the SEC. Use the "red herring" to do your homework on the kind of people who are running the business and how many shares they own. On the basis of your preliminary investigation you may decide to place a preliminary "order." You are under no obligation to place the actual purchase order even after you have received the final prospectus unless you decide to do so. Don't send in your check until you have reviewed the final prospectus carefully as to each of the above eight points.

Registered Limited Partnerships

We have recommended registered limited partnerships for years to our clients. Many of the real estate and oil and gas income partnerships have been offering partnerships for a number of years. Their prospectuses are now so heavy that when my clients leave my offices with one of each of the investments I have recommended, I sometimes have to provide them with a box to carry them in.

Every time we offer a limited partnership we are required also to present a prospectus. Every time a management group closes one partnership and wants to open another that for all practical purposes is identical, they must go through all the expense and delay of registering it again with both the SEC and all the fifty states.

Some states have securities commissions that pride themselves on making it difficult, expensive, and often impossible to clear the offerings. The residents of their states are being deprived of some excellent investment opportunities. Even if the state has approved the offering and the general partner wants to extend it, the commission often gleefully refuses.

Private Placements

In 1974, the SEC adopted Rule 146 to the Securities Act of 1933. The rule stated that it was "designed to provide more objective standards for determining when offers or sales of securities by an issuer would be deemed to be transactions not involving any public offering within the meaning of Section 4 (2) of the Act, and thus would be exempt from the registration provision of the Act."

In May of 1978, Rule 146 was amended to require an issuer to notify the SEC when an offering was made that relied on this exemption from registration, excluding offerings of less than $50,000 during any twelve-month period. One of the stated purposes of this filing was "the need to be able to perceive misuses of the rule and, thus, to become aware of, and prevent, frauds in their incipient stages." No explanation is given about how they can prevent fraud in its "incipient stage" by legislation or regulation.

One great difficulty for those who have tried to abide by the rules is that Rule 146 has prohibited any offering to be made by any form of general solicitation or general advertising.

The honest and bona fide issuers have gone to great lengths to live by the letter of the rules. As a result, the small and honest entrepreneur often has great difficulty reaching viable investors in the marketplace. Not so with those who have tried to mislead or defraud.

The SEC recently adopted Regulation D coordinating in a single regulation certain of the SEC's limited offering exemption rules by replacing Rules 146, 240, and 242. Without trying to make you a securities attorney, let me summarize what I think the regulation says. We have not as yet been able to determine what the SEC says it says.

Basically, Regulation D is a series of six rules, designated Rules 501 through 506, which establish three exemptions from the registration requirements of the 1933 act.

The most important definition in Rule 501 is that of an "accredited investor" and it lists eight categories that are not counted for purposes of limiting the number of purchasers. These are:

1. Any financial institution such as banks, insurance companies, and investment companies, as well as employee benefit plans.

2. Any private business development company.

3. Any college or university endowment funds, as well as other nonprofit organizations with assets of $5 million.

4. Any corporate or partnership "insider."

5. Any purchaser of at least $150,000 of the securities being offered, with the total purchase price not exceeding 20 percent of the purchaser's net worth at the time of sale (including joint net worth with

purchaser's spouse) for: (a) cash; (b) marketable securities; (c) a full recourse obligation, which must be discharged within five years of sale; or (d) cancellation of indebtedness.

6. Individuals with a net worth in excess of $1 million (including joint net worth with spouse).

7. Individuals with income in excess of $200,000 in each of the last two years, with a reasonable expectation of having income in excess of $200,000 in the year of purchase.

8. Any entity 100 percent owned by accredited investors.

Rule 502 (b) describes when and what type of disclosure must be furnished in Regulation D offerings, but when an issuer sells securities under Rule 504 or sells only to accredited investors, the rule does not mandate any specific disclosures. Rule 504 also exempts from registration certain offers and sales of securities up to $500,000 during a twelve-month period to an unlimited number of persons.

Rule 505 provides exemption for certain partnerships of sales of securities up to $5 million during any twelve-month period to no more than thirty-five purchasers who are not accredited and to an unlimited number of accredited investors.

I am convinced that private placements, if permitted to work effectively in the marketplace, can be a much needed source of capital for worthwhile business undertakings. We are at a critical point in the economic life of our nation. We have a tremendous need for capital formation. It is vital that we encourage investments in capital goods to provide employment for the new batch of youth who want to join the work force but cannot find employment. Let us hope that the SEC will try less in the future to "protect" us and place the burden for financial responsibility back on our individual shoulders, where many of us think it belongs. Financial responsibility can never be legislated.

Private placement offerings can be, and often are, superior to those offered by public registration. Many of them need only relatively small amounts of money, but the enormous legal and registration costs piled on to the offering would destroy its economic feasibility. Some of the best investments I've seen have been offered by private placement, and some of the worst have been, too.

Offering memorandums can provide the offeree with the same information that a full registration would disclose. They can contain all relevant and material facts. Unfortunately, these documents are written by lawyers who anticipate that the document may be reviewed by other lawyers; therefore they emphasize the risks while usually ignoring any potential rewards. The result is an offering memorandum that the average investor is not able to understand. The investor may take it to an advisor to interpret. Unfortunately, these advisors are often inexperienced in the particular field and are unable to comprehend totally the nature of the investment and its risks and rewards. Also, the memorandum is often an inch thick, and who wants to plow through all that? So, they recommend against it. C.P.A.s and attorneys can be helpful, but only if they understand the offering and the potential benefits, as well as the risks, and are not embarrassed to admit that they can't possibly know everything. I remind you again, if your advisor says he is never "wrong," of course he is never right, either, and you may be the loser by having to pay exorbitant taxes or you may be missing out on a good investment. Do not place the investment decision on him. That decision must be yours. That is not his expertise. He does not want to run the risk of losing you as a client if the investment is not as successful as you had hoped.

To me, one of the saddest aspects of most private placements has been that the suitability requirements for potential offerees have been so high that if their taxable income has been $44,000 instead of $45,800 (plus a certain net worth), I have had to let these clients pay their taxes, while I could cut the taxes down very low for the clients in the 49 percent bracket. Or, if a client has had $100,000 in taxable income but only $50,000 in net worth, and the suitability requirements state $150,000 net worth, again I have not been allowed to assist him.

In the past, private placements have limited the number of purchasers to thirty-five, exempting the $150,000 investor in most states. Regulation D appears to be a welcome and much needed change from these restrictions.

If you are a "knowledgeable" and "experienced" person with the necessary assets, you should definitely consider private placements. The exemption saves the general partner considerable legal and administrative expenses, which can run into hundreds of thousands of dollars, and allows flexibility in timing and tax considerations. Some offerings have been drawn up and placed within ten to thirty days. This flexibility could allow an investor group to take advantage of special situations offering temporary opportunities that would be unavailable by the time the public offering registration was completed.

The reduction in costs and the flexibility and speed of private placements can also allow investors to take advantage of smaller opportunities. This can be particularly important with regard to certain real estate opportunities.

Most private offerings place emphasis on tax-sheltered investments. However, you should avoid the offerings that emphasize only "write-offs" and that do not offer sound economic investment potential. There are legitimate opportunities under the tax code to partly shelter your income. Congress created these opportunities in order to funnel investment funds into high risk areas. There are reputable general partners who will use your investment funds in an honest and capable manner that should provide you with not only tax advantages but economic gain.

Seek out a competent financial planner who is a specialist in tax-sheltered investments. Tax shelters are very complex and require the attention of a knowledgeable individual. Begin early in the year. Study tax laws yourself, and learn to apply them to your own particular needs. You'll find the investment of time and energy very rewarding.

A Great Need

It has not been my intent to be unduly critical of the Securities and Exchange Commission. It does an admirable job with dedicated and limited personnel. I am, however, keenly aware of the great need for a simpler, more understandable prospectus that a person who has not had the benefit of legal training and considerable expertise in a wide range of subjects can read and grasp in order to make an informed investment decision.

There are already indications that this is occurring. In a recent speech reported in the *Wall Street Journal,* former SEC Chairman Ray Garrett said:

> We all know the somber, liturgical disclaimers that appear in corporate prospectuses. . . . There can be no assurance that a heavier-than-air machine can be made to fly, or that if it can, anyone will want to buy one, or if someone wants to buy one, he will be willing to pay enough to make production profitable.

> Or suppose General Eisenhower's D-Day order had to be filed with the SEC. . . . The officers who planned this assault, including myself, have never before planned anything like this. In fact, I have never commanded any troops in combat. The airborne and other methods being employed have never before been tried by our Army. The weather forecast is only slightly favorable, and such forecasts have a high degree of unreliability. Therefore, there is no assurance that any of you will reach Normandy alive, or, if you do, that you can secure the beach.

Go to a financial planner and obtain a prospectus and then answer the following questions.

Application

Registered Stock Offering

1. What industry is involved?
2. Is this an ascending industry?
3. What products or services are produced?
4. What is the demand-supply situation today regarding these products or services?
5. How many years experience does the chief executive officer have in this field?
6. How many shares are owned by management? What is management's compensation?

	Shares Owned	_Compensation_
President	_____	$ _____
Vice President	_____	$ _____
Secretary	_____	$ _____
Treasurer	_____	$ _____

7. Total net worth of the company?

8. What is the debt-equity ratio of the company?

9. What other alternative investments can you find that offer as much potential for the same or less risk?

10. Is it feasible to make an on-the-spot investigation of the company and its facilities?

Registered Limited Partnership Offering

1. Industry?

2. Demand-supply situation?

3. Years of experience of the general partner? Is the general partner a corporation or an individual, or both? What is their net worth?

4. Is this their first offering? If not, how many previous offerings have been made?

5. What is their track record to date?

6. Answer 9 and 10 above.

Rule 146—Private Placement Limited Partnerships

1. Do the tax provisions fit your needs?

2. Are the tax opinions well documented?

3. How many gray areas are there, and will they bother you enough to make you forego the investment?

4. Are the deductions presented overly aggressive?

5. What is the demand-supply ratio in this area of investment?

6. What is the performance record and experience of the general partner?

7. Is the program assessable?

8. Does the investment require additional investments over a period of years? If so, do you anticipate being in a sufficiently high bracket over that period of time to benefit?

9. If your tax return is audited, will it upset you? Which will upset you more—being audited or paying the tax?

Chapter 17

Where You Are
Now Financially

Financial planning is like navigation. If you know where you are and where you want to go, navigation isn't such a great problem. It's when you don't know the two points that it's difficult.

To find out where you are, take an in-depth financial inventory. Figure 17-1 is the personal planning data sheet that I hand out at the first session of my three-session financial planning seminars.

We require each person in attendance who wants an appointment to complete and return it to us together with all his life and disability insurance policies, plus his tax returns for the last three years, before our consultation. This gives us time to do an analysis of any stocks, bonds, and limited partnerships in his portfolio, and to make an appraisal of his retirement program and tax situation.

If we should grant an appointment to someone who has not completed the data sheet, we complete one together. Without this information, we are flying blind. If an individual does not choose to give us this information, we usually do not accept him as a client. It would be as if he had gone to his family doctor in pain and refused to tell where the pain was located. Please stop now and complete your personal planning data sheet.

FINANCIAL PLANNING DATA SHEET

DATE _____

NAME _____ AGE

ADDRESS _____ ZIP CODE

HOME PHONE NO. _____ BUSINESS PHONE NO.

EMPLOYER _____ OCCUPATION

NAME OF SPOUSE _____ AGE

EMPLOYER _____ SPOUSE'S BUSINESS PHONE NO.

OCCUPATION

DO YOU HAVE A CURRENT WILL? _____ DATE OF WILL _____

ARE YOU COVERED UNDER A PENSION PLAN?

DO YOU HAVE AN _____IRA? ___KEOGH? ___

My financial resources

I. LOANED DOLLARS:

   A. Checking Account $_____

   B. Amounts in Passbook Savings Accounts:

           Institution   Amount

           1. _____   _____

           2. _____   _____ $_____

C. Certificates of Deposit:

Institution   Rate %   Maturity   Amount

1. _____ _____ _____ _____

2. _____ _____ _____ _____

3. _____ _____ _____ _____ $_____

D. Credit Union_____% $_____

E. Money Market Mutal Funds
Fund   Amount

1. _____ $_____

2. _____ $_____ $_____

F. Government Bonds & Instruments

Description	% Rate	Maturity Date	Market Value	Cost
_____	_____	_____	_____	_____
_____	_____	_____	_____	_____
_____	_____	_____	_____	_____
			$_____	

G. Bonds—Corporate and Municipals

Name of Company or Munici- pality	No. of Bonds	Rate %	Maturity Date	Cost	Market Value
_____	_____	_____	_____	_____	_____
_____	_____	_____	_____	_____	_____
_____	_____	_____	_____	_____	$_____

H. Mortgages Receivable (Owed You) $_____

I. Loans Receivable $_____

J. Cash Value of

    Insurance Policies (see Worksheet) $_____

TOTAL LOANED DOLLARS $_____(1)

II. WORKING DOLLARS:

A.   Stocks and Mutual Funds

No. of Shares	Name of Company	Date of Purchase	Cost	Market Value
_____	_____	_____	_____	_____
_____	_____	_____	_____	_____
_____	_____	_____	_____	_____
_____	_____	_____	_____	_____
_____	_____	_____	_____	_____
_____	_____	_____	_____	_____
_____	_____	_____	_____	_____
_____	_____	_____	_____	_____
_____	_____	_____	_____	_____
_____	_____	_____	_____	_____
			$_____	

Total Market Value $_____

Real Estate

Home (Market Value Less Mortgage) $_____

Other Real Estate (Net After Mortgages):

_____ $_____

_____ $_____

_____ $_____

_____ $_____ $_____

Vested Retirement
Fund Benefits:

_____ $_____

_____ $_____ $_____

Limited Partnerships & Other:

_____ $_____

_____ $_____

_____ $_____ $_____

Investment Grade Tangible Assets:

_____ _____ $_____

_____ _____ $_____ $_____

Commodities:

_____ _____ $_____

Total Working Dollars $_____

Less Notes and Accounts Payable
(not already indicated) $_____

Total Loaned and working Dollars $_____

Financial Objective numbered in order of Importance:

_____ Income now

_____ Income at retirement

_____ Maximum tax advantage

_____ Educate children

_____ Travel

_____ Other _____
                (specify)

Estimated Gross Income this year $_____

Estimated taxable income $_____

Tax Bracket   _____%

Taxable Income last 3 years:

3 years ago	2 years ago	last year
$_____	$_____	$_____

Taxes Paid:

$_____	$_____	$_____

No. of Dependents_____

Amount you could save each month $_____

Retirement Data:

No. of years before: _____ years

Desired monthly income $_____
     Possible Sources:
     Social Security $_____

     Pensions $_____

     Investments $_____

     Other $_____

                        Total $_____

Additional needed if retiring today $_____

Anticipated inflation rate per year _____ %

Children Educational Cost Data:

Name of Child	Age	Years Before College	Estimated Cost
_____	_____	_____	_____
_____	_____	_____	_____
_____	_____	_____	_____
Total			_____
Amount set aside			_____
Additional needed			_____

Present Life Insurance, & Annuities Work Sheet
(to complete item J)

Company	Type	Face Amount	Cash Value	*Net Insurance	Annual Premium
_____	_____	_____	_____	_____	_____
_____	_____	_____	_____	_____	_____
_____	_____	_____	_____	_____	_____
_____	_____	_____	_____	_____	_____
TOTAL	_____	_____	_____	_____	_____

* Face Amount less Cash Value = Net Insurance

Disability Insurance

Company	Monthly Coverage	Premium
_____	$_____	$_____

Figure 17-1

Your Will

You will note that I ask if you have a will. This is a very important part of your financial planning. In reality, everyone has a will. It is the one that you have written to fit your own wishes or the one that the state would write for you after your death. However, the state's will most likely would not bear any resemblance to what you would have written, had you done so during your lifetime.

I urge you to obtain a properly drawn will prepared by a competent lawyer in the state where you are living. If your will was drawn before September of 1981, because of the changes in ERTA, you should return to your lawyer to be sure it fits your desires under our current tax laws.

I won't go into details about all the will should contain. However, let me make this one suggestion as to what you should *not* do. Do not, for example, will so many shares of XYZ company to your daughter Sally, nor your credit union account to your son Johnny. If you do, every time you change your investments (which you will need to do often in the world of change in which we live), you'll also need to alter your will. If you plan for all the disbursement of your assets equally among your four children, specify that 25 percent of your assets should go to each. If you want a portion to go to charity, reduce these percentages in order to have some left for this purpose.

In making these suggestions, I'm not trying to practice law. A competent lawyer in the state in which you reside should prepare your will. I'm a financial planner, and I should and will stick to recommending financial plans that can fulfill your needs. How often I've wished that lawyers would do likewise and stick to their profession and let me

practice mine. The temptation to give financial advice seems at times to be just too great for some of them. This may be especially true when a woman has lost a husband on whom she was very dependent. The lawyer may be the only man she knows to depend on at a time when she is very lonely and insecure. Unfortunately, many times her lawyer will take the easy way out and tell her just to put her funds where they will be "safe," meaning a savings account. Here the ravages of inflation will destroy the only value the money has—purchasing power—and she may have to lower her standard of living each year.

Men, prepare your wives to be widows. Most of them will be. Women live longer than men. You've worked together a lifetime to accumulate your assets. The shock will often be so great to your widow that she can't make rational decisions about money or many other things. Yet, some of her most crucial financial decisions must often be made at a time when she may be least prepared emotionally to make them.

If you are a woman who has been taught that it's "not nice to talk about money," let me assure you it is "nice" to talk about money. It is dumb not to be savvy about it!

Many a large law firm has very strong ties with a particular bank in its city. The firm secures clients for the bank's trust department by drawing up the will in such a way that the bank becomes the trustee. This may be a good arrangement if the heirs have a spendthrift nature and little or no knowledge of money management. It may be a very poor arrangement otherwise. Many bank trust departments are woefully understaffed—often with less than knowledgeable people. They are working for the bank and have a responsibility to make the bank a profit. This can influence the investments they choose. A certificate of deposit placed in their bank is much more valuable to the bank than if the trust funds were invested in stocks, mutual funds, or limited partnerships. They may also be forced by regulations to choose investments on the basis of what will please the bank examiners rather than what might be most advantageous to the beneficiaries.

Loaned Dollars

We have already listed many of the ways that you can loan money. I've covered these in detail. All of these ways of "lending" money offer you a reasonably good guarantee of return of principal and a stated rate of return, with the exception of the cash surrender value of your life insurance policies.

Checking Account. This item is self-explanatory. Add up all your checking accounts and list here, or if you have several, make a separate list.

Passbook Savings Account. List these by institutions and amounts. Then total.

Credit Union. List this amount.

Money Market Mutual Funds. List them. If funds are there temporarily, waiting to go back into one of their stock funds, so indicate. If this account is for your liquid money, so indicate.

Government Bonds and Instruments. If you have a variety of them, be sure to give a description, the interest rate, how much you paid for them, and their current value.

Bonds—Corporate and Municipal . Be sure to describe the bonds fully, or your financial planner will not be able to get a current quote for you. List the bonds, their rates, maturities, cost, and, if you know, their current value.

Mortgage Receivable. Have you carried back a mortgage when you sold some real estate? If so, list it here along with the payment schedule.

Loans Receivable. Have you loaned money that you anticipate will be paid back to you?

Cash Surrender Value of Life Insurance. In addition to this worksheet, there is one in the Appendix that you can use to calculate your cash surrender value. These funds do not technically belong to you. They belong to the life insurance company as a part of its reserve. However, you can obtain that portion designated as cash surrender value by borrowing it from the insurance company and paying interest to do so, or by surrendering your protection. If it is left with the insurance company and death occurs, the beneficiary receives only the face amount of the policy, regardless of how much you have "saved" using this method.

How Much in Cash Reserves?

As you make a total of your "loaned dollars" you may be asking, "How much should I keep in cash reserve?"

As I mentioned earlier, when I first started giving investment seminars, I suggested three months' expenses in cash reserve.

Now I suggest that my clients leave as much money idle as it takes to give them peace of mind, for peace of mind is a good investment. I don't seem to have peace of mind with any of my money idle, with the exception of a checking account and temporary funds in a money market mutual fund. You may not have any peace of mind without a lot in a "guaranteed" savings account where you can give it a comforting pat every now and then.

If you need cash and have your funds invested in good stocks, mutual funds, oil and gas income limited partnerships, and commercial income real estate limited partnerships, you can sell the first two any time you desire. However, it may not be the right time in the market, or you may not want to destroy this goose that is laying the golden eggs. If not, you can take your stock certificates to the bank and use them for collateral for a loan.

You can rent a lot of time (interest) and deduct the rent on your income tax return. Therefore, I don't think I need to keep money idle working for someone else while waiting for an emergency. I have cash any time I need it.

Working or "Owned" Dollars

The four main categories in this area are stocks, real estate through individual ownership or through limited partnerships, energy, and other areas of high demand through the same form, and investment-grade tangible assets.

Stocks

Under "stocks" you should list your common stocks, preferred stocks, convertible bonds, and any warrants or rights you may own. List the number of shares, the cost basis, date of purchase, and today's market value.

Knowing your cost basis is very important in doing good financial planning for two reasons. First of all, you need to unemotionally take a good hard look at your performance in the market. For example, let's say that you purchased 100 shares of XYZ Corporation five years ago for $10 per share. Today's market value is 14-5/8. Your average gain per year has been 8 percent compounded. If the stock pays a significant dividend that you are reinvesting, add this to your return after adjusting for your tax loss.

Is 8 percent gain per year within your investment results guideline? If you have calculated that you must have a result of 15 percent a year to reach your goal and your investments are not reaching this objective, you will need to consider making some changes in your investment program.

Another important reason for knowing your cost basis is that you need to know how much capital gains would be realized if you were to sell at a profit or capital loss if selling at a loss. You need to weigh how much you will have to gain from another investment to overcome the tax loss if you are selling at a profit, to come out ahead. On the other hand, if you have a loss, you may need to know how much you could save on your income taxes by establishing the loss.

Many have difficulty figuring cost basis, usually because of poor record keeping or because they become confused by stock splits. It only takes a small amount of time to keep good records if this is done as the transactions are made. Appendix Figure 1 shows a stock record sheet that you may want to consider using. I like to use this sheet in a looseleaf notebook, and then pull and file the sheets after the stock has been sold. Both the buy and sell confirmations that you receive from your broker should be kept in your permanent files.

Figuring the effect of stock splits and dividends is not difficult if done as they are made. Let's look at an example. You purchased 100 shares of XYZ Corp. at $50 per share, or $5,000, in 1970. You received a stock dividend of 2 percent or two shares in 1971, and a two-for-one stock split in 1972, which gives you a total of 204 shares. You have added no new money. Your cost basis is still $5,000. Your cost basis per share, however, has changed. You now have 204 shares. Your original 100 plus 2 = 102 x 2 = 204 shares. You paid $5,000, and you have 204 shares, so your new cost basis per share is $24.51. If you should sell 50 shares, your cost basis would be 50 x $24.51 or $1,225.50, and the cost basis for your remaining shares would be $3,774.50.

United Retirement Fund Benefits

The word *vested* means that you could take it with you if you left your job. You should bring any retirement benefit records you have when you are meeting with your financial planner.

Real Estate

First, list your home (its current market value less the mortgage). Then list your equity in other real estate holdings that are not limited partnerships.

Limited Partnerships

List here your limited partnerships in real estate, oil and gas, cinema, and so on, and indicate whether they are registered or private placements.

Investment-Grade Tangible Assets

List here your holdings in gold and silver bullion, rare coins and stamps, investment-grade art works, and any other collectibles.

Commodity Accounts

List amount of investments and other pertinent information.

Total Working Dollars

Add up your working dollars.

Money You Owe Others

Include here all your accounts and notes receivable that you owe (but exclude your charge accounts unless they are a meaningful percentage of your assets) and subtract this amount from your working dollars.

Total Loaned and Working Dollars

This figure should be reasonably close to your net worth, exclusive of your personal assets.

Your Financial Objectives

The last section of the personal data sheet is designed to help you determine your financial objectives. Number these in the order of their priority to you.

_____	Income now
_____	Income at retirement
_____	Maximum tax advantage
_____	Educate children
_____	Travel
_____	Other _____
	(specify)

Estimated Gross Income

Determine early in the year what you estimate your income from all sources will be. This is necessary if you want to do your tax planning earlier.

Estimated Taxable Income

Now list all the deductions you will be entitled to. Study last year's tax return. This will help you list many that you may otherwise overlook. What is your estimated taxable income? Do you want to be taxed on this amount? If not, start early to select tax-favored investments with good economic potential so that you can lower your taxable income. Always strive to turn your tax liabilities into assets. You don't increase your net worth through tax receipts. You increase it by avoiding the one-way trip to Washington.

Your Tax Bracket

Look at the tax schedule in the Appendix (Table 17). I find that many do not understand what is meant by tax bracket. For example, it does not mean that if you earned $45,800 on a joint return, you lost 44 percent, or $20,152 to taxes. Your tax would be $11,457. It means that if you have a taxable income of $45,801, you lose 44¢ of that last $1.00. We have a progressive tax system beginning at 12 percent and going to 50 percent. Your income is taxed at these various levels.

Your tax bracket is a very important item, for it should influence your selection of investments. If you are in the lower brackets, you can afford to invest for income that is taxable. The higher your bracket, the more you should consider tax-sheltered and tax-favored investments.

Amount You Can Save Monthly

Sit down with your family and determine how much you can comfortably save each month—not too comfortably, or you won't save anything. However, don't set the amount too high, but establish an amount you can actually save. If you set it too high, you may become discouraged, abandon the plan, and fail to reach your goal of financial independence.

Taxable Income Last Three Years

I ask this question for two reasons. I often find that estimates of current taxable income are too high or too low. This gives me a picture of what it has been and gives me an opportunity to inquire about what has caused the change. Also, there are investments that contain investment tax credit, energy tax credit, and certain business losses that under certain conditions can be carried back three years to allow us to recoup taxes already paid.

Number of Dependents

This, of course, is a number each of us can calculate. However, if you are using some tax-favored investments with good write-offs, you should fill out a W-4 form and claim a deduction for each $1,000 of write-off in January, or as early in the year as you know you will be making investments that entitle you to write-off. You are only required to send the IRS the taxes you owe. If the money won't be owed, why send it to them and wait for them to send it back? Remember, money has fantastic earning power. It will either work for the IRS or for you. Which do you choose?

If Retirement Is Your Objective

Determine when you plan to retire and map your plan accordingly. Sometimes I'll be counseling a couple age fifty who solemnly tell me that they plan to retire at age fifty-five. When I look at their assets, I realize that there is just no way. They are not being realistic. Regardless of how much they may want to retire in five years, they will not be able to do so with only the income from the assets they have accumulated. They didn't begin combining the three ingredients of time, money, and free enterprise soon enough.

Desired Monthly Income

Decide what you feel would be an adequate or desired monthly income and adjust for inflation. Use the inflation factor you feel is realistic. Do learn to look at circumstances the way they truly are, rather than the way you wish they were.

Sources of Monthly Income

Social Security. I suggest that you call your local Social Security office and request their latest booklet to determine your projected income from Social Security. You may want to consider whether you think Social Security will be solvent when it is time for you to retire.

Pension. If your company has a pension or profit-sharing plan, find out how much your pension will be and/or what has been credited to your profit-sharing account. Also find out how much is vested (meaning how much you could take with you if you should leave).

Be sure to read about the possible tax advantages of an IRS rollover in an earlier chapter.

College Financing Needs

Chapter 15 on financing a college education will be helpful in calculating how much you are going to need for your dependents' college expenses.

How Did You Do?

You've now completed your personal planning data sheet. You have, haven't you?

How did you do? How many years have you worked? How much have you earned? How much have you saved? How many years before retirement? What do you plan to do about your financial situation beginning today? Write down specific steps that you are going to take to reach your goal. Have a family council and plan your attack.

Financial planning should be a joint endeavor if a couple is involved and a family matter if there are children. When it comes to financial planning, I find that love is not so much looking into each other's eyes as looking in the same direction. If both have the financial vision, the chances for attaining financial goals are vastly improved.

Application

1. Complete the Financial Data Sheet.
2. Are you pleased with your results?
3. How many dollars do you have idle in a "guaranteed" position?
4. Should you have more of them idle?
5. Do you feel that these dollars are safe? (Safety means that you will be returned the same amount of purchasing power at a point of time in the future that you have today.)
6. Should you have more dollars working for you?
7. In what areas today is demand greater than supply?
8. Do these areas lend themselves to convenient and prudent investing?
9. Which are best for you?
10. What yield are you averaging on your fixed-dollar investments?

Fixed Dollar	Yield
_____	_____
_____	_____
_____	_____

11. What rate of return are you averaging on your working dollars?

Investment	Rate of Return
_____	_____
_____	_____
_____	_____

12. What date each year have you set aside to update your analysis and consider alternative courses? _____

Chapter 18

How to Choose
a Financial Planner

Reaching your predetermined worthwhile goal of financial independence will require from you creativity, determination, a willingness to change courses often, agility, sublimation of your ego, a reduction of your prejudices, an open mind, and the ability to act quickly.

If you are a success in your chosen profession, you are no doubt devoting many hours to keeping thoroughly informed and to implementing that knowledge. This leaves little time for the very specialized and demanding area of financial planning. Therefore, to obtain the maximum performance on your investable dollars you will need to search out and use the services of a dedicated, creative, knowledgeable, and caring financial planner who is backed up by a team of professionals.

You may not have heard of the profession of financial planner before or, if so, only for the last few years. The profession as such is only about fifteen years old. The national organization, the International Association of Financial Planners, was formed only eleven years ago.

It is a growing profession because the world of investment is growing more dynamic, the tax bite more oppressive, the laws more complex, the inflation rate more destructive, the rapidity of change in economic events nationally and internationally more intense, and individual professions more specialized.

The other day I heard this example of specialization. Two men were discussing the Nabisco factory out on Almeda in Houston and how each department was organized. One of the men said, "They are so departmentalized that they have a vice-president of Fig Newton cookies." The other replied, "Oh, you're just talking." They decided to call the company and see. When the operator answered, they asked for the vice-president of Fig Newtons, and she replied, "Bulk or packaged?" Perhaps your area of expertise is not that specialized, but the world of money is, so you will need to procure the best investment advice you can.

Many of the large Fortune 500 corporations now provide and pay for the services of financial planners for their top personnel. It is good business practice because it leaves these executives free to devote their full energy to the corporation's business. An employee with his own financial house in order is a more creative and happy individual who should in turn be more productive.

This service is becoming more and more entrenched as an executive perk. It is good for the corporation as well as the executive, because it allows their officers to devote more of their time to the corporation rather than taking the time required to do their own financial planning. If they are worrying about the proper utilization of their money, they are being distracted from the maximum utilization of their concentration on corporate matters.

If you are not fortunate enough to have this service provided for you, you will need to select a financial planner for yourself.

Where to Obtain Financial Advice

Lawyers

Do not go to a lawyer for financial advice. It is not his area of expertise. He usually has little or no training in this area, yet he will have difficulty admitting to his lack of expertise because the world has cast him in the role of all-knowing advisor. As a matter of fact, many lawyers are knowledgeable only about one small segment of the law, and you may have trouble even finding out what that segment is.

There is a growing concern that our society is being overburdened with lawyers and that their encouragement of law suits is miring our courts in litigation and causing our medical bills to soar as the cost of malpractice insurance premiums is passed on to each of us. I will not pronounce judgment on this matter, but will leave that appraisal to you. If this is the situation, it will not be remedied soon, because our law schools continue to pour more and more graduates onto the scene each new spring. Even though there is no other profession from which you'll have such a vast number to choose, you will probably find it most difficult to find the right attorney with the knowledge you need. Be prepared also to pay while he "researches" your question. Be as informed as you can before asking advice. Always ask his fees before the consultation begins and as you go along. If you do not, you may find your coffers diminished more than you had planned. This is by no means a condemnation of lawyers. I consult with them often and one of my best friends is an attorney. However, both my clients and I can recount some cases that would encourage caution.

Bankers

For banking advice, go to your own banker if he is well informed in the area in which you need advice. Your banker may be competent to make loans effectively enough to make a profit for the bank, and he may or may not have sufficient expertise to determine whether your ideas for a particular business will yield a profit. He is a money changer, money counter, and money lender. He is not a money manager. If you deposit your dollars in his bank through checking accounts, savings accounts, and certificates of deposit, his expertise is to lend your money out again at a higher rate. Always develop a close relationship with a very good banker who heads up or is a ranking officer of a bank that has sufficient funds to handle your bankable ideas. He can make a very important contribution toward your goal of financial independence.

Certified Public Accountants

It essential that you have an extremely sharp, creative, diligent, industrious, and accessible certified public accountant. You should go to him for tax advice—on certain points in the tax law or to see if the tax portion of a certain tax-favored investment fits your circumstances. Do not go to him for investment advice. You are not paying him for this. It's not his field, and if you place this burden on him, he will reject almost any tax-favored investment you present to him. If he should encourage you and the investment does not perform to your expectations, you will hold him responsible, and he may lose you as a client. He therefore won't take that risk. It's much safer for him to say no. In that way, he doesn't have to run the risk of losing you as a client, and he also doesn't have to read the private placement offering memorandum that is probably an inch thick written in legalese by lawyers for other lawyers to read. In this way he is never wrong. Of course, he is never right either, and it's the IRS that wins. But you lose!

Accountants are by nature "conservative." Orderly columns of figures that balance is their world. That is what attracted them to the profession. They deal in "black and white" matters and financial planning will always be various shades in between. They do not handle financial products such as securities, insurance, and tax shelters, and they generally don't much trust those who do. Therefore, don't expect accountants to go out on a limb. Most of the Big Eight firms have a few toes in the water, but their planning usually consists of elaborate analysis and little "implementation" of plans. Some of the smaller, more aggressive firms have taken a more active interest in helping to guide the complete planning process.

For advice on a legal question, go to a competent lawyer; for advice on taxes, go to a C.P.A.; for advice on banking, go to a banker. But don't expect good money management advice from any of them. Yes, I did intend to include the banker. As I said earlier, many bankers are trained to be money changers, money counters, and money lenders, but few are trained to be money managers. I say this even though I am a director of a national bank.

Why I Became a Financial Planner

For many years I was a stockbroker for a large brokerage firm that was a member of the New York Stock Exchange. However, I found myself frustrated by the feeling that I was not doing enough for my clients. I found that what most people needed was not someone to tout them on a stock that they felt might go up a few points; what they really needed was someone to sit down with them and help them analyze where they were and where they wanted to be at a certain period in their lives, and to give them some directional help as to how to arrive at their desired destination and to buy the time to acquire this desired living estate.

I found that the broker was trying to get all of his clients' money into securities, and the insurance agent was trying to get it all into the cash surrender value of whole life insurance policies and was recommending this as the solution for all his clients' money problems. If clients had a C.P.A., he was only telling them how much tax they owed on April 15—when it was almost five months too late to do anything about reducing their tax liabilities. Most of them did not have an attorney, and if they did, they did not even have a properly drawn will, to say nothing of any provision for reduction of estate taxes. There seemed to be a great need for a person or team that was competent and caring to pull these torn and fractured people together into a coordinated, guided, functioning whole. It also seemed that the client should be free to leave and to return as he saw fit.

I became convinced that this was a calling worthy of my life and talents. So, in 1968, at a very low spot in the stock market and at a time when nearly all the small brokerage houses were merging into the large ones, I left a large one to set up a small one. This was a scary move. You have no idea of the mass of regulations that entangle a stock brokerage firm, and the regulatory agencies make it especially difficult for smaller firms. But the need was so great and my dedication so strong that I made the move. It has gone well over these past years, and I have the satisfaction of knowing that I've made a truly worthwhile contribution to the financial future of thousands. Our seminars have grown and grown in attendance and so have the number of our clients. I feel we've done our bit to raise the level of financial independence in Houston and the surrounding cities.

At one of the three-session seminars that I conduct regularly in Houston, an editor of Reston Publishing, a subsidiary of Prentice-Hall, was in the audience. The next day he wrote me a letter that said, "You have the ability to make a difficult subject simple. Have you considered writing a book?" I had indeed thought of writing a book, but probably would never have done so if Reston had not signed me to a contract and kept after me until the book was completed.

After my first book, *Money Dynamics*, came out, a marvelous thing happened. Stockbrokers and financial planners across the country began to recommend and give it to their clients and use it in their investment seminars. Colleges began using it in their classrooms, financial writers began to praise the book, and bookstores began to have brisk sales. The sales increased with my second book, *The New Money Dynamics*, and it became a top seller. My third book, *Money Dynamics for the 1980s*, has already sold over a quarter of a million copies in hard back, and the sales are still brisk. This has been a gratifying experience for me, a sort of financial mission, because I now feel I've helped raise the level of financial independence across our nation—and abroad.

There are a number of reasons why I think my books have filled such a great need. First, most of the people in this country are financial illiterates. Even the basic rudiments of money management are not taught in our schools. We continue to spend millions teaching our youth how to earn a dollar, but not what to do with it once it has been obtained. There is a real dearth of knowledge about money. Second, my books are written in lay language from experience, not theory. These are the problems I've seen during my daily counseling with clients in my office. These are my observations of solutions from twenty years of experience. I have been able to see what these clients need and to appraise their temperaments and coordinate their investments with them in order to match their needs to their tax brackets, the amount of money they have to work with, and the time they have to accomplish their goals. My books have been how-to books based on experience, and they have been motivational books to get the readers to act on their new-found knowledge. You or any reader can glowingly say, after reading this book, "I can be financially independent." But unless you act on your new-found knowledge, I will have left you right where I found you.

This is my fourth book on this subject, because the world of money changes so rapidly that I must keep writing to keep you current. Also, Congress keeps changing our tax laws, which in turn changes the rules by which the money game is played. You must learn to play the game and play to win—and win you can.

"Money Dynamics Letter"

The response to my books has produced a joyful avalanche of mail. Your letters have touched me deeply and I've sincerely tried to respond to them, though I'll have to admit that it has become extremely difficult to keep up with the sheer volume.

Because of the many letters and telephone calls asking for a continuous update of information as our economy and tax laws change, my publisher is now making available for subscription my monthly newsletter. In it I will share with you new investment ideas, new tax-savings techniques, new life insurance products and uses, estate planning ideas that conform to our new tax laws, and my concept of where we are in the stock market and the economy.

For information about subscribing to the *Money Dynamics Letter* write to Reston Publishing Company, 11480 Sunset Hills Road, Reston, Virginia 22090, or call (703) 437-8900.

The other day I spoke to a Success Rally, and during the question and answer portion of the program I was asked why our firm has been so successful. I believe there are many reasons, but one that has been important is that we've always tried to visualize how the business will be done in ten years and do it that way now. It's very interesting to me to see some of our major brokerage houses begin to set up financial planning departments. Most of them are floundering, but they are trying. How we welcome them! The country needs more and more really top-quality financial planners.

Characteristics You'll Want
in Your Financial Planner

"Sixth Sense"

You will want him to have a sixth sense about money. I used the pronoun him but you'll remember from Chapter 1 that I'm using it as a neutral pronoun, with no reference to sex. Your financial planner can be either female or male. God was very fair. He handed out brains fairly equally between the sexes. The female planner, however, may be superior because she has had to become accepted in what has been until recently a male domain. I remember when I was first a broker with a large firm and my desk was out in front of the board like the desks of all the other male brokers. A man dropped into the office and selected me to open his account. He later told me, "You must be good or they would never have let you stay."

More and more men and women who are knowledgeable, caring, helping people are coming into the profession—and that's the way it should be. You'll want your planner to have the ability to stand back and analyze where demand is greater than the supply. This is a talent that can only be developed from being in the thick of financial undertakings and having contacts with some of the handful of people in this country who make the major decisions or influence those who do. You'll want your planner to be well informed about the economy here and abroad and to have the talent to predict trends before they occur, the acute perception to detect when the trends have changed, and the ability to act.

Questioning Technique

Your planner should be one who asks you a lot of in-depth questions, similar to the ones you've just completed in the data sheet. Then he'll want to talk to you to learn of your preferences, fears, prejudices, values, and goals. After I have the data and learn about a person's goals, I usually know what will be the best investments for him, but translating and applying my recommendations to fit his temperament is my great challenge. And even though one investment would be better for him from a money-making standpoint than others, it will not be the best investment if it does not provide him with sufficient peace of mind.

Investment Recommendations

Your financial planner should recommend investments that will help you accomplish your financial goals after he has become thoroughly familiar with your tax bracket, your time schedule, your assets, your diversification, and current events as he interprets them.

Tax Savings Techniques

He should be familiar with our tax laws as they apply to investments. He should be constantly attuned to each change and be cognizant of the IRS Letter Rulings. But he should not come unglued if one of them should occur that pertains to an investment you've already made. A ruling is really nothing more than the opinion of the IRS. Only Congress and the tax courts can determine or give the parameters of the law.

Every investment you make must be coordinated with your tax bracket or you are making the wrong investment.

How Is a Planner Compensated?

Fee-Only Planners

Your planner may be a fee-only planner, meaning he will charge you a fee for gathering all your financial data, analyzing it, and recommending a plan of action. He will receive his compensation whether you implement your plan or not. His role is to recommend objectively what he believes will accomplish your financial objectives. His fee may well range from $500 to $10,000. Many set the meter running at $100 an hour. Fee-only planners tend to be thorough and conscientious. Many of them are accustomed to dealing with the well-to-do and do not do cut-rate work. Some planners charge annual retainer or review fees to keep all of your documents updated and to keep you current on your performance. If yours is good (and do replace him if he is not), his fees should be insignificant compared to the potential value you will receive. Your fee to him is also tax deductible, so the IRS gets to share in his cost.

Fee and Commission Planners

Some financial planners charge both a fee and a commission when you implement your plan. Some fee-only planners have the mistaken opinion that a planner cannot be objective if he is receiving a commission. This is not true, because the planner cannot keep his clients unless he performs very well, nor will he receive any referrals from that client. Referrals are the greatest source of clients for a good planner.

It is perfectly acceptable for the planner to receive both a fee and a commission. It is quite costly to gather your data, process it, and make suitable recommendations. He deserves a fee for doing this. However, unless you implement your plan, it will not enhance your net worth. Most people prefer to have the planner, in whom they have already developed confidence and who has all their information, implement their plan. Because he receives a commission, he can usually afford to charge you a smaller fee than the fee-only planner can.

Commission-Only Planners

Your planner may charge only a commission. This is how the planners of our company receive their compensation. It is not superior to either of the other methods of compensation. It is just the way we've chosen to do our business. We may start charging a fee in the future, but we do not at present. However, our tax laws are becoming more and more complex, and many of our tax-favored investments require investments over three- and four-year periods with writeoffs over even longer periods of time; so the need for very sophisticated calculations are mushrooming and will eventually require more and more computer time. Computer time is expensive, so sooner or later at least a portion of that cost will and should be passed on to the client. Always remember your concern is not what something costs, but what it pays!

Seek out a financial planner who has an excellent reputation and in whom you truly have confidence. Then follow his advice. Don't make the mistake of going from person to person asking their opinions. This will only serve to confuse you, and cause you to make poor decisions. You'll always find those who are eager to give you free advice about your money. Often the more readily they give advice, the more miserable the job they have done with their own money.

Your financial planner should be experienced in investments, life insurance, tax shelters, and estate planning, and should have a close working relationship with a creative C.P.A. and a competent attorney.

All of these areas must be skillfully meshed in the complex money arena you will find yourself in today.

International Association for Financial Planners (IAFP)

Your planner, in my opinion, should definitely be a member of the International Association for Financial Planners, headquartered in Atlanta, at 5775 Peachtree Dunwoody Rd., Suite 120-C, Atlanta, Georgia 30342. Their telephone number is (404) 252-9600. The executive director is Vernon Gwynne.

The IAFP has grown into an internationally prominent organization representing 10,000 individual members, many of them the leading financial planners in the world. (There is interest in financial planning in western Europe, South Africa, and Canada. Otherwise, it is an American phenomenon.) Among its services, the IAFP will provide you with information about a financial planner in your area. I'm very pleased to have had the privilege of serving on their board. They are making a tremendous contribution to the field of financial planning. Their magazine, *The Financial Planner,* is an outstanding publication. Editor Forrest Wallace Cato and his staff do a superior job of keeping readers current on new investment ideas, tax shelters, estate planning, and new tax laws.

Certified Financial Planner

Many of the IAFP members have also received the accreditation of certified financial planner. I'm proud to say I have been awarded this very valued accreditation from the College for Financial Planning, headquartered in Denver.

The College for Financial Planning has graduated more than 3,500 certified financial planners who hold the CFP designation. Although this designation is not yet as well recognized by the public as is the C.P.A. (certified public accountant), it is rapidly gaining respect in the industry. For information about their code of ethics and for names of certified financial planners in your area, contact the College for Financial Planning, 9725 East Hamptden Avenue, Suite 200, Denver, Colorado 80231. Their telephone number is (303) 755-7101.

It might be helpful to take a look at some of the strengths and weaknesses of the different backgrounds you will find in the financial planning industry.

Insurance. More than any other financial industry, insurance has done an excellent job of teaching its salesmen to listen to people and answer their questions. Unfortunately, many insurance salesmen were trained to give the same answer to every question: "Buy whole life insurance." Whole life has been the insurance industry's big blind spot in financial planning, not only because it is an inferior product (see Chapter 13), but also because it has been billed as one easy solution to a host of problems and goals. Of course, we know financial planning is not that easy.

Most knowledgeable and conscientious financial planners from the insurance industry now recommend term insurance. They also may recommend annuities as savings and retirement vehicles. Unfortunately, some of them recommend only the mutual funds sponsored by their own insurance company, yet there is no one solution to your financial planning problems.

A good test of an insurance-financial planner is to ask how many insurance companies he represents. If he says, "Why, I represent only the finest, Gibraltar Life," you can be almost sure he is not a real financial planner. A creative insurance-financial planner should be free to select the best products available from a variety of companies.

Securities. You may have read in the newspaper that such and such a large brokerage house has established a financial planning subsidiary, called by a name such as Personal Capital Planning. However, if you call their local office and say, "Financial planning department, please," the switchboard operator will invariably ask, "Do you have a broker?" "No," you say, "I want a financial planner." "Just a second," she says, "I'll connect you with a broker." Don't blame the operator. She doesn't know the firm has a financial planning subsidiary and neither do some of the brokers, believe it or not. Right now, financial planning is just a quiet experiment with a number of the major stock exchange member firms. But, the interest is growing and we welcome them with open arms.

The old-line securities brokers, unfortunately, did not receive much training listening to people, except in thirty-second snatches over the telephone. Some of them have never met their best clients face-to-face. The reason is that if they leave their phone to meet people, they are not "writing tickets" (taking orders), and therefore, in the eyes of many securities firms, they are failing at their jobs.

This is unfortunate, because the securities industry has the best range of financial planning services to offer—including insurance, tax shelters, asset management programs, and even pension planning. They also have recognized images and "storefronts" so that people can walk in off the street and receive help quickly.

There are some praiseworthy bright spots in the recent financial planning efforts of stock exchange firms. Several firms now make relatively inexpensive financial plans available through their branch-office broker networks. Several regional firms have begun to more or less promote financial planning. If you already have a good broker, you may want to ask him about his interest in financial planning. Many of them have "caught the bug" and are moving ahead to help and listen to clients, whether their firm's officers are interested or not.

Independent Planners. Most real planning to date has been done by the smaller professional groups. In effect, they work for their clients, negotiating for them with many of the largest financial service companies in the United States. A good planner is neither a wholesaler nor a retailer. He will be representing you. You usually do not need to worry about whether he has a large amount of corporate assets and high capitalization, because most of the independent financial planners do not take possession of client securities or act as fiduciaries.

Everything depends on personal integrity and performance in accordance with your objectives. Therefore, you should not feel the least bit shy about doing some personal investigation of the independent planner before you hire him. What do other clients think of him? How is he viewed in the community? If your investigation turns up a bad egg, don't let that destroy your faith in all financial planners. The industry is still working on a system for keeping incompetent practitioners out of the business.

A good financial planner is like a good growth investment that keeps paying for a lifetime yet keeps growing in value. He should be one of your most valuable assets in projecting you progressively down the road to financial independence.

Application

1. Contact the International Association of Financial Planners and get the name of members in your area.

2. Contact the College for Financial Planning and do likewise.

3. Look in your telephone directory for a listing of financial planners, certified. Some cities now permit such as listing in the yellow pages.

4. Attend a financial planning seminar. Try to appraise the speaker's knowledge and personality, and determine if you should be able to work together.

5. Ask your associates if they have a good financial planner.

Chapter 19

Repositioning Can Maximize Your Money's Power

We've come a long way together, and it is now time to tie everything together and map your financial plan. To help you accomplish this I want to share with you my Diagram for Financial Independence. It is a diagram that I have designed, refined, tested, and embraced during my twenty years as a financial planner. The diagram has served my clients well. When we've diversified their assets over the diagram in correlation with their tax bracket, they have remained financially whole, with repositioning within the diagram, regardless of economic changes. I first published my diagram in the *Financial Planner Magazine* in February 1977. Since that time it has been used by many financial planners.

Figure 19-1 is my Diagram for Financial Independence. Study it, see how it ties together many of the areas you have studied, and then let's look at implementation. All the knowledge that ever existed will not benefit you if you do not apply it to your particular situation.

Life Insurance — The Umbrella of Time

Tax Bracket	Idle "Guaranteed"	American Industry	Energy	Real Estate	Other
Below 22%	Checking (all brackets) — Money Market Mutual Funds (all brackets) — Corp. Bonds[1]	Income Mutual Fund			
22% to 29%		Stocks & Mutual Funds Inc. Growth	Reg. Ltd. Ptshp. Oil & Gas Income (all brackets)	Reg. Ltd. Ptshp. Triple Net Leases	
29% to 44%	Sing. Premium Def. Annuities[1]	Growth Stocks & Mutual Funds w/Timing		Home — Reg. Ltd. Ptshp. Apts., Shopping, Office, Hotel, Motel, Mini-Warehouse, Etc.	Reg. Ltd. Ptshp. Cinema Marine Cont.
44% to 50%	Municipal Bonds: Funds Individual[1]	Aggressive Growth Stocks & Funds w/Timing — Inv. Adv. Serv. Speculation	Oil & Gas Drilling — Ltd. Ptshp. Development Exploratory	Reg. & Private Placements Apts., Shop., Office, Raw Land	Reg. & Private Placements Cinema, Cable, R&D, Horses, Leasing, Mining, Energy Mgt.

[1] Listed but not recommended

FAIL SAFE PLAN — GOLD, SILVER, CURRENCIES, HARD ASSETS

Figure 19-1. Diagram for financial independence.

The Umbrella of Time

Across the top of the diagram you will find "Life-Insurance—The Umbrella of Time." You learned earlier that the great mystery of life is the length of it and that you need a plan whether you live a "normal" lifetime or not. Since you do not know which it will be, you will want to provide an umbrella over your dependents in order to protect them until you have had time to substitute a living estate for a death estate. You have already discovered that the cost of buying time is not expensive if done properly and that the expense can be conveniently covered in the average budget.

We also agreed that you want a living estate rather than a death estate. Once you have provided this living estate, you have fulfilled your obligation to those dependent upon you and are free to stop wasting your hard after-tax dollars on life insurance premiums. (We also determined that if you wanted to pass on your estate intact, we could continue to carry sufficient life insurance for that purpose.)

After you have provided this umbrella or have become self-insured, you are free to devote your attention to making your assets grow. We've already concluded that although money will not bring you happiness, neither will poverty. Money will give you options in life that you will not have without it. No person is free, regardless of race or creed, until he is financially independent. He is an economic slave.

Tax Bracket

Now that we have bought you time, let's proceed with the building of your living estate, or if you've already acquired sufficient assets, let's plot where they are located on the diagram and then see if some of them should be repositioned for greater growth, tax advantage, safety, diversification, or increased spendable income.

Every investment you will ever make should be carefully correlated with your tax bracket. If it is not, you are probably making the wrong investment. The only money you'll ever spend is what the government lets you keep; therefore, you must learn to think in terms of "keepable" income or "after-tax" income, not pretax income.

Tax Equivalents

You must learn to think in tax equivalents: What would you have to earn on a taxable instrument, such as a certificate of deposit, to be equivalent to the after-tax, tax-sheltered, or tax-free return on an alternative investment? For example, if you are in the 33 percent tax bracket, you must earn $1,496 to have $1,000 left after taxes. You calculate this by taking 1.00 minus .33 (your bracket), which gives you .67, your reciprocal ($1,000 ÷ .67 = $1,496). If you are in a 44 percent tax bracket, you need to earn $1,786 ($1,000 ÷ .56).

Tax Categories

You will note that the diagram has four tax categories: below 22 percent, 22–29 percent, 29–44 percent, and 44–50 percent. Because we have a progressive tax schedule, you will have some of your income in all of these brackets, beginning at 12 percent. By now you should have determined your top tax bracket. If not, look at Appendix Table 17 and do so now.

The next column in the diagram is for Idle "Guaranteed" Dollars. You need some liquid assets. We all do. As a matter of fact, I encourage you to keep as much money there as it takes to give you peace of mind. You may need what I call "patting" money. Some people do, and you may be one of them, so you should keep some money in that position. Peace of mind is a good investment. However, throughout this book I've tried to educate you to the point where you will not have any peace of mind if you leave *too many* of your funds idle. The assets that you have in this column are "guaranteed" as to principal on maturity and rate of return. Unfortunately, today they are guaranteed to lose! After inflation and taxation you cannot win! You are like the little frog we've already learned about who is trying to get out of the financial well by hopping up one and sliding back two–you are losing the money game on all the funds you have positioned in this column.

Let's now analyze each category in the diagram in a general way, and then I'll go through the diagram using two hypothetical cases. I'll diagram where they are now and see if some of their assets could be repositioned to maximize their growth and safety.

Checking Accounts

Our first category under "guaranteed" dollars is a checking account. You will need one or more accounts for convenience and for a strong banking connection. Develop a superb relationship with the top people in the bank of your choice. Choose a bank large enough and progressive enough to fund any good bankable project that you may present to them. Your banking connections will be of immeasurable help to you in winning the money game. You will find that the wise use of leverage will be indispensable to you in the inflationary world in which we live. In addition, our tax laws subsidize a portion of its expense.

You may need more than one checking account to allocate your spending and investments properly. You will certainly need an account for the payment of your bills, whether for necessities or luxuries, but do not keep too large an amount there not earning interest. On the other hand, always keep enough there so that you can write a check whenever you want to. It's psychologically bad for you to feel poor. You won't feel like a winner. You won't feel that you have options in life. You want to think, feel, and act like a winner at all times–because you are!

Money Market Funds

In my opinion, there are only two places to have "idle" dollars. These are in a checking account and in one of the mutual fund money market funds. There will be times when you need liquid assets, such as when you're waiting for the right investment to become available, or when you have to set aside funds to pay taxes (not too many, I hope), or have temporarily withdrawn from the stock market and are waiting to return when conditions become more favorable. There are a number of money market funds from which to choose. Their rates will vary slightly, but most will be comparable. (I do recommend, however, that you avoid those that are heavy in commercial paper.) A money market fund gives you the convenience of opening an account for $1,000 or more with no cost to deposit the funds, no cost to take them out, and the privilege, if you request it, of writing checks for $500 or more while receiving approximately the same rate as a million dollars certificate of deposit. Your dollars even earn while your check is on its way to the fund. Any time you need money in your checking account, just write a check on the fund and deposit it into your checking account. If the amount you need is $500 or more, you can write a check on the fund itself. I transfer funds from my money market fund to my checking account for ease of recordkeeping.

If you have a mutual market fund account using timing, you will need two money market funds, because the computer won't know not to pop all your funds back into the market.

Certificates of Deposit

I know of no occasion when you should buy a certificate of deposit. Why tie up your money for a long period of time at a fixed rate and suffer a penalty if you should desire to withdraw it early? You also run the risk of the bank or savings and loan company refusing to allow you to withdraw it all. Withdrawal is at their option—read the fine print. Over a period of a few years you can usually obtain a higher rate on your money in money market mutual funds than in certificates of deposit, and you'll have flexibility, which is very important in this world of constant change.

Corporate Bonds

I do not recommend that you invest in corporate bonds, with perhaps the exception of short-term investments in selected discount corporate bonds. I have placed them in the guaranteed column. However, they are not guaranteed as to principal before their maturity date. If you should need your funds or find more attractive investments before that date and sell them, you will have a loss if interest rates have risen above the rate your bonds carry. On the other hand, you may obtain a premium if interest rates have dropped below the rate your bond carries. Corporate bonds have been a financial disaster over any of the past twenty-eight ten-year periods.

Single-Premium Deferred Annuity

There can be some uses for single-premium deferred annuities if you think that for your peace of mind you just have to have your funds guaranteed, yet you are in a 33 percent tax bracket or higher and would like to defer taxes. This type of "loaned" dollar fits this requirement. Or perhaps you have invested in an aggressive tax shelter that has used accelerated depreciation, which creates a negative cost basis. When the property is sold or a foreclosure takes place, you may owe a capital-gains tax. You can invest these tax dollars you have saved (you would not have had them anyway if you had not invested in the tax-favored investment and paid the tax) into an annuity where they can compound tax deferred. When and if the tax is due, you'll have the funds with which to pay the taxes, and because the annuity has been earning interest on interest without the dilution of taxes, you should have funds left over. Remember that until you withdraw from the annuity more than your original investment, there is no tax due.

Another possibility worthy of your consideration is that of refinancing your home and placing the funds in the annuity. (Unfortunately, you can't do this if you live in Texas.) You should definitely not leave idle capital in the equity of your home if attractive financing is available. Your home doesn't know whether it has a small or large mortgage on it. It will inflate just as much with a large mortgage as with a small one. Having a large equity in your home is like having that much money in a checking account not drawing interest.

If you need the peace of mind of knowing that money is available and guaranteed if you should ever desire to pay on or off the mortgage, you could place these funds into the annuity and let them compound tax deferred. You can always withdraw them whenever you choose to pay off the mortgage or to pay for expenses such as a college education, starting a business, participating in an investment, and so on.

Cash is severely hurt by inflation. Debt is the beneficiary. Also, you are entitled to deduct the interest while using the funds in alternative investments, and when you pay off the principal, you can do so with cheaper dollars. Again, I emphasize that inflation rewards those who owe money, not those who pay cash.

However, you must remember unless your annuity rate is greater than the inflation rate, you are still not winning the money game.

Municipal Bonds

On the diagram under "idle" guaranteed dollars in the 44–50 percent bracket, I have placed municipal bonds. These can be municipal bond funds, municipal bond trusts, or individual municipal bonds that you have selected. Regardless of which you choose, under present conditions you are not winning the race with inflation. The bonds also decline in market price when interest rates exceed the rates of the bonds. You are guaranteed to receive back at maturity each dollar of face amount, but it will be a dollar that has lost its purchasing power. In a 44 percent bracket or above, you may have more keepable income from a municipal than a corporate or a certificate, but your purchasing power is shrinking rather than growing.

Also remember that there is no such thing as a "tax free" bond. The spread between the corporate rate and the municipal rate is your tax. You've just paid it in advance.

American Industry

We now move into the area of putting your dollars to work for you as hard as you had to work to get them. You'll definitely want to consider stock of American corporations and, if you have developed sufficient expertise, that of foreign corporations.

Equities in stocks should be a viable part of your asset distribution. However, you should probably never have more than 25 percent of your assets in that position, and there will be periods of time when none should be there. The only reason you should ever have money invested in the stock market is to make money. When you can't make money, and there will be times when this will be extremely difficult to do, get out and sit on the sidelines in money market mutual funds.

If you have the three *T*s and an *M* and find the time spent selecting stocks is more enjoyable and more profitable than some leisure pursuits, select and manage your own portfolio. You'll remember that the *T*s are: time to study the market and the information about current companies and national and international affairs; training to interpret and decipher financial reports; and the temperament to make rational decisions quickly. The *M* is for sufficient funds to diversify in order to spread your risks and broaden your base for profits.

Mutual Funds

If you do not have the three *T*s and an *M*, don't take an ego trip. Let the professionals help you through either *private* professional management, using an investment advisory service if you have sufficient funds to obtain an excellent one or *public* professional management, using a well-managed family of mutual funds.

You'll note that I have placed the income funds in the 22 percent or below category (if you are warm, you are in at least a 22 percent bracket). If you are in that bracket you usually need income and will not be sacrificing as much to taxes. As you move up in bracket, you will want to move more and more toward growth. Actually, above this 22 percent bracket I like to jump all the way to an aggressive growth fund as my target fund, with a timing service superimposed to move my funds back and forth between its money market funds and aggressive growth fund. This allows your funds to be moved in the market freely without commission and gives you a safe harbor to run to and stay in until the storm has passed. (You could have a capital-gains tax and the timing service might charge a fee.)

Speculation

In the 44 to 50 percent category, there is nothing wrong with speculating with some of your money that you can afford to lose. Approach this area intelligently—try to predict a trend before it happens, and move out of it before it runs out. Some of my most productive investments (meaning I made money rapidly) were in the lower priced silver, gold, and oil stocks in 1979.

Registered Oil and Gas Income Limited Partnerships

To me, energy is gold—black gold. It's a product that everyone wants and needs and that is in short supply. If you can supply it, that's certainly a possibility worthy of your investment dollars. However, I would not recommend this type of investment for those below the 22 percent tax bracket. Not that you wouldn't enjoy the income (at present largely tax-sheltered) in this bracket, but you might need quicker access to your funds than these provide.

In the 22 to 50 percent bracket, these can be an excellent choice for your "serious" after-tax dollars. In the past we have done extremely well for our clients in this area, and they have naturally been pleased. I'm even more enthusiastic about this type of investment today. When I first presented this program in the early 1970s, I told my clients what I hoped to have this investment do for them. The results have far exceeded this hope, but I still use the same presentation as I did then. (I didn't know we would do so well, and OPEC certainly added its bit.) I told them then, as I still do now, that I hoped that they would receive a 7-9 percent cash flow the first twelve months with a write-off of 13-15 percent of their investment. The first year the general partner would be acquiring the properties. The second year and thereafter I had hoped to have them receive a cash flow of 10-12 percent. In reality we have moved up to 12 percent by the fifth quarter after their investment and have surpassed our hoped-for results each year thereafter.

As you will remember, you'll have three options regarding your cash flow if you use this type of investment. First, you may reinvest your distributions. This is an especially good choice if you are investing for growth or will be retiring in a few years and want to build your assets. At retirement you could choose option two or three. In option two you may withdraw a certain percent and reinvest the remainder in order to preserve your capital. The third option is to take everything in cash. Technically you should be receiving a return *on* capital as well as a return *of* capital when you choose this option, but as the price of energy has escalated, your balance would have grown rather than diminished.

If the OPEC alliance holds together, if there continues to be some semblance of deregulation, and if the demand for oil and gas keeps increasing, this type of investment should benefit. Also, the limited partnerships will have a definite advantage over the oil companies in acquiring properties, because the first 1,000 barrels a day of oil for each partner in the partnership will be taxed at a lower "windfall-profits tax" than will the oil of larger producing companies. This should place the limited partnership programs in a very advantageous position when it comes to acquiring future production. The windfall-profits tax is very burdensome to the oil companies and is an administrative and computer nightmare.

As you are already aware, corporate earnings bear the burden of double taxation. First, corporate earnings are taxed. A portion of what is left is then paid out to shareholders and is taxed again. This added tax burden is causing stock in many corporations to sell at a discount on assets.

The limited partnership escapes this double taxation. All the tax advantages flow through to the investor as an individual. To date, not only has there been no double taxation, but very little or no taxation has been due on the cash flow.

Registered Oil and Gas Drilling Programs

If you are in the 44 percent bracket or above, you may want to consider investing in a drilling program. You will usually have a wide range of programs to choose from (exploration, development, royalty, and so on, as you learned earlier).

For this approach to energy you should use as much "tax cash" as you can, rather than "cash cash", meaning you should consider using some of you "soft" dollars—those that will be making that one-way trip to Washington, if you don't invest in some tax-favored investment. Most registered programs will have little or no leverage in them, so for each $1 you put up you'll write off nearly $1. This means that if you are in a 50 percent bracket, half of the money you invest will be yours and half will be IRS's.

Private Placement Drilling Programs

I've seen some of the best *and* some of the worst drilling programs structured as private offering. These offerings can usually be more creatively financed to offer write-offs in excess of 100 percent using recourse financing. This means that you will be signing recourse notes that you will be required to pay if they aren't paid off out of production. Even if they are, any money paid on your loan is taxable to you.

Some programs have been structured with leverage, plus mining prospects for precious metals. This combination can be more favorable tax-wise in the year the investment is made if properly financed and structured with a general partner who has outstanding know-how. If the program is structured with a two-for-one write-off, you may be using, for the present, only tax dollars. But don't be deceived, the day of reckoning comes rather soon, and when and if this loan is paid off, a taxable event does occur. Most of the combination programs I've seen have been very high risk.

Real Estate

In the next column you will find real estate. Our tax laws in the past have unquestionably favored commercial and residential income-producing real estate and ERTA gave it even greater advantages.

Nonrecourse financing can still be used (meaning the lender looks to the value of the property rather than to you for his collateral). You receive the appreciation on the total value of the buildings, not just on your cash contribution. You are permitted to deduct the interest and at the same time you are allowed to take depreciation on the total cost basis of the property, not just on your down payment. There are a number of possibilities in real estate you will want to investigate.

Home

Your first consideraton may be the purchase of your own home. I have positioned your home in the 29 through 50 percent category in the real estate column. This does not mean that you should not consider owning your own home in the lower brackets. However, your tax advantage is not as great at this level and it may be cheaper to rent.

Housing is one of the necessities of life and can also be an "investment in living" if it fits your lifestyle. A home in most instances has also been an excellent financial investment over the past few years, but may be less attractive in the future.

Triple-Net Leases of Registered Limited Partnerships

If you are in the 22 to 29 percent bracket, you may want to consider investing in registered limited partnerships that put your money to work in triple-net leases of the building of our major corporations. These are conservative nonoperating parnerships that provide capital for business expansion. As you will remember from our real estate chapter in times of tight or expensive money, major corporations such as J.C. Penney, General Motors, Sears, and Safeway sell their buildings and then lease them back. This allows them to continue their program of growth unhampered by a shortage of funds, and it also provides them with some financing and tax advantages. Under this arrangement, they make a lease payment each month and pay all other expenses.

I much prefer these to the bonds of the same corporation, because the corporation must pay the rent or it will have to move. Their objective is an 8 to 9 percent cash flow with all or most of it tax sheltered. At present we are obtaining shelter on nearly all of the cash flow. You should consider this as your "now" benefit. Your "later" potential benefits could be equity build-up of perhaps 4 percent a year (mortgage paydown) and appreciation (as much as inflation, one hopes) on both your investment and the mortgaged portion. As properties have been sold from these partnerships, the appreciation on these buildings has far exceeded what we had hoped for.

Registered Limited Partnerships in Multifamily Housing

For your dollars in the 20–44 percent bracket, you should consider registered limited partnerships that invest in multifamily housing. Since we have a progressive tax system, some of your dollars are in this category, even if you are in a higher bracket. A number of excellent limited partnerships investing in this type of housing are available.

The housing shortage of the 1980s will probably be the worst we've ever had in the United States. As we enter this decade, vacancy rates of multifamily garden-type apartments are below 4-1/2 pecent, and there will be no units under construction until rents escalate considerably. This is occurring when the average family cannot qualify for a home loan and will have no choice but to rent housing or to buy or rent a mobile or premanufactured home.

Investments in this type of already-occupied housing should offer you an excellent potential for gain as rents increase, construction costs for new units escalate, and family units rise in number. I think that housing is one of the most viable investments that you should be considering today, and it certainly should have a priority position on your diagram. Your "now" benefits will be greater in the 29 percent and above bracket because of the excess deductions to which you will be entitled. Your "later" benefits should be excellent as rents and replacement costs increase. This provides a possibility for deferring taxes and converting to capital gains. It's an excellent way to play the D.C. game—defer and convert.

Tax Equivalent

In deciding which is best for you currently—the triple-net lease or the multifamily partnership—remember to use tax equivalents. (You may, however, want to use both investments.) If you invested $10,000 in triple-net-lease partnerships and received an 8 percent cash flow (we are receiving more) and all of it is tax-sheltered, your keepable cash distribution would be $800 for your "now" benefit. If, on the other hand, you had invested $10,000 in the multifamily housing partnership that is leveraged, and they paid out a 5 percent cash flow tax-sheltered, you would receive $500. Let's also assume that you have an excess deduction of 14 percent because of additional depreciation and interest expense. This would entitle you to save $616 in taxes in a 44 percent bracket ($1,400 × .44). You would then have $500 plus $616 of taxes saved, or a total of $1,116. Your net keepable cash flow would be $684 more, even though the cash distribution sent to you was $500 instead of $800. I often find that my clients forget about the $616 they didn't have to send to Washington, and I have to remind them that if they didn't have to send it to Washington they still have it in their pockets.

There is a wide range of registered limited partnerships offered by general partners who have excellent past performance records. Some of these have larger write-offs and larger cash flow. Some even have write-offs going in. They may invest in office buildings and shopping centers in addition to apartments. Even those that invest primarily in apartments will often add an office building, hotel, or shopping center to give the program added diversification.

Real Estate Private Placements

You should consider real estate private placements if you have some of your income in the 44 percent and above bracket. If these are properly and fairly structured with the right general partner buying, managing, and selling the properties, he can offer you tremendous investment potential while providing write-offs going in and tax shelter on cash flow during your holding period. You will give up the wide diversification of the registered program, for there will usually be only one property in the program. You will also not have the watchful eye of the Securities and Exchange Commission, nor will you have the added expense of registration costs. These offerings are usually structured so that you can use most or all "tax-cash"! Your write-off could run from 30 to 150 percent of your investment, and as high as 200 percent in certain two-tiered partnerships. The properties may be apartment buildings, shopping centers, motels, hotels, community home parks, or office buildings. They may be new construction or second- or third-owner properties. If you invest in new construction, you could have more risk because you could have building cost overruns, interim financing rates could escalate while the buildings are under construction, and there could be a lag in rent-up time. You could also have added tax advantage and more profit when they are sold. I have found partnerships that invested in new construction properties to be extremely profitable.

We have done the equity financing for a number of office buildings and shopping centers for a particular Houston builder and our clients have been very pleased with the results that they have received.

Suitability requirements on private placements usually run very high. You always have to be in a 44 percent tax bracket or above and/or have a substantial net worth.

Raw Land

Raw land for investment purposes may not be a viable investment for you unless your bracket is very high and you anticipate having sufficient future income to service the mortgage and pay the taxes. You must be in a position to support the land over a period of time rather than the reverse situation.

If you purchase a small bit of acreage in the country as a get-away retreat, you should consider that as an investment in living, rather than an investment for increasing your net worth. It may do the latter, but that's not your main purpose.

Other Investments

I have placed a wide variety of investments. One of my favorites in the 29-40 percent tax bracket is a registered limited partnership that invests in movies. In one offering that I like particularly, the proceeds will be used to produce five major motion pictures and distribute ten more. We anticipate a 60-65 percent write-off going in and a cash flow that will return all of our investors' money in one to two years and still retain their interest in the movies produced. In this way, we should have the funds available to reposition again with very little time lag and we should greatly increase our internal rate-of-return potential.

I have also placed cinema in the 44 percent and above category, but for these tax-cash dollars we may want to consider a leveraged movie program with higher risks and higher write-offs. With letters of credit, these write-offs can run in excess of three to one—but, remember, the piper must be paid later.

In this category you'll also find private placement offerings in limited partnerships investing in cable television systems, research and development projects, race horses, cattle and horse breeding programs, mining, leasing, energy management, franchises, television and movie production companies, and the like. All of these can provide from 50 percent to over 200 percent write-offs going in.

Fail-Safe Plan

As I've discussed earlier, I have used gold as my "fail-safe fire insurance" program in case my other areas of investing ran into difficulties. I do believe that a portion of your funds should be in this type of hard asset. The more that inflation increases and the world's stability is threatened, the more you should look at gold, silver, gemstones, and collectibles. Gold could be remonetized in the 1980s.

I hope you have received some practical guidance for tying your financial plan together and will plot your assets on the diagram in order to determine if you have sufficient diversification and if their location fits your tax bracket and your financial objectives.

It may now be helpful for you to examine the finances of two hypothetical families to see how their assets are positioned and to consider whether or not they should be repositioned to accomplish their financial goals.

The Jones Family

Figure 19-2 is the data sheet of the Jones family. Look it over at this time.

Now that you've studied Jack and Jill Jones' data sheet, what suggestions would you make? First, you'll note that if Jack should die, Jill could probably continue working; but her income would not be sufficient to enable the family to continue living at their present standard of living.

Jack's present income from salary is $3,333 per month. Let's assume the family would continue to need 75 percent of that amount. Social Security could provide $929 (reduced if she continues to work), leaving a balance needed of $1,571 per month. How much capital will it take to provide $1,571 per month? Widows tend to be extremely conservative, so let's use a rate of 6 percent. Multiply 1,571 × 200 (12 divided by .06) = $314,200 of principal. Subtract from this their

Figure 19-2

FINANCIAL PLANNING DATA SHEET

DATE _____

Jack T. Jones   35

NAME   **AGE**

1234 Briar Lane, Houston, TX 77027

ADDRESS   **ZIP CODE**

123-4567   891-2345

HOME PHONE NO.   **BUSINESS PHONE NO.**

Self   Architect

EMPLOYER   **OCCUPATION**

Jill B.   33

NAME OF SPOUSE   **AGE**

Texas Corp.   678-9101

EMPLOYER   **SPOUSE'S BUSINESS PHONE NO.**

Secretary

OCCUPATION

DO YOU HAVE A CURRENT WILL? ___no_____

ARE YOU COVERED UNDER A PENSION PLAN? _no_ –

IRA_no__KEOGH__no_

My financial resources

I. **LOANED DOLLARS:**

A. Checking Account $___2,000___

B. Amounts in Passbook Savings Accounts:

Institution	Amount	
1. Gibraltar S&L	3,000	
2. Capital Nat'l	4,000	$___7,000

C. Certificates of Deposit:

	Institution	Rate %	Maturity	Amount	
1.	Gibraltar	7-3/4	11/3/84	10,000	
2.	Home S&L	7-1/2	12/2/83	10,000	
3.	Am. S&L	7-1/2	12/1/82	5,000	$ 25,000

D. Credit Union __8__ % $_____

E. Government Bonds & Instruments

Type	Rate %	Maturity Date	Current Value	
Series E	6	various	5,000+	
				$ 5,000

F. Bonds—Corporate and Municipals

Name of Company or Munici- pality	No. of Bonds	Rate %	Maturity Date	Cost	Market Value	
AT&T	2	7-1/8	2003	1,960	1,086	
Nuveen Bond Fd.				21,126	12,831	
						$ 13,917

G. Mortgages You Carry $_____

H. Loans Receivable $_____

I. Cash Value of

Insurance Policies (see Worksheet) $ 9,790

TOTAL LOANED DOLLARS $ 62,707 __(1)

II. WORKING DOLLARS:

A. Stocks and Mutual Funds

No. of Shares	Name of Company	Date of Purchase	Cost	Market Value
200	Southern Co.	1977	3600	2650
200	Houston Ind.	1977	7220	3850
300	Gen Pub Ut	1977	6480	1538
			$ 17,300	

Total Market Value $ 8038 _____(2)

Real Estate

Home (Market Value Less Mortgage) $ 40,000
   $70,000 mkt. $30,000 mtg.
Other Real Estate (Net After Mortgages):

Lake Lot $ 10,000

_____ $_____

_____ $_____

_____ $_____ $ 10,000

Limited Partnerships:

_____ $_____

_____ $_____

_____ $_____ $_____

                          Total Loaned and
                          Working Dollars $ 120,745

Financial Objective numbered in order of Importance:

_____ Income now

___3___ Income at retirement

___2___ Maximum tax advantage

___1___ Educate children

___4___ Travel

_____ Other _____
                          (specify)

Estimated Gross Income this year $___61,160___

Estimated taxable income $_____

Tax Bracket   _____%

Taxable Income last 3 years:

$___28,129___ $___29,900___ $___32,246___

Taxes Paid:

$___5,634___ $___6,201___ $___7,069___

No. of Dependents___4___

Amount you could save each month $___$200___

Retirement Data:

     No. of years before: ___30___ years

     Desired monthly income $___8,000___

        Possible Sources:

        Social Security $___?___

        Pensions $___--___

        Investments $___?___

        Other $_____

                   Total $_____

     Additional needed if retiring today $_____

Children Educational Cost Data:

Name of Child	Age	Years Before College	Estimated Cost
Jim	10	7	30,000
Jan	8	9	35,000
	Total		65,000
	Amount set aside		25,000
	Additional needed		40,000

Present Life Insurance, & Annuities Work Sheet
(to complete item I-H)

Company	Type	Face Amount	Cash Value	*Net Insurance	Annual Premium
Blessed Assurance	WL	80,000	6280	73,720	1258
"	WL	5,000	1455	3545	93
"	WL	5,000	1040	3960	125
"	WL	5,000	1015	3985	98
TOTAL		95,000	9790	85,210	1572

* Face Amount less Cash Value = Net Insurance

Disability Insurance

Company	Monthly Coverage	Premium
none	$	$

Jack has one employee who has worked one year. He has had his own firm for 7 years.

Jill works for a corporation with no pension plan.

Figure 19-2

present living estate of $88,845, exclusive of their home, and you arrive at a figure of $225,355. Since Jill has employable skills, let's reduce the coverage required by $25,355, leaving the amount of life insurance Jack should carry of around $200,000. Since the children are ten and eight years of age, he will probably need this coverage for at least ten years. If he were to obtain a $50,000 ten-year deposit term policy with a $150,000 term rider, this could be purchased for $418 per annum with an added first-year deposit of $500 to be returned to him doubled and tax-free in ten years.

Jack's present annual life insurance premiums are $1,572 for a face amount of $95,000. His net amount of insurance is $85,210 because there is $9,790 of cash value in the policies. This change would reduce his premium that year by $1,154, increase his coverage by $105,000, and release $9,790 to be repositioned. At only 10 percent return, this would produce $979 of income per year.

Disability Income

Jack is much more likely to be disabled than he is to die. He should also obtain a disability income policy that would pay the family $2,000 per month. If we use a ninety-one-day elimination period, we could obtain for him a sickness and accident policy for $502 per year.

Now that we've placed the umbrella of time over the family in case the main breadwinner should die or become disabled, let's turn our attention to the family's other assets and see if they are positioned in the best way to accomplish the family's financial goal. Let's examine their data sheet item by item.

Checking Account. Two thousand dollars is a reasonable average amount to keep in this position and should be left there.

Savings Account. Passbook savings accounts are obsolete today. We would recommend that they open a money market mutual fund with check-writing privileges and move the $3,000 now in the Gibraltar Savings and Loan into the account. The Capital National account of $4,000 should be moved to their reposition list.

Certificates of Deposit. There are three. Let's leave his American Savings and Loan certificate for $5,000 in place until it matures and then move it to a money market fund. Since neither their Gibraltar Savings and Loan account of $10,000 nor their Home Savings and Loan account of $10,000 is keeping up with inflation and taxes, and both have a long time before maturity, Jack and Jill should take their penalty and redeem them, moving the proceeds to their reposition list.

Series E Bonds. There has never been a period of time when Series E bonds have been a good investment, so these should be repositioned.

Bonds. Bonds do not fit the family's objective. Bonds are vulnerable to inflation, taxes, and increasing interest rates. The Joneses have a loss of $874 on their AT&T bonds. These should be sold and the loss realized, freeing $1,086 to be put to work more productively. These proceeds should be added to their reposition list.

Municipal Bond Fund. This couple, in my opinion, should never have been sold a municipal bonds fund. They should redeem it and put the funds to work more productively. A sale would release $12,831 and establish a loss of $8,295.

Cash Value of Insurance. By obtaining a new $200,000 policy, $9,790 will be released to be put to work for the Joneses while obtaining $105,000 more coverage, at a savings of $96.17 per month.

Stocks. For several years the Joneses have been following the advice of a particular financial writer who recommended utility stocks. This has proved to be poor advice. I do not usually recommend buying utilities because they are composed basically of two things—raw materials and money—both of which are expensive and could continue to be so. Add to this an angry consumer, and you have an industry with reduced opportunity for growth. These funds should be repositioned. This would release $8,038 and establish a loss of $9,262.

Home. The Joneses are looking for a new home. If they should decide to buy one for $80,000, I would advise them to make the minimum down payment. If they can obtain 80 percent financing, this would require $16,000 down and release another $24,000 for investment to help make the added payments and produce some growth of capital.

Recreational Lot. Since the lot was bought as an investment and not as a recreational spot and since prices have not risen on lots in the area for two years, they might consider placing it on the market.

Retirement Program. Jack is self-employed and has been for seven years. He has one employee who has worked for him for one year. I recommend that he establish a Keogh Plan. He will be allowed to contribute $6,000 (15 percent of $40,000). This now becomes a deductible item on his income tax return, and the funds are allowed to compound tax-sheltered. He should also place $2,000 in an IRA account, receive a deduction, and let these earnings compound tax-deferred. Jill should also place $2,000 in an IRA account.

Will. They both should have wills prepared by a competent attorney practicing in the state in which they reside.

Now let's look at ways they could reposition their assets to maximize their potential.

The Jones's Gross Income Before Repositioning

Jack's Salary	$40,000
Jill's Salary	18,000
Gibraltar Savings Account, $3,010 at 5-1/2%	165
Capital National Savings Account, $4,525 at 5-1/4%	238
Gibraltar C.D. $10,000 at 7-3/4%	734
Home S&L C.D. $10,000 at 7-1/2%	750
Am. S&L C.D. $5,000 at 7-1/2%	375
AT&T Bond 2,000 shares at 7-1/8%	142
Southern Co. 200 shares at 1.62	324
Ho. Ind. 200 shares at 2.16	432
Gen Pub. Util. 300 shares at 0	0
Gross income	$61,160

The Jones's Deductions Before Repositioning

CPA fee for preparing tax return	$300
Dividend exclusion	200
Taxes on home	1,400
Interest on home	2,550
Taxes on recreational lot	275
Safe-deposit box	48
Contributions	2,000
Medical	150
Sales taxes	271
Interest expense on charge accounts	363
Miscellaneous	200
Professional fees and trade publications	225
	$ 7,982
Exemptions	4,000
	$11,982
Zero bracket	(3,400)
	$ 8,582

Funds for Repositioning

Source	Cost	Mkt	Gain/Loss	Funds for Repositioning
AT&T Bonds	1,960	1,086	(874)	1,086
Nuveen Bond Fund	21,126	12,831	(8,295)	12,831
Utility Stock	17,300	8,038	(9,262)	8,038
Gibraltar Passbook				3,000
Capital National Passbook				4,000
Gibraltar S&L C.D.				10,000
Home S&L C.D.				10,000
Series E Bonds				5,000
Cash value of insurance				9,790
Savings on insurance premium				1,154
				$ 64,899
If home is sold				24,000
If lot is sold				10,000
			(18,431)	$ 98,899
Savings on taxes				9,287
				$108,186

Repositioning of Assets
(Without Sale of Home and Lot)

Placement	Amount	Deductible
1. Deposit for life insurance	$ 500	
2. Money market mutual fund	3,000	
3. Growth mutual, Keogh (Jack)	6,000	$ 6,000
4. Growth mutual, IRA (Jack)	2,000	2,000
5. Growth mutual, IRA (Jill)	2,000	2,000
6. Growth mutual, joint	15,000	
7. Oil & Gas Income Partnership	15,000	1,400
8. Multifamily housing—leveraged	10,000	2,250
9. Multifamily housing—all cash	9,000	
10. Cinema	10,000	6,500
11. $6,000 of capital loss against $3,000 ordinary income		3,000
		$23,150

Jones's Deductions After Repositioning

CPA fee	$ 300
Dividend exclusion	200
Taxes on home	1,400
Interest on home	2,550
Taxes on recreational lot	275
Safe-deposit box	48
Contributions	2,000
Medical	150
Sales taxes	271
Interest expense on charge accounts	363
Miscellaneous	200
Professional fees and trade publications	225
Keogh contribution	6,000
IRA (Jack)	2,000
IRA (Jill)	2,000
Oil & Gas	1,400
Multifamily	2,250
Cinema	6,500
($6,000 of capital loss against $3,000 ordinary income $12,431 of capital loss to be carried forword)	3,000
Deductions	$31,132
Exemptions	4,000
Deductions	$35,132
Zero bracket	(3,400)
Net deductions	$31,732

Jones's Taxable Income After Repositioning

Jack's salary	$40,000
Jill's salary	18,000
Money market fund $3,000 at 14%	420
American S&L	395
Mutual fund open account $15,000 at 2%	300
Taxable before deductions	$59,115
Deductions	31,732
Taxable	$27,383
Taxes due	4,844

Tax Savings by Repositioning

Taxes due before repositioning	$14,131
Taxes due after repositioning	4,844
Tax savings from repositioning	$9,287

Let's discuss why the Jones's assets were repositioned the way they were:

1. The $500 deposit was for the $5,000 ten-year deposit level portion of his new life insurance policy. This entitles him to a $150,000 low-cost term rider for $1.03 per thousand.

2. The $3,000 in the money market funds is for liquidity in case of an emergency. In this position, access is easier than in the passbook because the Joneses have check-writing privileges and the yield is three times higher.

3., 4., and 5. Jack is eligible for a Keogh contribution of $6,000 without including his employee for two more years. Both Jack and Jill are eligible for IRA accounts.

6. With $15,000 in a joint mutual fund account, they qualify for the $25,000 quantity discount because their $10,000 IRA and Keogh contributions were made into the same family of funds. Cash flow from their real estate and cinema partnerships should also be invested in their joint account. A timing service will be superimposed on the fund.

7. The oil and gas income limited partnership provides a small deduction, and for the first few years most of the cash flow will not be taxable. It provides them diversification and an opportunity for growth. The $200 per month they can save can be added to this partnership. After the original investment, the partnership accepts amounts as small as $50. Another choice would be their IRA account in the mutual funds for next year's contribution.

8. The $10,000 plus the $9,000 in tax savings in a multifamily housing limited partnership should provide tax-sheltered cash flow, excess deductions, and, they hope, equity buildup and appreciation.

9. The $10,000 invested in the cinema limited partnership should provide a $6,500 write-off and, they hope, all of the original investment back over the first year or two.

10. Losses of $18,431 were established by repositioning; $6,000 can be used against $3,000 of ordinary income this year and the remainder carried forward. If the recreation lot can be sold at a capital gains, the loss can be used dollar for dollar against the gain and save the capital gains taxes.

If the Joneses buy a new home and sell their lot, they will have an additional $34,000 to invest. They should consider investments of $10,000 in a miniwarehouse limited partnership, an additional $14,000 in a multifamily real estate limited partnership, and $10,000 additional investment in an oil and gas income partnership.

Figure 19-3 shows their assets before and after repositioning and before the sale of the home and lot. As you will note, their diversifica-

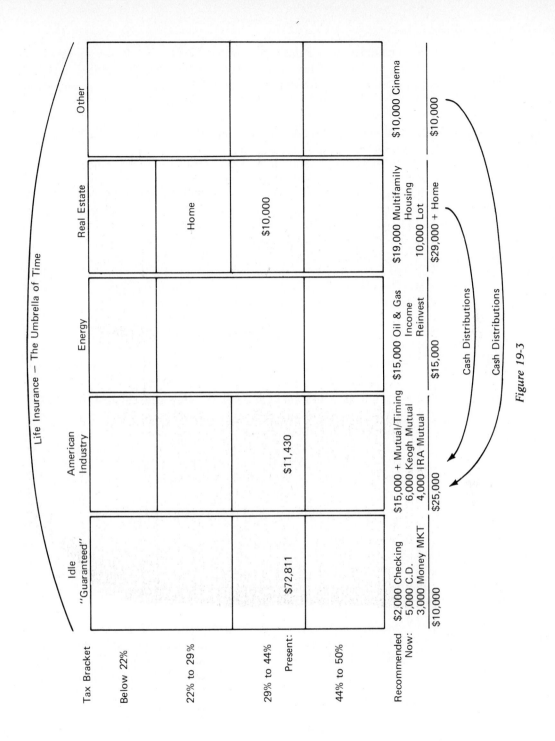

Figure 19-3

tion, balance, opportunity for growth, and their losses to taxes are greatly improved. They have $10,000 in "guaranteed" dollars, $25,000 in mutual funds under timing, $15,000 in energy, $29,000 in real estate (plus their home and lot), and $10,000 in cinema.

If the lot and home are sold and the proceeds invested as recommended above, $24,000 would be added to real estate and $10,000 to the oil and gas.

Although their liquidity is somewhat lessened, it should be adequate. They have $10,000 in checking, money market funds, and certificates of deposit. They also have $15,000 in redeemable mutual funds. (There would be a penalty if they redeemed their $10,000 in their Keogh and IRA accounts.) Their $15,000 in the oil and gas can be liquidated at the oil company's repurchase price and their cinema is self-liquidating. They should also be receiving cash distributions from the real estate limited partnerships, which we plan to flow to their redeemable mutual funds, or which the Joneses could use if cash is needed. The real estate partnership funds could be tied up for three to seven years.

The Smiths

Let's examine the data sheet of Bob and Jane Smith (Figure 19-4). Their two children are both married and self-sufficient. Bob is taking early retirement and setting up a consulting firm. His close friend did so three years ago and is now earning more than when he worked for the corporation. Bob has already received offers of more assignments than he feels he can handle. Let's look at the Smiths' income, deductions, and taxes due before any repositioning of assets.

Now let's see how the Smiths might reposition their assets so that they would work harder for them, reduce their tax burden, and better fit their new employment circumstances.

Checking Account. The $2,500 is a reasonable amount in checking, for they may be doing some personal and business travel after Bob retires.

Savings Account. Passbook savings accounts are obsolete. Since Bob is beginning a new consulting business and may need some liquidity for expenses, he should open a money market mutual fund account with check-writing privileges and deposit the $8,000 from the Spring Branch Savings and Loan into the account. He should move the $7,000 from Pasadena Savings and Loan to the repositioning list.

Figure 19-4

FINANCIAL PLANNING DATA SHEET

DATE _____

Robert A. Smith   55
NAME   **AGE**

5678 Roaring Brook   Houston, TX 77012
ADDRESS   **ZIP CODE**

891-2345   678-9123
HOME PHONE NO.   **BUSINESS PHONE NO.**

Ho-Tex Energy   Engineer
EMPLOYER   **OCCUPATION**

Jane B. Smith   54
NAME OF SPOUSE   **AGE**

_____   _____
EMPLOYER   **SPOUSE'S BUSINESS PHONE NO.**

Homemaker
OCCUPATION

DO YOU HAVE A CURRENT WILL? _____ yes _____

ARE YOU COVERED UNDER A PENSION PLAN?

IRA no **KEOGH** no

My financial resources

I. **LOANED DOLLARS:**

   A. Checking Account $ 2,500

   B. Amounts in Passbook Savings Accounts:

Institution	Amount	
1. Pasadena S&L	7,000	
2. Spring Br. S&L	8,000	$ 15,000

C. Certificates of Deposit:

	Institution	Rate %	Maturity	Amount	
1.	Am. S&L	7-3/4	1/1/85	15,000	
2.	Home S&L	7-1/2	1/1/84	17,000	
3.	1st City Bk	7-1/2	12/1/82	5,000	$ 37,000

D. Credit Union __12__ % $ __5,000__

E. Government Bonds & Instruments

Type	Rate %	Maturity Date	Current Value
_____	_____	_____	_____
_____	_____	_____	_____
_____	_____	_____	_____

$_____

F. Bonds—Corporate and Municipals

Name of Company or Municipality	No. of Bonds	Rate %	Maturity Date	Cost	Market Value
Exxon	5	8-1/4	2001	5200	3025
RCA	10	9-1/4	1990	10,020	6762
_____	_____	_____	_____	_____	_____
_____	_____	_____	_____	_____	_____

$ 9,787

G. Mortgages You Carry $ 10,500

H. Loans Receivable $_____

I. Cash Value of

Insurance Policies (see Worksheet) $ 18,209

TOTAL LOANED DOLLARS $ 97,996 ___(1)

II. WORKING DOLLARS:

A. Stocks and Mutual Funds

No. of Shares	Name of Company	Date of Purchase	Cost	Market Value
300	Am. Elec. Pwr.	1977	7725	5250
400	Gen. Pub. Ut.	1977	8640	2050
300	Gulf States Ut.	1977	4470	3877
400	AT&T	1978	25,890	22,100
200	Safeway	1978	9200	5700
200	Gen. Motors	1977	15,700	8465
300	Exxon	1978	16,080	8550

$ 37,705

Total Market Value $ 55,992 (2)
Pension Funds 189,000
244,992

Real Estate

Home (Market Value Less Mortgage) $ 155,000
$175,000 − $20,000 mtg.
Other Real Estate (Net After Mortgages):

Commercial lot $ 50,000

$

$

$ $ 50,000

Limited Partnerships:

$

$

$ $

Total Loaned and
Working Dollars $ 547,988

Financial Objective numbered in order of Importance:

_____ Income now

___2___ Income at retirement

___1___ Maximum tax advantage

_____ Educate children

___3___ Travel

_____ Other _____
                    (specify)

Estimated Gross Income this year .... $ 72,680

Estimated taxable income .... $ 62,000

Tax Bracket .... 50 %

Taxable Income last 3 years:

$ 57,123 $ 61,291 $ 63,210

Taxes Paid:

$ 18,268 $ 20,375 $ 21,411

No. of Dependents ___2___

Amount you could save each month .... $ _____

Retirement Data:

    No. of years before: ___0___ years

    Desired monthly income .... $ _____

      Possible Sources:

      Social Security $ _____

      Pensions $ have 189,000 in acct.

      Investments $ _____

      Other $ _____

                           Total $ _____

Additional needed if retiring today $ _____

Anticipated inflation rate per year _____ %

Children Educational Cost Data:

Name of Child	Age	Years Before College	Estimated Cost
_____	_____	_____	_____
_____	_____	_____	_____
_____	_____	_____	_____

Children ages 30 and 32; married, self-sufficient

Total _____

Amount set aside _____

Additional needed _____

Present Life Insurance, & Annuities Work Sheet
(to complete item I-H)

Company	Type	Face Amount	Cash Value	*Net Insurance	Annual Premium
Group		70,000	0	70,000	---
XYZ		10,000	4025	5975	100
ABC		28,000	14,184	13,816	464
TOTAL		108,000	18,209	89,791	564

* Face Amount less Cash Value = Net Insurance

Disability Insurance

Company	Monthly Coverage	Premium
_____	$_____	$_____

Is taking early retirement and setting up a consulting practice. He expects to earn as much or more than he does now.

Figure 19-4

Certificates of Deposit. They should reposition the $15,000 and $17,000 certificates due in 1985 and 1984. They should leave the $5,000 certificate at First City Bank until it matures and then move it to their repositioning list.

Corporate Bonds. Corporate bonds, regardless of the fact that many financial writers advise them for retirement, the just won't make it in a world of high inflation and high taxes. The Smiths should reposition the proceeds from their bonds. This frees $9,787 to work for them and establishes a $5,433 capital loss to be charged off at tax time.

Cash Value of Life Insurance. Bob's group policy will be carried by his company with reduced coverage. This could be sufficient for Jane's needs, since they alread have a living estate of $547,988. If, however, they would like to carry some insurance, this can be done. His coverage outside of his company is $38,000, $18,709 of which is cash value, or a net coverage of only $20,000. This amount of insurance $18,709 of which is cash value, or a net coverage of only $20,000. could be obtained at a relatively low cost and would free $18,209 to go to work for them.

Mortgage Receivable. This asset is locked in and all they can do is to accept the monthly payment of principal and interest. They sold some land that was appreciating, so in reality they traded an appreciating asset for one that is depreciating in purchasing power.

Stocks. Again we find a couple who believed the financial writers who advised their readers to invest in high-quality corporate bonds and utility stocks for income at retirement. Don't be lured into this trap, for the same reasons that I pointed out in the Jones case. The Smiths have a quality portfolio of utilities and three "blue chips," none of which show a profit.

The Smiths do not enjoy studying and investing in the market, so it was decided that it would be best to put their portfolio under professional management by repositioning these funds. This would release $55,992 and establish a loss of $31,713.

Home. The Smiths live in a large home in the suburbs. Bob does not want to commute, and Jane and Bob are both tired of yard work. There is a very nice high-rise being built near the office complex where Bob will establish his new office. The condominium will cost $120,000 and can be financed with 25 percent down or $30,000. Their present home cost them $50,000. They can sell it for $175,000, which would be a capital gain of $125,000. Since Bob is fifty-five and they have lived in their home for fifteen years, this gain will not be taxable.

Commercial Lot. The Smiths bought the commercial lot ten years ago for $21,000. They have an offer to sell it for $50,000. They think the property has matured and that this is the maximum amount they can obtain for several years. They should sell the lot. This will establish a $29,000 long-term capital gain. There should not be any tax due, since they will have established a $31,713 long-term capital loss from the sale of their stocks and bonds.

Pension Fund. Bob should take a lump sum payout from his pension plan and roll it over into an IRA. He must do this within sixty days of receipt of the proceeds. No tax will be due and his investment will be allowed to compound tax-sheltered.

If he does not roll over his funds, they will be substantially diluted by taxes (even with averaging). We recommend that he invest his funds for the present in a mutual fund, investing $100,000 in fund 1 and $89,000 in fund 2. (We will place another $11,000 in the same family of funds within a thirteen-month period to qualify for the $100,000 discount.)

Inside of IRA, his funds are tax-sheltered. We recommend that he superimpose a timing service to move his funds between the aggressive growth fund and the money market fund within the family of funds, as economic conditions dictate. This can be done without commission and without tax consequences.

Now let's look at the assets to be repositioned and the effect on their tax liabilities:

Smiths' Gross Income Before Repositioning

Robert's salary	$60,000
Pasadena S&L, $7,000 at 5-1/2%	385
Spring Br. S&L, $8,000 at 5-1/2%	440
American S&L, $15,000 C.D. at 7-3/4%	1,162
Home S&L, $17,000 C.D. at 7-1/2%	1,275
First City Bank, $5,000 C.D. at 7-1/2%	375
Credit Union, $5,000 at 10%	500
Exxon Bonds, 5 at 8-1/4%	412
RCA Bonds, 10 at 9-1/4%	925
Am. Elec. Power, 300 shares at $2.26	678
Gulf States Ut. 300 shares at $1.56	468
AT&T, 400 shares at $5.40	2,160
Safeway, 200 shares at $2.60	520
GM, 200 shares at $2.40	480
Exxon, 300 shares at $3.00	900
Mortgage interest	2,000
Total Taxable Income Before Deductions	$72,680

Smiths' Deductions Before Repositioning

CPA fees	$ 1,000
Dividend exclusion	200
Taxes on home	3,500
Interest on home	1,600
Taxes on lot	1,000
Safe-deposit box	48
Contributions	3,000
Medical	150
Sales taxes	372
Interest Expense	342
Professional fees and publications	300
Miscellaneous	200
	11,712
Exemptions	2,000
	13,712
Zero bracket	(3,400)
Total deductions	$10,312
Gross income	$72,680
Deductions	10,312
Taxable	$62,368
Taxes due	$17,714

Smiths' Assets To Be Repositioned

Source	Cost	Market	Gain & Loss	Reposition
Cash value of life insurance				18,209
Pasadena S&L				7,000
Spring Branch S&L				8,000
Am. S&L C.D.				15,000
Home S&L C.D.				17,000
Exxon 5 Bonds	5,200	3,025	(2,175)	3,025
RCA 10 Bonds	16,020	6,762	(9,258)	6,762
Am. Elec. Power	7,725	5,250	(2,475)	5,250
Gen. Pub. Utilities	8,640	2,050	(6,590)	2,050
Gulf States Utilities	4,470	3,877	(593)	3,877
AT&T	25,890	22,100	(3,790)	22,100
Safeway	9,200	5,700	(3,500)	5,700
General Motors	15,700	8,465	(7,235)	8,465
Exxon	16,080	8,550	(7,530)	8,550
			(43,146)	130,988
Home sale	50,000	175,000 [1]	—	155,000
Commercial lot sale	21,000	50,000	29,000	50,000
			(14,146)	335,988
Pension plan				189,000
				$524,988

1 Mortgage $20,000

Recommended Repositioning

	Amount	Deductions
1. Money market mutual funds	25,000	——
2. Cinema limited partnership	20,000	(13,000)
3. Community home park partnership	30,000	—
4. Nonleveraged multifamily limited partnership	40,000	—
5. Leveraged multifamily limited partnership	30,000	(6,000)
6. Miniwarehouse limited partnership	30,000	—
7. Oil and gas income limited partnership – leveraged	50,000	(5,600)
8. Oil and gas income – not leveraged	40,000	—
9. IRA rollover:		
Family of mutual funds/timing #1	100,000	—
Family of mutual funds/timing #2	89,000	—
10. Family of mutual funds #2 joint	11,000	—
11. IRA (Bob)	2,000	(2,000)
12. IRA (Jane)	2,000	(2,000)
13. Triple-net lease partnership	25,000	—
14. Condo downpayment	30,000	—
	524,000	(28,600)

Smiths' Estimated Taxable Income After Repositioning and Before Deductions

Robert's income	$58,700
Jane's income	2,000
$25,000 money market at 15%	3,750
$11,000 mutual funds at 3%	330
Nonleverage oil and gas income	3,000
Miniwarehouses	1,500
Mortgage interest	1,000
Total before deductions	$70,280

Smiths' Deductions After Repositioning

Cinema	$13,000
Community home park	3,600
Leveraged real estate	6,000
Oil and gas income–leveraged	5,600
IRA (Robert)	2,000
IRA (Jane)	2,000
Used $6,000 of capital losses after sheltering gain on lot. Will carry forward $19,854.	3,000
	($35,200)

Taxable income before deductions	$70,280
Deductions	(35,200)
Taxable	$35,080
Taxes due	$ 6,993

Tax Savings

Taxes due before repositioning	$18,694
Taxes due after repositioning	-6,993
Tax savings	$11,701

Reasons for Recommended Repositioning

1. The $25,000 in money market mutual funds plus $2,500 in checking and $5,000 left in the certificate of deposit for a total of $32,500 in cash is too much in an idle guaranteed position. However, Jane will probably want some new furnishings for the condo and Bob's new consulting business may not produce income for several months. With this much cash, there will be no pressure on Bob to go to work any sooner than he desires nor Jane to postpone buying furnishings for the condo. Later, a good portion of these funds should be added to their limited partnership.

2. The $20,000 in cinema partnership should be ideal for their situation. It should give a 65 percent or $13,000 write-off now to reduce their taxes and should give them a rapid return of capital to be repositioned later.

3. The $30,000 invested in the community home park partnership should produce 4 percent tax-sheltered cash flow, with excess deductions of around 12 percent to shelter other income, with the potential for increasing cash flow to around 10 to 12 percent by the fifth year plus equity buildup and appreciation potential.

4. The $40,000 invested in nonleveraged multifamily housing lets them take advantage of the shortage of capital that exists at certain times. Cash is king at such times, so the partnerships should be able to make some excellent buys, and with no mortgages to service, they should have an excellent tax-sheltered cash flow beginning at 8–9 percent and increasing each year. If interest rates go down in a few years, the management will probably finance the properties, returning to the Smiths all or a portion of their original investment (not taxable). If interest rates go up, rents should also go up, so they should be able to sell the properties at a gain.

5. The $30,000 invested in leverage multifamily housing should provide the Smiths around a 3 percent tax-sheltered cash flow the first year, plus a 20 percent deduction, with the cash flow going up each year to perhaps around 9 percent by the fifth year—all tax-sheltered and still with excess deductions and growth potential.

6. The $30,000 invested in miniwarehouse partnerships should provide the Smiths a good way to obtain warehouse prime property plus receive a good cash flow beginning around 10 percent after completion and increasing each year, with 35–40 percent of distributions tax-sheltered.

7. The leveraged oil and gas income programs should provide a 7–9 percent cash flow the first twelve months plus a 14 percent write-off, with an increasing tax-sheltered cash flow of 12 percent and above projected thereafter.

8. The nonleveraged oil and gas programs should provide more cash flow than the leveraged one—perhaps yielding around 15 percent, with less tax shelter and perhaps without much appreciation potential.

9. The $189,000 IRA rollover avoids current taxation on Bob's pension plan distributions. By placing $100,000 in one family of funds, Bob and Jane qualify for the $100,000 discount, and by placing $89,000 in another family of funds, they not only have greater diversification of stocks but also greater diversification of brains. They can receive a check a month from the funds when he reaches 59-1/2 years of age. These distributions would be taxed as ordinary income. They should, however, delay these withdrawals as long as they can, because all of their yield is compounding inside the rollover without taxes.

10. The $11,000 in the second family of funds in their joint account gives them the $100,000 discount on the $89,000 in their rollover account, and the $11,000 in their joint account provides liquidity and a place to deposit their cash flow from those partnerships that do not provide reinvestment privileges.

11. and 12. Jane is planning to keep books for Bob's new consulting firm and he'll pay her at least $2,000 per year. From her earnings she'll set up an IRA account of $2,000, and Bob will also contribute $2,000 to his IRA account. Later he may also set up a Keogh account using 15 percent of his self-employment income from his consulting business. This would also provide him with another tax deduction.

13. The $25,000 in the triple-net lease partnership should provide a 9 percent tax-sheltered beginning cash flow.

14. The $30,000 is reserved for a down payment on the condominium.

If Bob decides he doesn't want to work at consulting after they have done the above repositioning, they should have sufficient income

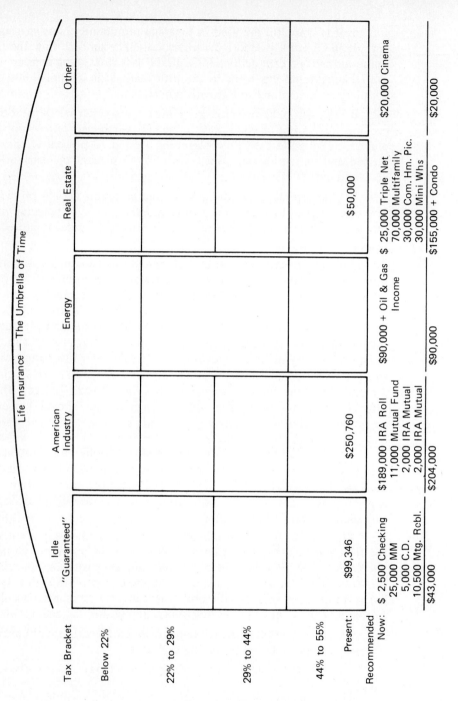

Figure 19-5

after taxes to continue their present standard of living. If he does want to go into consulting, they can reinvest their cash flow and have it compound until they do decide to use it.

This repositioning saved them $11,701 in taxes, which could be invested in a real estate investment trust or could be used to invest in a tax shelter if Bob's consulting practice produces as much income as he is anticipating. Figure 19-5 will allow you to compare the Smiths' assets before and after repositioning.

Summary of Case Studies

I hope these two case studies will be helpful to you in repositioning your own assets. I find that most of the people who come to our team of financial planners for counseling have already accumulated some assets, but these assets are being employed less productively than they should be and often work harder for someone else than they do for these people. I also find that many are not knowledgeable about our tax laws and could, with proper guidance, greatly reduce their tax drains.

Application

Get busy now and take your own financial inventory if you have not already done so. Use the blank diagram in the Appendix (Figure 14). Plot where you are now opposite your tax bracket. Then see how you might reposition your assets to your maximum advantage. Do your tax planning early in the year and always keep good records. Many items are legitimate deductions, but the IRS requires a record for proof.

Take a comprehensive inventory of your financial progress at least once a year, and if you are in a high enough tax bracket to make the use of tax shelters worthwhile, you will want to keep a running score.

After a while, you'll find this process fun and not such a chore. I have clients who actually have more fun saving their money and bringing it to me to invest than they do spending it. The other day I told a couple who had been our faithful clients for over fifteen years to take a trip and spend some of their money. They had enough.

You and I have had a pleasant journey together. I sincerely hope that you now have five ingredients for financial independence: that you have some time, that you have some money, and that you already know how blessed you are to live in a country where you have the privilege of owning a part of American industry, energy, real estate, and other areas where demand is greater than supply. I hope from our time together you've added two more ingredients—a little more knowledge of how to combine these three ingredients and the motivation to do something now in order to make the most of the time that you have left.

To survive in our economic climate you must be willing to accept change. Agility continues to be the order of the day. If you are abiding by the "prudent man's rule" of yesteryear, you will lose. The "prudent man's rule" during times of inflation and high taxation becomes the "stupid man's rule." Do not expect this to change during the decade of the 1980s. It will not.

For inflation to subside, government spending and costly regulations must be reduced. Attempts are being made in these directions, but the spenders outnumber those who understand that the free enterprise system must have capital and incentives to survive and prosper, and that people do not work to pay taxes, but work to be able to have money after taxes.

There will be token speeches made in the halls of Congress about reducing government spending, but the Congressmen do not mean cuts in their own districts. They mean that spending should be reduced in someone else's district. Our greatest need today is for statesmen who are more concerned about the future of the nation than about reelection. We must fill the void that exists in our educational system and at least teach personal finance, the rudiments of capitalism, and basic economics. Only when we educate our people and elect men and women to Congress who understand and love our free enterprise system will our strangling bureaucracy be diminished and free people be allowed to rise to their highest levels of potential.

My creed, which is also that of some of our leading financial planners, is as follows:

I DO NOT CHOOSE TO BE A COMMON MAN. It is my right to be uncommon–if I can.

I seek opportunity—not security. I do not wish to be a kept citizen, humbled and dulled by having the state look after me. I want to take the calculated risk: to dream and to build, to fail and to succeed.

I refuse to barter incentive for a dole. I prefer the challenges of life to the guaranteed existence and the thrill of fulfillment to the stale calm of utopia.

I will not trade freedom for beneficence, nor my dignity for a handout. I will never cower before any master, nor bend to any threat. It is my heritage to stand erect, proud and unafraid; to think and act for myself; to enjoy the benefits of my creations; and to face the world boldly and say, "This, I have done."

As you lay down this book and go forth to implement you plan for financial independence, remember that the world could be your oyster.

All you'll need to do is approach it with enthusiasm, intelligence, a willingness to change, and true gusto. If you implement what you have learned, you should have the financial means by which to live the good life, enjoy the beautiful world around you, and someday be able to retire in financial dignity.

If you accomplish this worthy predetermined goal, you will say, "It was good that Venita passed my way." God bless!

Glossary of Investing

Accrued Interest: Interest accrued on a bond since the last interest payment was made. The buyer of the bond pays the market price plus accrued interest.

Accumulation Plan: A plan for the systematic accumulation of mutual fund shares through periodic investments and reinvestments of income dividends and capital gains distributions.

Amortization: Accounting for expenses or charges as applicable rather than as paid. Includes such practices as depreciation, depletion, write-off of intangibles, prepaid expenses, and deferred charges.

Annual Report: The formal financial statement issued yearly by a corporation. The annual report shows assets, liabilities, earnings, standing of the company at the close of the business year, performance of the company profit-wise during the year, and other information of interest to shareowners.

Arbitrage: Dealing in differences. Example: Buying on one exchange while simultaneously selling short on another at a higher price.

Asked Price: The price asked for a security offered for sale. Quoted, bid, and asked prices are wholesale prices for interdealer trading, and do not represent prices for the public.

Asset: On a balance sheet, that which is owned or receivable.

Auction Market: Dealings on a securities exchange where a two-way auction is continuously in effect.

Authorized Stock: The total number of shares of stock authorized for issue by a company's shareholders.

Averages: Various ways of measuring the trend of stocks listed on exchanges. Formulas, some very elaborate, have been devised to compensate for stock splits and stock dividends and thus give continuity to the average. In the case of the Dow-Jones Industrial Average, the prices of the thirty stocks are totaled and then divided by a figure that is intended to compensate for past stock splits and stock dividends and that is changed from time to time.

Balance Sheet: A condensed financial statement showing the nature and amount of a company's assets, liabilities, and capital on a given date. The balance sheet shows in dollar amounts what the company owned, what it owes, and its stockholders' ownership in the company.

Balanced Fund: A mutual fund that is required to keep a specified percentage of its total assets invested in senior securities.

Bear: One who believes the stock market will decline.

Bear Market: A declining stock market.

Bearer Bond: A bond that does not have the owner's name registered on the books of the issuing company and that is payable to the holder.

Bid and Asked: Often referred to as a quotation or quote. The bid is the highest price anyone has declared that he wants to pay for a security at a given time; the asked is the lowest price anyone will take at the same time.

Big Board: A popular term for the New York Stock Exchange, Inc.

Block: A large holding or transaction of stock, popularly considered to be 10,000 shares or more.

Blue Chip: A company known nationally for the quality and wide acceptance of its products or services, and for its ability to make money and pay dividends.

Blue Sky Laws: A popular name for laws enacted by various states to protect the public against securities frauds. The term is believed to have originated when a judge ruled that a particular stock had about the same value as a patch of blue sky.

Bond: Basically an IOU or promissory note of a corporation, usually issued in multiples of $1,000. A bond is evidence of a debt on which the issuing company usually promises to pay the bondholders a specified amount of interest for a specified length of time, and to repay the loan on the expiration date. In every case, a bond represents debt—its holder is a creditor of the corporation and not a part owner, as is the shareholder.

Bond Fund: A mutual fund invested completely in bonds.

Book Value: An accounting term for the value of a stock determined from a company's records by adding all assets and then deducting all debts and other liabilities, plus the liquidation price of any preferred issues. The sum arrived at is divided by the number of common shares outstanding, and the result is book value per common share. Book value of the assets of a company or a security may have little or no significant relationship to market value.

Broker: An agent who handles the public's orders to buy and sell securities, commodities, or other property. A commission is charged for this service.

Bull: One who believes the stock market will rise.

Bull Market: An advancing stock market.

Business Cycle: The long-term boom-recession cycle that has been characteristic of business conditions not only nationally, but on a world-wide basis.

Call: An option to buy a specified number of shares of a certain security at a definite price within a specified period of time.

Callable: A bond issue, all or part of which may be redeemed by the issuing corporation under definite conditions before maturity. The term also applies to preferred shares, which may be redeemed by the issuing corporation.

Capital Gain or Capital Loss: Profit or loss from the sale of a capital asset. A capital gain, under current federal income tax laws, may be either short-term (six months or less) or long-term (more than six months). A short-term capital gain is taxed at the reporting individual's full income tax rate. A long-term capital gain is subject to a lower tax.

Capital Market: The market that deals in long-term securities issues of both debt and equity.

Capital Shares: When referring to a dual- or leveraged-type closed-end investment company, those shares to which all gains or losses accrue and which have no claim on dividends.

Capital Stock: All shares representing ownership of a business, including preferred and common.

Capitalization: Total amount of the various securities issued by a corporation. Capitalization may include bonds, debentures, preferred and common stock, and surplus.

Certificate: The actual piece of paper that is evidence of ownership of stock in a coporation. Loss of a certificate may cause, at least, a great deal of inconvenience; at worse, financial loss.

Closed-End Investment Company: An investment company that issues a fixed number of shares and does not redeem them. It may also issue senior securities and/or warrants.

Collateral: Securities or other property pledged by a borrower to secure repayment of a loan.

Commission: The broker's basic fee for purchasing or selling securities or property as an agent.

Common Stock: Securities that repesent an ownership interest in a corporation. If the company has also issued preferred stock, both common and preferred have ownership rights. Claims of both common and preferred stockholders are junior to claims of bondholders or other creditors of the company. Common stockholders assume the greater risk, but generally they also excercise the greater control and may gain the greater reward in the form of dividends and capital appreciation.

Common Stock Fund: A mutual fund that has a stated policy of investing all of its assets in common stocks. The term is also applied to funds that normally invest only in common stocks, though are not restricted to them by charter.

Confirmation: A written description of the terms of a transaction in securities supplied by a broker/dealer to his customer or to another broker/dealer.

Conglomerate: A corporation that has diversified its operations, usually by acquiring enterprises in widely varied industries.

Constructive Receipt: A doctrine of the Internal Revenue Service that requires the reporting of income (including capital gains) in the year in which it could have been received had the taxpayer so wished. Thus, dividends of a mutual fund automatically reinvested are taxable in the year in which reinvested on the basis that the taxpayer could have received them by check and then reinvested them or not at his option.

Convertible: A bond, debenture, or preferred share that may be exchanged by the owner for common stock or another security, usually of the same company, in accordance with the terms of the issue.

Corporate Bond: An evidence of indebtedness issued by a corporation, rather than by the U.S. Government or municipality.

Corporation: An organization chartered by a state government. When the term is used without qualification, it generally refers to an organization carrying on a business for profit. However, there are nonprofit corporations and municipalities, which differ from corporations organized for profit in that they do not issue stock.

Coupon Bond: Bond with interest coupons attached. The coupons are clipped as they come due and are presented by the holder for payment of interest.

Cumulative Preferred: A stock with a provision that if one or more dividends are omitted, the omitted dividends must be paid before dividends may be paid on the company's common stock.

Cumulative Voting: A type of shareholder voting in which the number of shares held is multiplied by the number of directors to be elected to determine the number of votes a shareholder may cast. He may cast all votes for one director or may allocate them in any way he sees fit.

Current Assets: Those assets of a company that are reasonably expected to be realized in cash, or sold, or consumed during the normal operating cycle of the business.

Current Liabilities: Money owned and payable by a company, usually within one year.

Custodian: The corporation, usually a bank, charged with the safekeeping of an investment company's portfolio securities.

Dealer: An individual or firm in the securities business acting as a principal rather than as an agent. Typically, a dealer buys for his own account and sells to a customer from his own inventory. The dealer's profit or loss is the difference between the price he pays and the price he receives for the same security. The dealer's confirmation must disclose to his customer that he has acted as principal. The same individual or firm may function, at different times, as either a broker or dealer.

Debenture: A promissory note backed by the general credit of a company and usually not secured by a mortgage or lien on any specific property.

Depletion: Natural resources, such as metals, oils and gas, and timber that conceivably can be reduced to zero over the years, present a special problem in capital management. Depletion is an accounting practice consisting of charges against earnings based upon the amount of the assets taken out of the total reserves in the period for which accounting is made. A bookkeeping entry, it does not represent any cash outlay, nor are any funds earmarked for the purpose.

Depreciation: Normally, charges against earnings to write off the cost, less salvage value, of an asset over its estimated useful life. A bookkeeping entry, it does not represent any cash outlay, nor are any funds earmarked for the purpose.

Director: A person elected by shareholders to establish company policies. The directors elect the president, vice-president, and all other operating officers. Directors decide, among other matters, if and when dividends will be paid.

Discount: The amount of money by which a preferred stock or bond may sell below its par value.

Discretionary Account: An account in which the customer gives the broker or someone else discretion, either complete or within specific limits, as to the purchase and sale of securities or commodities, including selection, timing, amount, and price to be paid or received.

Diversification: Spreading investments among different companies in different fields. Another type of diversification is also offered by the securities of many individual companies because of the wide range of their activities.

Diversified Investment Company: An investment company which, under the Investment Company Act of 1940, must invest 75 percent of its total assets so that not more than 5 percent of total assets are invested in the securities of any one issuer. Also, the company may not own more than 10 percent of the voting securities of any one issuer.

Dividend: The payment designated by the board of directors to be distributed pro rata among the shares outstanding. On preferred shares, it is generally a fixed amount. On common shares, the dividend varies with the fortunes of the company and the amount of cash on hand, and it may be omitted if business is poor or the directors determine to withhold earnings to invest in plant and equipment. Sometimes a company will pay a dividend out of past earnings even if it is not currently operating at a profit.

Dividend Reinvestment Plan: A mutual fund share account in which dividends are automatically reinvested in additional shares. With this type of account, capital gains distributions are also automatically reinvested. Dividends (but not capital gains) may be invested at offering price (i.e., with a sales charge), but are more commonly reinvested at asset value.

Dollar-Cost-Averaging: A system of buying securities at regular intervals with a fixed dollar amount. Under this system the investor buys by the dollars' worth rather than by the number of shares. If each investment is of the same number of dollars, payments buy more when the price is low and fewer when it rises. Temporary downswings in price thus benefit the investor if he continues to make periodic purchases in both good times and bad, and the price at which the shares are sold is more than their average cost.

Double Taxation: The federal government taxes corporate profits once as corporate income; any part of the remaining profits distributed as dividends to stockholders may be taxed again as income to the recipient stockholder.

Dow-Jones Average: Widely quoted stock averages computed regularly. They include an industrial stock average, a rail average, a utility average, and a combination of the three.

Dow Theory: A theory of market analysis based upon performance of the Dow-Jones industrial and transportation stock price averages. The theory says that the market is in a basic upward trend if one of these averages advances above a previous important high, accompanied or followed by a similar advance in the other. A dip in both averages below previous important lows is regarded as confirmation of a basic downward trend. The theory does not attempt to predict how long either trend will continue, although it is widely misinterpreted as a method of forecasting future action.

Dual Fund: A closed-end investment company with two classes of shares: income and capital outstanding. Also designated as a *leveraged fund.*

Equity: The ownership interest of common and preferred stockholders in a company. Also refers to excess of value of securities over the debit balance in a margin account. Also, the value of a property that remains after all liens and other charges against the property are paid. A property owner's equity generally consists of his or her monetary interest in the property in excess of the mortgage indebtedness. In the case of long-term mortgage, the owner's equity builds up quite gradually during the first several years because the bulk of each monthly payment is applied, not to the principal amount of the loan, but to the interest.

Ex-Dividend: A synonym for "without dividend." The buyer of a stock selling ex-dividend does not receive the recently declared dividend. Every dividend is payable on a fixed date to all shareholders recorded on the books of the company as of a previous date or record. For example, a dividend may be declared as payable to holders of record on the books of the company on a given Friday. Since five business days are allowed for delivery of stock in a "regular way" transaction on the stock exchange, the exchange would declare the stock "ex-dividend" as of the opening of the market on the preceding Monday. That means anyone who bought it on or after Monday would not be entitled to that dividend. When stocks go ex-dividend, the stock tables include the symbol "x" following the name.

Ex-Rights: Without the rights. Corporations raising additional money may do so by offering stockholders the right to subscribe to new or additional stock, usually at a discount from the prevailing market price. The buyer of a stock selling ex-rights is not entitled to the rights.

Extra: The short form of "extra dividend." A dividend in the form of stock or cash in addition to the regular or usual dividend the company has been paying.

Face Value: The value of a bond that appears on the face of the bond, unless the value is otherwise specified by the issuing company. Face value is ordinarily the amount the issuing company promises to pay at maturity. Face value is not an indication of market value. It is sometimes referred to as par value.

Fiduciary: One who acts for another in financial matters.

Floor: The huge trading area of a stock exchange where stocks and bonds are bought and sold.

Floor Broker: A member of the stock exchange who executes orders on the floor of the exchange to buy or sell any listed securities.

Fully Managed Fund: A mutual fund whose investment policy gives its management complete flexibility as to the types of investments made and the proportions of each. Management is restricted only to the extent that federal or blue sky laws require.

Gilt-Edged: High-grade bond issued by a company that has demonstrated its ability to earn a comfortable profit over a period of years and pay its bondholders their interest without interruption.

Good Delivery: Certain basic qualifications must be met before a security sold on the exchange may be delivered. The security must be in proper form to comply with the contract of sale and to transfer title to the purchaser.

Good 'til Cancelled Order (GTC) or **Open Order:** An order to buy or sell that remains in effect until it is either executed or cancelled.

Government Bonds: Obligations of the U.S. government, regarded as the highest grade issues in existence.

Growth Fund: A fund whose rate of growth over a period of time is considerably greater than that of business generally. An average rate of 10 percent per year is used by some analysts as definitive.

Growth Stock: Stock of a company with a record of relatively rapid growth earnings.

Holding Company: A corporation that owns the securities of another, in most cases with voting control.

Income Fund: A mutual fund with a primary objective of current income.

Indenture: A written agreement under which bonds and debentures are issued, setting forth maturity date, interest rate, and other terms.

Institution: An organization holding substantial investing assets, often for others. Includes banks, insurance companies, investment companies, and pension funds.

Interest: Payments made by a borrower to a lender for the use of his money. A corporation pays interest on its bonds to its bondholders.

Investment: The use of money for the purpose of making more money: to gain income or increase capital or both.

Investment Banker: Also known as an *underwriter.* The middleman between the corporation issuing new securities and the public. The usual practice is for one or more investment bankers to buy outright from a corporation a new issue of stocks or bonds. The group forms a syndicate to sell the securities to individuals and institutions. Investment bankers also distribute very large blocks of stocks or bonds (perhaps held by an estate).

Investment Company: A company or trust that uses its capital to invest in other companies. There are two principal types: the closed-end and the open-end, or mutual fund. Shares in closed-end investment companies are readily transferrable in the open market and are bought and sold like other shares. Capitalization of these companies remains the same unless action is taken to change, which seldom occurs. Open-end funds sell their own new shares to investors, stand ready to buy back their old shares, and are not listed. Open-end funds are so named because their capitalization is not fixed; they issue more shares as people want them.

Investment Company Act of 1940: An act passed by the Congress for the specific purpose of empowering the Securities and Exchange Commission to regulate investment companies.

Investment Counsel: One whose principal business consists of acting as investment advisor, and a substantial part of whose business consists of rendering investment supervisory services.

Investor: An individual whose principal concerns in the purchase of a security are regular dividend income, safety of the original investment, and, if possible, capital appreciation.

Issue: Any of a company's securities, or the act of distributing such securities. Upon the death of a joint tenant, his interest passes, not to his heirs, but to his co-owner.

Legal List: A list of investments selected by various states in which certain institutions and fiduciaries, such as insurance companies and banks, may invest. Legal lists are often restricted to high-quality securities and, if possible, capital appreciation.

Leverage: The effect on the per-share earnings of the common stock of a company when large sums must be paid for bond interest or preferred stock dividends, or both, before the common stock is entitled to share in earnings. Leverage may be advantageous for the common stock when earnings are good, but may work against the common stock when earnings decline. Leverage also refers to mortgage funds used in financing of real estate and oil limited partnerships.

Liabilities: All the claims against a corporation. Liabilities include accounts and wages and salaries payable, dividends declared payable, accrued taxes payable, fixed or long-term liabilities such as mortgage bonds, debentures, and bank loans.

Lien: A claim against property that has been pledged or mortgaged to secure the performance of an obligation. A bond may be secured by a lien against specified property of a company.

Limited Order: An order to buy or sell a stated amount of a security at a specified price, or at a better price.

Liquidating Value: When referring to the shares of an open-end investment company, the value at redemption. Usually the net asset value.

Listed Stock: The stock of a company that is traded on a securities exchange.

Locked In: An investor is said to be locked in when he has a profit on a security he owns, but does not sell because his profit would immediately become subject to the capital gains tax.

Management: The board of directors, elected by the stockholders, and the officers of the corporation, appointed by the board of directors.

Management Fee: The fee paid to the investment manager of a mutual fund. It is usually about one-half of one percent of average net assets annually. Not to be confused with the sales charge, which is the one-time commission paid at the time of purchase as a part of the offering price.

Manipulation: An illegal operation. Buying or selling a security for the purpose of creating false or misleading appearance of active trading or for the purpose of raising or depressing the price to induce purchase or sale by others.

Margin: The amount paid by the customer when he uses his broker's credit to buy security.

Margin Call: A demand upon a customer to put up money or securities with the broker. The call is made when a purchase is made or when a customer's equity in a margin account declines below a minimum standard set by the exchange or by the firm.

Market Order: An order to buy or sell a slated amount of a security at the most advantageous price obtainable.

Market Price: In the case of a security, market price is usually considered the last reported price at which the stock or bond sold.

Maturity: The date on which a loan or a bond or a debenture comes due and is to be paid off.

Member Firm: A securities brokerage firm organized as a partnership or corporation and owning at least one seat on the exchange.

Mortgage Bond: A bond secured by a mortgage on a property. The value of the property may or may not equal the value of the so-called mortgage bonds issued against it.

Municipal Bond: A bond issued by a state or a political subdivision, such as a county, city, town, or village. The term also designates bonds issued by state agencies and authorities. In general, interest paid on municipal bonds is exempt from federal income taxes and from state and local income taxes within the state of issue.

Mutual Fund: An open-end investment company that continuously offers new shares to the public in addition to redeeming shares on demand as required by law. While in common use, the term mutual fund has no meaning in law.

NASD: The National Association of Securities Dealers, Inc. An association of brokers and dealers in the over-the-counter securities business. The association has the power to expel members who have been declared guilty of unethical practices. NASD is dedicated to, among other objectives, "adopt, administer and enforce rules of fair practice and rules to prevent fraudulent and manipulative acts and practices, and in general to promote just and equitable principles of trade for the protection of investors."

NASDAQ: An acronym for National Association of Securities Dealers Automated Quotations. An automated information network that provides brokers and dealers with price quotations on securities traded over the counter.

Negotiable: Refers to a security, title to which is transferable by delivery.

Net Asset Value: A term usually used in connection with investment companies, meaning net asset value per share. It is common practice for an investment company to compute its assets daily by totaling the market value of all securities owned. All liabilities are deducted, and the balance is divided by the number of shares outstanding. The resulting figure is the net asset value per share.

Net Change: The change in the price of a security from the closing price on one day to the closing price on the following day on which the stock is traded. The net change is ordinarily the last figure on the stock price list. The mark +2-1/8 means up $2.125 a share from the last sale on the previous day the stock traded.

New Issue: A stock or bond sold by a corporation for the first time. Proceeds may be issued to retire outstanding securities of the company, for new plant or equipment, or for additional working capital.

Noncumulative: A preferred stock on which unpaid dividends do not accrue. Omitted dividends are, as a rule, gone forever.

NYSE Common Stock Index: A composite index covering price movements of all common stocks listed on the "Big Board." It is based on the close of the market December 31, 1965, as 50.00 and is weighted according to the number of shares listed for each issue. The index is computed continuously and printed on the ticker tape each half hour. Point changes in the index are converted to dollars and cents to provide a meaningful measure of changes in the average price of listed stocks.

Odd Lot: An amount of stock less than the established 100-share unit of 10-share unit of trading: from 1 to 99 shares for the great majority of issues, 1 to 9 for so-called inactive stocks. Odd-lot prices are geared to the auction market. On an odd-lot market order, the odd-lot dealer's price is based on the first round-lot transaction that occurs on the floor following receipt at the trading post of the odd-lot order. The differential between the odd-lot price and the "effective" round-lot price is 12-1/2 cents a share. For example: You decide to buy 20 shares of ABC common at the market. Your order is transmitted by your commission broker to the representative of an odd-lot dealer at the post where ABC is traded. A few minutes later there is a 100-share transaction in ABC at $10 a share. The odd-lot price at which your order is immediately filled by the odd-lot dealer is $10.125 a share. If you had sold 20 shares of ABC, you would have received $9.875 a share.

Offer: The price at which a person is ready to sell. Opposite of bid, the price at which one is ready to buy.

Open Account: When referring to a mutual fund, a type of account in which the investor may add or withdraw shares at any time. In such an account, dividends may be paid in cash or reinvested at the account holder's option.

Open-End Investment Company: By definition under the 1940 act, an investment company that has outstanding redeemable shares. Also generally applied to those investment companies which continuously offer new shares to the public and stand ready at any time to redeem their outstanding shares.

Option: A right to buy or sell specific securities or properties at a specified price within a specified time.

Overbought: An opinion as to price levels. May refer to a security that has had a sharp rise or to the market as a whole after a period of vigorous buying which, it may be argued, has left prices "too high."

Oversold: An opinion, the reverse of overbought. A single security or a market that, it is believed, has declined to an unreasonable level.

Over-the-Counter: A market for securities made up of securities dealers who may or may not be members of a securities exchange.

Over-the-counter is mainly a market made over the telephone. Thousands of companies have insufficient shares outstanding, stockholders, or earnings to warrant application for listing on an exchange. Securities of these companies are traded in the over-the-counter market between dealers who act either as principals or as brokers for customer.

Paper Profit: An unrealized profit on a security still held. Paper profits become realized profits only when the security is sold.

Par: In the case of a common share, par means a dollar amount assigned to the share by the company's charter. Par value may also be used to compute the dollar amount of the common shares on the balance sheet. Par value has little significance so far as market value of common stock is concerned.

Penny Stocks: Low-priced issues, often highly speculative, selling at less than $1 a share. Frequently used as a term of disparagement, although a few penny stocks have developed into investment-caliber issues.

Point: In the case of shares of stock, a point means $1. If ABC shares rise three points, each share has risen $3. In the case of bonds, a point means $10, since a bond is quoted as a percentage of $1,000. A bond that rises three points gains 3 percent of $1,000, or $30 in value. An advance from 87 to 90 would mean an advance in dollar value from $870 to 900 for each $1,000 bond. In the case of market averages, the work point means merely that and no more. If, for example, the Dow-Jones Industrial Average rises from 870.25 to 871.25, it has risen a point. A point in this average, however, is not equivalent to $1.

Portfolio: Holdings of securities by an individual or institution. A portfolio may contain bonds, preferred stocks, and common stocks of various types of enterprises.

Preferred Stock: A class stock with a claim on the company's earnings before payment may be made on the common stock and usually entitled to priority over common stock if the company liquidates. Usually entitled to dividends at a specified rate, when declared by the board of directors and before payment of a dividend on the common stock, depending upon the term of the issue.

Premium: The amount by which a preferred stock or bond may sell above its par value. In the case of a new issue of bonds or stocks, premium is the amount the market price rises over the original selling price.

Price–Earnings Ratio: The price of a share of stock divided by earnings per share for a twelve-month period. For example, a stock selling for $100 a share and earning $5 a share is said to be selling at a price-earnings ratio of 20 to 1.

Primary Distribution: Also called *primary offering.* The original sale of a company's securities.

Principal: The person for whom a broker executes an order, or a dealer buying or selling for his own account. The term "principal" may also refer to a person's capital or to the face amount of a bond.

Profit-Taking: Selling stock that has appreciated in value since purchase to realize the profit that has been made possible. The term is often used to explain a downturn in the market following a period of rising prices.

Prospectus: The document that offers a new issue of securities to the public. It is required under the Securities Act of 1933.

Proxy: Written authorization given by a shareholder to someone else to represent him and vote his shares at a shareholders' meeting.

Proxy Statement: Information required by the SEC to be given to stockholders as a prerequisite to solicitation of proxies for a security subject to the requirements of the Securities Exchange Act.

Prudent Man's Rule: An investment standard. In some states, the law requires that a fiduciary, such as a trustee, may invest the fund's money only in a list of securities designated by the state—the so-called legal list. In other states, the trustee may invest in a security if it is one that a prudent man of discretion and intelligence, who is seeking a reasonable income and preservation of capital, would buy.

Put: An option to sell a specified number of shares at a definite price within a specified period of time. The opposite of a call.

Quotation: Often shortened to *quote.* The highest bid to buy and the lowest offer to sell a security in a given market at a given time. If you ask your broker for a quote on a stock, he may come back with something like "45-1/4 to 45-1/2." This means that $45.25 is the highest price any buyer wanted to pay at the time the quote was given on the floor of the exchange, and that $45.50 was the lowest price any seller would take at the same time.

Rally: A brisk rise following a decline in the general price level of the market or in an individual stock.

Record Date: The date on which you must be registered as a shareholder on the stock book of a company to receive a declared dividend or, among other things, to vote on company affairs.

Red Herring: A preliminary prospectus used to obtain indications of interest from prospective buyers of a new issue.

Redemption Price: The price at which a bond may be redeemed before maturity, at the option of the issuing company. Redemption value also applies to the price an open-end investment company must pay to call in certain types of preferred stock. It is usually the net asset value per share—it fluctuates with the value of the company's investment portfolio.

Registered Bond: A bond that is registered on the books of the issuing company in the name of the owner. It can be transferred only when endorsed by the registered owner.

Registered Representative: A full-time employee who has met the requirements of an exchange as to background and knowledge of the securities business. Also known as an *account exchange* or *customer's broker.*

Registrar: Usually a trust company or bank charged with the responsibility of preventing the issuance of more stock than authorized by a company.

Registration: Before a public offering may be made of new securities by controlling stockholders, through the mails or in interstate commerce, the securities must be registered under the Securities Act of 1933. Registration statement is filed with the SEC by the issuer. It must disclose pertinent information relating to the company's operations, securities, management, and purpose of the public offering. On security offerings involving less than $300,000, less information is required. Before a security may be admitted to dealings on a national securities exchange, it must be registered under the Securities Exchange Act of 1934. The application for registration must be filed with the exchange and the SEC by the company issuing the securities. It must disclose pertinent information relating to the company's operations, securities, and management.

Regulation T: The federal regulation governing the amount of credit that may be advanced by brokers and dealers to customers for the purchase of securities.

Regulation U: The federal regulation governing the amount of credit that may be advanced by a bank to its customers for the purchase of listed stocks.

REIT: Real estate investment trust, an organization similar to an investment company in some respects, but concentrating its holdings in real estate investments. The yield is generally liberal, since REITs are requested to distribute as much as 90 percent of their income.

Return: Another term for *yield.*

Rights: When a company wants to raise more funds by issuing additional securities, it may give its stockholders the opportunity, ahead of others, to buy the new securities in proportion to the number of shares each owns. The piece of paper evidencing this privilege is called a right. Because the additional stock is usually offered to stockholders below the current market price, rights ordinarily have a market value of their own and are actively traded. In most cases they must be exercised within a relatively short period. Failure to exercise or sell rights may result in actual loss to the holder.

Round Lot: A unit of trading or a multiple thereof. On most exchanges the unit of trading is 100 shares in the case of stocks and $1,000 par value in the case of bonds. In some inactive stocks, the unit of trading is 10 shares.

Seat: A traditional figure of speech for a membership on an exchange. Price and admission requirements vary.

SEC: Securities and Exchange Commission, established by Congress to help protect investors. The SEC administers the Securities Act of 1933, the Securities Exchange Act of 1934, the Trust Indenture Act, the Investment Company Act, the Investment Advisers Act, and the Public Utility Holding Company Act.

Secondary Distribution: Also known as a *secondary offering.* The redistribution of a block of stock some time after it has been sold by the issuing company. The sale is handled off the exchange by a securities firm or group of firms, and the shares are usually offered at a fixed price that is related to the current market price of the stock. Usually the block is a large one, such as might be involved in the settlement of an estate. The security may be listed or unlisted.

Sinking Fund: Money regularly set aside by a company to redeem its bonds, debentures, or preferred stock from time to time as specified in the indenture or charter.

Special Offering: Occasionally a large block of stock becomes available for sale that, due to its size and the market in that particular issue, calls for special handling. A notice is printed on the ticker tape announcing that the stock will be offered for sale on the floor of the exchange at a fixed price. Member firms may buy this stock for customers directly from the seller's broker during trading hours. The price is usually based on the last transaction in the regular auction market. If there are more buyers than stock, allotments are made. Only the seller pays a commission on a special offering.

Specialist: A member of an exchange who has two functions. The first is to maintain an orderly market, insofar as reasonably practicable, in the stocks in which he is registered as a specialist. The exchange expects the specialist to buy or sell for his own account, to a reasonable degree, when there is a temporary disparity between supply and demand. The specialist also acts as a broker's broker. When a commission broker on the exchange floor receives a limit order, say, to buy at $50 a stock then selling at $60, he cannot wait at the post where the stock is traded to see if the price reaches the specified level. So he leaves the order with the specialist, who will try to execute it in the market if and when the stock declines to the specified price. The specialist must put his customers' interest above his own at all times.

Speculator: One who is willing to assume a relatively large risk in the hope of gain. His principal concern is to increase his capital rather than his dividend income. The speculator may buy and sell the same day or speculate in an enterprise he does not expect to be profitable for years.

Split: The division of the outstanding shares of a corporation into a larger number of shares. A 3-for-1 split by a company with 1 million shares outstanding results in 3 million shares outstanding. Each holder of 100 shares before the 3-to-1 split would have 300 shares, although his proportionate equity in the company would remain the same; 100 parts of 1 million are the equivalent of 300 parts of 3 million.

Spread: The difference between the bid price and the offering price. Also, the combination of a put and a call "points away" from the market.

Statement of Policy: The SEC's statement of its own position as to those things considered "materially misleading" in the offer of shares of open-end investment companies.

Stock: Ownership shares of a corporation.

Stock Certificate: A certificate that provides physical evidence of stock ownership.

Stock Dividend: A dividend paid in securities rather than cash. The dividend may be additional shares of the issuing company or shares of another company (usually a subsidiary) held by the issuing company.

Stock Exchange: An organization registered under the Securities Exchange Act of 1934 with physical facilities for the buying and selling of securities in a two-way auction.

Stock Power: An assignment and power of substitution separate from a stock certificate authorizing transfer of the stock on the books of the corporation.

Stockholder of Record: A stockholder whose name is registered on the books of the issuing corporation.

Stop Order: An order to buy at a price above or to sell below the current market. Stop buy orders are generally used to limit loss or protect unrealized profits on a short sale. Stop sell orders are generally used to protect unrealized profits or limit loss on a holding.

Street Name: Securities held in the name of a broker instead of his customer's name are said to be carried in a street name. This occurs when the securities have been bought on margin or when the customer wishes the security to be held by the broker.

Suitability Rule: The rule of fair practice that requires a member to have reasonable grounds for believing that a recommendation to a customer is suitable on the basis of his financial objectives and abilities.

Tenants in Common: A form of registration of property, frequently used with securities. An undivided estate in property where, upon the death of the owner, the undivided estate becomes the property of his heirs or divisees and not of his surviving co-owner.

Tenants by the Entirety: A form of registration of property, usually real estate.

Tips: Supposedly "inside" information on corporation affairs.

Trader: One who buys and sells for his own account for short-term profit.

Transfer: This term may refer to two different operations. For one, the delivery of a stock certificate from the seller's broker to the buyer's broker and legal change of ownership, normally accomplished within a few days. For another, to record the change of ownership on the books of the corporation by the transfer agent. When the purchaser's name is recorded on the books of the company, dividends, notices of meetings, proxies, financial reports, and all pertinent literature sent by the issuer to its securities holders are mailed directly to the new owner.

Transfer Agent: One who keeps a record of the name of each registered shareowner, his or her address, and the number of shares owned, and sees that certificates presented to his office for transfer are properly cancelled and that new certificates are issued in the name of the transferee.

Treasury Bill: Short-term U.S. government paper with no stated interest rate. It is sold at a discount in competitive bidding and reaches maturity in ninety days or less.

Treasury Bond: U.S. government bonds issued in $1,000 units with maturity of five years or longer. They are traded on the market like other bonds.

Treasury Note: U.S. government paper, not legally restricted as to interest rates, with maturities from one to five years.

Treasury Stock: Stock issued by a company but later reacquired. It may be held in the company's treasury indefinitely, reissued to the public, or retired. Treasury stock receives no dividends and has no vote while held by the company.

Underwriter's Fee: In the sale of mutual funds shares, the difference between the total sales charge and the underwriter's reallowance to the dealer.

Unlisted: A security not listed on a stock exchange.

Voting Right: The stockholder's right to vote his stock in the affairs of his company. Most common shares have one vote each. Preferred stock usually has the right to vote when preferred dividends are in default for a specified period. The right to vote may be delegated by the stockholder to another person.

Warrant: A certificate giving the holder the right to purchase securities at a stipulated price within a specified time limit or perpetually. Sometimes a warrant is offered with securities as an inducement to buy.

When Issued: A short form of "when, as, and if issued." The term indicates a conditional transaction in a security authorized for issuance but not yet actually issued. All "when issued" transactions are on an "if" basis, to be settled if and when the actual security is issued and the exchange or National Association of Securities Dealers rules that the transactions are to be settled.

Withdrawal Plan: A mutual fund plan that permits monthly or quarterly withdrawal of specified dollar amounts, usually involving the invasion of principal. Alternately, a plan may permit varying withdrawals based on the liquidation of a fixed number of shares monthly or quarterly.

Working Control: Theoretically, ownership of 51 percent of a company's voting stock is necessary to exercise control. In practice— and this is particularly true in the case of a large corporation— effective control sometimes can be exerted through ownership, individually or by a group acting in concert, of less than 50 percent.

Yield: Also known as *return*. The dividends or interest paid by a company expressed as a percentage of the current price. A stock with a current market value of 20 a share that has paid $1 in dividends in the preceding twelve months is said to return 5 percent ($1.00/$20.00). The current return on a bond is figured the same way.

Appendix

Table 1. $10,000 Lump Sum at Varying Rates Compounded Annually—End of Year Values

	5th Yr.	10th Yr.	15th Yr.	20th Yr.	25th Yr.	30th Yr.	35th Yr.	40th Yr.
1%	10,510	11,046	11,609	12,201	12,824	13,478	14,166	14,888
2%	11,040	12,189	13,458	14,859	16,406	18,113	19,998	22,080
3%	11,592	13,439	15,579	18,061	20,937	24,272	28,138	32,620
4%	12,166	14,802	18,009	21,911	26,658	32,433	39,460	48,010
5%	12,762	16,288	20,789	26,532	33,863	43,219	55,160	70,399
6%	13,382	17,908	23,965	32,071	42,918	57,434	76,860	102,857
7%	14,025	19,671	27,590	38,696	54,274	76,122	106,765	149,744
8%	14,693	21,589	31,721	46,609	68,484	100,626	147,853	217,245
9%	15,386	23,673	36,424	56,044	86,230	132,676	204,139	314,094
10%	16,105	25,937	41,772	67,274	108,347	174,494	281,024	452,592
11%	16,850	28,394	47,845	80,623	135,854	228,922	385,748	650,008
12%	17,623	31,058	54,735	96,462	170,000	299,599	527,996	930,509
13%	18,424	33,945	62,542	115,230	212,305	391,158	720,685	1,327,815
14%	19,254	37,072	71,379	137,434	264,619	509,501	981,001	1,888,835
15%	20,113	40,455	81,370	163,665	329,189	662,117	1,331,755	2,678,635
16%	21,003	44,114	92,655	194,607	408,742	858,498	1,803,140	3,787,211
17%	21,924	48,068	105,387	231,055	506,578	1,110,646	2,435,034	5,338,687
18%	22,877	52,338	119,737	273,930	626,686	1,433,706	3,279,972	7,503,783
19%	23,863	56,946	135,895	324,294	773,880	1,846,753	4,407,006	10,516,675
20%	24,883	61,917	154,070	383,375	953,962	2,373,763	5,906,682	14,697,715
21%	25,937	67,274	174,494	452,592	1,173,908	3,044,816	7,897,469	20,484,002
22%	27,027	73,046	197,422	533,576	1,442,101	3,897,578	10,534,018	28,470,377
23%	28,153	79,259	223,139	628,206	1,768,592	4,979,128	14,017,769	39,464,304
24%	29,316	85,944	251,956	738,641	2,165,419	6,348,199	18,610,540	54,559,126
25%	30,517	93,132	284,217	867,361	2,646,698	8,077,935	24,651,903	75,231,638

Table 2. $1200 Per Year at Varying Rates Compounded Annually—End of Year Values

	5th Yr.	10th Yr.	15th Yr.	20th Yr.	25th Yr.	30th Yr.	35th Yr.	40th Yr.
1%	6,182	12,680	19,509	26,686	34,231	43,359	50,492	59,250
2%	6,369	13,402	21,168	29,739	39,205	49,654	61,192	73,932
3%	6,561	14,169	22,988	33,211	45,063	58,803	74,731	93,195
4%	6,760	14,983	24,990	37,162	51,974	69,993	91,917	118,592
5%	6,962	15,848	27,188	41,662	60,135	83,713	113,803	152,208
6%	7,170	16,766	29,607	46,791	69,787	100,562	141,745	196,857
7%	7,383	17,740	32,265	52,638	81,211	121,287	177,495	256,332
8%	7,603	18,774	35,188	59,307	94,744	146,815	223,322	335,737
9%	7,827	19,872	38,403	66,918	110,788	178,290	282,150	441,950
10%	8,059	21,037	41,940	75,602	129,818	217,131	357,752	584,222
11%	8,295	22,273	45,828	85,518	152,398	265,095	454,996	774,992
12%	8,538	23,586	50,103	96,838	179,200	324,351	581,355	1,030,970
13%	8,786	24,976	54,806	112,164	211,020	397,578	741,298	1,374,583
14%	9,043	26,454	59,976	124,521	248,799	488,084	948,807	1,835,890
15%	9,304	28,018	65,660	141,372	293,654	599,948	1,216,015	2,455,144
16%	9,572	29,679	71,910	160,609	346,905	726,194	1,560,032	3,286,173
17%	9,848	31,440	78,778	182,566	410,115	909,004	2,002,792	4,400,869
18%	10,130	33,306	86,326	207,625	485,126	1,119,982	2,572,378	5,895,109
19%	10,419	35,284	94,620	236,216	574,117	1,380,464	3,304,696	7,896,595
20%	10,716	37,380	103,730	268,831	679,652	1,701,909	4,245,610	10,575,154
21%	11,019	39,601	113,736	306,021	804,759	2,098,358	5,453,622	14,156,310
22%	11,330	41,954	124,722	348,416	952,998	2,587,006	7,003,256	18,939,087
23%	11,649	44,446	136,779	396,727	1,128,558	3,188,884	8,989,333	25,319,371
24%	11,976	47,085	150,013	451,758	1,336,360	3,929,683	11,532,334	33,820,458
25%	12,310	49,879	164,530	514,417	1,582,186.	4,840,641	14,666,342	45,132,982

Table 3. Approximate Annual Investment Required to Equal $100,000 at the End of a Specified Period—Varying Rates

	5 Yrs.	10 Yrs.	15 Yrs.	20 Yrs.	25 Yrs.	30 Yrs.	35 Yrs.	40 Yrs.
1%	19,380	9,464	6,151	4,497	3,506	2,768	2,378	2,026
2%	18,841	8,954	5,669	4,036	3,061	2,417	1,961	1,624
3%	18,290	8,470	5,220	3,613	2,663	2,041	1,606	1,288
4%	17,751	8,009	4,802	3,229	2,309	1,714	1,306	1,011
5%	17,236	7,572	4,414	2,880	1,966	1,433	1,054	788.39
6%	16,736	7,157	4,053	2,565	1,720	1,193	846.59	609.58
7%	16,254	6,764	3,719	2,280	1,478	989.39	676.08	468.14
8%	15,783	6,392	3,410	2,024	1,267	817.36	537.34	357.42
9%	15,332	6,039	3,125	1,793	1,083	673.06	425.31	271.52
10%	14,890	5,704	2,861	1,587	924.37	552.66	335.43	205.40
11%	14,467	5,388	2,618	1,403	787.41	452.67	263.74	154.84
12%	14,055	5,088	2,395	1,239	669.64	369.97	206.41	116.40
13%	13,658	4,805	2,190	1,070	568.67	301.83	168.00	87.29
14%	13,270	4,536	2,001	963.69	482.32	245.86	126.47	65.36
15%	12,898	4,283	1,828	848.82	408.64	200.02	98.68	48.88
16%	12,537	4,043	1,669	747.16	345.92	165.25	76.92	36.52
17%	12,185	3,817	1,523	657.30	292.60	132.02	59.92	27.27
18%	11,846	3,603	1,390	577.97	247.36	107.14	46.65	20.36
19%	11,517	3,401	1,268	508.01	209.02	86.93	36.31	15.20
20%	11,198	3,210	1,157	446.38	176.56	70.51	28.26	11.35
21%	10,802	3,030	1,056	392.13	149.11	57.19	22.00	8.48
22%	10,591	2,860	962.14	344.42	125.92	46.39	17.13	6.34
23%	10,301	2,700	877.33	302.48	106.33	37.63	13.35	4.74
24%	10,020	2,549	799.93	265.63	89.80	30.53	10.41	3.55
25%	9,749	2,406	729.35	233.27	75.84	24.79	8.18	2.66

Table 4. Lump Sum Required to Equal $100,000 at the End of a Specified Period—Varying Rates

	5 Yrs.	10 Yrs.	15 Yrs.	20 Yrs.	25 Yrs.	30 Yrs.	35 Yrs.	40 Yrs.
1%	95,147	90,529	86,135	81,954	77,977	74,192	70,591	67,165
2%	90,573	82,348	74,301	67,297	60,953	55,207	50,003	45,289
3%	86,261	74,409	64,186	55,367	47,761	41,199	35,538	30,656
4%	82,193	67,556	55,526	45,639	37,512	30,832	25,341	20,829
5%	78,353	61,391	48,102	37,689	29,530	23,138	18,129	14,205
6%	74,726	55,839	41,727	31,180	23,300	17,411	13,011	9,722
7%	71,299	50,835	36,245	25,842	18,425	13,137	9,367	6,678
8%	68,058	46,319	31,524	21,455	14,602	9,938	6,763	4,603
9%	64,993	42,241	27,454	17,843	11,597	7,537	4,899	3,184
10%	62,092	38,554	23,940	14,864	9,230	5,731	3,558	2,209
11%	59,345	35,218	20,900	12,403	7,361	4,368	2,592	1,538
12%	56,743	32,197	18,270	10,367	5,882	3,340	1,894	1,075
13%	54,276	29,460	15,989	8,678	4,710	2,557	1,388	753.12
14%	51,937	26,974	14,010	7,276	3,780	1,963	1,019	529.43
15%	49,718	24,718	12,289	6,110	3,040	1,510	750.89	373.32
16%	47,611	22,683	10,792	5,139	2,447	1,165	554.59	264.05
17%	45,611	20,804	9,489	4,329	1,974	900.38	410.67	187.31
18%	43,711	19,107	8,352	3,651	1,596	697.49	304.88	133.27
19%	41,905	17,560	7,359	3,084	1,292	541.49	226.91	95.10
20%	40,188	16,151	6,491	2,610	1,048	421.27	169.30	68.04
21%	38,554	14,864	5,731	2,209	851.85	328.43	126.62	48.82
22%	37,000	13,690	5,065	1,874	693.43	256.57	94.93	35.12
23%	35,520	12,617	4,482	1,592	565.42	200.84	71.34	25.34
24%	34,112	11,635	3,969	1,354	461.80	157.52	53.72	18.33
25%	32,768	10,737	3,512	1,153	377.78	123.79	40.56	13.30

Table 5. One Dollar Principal Compounded Annually

End of Year	2½%	3%	5%	6%	8%	10%	12%	15%
1	$ 1.0250	$ 1.0300	$ 1.0500	$ 1.0600	$ 1.0800	$ 1.1000	$ 1.1200	1.1500
2	1.0506	1.0609	1.1025	1.1236	1.1664	1.2100	1.2544	1.3225
3	1.0769	1.0927	1.1576	1.1910	1.2597	1.3310	1.4049	1.5209
4	1.1038	1.1255	1.2155	1.2625	1.3605	1.4641	1.5735	1.7490
5	1.1314	1.1593	1.2763	1.3382	1.4693	1.6105	1.7623	2.0114
6	1.1597	1.1941	1.3401	1.4185	1.5869	1.7716	1.9738	2.3131
7	1.1887	1.2299	1.4071	1.5036	1.7138	1.9487	2.2107	2.6600
8	1.2184	1.2668	1.4775	1.5938	1.8509	2.1436	2.4760	3.0590
9	1.2489	1.3048	1.5513	1.6895	1.9990	2.3579	2.7731	3.5179
10	1.2801	1.3439	1.6289	1.7908	2.1589	2.5937	3.1058	4.0456
11	1.3121	1.3842	1.7103	1.8983	2.3316	2.8531	3.4785	4.6524
12	1.3449	1.4258	1.7959	2.0122	2.5182	3.1384	3.8960	5.3503
13	1.3785	1.4685	1.8856	2.1329	2.7196	3.4523	4.3635	6.1528
14	1.4130	1.5126	1.9799	2.2609	2.9372	3.7975	4.8871	7.0757
15	1.4483	1.5580	2.0789	2.3966	3.1722	4.1772	5.4736	8.1371
16	1.4845	1.6047	2.1829	2.5404	3.4259	4.5950	6.1304	9.3576
17	1.5216	1.6528	2.2920	2.6928	3.7000	5.0545	6.8660	10.7613
18	1.5597	1.7024	2.4066	2.8543	3.9960	5.5599	7.6900	12.3755
19	1.5987	1.7535	2.5270	3.0256	4.3157	6.1159	8.6128	14.2318
20	1.6386	1.8061	2.6533	3.2071	4.6610	6.7275	9.6463	16.3665
21	1.6796	1.8603	2.7860	3.3996	5.0338	7.4002	10.8038	18.8215
22	1.7216	1.9161	2.9253	3.6035	5.4365	8.1403	12.1003	21.6447
23	1.7646	1.9736	3.0715	3.8197	5.8715	8.9543	13.5523	24.8915
24	1.8087	2.0328	3.2251	4.0489	6.3412	9.8497	15.1786	28.6252
25	1.8539	2.0938	3.3864	4.2919	6.8485	10.8347	17.0001	32.9190

End of Year	2½%	3%	5%	6%	8%	10%	12%	15%
26	$ 1.9003	$ 2.1566	$ 3.5557	$ 4.5494	$ 7.3964	$ 11.9182	$ 19.0401	$ 37.8568
27	1.9478	2.2213	3.7335	4.8223	7.9881	13.1100	21.3249	43.5353
28	1.9965	2.2879	3.9201	5.1117	8.6271	14.4210	23.8839	50.0656
29	2.0464	2.3566	4.1161	5.4184	9.3173	15.8631	26.7499	57.5755
30	2.0976	2.4273	4.3219	5.7435	10.0627	17.4494	29.9599	66.2218
31	2.1500	2.5001	4.5380	6.0881	10.8677	19.1943	33.5551	76.1435
32	2.2038	2.5751	4.7649	6.4534	11.7371	21.1138	37.5817	87.5651
33	2.2589	2.6523	5.0032	6.8406	12.6760	23.2252	42.0915	100.6998
34	2.3153	2.7319	5.2533	7.2510	13.6901	25.5477	47.1425	115.8048
35	2.3732	2.8139	5.5160	7.6861	14.7853	28.1024	52.7996	133.1755
36	2.4325	2.8983	5.7918	8.1473	15.9682	30.9127	59.1356	153.1519
37	2.4933	2.9852	6.0814	8.6361	17.2456	34.0039	66.2318	176.1246
38	2.5557	3.0748	6.3855	9.1543	18.6253	37.4043	74.1797	202.5433
39	2.6196	3.1670	6.7048	9.7035	20.1153	41.1448	83.0812	232.9248
40	2.6851	3.2620	7.0400	10.2857	21.7245	45.2593	93.0510	267.8635
41	2.7522	3.3599	7.3920	10.9029	23.4625	49.7852	104.2171	308.0431
42	2.8210	3.4607	7.7616	11.5570	25.3395	54.7637	116.7231	354.2495
43	2.8915	3.5645	8.1497	12.2505	27.3666	60.2401	130.7299	407.3870
44	2.9638	3.6715	8.5572	12.9855	29.5560	66.2641	146.4175	468.4950
45	3.9379	3.7816	8.9850	13.7646	31.9204	72.8905	163.9876	538.7693
46	3.1139	3.8950	9.4343	14.5905	34.4741	80.1795	183.6661	619.5847
47	3.1917	4.0119	9.9060	15.4659	37.2320	88.1975	205.7061	712.5224
48	3.2715	4.1323	10.4013	16.3939	40.2106	97.0172	230.3908	819.4007
49	3.3533	4.2562	10.9213	17.3775	43.4274	106.7190	258.0377	942.3103
50	3.4371	4.3839	11.4674	18.4202	46.9016	117.3909	289.0022	1083.6574

Table 6. One Dollar Per Annum Compounded Annually

End of Year	3%	5%	6%	8%	10%	12%	15%
1	$ 1.0300	$ 1.0500	$ 1.0600	$ 1.0800	$ 1.1000	$ 1.1200	$ 1.1500
2	2.0909	2.1525	2.1836	2.2464	2.3100	2.3744	2.4725
3	3.1836	3.3101	3.3746	3.5061	3.6410	3.7793	3.9934
4	4.3091	4.5256	4.6371	4.8666	5.1051	5.3528	5.7424
5	5.4684	5.8019	5.9753	6.3359	6.7156	7.1152	7.7537
6	6.6625	7.1420	7.3938	7.9228	8.4872	9.0890	10.0668
7	7.8923	8.5491	8.8975	9.6366	10.4359	11.2297	12.7268
8	9.1591	10.0266	10.4913	11.4876	12.5795	13.7757	15.7858
9	10.4639	11.5779	12.1808	13.4866	14.3974	16.5487	19.3037
10	11.8078	13.2068	13.9716	15.6455	17.5312	19.6546	23.3493
11	13.1920	14.9171	15.8699	17.9771	20.3843	23.1331	28.0017
12	14.6178	16.7130	17.8821	20.4953	23.5227	27.0291	33.3519
13	16.0863	18.5986	20.0151	23.2149	26.9750	31.3926	39.5047
14	17.5989	20.5786	22.2760	26.1521	30.7725	36.2797	46.5804
15	19.1569	22.6575	24.6725	29.3243	34.9497	41.7533	54.7175
16	20.7616	24.8404	27.2129	32.7502	39.5447	47.8837	64.0751
17	22.4144	27.1324	29.9057	36.4502	44.5992	54.7497	74.8364
18	24.1169	29.5390	32.7600	40.4463	50.1591	62.4397	87.2118
19	25.8704	32.0660	35.7856	44.7620	56.2750	71.0524	101.4436
20	27.6765	34.7193	38.9927	49.4229	63.0025	80.6987	117.8101
21	29.5368	37.5052	42.3923	54.4568	70.4027	91.5026	136.6316
22	31.4529	40.4305	45.9958	59.8933	78.5430	103.6029	158.2764
23	33.4265	43.5020	49.8156	65.7648	87.4973	117.1552	183.1678
24	35.4593	46.7271	53.8645	72.1059	97.3471	132.3339	211.7930
25	37.5530	50.1135	58.1564	78.9544	108.1818	149.3339	244.7120

End of Year	3%	5%	6%	8%	10%	12%	15%
26	$ 39.7096	$ 53.6691	$ 62.7058	$ 86.3508	$ 120.0999	$ 168.3740	$ 282.5688
27	41.9309	57.4026	67.5281	94.3388	133.2099	189.6989	326.1041
28	44.2189	61.3227	72.6398	102.9659	147.6309	213.5828	376.1697
29	46.5754	65.4388	78.0582	112.2832	163.4940	240.3327	433.7451
30	49.0027	69.7608	83.8017	122.3459	180.9434	270.2926	499.9569
31	51.5028	74.2988	89.8898	133.2135	200.1378	303.8477	576.1005
32	54.0778	79.0638	96.3432	144.9506	221.2515	341.4294	663.6655
33	56.7302	84.0670	103.1838	157.6267	244.4767	383.5210	764.3654
34	59.4621	89.3203	110.4348	171.3168	270.0244	430.6635	880.1702
35	62.2759	94.8363	118.1209	186.1021	298.1268	483.4631	1013.3757
36	65.1742	100.6281	126.2681	202.0703	329.0395	542.5987	1166.4975
37	68.1594	106.7095	134.9042	219.3158	363.0434	608.8305	1342.6222
38	71.2342	113.0950	144.0585	237.9412	400.4478	683.0102	1545.1655
39	74.4013	119.7998	153.7620	258.0565	441.5926	766.0914	1778.0903
40	77.6633	126.8398	164.0477	279.7810	486.8518	859.1424	2045.9539
41	81.0232	134.2318	174.9505	303.2435	536.6370	963.3595	2353.9969
42	84.4839	141.9933	186.5076	328.5830	591.4007	1080.0826	2708.2465
43	88.0484	150.1430	198.7580	355.9496	651.6408	1210.8125	3115.6334
44	91.7199	158.7002	211.7435	385.5056	717.9048	1357.2300	3584.1285
45	95.5015	167.6852	225.5081	417.4261	790.7953	1521.2176	4122.8977
46	99.3965	177.1194	240.0986	451.9002	870.9749	1704.8838	4742.4824
47	103.4084	187.0254	255.5645	489.1322	959.1723	1910.5898	5455.0047
48	107.5406	197.4267	271.9584	529.3427	1056.1896	2140.9806	6274.4055
49	111.7969	208.3480	289.3359	572.7702	1162.9085	2399.0182	7216.7163
50	116.1808	219.8154	307.7561	619.6718	1280.2994	2688.0204	8300.3737

Table 7.

If you're interested in growth

Summaries of assumed $10,000 investments

Here's what would have happened if you had invested $10,000 in The Seminar Fund and taken all income dividends and capital gain distributions in additional shares...

10-Year Periods

	Jan. 1-Dec. 31	Income Dividends Reinvested	Total Investment Cost	Ending Value of Shares	Capital Gain Distributions Taken in Shares*
...here's how you would have done in any of these 39 periods:	1934-1943	$6,367	$16,367	$34,334	$6,853
	1935-1944	6,038	16,038	33,734	6,640
	1936-1945	3,801	13,801	25,192	5,337
	1937-1946	3,005	13,005	16,853	3,598
	1938-1947	5,545	15,545	27,612	6,993
	1939-1948	5,273	15,273	21,577	5,779
	1940-1949	6,006	16,006	23,416	6,297
MEDIAN PERIOD	1941-1950	7,002	17,002	28,746	7,154
	1942-1951	8,421	18,421	36,562	9,256
	1943-1952	8,026	18,026	35,134	9,383
	1944-1953	6,783	16,783	26,579	7,691
	1945-1954	6,106	16,106	33,648	7,482
	1946-1955	5,072	15,072	30,844	6,976
	1947-1956	5,805	15,805	34,995	9,056
	1948-1957	6,351	16,351	30,558	10,432
	1949-1958	6,935	16,935	44,084	11,638
BEST PERIOD	1950-1959	6,959	16,959	46,002	11,339
	1951-1960	6,404	16,404	40,139	13,026
	1952-1961	5,938	15,938	41,912	12,831
	1953-1962	5,801	15,801	32,421	12,945
	1954-1963	6,286	16,286	39,662	13,821
	1955-1964	4,407	14,407	29,537	10,119
	1956-1965	3,834	13,834	29,872	9,225
	1957-1966	3,870	13,870	27,238	9,741
	1958-1967	4,968	14,968	39,877	12,382
	1959-1968	3,956	13,956	32,214	9,400
	1960-1969	3,985	13,985	25,196	9,333
	1961-1970	4,334	14,334	24,736	9,495
	1962-1971	3,966	13,966	23,508	7,660
	1963-1972	5,102	15,102	31,400	9,352
	1964-1973	4,645	14,645	21,257	7,795
WORST PERIOD	1965-1974	4,734	14,734	14,994	6,177
	1966-1975	4,260	14,260	16,002	4,411
	1967-1976	4,646	14,646	20,523	3,986
	1968-1977	3,949	13,949	15,523	2,972
	1969-1978	3,682	13,682	15,215	2,209
	1970-1979	4,583	14,583	20,299	2,060
	1971-1980	5,113	15,113	23,992	2,084
	1972-1981	5,120	15,120	20,673	3,014

15-Year Periods

	Jan. 1-Dec. 31	Income Dividends Reinvested	Total Investment Cost	Ending Value of Shares	Capital Gain Distributions Taken in Shares*
...here's how you would have done in any of these 34 periods:	1934-1948	$15,397	$25,397	$57,089	$20,336
	1935-1949	14,332	24,332	49,772	17,919
	1936-1950	9,162	19,162	32,569	10,739
	1937-1951	7,149	17,149	26,303	7,323
	1938-1952	12,808	22,808	47,929	13,854
	1939-1953	11,428	21,428	37,573	11,524
	1940-1954	12,638	22,638	58,174	13,894
	1941-1955	14,538	24,538	74,744	19,262
BEST PERIOD	1942-1956	17,453	27,453	89,365	27,177
	1943-1957	16,695	26,695	67,439	27,353
	1944-1958	13,996	23,996	73,532	23,037
	1945-1959	12,569	22,569	68,078	22,827
MEDIAN PERIOD	1946-1960	10,263	20,263	52,022	18,862
	1947-1961	11,563	21,563	65,590	22,118
	1948-1962	12,512	22,512	56,391	24,019
	1949-1963	13,557	23,557	69,051	26,499
	1950-1964	13,540	23,540	73,362	28,102
	1951-1965	12,370	22,370	77,732	27,859
	1952-1966	11,723	21,723	66,593	28,299
	1953-1967	11,794	21,794	76,532	28,446
	1954-1968	13,422	23,422	89,115	31,288
	1955-1969	9,820	19,820	50,985	23,062
	1956-1970	8,844	18,844	41,685	19,525
	1957-1971	8,935	18,935	44,049	17,770
	1958-1972	11,265	21,265	57,963	21,332
	1959-1973	8,654	18,654	33,301	15,298
WORST PERIOD	1960-1974	8,864	18,864	23,928	12,795
	1961-1975	9,615	19,615	30,992	11,927
	1962-1976	8,649	18,649	32,616	9,707
	1963-1977	11,010	21,010	36,636	11,520
	1964-1978	9,923	19,923	34,198	8,997
	1965-1979	9,588	19,588	35,032	7,563
	1966-1980	8,669	18,669	35,480	6,062
	1967-1981	9,977	19,977	33,424	7,574

20-Year Periods

...here's how you would have done in any of these 29 periods:

1934-1953	$31,576	$41,576	$99,201	$35,435
1935-1954	28,345	38,345	123,418	33,970
1936-1955	17,651	27,651	84,521	24,379
1937-1956	13,615	23,615	64,174	20,149
1938-1957	24,579	34,579	91,846	38,256
1939-1958 (MEDIAN PERIOD)	21,625	31,625	103,944	33,217
1940-1959	23,815	33,815	117,703	40,426
1941-1960	27,120	37,120	126,064	48,064
1942-1961 (BEST PERIOD)	32,157	42,157	167,493	60,535
1943-1962	30,292	40,292	124,450	57,336
1944-1963	25,040	35,040	115,177	47,824
1945-1964	22,306	32,306	108,571	44,673
1946-1965	17,996	27,996	100,743	38,084
1947-1966	20,616	30,616	104,215	46,325
1948-1967	22,934	32,934	133,109	51,763
1949-1968	25,980	35,980	155,150	56,909
1950-1969	26,986	36,986	126,637	60,252
1951-1970	25,406	35,406	108,473	54,662
1952-1971	24,105	34,105	107,694	47,929
1953-1972	23,878	33,878	111,244	45,624
1954-1973	26,417	36,417	92,123	47,606
1955-1974 (WORST PERIOD)	19,692	29,692	48,421	30,068
1956-1975	17,741	27,741	52,228	23,623
1957-1976	17,710	27,710	61,116	21,606
1958-1977	22,171	32,171	67,632	25,334
1959-1978	16,921	26,921	53,573	17,181
1960-1979	16,609	26,609	55,905	15,008
1961-1980	18,156	28,156	64,841	15,124
1962-1981	17,121	27,121	53,116	15,406

25-Year Periods

...here's how you would have done in any of these 24 periods:

1934-1958	$58,378	$68,378	$274,006	$92,456
1935-1959	51,959	61,959	249,340	90,027
1936-1960	31,827	41,827	142,370	56,830
1937-1961	24,140	34,140	120,145	44,024
1938-1962	43,042	53,042	169,326	78,968
1939-1963 (MEDIAN PERIOD)	37,238	47,238	162,816	68,257
1940-1964	40,650	50,650	187,710	78,196
1941-1965	45,860	55,860	244,133	94,648
1942-1966	55,276	65,276	266,129	122,350
1943-1967 (BEST PERIOD)	53,293	63,293	293,762	118,563
1944-1968	45,761	55,761	258,788	98,548
1945-1969	42,202	52,202	187,411	92,252
1946-1970	34,891	44,891	140,585	72,821
1947-1971	39,993	49,993	168,537	77,045
1948-1972	43,951	53,951	193,484	81,640
1949-1973	48,604	58,604	160,386	85,318
1950-1974	51,507	61,507	120,265	77,652
1951-1975	48,559	58,559	135,906	65,323
1952-1976	45,560	55,560	149,420	57,308
1953-1977	44,809	54,809	129,796	53,306
1954-1978	49,288	59,288	148,202	52,814
1955-1979	35,366	45,366	113,131	34,544
1956-1980	32,134	42,134	109,270	29,012
1957-1981 (WORST PERIOD)	33,585	43,585	99,531	32,286

48 Years

ICA's Lifetime	1934-1981	$832,622	$842,622	$2,331,160	$827,555

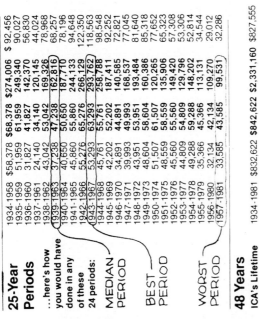

*The value of the shares acquired with these capital gain distributions is reflected in "Ending Value of Shares."

Table 8. $10,000 Initial Investment in The Seminar Fund—20 Years

DATE	INITIAL INVESTMENT	OFFERING PRICE	SALES CHARGE INCLUDED	SHARES PURCHASED	NET ASSET VALUE PER SHARE	INITIAL NET ASSET VALUE
1/ 1/52	$10,000.00	$3.26	8.50%	3,067.485	$2.983	$9,149

MONTHLY INVESTMENTS OF $100.00 — SAME DAY AS INITIAL INVESTMENT
DIVIDENDS AND CAPITAL GAINS REINVESTED

CUMULATIVE VOLUME DISCOUNT REFLECTED WHERE APPLICABLE IN THIS ILLUSTRATION

	=====COST OF SHARES=====					=====VALUE OF SHARES=====					
DATE	CUM INV'M'T	ANNUAL INCOME DIVS	CUM INCOME DIVS	TOTAL INV'M'T COST	ANNUAL CAP GAIN DISTRIB'N	FROM INV'M'T	FROM CAP GAINS REINV'D	SUB-TOTAL	FROM DIVS REINV'D	TOTAL VALUE	SHARES HELD
12/31/52	11,100	381	381	11,481	492	10,476	498	10,974	386	11,360	3,688
12/31/53	12,300	468	849	13,149	341	10,917	805	11,722	831	12,253	4,343
12/31/54	13,500	530	1,379	14,879	974	17,671	1,800	19,226	1,800	21,026	5,048
12/31/55	14,700	700	2,080	16,780	1,889	20,481	2,155	24,876	2,755	27,631	5,866
12/31/56	15,900	798	2,877	18,777	2,274	21,593	4,395	26,250	3,538	31,788	6,741
12/31/57	17,100	918	3,795	20,895	1,488	18,309	6,257	25,363	3,664	29,027	7,658
12/31/58	18,300	997	4,792	23,092	314	26,163	7,054	33,363	6,105	43,438	8,452
12/31/59	19,500	1,098	5,890	25,390	2,889	28,357	11,170	37,333	8,458	54,331	9,505
12/31/60	20,700	1,304	7,194	27,895	3,511	28,422	14,484	42,751	8,505	68,126	10,580
12/31/61	21,900	1,372	8,566	30,466	3,672	33,600	17,404	45,826	11,110	60,57	10,635
12/31/62	23,100	1,521	10,087	33,187	3,094	38,342	23,416	54,704	10,553	75,317	11,699
12/31/63	24,300	1,634	11,721	36,021	3,074	33,761	27,362	61,489	13,828	88,772	13,819
12/31/64	25,500	1,846	13,567	39,067	6,839	37,310	27,228	72,133	16,639	114,008	15,200
12/31/65	26,700	2,115	15,682	42,382	8,789	44,711	34,823	92,348	21,482	116,303	16,753
12/31/66	27,900	2,737	18,418	46,318	7,124	41,978	47,637	93,821	22,482	151,179	16,698
12/31/67	29,100	3,268	21,686	50,786	6,405	51,486	51,843	140,924	30,255	178,128	18,292
12/31/68	30,300	4,060	25,746	56,046	10,773	57,344	69,438	140,837	30,291	160,198	20,292
12/31/69	31,500	4,574	30,321	61,821	7,047	47,733	83,493	125,391	34,807	165,694	24,254
12/31/70	32,700	4,968	35,288	67,988	3,532	46,534	80,787	129,321	38,373	195,163	26,447
12/31/71	33,900	5,233	40,522	74,422		53,164	93,791	146,955	48,208		27,900
					TOTAL	80,294					

DATE	INITIAL INVESTMENT	OFFERING PRICE	SALES CHARGE INCLUDED	SHARES PURCHASED	NET ASSET VALUE PER SHARE	INITIAL NET ASSET VALUE
1/ 1/72	$195,163.00	$6.99	0.00%	27,900.360	$6.995	$195,163

SYSTEMATIC WITHDRAWAL PLAN
DIVIDENDS AND CAPITAL GAINS REINVESTED
MONTHLY WITHDRAWALS OF $975.81 (6.0% ANNUALLY) BEGINNING 1/31/72

| | =========AMOUNTS WITHDRAWN========= | | | | | ====VALUE OF REMAINING SHARES==== | | | |
DATE	FROM INCOME DIVS	FROM PRINCIPAL	ANNUAL TOTAL	CUM TOTAL	ANNUAL CAP GAIN DISTRIB'N	REMAINING ORIGINAL SHARES	CAP GAIN SHARES	TOTAL VALUE	SHARES HELD
12/31/72	5,328	6,381	11,710	11,710	6,339	207,026	6,461	213,487	27,888
12/31/73	5,585	6,125	11,710	23,420	4,132	156,783	9,645	166,428	27,761
12/31/74	8,055	3,655	11,710	35,130	0	118,365	9,449	152,814	27,173
12/31/75	7,108	4,602	11,710	46,840	910	147,417	10,495	157,912	26,517
12/31/76	6,224	5,486	11,710	58,550	2,948	175,965	15,971	191,636	26,131
12/31/77	6,257	5,453	11,710	70,260	3,534	156,711	18,270	174,981	25,865
12/31/78	6,570	5,140	11,710	81,970	0	168,118	20,228	188,346	25,146
12/31/79	7,722	3,988	11,710	93,680	2,263	186,305	25,394	211,699	24,905
12/31/80	9,532	2,177	11,710	105,390	4,981	209,156	34,267	243,423	25,225
12/31/81	11,531	179	11,710	117,100	16,649	187,052	46,734	233,786	27,058
TOTALS	73,912	43,188	117,100		42,055				

Table 9

Investing in common stocks requires skill

The difficulty of selecting individual stocks is illustrated by the wide variation in the results of assumed investments made 48 years ago in each of the 30 stocks now in the Dow Jones Industrial Average.

Dow Jones Industrial Stocks	Market Value of Investment*		
	December 31, 1933	December 31, 1981	Percent Change
Minnesota Mining & Manufacturing	$10,000	$6,540,000	+ 65,300%
Merck	**	3,813,753	38,038
International Business Machines	10,000	2,704,208	26,942
Eastman Kodak	10,000	569,533	5,595
International Paper	10,000	485,908	4,759
Standard Oil Company of California	10,000	259,563	2,496
Texaco	10,000	247,401	2,374
Procter & Gamble	10,000	247,347	2,373
Exxon	10,000	221,562	2,116
United Technologies	10,000	215,079	2,051
Sears, Roebuck	10,000	185,778	1,758
General Electric	10,000	176,539	1,665
Goodyear Tire & Rubber	10,000	155,351	1,454
Aluminum Company of America	10,000	124,687	1,147
Westinghouse Electric	10,000	111,743	1,017
General Foods	10,000	78,154	682
Bethlehem Steel	10,000	75,405	654
du Pont	10,000	68,971	590
General Motors	10,000	65,070	551
Union Carbide	10,000	64,895	549
Owens-Illinois	10,000	58,518	485
United States Steel	10,000	56,309	463
American Brands	10,000	43,556	336
Inco	10,000	32,386	224
American Telephone & Telegraph	10,000	31,579	216
Manville Corporation	10,000	29,504	195
Allied Corporation	10,000	27,173	172
American Can	10,000	13,889	39
Woolworth	10,000	12,486	25
International Harvester	10,000	10,688	7

*It was assumed that the entire $10,000 was invested in each stock and that fractional shares were purchased where required to use up the full amount. No brokerage charges were included in the cost. Adjustments were made for all stock splits and stock dividends.
**This $10,000 investment was made one year later, December 31, 1934, when the stock of the company was first available for purchase by the public.

Table 10. Seminar Fund vs. Leading Stock Market Indexes

	Seminar Fund	S&P 500	DJIA	NYSE
1934	+ 25.4%	− 5.9%	+ 4.1%	na
1935	+ 83.1	+ 41.4	+ 38.5	na
1936	+ 43.4	+ 27.9	+ 24.8	na
1937	− 40.9	− 38.6	− 32.8	na
1938	+ 26.3	+ 25.2	+ 28.1	na
1939	− 1.4	− 5.4	− 2.9	na
1940	− 6.1	− 15.3	− 12.7	− 12.9%
1941	− 12.3	− 17.9	− 15.4	− 18.0
1942	+ 11.0	+ 12.4	+ 7.6	+ 12.5
1943	+ 28.5	+ 19.4	+ 13.8	+ 20.4
1944	+ 19.6	+ 13.8	+ 12.1	+ 14.0
1945	+ 33.6	+ 30.7	+ 26.6	+ 31.1
1946	− 5.3	− 11.9	− 8.1	− 11.5
1947	− 3.4	0	+ 2.2	− 2.0
1948	− 4.1	− 0.6	− 2.1	− 2.8
1949	+ 4.5	+ 10.3	+ 12.9	+ 10.2
1950	+ 14.5	+ 21.8	+ 17.6	+ 21.2
1951	+ 13.2	+ 16.5	+ 14.4	+ 13.2
1952	+ 8.1	+ 11.8	+ 8.4	+ 6.5
1953	− 3.5	− 6.6	− 3.8	− 6.1
1954	+ 51.3	+ 45.0	+ 44.0	+ 42.6
1955	+ 21.9	+ 26.4	+ 20.8	+ 22.2
1956	+ 7.8	+ 2.6	+ 2.3	+ 2.7
1957	− 14.5	− 14.3	− 12.8	− 13.3
1958	+ 40.8%	+ 38.1%	+ 34.0%	+ 36.7%
1959	+ 11.5	+ 8.5	+ 16.4	+ 11.4
1960	+ 1.9	− 3.0	− 9.3	− 3.8
1961	+ 20.4	+ 23.1	+ 18.7	+ 24.1
1962	− 15.5	− 11.8	− 10.8	− 11.9
1963	+ 20.0	+ 18.9	+ 17.0	+ 18.1
1964	+ 13.8	+ 13.0	+ 14.6	+ 14.4
1965	+ 24.3	+ 9.1	+ 10.9	+ 9.5
1966	− 1.4	− 13.1	− 18.9	− 12.6
1967	+ 26.0	+ 20.1	+ 15.2	+ 23.1
1968	+ 14.1	+ 7.7	+ 4.3	+ 9.4
1969	− 13.2	− 11.4	− 15.2	− 12.5
1970	− 0.7	+ 0.1	+ 4.8	− 2.5
1971	+ 13.8	+ 10.8	+ 6.1	+ 12.3
1972	+ 12.8	+ 15.6	+ 14.6	+ 14.3
1973	− 19.5	− 17.4	− 16.6	− 19.6
1974	− 22.8	− 29.7	− 27.6	− 30.3
1975	+ 29.4	+ 31.5	+ 38.3	+ 31.9
1976	+ 25.3	+ 19.1	+ 17.9	+ 21.5
1977	− 6.0	− 11.5	− 17.3	− 9.3
1978	+ 10.7	+ 1.1	− 3.1	+ 2.1
1979	+ 14.8	+ 12.3	+ 4.2	+ 15.5
1980	+ 16.1	+ 25.8	+ 14.9	+ 25.7
1981	− 4.0	− 9.7	− 9.2	− 8.7

Results are based on the assumption that the current maximum sales charge was paid, while results for the indices were computed without sales charge.

Figures reflect change in net asset value per share adjusted for capital gain distributions.

**   Prior to June 1964 this index was calculated weekly. Therefore, some of the "years" before 1964 actually represent periods of 52 or 53 weeks.

na   Index not computed for this period.

595

Table 11

If you're interested in a retirement program

Many shareholders who reinvest all of their income dividends and capital gain distributions while they are accumulating shares find it helpful to begin taking these dividends and distributions in cash when they retire.

Such was the case with John and Martha Thomas. This fictional couple began an accumulation program by investing $250 on January 1, 1947. They added $100 each month thereafter until John retired 15 years later at the end of 1961. By this time, the value of their investment (as shown by the circled number below) had grown to $63,674.

Now John and Martha began to take all their dividends and capital gain distributions in cash. The right-hand table shows what they would have received each year and the fluctuations in the year-end value of their shares for the past 20 years. As you can see, over the past two decades they would have received $48,395 in dividends and $54,325 in capital gain distributions — a total of $102,720 in cash. And by the end of 1981 the value of their holdings would have grown to $93,961.

15-Year Share Accumulation Illustrations
Total Investments: $18,150

Jan. 1-Dec. 31	Dividends Reinvested	Total Cost (including dividends)	Capital Gain Distributions Taken in Shares*	Ending Value of Shares
1934-1948	$8,722	$26,872	$10,879	$39,313
1935-1949	8,613	26,763	9,989	37,673
1936-1950	8,592	26,742	9,107	39,599
1937-1951	9,153	27,303	9,737	43,433
1938-1952	9,928	28,078	10,915	46,488
1939-1953	9,942	28,092	10,359	41,889
1940-1954	9,949	28,099	11,599	59,097
1941-1955	9,997	28,147	14,336	65,869
1942-1956	9,810	27,960	16,509	63,802

20-Year Use of Investment

$63,674 — Net asset value of shares accumulated as of December 31, 1961†

Year Ended Dec. 31	Dividends in Cash	Capital Gains in Cash	Value at Year End
1962	$ 1,359	$ 2,447	$ 51,603
1963	1,359	2,556	59,270
1964	1,414	3,861	63,511
1965	1,468	4,731	74,005
1966	1,686	5,546	67,643
1967	1,849	4,024	81,020
1968	2,066	3,426	88,252
1969	2,121	5,329	71,830
1970	2,121	3,154	68,133

1943-1957	9,238	27,388	16,166	47,725
1944-1958	8,918	27,068	15,423	60,401
1945-1959	8,656	26,806	16,787	60,688
1946-1960	8,623	26,773	17,254	56,815
1947-1961	8,712	26,862	18,326	(63,674)
1948-1962	8,513	26,663	17,724	49,139
1949-1963	8,164	26,314	17,008	53,243
1950-1964	7,600	25,750	16,754	53,147
1951-1965	7,090	25,240	16,916	57,799
1952-1966	6,896	25,046	17,577	50,661
1953-1967	6,718	24,868	16,846	56,274
1954-1968	6,525	24,675	15,277	55,876
1955-1969	6,334	24,484	14,817	42,582
1956-1970	6,404	24,554	13,891	39,104
1957-1971	6,486	24,636	12,380	41,325
1958-1972	6,437	24,587	11,505	42,886
1959-1973	6,225	24,375	10,017	31,431
1960-1974	6,695	24,845	8,279	23,664
1961-1975	6,865	25,015	6,889	29,207
1962-1976	6,889	25,039	6,124	34,631
1963-1977	6,755	24,905	5,435	30,531
1964-1978	6,584	24,734	4,155	31,470
1965-1979	6,688	24,838	3,496	34,172
1966-1980	7,065	25,215	3,378	37,978
1967-1981	7,701	25,851	5,006	35,300

1971	2,121	1,414	76,072
1972	2,121	2,556	83,249
1973	2,229	1,794	65,197
1974	3,263	–	50,352
1975	2,936	381	64,762
1976	2,610	1,251	79,878
1977	2,664	1,523	73,570
1978	2,828	–	81,455
1979	3,371	979	92,439
1980	4,133	2,175	104,945
1981	4,676	7,178	93,961
Totals:	$48,395	$54,325	

†If all the shares had been purchased at offering price (which includes the sales commission as described in the prospectus) on December 31, 1961 instead of accumulated in the shareholder account, the cost would have been $66,665.

*The value of the shares acquired with these capital gain distributions is reflected in "Ending Value of Shares."

Table 12

If you're interested in investing monthly

Here's what would have happened if you had invested $250 in The Seminar Fund and added $100 every month . . .

...for 10 Years

(Total Investments: $12,150)

Here's how you would have done in every 10-year period in the Fund's history:

Jan.1-Dec. 31	Dividends Reinvested	Total Cost (including dividends reinvested)	Capital Gain Distributions Taken in Shares*	Ending Value of Shares
1934-1943	$2,808	$14,958	$2,113	$19,703
1935-1944	2,719	14,869	2,111	21,129
1936-1945	2,526	14,676	3,061	24,980
1937-1946	2,776	14,926	3,938	22,630
1938-1947	3,328	15,478	4,550	22,023
1939-1948	3,540	15,690	4,312	19,783
1940-1949	3,653	15,803	4,248	19,770
1941-1950	3,744	15,894	4,069	21,297
1942-1951	3,704	15,854	4,129	22,083
1943-1952	3,425	15,575	3,940	21,057
1944-1953	3,311	15,461	3,490	18,667
1945-1954	3,209	15,359	3,827	25,890
1946-1955	3,275	15,425	4,979	29,026
1947-1956	3,427	15,577	6,261	29,355
1948-1957	3,437	15,587	6,530	23,022
1949-1958	3,353	15,503	6,275	29,393
1950-1959	3,120	15,270	6,686	28,533
1951-1960	2,921	15,071	6,460	25,378
1952-1961	2,748	14,898	6,367	26,913
1953-1962	2,554	14,704	5,717	20,136
1954-1963	2,292	14,442	5,018	21,003
1955-1964	2,067	14,217	4,747	20,747
1956-1965	2,011	14,161	5,025	23,435
1957-1966	2,068	14,218	5,530	21,302
1958-1967	2,126	14,276	5,498	24,422
1959-1968	2,151	14,301	5,017	24,725
1960-1969	2,265	14,415	5,242	19,841
1961-1970	2,317	14,467	4,863	18,394
1962-1971	2,361	14,511	4,191	19,524
1963-1972	2,303	14,453	3,763	20,096
1964-1973	2,212	14,362	3,120	14,844
1965-1974	2,384	14,534	2,262	11,231
1966-1975	2,466	14,616	1,665	14,139
1967-1976	2,479	14,629	1,431	17,050
1968-1977	2,521	14,671	1,335	15,618
1969-1978	2,626	14,776	1,018	16,991
1970-1979	2,841	14,991	968	19,195
1971-1980	3,052	15,202	1,123	21,316
1972-1981	3,422	15,572	2,163	19,850

...for 20 Years

(Total Investments: $24,150)

Here's how you would have done in every 20-year period in the Fund's history:

1934-1953	$20,706	$44,856	$22,138	$ 76,013
1935-1954	19,967	44,117	23,135	103,655
1936-1955	19,635	43,785	27,075	113,533
1937-1956	20,533	44,683	32,583	116,063
1938-1957	22,022	46,172	36,166	96,643
1939-1958	21,860	46,010	35,720	124,788
1940-1959	21,782	45,932	39,722	128,003
1941-1960	21,555	45,705	40,827	118,964
1942-1961	20,772	44,922	41,451	128,247
1943-1962	19,302	43,452	38,360	94,830
1944-1963	18,394	42,544	36,623	101,930
1945-1964	17,742	41,892	37,189	104,552
1946-1965	17,455	41,605	39,302	118,599
1947-1966	17,924	42,074	43,082	109,020
1948-1967	18,047	42,197	43,149	124,915
1949-1968	18,207	42,357	41,487	128,493
1950-1969	17,814	41,964	41,043	98,650
1951-1970	17,257	41,407	37,648	87,183
1952-1971	16,780	40,930	33,092	88,925
1953-1972	16,068	40,218	30,012	89,317
1954-1973	15,153	39,303	25,994	63,756
1955-1974	15,176	39,326	20,983	45,341
1956-1975	15,385	39,535	17,956	55,258
1957-1976	15,367	39,517	16,215	64,995
1958-1977	15,187	39,337	14,755	57,235
1959-1978	14,728	38,878	11,993	58,273
1960-1979	15,037	39,187	10,666	63,355
1961-1980	15,623	39,773	10,159	69,600
1962-1981	16,689	40,839	12,780	64,046

...for 25 Years

(Total Investments: $30,150)

Here's how you would have done in every 25-year period in the Fund's history:

1934-1958	$41,888	$72,038	$67,212	$219,276
1935-1959	40,340	70,490	71,529	218,130
1936-1960	39,206	69,356	71,911	199,360
1937-1961	40,089	70,239	77,023	226,244
1938-1962	41,949	72,099	80,109	185,151
1939-1963	41,010	71,160	78,633	202,859
1940-1964	40,501	70,651	81,734	211,977
1941-1965	39,647	69,797	85,896	239,262
1942-1966	38,919	69,069	90,097	211,896
1943-1967	37,286	67,436	86,276	232,838
1944-1968	37,200	67,350	82,555	237,963
1945-1969	37,380	67,530	84,016	187,449
1946-1970	37,823	67,973	81,006	172,096
1947-1971	38,665	68,815	75,806	183,375
1948-1972	38,342	68,392	71,728	189,186
1949-1973	37,431	67,581	65,505	138,898
1950-1974	37,522	67,672	54,918	98,659
1951-1975	36,510	66,660	46,443	115,598
1952-1976	35,155	65,305	41,077	131,154
1953-1977	33,566	63,716	36,472	111,512
1954-1978	31,691	61,841	29,801	110,394
1955-1979	30,544	60,694	25,378	114,106
1956-1980	31,333	61,483	23,916	124,217
1957-1981	33,066	63,216	28,185	113,598

Table 13.

All it takes is $250 to start your investment program now

If you had invested $250 in The Seminar Fund and then added $100 every month through the 48-year lifetime of the Fund, here's how you would have done . . .

Total Invested since January 1, 1934	**$ 57,750**
Income Dividends (reinvested)	**689,013**
Total Cost (including dividends reinvested)	**$ 746,763**
Value of Investment on December 31, 1981	**$1,963,312**

*Includes value of shares taken as capital gain distributions

This table covers the period from January 1, 1934 through December 31, 1981. While this period, on the whole, was one of generally rising common stock prices, it also included some interim periods of substantial market decline. Results shown should not be considered as a representation of the dividend income or capital gain or loss that may be realized from an investment made in the Fund today. A program of the type illustrated does not ensure a profit or protect against depreciation in declining markets.

COST OF SHARES

Year Ended Dec. 31	Monthly Investments (cumulative)	Dividends Reinvested (cumulative)	Total Cost (including dividends)
1934	$ 1,350	—	$ 1,350
1935	2,550	—	2,550
1936	3,750	$ 97	3,847
1937	4,950	368	5,318
1938	6,150	425	6,575
1939	7,350	629	7,979
1940	8,550	1,005	9,555
1941	9,750	1,591	11,341

VALUE OF SHARES ACQUIRED

Monthly Investments	Capital Gain Distributions (cumulative)	Dividends Reinvested (cumulative)	Total Value
$ 1,375	—	—	$ 1,375
4,305	—	—	4,305
6,389	$ 1,199	$ 127	7,715
4,428	743	286	5,457
6,681	1,271	414	8,366
7,549	1,493	603	9,645
8,087	1,533	947	10,567
8.086	1,374	1,389	10,849

1942	10,950	2,200	13,150	10,094	1,644	2,188	13,926
1943	12,150	2,808	14,958	14,002	2,312	3,389	19,703
1944	13,350	3,533	16,883	17,316	3,583	4,651	25,550
1945	14,550	4,255	18,805	22,778	6,971	6,564	36,313
1946	15,750	5,370	21,120	21,149	8,516	6,858	36,523
1947	16,950	6,931	23,881	20,584	9,607	7,859	38,050
1948	18,150	8,722	26,872	20,169	10,137	9,007	39,313
1949	19,350	10,547	29,897	21,528	11,762	10,989	44,279
1950	20,550	12,768	33,318	25,126	14,688	14,532	54,346
1951	21,750	15,206	36,956	28,354	18,723	18,193	65,270
1952	22,950	17,789	40,739	30,453	22,627	21,407	74,487
1953	24,150	20,706	44,856	29,709	23,294	23,010	76,013
1954	25,350	23,797	49,147	44,206	39,285	36,671	120,162
1955	26,550	27,696	54,246	51,207	55,308	45,481	151,996
1956	27,750	31,995	59,745	52,381	67,453	49,730	169,564
1957	28,950	36,802	65,752	43,084	63,110	44,269	150,463
1958	30,150	41,888	72,038	59,765	93,713	65,798	219,276
1959	31,350	47,367	78,717	63,374	114,260	73,996	251,630
1960	32,550	53,756	86,306	62,082	124,556	77,651	264,289
1961	33,750	60,364	94,114	72,008	159,218	95,345	326,571
1962	34,950	67,585	102,535	59,495	140,389	84,626	284,510
1963	36,150	75,232	111,382	69,571	176,152	105,186	350,909
1964	37,350	83,770	121,120	75,712	212,351	121,139	409,202
1965	38,550	93,455	132,005	89,490	279,737	151,563	520,790
1966	39,750	105,889	145,639	82,932	293,444	150,729	527,105
1967	40,950	120,632	161,582	100,566	384,580	195,544	680,690
1968	42,150	138,839	180,989	110,831	454,226	232,444	797,501
1969	43,350	159,242	202,592	91,286	413,084	209,060	713,430
1970	44,550	181,280	225,830	87,866	423,511	222,071	733,448
1971	45,750	204,372	250,122	99,332	488,677	271,614	859,623
1972	46,950	228,591	275,541	109,930	564,827	322,403	997,160
1973	48,150	255,628	303,778	87,145	465,090	278,347	830,582
1974	49,350	298,002	347,352	68,318	359,194	255,094	682,606
1975	50,550	338,496	389,046	89,103	467,314	369,016	925,433
1976	51,750	376,298	428,048	111,167	595,230	494,245	1,200,642
1977	52,950	416,908	469,858	103,550	571,917	495,466	1,170,933
1978	54,150	462,558	516,708	115,883	633,209	595,172	1,344,264
1979	55,350	519,673	575,023	132,784	735,998	734,488	1,603,270
1980	56,550	594,267	650,817	152,065	876,757	916,232	1,945,054
1981	57,750	689,013	746,763	137,285	913,278	912,749	1,963,312

The total cost column represents the initial investment of $250, plus the cumulative total of monthly investments of $100, plus the cumulative amount of dividends reinvested. A sales charge, as described in the prospectus, was included in the price of the shares purchased through periodic investments with right of accumulation reflected where applicable. There is no sales charge on shares acquired through reinvestment of dividends and capital gain distributions.

Capital gain distributions taken in shares totaled $678,183.

Table 14. Hypothetical Illustration—$100 Investment in The Seminar Fund

PREPARED FOR: MR. SAM. STEADY

DATE	INITIAL INVESTMENT	OFFERING PRICE	SALES CHARGE INCLUDED	SHARES PURCHASED	NET ASSET VALUE PER SHARE	INITIAL NET ASSET VALUE
1/ 1/52	$100.00	$3.26	8.50%	30.675	$2.963	$91

MONTHLY INVESTMENTS OF $100.00 -- SAME DAY AS INITIAL INVESTMENT
DIVIDENDS AND CAPITAL GAINS REINVESTED

CUMULATIVE VOLUME DISCOUNT REFLECTED WHERE APPLICABLE IN THIS ILLUSTRATION

	=========COST OF SHARES=========					=========VALUE OF SHARES=========					
DATE	ANNUAL INCOME DIVS	CUM. INCOME DIVS	TOTAL INV'M'T COST	CUM. INV'M'T	ANNUAL CAP GAIN DISTRIB'N	FROM INV'M'T	FROM CAP GAINS REINV'D	SUB-TOTAL	FROM DIVS REINV'D	TOTAL VALUE	SHARES HELD
12/31/52	26	26	1,226	1,200	47	1,122	48	1,170	27	1,197	386
12/31/53	74	100	2,500	2,400	61	2,141	105	2,246	99	2,345	811
12/31/54	119	219	3,819	3,600	231	4,414	387	4,801	277	5,078	1,219
12/31/55	185	404	5,204	4,800	505	6,146	960	7,106	503	7,609	1,615
12/31/56	234	638	6,638	6,000	677	7,214	1,635	8,849	732	9,581	2,031
12/31/57	290	928	8,128	7,200	565	6,727	1,857	8,584	848	9,432	2,488
12/31/58	337	1,265	9,665	8,400	507	10,433	3,064	13,497	1,534	15,031	2,927
12/31/59	390	1,655	11,255	9,600	1,184	11,975	2,388	14,363	1,989	16,352	3,433
12/31/60	482	2,137	12,937	10,800	1,061	12,648	5,320	17,968	2,406	20,374	3,967
12/31/61	524	2,661	14,661	12,000	1,344	15,579	7,446	23,025	3,270	26,295	4,491
12/31/62	598	3,259	16,459	13,200	1,044	13,707	6,783	20,490	3,444	23,934	5,043
12/31/63	660	3,919	18,319	14,400	1,255	16,931	8,215	25,146	5,513	30,659	5,625
12/31/64	761	4,680	20,280	15,600	2,099	19,258	10,199	29,457	7,377	36,834	6,307
12/31/65	887	5,567	22,367	16,800	2,875	23,652	16,515	40,167	7,884	48,051	7,061
12/31/66	1,164	6,730	24,730	18,000	3,730	22,705	16,092	38,797	10,875	49,672	7,985
12/31/67	1,406	8,136	27,336	19,200	3,069	26,388	25,164	51,552	13,730	65,282	8,762
12/31/68	1,765	9,901	30,301	20,400	2,773	31,743	32,073	63,816	13,828	77,644	9,567
12/31/69	2,006	11,907	33,507	21,600	4,706	32,171	23,442	55,613	14,823	70,436	10,664
12/31/70	2,197	14,104	36,904	22,800	3,706	27,234	30,388	57,622	15,943	73,565	11,742
12/31/71	2,335	16,439	40,439	24,000	1,581	31,425	32,601	64,026	23,305	87,331	12,484
12/31/72	2,478	18,917	44,117	25,200	3,027	35,582	45,916	81,498	20,926	102,424	13,380
12/31/73	2,797	21,714	48,114	26,400	2,284	28,693	37,213	65,906	20,371	86,277	14,391
12/31/74	4,443	26,157	53,757	27,600		23,302	17,986	41,288	30,542	71,830	15,514
12/31/75	4,297	30,454	59,254	28,800	564	31,174	25,468	56,642	41,856	98,498	16,540
12/31/76	4,047	34,501	64,501	30,000	1,971	39,688	45,350	85,038	41,897	126,935	17,554
12/31/77	4,384	38,885	70,085	31,200	2,546	37,689	36,545	74,234	52,566	126,800	18,743
12/31/78	4,969	43,854	76,254	32,400		42,936	39,605	82,541	64,127	146,668	19,581
12/31/79	6,260	50,114	83,714	33,600	1,764	49,972	59,966	109,938	66,127	176,065	20,713
12/31/80	8,223	58,337	93,137	34,800	4,145	58,020	72,604	130,624	84,153	214,777	22,256
12/31/81	10,492	68,829	104,829	36,000	14,696	53,054	79,176	132,230	85,432	217,662	25,192
TOTAL					63,414						

PREPARED FOR: MR. GEORGE GENIUS

	COST OF SHARES				VALUE OF SHARES					
DATE	INVESTMENT	ANNUAL INCOME DIVS	CUM. INCOME DIVS	TOTAL INV'M'T COST	ANNUAL CAP GAIN DISTRIB'N	FROM INV'M'T	FROM CAP GAINS REINV'D	FROM DIVS REINV'D	SUB-TOTAL	TOTAL VALUE	SHARES HELD
5/ 1/52	1,200.00	35	35	1,235	54	1,177	54	35	1,231	1,266	411
9/14/53	1,200.00	62	97	2,497	67	2,292	117	95	2,409	2,504	866
1/11/54	1,200.00	145	242	3,842	262	4,880	436	302	5,316	5,616	1,348
1/ 6/55	1,200.00	218	460	5,260	586	6,803	1,101	566	7,904	8,470	1,798
1/23/56	1,200.00	271	731	6,731	766	7,973	1,863	831	9,836	10,667	2,262
12/23/57	1,200.00	301	1,032	8,232	580	7,526	2,054	937	9,580	10,517	2,774
1/ 2/58	1,200.00	391	1,423	9,823	580	11,667	3,412	1,717	15,079	16,796	3,270
2/ 9/59	1,200.00	447	1,870	11,470	1,344	13,321	4,914	2,236	18,235	20,471	3,629
3/ 8/60	1,200.00	542	2,412	13,212	1,177	14,018	5,945	2,705	19,963	22,668	4,414
1/ 3/61	1,200.00	593	3,005	15,005	1,517	17,258	8,323	3,695	25,581	29,276	5,000
6/25/62	1,200.00	663	3,669	16,869	1,154	15,272	7,776	3,671	23,048	26,719	5,630
3/ 1/63	1,200.00	739	4,408	18,808	1,396	18,844	10,371	4,968	29,215	34,203	6,275
1/ 2/64	1,200.00	858	5,266	20,866	2,352	21,394	13,482	6,192	34,876	41,068	7,032
6/28/65	1,200.00	985	6,251	23,051	3,199	26,274	19,011	8,213	45,285	53,558	7,870
10/ 7/66	1,200.00	1,287	7,539	25,539	3,444	25,304	21,292	8,625	46,596	55,421	8,910
1/ 4/67	1,200.00	1,581	9,119	28,319	3,443	31,688	29,051	12,179	60,739	72,918	9,787
3/ 5/68	1,200.00	1,975	11,095	31,495	3,083	35,970	35,427	15,374	71,397	86,771	10,692
12/17/69	1,200.00	2,218	13,312	34,912	5,239	30,454	33,553	14,673	64,007	78,680	11,912
5/26/70	1,200.00	2,461	15,773	38,573	1,767	30,400	35,319	16,573	65,719	82,292	13,135
1/ 4/71	1,200.00	2,625	18,398	42,398	3,383	35,233	41,231	21,195	76,464	97,659	13,961
1/ 3/72	1,200.00	2,782	21,180	46,380	2,521	39,814	48,570	26,085	88,384	114,469	14,953
12/13/73	1,200.00	3,101	24,281	50,681		32,392	40,645	23,394	73,037	96,431	16,085
10/ 3/74	1,200.00	3,954	29,236	56,836	632	26,254	31,391	22,761	57,645	80,406	17,366
1/ 2/75	1,200.00	4,831	34,067	62,867	2,209	35,207	41,010	34,158	76,217	110,375	18,534
1/ 2/76	1,200.00	4,553	38,620	68,620	2,853	44,842	52,850	46,839	97,692	144,531	19,677
10/25/77	1,200.00	4,897	43,517	74,717		42,514	51,550	47,994	94,064	142,058	20,998
3/ 1/78	1,200.00	5,572	49,089	81,489	1,975	48,450	57,075	58,525	105,525	164,350	21,942
2/27/79	1,200.00	7,029	56,118	89,718	4,641	56,338	66,899	74,026	123,237	197,263	23,207
4/21/80	1,200.00	9,222	65,340	100,140	16,464	65,484	81,016	94,223	146,500	240,723	24,945
9/25/81	1,200.00	11,738	77,078	113,078		59,847	88,413	95,645	148,260	243,905	28,229

Table 15. Consumer Price Indexes for
Cost of Home Ownership and Apartment Rents

	Apartment Rents	Home Ownership Costs	Consumer Price Index
1970	100.0	100.0	100.0
1971	104.6	104.0	104.3
1972	108.3	109.0	107.7
1973	112.9	114.2	114.4
1974	118.6	127.0	127.0
1975	124.7	141.4	138.6
1976	131.4	149.2	146.6
1977	139.4	159.5	156.1
1978	149.0	176.8	168.0
1979	159.9	204.2	186.9
1980	180.8	258.4	221.9
1982(JAN)	197.8	286.5	242.9

Index series underwent a change in definition effective with the 1978 revision. Therefore these data differ from those previously published.

Source: U.S. Bureau of Labor Statistics, *Monthly Labor Review*

To arrive at the above figures the following formulas were used. 100/(value from the chart for 1970) times the value from the year. Straight line interpolation was used to calculate the data for 1980.

Table 16. Tax Exempt/Taxable Yield Equivalent

SINGLE RETURN Under Federal Income taxes effective for 1982

Taxable Income	$8,500-10,800	$10,800-12,900	$12,900-15,000	$15,000-18,200	$18,200-23,500	$23,500-28,000	$28,800-34,100	$34,100-41,500	Over $41,500
Tax Bracket	19%	22%	23%	27%	31%	35%	40%	44%	50%
7.00	8.64	8.97	9.09	9.59	10.14	10.77	11.67	12.50	14.00
7.25	8.95	9.29	9.42	9.93	10.51	11.15	12.08	12.95	14.50
7.50	9.26	9.62	9.74	10.27	10.87	11.54	12.50	13.39	15.00
7.75	9.57	9.94	10.06	13.36	11.23	11.92	12.92	13.84	15.50
8.00	9.88	10.26	10.39	10.96	11.59	12.31	13.33	14.29	16.00
8.25	10.19	10.58	10.71	11.30	11.96	12.69	13.75	14.73	16.50
8.50	10.49	10.90	11.04	11.64	12.32	13.08	14.17	15.18	17.00
8.75	10.80	11.22	11.36	11.99	12.68	13.46	14.58	15.63	17.50
9.00	11.11	11.54	11.69	12.33	13.04	13.85	15.00	16.07	18.00
9.25	11.42	11.86	12.01	12.67	13.41	14.23	15.42	16.52	18.50
9.50	11.83	12.18	12.34	13.01	13.77	14.62	15.83	16.96	19.00
9.75	12.04	12.50	12.66	13.36	14.13	15.00	16.25	17.41	19.50
10.00	12.35	12.82	12.99	13.70	14.49	15.38	16.67	17.86	20.00
10.25	12.65	13.14	13.31	14.04	14.86	15.77	17.08	18.30	20.50
10.50	12.96	13.46	13.64	14.38	15.22	16.15	17.50	18.75	21.00
10.75	13.25	13.78	13.96	14.73	15.58	16.54	17.92	19.20	21.50
11.00	13.58	14.10	14.29	15.07	15.94	16.92	18.33	19.64	22.00
11.25	13.89	14.42	14.61	15.41	16.30	17.31	18.75	20.09	22.50
11.50	14.20	14.74	14.94	15.75	16.67	17.69	19.17	20.54	23.00
11.75	14.51	15.06	15.26	16.10	17.03	18.08	19.58	20.98	23.50
12.00	14.81	15.38	15.58	16.44	17.39	18.46	20.00	21.43	24.00
12.25	15.12	15.71	15.91	16.78	17.75	18.85	20.42	21.88	24.50
12.50	15.43	16.03	16.23	17.12	18.12	19.23	20.83	22.32	25.00
12.75	15.74	16.35	16.56	17.47	18.48	19.62	21.25	22.77	25.50
13.00	16.05	16.67	16.88	17.81	18.84	20.00	21.67	23.21	26.00
13.25	16.36	16.99	17.21	18.15	19.20	20.38	22.08	23.66	26.50
13.50	16.67	17.31	17.53	18.49	19.57	20.77	22.50	24.11	27.00
13.75	16.98	17.63	17.86	18.84	19.93	21.15	22.92	24.55	27.50
14.00	17.28	17.95	18.18	19.18	20.29	21.54	23.33	25.00	28.00
14.25	17.59	18.27	18.51	19.52	20.65	21.92	23.75	25.45	28.50
14.50	17.90	18.59	18.83	19.86	21.01	22.31	24.17	25.89	29.00
14.75	18.21	18.91	19.16	20.21	21.38	22.69	24.58	26.34	29.50
15.00	18.52	19.23	19.48	20.55	21.74	23.08	25.00	26.79	30.00
15.25	18.83	19.55	19.81	20.89	22.10	23.46	25.42	27.23	30.50
15.50	19.14	19.87	20.13	21.23	22.46	23.85	25.83	27.68	31.00
15.75	19.44	20.19	20.45	21.58	22.83	24.23	26.25	28.13	31.50
16.00	19.75	20.50	20.78	21.92	23.19	24.62	26.67	28.57	32.00

Tax-Exempt Yields (%)

Taxable Income	$11,900-16,000	$16,000-20,200	$20,200-24,600	$24,600-29,900	$29,900-35,200	$35,200-45,800	$45,800-60,000	$60,000-85,600	Over $85,600
Tax Bracket	19%	22%	25%	29%	33%	39%	44%	49%	50%
7.00	8.64	8.97	9.33	9.86	10.45	11.48	12.50	13.73	14.00
7.25	8.95	9.29	9.67	10.21	10.82	11.89	12.95	14.22	14.50
7.50	9.26	9.62	10.00	10.56	11.19	12.30	13.39	14.71	15.00
7.75	9.57	9.94	10.33	10.92	11.57	12.70	13.84	15.20	15.50
8.00	9.88	10.26	10.67	11.27	11.94	13.11	14.29	15.69	16.00
8.25	10.19	10.58	11.00	11.62	12.31	13.52	14.73	16.18	16.50
8.50	10.49	10.90	11.33	11.97	12.69	13.93	15.18	16.67	17.00
8.75	10.80	11.22	11.67	12.32	13.06	14.34	15.63	17.16	17.50
9.00	11.11	11.54	12.00	12.68	13.43	14.75	16.07	17.65	18.00
9.25	11.42	11.86	12.33	13.03	13.81	15.16	16.52	18.14	18.50
9.50	11.83	12.18	12.67	13.38	14.18	15.57	16.96	18.63	19.00
9.75	12.04	12.50	13.00	13.73	14.55	15.98	17.41	19.12	19.50
10.00	12.35	12.82	13.33	14.08	14.93	16.39	17.86	19.61	20.00
10.25	12.65	13.14	13.67	14.44	15.30	16.80	18.30	20.10	20.50
10.50	12.96	13.46	14.00	14.79	15.67	17.21	18.75	20.59	21.00
10.75	13.25	13.78	14.33	15.14	16.04	17.62	19.20	21.08	21.50
11.00	13.58	14.10	14.67	15.49	16.42	18.03	19.64	21.57	22.00
11.25	13.89	14.42	15.00	15.85	16.79	18.44	20.09	22.06	22.50
11.50	14.20	14.74	15.33	16.20	17.16	18.85	20.54	22.55	23.00
11.75	14.51	15.06	15.67	16.55	17.54	19.26	20.98	23.04	23.50
12.00	14.81	15.38	16.00	16.90	17.91	19.67	21.43	23.53	24.00
12.25	15.12	15.71	16.33	17.25	18.28	20.08	21.88	24.02	24.50
12.50	15.43	16.03	16.67	17.61	18.66	20.49	22.32	24.51	25.00
12.75	15.74	16.35	17.00	17.96	19.03	20.90	22.77	25.00	25.50
13.00	16.05	16.67	17.33	18.37	19.40	21.31	23.21	25.49	26.00
13.25	16.36	16.99	17.67	18.66	19.78	21.72	23.66	25.98	26.50
13.50	16.67	17.31	18.00	19.01	20.15	22.13	24.11	26.47	27.00
13.75	16.98	17.63	18.33	19.37	20.52	22.54	24.55	26.96	27.50
14.00	17.28	17.95	18.67	19.72	20.90	22.95	25.00	27.45	28.00
14.25	17.59	18.27	19.00	20.07	21.27	23.36	25.45	27.94	28.50
14.50	17.90	18.59	19.33	20.42	21.64	23.77	25.89	28.43	29.00
14.75	18.21	18.91	19.67	20.77	22.01	24.18	26.34	28.92	29.50
15.00	18.52	19.23	20.00	21.13	22.39	24.59	26.79	29.21	30.00
15.25	18.83	19.55	20.33	21.48	22.76	25.00	27.23	29.90	30.50
15.50	19.14	19.87	20.67	21.83	23.13	25.41	27.68	30.39	31.00
15.75	19.44	20.19	21.00	22.18	23.51	25.82	28.13	30.88	31.50
16.00	19.75	20.50	21.33	22.45	23.88	26.23	28.57	31.37	32.00

Tax-Exempt Yields (%)

Table 17. Tax Rate Schedules

TAX RATE SCHEDULES FOR MARRIED INDIVIDUALS FILING JOINT RETURNS AND SURVIVING SPOUSES

¶ 5

Taxable Income	1981*		1982		1983		1984	
	Pay +	% on Excess**	Pay +	% on Excess**	Pay +	% on Excess**	Pay +	% on Excess**
0— $3,400	-0-	-0-	-0-	-0-	-0-	-0-	-0-	-0-
$3,400— 5,500	-0-	14	-0-	12	-0-	11	-0-	11
5,500— 7,600	$294	16	$252	14	$231	13	$231	12
7,600— 11,900	630	18	546	16	504	15	483	14
11,900— 16,000	1,404	21	1,234	19	1,149	17	1,085	16
16,000— 20,200	2,265	24	2,013	22	1,846	19	1,741	18
20,200— 24,600	3,273	28	2,937	25	2,644	23	2,497	22
24,600— 29,900	4,505	32	4,037	29	3,656	26	3,465	25
29,900— 35,200	6,201	37	5,574	33	5,034	30	4,790	28
35,200— 45,800	8,162	43	7,323	39	6,624	35	6,274	33
45,800— 60,000	12,720	49	11,457	44	10,334	40	9,772	38
60,000— 85,600	19,678	54	17,705	49	16,014	44	15,168	42
85,600—109,400	33,502	59	30,249	50	27,278	48	25,920	45
109,400—162,400	47,544	64	42,149	50	38,702	50	36,630	49
162,400—215,400	81,464	68	68,649	50	65,202	50	62,600	50
215,400—	117,504	70	95,149	50	91,702	50	89,100	50

* The CCH-prepared rate schedule shown above for 1981 is the same rate schedule that applied for 1980 taxes. A taxpayer may use this schedule to find the approximate taxes due for 1981 by computing the tax under the schedule and reducing the result by 1.25%.
** The amount by which the taxpayer's taxable income exceeds the base of the bracket.

TAX RATE SCHEDULES FOR SINGLE INDIVIDUALS

¶7

Taxable Income	1981*		1982		1983		1984	
	Pay +	% on Excess**	Pay +	% on Excess**	Pay +	% on Excess**	Pay +	% on Excess**
0— $2,300	-0-	-0-	-0-	-0-	-0-	-0-	-0-	-0-
$2,300— 3,400	-0-	14	-0-	12	-0-	11	-0-	11
3,400— 4,400	$154	16	$132	14	$121	13	$121	12
4,400— 6,500	314	18	272	16	251	15	241	14
6,500— 8,500	692	19	608	17	566	15	535	15
8,500— 10,800	1,072	21	948	19	866	17	835	16
10,800— 12,900	1,555	24	1,385	22	1,257	19	1,203	18
12,900— 15,000	2,059	26	1,847	23	1,656	21	1,581	20
15,000— 18,200	2,605	30	2,330	27	2,097	24	2,001	23
18,200— 23,500	3,565	34	3,194	31	2,865	28	2,737	26
23,500— 28,800	5,367	39	4,837	35	4,349	32	4,115	30
28,800— 34,100	7,434	44	6,692	40	6,045	36	5,705	34
34,100— 41,500	9,766	49	8,812	44	7,953	40	7,507	38
41,500— 55,300	13,392	55	12,068	50	10,913	45	10,319	42
55,300— 81,800	20,982	63	18,968	50	17,123	50	16,115	48
81,800—108,300	37,677	68	32,218	50	30,373	50	28,835	50
108,300—	55,697	70	45,468	50	43,623	50	42,085	50

* The CCH-prepared rate schedule shown above for 1981 is the same rate schedule that applied for 1980 taxes. A taxpayer may use this schedule to find the approximate taxes due for 1981 by computing the tax under the schedule and reducing the result by 1.25%.

** The amount by which the taxpayer's taxable income exceeds the base of the bracket.

TAX RATE SCHEDULES FOR HEAD OF HOUSEHOLD

¶ 8

Taxable Income	1981* Pay +	% on Excess**	1982 Pay +	% on Excess**	1983 Pay +	% on Excess**	1984 Pay +	% on Excess**
0— $2,300	-0-	-0-	-0-	-0-	-0-	-0-	-0-	-0-
$2,300— 4,400	-0-	14	-0-	12	-0-	11	-0-	11
4,400— 6,500	$294	16	$252	14	$231	13	$231	12
6,500— 8,700	630	18	546	16	504	15	483	14
8,700— 11,800	1,026	22	898	20	834	18	791	17
11,800— 15,000	1,708	24	1,518	22	1,392	19	1,318	18
15,000— 18,200	2,476	26	2,222	23	2,000	21	1,894	20
18,200— 23,500	3,308	31	2,958	28	2,672	25	2,534	24
23,500— 28,800	4,951	36	4,442	32	3,997	29	3,806	28
28,800— 34,100	6,859	42	6,138	38	5,534	34	5,290	32
34,100— 44,700	9,085	46	8,152	41	7,336	37	6,986	35
44,700— 60,600	13,961	54	12,498	49	11,258	44	10,696	42
60,600— 81,800	22,547	59	20,289	50	18,254	48	17,374	45
81,800—108,300	35,055	63	30,889	50	28,430	50	26,914	48
108,300—161,300	51,750	68	44,139	50	41,680	50	39,634	50
161,300—	87,790	70	70,639	50	68,180	50	66,134	50

* The CCH-prepared rate schedule shown above for 1981 is the same rate schedule that applied for 1980 taxes. A taxpayer may use this schedule to find the approximate taxes due for 1981 by computing the tax under the schedule and reducing the result by 1.25%.

** The amount by which the taxpayer's taxable income exceeds the base of the bracket.

Table 18. Projected Investment Performance for a Limited Partner in a 50% Tax Bracket for a $57,250 Investment

(1/35th OF TOTAL OFFERING AMOUNT)

YEAR	INVESTMENT	ANNUAL (TAX LOSSES) OR TAXABLE INCOME	RATIO OF TAX LOSSES TO INVESTMENT	ANNUAL TAX SAVINGS OR (TAX LIABILITY)	ANNUAL SHELTERED CASH DISTRIBUTION	TOTAL ANNUAL BENEFITS	CUMULATIVE AFTER TAX BENEFITS
1979	$6,500	$(7,193)	111%	$ 3,597		$ 3,597	$ 3,597
1980	15,500	(25,589)	165%	12,794		12,794	16,391
1981	13,000	(19,946)	153%	9,973	$ 2,096	12,069	28,460
1982	12,000	(16,783)	140%	8,392	2,739	11,131	39,591
1983	10,250	(14,873)	145%	7,436	3,384	10,820	50,411
1984		(3,869)		1,935	4,104	6,039	56,450
1985		402		(201)	4,782	4,581	61,031
1986		1,222		(611)	5,383	4,772	65,803
1987		2,040		(1,020)	6,014	4,994	70,797
1988		2,861		(1,431)	6,676	5,245	76,042
	$57,250	$ 81,728		$40,864	$35,178	$76,042	

PROJECTION OF RESALE ON JANUARY 1, 1989

ASSUMPTIONS	PRETAX RESALE PROCEEDS	RESALE TAX LIABILITY	YEAR OF RESALE AFTER TAX BENEFITS	PREVIOUS AFTER TAX BENEFITS		CUMULATIVE AFTER TAX BENEFITS THROUGH RESALE
A. Abandonment on 1/1/89	None	- $19,243	= $(19,243)	+ $76,042	=	$ 56,799
B. Resale of property at the Partnership's original purchase price	$44,544	- 30,379	= 14,165	+ 76,042	=	91,042
C. Resale of property at estimated market value	87,186	- 41,040	= 46,146	+ 76,042	=	122,188

THE ACCOMPANYING NOTES AND ASSUMPTIONS ARE AN INTEGRAL PART OF THIS STATEMENT.

(The above represents a mere prediction of future events based on assumptions which may or may not occur and may not be relied upon to indicate the actual results which may be obtained.)

Table 19. Hypothetical Composite Pro-Forma for Every
$10,000 of Investment - 30% Bracket

Year	A I.T.C.	B Write Off	C Tax Savings	D Gross Cash Distributions	E Taxable Income	F Tax	G Net After-Tax Cash Distributions	H Equivalent Taxable Return
'82	$ 574	$ 4,190	$ 1,831	$ 0	$ 0	$ 0	$ 0	$ 2,616
'83		562	169	0	0	0	0	241
'84		1,117	335	656	0	0	656	1,416
'85		864	259	2,425	0	0	2,425	3,834
'86				2,192	2,006	602	1,590	2,271
'87				1,552	1,552	466	1,086	1,552
'88				935	935	281	654	934
'89				* 1,611	1,611	483	1,128	* 1,611
'90				** 1,852	1,852	556	1,296	** 1,851
'91				598	598	179	419	599
'92				***14,655	14,677	4,403	10,252	***14,646
Totals			$2,594	$26,476			$19,506	$31,570

This hypothetical portfolio includes 50% of equity invested in one aircraft, 40% in vendor lease agreements, 6% in an oil rig and 4% in over-the-road trailers.

*Assumes the sale of vendor leasing equipment at a net 10% residual value ($1,078)
**Assumes the sale of over-the-road trailers at a net 70% residual value ($1,801)
***Assumes the sale of the aircraft at a net 100% residual value ($13.333) and the sale of the oil rig at a net 100% residual value ($1,766)

A. *I.T.C.* (Investment Tax Credit) estimated in ALI IV-A portfolio
B. *Write-off* from depreciation and interest deductions
C. *Tax Savings* equals write-off times tax bracket, plus ITC
D. *Gross Cash Distribution* is the rental income, less debt service, plus cash from sale of equipment, less any cash held in reserve
E. *Taxable Income* is that portion of the Gross Cash Distribution on which taxes are paid
F. *Tax* equals Taxable Income times tax bracket
G. *Net After-Tax Cash Distribution* is Gross Cash Distributions less Taxes - it is the after-tax return
H. *Equivalent Taxable Return* equals the Tax Savings, if appropriate, plus the Net After-Tax Cash Distributions, divided by the complement of the tax bracket (complement is the difference between tax bracket and 100)

611

Hypothetical Composite Pro-Forma
for Every $10,000 of Investment - 50% Bracket

Year	A I.T.C.	B Write Off	C Tax Savings	D Gross Cash Distributions	E Taxable Income	F Tax	G Net After-Tax Cash Distributions	H Equivalent Taxable Return
'82	$ 574	$ 4,190	$ 2,669	$ 0	$ 0	$ 0	$ 0	$ 5,338
'83		562	281	0	0	0	0	562
'84		1,117	559	656	0	0	656	2,430
'85		864	432	2,425	0	0	2,425	5,714
'86				2,192	2,006	1,003	1,189	2,378
'87				1,552	1,552	776	776	1,552
'88				935	935	467	468	936
'89				* 1,611	1,611	806	805	* 1,610
'90				** 1,852	1,852	926	926	** 1,852
'91				598	598	299	299	598
'92				***14,655	14,677	7,338	7,317	***14,634
Totals			$3,941	$26,476			$14,861	$37,604

*This hypothetical portfolio includes 50% of equity invested in one aircraft, 40% in vendor lease agreements, 6% in an oil rig and 4% in over-the-road trailers.

*Assumes the sale of vendor leasing equipment at a net 10% residual value ($1,078)
**Assumes the sale of over-the-road trailers at a net 70% residual value ($1,801)
***Assumes the sale of the aircraft at a net 100% residual value ($13,333) and the sale of the rig at a net 100% residual value ($1,766)

A. I.T.C. (Investment Tax Credit) estimated in ALI IV-A portfolio

B. Write-off from depreciation and interest deductions

C. Tax Savings equals write-off times tax bracket, plus ITC

D. Gross Cash Distribution is the rental income, less debt service, plus cash from sale of equipment, less any cash held in reserve

E. Taxable Income is that portion of the Gross Cash Distribution on which taxes are paid

F. Tax equals Taxable Income times tax bracket

G. Net After-Tax Cash Distribution is Gross Cash Distributions less Taxes - it is the after-tax return

H. Equivalent Taxable Return equals the Tax Savings, if appropriate, plus the Net After-Tax Cash Distributions, divided by the complement of the tax bracket (complement is the difference between tax bracket and 100)

612

Table 20. Marine Containers—Hypothetical Example of Limited Partner's Share of Distributions, Taxable Income or Loss, and Investment Tax Credit for a $10,000 Investment.*

Year	Cash Distributions To Limited Partner	Partnership Tax Calculations Add Repayment of Principal on Loans	Depreciation & Other Adjustments	Taxable Income (Loss) Reported To Limited Partner	Investment Tax Credit	Limited Partner's After-Tax Cash Flow**	Unrecovered Investment	Ending Balance of Reinvestment Fund***
'82	$ 250	$ –	$ (820)	$ (570)	$ 650	$ 1,185	$8,815	$ 1,244
'83	1,160	234	(2,364)	(970)	410	2,055	6,760	3,526
'84	1,710	354	(2,864)	(800)	–	2,110	4,650	6,094
'85	1,800	411	(2,781)	(570)	–	2,085	2,565	8,893
'86	1,900	476	(2,786)	(410)	–	2,105	460	11,993
'87	2,000	552	(1,792)	760	–	1,620	–	14,893
'88	2,110	639	1	2,750	–	735	–	17,154
'89	2,220	740	–	2,960	–	740	–	19,646
'90	2,340	858	2	3,200	–	740	–	22,388
'91	2,730	235	15	2,980	–	1,240	–	25,772
'92	2,980	–	20	3,000	–	1,480	–	29,903
'93	3,110	–	20	3,130	–	1,545	–	34,516
'94	3,250	–	20	3,270	–	1,615	–	39,663
'95	3,390	–	30	3,420	–	1,680	–	45,393
'96	3,550	–	20	3,570	–	1,765	–	51,786
'97	5,050	–	(250)	4,800	–	2,650	–	59,747
'98	6,280	–	(1,100)	5,180	–	3,690	–	69,596
Total	$45,830	$4,499	$(14,629)	$35,700	$1,060	$29,040		$69,596

* The figures in this hypothetical example are based on a complicated set of assumptions, the key ones being 1) annual gross rental equal to 26% of equipment cost during the first year and increasing 5% per year thereafter, and 2) the acquiring of about 1/3 of the containers with debt.

** 50% tax bracket assumed.

*** 10% earnings rate on reinvestment fund assumed.

613

Table 21. Cinema—Hypothetical Investor Benefits
Sucessful Case
40% taxpayer—$10,000 investment

Year	Share of Cash Flow	Share of Taxable Income (Loss)	Tax Saving (Liability)	ITC	Total Benefit	Cumulative Benefit
1982	$ -	$(6398)	$ 2559	$ 67	$2626	$ 2626
1983	13900	13993	(5597)	409	8712	11338
1984	5005	1853	(741)		4264	15602
1985	223	1499	(600)		1633	17235
	$21138*	$ 10947*	$(4379)	$476	$17235*	

*Does not include any income from residual value of films.

Assumptions:

(1) Four films are produced. Net film rentals average $15,000,000 each in U.S. and $6,000,000 each in Foreign Markets.

(2) Four films sold to all televisions sources for an average of $5,000,000 each.

(3) Film distribution advance is recouped.

After-tax internal rate of return = 49.69%

The internal rate of return is high due to the receipt of a major portion of total benefits in the early years. This emphasizes the time value of money.

The after-tax rate of return has been calculated in the following manner:

1. Cash flows are quarterly, in keeping with the Partnership quarterly distributions of cash.

2. Tax benefits or liabilities occur in the second quarter of the year following the taxable income or loss upon which they are calculated.

Table 22. Analysis of Presidential 100 Life Insurance Plan

AGE 40 MALE   AMOUNT OF POLICY $25000

	ANNUAL RESULTS				CUMULATIVE RESULTS			
(1) Your Annual Payment	(2) The Savings Portion of Your Insurance Will Increase By	(3) Therefore, Your Annual Cost Is Only	(4) The Total of Your Payments	(5) The Total Savings Portion of Your Insurance	(6) You May Elect Paid-Up Insurance in the Amount of	(7) Therefore, Your Cumulative Cost Is Only	(8) If You Should Die, Your Beneficiary Will Receive Tax Free *	INSURANCE YEAR
$525.50	$ NONE	$525.50	$ 525.50	$ NONE	$ NONE	$ 525.50	$25000	1
525.50	250	275.50	1051.00	250	600	801.00	25000	2
525.50	450	75.50	1576.50	700	1600	876.50	25000	3
525.50	475	50.50	2102.00	1175	2600	927.00	25000	4
525.50	475	50.50	2627.50	1650	3575	977.50	25000	5
525.50	475	50.50	3153.00	2125	4475	1028.00	25000	6
525.50	500	25.50	3678.50	2625	5400	1053.50	25000	7
525.50	475	50.50	4204.00	3100	6250	1104.00	25000	8
525.50	500	25.50	4729.50	3600	7075	1129.50	25000	9
525.50	500	25.50	5255.00	4100	7900	1155.00	25000	10
525.50	500	25.50	5780.50	4600	8650	1180.50	25000	11
525.50	500	25.50	6306.00	5100	9400	1206.00	25000	12
525.50	525	.50	6831.50	5625	10150	1206.50	25000	13
525.50	500	25.50	7357.00	6125	10825	1232.00	25000	14
525.50	525	.50	7882.50	6650	11500	1232.50	25000	15
525.50	500	25.50	8408.00	7150	12125	1258.00	25000	16
525.50	525	.50	8933.50	7675	12750	1258.50	25000	17
525.50	525	.50	9459.00	8200	13350	1259.00	25000	18
525.50	500	25.50	9984.50	8700	13900	1284.50	25000	19
525.50	525	.50	10510.00	9225	14475	1285.00	25000	20
525.50	525	.50	10510.00	9225	14475	1285.00	25000	AGE 60
525.50	500	25.50	13137.50	11725	16875	1412.50	25000	AGE 65

This Column Shows The Most That You Could Lose If You Surrendered This Plan

* Federal Income Tax

615

Table 23. Without IRA Rollover

$88,201 distribution | January 1, 1944 - December 31, 1954
$14,056 taxes due | Self-Liquidating for the next 21 years
$74,145 Balance Invested in The Seminar Fund | January 1, 1955 - January 1, 1976
9% withdrawal for first 11 years

DATE	INITIAL INVESTMENT	OFFERING PRICE	SALES CHARGE INCLUDED	SHARES PURCHASED	NET ASSET VALUE PER SHARE	INITIAL NET ASSET VALUE
1/ 1/44	$74,145.00	$4.75	4.50%	15,609.470	$4.532	$70,742

SYSTEMATIC WITHDRAWAL PLAN
DIVIDENDS AND CAPITAL GAINS REINVESTED
MONTHLY WITHDRAWALS OF $556.09 (9.0% ANNUALLY) BEGINNING 1/31/44

	=========AMOUNTS WITHDRAWN=========					====VALUE OF REMAINING SHARES====			
DATE	FROM INCOME DIVS	FROM PRINCIPAL	ANNUAL TOTAL	CUM TOTAL	ANNUAL CAP GAIN DISTRIB'N	REMAINING ORIGINAL SHARES	CAP GAIN SHARES	TOTAL VALUE	SHARES HELD
12/31/44	1,920	4,753	6,673	6,673	2,536	76,330	2,609	78,939	15,116
12/31/45	1,640	5,033	6,673	13,346	6,235	89,410	9,567	98,977	15,245
12/31/46	2,243	4,430	6,673	20,019	5,407	75,400	13,751	89,151	15,509
12/31/47	2,869	3,804	6,673	26,692	3,446	65,696	16,066	81,782	15,448
12/31/48	2,854	3,819	6,673	33,365	2,108	57,444	17,047	74,491	15,152
12/31/49	2,556	4,117	6,673	40,038	2,311	53,652	19,522	73,174	14,752
12/31/50	2,715	3,958	6,673	46,711	2,134	55,373	23,854	79,227	14,378
12/31/51	2,668	4,005	6,673	53,384	3,327	55,971	29,189	85,160	14,276
12/31/52	2,550	4,123	6,673	60,057	3,514	53,577	33,694	87,271	14,167
12/31/53	2,637	4,036	6,673	66,730	1,956	46,278	33,551	79,829	13,811
12/31/54	2,526	4,148	6,673	73,403	4,844	61,744	53,290	115,034	13,809
TOTALS	27,178	46,225	73,403		37,818				

NOTE: 20.0% SUBTRACTED FROM DIVIDENDS AND 10.0% SUBTRACTED FROM CAPITAL GAIN
DISTRIBUTIONS AS PAID TO REFLECT LIABILITY FOR FEDERAL INCOME TAXES.

SYSTEMATIC WITHDRAWAL PLAN
DIVIDENDS AND CAPITAL GAINS REINVESTED
MONTHLY WITHDRAWALS BEGINNING 1/31/55 BASED ON A 21-YEAR SELF-LIQUIDATING PROGRAM DESIGNED TO EXHAUST PRINCIPAL

DATE	INITIAL INVESTMENT	OFFERING PRICE	SALES CHARGE INCLUDED	SHARES PURCHASED	NET ASSET VALUE PER SHARE	INITIAL NET ASSET VALUE
1/ 1/55	$115,034.00	$8.33	0.00%	13,809.600	$8.330	$115,034

DATE	=====AMOUNTS WITHDRAWN=====				ANNUAL CAP GAIN DISTRIB'N	=====VALUE OF REMAINING SHARES=====			SHARES HELD
	FROM INCOME DIVS	FROM PRINCIPAL	ANNUAL TOTAL	CUM TOTAL		REMAINING ORIGINAL SHARES	CAP GAIN SHARES	TOTAL VALUE	
12/31/55	2,875	3,313	6,188	6,188	8,659	126,629	8,995	135,624	14,397
12/31/56	2,958	4,240	7,198	13,386	9,286	122,702	18,229	140,931	14,945
12/31/57	3,080	4,083	7,164	20,550	6,642	95,234	21,012	116,246	15,332
12/31/58	3,035	4,692	7,727	28,277	5,028	123,528	33,939	157,467	15,651
12/31/59	3,034	6,923	9,956	38,233	10,188	121,668	45,649	167,317	15,793
12/31/60	3,265	6,917	10,182	48,415	8,273	109,723	52,479	162,202	15,758
12/31/61	3,110	9,242	12,352	60,767	8,904	115,628	68,904	184,532	15,519
12/31/62	3,113	8,187	11,300	72,067	6,286	85,837	61,439	147,276	15,188
12/31/63	3,015	9,746	12,761	84,828	6,304	88,472	77,080	165,552	14,952
12/31/64	3,055	12,318	15,373	100,201	9,260	82,725	91,923	174,648	14,653
12/31/65	3,116	14,800	17,916	118,117	11,159	80,791	118,649	199,440	14,394
12/31/66	3,563	16,289	19,852	137,969	13,120	58,249	154,042	179,069	13,638
12/31/67	3,739	20,086	23,825	161,794	9,036	49,174	177,080	203,216	12,694
12/31/68	3,992	22,827	26,819	188,613	7,572	28,944	153,972	206,024	11,798
12/31/69	3,615	23,521	27,336	215,949	10,930	1,893	131,831	155,865	10,521
12/31/70	3,483	20,319	23,802	239,751	5,988	0	122,503	131,831	8,756
12/31/71	2,957	25,919	28,876	268,627	2,044	0	105,567	122,503	6,895
12/31/72	2,366	30,509	32,895	301,522	2,899	0	58,008	105,567	4,838
12/31/73	1,862	28,842	30,704	332,226	1,447	0	23,515	58,008	2,539
12/31/74	1,562	24,489	26,071	358,297	0	0	0	23,515	0
12/31/75	414	29,620	30,034	388,331	14	0	0	0	0
TOTALS	61,451	326,860	386,331		143,040				

NOTE: 20.0% SUBTRACTED FROM DIVIDENDS AND 10.0% SUBTRACTED FROM CAPITAL GAIN DISTRIBUTIONS AS PAID TO REFLECT LIABILITY FOR FEDERAL INCOME TAXES.

Table 24. With IRA Rollover

$88,201 Invested in The Seminar Fund

Self-Liquidating for the next 21 years

9% withdrawal for 11 years

January 1, 1955 through January 1, 1976

DATE						NET ASSET VALUE PER SHARE	INITIAL NET ASSET VALUE
1/ 1/44	$88,201.00	$4.75	4.50%	18,568.630		$4.532	$84,153

SYSTEMATIC WITHDRAWAL PLAN
DIVIDENDS AND CAPITAL GAINS REINVESTED
MONTHLY WITHDRAWALS OF $661.51 (9.0% ANNUALLY) BEGINNING   1/31/44

| | ===========AMOUNTS WITHDRAWN=========== | | | | | =====VALUE OF REMAINING SHARES===== | | | |
DATE	FROM INCOME DIVS	FROM PRINCIPAL	ANNUAL TOTAL	CUM TOTAL	ANNUAL CAP GAIN DISTRIB'N	REMAINING ORIGINAL SHARES	CAP GAIN SHARES	TOTAL VALUE	SHARES HELD
12/31/44	2,864	5,074	6,350	6,350	3,367	91,396	3,464	94,860	18,165
12/31/45	2,471	5,467	6,350	12,701	8,365	107,664	12,790	120,454	18,554
12/31/46	3,425	4,513	6,350	19,051	7,346	91,560	18,498	110,058	19,147
12/31/47	4,451	3,487	6,350	25,402	4,766	80,893	21,769	102,662	19,392
12/31/48	4,506	3,432	6,350	31,752	2,969	71,941	23,185	95,126	19,350
12/31/49	4,112	3,826	6,350	38,102	3,319	68,577	26,728	95,305	19,214
12/31/50	4,459	3,479	6,350	44,453	3,126	72,437	32,869	105,306	19,111
12/31/51	4,469	3,469	6,350	50,803	4,980	75,002	40,618	115,620	19,383
12/31/52	4,363	3,575	6,350	57,154	5,375	73,777	47,378	121,155	19,667
12/31/53	4,621	3,317	6,350	63,504	3,064	65,961	47,488	113,449	19,627
12/31/54	4,527	3,411	6,350	69,854	7,764	90,907	76,351	167,258	20,078
TOTALS	44,267	43,051	69,854		54,442				

NOTE: 20.0% SUBTRACTED FROM TOTAL AMOUNTS WITHDRAWN TO REFLECT LIABILITY FOR FEDERAL INCOME TAXES.

DATE	INITIAL INVESTMENT	OFFERING PRICE	SALES CHARGE INCLUDED	SHARES PURCHASED	NET ASSET VALUE PER SHARE	INITIAL NET ASSET VALUE
1/ 1/55	$167,258.00	$8.33	0.00%	20,078.990	$8.330	$167,258

SYSTEMATIC WITHDRAWAL PLAN
DIVIDENDS AND CAPITAL GAINS REINVESTED
MONTHLY WITHDRAWALS BEGINNING   1/31/55 BASED ON A 21-YEAR SELF-LIQUIDATING PROGRAM
DESIGNED TO EXHAUST PRINCIPAL

| | ===========AMOUNTS WITHDRAWN=========== | | | | | =====VALUE OF REMAINING SHARES===== | | | |
DATE	FROM INCOME DIVS	FROM PRINCIPAL	ANNUAL TOTAL	CUM TOTAL	ANNUAL CAP GAIN DISTRIB'N	REMAINING ORIGINAL SHARES	CAP GAIN SHARES	TOTAL VALUE	SHARES HELD
12/31/55	5,248	3,797	7,236	7,236	14,050	185,168	14,592	199,760	21,205
12/31/56	5,462	5,180	8,514	15,750	15,259	180,421	29,767	210,188	22,289
12/31/57	5,762	4,972	8,587	24,337	11,050	140,959	34,508	175,467	23,148
12/31/58	5,744	5,975	9,376	33,713	8,466	183,947	55,963	239,910	23,360
12/31/59	5,796	9,447	12,194	45,907	17,312	182,044	75,792	257,836	24,119
12/31/60	6,320	9,472	12,633	58,541	14,201	165,071	87,615	252,686	24,604
12/31/61	6,076	13,249	15,461	74,002	15,462	174,631	115,644	290,275	24,788
12/31/62	5,146	11,712	14,286	88,288	11,005	130,332	103,523	233,855	24,642
12/31/63	6,001	14,332	16,266	104,554	11,161	134,828	130,432	265,260	24,335
12/31/64	6,134	18,581	19,772	124,326	16,541	126,264	156,428	282,692	24,203
12/31/65	6,324	22,786	23,288	147,614	20,138	123,137	203,093	326,230	23,969
12/31/66	7,324	25,342	26,133	173,748	23,910	88,313	208,183	296,496	23,834
12/31/67	7,762	31,838	31,680	205,428	16,683	73,127	266,570	339,697	22,798
12/31/68	8,387	36,714	36,081	241,509	14,064	40,049	307,617	347,666	21,421
12/31/69	8,103	38,361	37,171	278,679	20,493	0	266,168	266,168	20,148
12/31/70	7,475	33,447	32,737	311,417	11,362	0	227,621	227,621	18,166
12/31/71	6,395	43,606	40,001	351,418	3,937	0	213,107	213,107	15,232
12/31/72	5,198	52,185	45,907	397,324	5,625	0	185,164	185,164	12,094
12/31/73	4,091	49,925	43,213	440,537	2,832	0	102,684	102,684	8,564
12/31/74	3,513	42,802	37,052	477,588	0	0	42,129	42,129	4,549
12/31/75	929	53,073	43,201	520,789	27	0	0	0	0
TOTALS	124,190	526,796	520,789		253,578				

NOTE: 20.0% SUBTRACTED FROM TOTAL AMOUNTS WITHDRAWN TO REFLECT LIABILITY FOR FEDERAL INCOME TAXES.

Table 25. Hypothetical Illustration—Growth Seminar Fund, Inc.

PREPARED FOR: DR. HENRY KATZ KEOGH PLAN

DATE	INITIAL INVESTMENT	OFFERING PRICE	SALES CHARGE INCLUDED	SHARES PURCHASED	NET ASSET VALUE PER SHARE	INITIAL NET ASSET VALUE
1/ 1/72	$15,000.00	$3.60	6.00%	4,166.664	$3.380	$14,083

ANNUAL INVESTMENTS OF $15,000.00 - SAME DAY AS INITIAL INVESTMENT
DIVIDENDS AND CAPITAL GAINS REINVESTED

CUMULATIVE VOLUME DISCOUNT REFLECTED WHERE APPLICABLE IN THIS ILLUSTRATION

| | =====COST OF SHARES===== | | | | | =========VALUE OF SHARES========= | | | | | |
DATE	CUM INV'M'T	ANNUAL INCOME DIVS	CUM INCOME DIVS	TOTAL INV'M'T COST	ANNUAL CAP GAIN DISTRIB'N	FROM INV'M'T	FROM CAP GAINS REINV'D	SUB-TOTAL	FROM DIVS REINV'D	TOTAL VALUE	SHARES HELD
12/31/72	15,000	229	229	15,229	500	15,208	510	15,718	234	15,952	4,370
12/31/73	30,000	371	600	30,600	2,224	17,351	2,219	19,570	458	20,028	9,272
12/31/74	45,000	948	1,547	46,547	0	21,831	1,541	23,372	1,022	24,394	16,262
12/31/75	60,000	1,666	3,214	63,214	0	53,003	2,276	55,279	3,198	58,477	26,400
12/31/76	75,000	1,315	4,529	79,529	0	86,474	2,923	89,397	5,532	94,929	33,366
12/31/77	90,000	1,923	6,451	96,451	0	115,309	3,339	118,648	8,656	127,304	39,170
12/31/78	105,000	2,726	9,177	114,177	0	155,730	4,007	159,737	13,720	173,457	44,476
12/31/79	120,000	3,855	13,033	133,033	0	254,005	5,980	259,985	25,551	285,536	49,061
12/31/80	135,000	6,705	19,737	154,737	16,504	314,093	30,340	344,433	39,360	383,793	56,398
12/31/81	150,000	24,925	44,662	194,662	41,276	293,695	68,726	362,421	60,566	422,987	69,570
TOTAL					60,503						

619

Table 26. Summary of Tax-Sheltered Retirement Plans

Type of Taxpayer	Type of Plan	Eligibility Requirements	Maximum Annual Contributions
Self-employed person (sole proprietor or partner). Part-time self-employed person (with special provisions when adjusted gross income $15,000 or less).	Keogh	All employees with 3 years of service must be included, with contributions made on same percentage basis as employer's.	15% of self-employment income but not more than $15,000 a year per self-employed. (Only first $200,000 of self-employment income may be basis for determining percentage contribution for employees—if over $100,000, then rate for employees must be at least 7½% of compensation.) (For tax years beginning after 1981.)
Individual	IRA (Individual Retirement Account)	Earned income and under age 70½.	100% of earned income, but not more than $2,000. (For tax years beginning after 1981.)
Individual with non-working spouse.	Marital IRA	Married couple filing joint return, each under age 70½ and only one has earned income.	100% of earned income, but not more than $2,250. Separate account for each spouse with maximum of $2,000 to any account. (For tax years beginning after 1981.)
Recipient of a qualifying rollover distribution from a tax-sheltered retirement plan either: a) through retirement or termination of employment b) through termination of plan while still employed c) death of employee (spouse).	Rollover IRA	Recipient must receive entire balance within 1 taxable year.	No limit. *Entire* distribution may be rolled over except for non-deductible employee contributions. Partial rollovers are allowed; the amount not rolled over is taxed as ordinary income.
Employee of non-profit organization (educational, medical, religious, plus others).	403(b)	Generally, participation by employee voluntary.	$45,475 or 20% of compensation from employer, whichever is less... plus catch-up provision for prior low-contribution years.
Employee of state & local governments. Independent contractor to state & local government.	Deferred Compensation Plan	Performs services for state/local government as employee or independent contractor—participation is voluntary.	$7,500 or 25% of gross compensation, whichever is less... plus limited catch-up provision.
Corporation	Profit Sharing (contributions come from profits at employer's discretion) Money Purchase Pension (contributions are required, based on salary) Defined Benefit Pension (contributions are required)	Employees meeting specified age (25) and service (1 yr.) requirements—certain classes can be excluded if non-discriminatory.	$45,475 or 15% (profit sharing), $45,475 or 25% (pension), $45,475 or 25% (combined pension and profit sharing) of compensation, whichever is less, per participant. Determined on actuarial basis designed to create assets sufficient to pay plan's predetermined benefit, but not to yield more than $136,425 a year or 100% of salary (whichever is less) per participant (defined benefit).
Subchapter S Corporation (corporation taxed as if a partnership).			15% of compensation but not more than $15,000 a year per participant. (Only first $200,000 of a stockholder's compensation may be basis for determining percentage contribution for all employees.) (For tax years beginning after 1981.)
Employers (and their employees).	Simplified Employee Pension (SEP) (a form of IRA with higher maximum contribution)	Generally, all employees over age 25 who have worked for employer for 3 of last 5 calendar years.	15% of compensation but not more than $15,000 a year per participant. (Only first $200,000 of compensation may be used as basis for determining percentage contribution—if over $100,000, then rate for employees must be at least 7½% of compensation.) (For tax years beginning after 1981.)

Financial Benefits for Planholder	Benefits for Planholder's Heirs	Set-up Deadline	Contribution Deadline	Distributions Start at
1. The contribution is tax deductible. 2. Growth and income generated by funds in plan are not subject to current taxes. 3. Assets in plan are not attachable in event of personal bankruptcy. 4. Benefits are 100% vested at all times.	Accounts are excluded from gross estate if paid to a named beneficiary over 2 or more taxable years.	Dec. 31 (or end of tax-payer's fiscal year).	Apr. 15 (or applicable tax-filing date including extensions).*	Earliest: 59½ years or disability or death Latest: 70½ years.
	Accounts are excluded from gross estate if paid to a named beneficiary over at least 36 months.	Apr. 15 (or applicable tax-filing date including extensions).*		
In addition to Benefits 2, 3 and 4 (above), **no taxes are paid on distribution—full amount is available for investment.** Without rollover, distribution is immediately taxable according to special 10-year averaging formula or as capital gains. Terminated plans are taxable as ordinary income.		No later than 60 days after receipt of lump sum distribution.		
1. The contribution is subtracted from the total taxable income of the planholder. 2. Growth and income generated by funds in plan are not subject to current taxes. 3. Assets in plan are not attachable in event of personal bankruptcy. 4. Benefits are 100% vested at all times.	Accounts are excluded from gross estate if paid to a named beneficiary over 2 or more taxable years.	Any time, but salary reduction applies only after salary reduction agreement is entered into.		Retirement or termination of employment or financial hardship or 59½ years.
1. The contribution is subtracted from the total taxable income of the planholder. 2. Growth and income generated by funds in plan are not subject to current taxes. **NOTE: Assets are subject to claims of creditors of employee as well as creditors of the government-employer.**	No special exclusion.			Retirement or termination of employment or unforeseen emergency or death.
1. Contributions to plan are not included in employees' taxable incomes. 2. Growth and income generated by funds in plan are not subject to current taxes. 3. Assets in plan are not attachable in event of personal bankruptcy.	Accounts are excluded from gross estate if paid to a named beneficiary over 2 or more taxable years or recipient elects not to use the special 10-year averaging formula or capital gains treatment if proceeds received in lump sum.	End of fiscal year.	Date for filing federal tax returns (including extensions).*	Retirement or disability or termination of employment or termination of plan. Certain profit-sharing plans permit "hardship" withdrawals.
1. The contribution is tax deductible. 2. Growth and income generated by funds in plan are not subject to current taxes. 3. Assets in plan are not attachable in event of personal bankruptcy. 4. Benefits are 100% vested at all times.	Accounts are excluded from gross estate if paid to a named beneficiary over at least 36 months.	April 15*	April 15*	Earliest: 59½ years or disability or death Latest: 70½ years.

Table 27. Incidental Cost of P.S. 58

The Incidental Cost of P.S. 58 when Life Insurance is included in a Pension or Profit Sharing Plan just may not be so incidental.

The following shows the cumulative Income Tax Liability passed through to the Insured "For the Premature Death Benefit" when it is included in a Pension or Profit Sharing Program.

TAX LIABILITY PER $100,000 INSURANCE FACE AMOUNT

Issue Age	P.S. 58
65	$ 3,151
64	6,049
63	8,712
62	11,162
61	13,415
60	$15,488
59	17,396
58	19,152
57	20,770
56	22,261
55	$23,635
54	24,902
53	26,071
52	27,150
51	28,147
50	$29,069
49	29,922
48	30,711
47	31,443
46	32,121
45	$32,751
44	33,336
43	33,880
42	34,387
41	34,860
40	35,302

Table 28. P.S. No. 58 Rates

The following rates are used in computing the "cost" of pure life insurance protection that is taxable to the employee under: qualified pension and profit-sharing plans (Q&A 179); split-dollar plans (Q&A 76); and tax-sheltered annuities (Q&A 123). Rev. Rul. 55–747, 1955–2 CB 228; Rev. Rul. 66–110, 1966–1 CB 12.

ONE YEAR TERM PREMIUMS FOR $1,000 OF LIFE INSURANCE PROTECTION

Age	Premium	Age	Premium	Age	Premium
15	$ 1.27	37	$ 3.63	59	$ 19.08
16	1.38	38	3.87	60	20.73
17	1.48	39	4.14	61	22.53
18	1.52	40	4.42	62	24.50
19	1.56	41	4.73	63	26.63
20	1.61	42	5.07	64	28.98
21	1.67	43	5.44	65	31.51
22	1.73	44	5.85	66	34.28
23	1.79	45	6.30	67	37.31
24	1.86	46	6.78	68	40.59
25	1.93	47	7.32	69	44.17
26	2.02	48	7.89	70	48.06
27	2.11	49	8.53	71	52.29
28	2.20	50	9.22	72	56.89
29	2.31	51	9.97	73	61.89
30	2.43	52	10.79	74	67.33
31	2.57	53	11.69	75	73.23
32	2.70	54	12.67	76	79.63
33	2.86	55	13.74	77	86.57
34	3.02	56	14.91	78	94.09
35	3.21	57	16.18	79	102.23
36	3.41	58	17.56	80	111.04
				81	120.57

The rate at insured's attained age is applied to the excess of the amount payable at death over the cash value of the policy at the end of the year.

Table 29

SOCIAL SECURITY BENEFITS

The information below will give you a rough estimate of what your retirement check will be. If retirement is some years away benefits will likely be higher because maximum covered earnings grew as follows, and because of automatic increases as the cost of living goes up.

1951-1954	$ 3,600	1974	$13,200
1955-1958	4,200	1975	14,100
1959-1965	4,800	1976	15,300
1966-1967	6,600	1977	16,500
1968-1971	7,800	1978	17,700
1972	9,000	1979	22,900
1973	10,800	1980	25,900
		1981	29,700

Social Security checks are not subject to Federal Income taxes. Benefits will be paid regardless of retirement income received from other sources.

Table 30

LIFE EXPECTANCY TABLES

Present Age	Life Expectancy No. of Years Males	Females	Present Age	Life Expectancy No. of Years Males	Females	Present Age	Life Expectancy No. of Years Males	Females	Present Age	Life Expectancy No. of Years Males	Females
20	52.1	56.7	35	38.2	42.8	50	25.5	29.6	65	15.0	18.2
21	51.1	55.8	36	37.3	41.9	51	24.7	28.7	66	14.4	17.5
22	50.2	54.9	37	36.5	41.0	52	24.0	27.9	67	13.8	16.9
23	49.3	53.9	38	35.6	40.0	53	23.2	27.1	68	13.2	16.2
24	48.3	53.0	39	34.7	39.1	54	22.4	26.3	69	12.6	15.6
25	47.4	52.1	40	33.8	38.2	55	21.7	25.5	70	12.1	15.0
26	46.5	51.1	41	33.0	37.3	56	21.0	24.7	71	11.6	14.4
27	45.6	50.2	42	32.1	36.5	57	20.3	24.0	72	11.0	13.8
28	44.6	49.3	43	31.2	35.6	58	19.6	23.2	73	10.5	13.2
29	43.7	48.3	44	30.4	34.7	59	18.9	22.4	74	10.1	12.6
30	42.8	47.4	45	29.6	33.8	60	18.2	21.7	75	9.6	12.1
31	41.9	46.5	46	28.7	33.0	61	17.5	21.0	76	9.1	11.6
32	41.0	45.6	47	27.9	32.1	62	16.9	20.3	77	8.7	11.0
33	40.0	44.6	48	27.1	31.2	63	16.2	19.6	78	8.3	10.5
34	39.1	43.7	49	26.3	30.4	64	15.6	18.9	79	7.8	10.1
									80	7.5	9.6

Source: Internal Revenue Code

625

Table 31
Clifford Trust
Amount That Can Be Transferred to a Fourteen Year
Clifford Trust Without Adverse Gift Tax Consequences

I	II	III	IV
		Zero Value	*Zero Value*
Term of	*Table B*	*Gift After*	*Gift After*
Years	*Valuation Factor*	*$10,000 Exclusion*	*$20,000 Exclusion*
14	.557699	$ 17,930	$ 35,861
13	.531161	18,826	37,653
12	.503031	19,879	39,758
11	.473212	21,132	42,264
10	.441605	22,644	45,289
Total Tax Free			
Over 5 Years...		$100,411	$200,825

Present Value of the Income Trust

Number of Years *(Term Certain)*	*Value of* *Income Interest*
10	.441605
11	.473212
12	.503031
13	.531161
14	.557699
15	.582735
16	.606354
17	.628636
18	.649656
19	.669487
20	.688195

Example of Taxable Value of Income Interest from $100,000
Placed in a 10-year Clifford Trust

1) Value of property transferred to trust	$100,000
2) Times "Table B" value for ten year term certain income interest	x.441605
3) Equals	$44,160.50

Table 32

Unified Estate and Gift Tax
Rate Schedule

Taxable Transfers From	To	Tax =	%	Of Excess Over
$ 0	$ 10,000	$ 0	18	$ 0
10,000	20,000	1,800	20	10,000
20,000	40,000	3,800	22	20,000
40,000	60,000	8,200	24	40,000
60,000	80,000	13,000	26	60,000
80,000	100,000	18,200	28	80,000
100,000	150,000	23,800	30	100,000
150,000	250,000	38,800	32	150,000
250,000	500,000	70,800	34	250,000
500,000	750,000	155,800	37	500,000
750,000	1,000,000	248,300	39	750,000
1,000,000	1,250,000	345,800	41	1,000,000
1,250,000	1,500,000	448,300	43	1,250,000
1,500,000	2,000,000	555,800	45	1,500,000
2,000,000	2,500,000	780,800	49	2,000,000
2,500,000	3,000,000	1,025,800	53	2,500,000
3,000,000	3,500,000	1,290,800	57	3,000,000
3,500,000	4,000,000	1,575,800	61	3,500,000
4,000,000	4,500,000	1,880,800	65	4,000,000

The cumulative transfers to which the tax applies are the sum of (a) the amount of the taxable estate and (b) the amount of the taxable gifts made by the decedent after 1976 other than gifts includible in the gross estate.

Unified Estate and Gift Tax Credit

Year	Amount of Credit	Amount of Exemption Equivalent
1982	$ 62,800	$225,000
1983	79,300	275,000
1984	96,300	325,000
1985	121,800	400,000
1986	155,800	500,000
1987 and thereafter	192,800	600,000

STOCKS

Company _____

Date Bought	No. of Shares	Price Per Share	Total Cost	Date Sold	No. of Shares	Price Per Share						Total Net Proceeds					

Figure 1. Recordkeeping Form for Stocks

DIVIDEND RECORD

Company _____

Date Dividend Paid	Number of Shares	Rate per Share	Total Amount of Dividend

Figure 2. Dividend Record

Figure 3. Motivational Tapes From Nightingale-Conant

Great Ideas by Earl Nightingale
Lead the Field by Earl Nightingale
The Psychology of Winning by D. Denis Waitley
Possibility Thinking by Dr. Robert H. Schuller
The Science of Getting Rich by Dr. Sidney Lecker
Direct Line by Earl Nightingale
Creative Thinking by Mike Vance
How to Be a No-Limit Person by Dr. Wayne Dyer
Kop's Keys to Success and Happiness by M.R. Kopmeyer
Communicate What You Think by Earl Nightingale
The Compleat Speaker by Earl Nightingale

All tapes are available from Nightingale-Conant Corporation, 3730 West Devon Avenue, Chicago, ILL 60659, phone (312) 677-3100

Figure 4

TEN YEAR APPRECIATION OF INVESTMENT QUALITY-RARE COINS

	1971	1972	1973	1974	1975	1976	1977	1978	1979	1980
	$1,500	$1,680	$3,480	$4,900	$6,125	$6,385	$6,355	$6,395	$6,840	$15,525

Source: (Redbook) A Guide Of United States Coins by R. S. Yeaman

GIA COLOR-GRADING SCALE

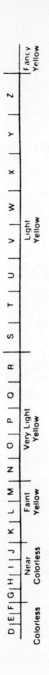

D E F G H I J K L M N O P Q R S T U V W X Y Z

Colorless | Near Colorless | Faint Yellow | Very Light Yellow | Light Yellow | Fancy Yellow

GIA CLARITY-GRADING SCALE

Flawless | VVS₁ VVS₂ | VS₁ VS₂ | S₁₁ | S₁₂ | I₁ I₂ I₃

Internally Flawless

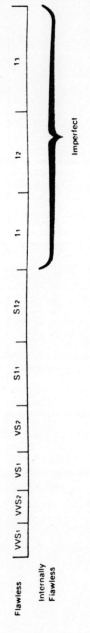

Imperfect

Figure 5

* Reflectance Spectrophotometer Units	C.M.	P.M.	Original Name Terms	U.K.	G.I.A.	A.G.S.	Deutsche RAL560QA5 Scan.D.N. 0.50 Ct. & Above	Scan.D.N. Less Than 0.50 Ct.	
0 - 50	0.25		Jager	Blue White					
51 - 80									
81 - 120	0.75				D	0			
121 - 160			River	Top Fine White	E		River	Rarest White	Colorless
161 - 200	1.25								
201 - 275		0.90			F				
276 - 350						1			
351 - 425									
426 - 500				Fine White					
501 - 750	2.25	0.95	Top Wesselton		G		Top Wesselton	White	
751 - 1000						2			Nearly Colorless
1001 - 2000	2.75	1.00	Wesselton	White	H		Wesselton		
2001 - 3000		1.03	Top Crystal	Commercial White	I	3	Top Crystal		
3001 - 4000	3.25	1.10	Crystal	Crystal	J	4	Crystal	Tinted White	
4001 - 5000	3.75		Top Cape		K	5			
5001 - 6000	4.25	1.15	Cape	Top Cape	L	6	Top Cape		Slightly Tinted
6001 - 7000	4.75		Low Cape		M		Cape	Yellowish	
7001 - 8000	5.25	1.20	Lt. Yellow	Cape	N	7			
8001 - 9000	5.75				O				
9001 - 10000	6.25		Yellow	Light Yellow	P	8	Light Yellow		Very Light Yellow
10001 - 11000	6.75				Q				
11001 - 12000	7.25	1.30			R				Light Yellow
12001 - 18000	7.75 10.00	1.50		Yellow	S - Z	9-10	Yellow	Yellow	

All the systems on this chart are based on master stones and opinion and are, therefore, open to different interpretations within each system. This means that they are not precisely comparable with each other

* Reflectance Spectrophotometer PMQ II using grating monochrometer M20; System covers 0 to 18,000+ points for Cape series stones only.

G.I.A. - Gemological Institute of America   P.M. - Photometer
A.G.S. - American Gem Society   Scan.D.N. - Scandinavian Diamond Nomenclature
C.M. - Colorimeter   U.K. - United Kingdom

Figure 6

Figure 7

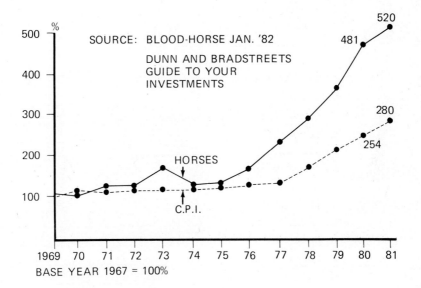

Figure 8. Comparison of Consumer Price Index vs. Horses

Program:

Investment Schedule: _____ _____ _____   TOTAL _____

TAX SAVINGS WORKSHEET

WITHOUT INVESTMENT:

1. Taxable Income $_____ Bracket _____%

2. Tax Due. $_____

WITH INVESTMENT:

3. Amount of Investment $_____ $_____ $_____

4. Write-off   _____ _____ _____

5. Net Taxable Income After Investment   _____ _____ _____

6. Tax Due   _____ _____ _____

7. Net Tax Savings $_____ $_____ $_____

8. Investment Tax Credit   _____ _____ _____

9. TOTAL TAX SAVINGS   _____ _____ _____

10. Amount Invested $_____ $_____ $_____

11. Less Tax Saved   _____ _____ _____

12. Net Cost of Investment   _____ _____ _____

Figure 9

ALTERNATIVE MINIMUM TAX

Taxable Income _____

Excess Adjusted Itemized Deductions[1] _____

60% (Excluded Portion) of Net LTCG _____

Less Exemption ___(20,000)___

   TOTAL _____

Next $40,000[2] _____ x 10% = _____

Balance[3] _____ x 20% = _____

Less Regular Tax (_____)

      TOTAL ALTERNATIVE MINIMUM TAX _____

[1]Those itemized deductions which exceed 60% of AGI.
[2]After $20,000 exemption.
[3]After $60,000.

Figure 10

WORKSHEET FOR CALCULATING
MINIMUM TAX ON OTHER
TAX PREFERENCE ITEMS

Total tax preference items $_____

Less: the greater or 1/2 of your
       regular tax liability
       or $10,000 $_____

Difference $_____

Rate ___15%___

Add on Minimum Tax $_____

Figure 11

COMPARISON STATEMENT

NAME OF APPLICANT		STREET	CITY	STATE	ZIP CODE
John W. Doe					
NAME OF INSURED IF OTHER THAN APPLICANT			DATE OF BIRTH OF INSURED		

1. COMPARATIVE INFORMATION	†Existing Life Insurance	†Existing Life Insurance	†Existing Life Insurance	Total Existing Life Insurance	Proposed Life Insurance
Policy Number					XXXXXXXXXXXX
Insurance Company					
Amount of Basic Insurance					
Currently	$ 15,000	$ 15,000	$ 16,000	$ 46,000	$ 200,000
10 Years Hence	$ 15,000	$ 15,000	$ 16,000	$ 46,000	$ 200,000
20 Years Hence	$ 15,000	$ 15,000	$ 16,000	$ 46,000	$ 200,000 [1]
At age 65	$ 15,000	$ 15,000	$ 16,000	$ 46,000	$ 200,000 [1]
Basic Plan of Insurance	Adj W.L.	Adj W.L.	Adj W.L.	Adj W.L.	ART
Present Amount of Term Rider(s)	$	$	$	$	$
Issue Age	30	30	34	Various	51
Issue Date	4-25-56	4-25-56	6-1-60	Various	XXXXXXXXXXXX

Premium For:	Premium / Payable To Age / Age Cov. Ceases	Premium / Payable To Age / Age Cov. Ceases	Premium / Payable To Age / Age Cov. Ceases	Premium / Payable To Age / Age Cov. Ceases	Premium / Payable To Age / Age Cov. Ceases
Basic Policy	$316.20 Life	$316.20 Life	$384.00 Life	$1,016.40 Life	$ 650 [2]
*Accidental Death Benefit	$	$	$	$	$
*Waiver of Premium Benefit	$	$	$	$	$
*Disability Income Benefit	$	$	$	$	$
Family Income or Increased Protection Rider	$	$	$	$	$
Option to Purchase Additional Insurance	$	$	$	$	$
Other Benefits (Explain)	$	$	$	$	$
Total Current Premium	$316.20	$316.20	$384.00	$1,016.40	$ 650 [2]
Frequency of Premium Payment	Annual	Annual	Annual	Annual	Annual
Tabular Cash Values:					
At Present	$ 5,145	$ 5,145	$ 4,832	$ 15,122 [2]	$ 0
1 Year Hence	$ 5,415	$ 5,415	$ 5,136	$ 15,966	$ 0
5 Years Hence	$ 6,489	$ 6,489	$ 6,352	$ 19,330	$ 0
10 Years Hence	$ 7,800	$ 7,800	$ 7,850	$ 23,450	$ 1,610 [2]
At age (Highest age shown in Cash Value Table of existing policy) Age 65	$ 8,820	$ 8,820	$ 8,976	$ 26,616	$ 0 [3]
Cash Value of any existing Dividend Additions or Accumulations (if available from applicant)	$	$	$	$	$
Amount of any Loan Now Outstanding	$	$	$	$	$
Amount of Annual Loan Interest	$ 5%	$ 5%	$ 5%	$ 5%	$
Date Contestable Period Expires	Expired	Expired	Expired	Expired	1985
Date Suicide Clause Expires	Expired	Expired	Expired	Expired	1985
Dividends					
Is Policy Participating?	Yes	Yes	Yes	Yes	No
Annual Dividend (current scale)					
1 Year Hence	$ 196	$ 196	$ 207	$ 599	$ 0
2 Years Hence	$ 204	$ 204	$ 217	$ 625	$ 0
5 Years Hence	$ 236	$ 236	$ 257	$ 729	$ 0
10 Years Hence	$ 276	$ 276	$ 304	$ 856	$ 0
Total 10 Years	$ 2,405	$ 2,405	$ 2,595	$ 7,405	$ 0

[1] If needed.

[2] Age 61 - $7.19/th re-entry; $15.23 without
65 - $9.51/th re-entry; $16.49 without.

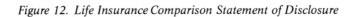

Figure 12. Life Insurance Comparison Statement of Disclosure

638

*If Premium for Benefits: (A) is not separable from basic policy premium, insert "Included in Basic Policy Premium," or (B) is an aggregate premium, show the aggregate premium.

**Dividends are based on the 19_____ dividend scale. The dividends shown are not to be construed as guarantees or estimates of dividends to be paid in the future. Dividends depend on mortality experience, investment, investment earnings and other factors, and are determined each year in the sole discretion of the Company's board of directors.

The agent is responsible for furnishing required dividend information. It is recommended that he obtain this for the policy being replaced from the Company issuing the original insurance. As an alternative, however, he may show dividends on closest comparable policy, amount, age and duration from current statistical manuals. (Interpolating where necessary). It is to be recognized that dividend information under this alternative method, with respect to existing insurance is not likely to be as accurate as dividend information obtained directly from the Company issuing the original insurance.

Source of dividend information used: _____

†If more than one existing life insurance policy is to be affected by a transaction included within the definition of a replacement contained in the Regulation, (1) the existing life insurance column of a separate signed Comparison Statement form must be completed for each such policy providing the information required by the form with respect to existing policies, and (II) a separate signed Comparison Statement form must be completed for the proposed policy. The latter form must summarize, to the extent possible, the information concerning the existing policies set forth on the separate forms, and must include the information required in Sections 2 through 5 of the Comparison Statement:

2. Advantages of Continuing the Existing Life Insurance:

3. Advantages of the Proposed Replacement of the Existing Life Insurance:

4. Additional information:
    (A)   The Existing Life Insurance Cannot fulfill Your Intended Objectives for the Following Reason(s):

    (B)   Under the Proposal, the Existing Insurance Policy Will be Treated as Follows:

5. The Primary Reason for the Proposed Replacement of the Existing Life Insurance by New Insurance is as Follows:

_____   _____
(DATE)   (SIGNATURE OF AGENT)

                                     _____
                                     (ADDRESS)

I hereby acknowledge that I received the above "Comparison Statement" and the "Notice to Applicants Regarding Replacement of Life Insurance" before I signed the application for the proposed new insurance.

_____   _____
(DATE)   (SIGNATURE OF APPLICANT)

ON $100 A MONTH

You can live in the famous

HOT SPRINGS *Region*

● Of the many attractive localities, where it is possible to live on $100 a month, Hot Springs, Ark., has a special appeal. By the time you are ready to retire from active work, its famous hot spring baths might prove a great boon to you physically.

Here in a land of scenic beauty— a favorite playground of the American people—and where there's just enough cold weather to make it welcome—you could have a cozy home, and live comfortably on a very moderate income.

That's the kind of life you can lead, when you're ready to retire. Whether it's Hot Springs, or another of the nation's wonder spots—

or perhaps your own home town —it would be possible to live comfortably on $100 a month. And what a great satisfaction it is to know that at 55, or later, you can have that income, or more, for the rest of your life! That's what you can do if you own ▮▮▮▮ ▮▮▮ *retirement insurance.*

Decide now that you will have a worry-proof income for your less productive years . . . a sure, dependable check every month from one of America's oldest, strongest life insurance companies. Mail us the coupon below for the booklet— "EARNED LEISURE." Play safe with your future!

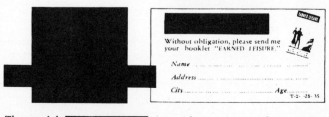

Without obligation, please send me your booklet "EARNED LEISURE."

Name ....

Address ....

City.................... Age..........

T-2- -25- 35

The assets of the ▮▮▮▮▮▮▮▮ *as reported to state insurance departments, now total a billion dollars—a great estate administered for the mutual welfare and protection of more than 600,000 policyholders.*

Figure 13. Annuity Advertisements

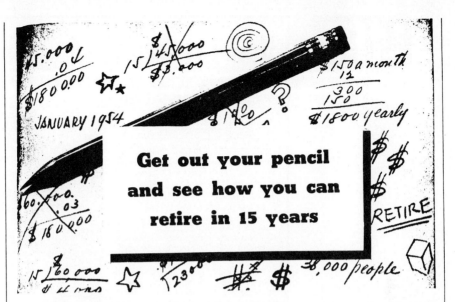

Get out your pencil and see how you can retire in 15 years

An advertisement that will help you get the things you want

IF YOU WANT an income for life — that will support you after you reach 55 or 60 — here are facts you should know.

Let's assume you are 40 now. Perhaps you are saving regularly — hoping you will have enough money some day to let you retire.

But will you? Let's see. In order to retire on $150 a month, you will have to save $45,000 and invest it at 4%. If you can get only 3%, you must save $60,000 to get the same income! Can you set aside that much in the next 15 years? It's a good way to retire, but it takes too much money for most of us.

That's why the ▆▆▆▆▆ Retirement Income Plan was started. It is now being used by over 38,000 people. Through this Plan, you can get a guar-

anteed income for life, you can guard against emergencies, you can avoid investment risks and uncertainties. And you can do all this with much less money than other investment plans require.

Get $150 a Month for Life

Here's how it works. Suppose you are 40 now, and you qualify for the following ▆▆▆▆▆ Plan which pays you $150 a month for life, beginning at age 55. Here is what the Plan provides:

1. A check for $150 when you reach 55, and a check for $150 every month thereafter as long as you live.

2. A life income to your wife in case of your death before age 55, and

3. A monthly Disability Income to you if, before age 55, total disability stops your earning power for six months or more.

Of course, you need not be 40 now. You may be older or younger. The income need not be $150 a month. It can be any amount from $10 to $200 a month or

more. And you can have it start at any age: 55, 60, 65 or 70. Similar Plans are available to women.

You don't have to be rich to retire this way. Since you start the Plan 15 years or more before you need the retirement income, you receive all the benefits of compound interest, long-range investments and *mutual* operation. You get a retirement income for far less money than ordinary investments require.

Send for Free Booklet

Let us mail you an important booklet giving the complete facts about the Retirement Income Plan. In a simple, illustrated way, this booklet shows you exactly how thousands of people are providing their own life incomes, tells you how the Plan protects against such emergencies as death or disability. Send the coupon below and we will mail you this booklet without cost or obligation. Discover for yourself the secret of getting your own life income!

TIME
THE WEEKLY NEWSMAGAZINE

TIME, May 15, 1939

Vol. 39, No. 21

November 21 1955

How I retired in 15 years with $250 a month

"Sometimes I have to smile. It's hard to believe that I'm retired today—retired with a life income. You see, I never had more than my salary, never inherited a dime, or even had luck in business! Yet a check for $250 a month arrives on the dot. And I'm my own boss for keeps!

"I left the office two years ago. And when I explained how I was doing it, though I was only 55, more than one of my friends said he only wished I'd told him years before. He'd be retiring, too.

"There's only one secret. Seventeen years ago, back in 1938, I had saved a little money. So I went into partnership with a friend. We thought it was going to pay off very well.

"Well, it didn't. But it was the most profitable investment I ever made. It showed me that there was no easy way for *me*, with *my* limited experience, to make a lot of money.

"I had to find a way that was systematic and sure. I was 40 then.

"It was shortly after that that I read an advertisement that told of a modern way for people of moderate means to retire. It didn't call for any great capital. It simply required fifteen or twenty working years ahead. One thing I liked particularly was that my family was protected with life insurance from the first day I took out my plan. (This, surely, was better than any ordinary savings method!) And the income was guaranteed—whatever happened to the business world—each month, every month, from the day it began as long as I live. The plan was called the ▮▮▮▮▮▮▮ Retirement Income Plan.

"The ad offered more information. So, I mailed in the coupon. It brought a booklet describing the various plans.

"Soon after, I applied and qualified for a ▮▮▮▮▮▮▮▮ Plan. And from that day on I've honestly felt like a rich man. Because I knew I wouldn't just simply live and work and die. I had a future I'd really enjoy. And that's what I'm doing today—with many, many thanks to my ▮▮▮▮▮▮ ▮▮▮▮ check for $250 a month that means financial independence for life."

Send for Free Booklet

This story is typical. Assuming you start at a young enough age, you can plan to have an income of $10 a month to $3,000 a year or more—beginning at age 55, 60, 65 or older. Send the coupon and receive, by mail and without charge, a booklet which tells about ▮▮▮▮▮▮▮▮ Plans. Similar plans are available for women—and for employee pension programs. Don't put it off. Send for your copy now.

Vol. 60, No. 3

January 21 1966

"How we retired in 15 years with $300 a month"

"Look at us! We're retired and having the time of our lives. A fish story? It sure isn't! Let me tell you about it.

"I started thinking about retiring in 1950. Nancy thought I was silly. It all seemed so far away. 'And besides,' she said, 'it makes me feel old.' It didn't seem silly to me, though. We'd just spent the afternoon with Nancy's aunt and uncle. Uncle Will had turned 65 during the war, and, by 1945, his working days were over.

"Now, life seemed to be standing still for them. They couldn't take even the short weekend trips that their friends could easily afford; they couldn't visit their children as often as they'd like.

"A pretty grim existence, I thought. But why? He'd had a good job. Then Nancy reminded me . . . they'd never planned ahead. During her uncle's working years, his paycheck was spent almost as soon as it arrived.

"Fortunately, they had put some money aside for a rainy day. But they hadn't planned ahead enough to make those retirement days sunny!

"Not for me, I decided. When it's time for me to retire, I want to be able to do the things we've always dreamed of doing instead of counting every penny.

"I showed Nancy a advertisement I'd seen in Life magazine a week or so before. It described their retirement income plan, telling how a man of 40 could retire in 15 years with a guaranteed income of $300 or more for life!

"Nancy agreed it was a great idea. The thought of retiring at 55 didn't make her feel old at all! So I filled out the coupon that day and sent it right off.

"A few days later the booklet describing the ▮▮▮▮▮▮ Plans arrived. I picked the right one for us and signed up right away. Three months ago my first check arrived—right on time.

"Last month we moved down here to Florida, and we love it. Nancy looks great with her tan, and she's thrilled at the thought of keeping it all year long!

"My tan suits me fine, but I'm really hooked on the fish. Whether I catch one a day or ten (or none), I'm having the time of my life, because we saved for a sunny day with ▮▮▮▮▮▮ "

Send for free booklet

This story is typical. Assuming you start early enough, you can plan to have an income of from $50 to $300 a month or more—beginning at age 55, 60, 65 or older. Send the coupon and receive by mail, without charge or obligation, a booklet which tells about ▮▮▮▮▮▮ Plans. Similar plans are available for women—and for Employee Pension Programs. Send for your free copy now. In 15 years you'll be glad you did!

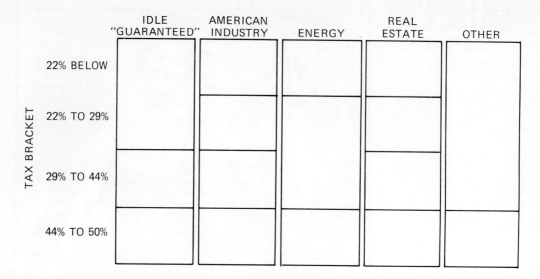

Figure 14. Personal Financial Inventory Form.

Worksheet 1.
My Life Insurance & Annuity Worksheet
(Use separate sheet for Term, Term Riders & Family Plan Riders)

NAME _____

BIRTHDATE _____ AGE _____

DATE _____

Company	Type Policy	Mortality table	Face amt. Basic policy	(2) Cash value	(3) Rate to borrow	(4) Actual ins	(5) Annual premium	(6) Last year's refund (dividend)	(7) Net premium	(8) Lost earnings @ __% on cash value	(9) Total cost	(10) Cost per thousand
TOTALS												

Example:

| Blessed Assurance Company | Whole Life | 1941 CSO | $10,000 | $4,000 | 5½% | $6000 (1) − (2) | $245 | $40 | $205 | $240 (2) × 6% | $445 (7) + (8) | $74.16 (9) ÷ (4) ($445÷6̶0̶ $74.19 |

645

Worksheet 2.

A Picture of My Present Life Insurance Program

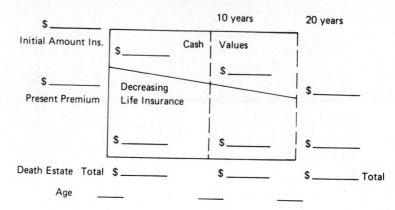

$ _____
Initial Amount Ins.

$ _____
Present Premium

10 years   20 years

$ _____   Cash ┊ Values

        ┊ $ _____

Decreasing
Life Insurance $ _____

$ _____   ┊ $ _____ $ _____

Death Estate Total $ _____ $ _____ $ _____ Total

Age   _____   _____   _____

Worksheet 3.

My age: _____

My Life Insurance Cost Worksheet

Present Plan

Face amount of policies $ _____
Less cash surrender value $ _____
Net insurance $ _____(1)
Present premium $ _____
Less dividend $ _____
  (last year)
Net premium $ _____
Plus lost earnings on
  cash value of $ _____ $ _____
  @ _____ %

TOTAL COST $ _____(2)
Cost per thousand @ age _____ $ _____(3)
    [(2) ÷ per thousand of (1)]

Recommended Plan

Plan _____
Cost per thousand @ age _____ $ _____

646

Worksheet 4.

Replacement Cost Index Worksheet

Present Program:

(1) Face amount $_____

(2) Less cash surrender value $_____

(3) Net insurance $_____

(4) Present Premium $_____

(5) Less cash value increase
     for the year $_____

(6) Plus lost earnings on $_____
     @ ____ % (2) $_____

(7) Less current dividend $_____

(8) Total cost $_____

(9) Replacement cost per thousand $_____
     @ ____ age [(8) ÷ no. of thousand in (3)]

Recommended Program:

Plan _____

Cost per thousand @ age ____ $_____

Addresses You'll Need to Know

American Birthright Trust Management
247 Royal Palm Way
Palm Beach, FL 33480
(305) 655-3481; also (800) 327-4508

American Funds Distributors, Inc.
333 South Hope Street
Los Angeles, CA 90071
(213) 486-9651

American General Capital Distributors
2777 Allen Parkway
Houston, TX 77019
(713) 526-8561; also (800) 231-3638

Anchor National Life Insurance Co.
2202 E. Camelback Rd.
Phoenix, AZ 85016
(602) 263-0363

Angeles Realty Corp.
10301 West Pico Blvd.
Los Angeles, CA 90064
(800) 421-4374

Arens's (Kurt) Gem Market Reporter
P.O. Box 39890
Phoenix, AZ 85069

The Balcor Company
The Balcor Building
10024 Skokie Boulevard
Skokie, IL 60066
(312) 677-2900

The Brennan Reports
William Brennan, Editor
P.O. Box 882
Valley Forge, PA 19482
(215) 783-0647

Brigham Young University
1222 SFLC
Provo, UT 84602
(801) 374-1211

College for Financial Planning
9725 East Hamptden Ave. Suite 200
Denver, CO 80231
(303) 755-7107

Consolidated Capital Equities Corp.
Suite 701, 333 Hegenberger Road
Oakland, CA 94621
(800) 227-1870; in California (800) 772-2443

Continental Trust Company
P.O. Box 367
Plano, TX 75074
(214) 422-1075

The Financial Planner Magazine
Forrest Wallace Cato, Editor
5775 Peachtree Dunwoody Rd., Suite 120-C
Atlanta, GA 30342
(404) 252-9600

Fireman's Fund American Life Insurance
Company
1600 Los Gamos Road
San Rafael, CA 94911
(415) 492-6953

First Trust Corporation
Genro Building
444 Sherman St.
Denver, CO 80203
(800) 525-8188 or (303) 744-2944

Fox & Carskadon
2755 Campus Drive, Suite 300
San Mateo, CA 94403
(415) 574-3333

Institute of Certified Financial
  Planners
9725 East Hamptden Ave, Suite 245
Denver, CO 80231
(303) 751-7600

Integrated Marketing, Inc.
660 Newport Center Dr., Suite 1420
Newport Beach, CA 92660
(714) 759-0451
National toll free (800) 854-3891
California toll free (800) 432-7203

International Association For
  Financial Planners
5775 Peachtree Dunwoody Rd.,
Suite 120
Atlanta, GA 30342
(404) 252-9600

Investment Company Institute
1775 K Street, N.W.
Washington, D.C. 20006
(202) 293-7700

Investment Timing Services, Inc.
Boyce Plaza, Suite 120
1035 Boyce Road
Pittsburgh, PA 15241
(412) 257-0100

Jones Intercable, Inc.
880 Continental National Bank Bldg.
Englewood, CO 80110
(303) 761-3183

Life Insurance RX Corporation
P.O. Box O
Sausalito, CA 94965
(415) 332-2266

Lincoln Trust Company
P.O. Box 5831 T.A.
Denver, CO 80217
(303) 771-1900

Massachusetts Financial Services Company
200 Berkeley St.
Boston, MA 02116
(800) 343-2829; also (617) 423-3500

The Robert A. McNeil Corporation
2855 Campus Drive
San Mateo, CA 94403
(415) 572-0660; also (800) 227-6709

Money Dynamics Letter
Venita VanCaspel, Editor
Reston Publishing Company, Inc.
11480 Sunset Hills Road
Reston, Virginia 22090
(703) 437-8900

Morgan Petroleum Securities
Gary Stellow, President
700 Cass St.
Monterey, CA 93940
(408) 649-1111

National Tax Shelter Digest
Marilyn Passell Goldsmith, Editor
1720 Regal Row, Suite 242
Dallas, TX 75234
(214) 630-0684

New England Rare Coin Galleries
89 Devonshire Street
Boston, MA 02109
(800) 225-6794
In Massachusetts: (617) 227-8000

New York Institute of Finance
70 Pine Street, 2nd Floor
New York, NY 10005
(212) 344-2900

John Nuveen & Co., Inc.
61 Broadway
New York, NY 10006
(212) 668-9500

Oppenheimer Management Corporation
One New York Plaza
New York, NY 10004
(212) 825-8260

The Pioneer Group, Inc.
60 State Street
Boston, MA 02109
(617) 742-7825; also (800) 225-6292

Pioneer Western Corporation
P.O. Box 5068
Clearwater, FL 33518
(813) 585-6565, ext. 212

Public Storage
94 So. Los Robles
Pasadena, CA 91101
(213) 681-6731

Putnam Fund Distributors, Inc.
265 Franklin St.
Boston, MA 02110
(617) 423-4960, ext. 405-406

Research Institute Master Federal Tax
Manual
Mt. Kisco, NY 10549

Reston Publishing Company, Inc.
11480 Sunset Hills Road
Reston, VA 22090
(703) 437-8900

Success, The Magazine of Achievers
Dwight L. Chapin, Editor
401 N. Wabash Ave.
Chicago, ILL 60611
(312) 828-9100

U.S. Tangible Investment Corp.
Burnett Marus, President
7950 Elmbrook Dr., Suite 100
Dallas, TX 75247
(214) 631-1110; also (800) 527-9250

Universal Stamp Corp.
12 Richmond St. E, Suite 324
Toronto, Ontario, Canada M5C 1N1
(416) 862-1018

Van Caspel & Co., Incorporated
5051 Westheimer
1540 Post Oak Tower
Houston, TX 77056
(713) 621-9733

Waddell and Reed, Inc.
P. O. Box 1343
Kansas City, MO 64141
(816) 283-4021

Warren, Gorham & Lamont
210 South St.
Boston, MA 02111

Index

Annuities
  fixed, 315-16
  nonprofit-institution employees,
    453-54
  private, 377-78
  retirement, 315-18, 458-59
  single-premium deferred, 316-18,
    333, 414, 520-21
Antiques, 291, 395
Appreciation
  hard tangible assets, 263-293
    passim
  real estate, 164, 165, 174-75,
    182, 185, 187, 188, 190, 199, 393, 526
Arabian horses, 356-57
Art, 290-91, 395
Assessments, by general partner, 257
Assets
  daily fluctuation of, 130-31
  repositioning, 515-55
Assumable mortgages, 216, 221
Attitude, winning mental, 3, 9-15, 405
Attorney, selection of, 462, 493-94,
    504-05
Averaging down, 88-89

Balanced mutual funds, 110
Balloon mortgage, 211, 222
Bank of America, 193
Bank/banker
  bank draft authorization, 155
  rates of return, 35-36
  selection of, 296-97, 505, 519
Bankruptcy, 43
Bargains, stock, 83
*Barrons National Business &
  Financial Weekly,* 400
Baruch, Bernard (quoted), 82, 171, 200,
    322
Before-tax dollars, investment of, 335
  oil/gas drilling programs, 249-59,
    335, 349-50
  real estate, private placements,
    184-87, 335
"Bid" and "asked" price, 65
Blended mortgages, 221-22
Blind pool, 171
Blue chip
  stocks, 73, 140
  syndrome, 390-91
"Bombing" a stock, 89, 193
Bond ratings, 304-05, 308, 313
Bond(s), 60, 61-62, 454, 459

corporate, 62-63, 73, 110,
    302, 307-13, 495, 520, 536, 548
  federal agency, 301-02
  federal government, 41, 299-
    303, 535
  municipal, 112, 303-07, 308, 375,
    414, 495, 521-22, 536
Book value, 91
Born to Win (James), 99
Borrowing
  as investment tool, 53, 136, 322-25
  on insurance policy, 324-25,
    409, 411, 412
Bracket creep, 7, 52-53, 338
Brokerage accounts, 66-67
Brokers/dealers, 286
  coin, rare, 269
  diamond, 281-82
  gemstone, colored, 283
  gold, 268
Brookings Institution, 208
Buildings/structures, preservation/
  rehabilitation, 340, 349
Business Week, 400
Buying, timing of, 87-88

Cable television, 350-52, 529
California, taxes in, 53
Call option, 85-86
Capital
  accumulation of, 11
  future allocation of, 92
Capital gains, 74, 199, 329-70 passim,
    371-73, 496
  long-term, 329-85 passim
Capital gains tax, 88, 92, 99, 288
  exemption from sale of dwelling, 183,
    208
  rate, 355
  reduction of, 162
Carter, Jimmy, 76, 230
Cash flow, 179-80, 182, 184
  negative, 185
  oil/gas programs, 237, 238-41, 246-47,
    252-53, 523
  tax-sheltered, 182, 184, 185, 187, 188,
    190, 246, 345
Cash reserves, 495-96
Cash surrender value, life insurance
  policy, 314-15, 409, 430, 495, 536, 548
Cattle breeding, 353-54, 529
Cattle feeding, 352-53